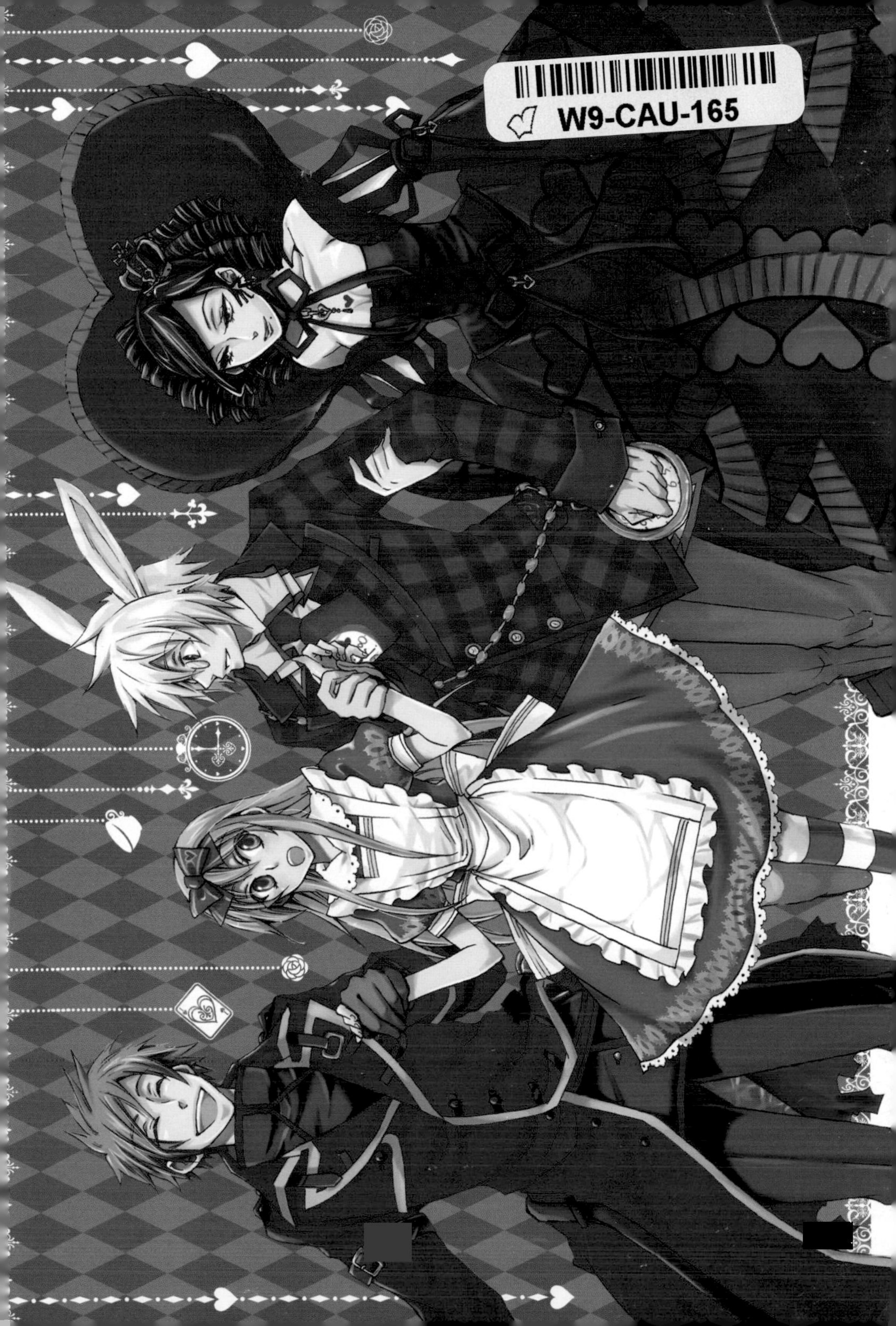

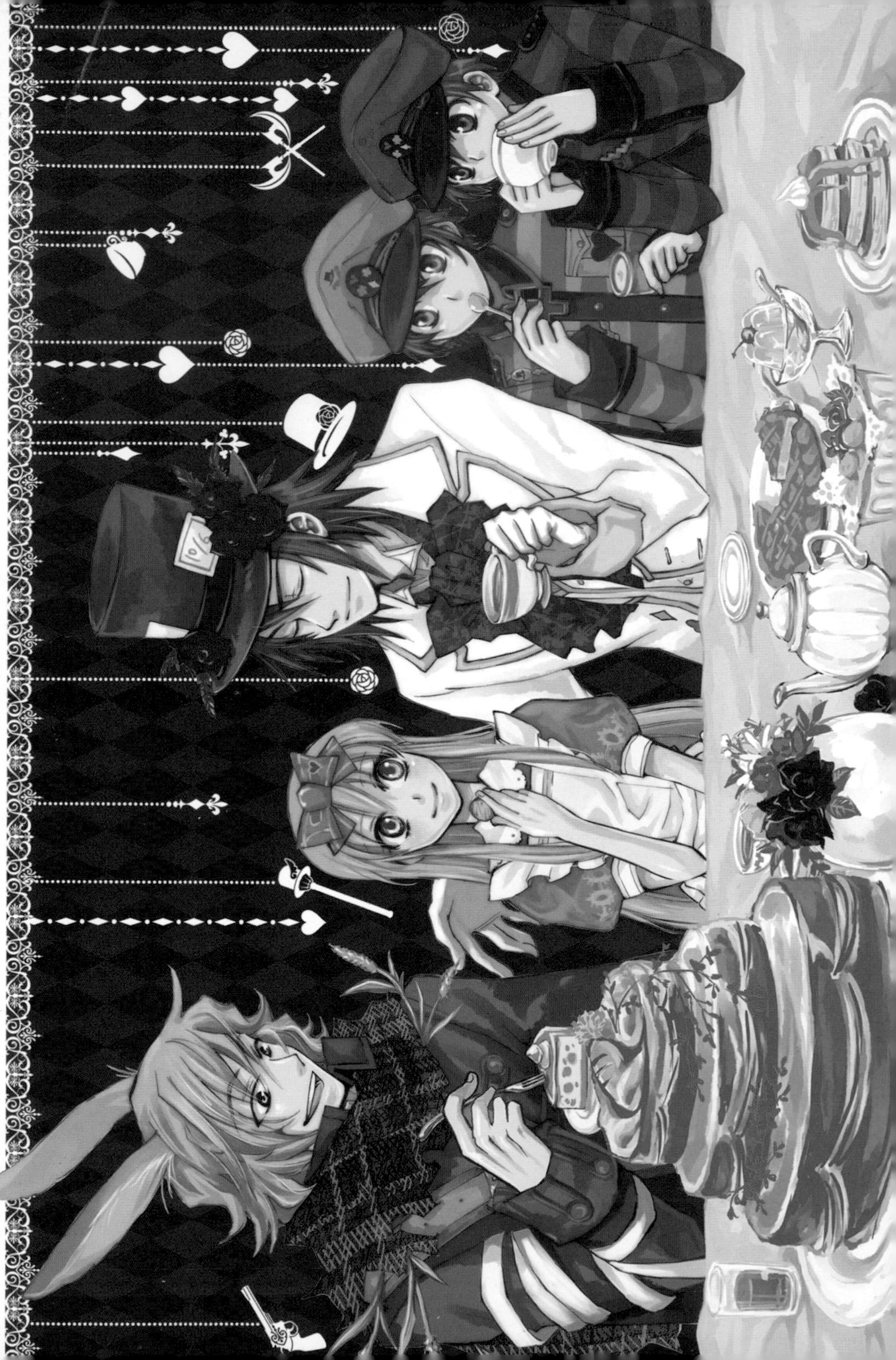

ALICE IN THE COUNTRY OF HEARTS

1

QuinRose ✕ Soumei Hoshino

ALICE IN THE COUNTRY OF HEARTS

1

CONTENTS

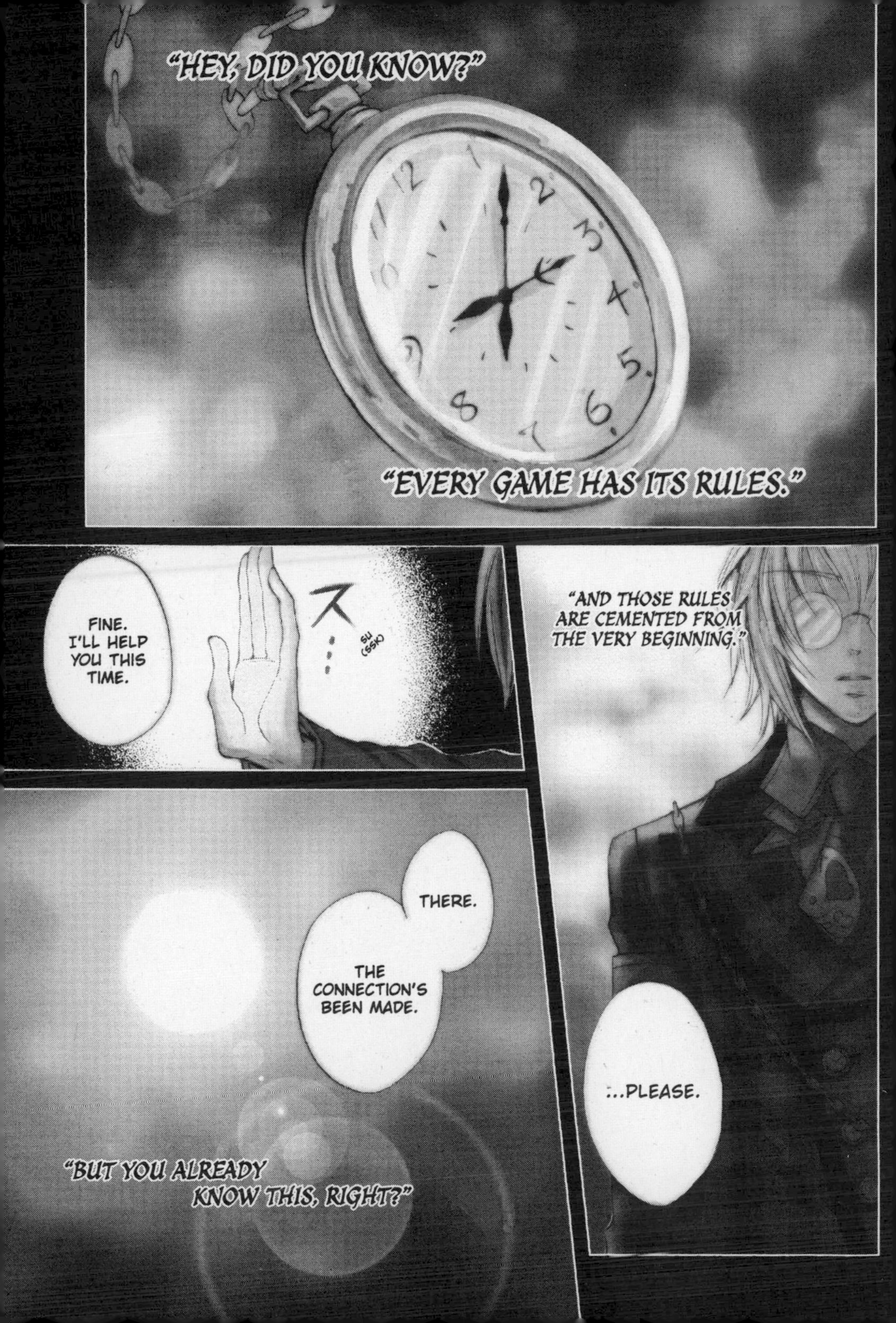
"HEY, DID YOU KNOW?"
"EVERY GAME HAS ITS RULES."
"AND THOSE RULES ARE CEMENTED FROM THE VERY BEGINNING."
...PLEASE.
FINE. I'LL HELP YOU THIS TIME.
ス...
SU (SSK)
THERE.
THE CONNECTION'S BEEN MADE.
"BUT YOU ALREADY KNOW THIS, RIGHT?"

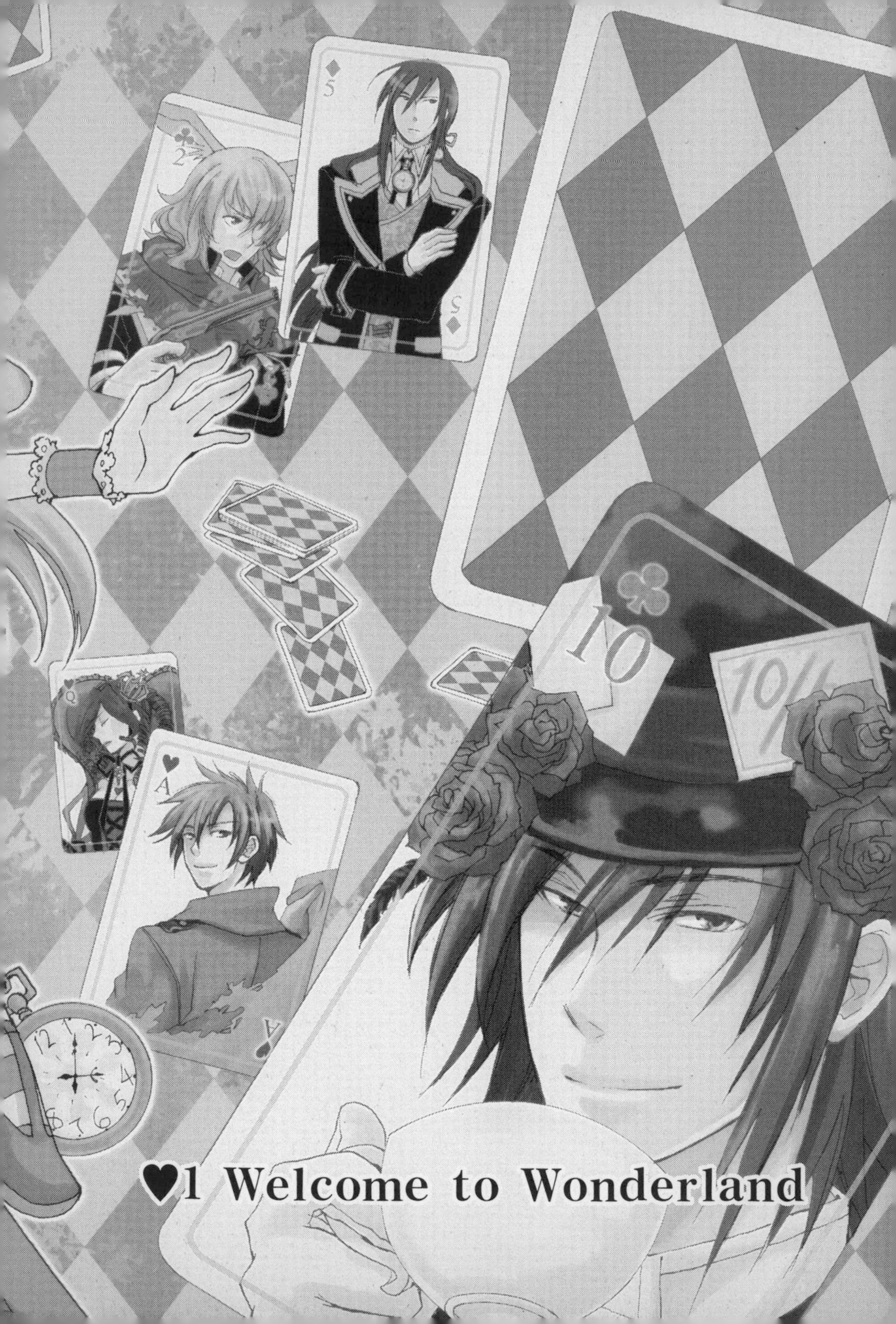

♥1 Welcome to Wonderland

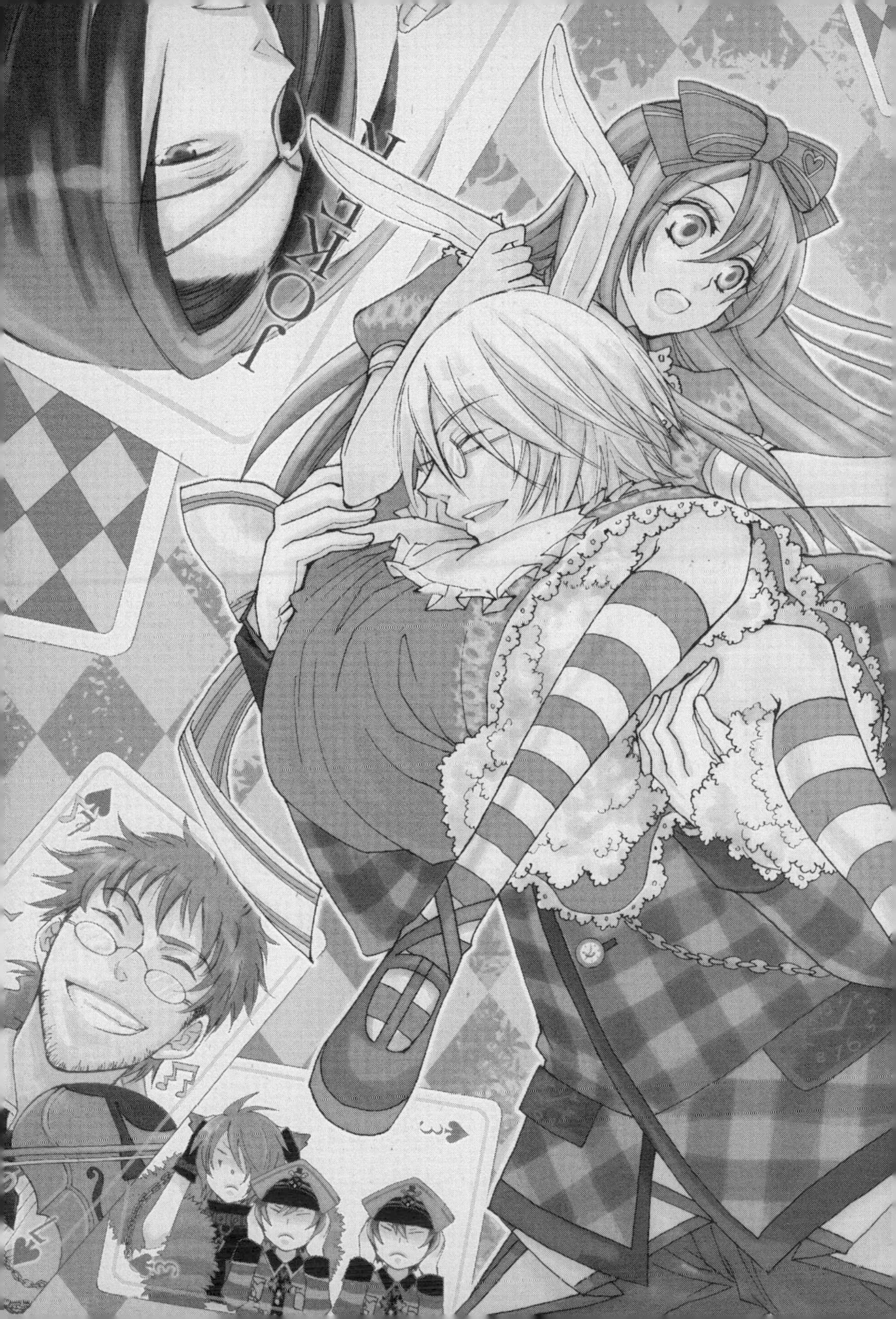

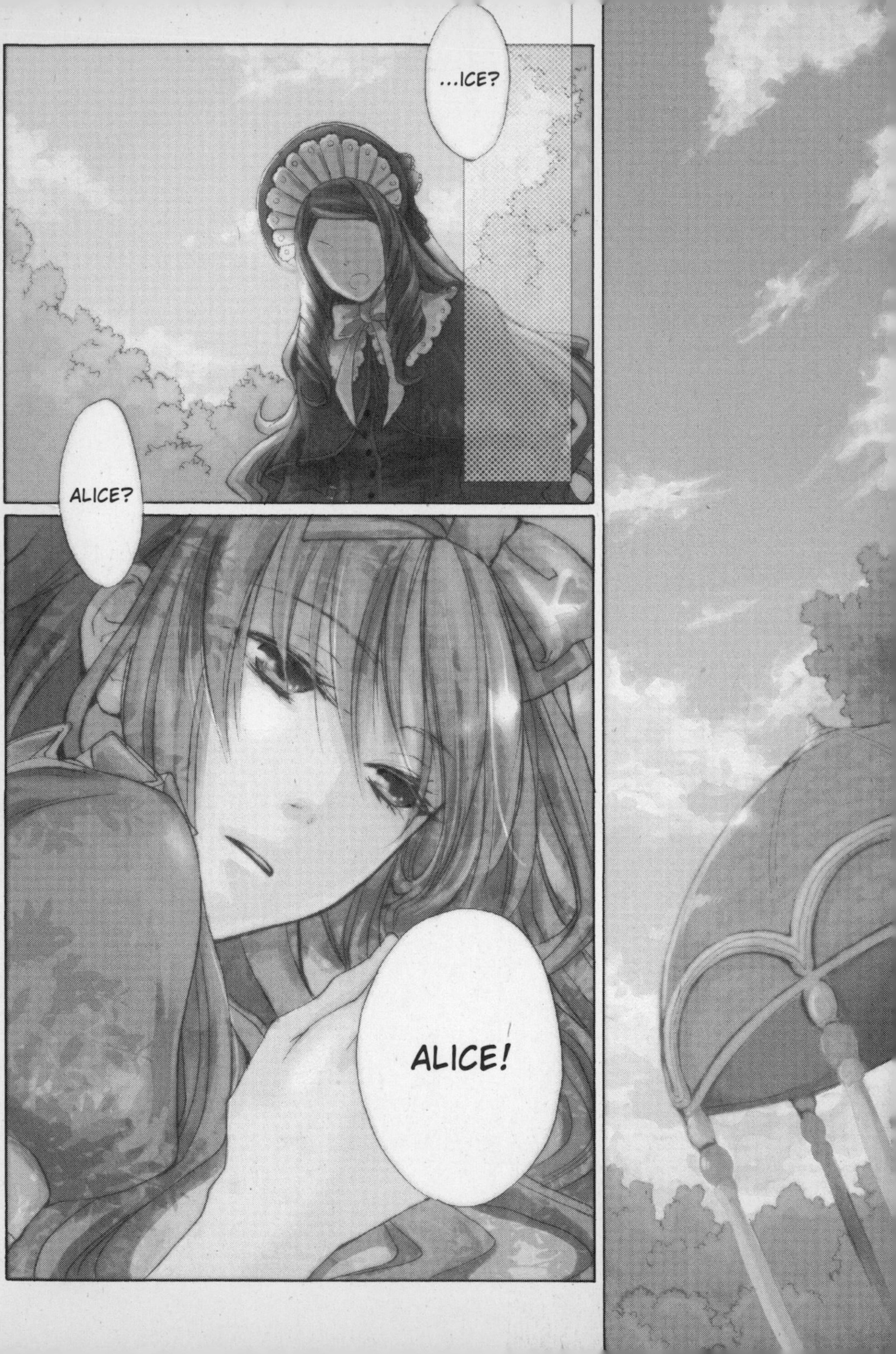
...ICE?
ALICE?
ALICE!

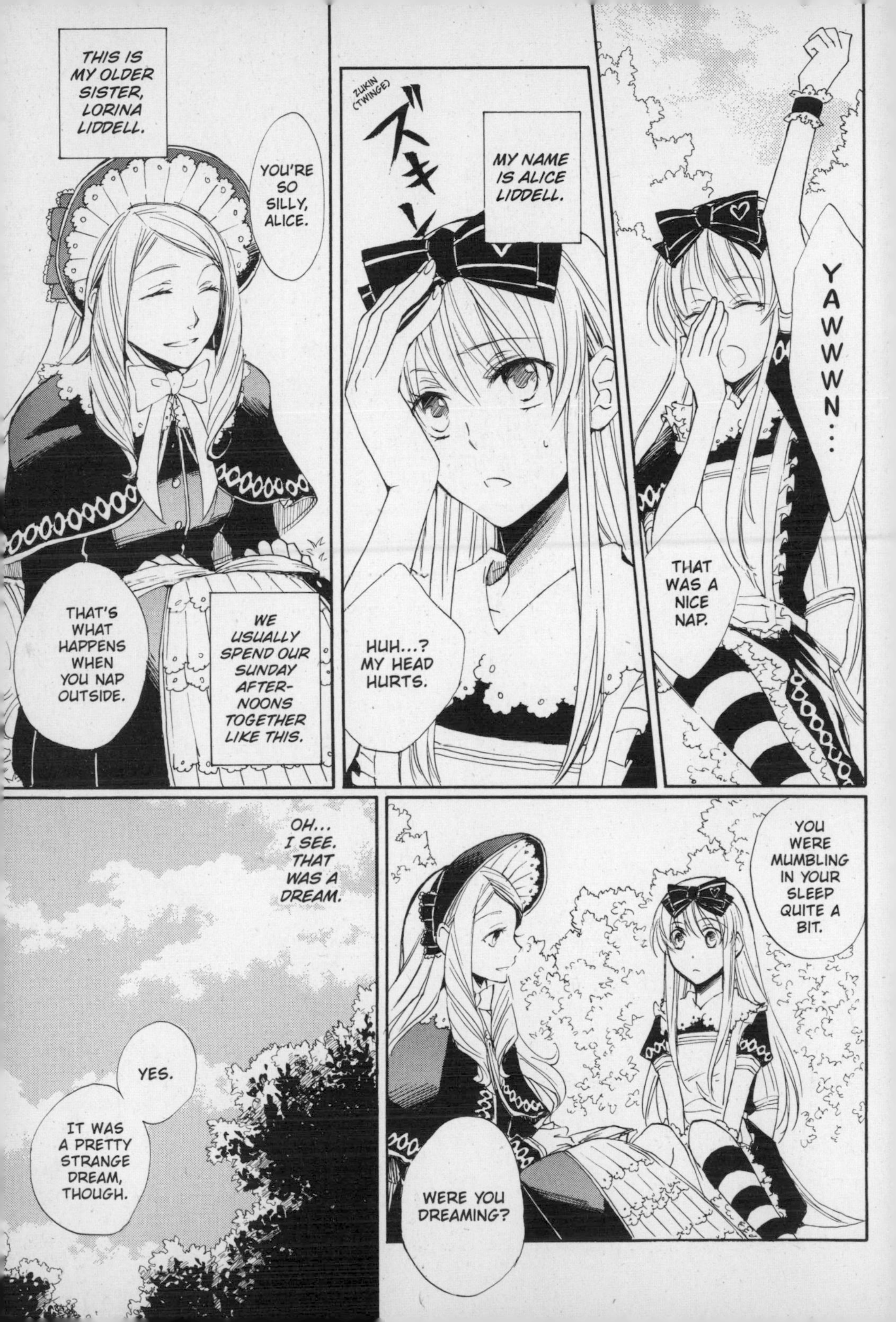
YAWWWN...
THAT WAS A NICE NAP.
ZUKIN (TWINGE)
ズキン
MY NAME IS ALICE LIDDELL.
HUH...? MY HEAD HURTS.
THIS IS MY OLDER SISTER, LORINA LIDDELL.
YOU'RE SO SILLY, ALICE.
THAT'S WHAT HAPPENS WHEN YOU NAP OUTSIDE.
WE USUALLY SPEND OUR SUNDAY AFTER-NOONS TOGETHER LIKE THIS.
YOU WERE MUMBLING IN YOUR SLEEP QUITE A BIT.
WERE YOU DREAMING?
OH... I SEE. THAT WAS A DREAM.
YES.
IT WAS A PRETTY STRANGE DREAM, THOUGH.

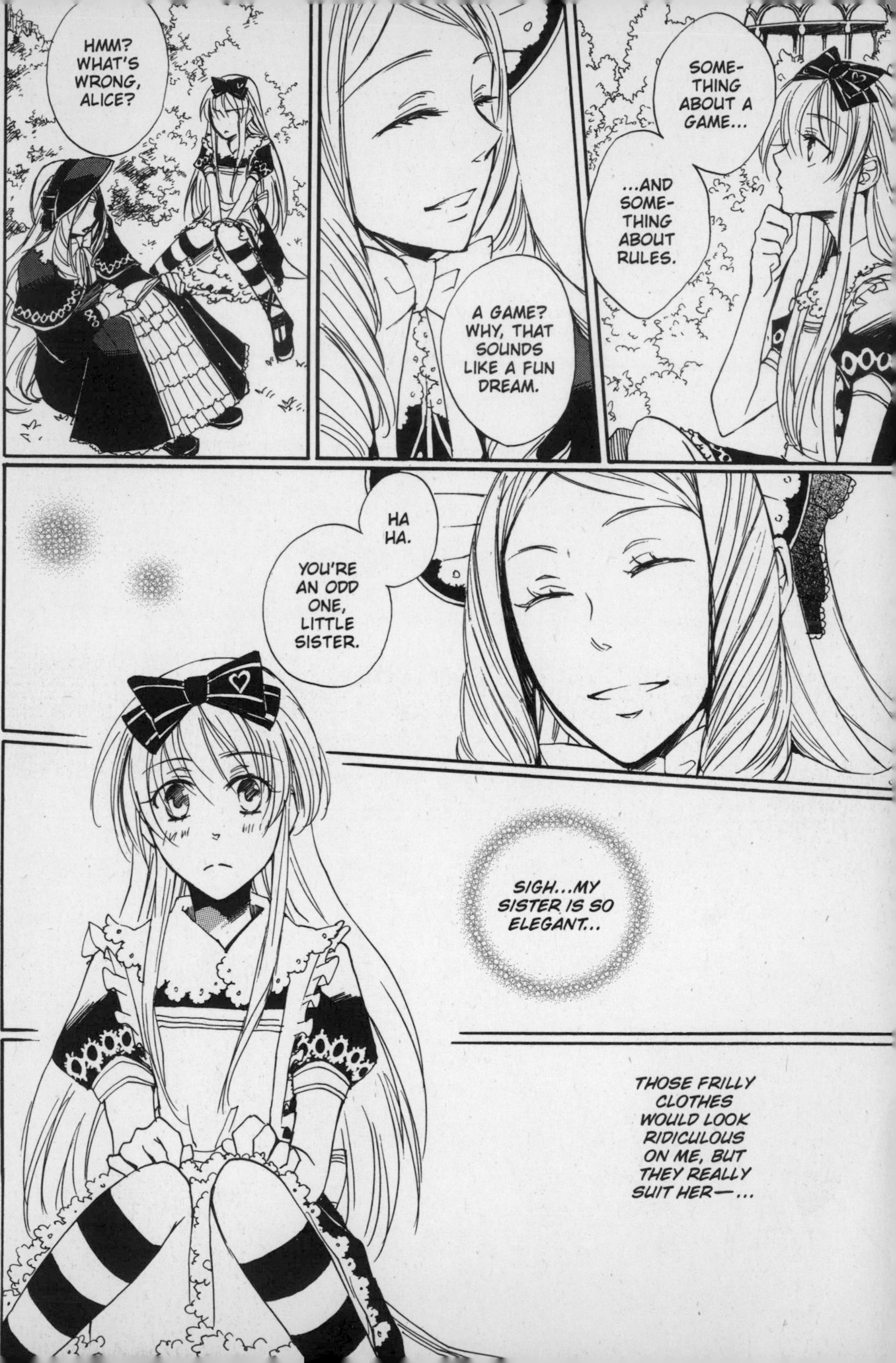
SOME-THING ABOUT A GAME...
...AND SOME-THING ABOUT RULES.
A GAME? WHY, THAT SOUNDS LIKE A FUN DREAM.
HMM? WHAT'S WRONG, ALICE?
HA HA.
YOU'RE AN ODD ONE, LITTLE SISTER.
SIGH...MY SISTER IS SO ELEGANT...
THOSE FRILLY CLOTHES WOULD LOOK RIDICULOUS ON ME, BUT THEY REALLY SUIT HER—...

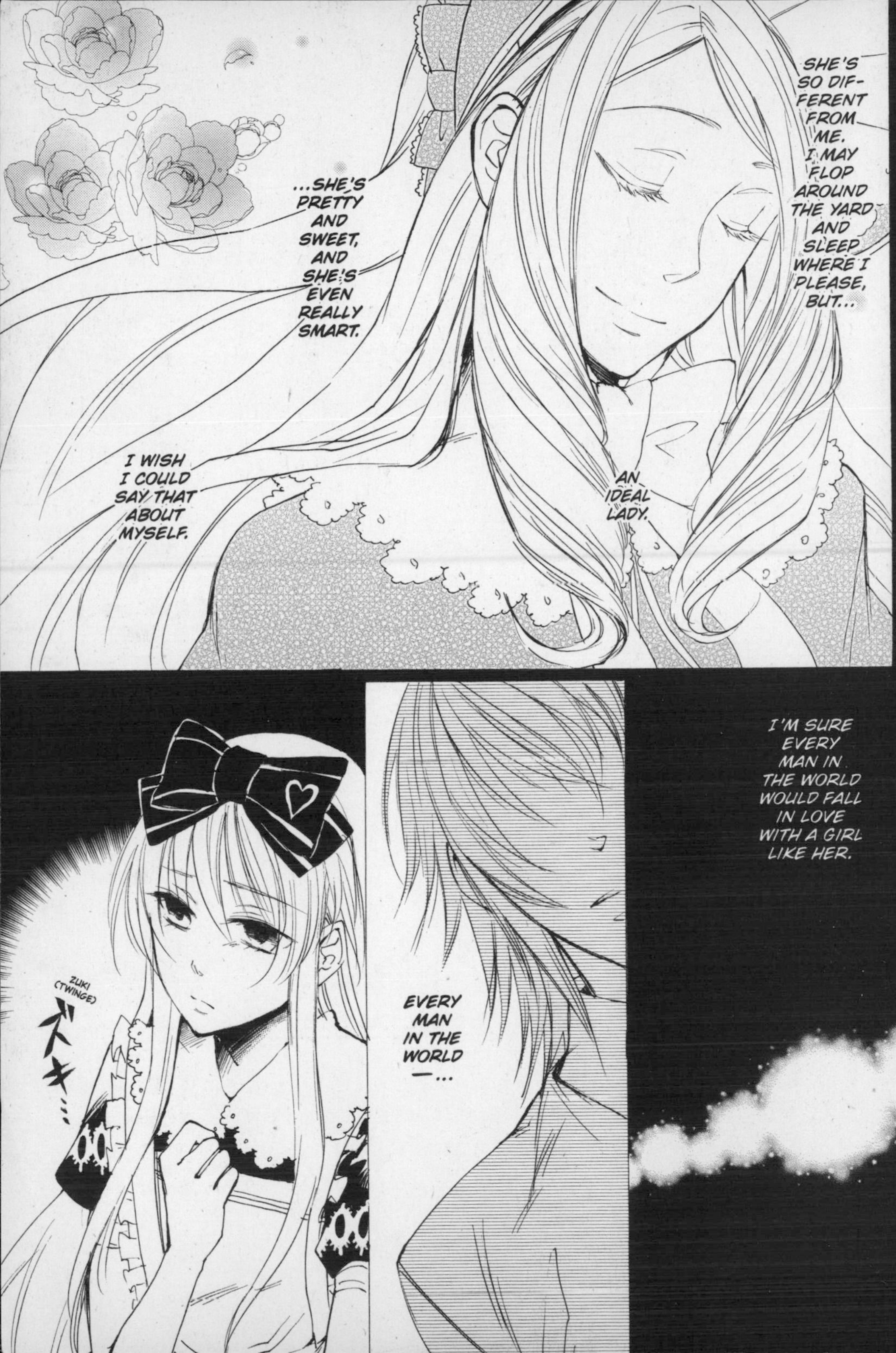
SHE'S SO DIFFERENT FROM ME. I MAY FLOP AROUND THE YARD AND SLEEP WHERE I PLEASE, BUT...
...SHE'S PRETTY AND SWEET, AND SHE'S EVEN REALLY SMART.
AN IDEAL LADY.
I WISH I COULD SAY THAT ABOUT MYSELF.
I'M SURE EVERY MAN IN THE WORLD WOULD FALL IN LOVE WITH A GIRL LIKE HER.
EVERY MAN IN THE WORLD —...
ZUKI (TWINGE)

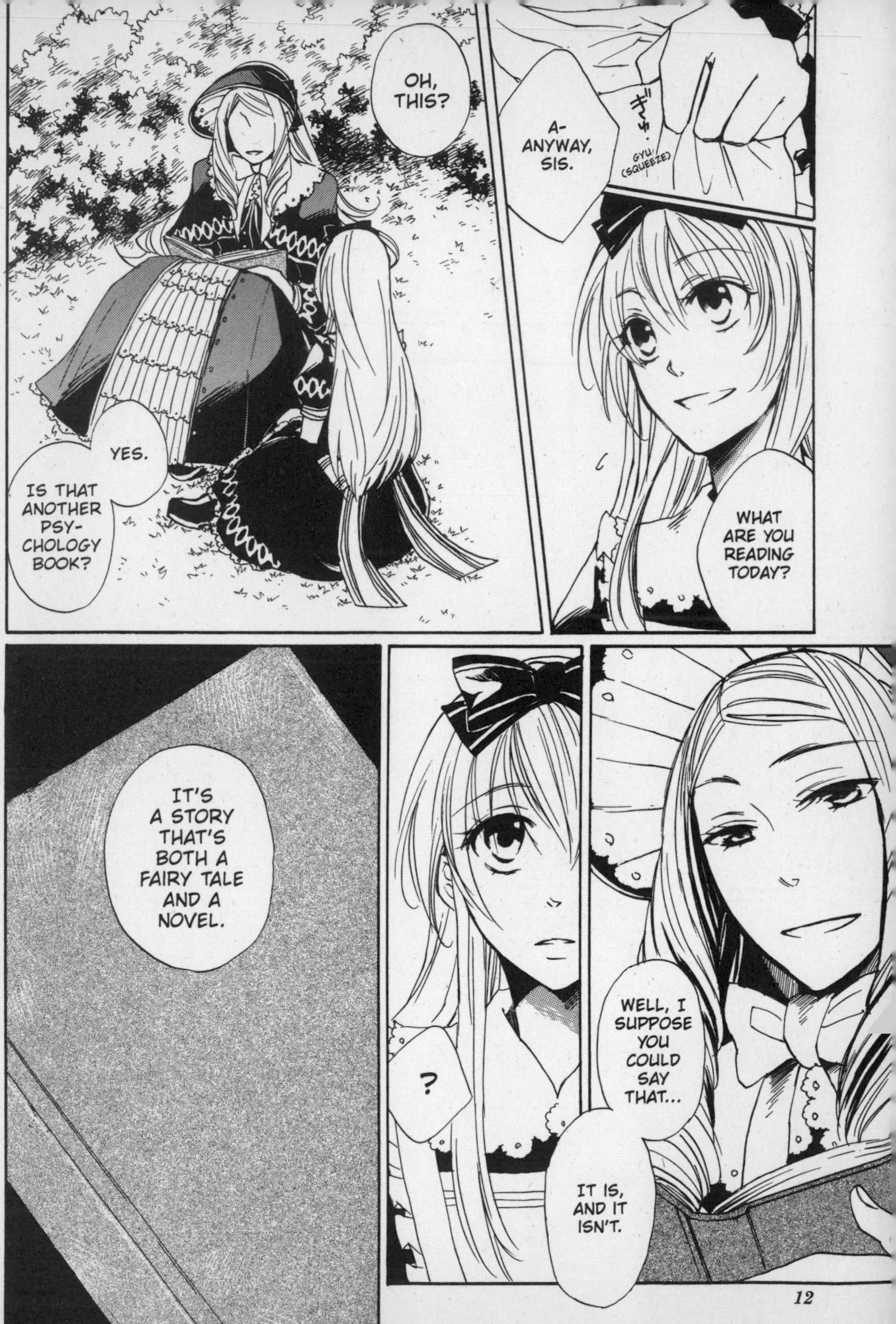
ギュッ
GYU (SQUEEZE)
A- ANYWAY, SIS.
WHAT ARE YOU READING TODAY?
OH, THIS?
YES.
IS THAT ANOTHER PSY- CHOLOGY BOOK?
WELL, I SUPPOSE YOU COULD SAY THAT...
IT IS, AND IT ISN'T.
?
IT'S A STORY THAT'S BOTH A FAIRY TALE AND A NOVEL.

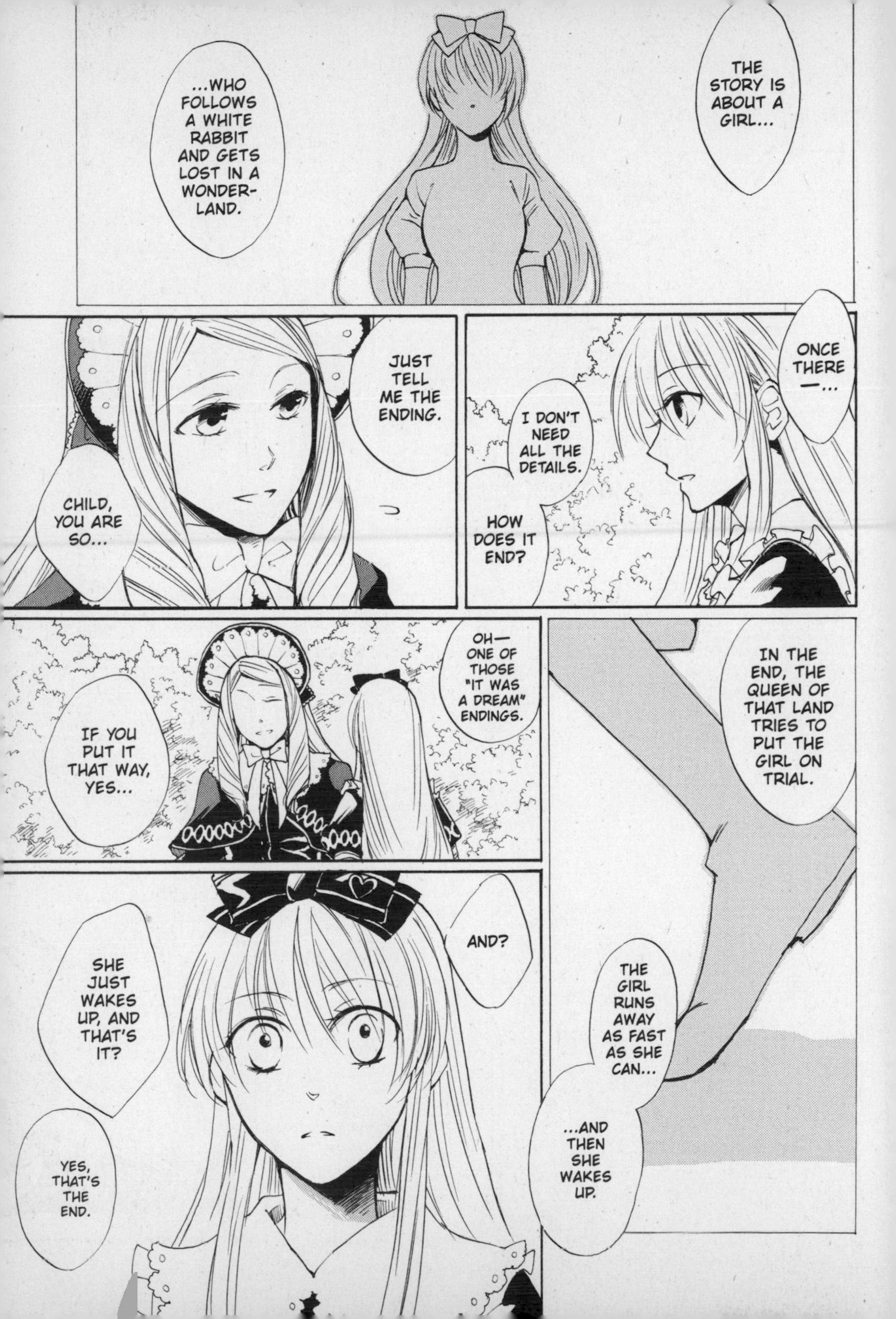
THE STORY IS ABOUT A GIRL...
...WHO FOLLOWS A WHITE RABBIT AND GETS LOST IN A WONDER-LAND.
ONCE THERE—...
I DON'T NEED ALL THE DETAILS.
HOW DOES IT END?
JUST TELL ME THE ENDING.
CHILD, YOU ARE SO...
IN THE END, THE QUEEN OF THAT LAND TRIES TO PUT THE GIRL ON TRIAL.
THE GIRL RUNS AWAY AS FAST AS SHE CAN...
...AND THEN SHE WAKES UP.
OH— ONE OF THOSE "IT WAS A DREAM" ENDINGS.
IF YOU PUT IT THAT WAY, YES...
AND?
SHE JUST WAKES UP, AND THAT'S IT?
YES, THAT'S THE END.

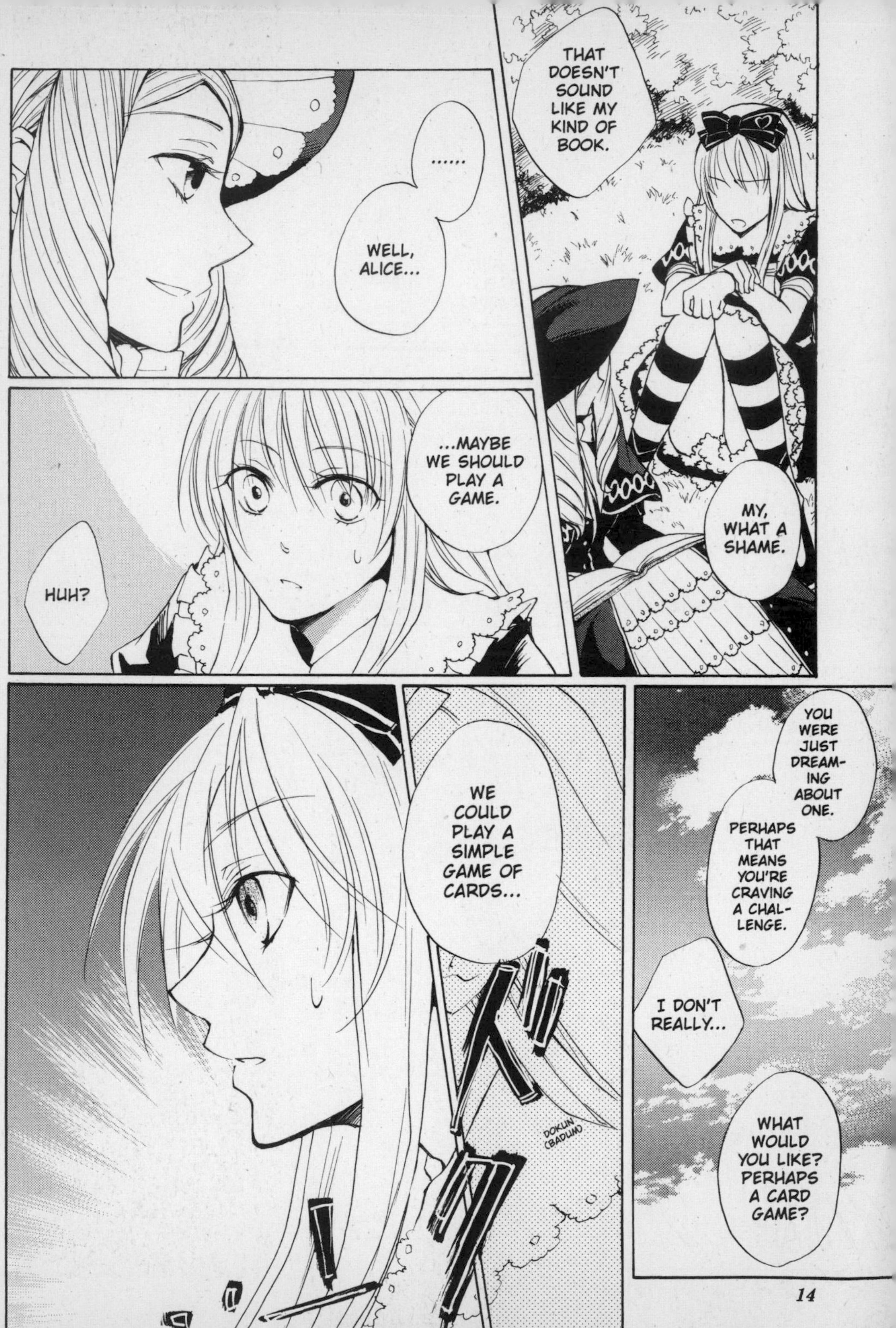
THAT DOESN'T SOUND LIKE MY KIND OF BOOK.
MY, WHAT A SHAME.
......
WELL, ALICE...
...MAYBE WE SHOULD PLAY A GAME.
HUH?
YOU WERE JUST DREAMING ABOUT ONE.
PERHAPS THAT MEANS YOU'RE CRAVING A CHALLENGE.
I DON'T REALLY...
WHAT WOULD YOU LIKE? PERHAPS A CARD GAME?
WE COULD PLAY A SIMPLE GAME OF CARDS...
DOKUN (BADUM)

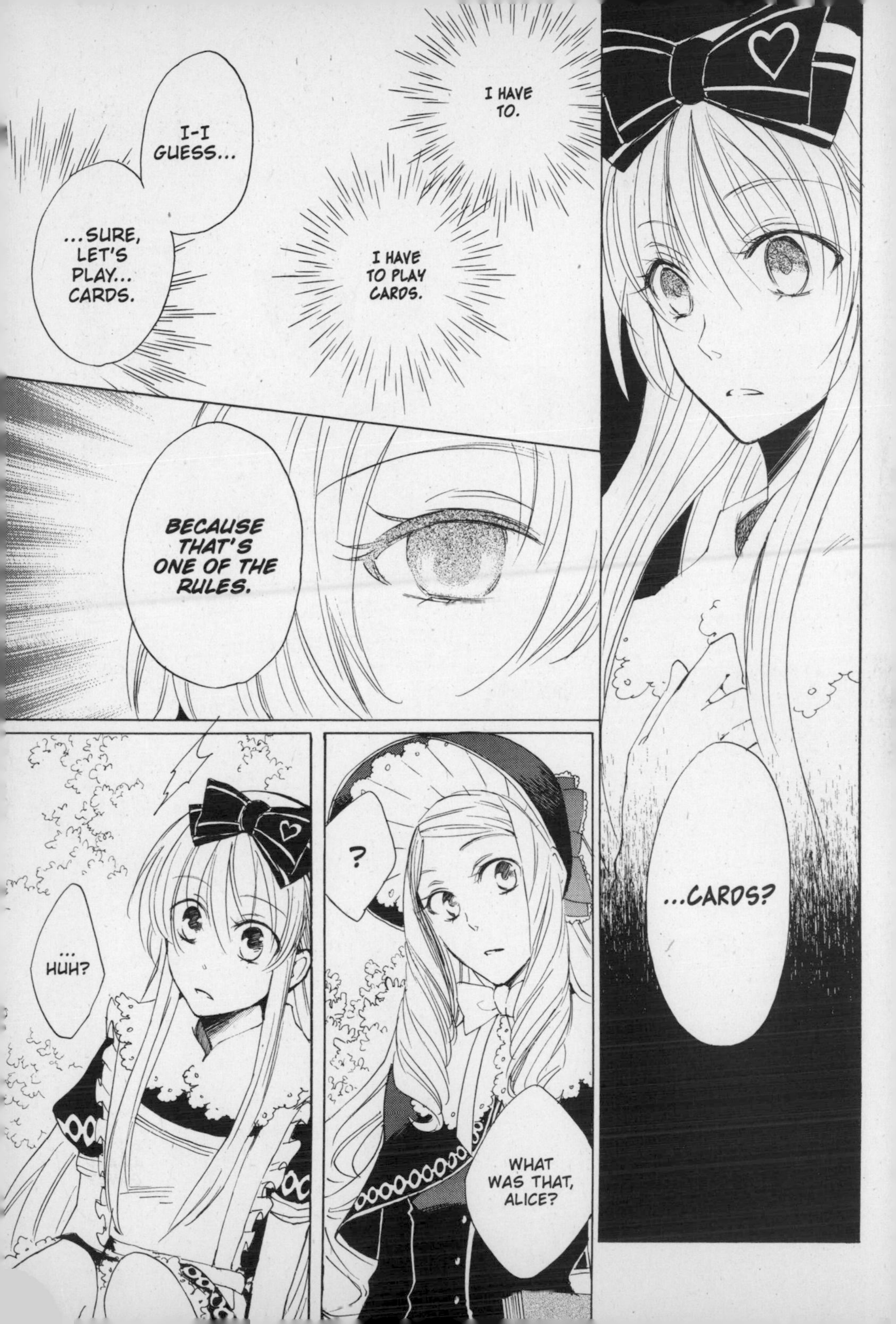
...CARDS?
I HAVE TO.
I HAVE TO PLAY CARDS.
I-I GUESS...
...SURE, LET'S PLAY... CARDS.
BECAUSE THAT'S ONE OF THE RULES.
?
WHAT WAS THAT, ALICE?
... HUH?

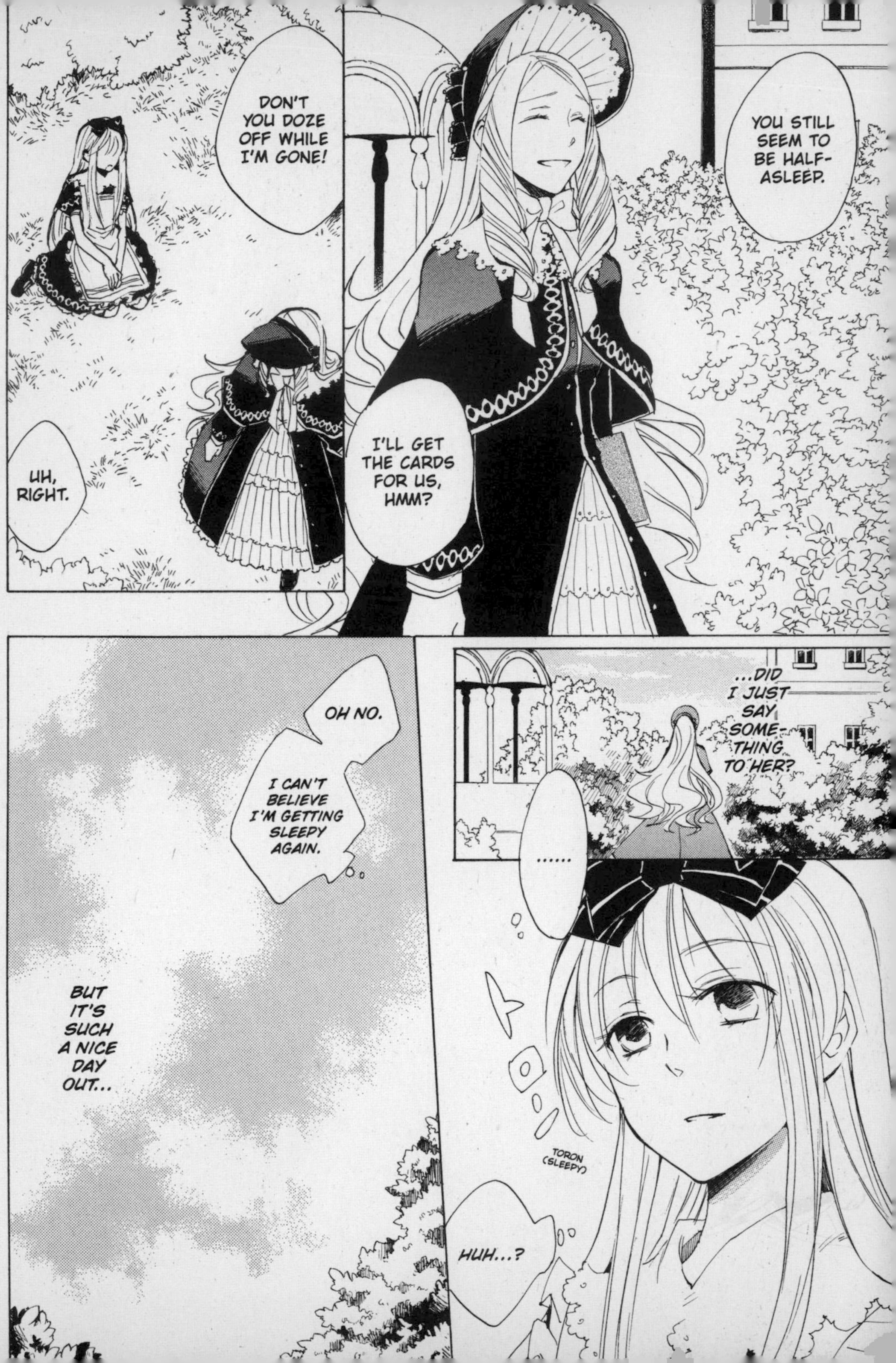
YOU STILL SEEM TO BE HALF-ASLEEP.
I'LL GET THE CARDS FOR US, HMM?
DON'T YOU DOZE OFF WHILE I'M GONE!
UH, RIGHT.
...DID I JUST SAY SOME-THING TO HER?
......
TORON (SLEEPY)
HUH...?
OH NO.
I CAN'T BELIEVE I'M GETTING SLEEPY AGAIN.
BUT IT'S SUCH A NICE DAY OUT...

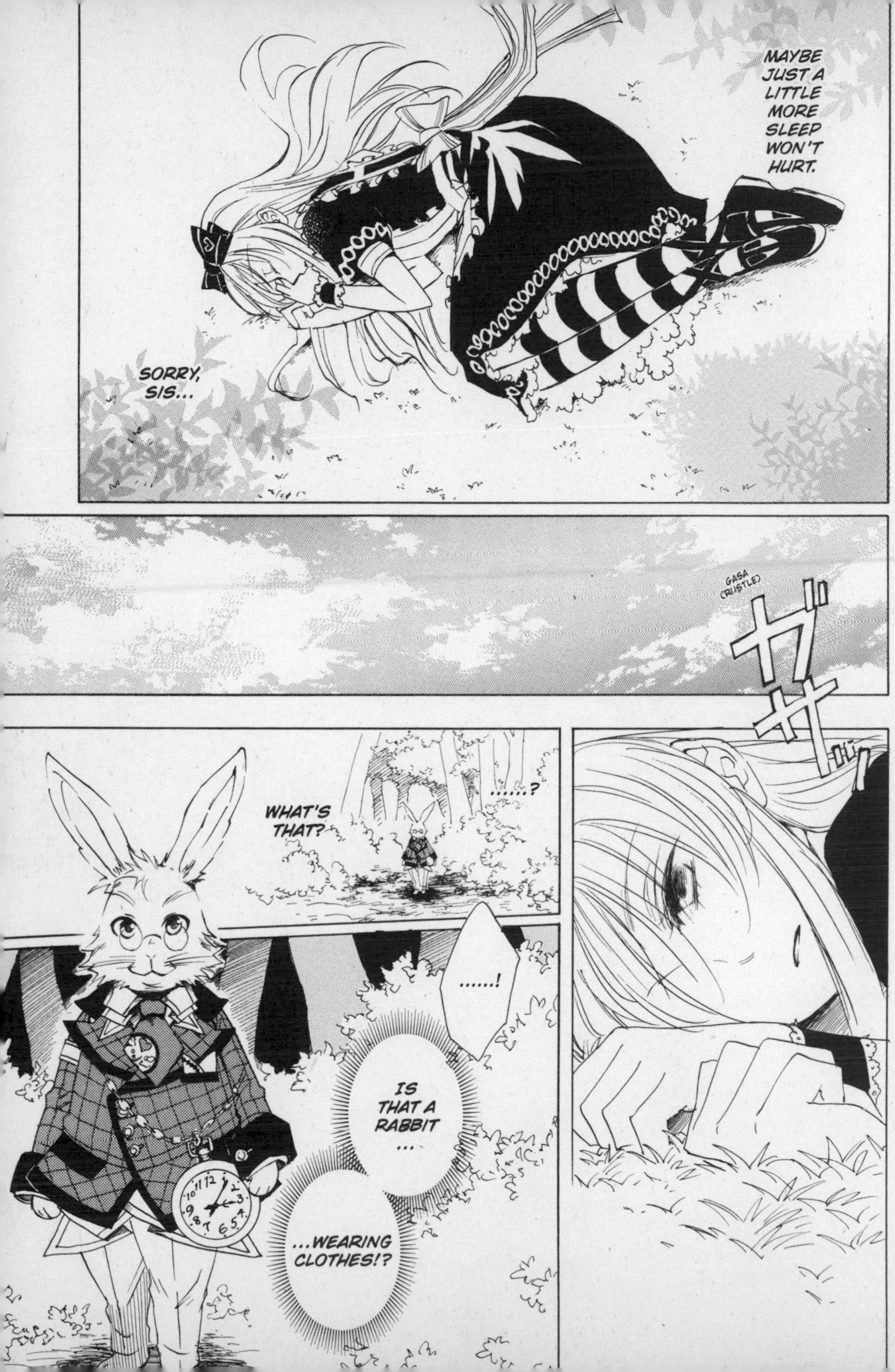
MAYBE JUST A LITTLE MORE SLEEP WON'T HURT.
SORRY, SIS...
GASA (RUSTLE)
......!
......?
WHAT'S THAT?
IS THAT A RABBIT ...
...WEARING CLOTHES!?

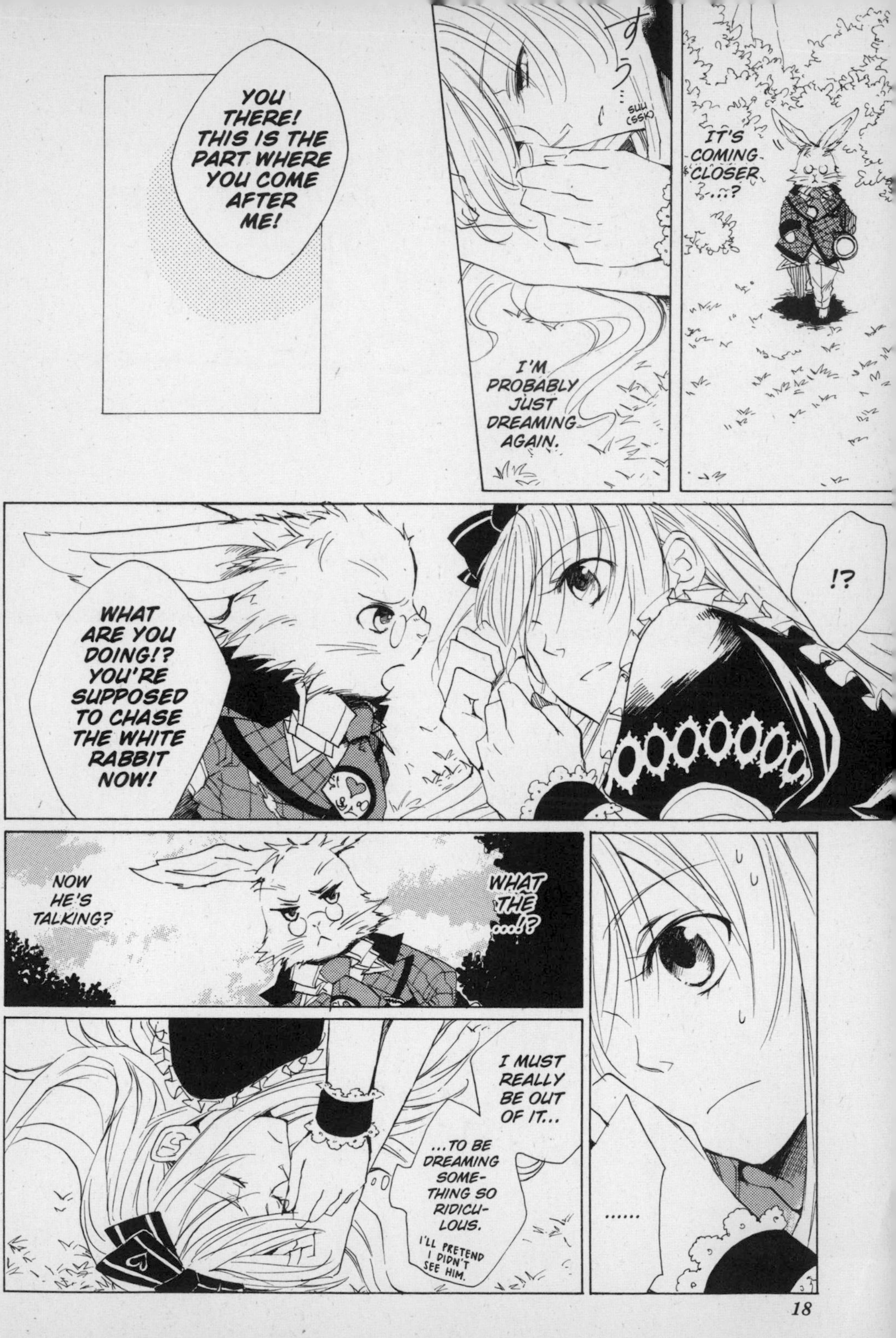
IT'S COMING CLOSER...?
すぅ…
SUU (SSK)
I'M PROBABLY JUST DREAMING AGAIN.
YOU THERE! THIS IS THE PART WHERE YOU COME AFTER ME!
!?
WHAT ARE YOU DOING!? YOU'RE SUPPOSED TO CHASE THE WHITE RABBIT NOW!
......
WHAT THE...!?
NOW HE'S TALKING?
I MUST REALLY BE OUT OF IT...
...TO BE DREAMING SOMETHING SO RIDICULOUS.
I'LL PRETEND I DIDN'T SEE HIM.

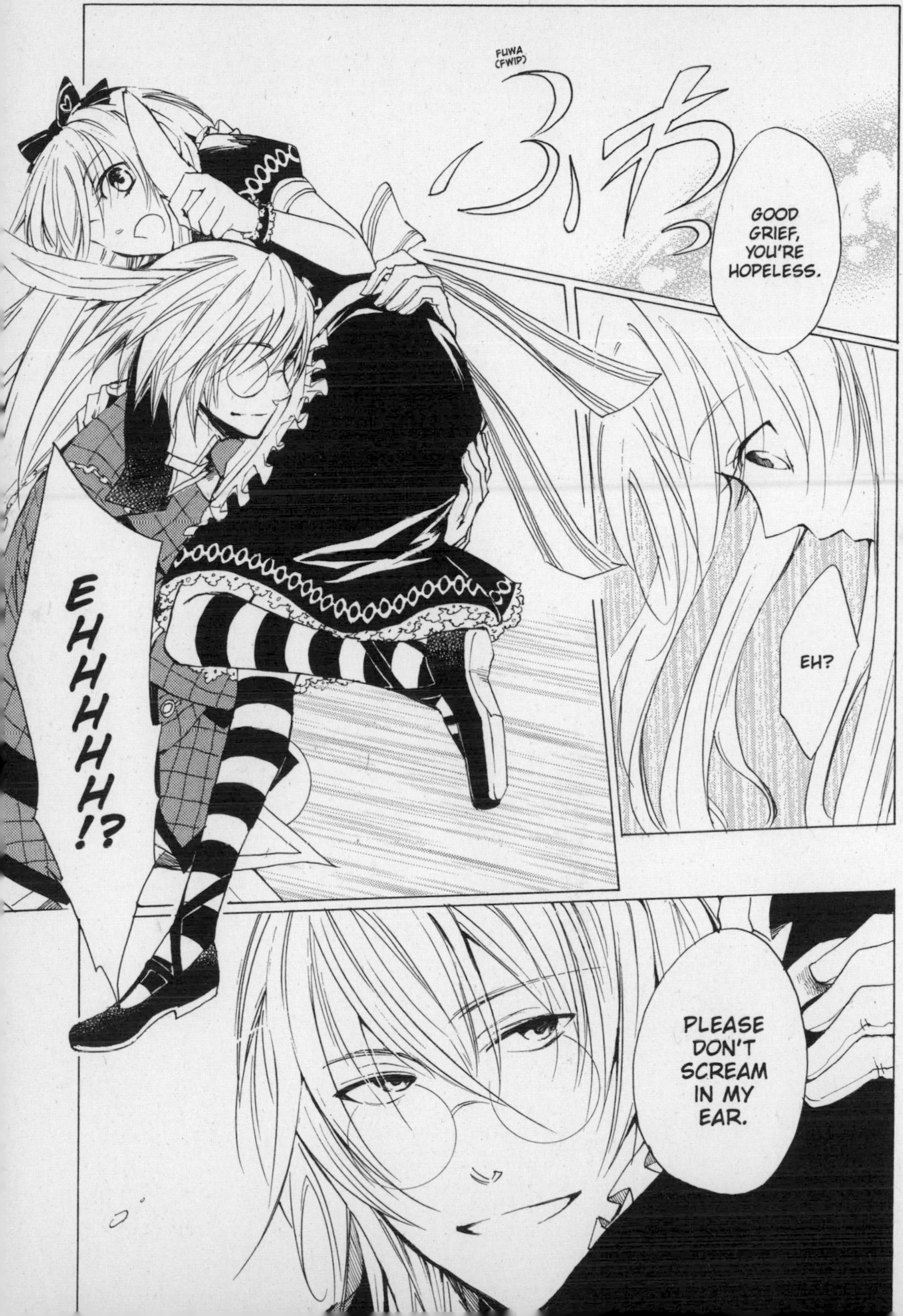
GOOD GRIEF, YOU'RE HOPELESS.
FUWA (FWIP)
EH?
EHHHHH!?
PLEASE DON'T SCREAM IN MY EAR.

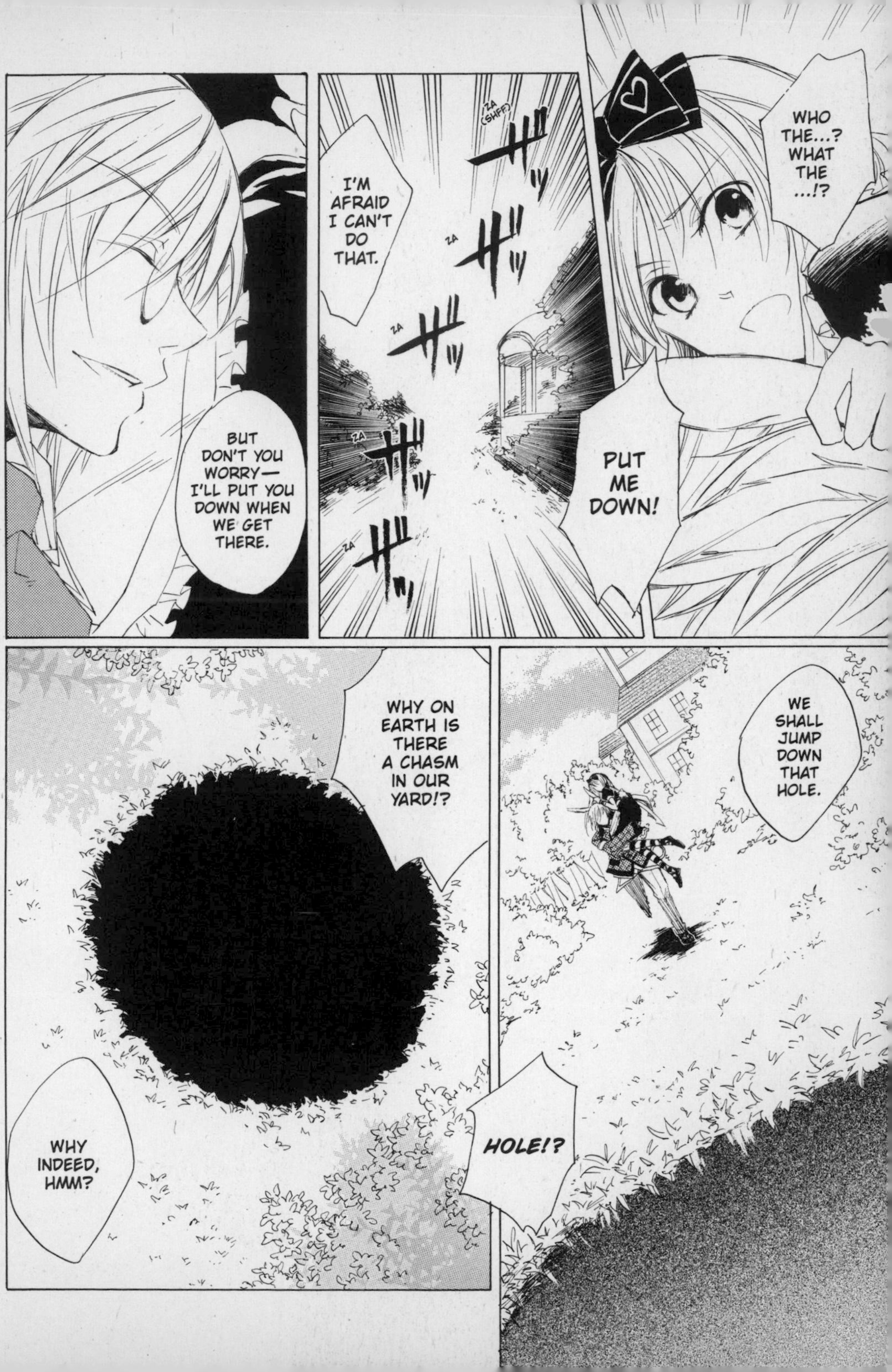
WHO THE...? WHAT THE...!?
PUT ME DOWN!
ZA (SHFF)
I'M AFRAID I CAN'T DO THAT.
ZA
ZA
ZA
ZA
BUT DON'T YOU WORRY— I'LL PUT YOU DOWN WHEN WE GET THERE.
WE SHALL JUMP DOWN THAT HOLE.
HOLE!?
WHY ON EARTH IS THERE A CHASM IN OUR YARD!?
WHY INDEED, HMM?

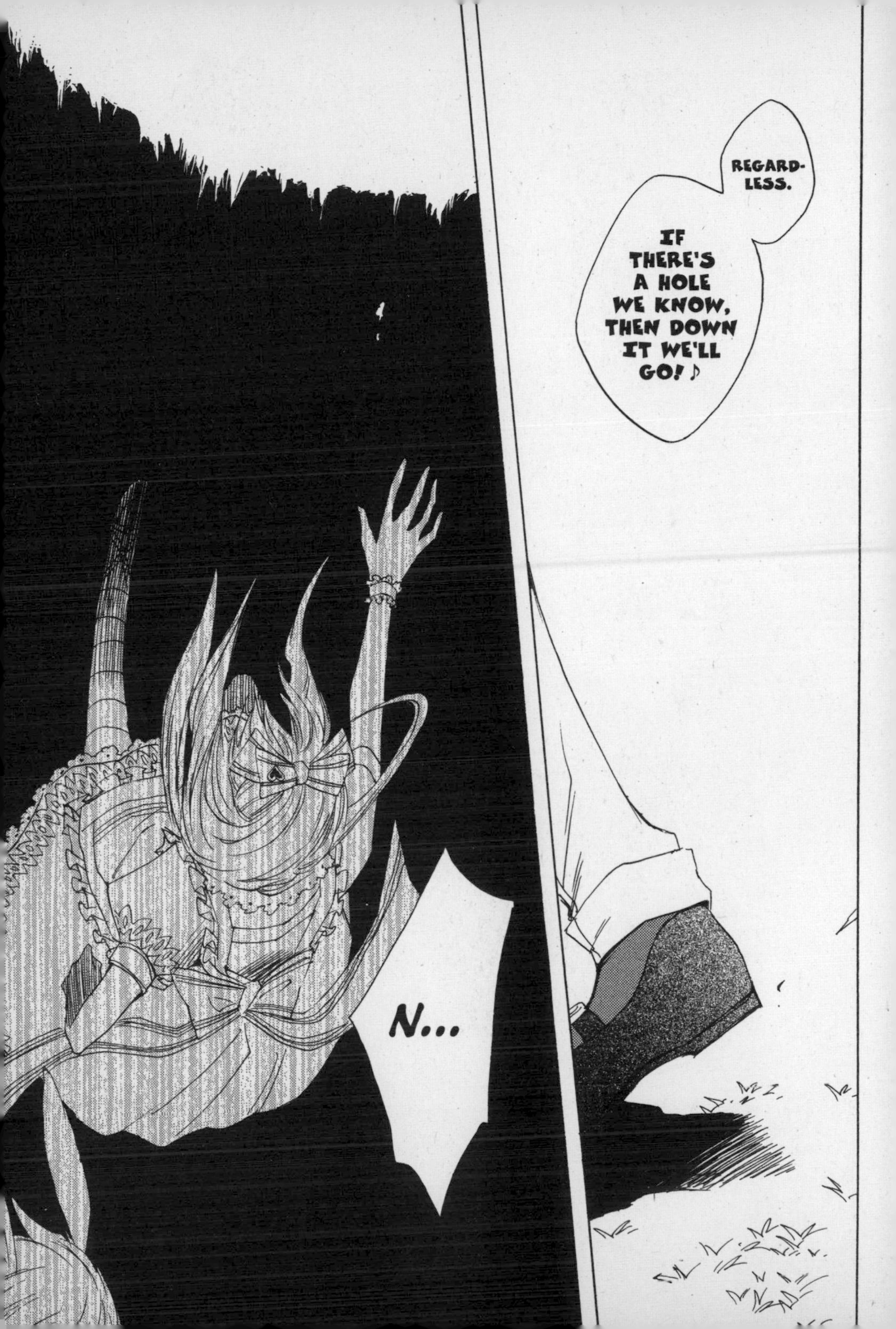
REGARD-LESS.
IF THERE'S A HOLE WE KNOW, THEN DOWN IT WE'LL GO! ♪
N...

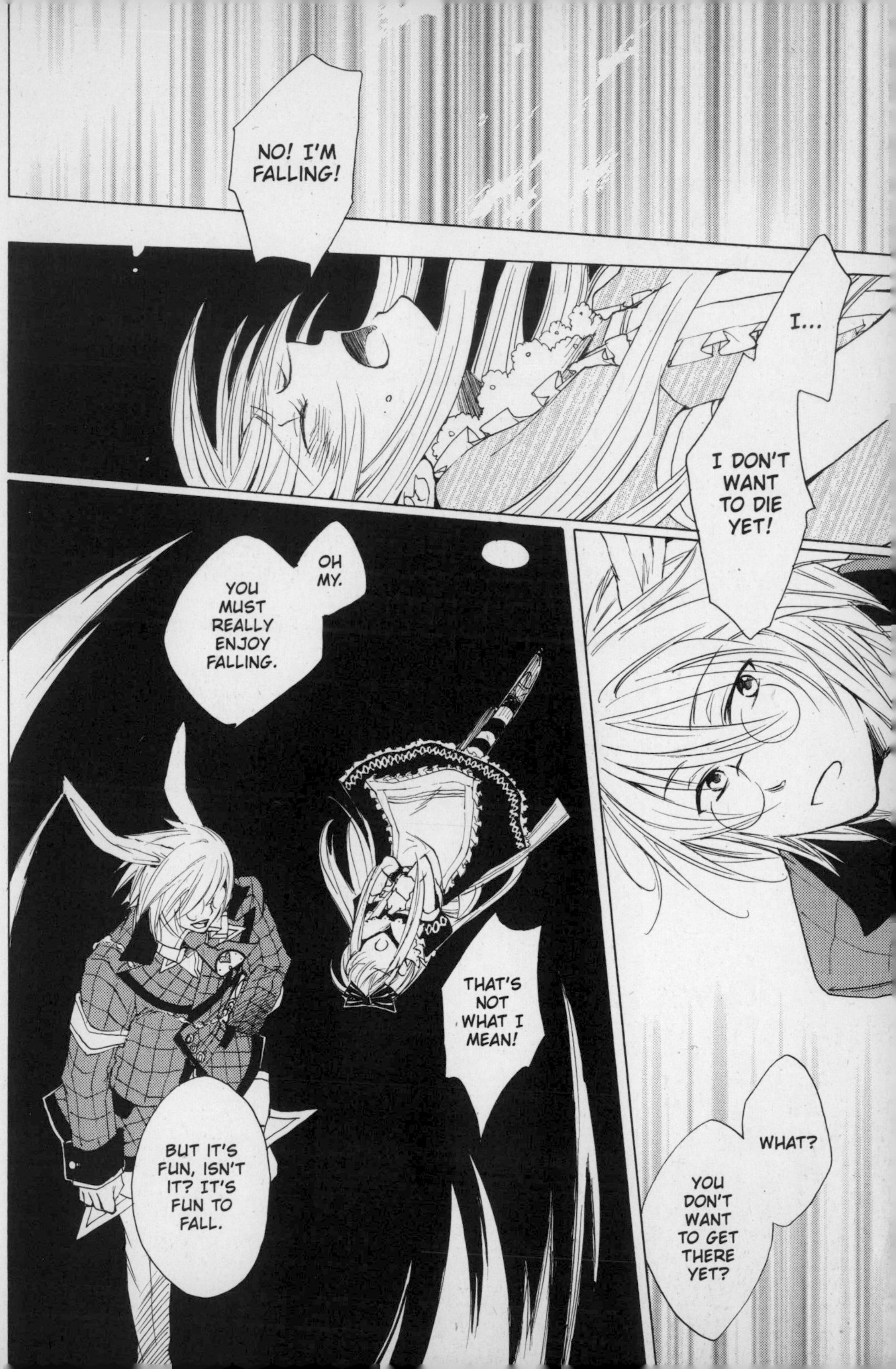
NO! I'M FALLING!
I...
I DON'T WANT TO DIE YET!
WHAT?
YOU DON'T WANT TO GET THERE YET?
OH MY.
YOU MUST REALLY ENJOY FALLING.
THAT'S NOT WHAT I MEAN!
BUT IT'S FUN, ISN'T IT? IT'S FUN TO FALL.

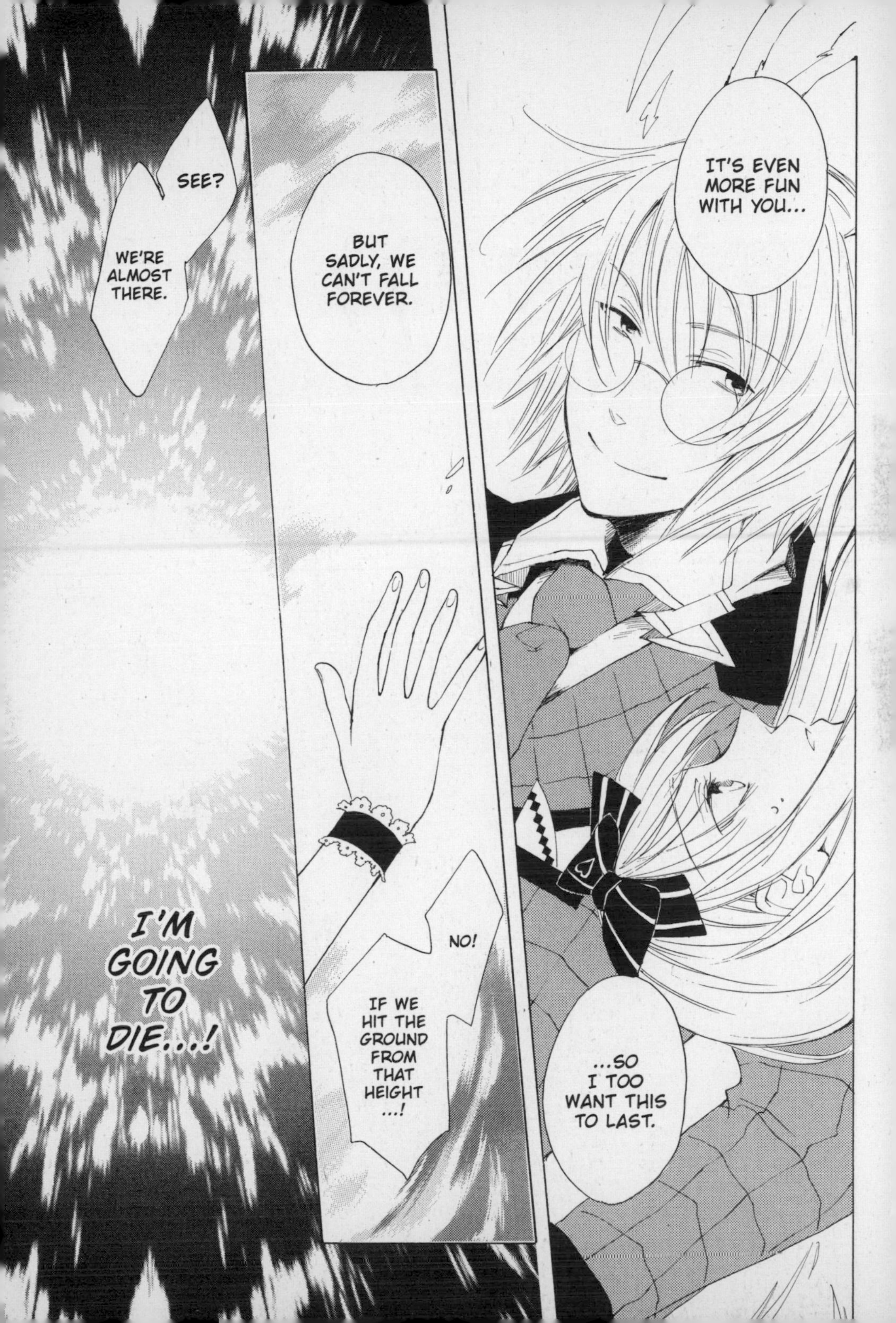
IT'S EVEN MORE FUN WITH YOU...
...SO I TOO WANT THIS TO LAST.
BUT SADLY, WE CAN'T FALL FOREVER.
NO!
IF WE HIT THE GROUND FROM THAT HEIGHT ...!
SEE?
WE'RE ALMOST THERE.
I'M GOING TO DIE...!

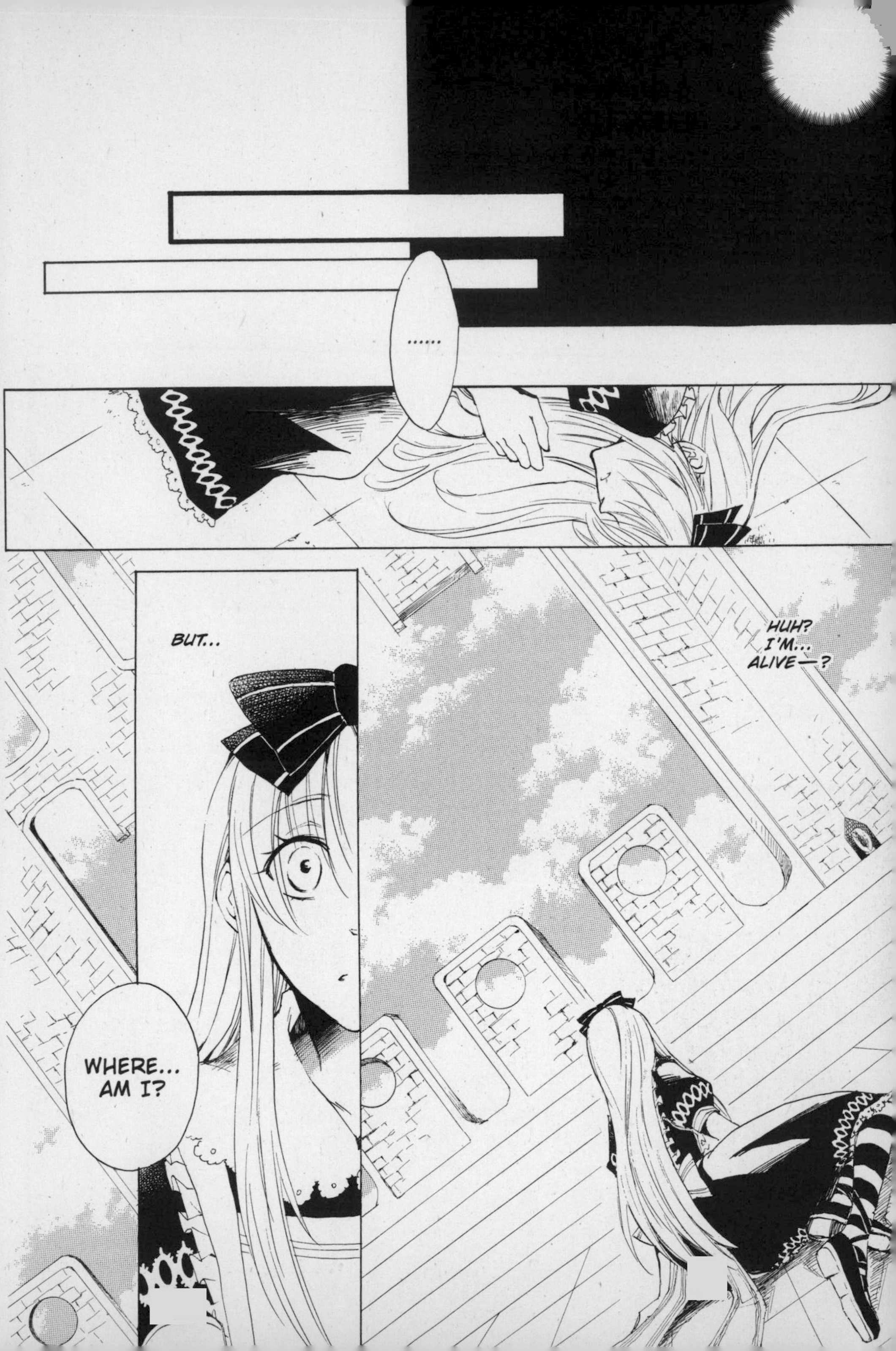
......
HUH? I'M... ALIVE—?
BUT...
WHERE... AM I?

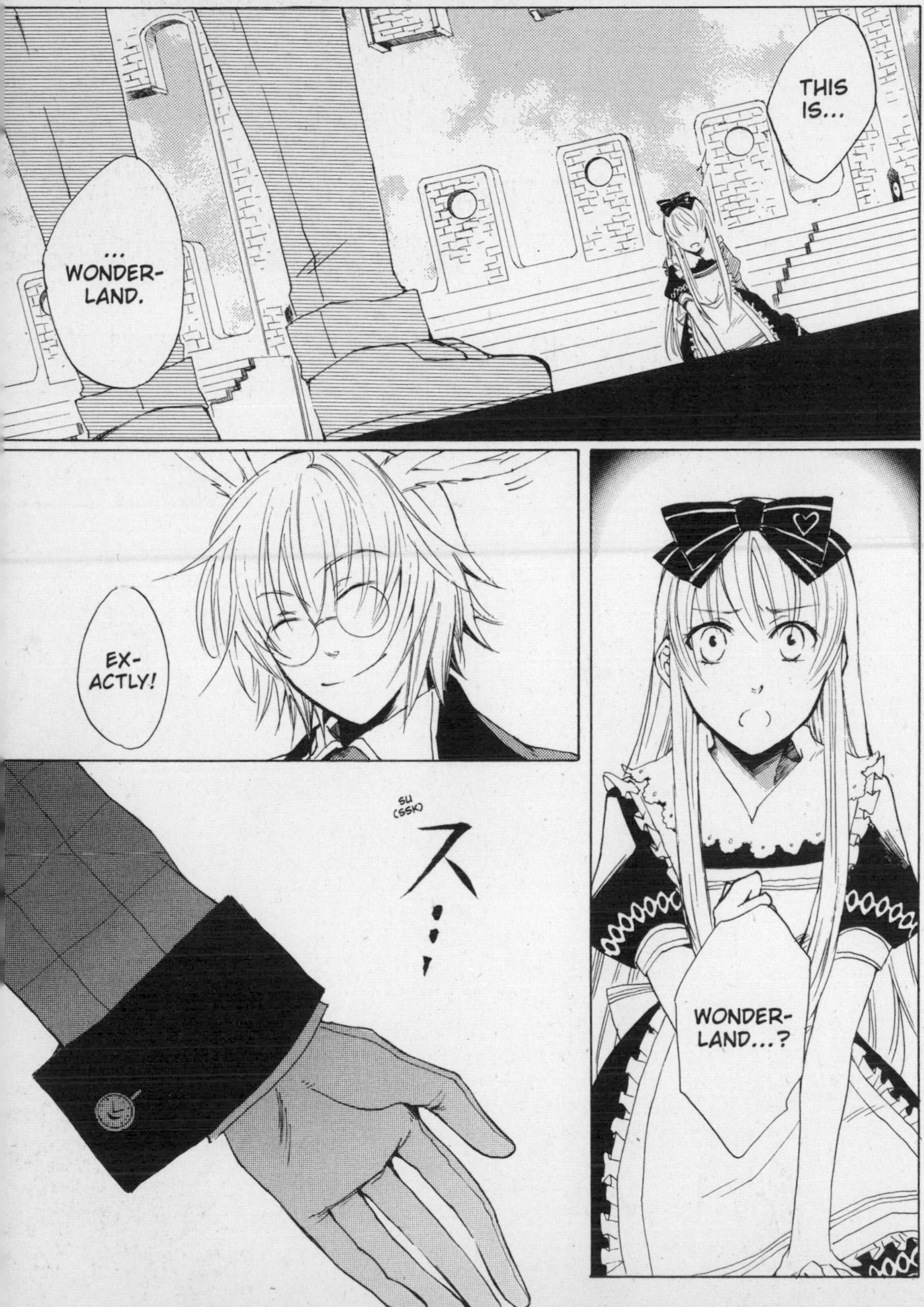
THIS IS...
...WONDERLAND.
WONDERLAND...?
EX-ACTLY!
SU (SSK)
ス...

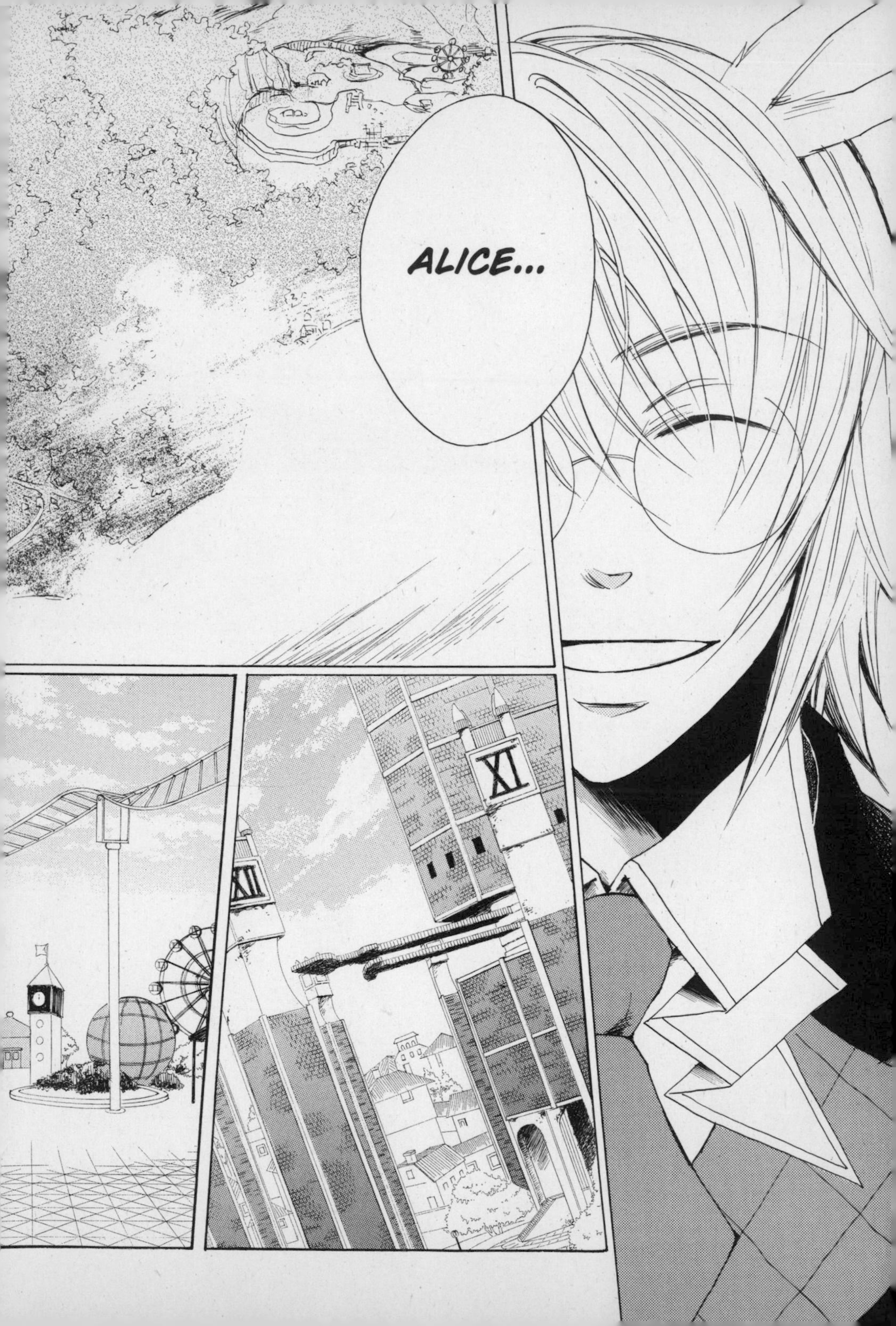
ALICE...

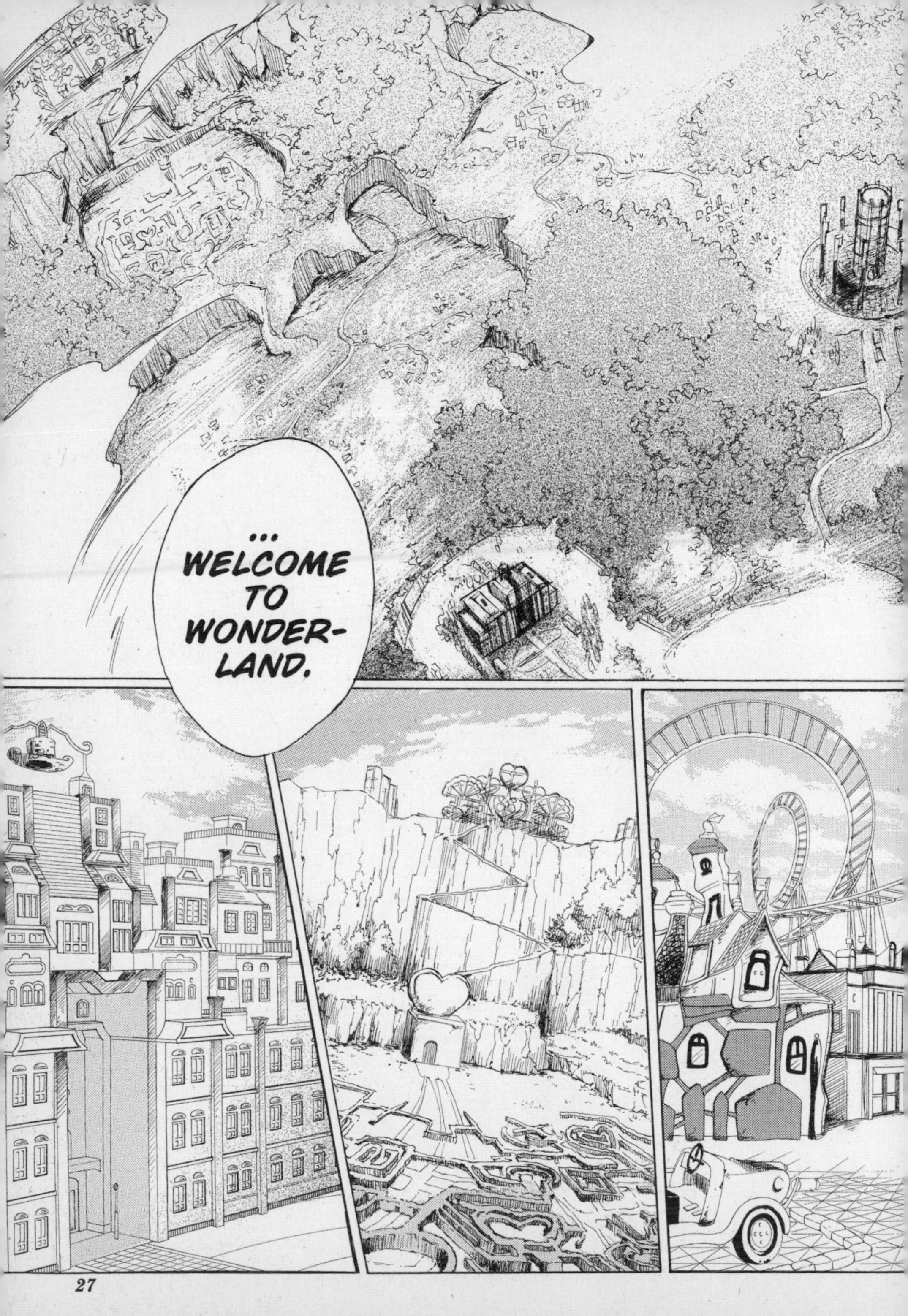
... WELCOME TO WONDER-LAND.

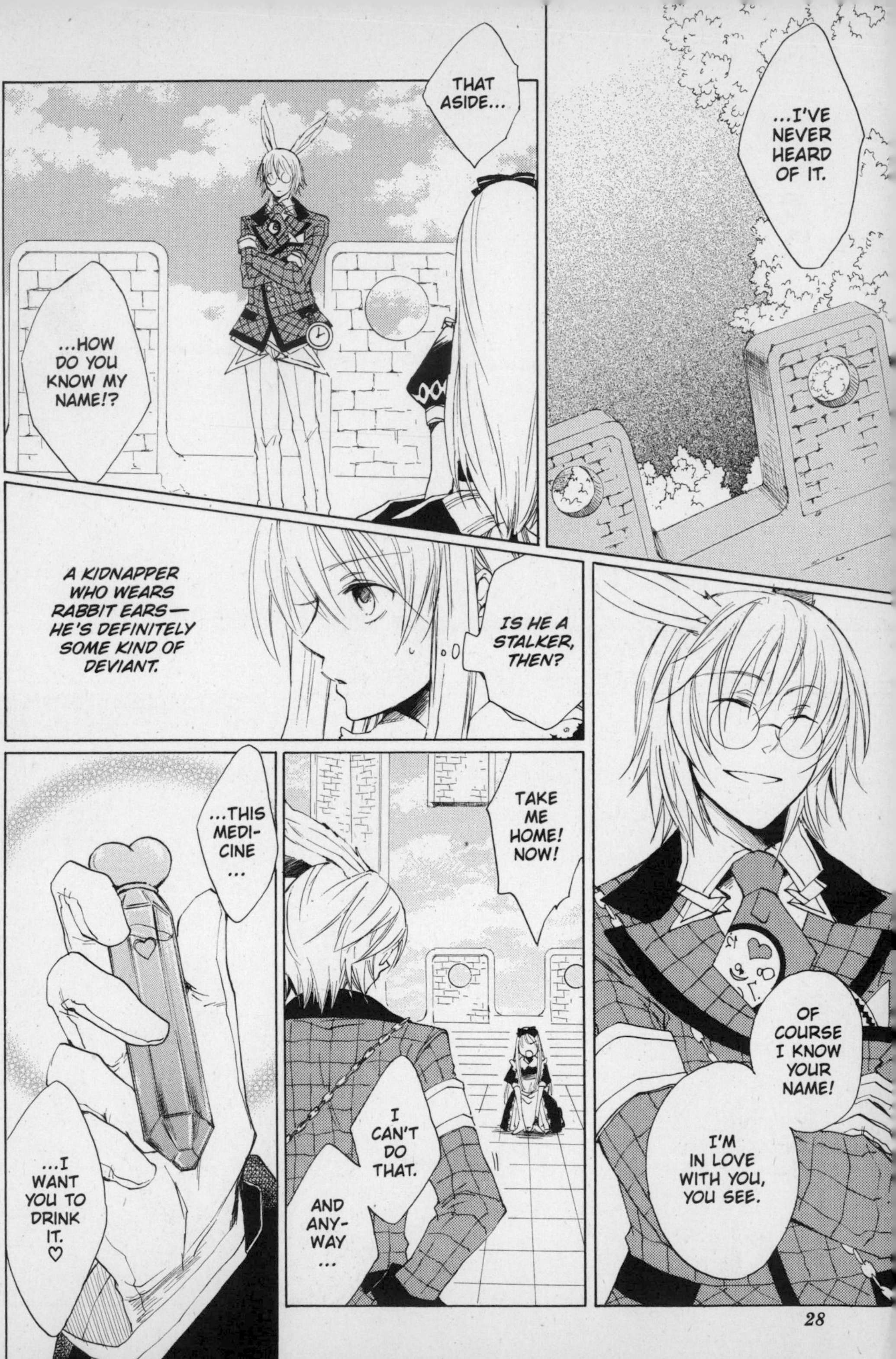
...I'VE NEVER HEARD OF IT.
THAT ASIDE...
...HOW DO YOU KNOW MY NAME!?
OF COURSE I KNOW YOUR NAME!
I'M IN LOVE WITH YOU, YOU SEE.
IS HE A STALKER, THEN?
A KIDNAPPER WHO WEARS RABBIT EARS—HE'S DEFINITELY SOME KIND OF DEVIANT.
TAKE ME HOME! NOW!
I CAN'T DO THAT.
AND ANY-WAY...
...THIS MEDI-CINE...
...I WANT YOU TO DRINK IT. ♡

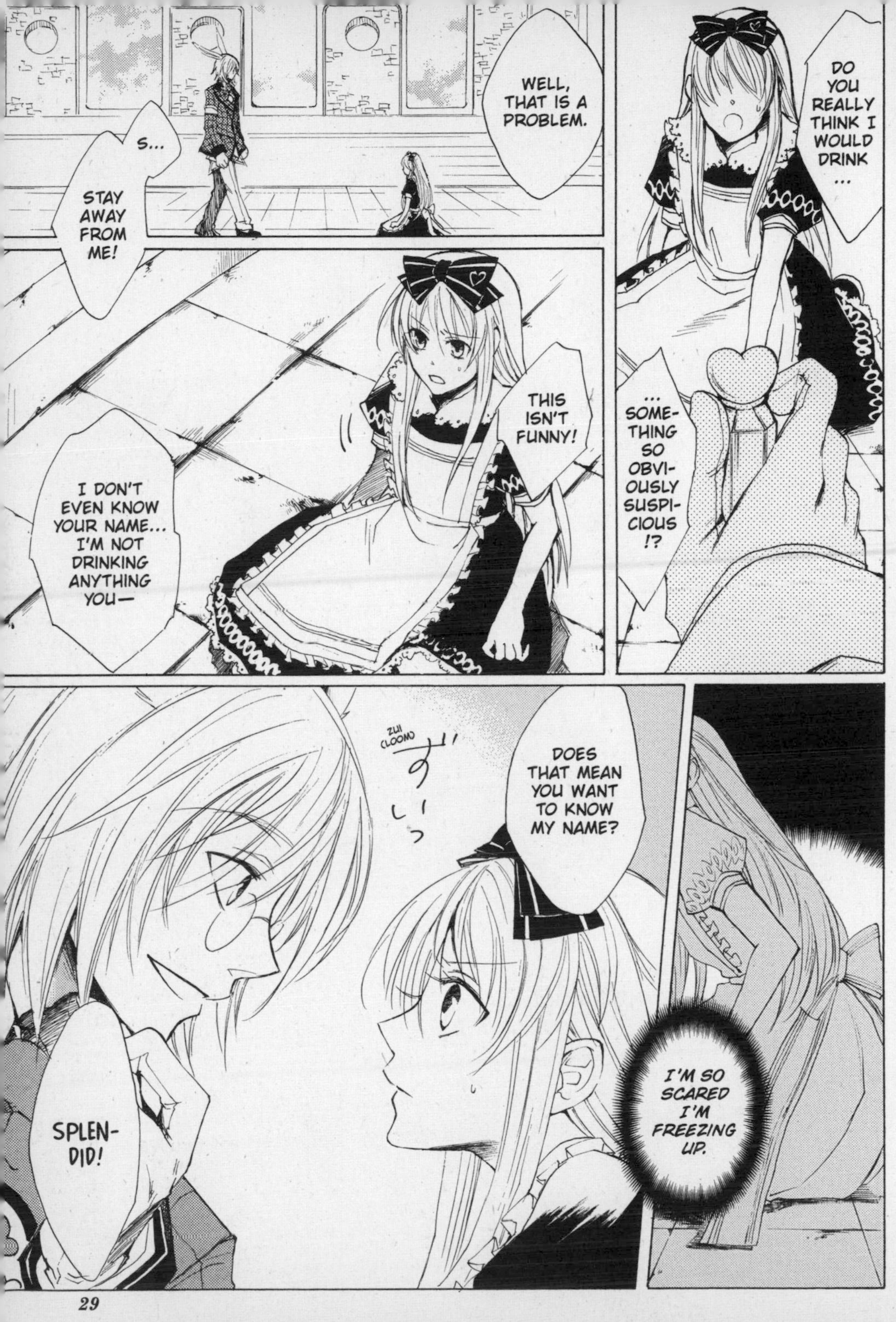
DO YOU REALLY THINK I WOULD DRINK ...
... SOMETHING SO OBVIOUSLY SUSPICIOUS !?
WELL, THAT IS A PROBLEM.
S...
STAY AWAY FROM ME!
THIS ISN'T FUNNY!
I DON'T EVEN KNOW YOUR NAME... I'M NOT DRINKING ANYTHING YOU—
I'M SO SCARED I'M FREEZING UP.
DOES THAT MEAN YOU WANT TO KNOW MY NAME?
ZUI (LOOM)
SPLEN- DID!

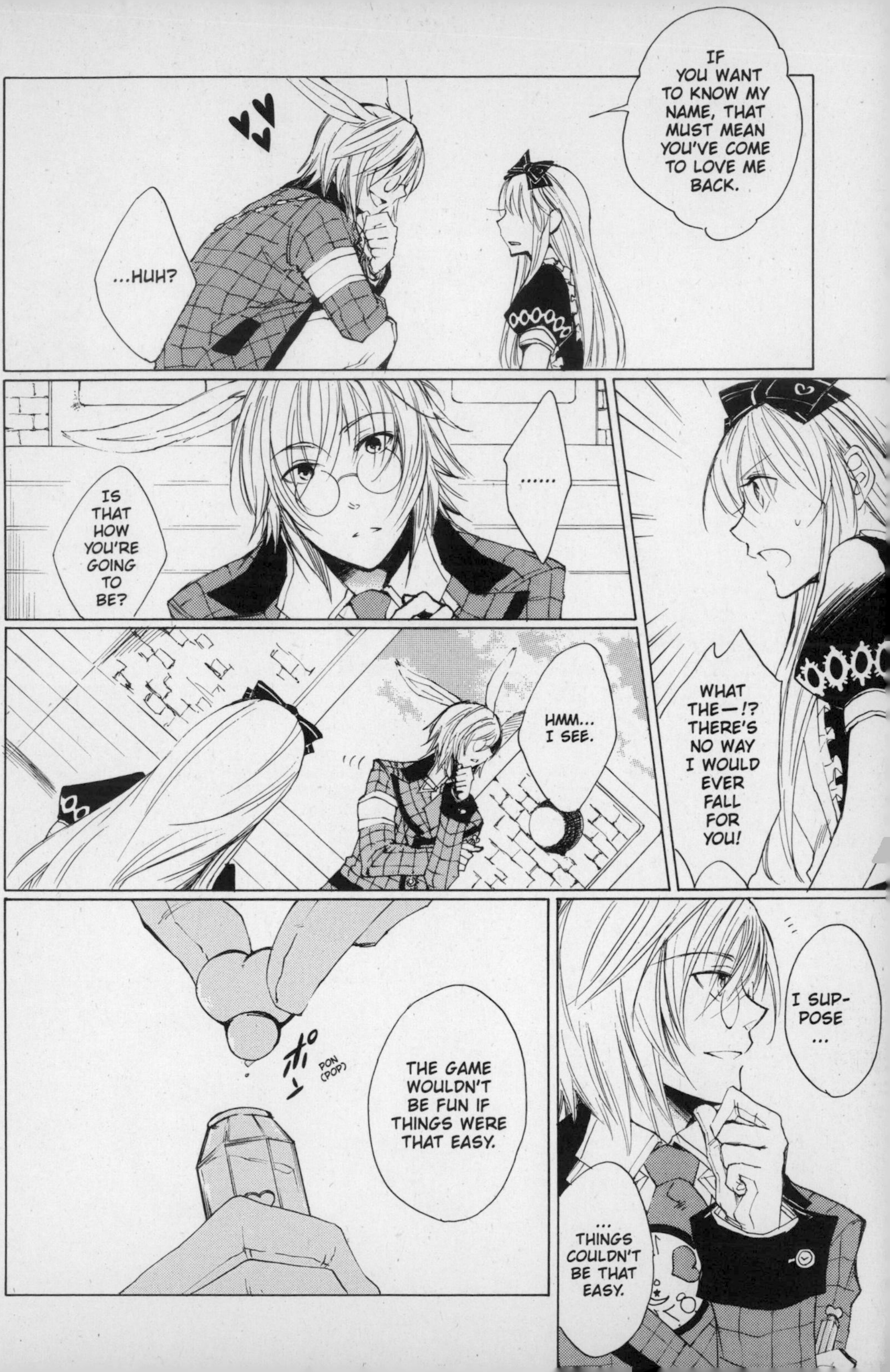
IF YOU WANT TO KNOW MY NAME, THAT MUST MEAN YOU'VE COME TO LOVE ME BACK.
...HUH?
WHAT THE—!? THERE'S NO WAY I WOULD EVER FALL FOR YOU!
......
IS THAT HOW YOU'RE GOING TO BE?
HMM... I SEE.
I SUP-POSE ...
... THINGS COULDN'T BE THAT EASY.
THE GAME WOULDN'T BE FUN IF THINGS WERE THAT EASY.
PON (POP)

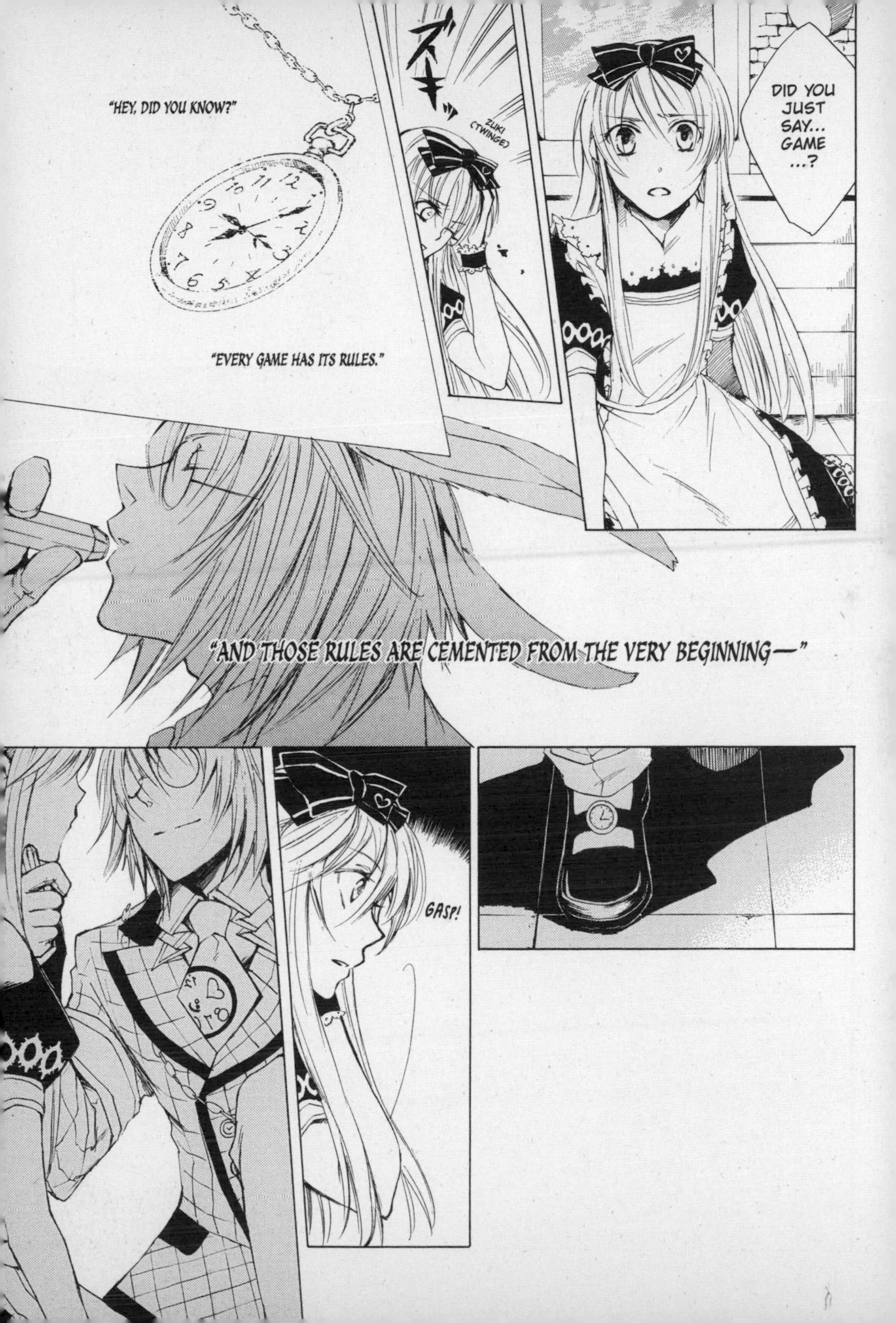
DID YOU JUST SAY... GAME ...?
ズキッ
ZUKI (TWINGE)
"HEY, DID YOU KNOW?"
"EVERY GAME HAS ITS RULES."
"AND THOSE RULES ARE CEMENTED FROM THE VERY BEGINNING—"
GASP!

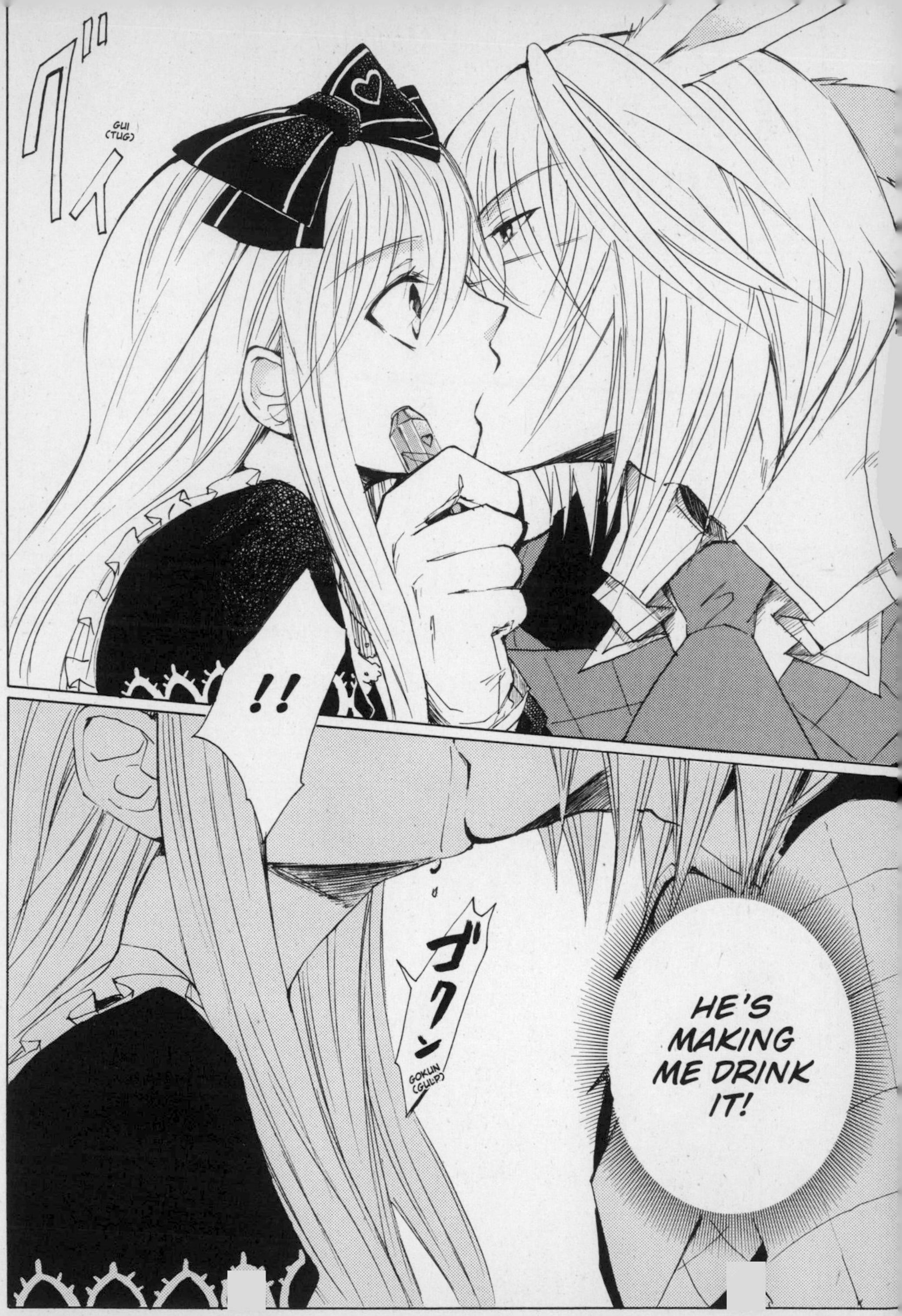
グイ
GUI (TUG)
!!
HE'S MAKING ME DRINK IT!
ゴクン
GOKUN (GULP)

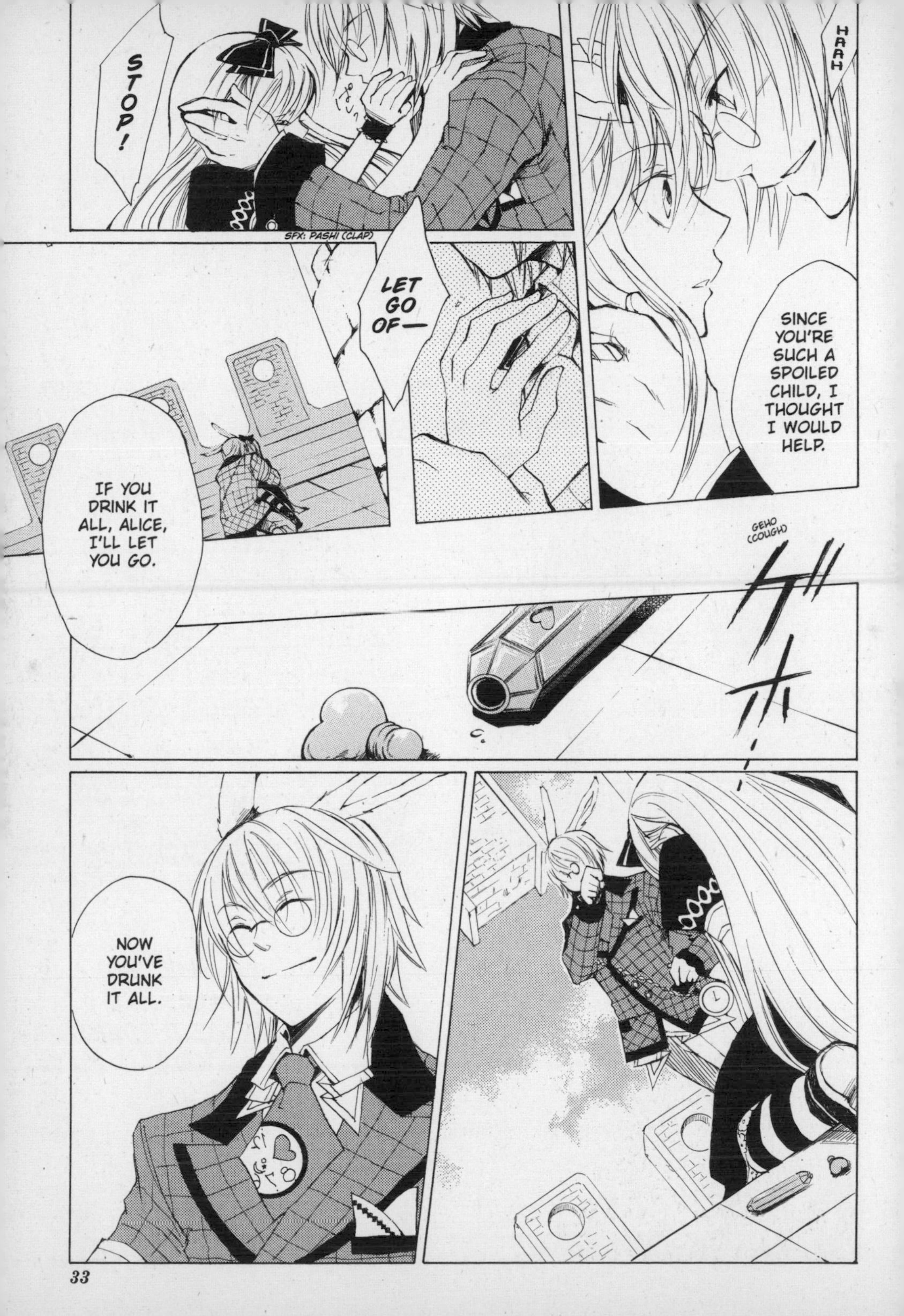
HAAH
SINCE YOU'RE SUCH A SPOILED CHILD, I THOUGHT I WOULD HELP.
STOP!
SFX: PASHI (CLAP)
LET GO OF—
IF YOU DRINK IT ALL, ALICE, I'LL LET YOU GO.
GEHO (COUGH)
NOW YOU'VE DRUNK IT ALL.

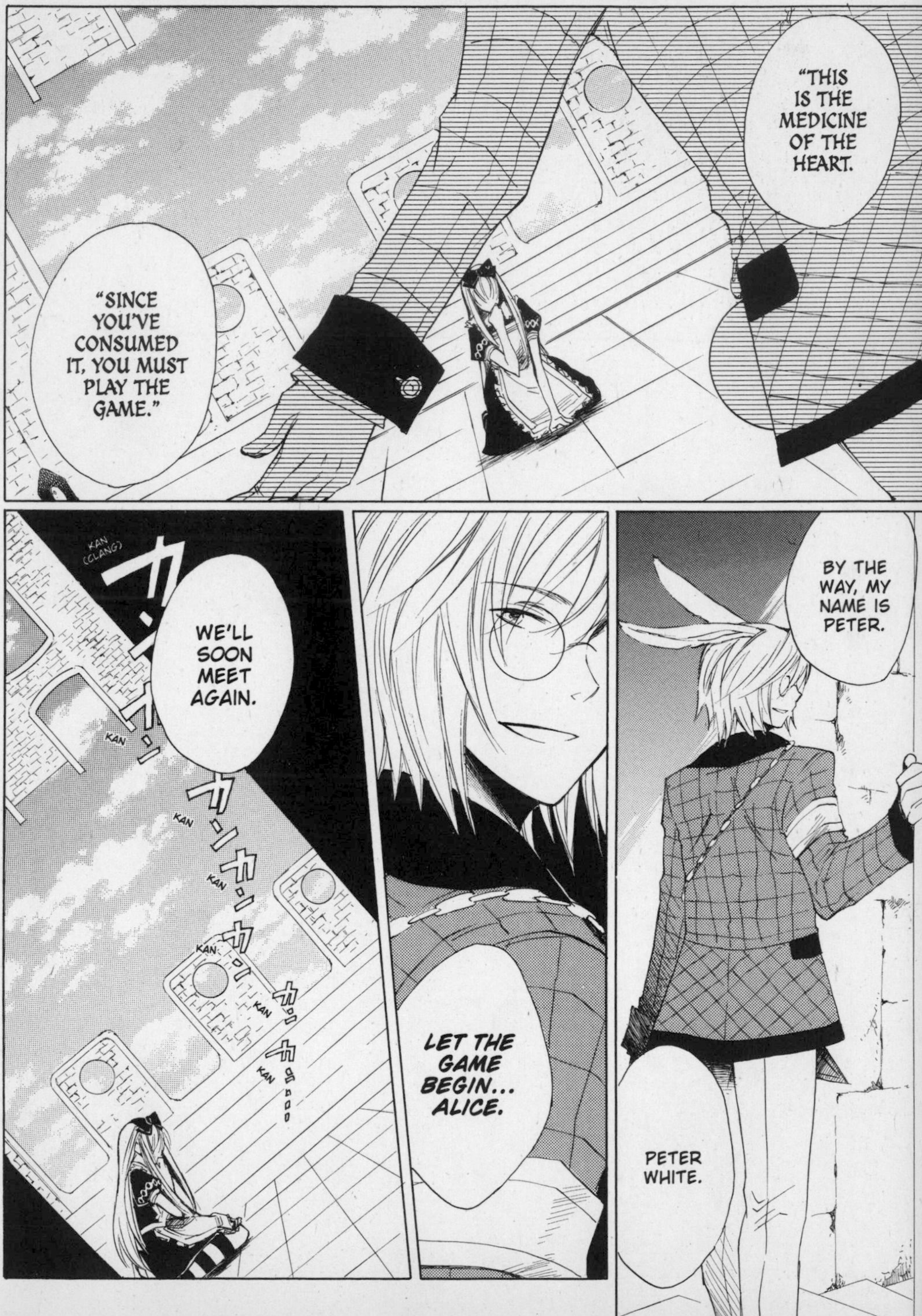
"THIS IS THE MEDICINE OF THE HEART.
"SINCE YOU'VE CONSUMED IT, YOU MUST PLAY THE GAME."
BY THE WAY, MY NAME IS PETER.
PETER WHITE.
LET THE GAME BEGIN... ALICE.
KAN (CLANG)
WE'LL SOON MEET AGAIN.
KAN
KAN
KAN
KAN
KAN
KAN

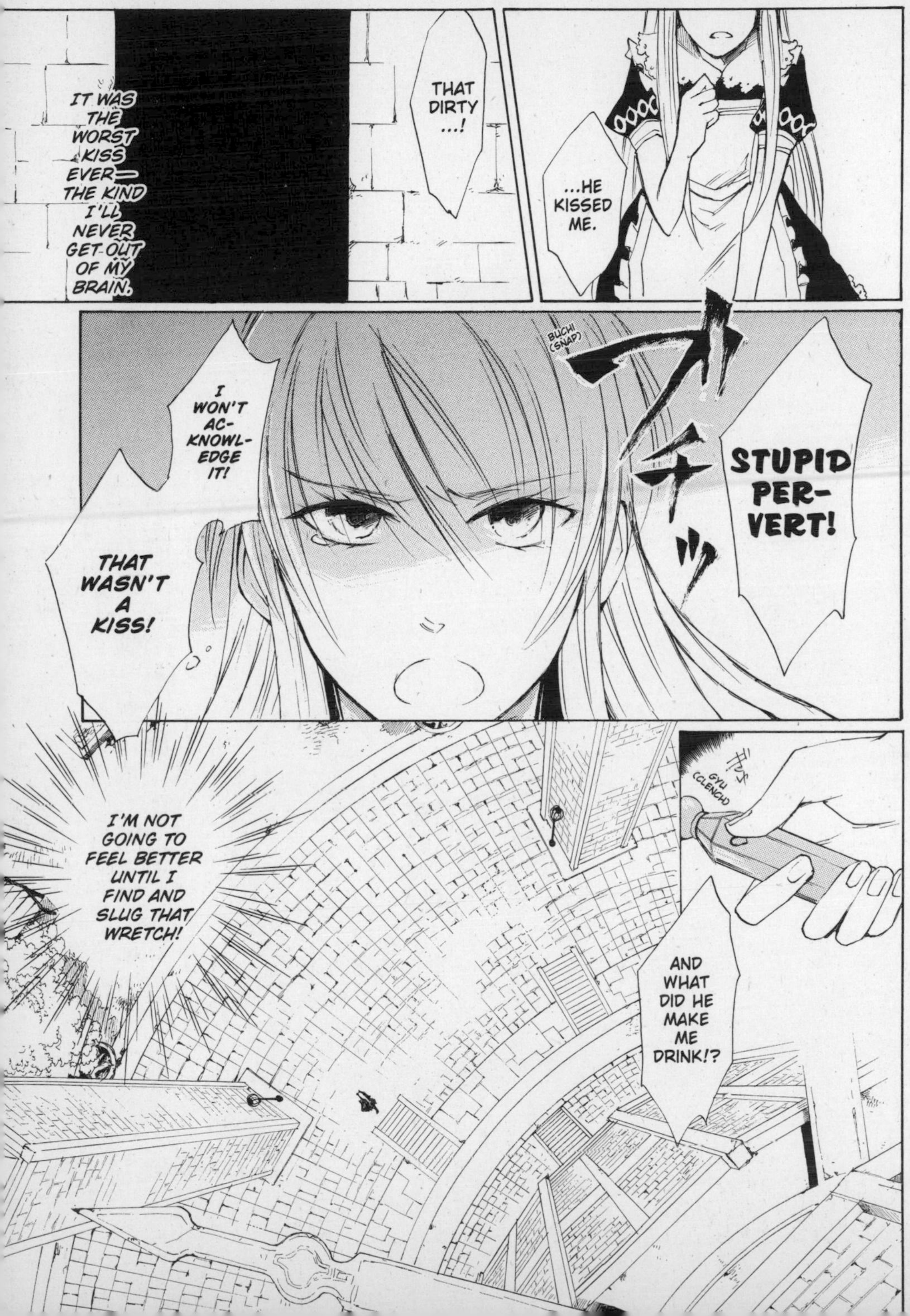
...HE KISSED ME.
THAT DIRTY ...!
IT WAS THE WORST KISS EVER—THE KIND I'LL NEVER GET OUT OF MY BRAIN.
BUCHI (SNAP)
STUPID PER-VERT!
I WON'T AC-KNOWL-EDGE IT!
THAT WASN'T A KISS!
GYU (CLENCH)
AND WHAT DID HE MAKE ME DRINK!?
I'M NOT GOING TO FEEL BETTER UNTIL I FIND AND SLUG THAT WRETCH!

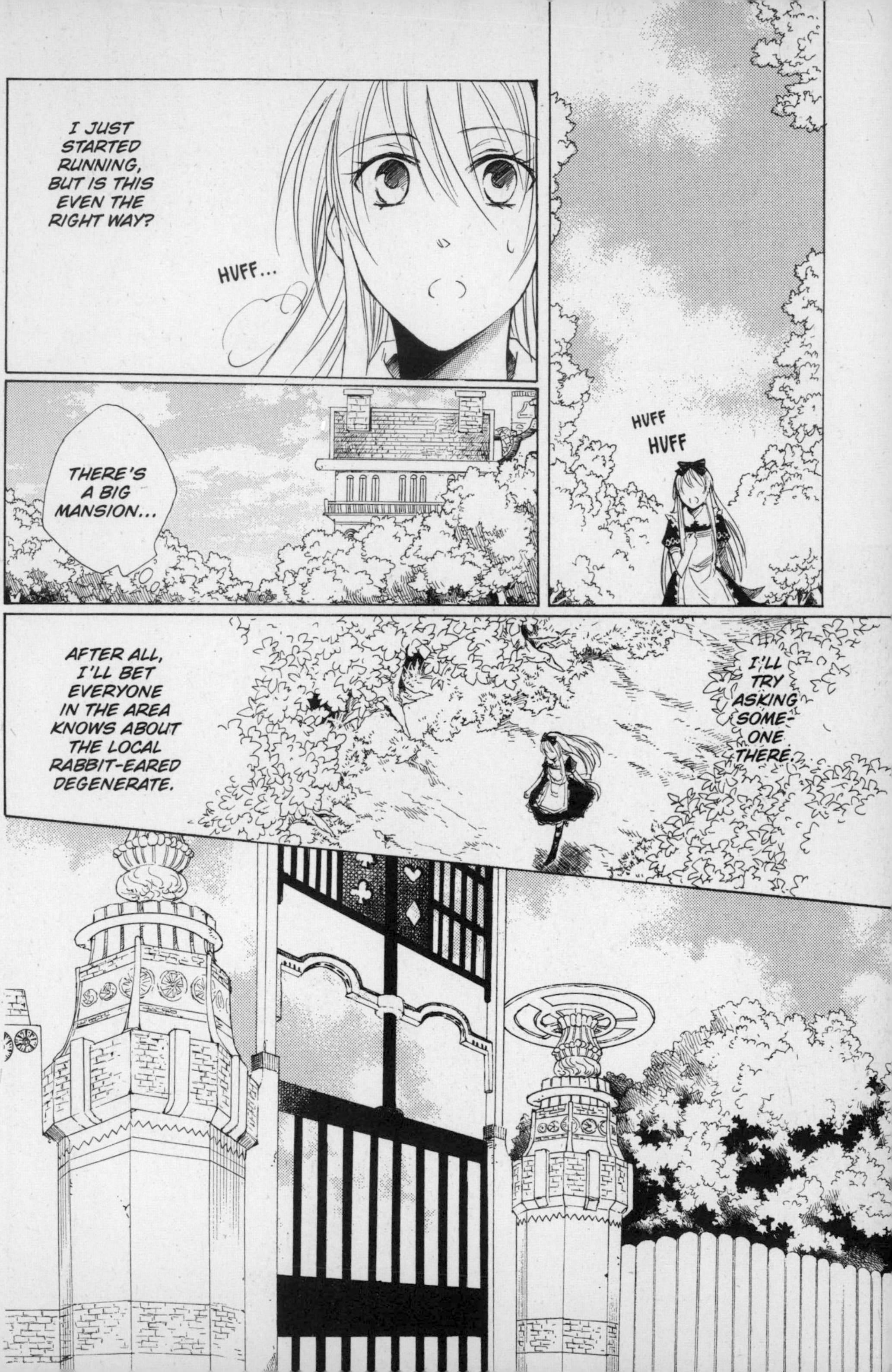
HUFF
HUFF
I JUST STARTED RUNNING, BUT IS THIS EVEN THE RIGHT WAY?
HUFF...
THERE'S A BIG MANSION...
I'LL TRY ASKING SOME-ONE THERE.
AFTER ALL, I'LL BET EVERYONE IN THE AREA KNOWS ABOUT THE LOCAL RABBIT-EARED DEGENERATE.

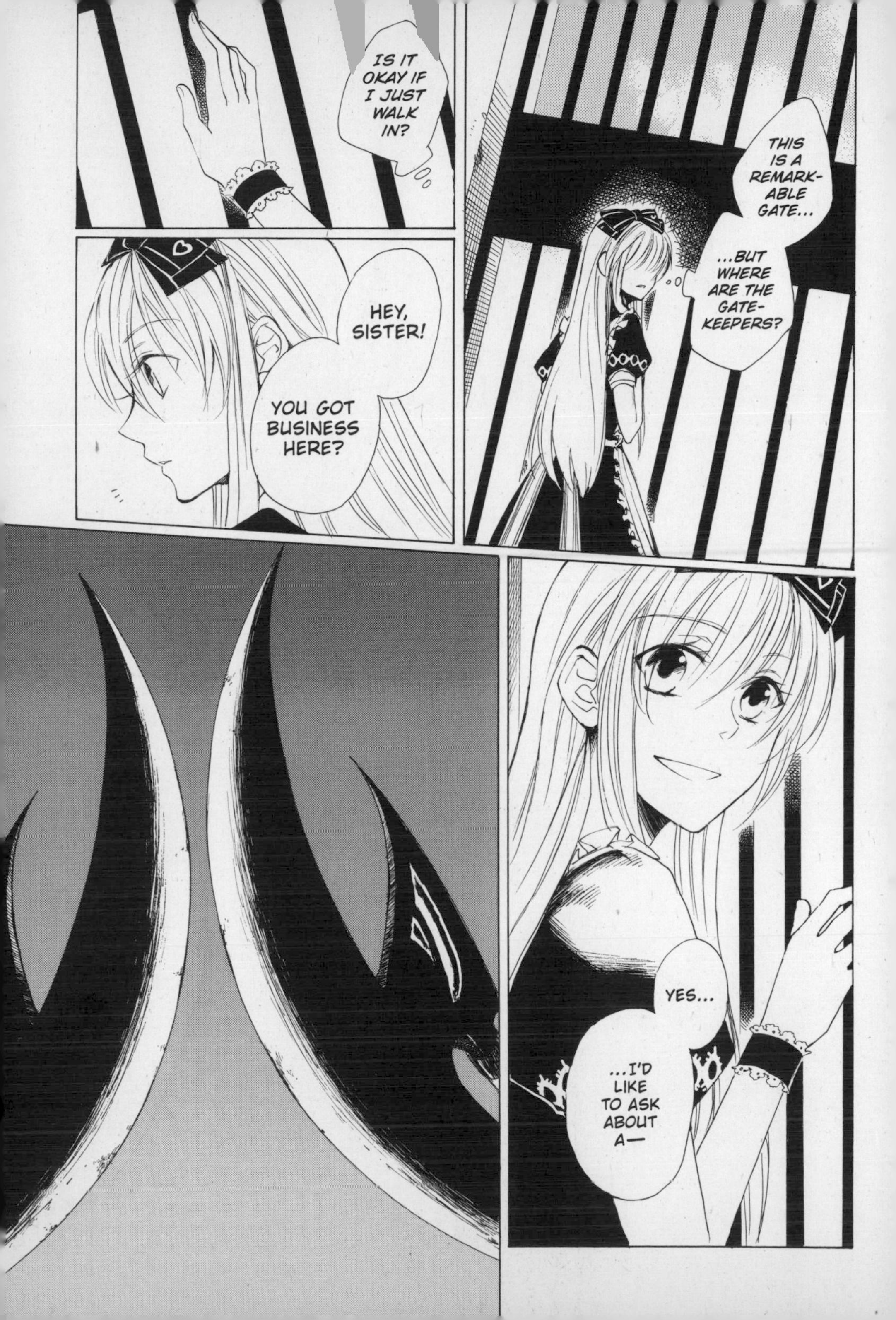
THIS IS A REMARK-ABLE GATE...
...BUT WHERE ARE THE GATE-KEEPERS?
IS IT OKAY IF I JUST WALK IN?
HEY, SISTER!
YOU GOT BUSINESS HERE?
YES...
...I'D LIKE TO ASK ABOUT A—

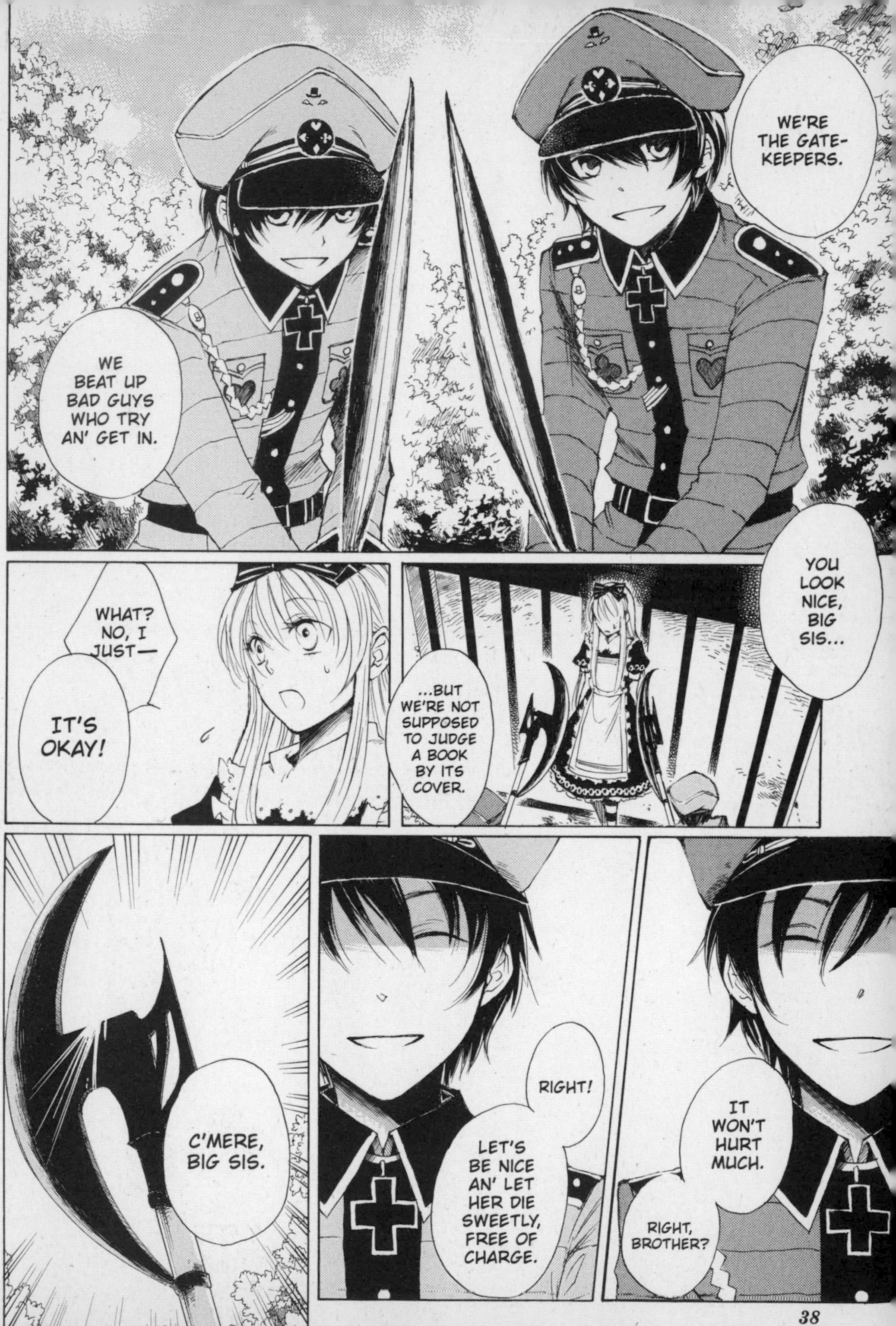
WE'RE THE GATE-KEEPERS.
WE BEAT UP BAD GUYS WHO TRY AN' GET IN.
YOU LOOK NICE, BIG SIS...
...BUT WE'RE NOT SUPPOSED TO JUDGE A BOOK BY ITS COVER.
WHAT? NO, I JUST—
IT'S OKAY!
IT WON'T HURT MUCH.
RIGHT, BROTHER?
RIGHT!
LET'S BE NICE AN' LET HER DIE SWEETLY, FREE OF CHARGE.
C'MERE, BIG SIS.

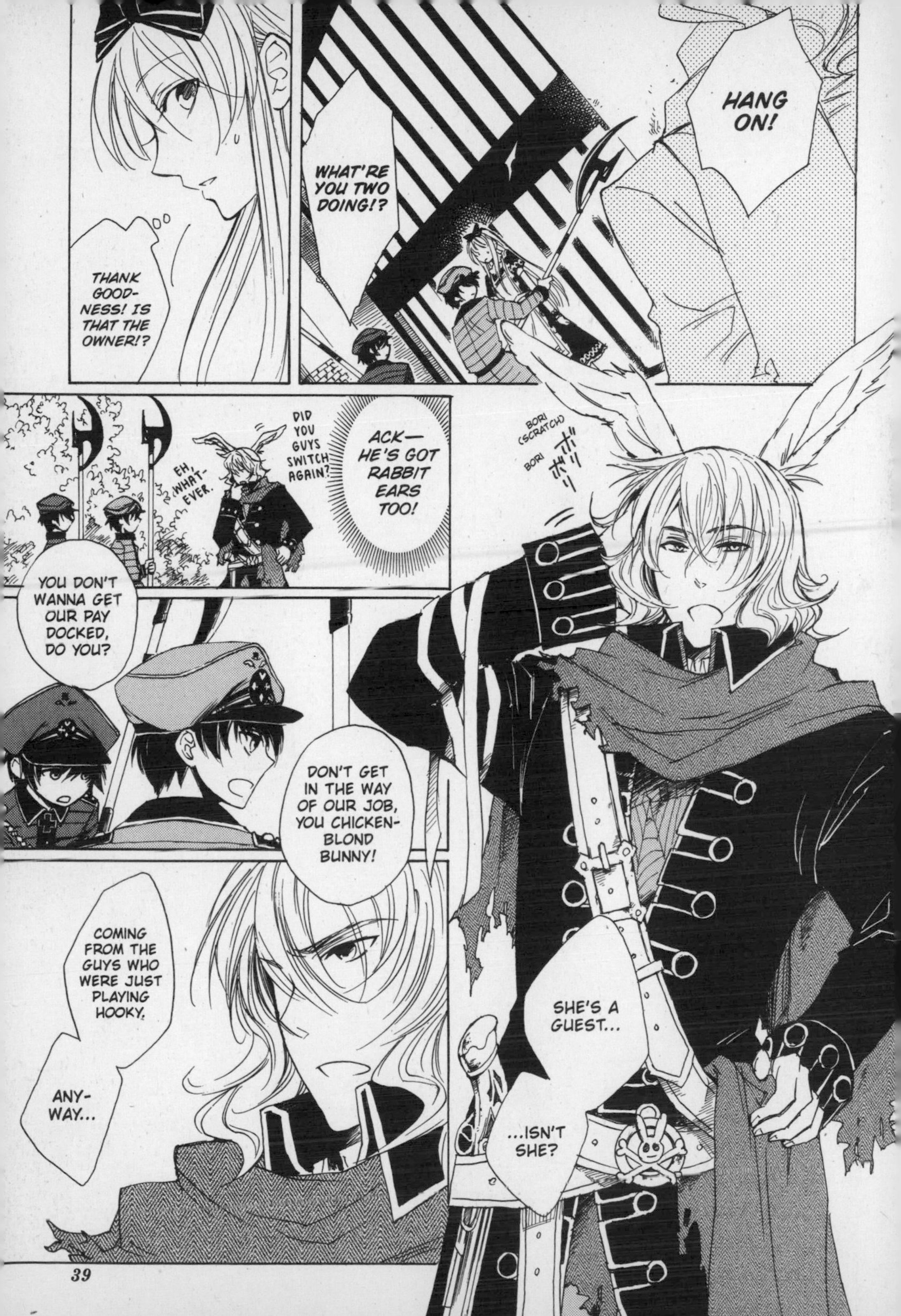

HANG ON!
WHAT'RE YOU TWO DOING!?
THANK GOODNESS! IS THAT THE OWNER!?
ACK— HE'S GOT RABBIT EARS TOO!
DID YOU GUYS SWITCH AGAIN?
EH, WHATEVER.
DON'T GET IN THE WAY OF OUR JOB, YOU CHICKEN-BLOND BUNNY!
YOU DON'T WANNA GET OUR PAY DOCKED, DO YOU?
COMING FROM THE GUYS WHO WERE JUST PLAYING HOOKY.
ANYWAY...
BORI (SCRATCH) BORI
ボリ ボリ
SHE'S A GUEST...
...ISN'T SHE?

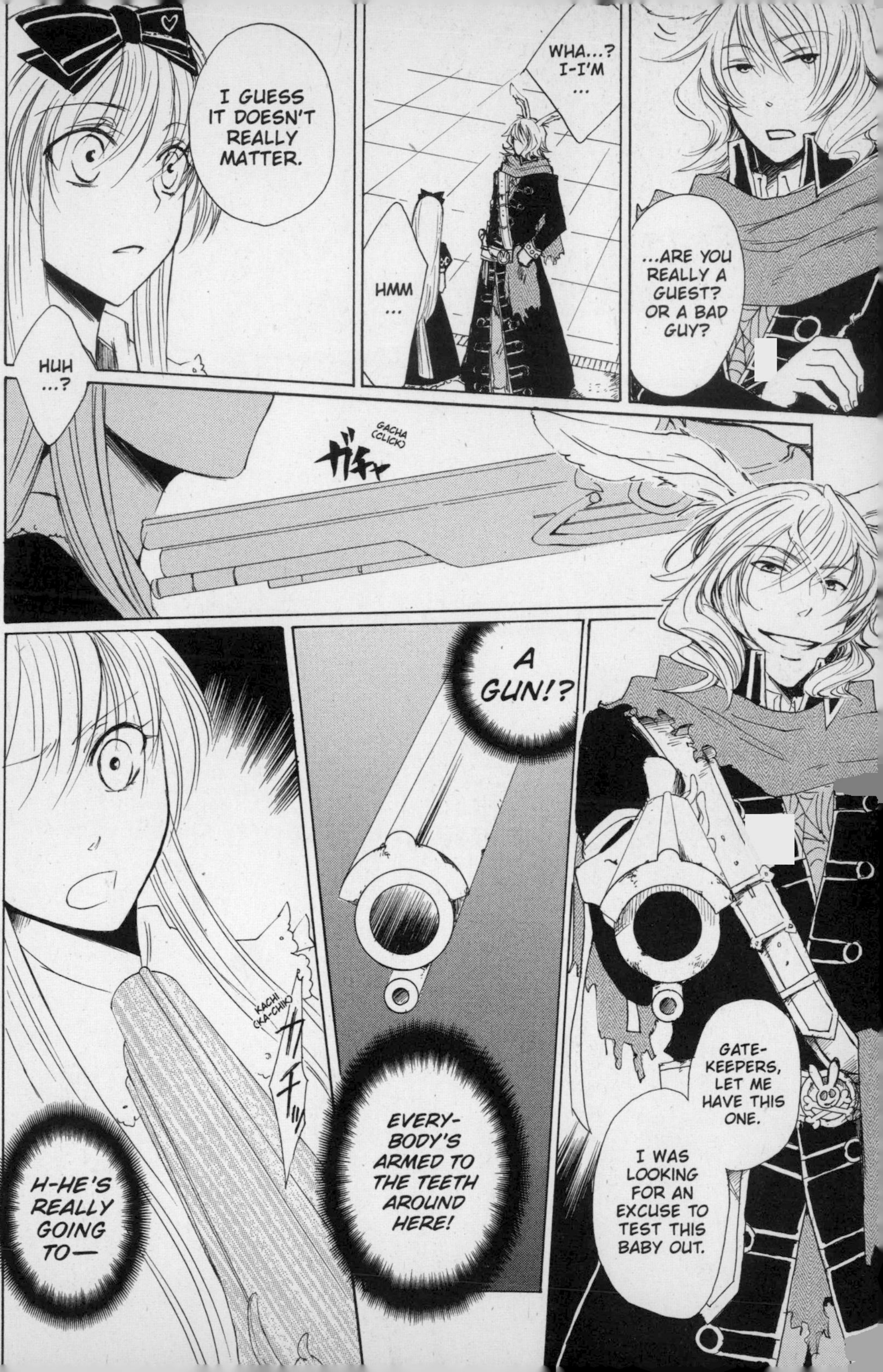
...ARE YOU REALLY A GUEST? OR A BAD GUY?
WHA...? I-I'M ...
HMM ...
I GUESS IT DOESN'T REALLY MATTER.
HUH ...?
GACHA (CLICK)
ガチャ
GATE-KEEPERS, LET ME HAVE THIS ONE.
I WAS LOOKING FOR AN EXCUSE TO TEST THIS BABY OUT.
A GUN!?
EVERY-BODY'S ARMED TO THE TEETH AROUND HERE!
KACHI (KA-CHIK)
カチ
H-HE'S REALLY GOING TO—

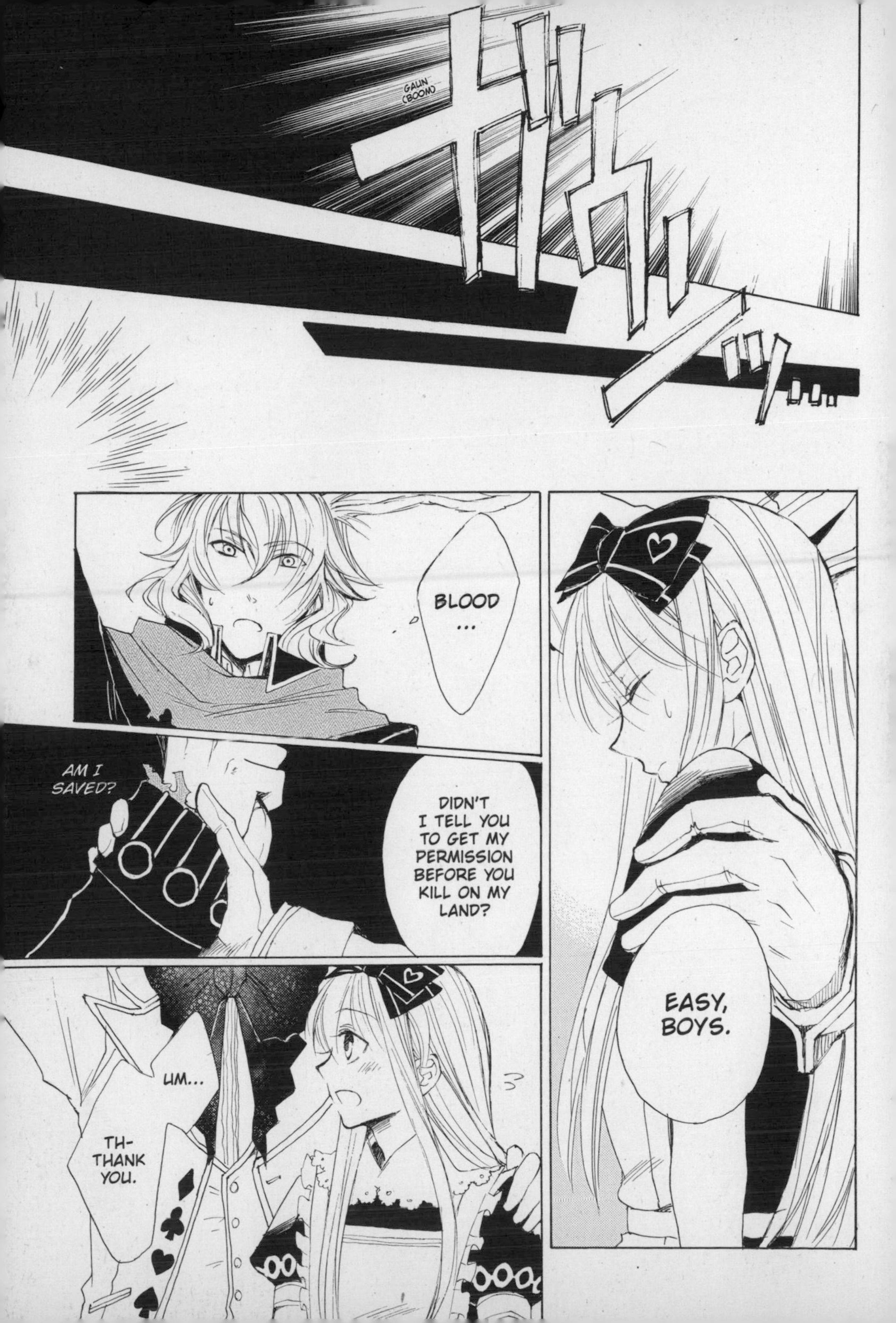
GAUN (BOOM)
EASY, BOYS.
BLOOD ...
AM I SAVED?
DIDN'T I TELL YOU TO GET MY PERMISSION BEFORE YOU KILL ON MY LAND?
UM...
TH-THANK YOU.

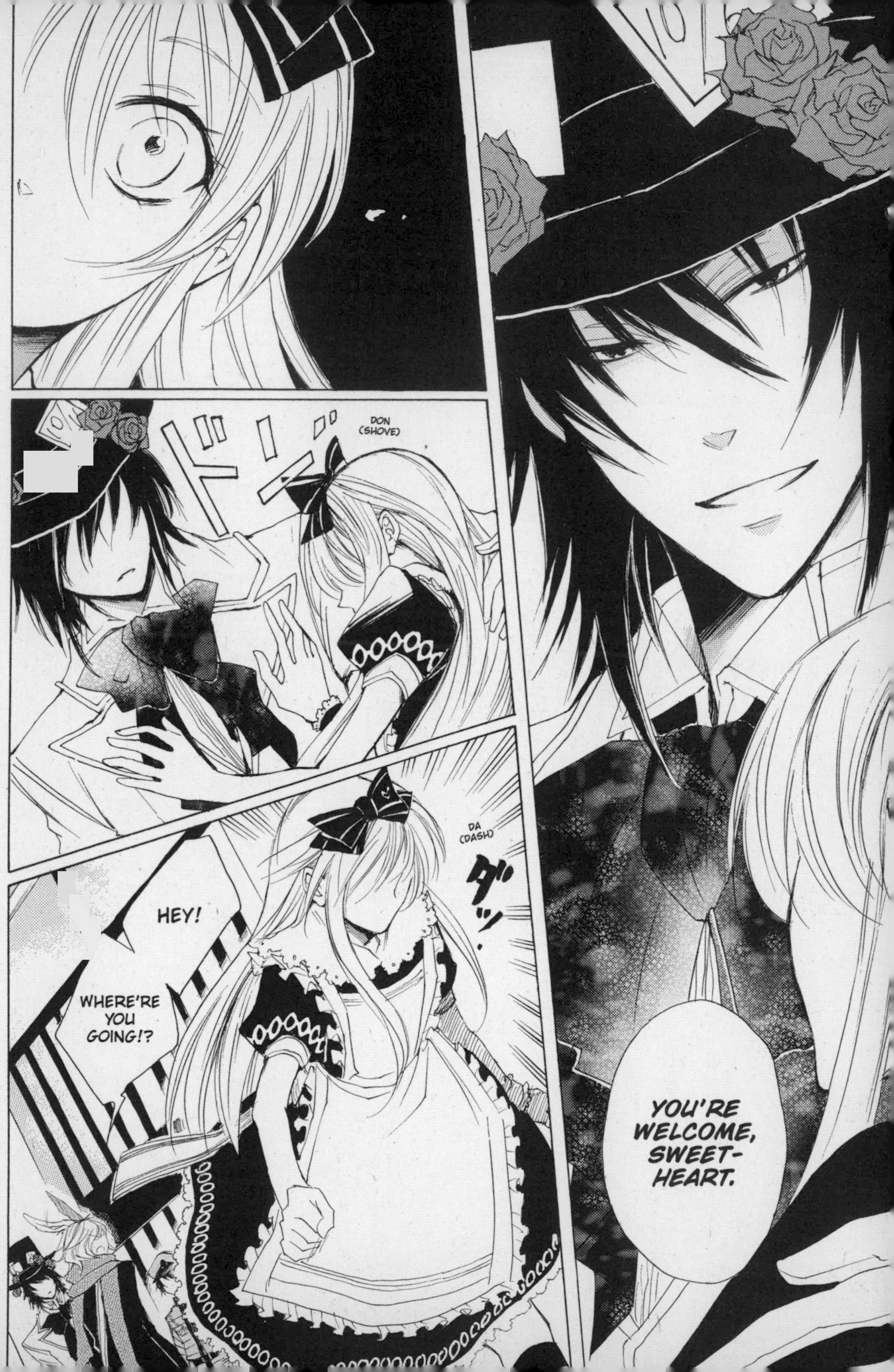
YOU'RE WELCOME, SWEET-HEART.
DON (SHOVE)
DA (DASH)
HEY!
WHERE'RE YOU GOING!?

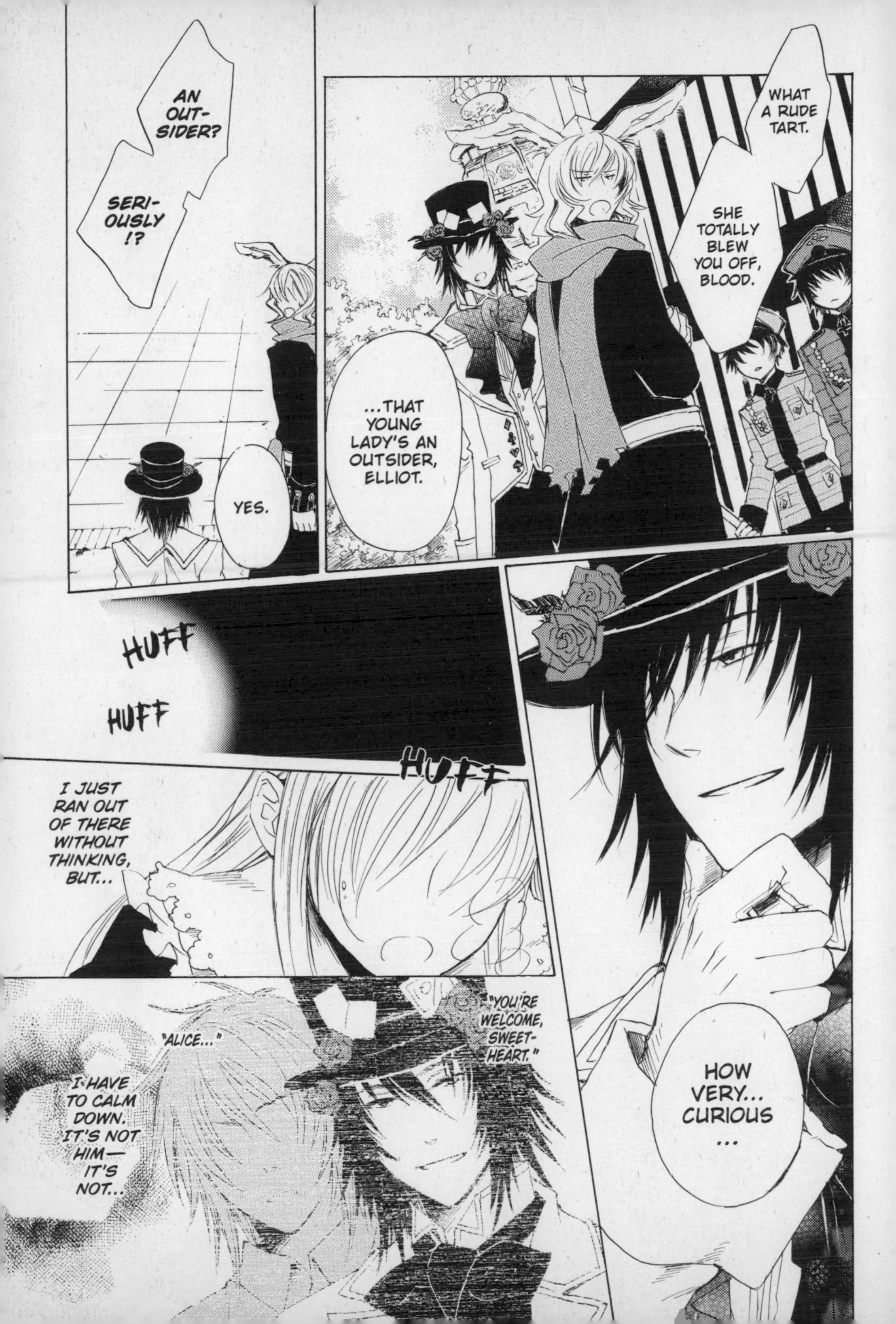
WHAT A RUDE TART.
SHE TOTALLY BLEW YOU OFF, BLOOD.
...THAT YOUNG LADY'S AN OUTSIDER, ELLIOT.
AN OUTSIDER?
SERIOUSLY!?
YES.
HOW VERY... CURIOUS ...
HUFF
HUFF
HUFF
I JUST RAN OUT OF THERE WITHOUT THINKING, BUT...
"YOU'RE WELCOME, SWEETHEART."
"ALICE..."
I HAVE TO CALM DOWN. IT'S NOT HIM—IT'S NOT...

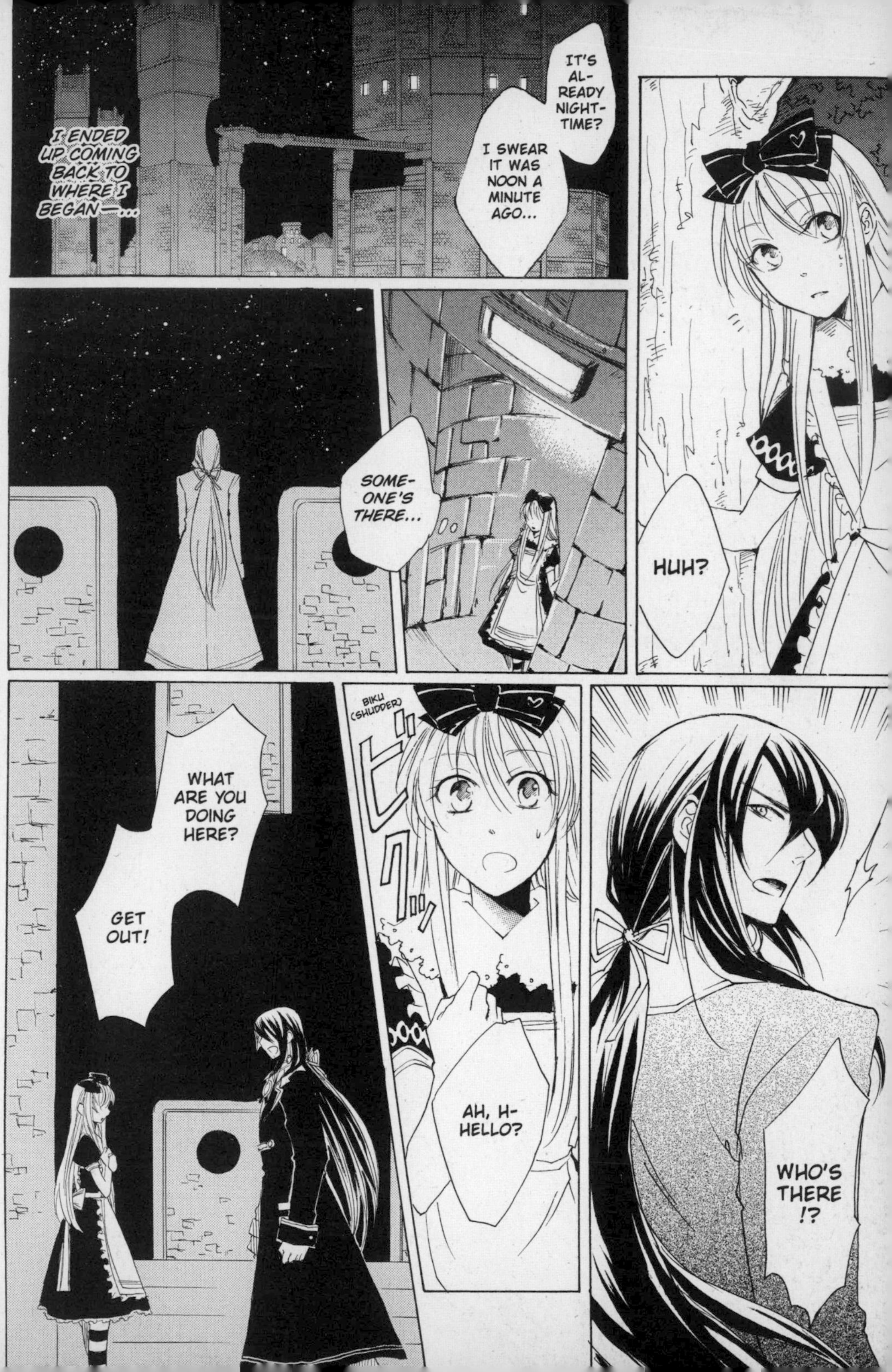
HUH?
IT'S AL-READY NIGHT-TIME?
I SWEAR IT WAS NOON A MINUTE AGO...
I ENDED UP COMING BACK TO WHERE I BEGAN—...
SOME-ONE'S THERE...
WHO'S THERE !?
BIKU (SHUDDER)
AH, H-HELLO?
WHAT ARE YOU DOING HERE?
GET OUT!

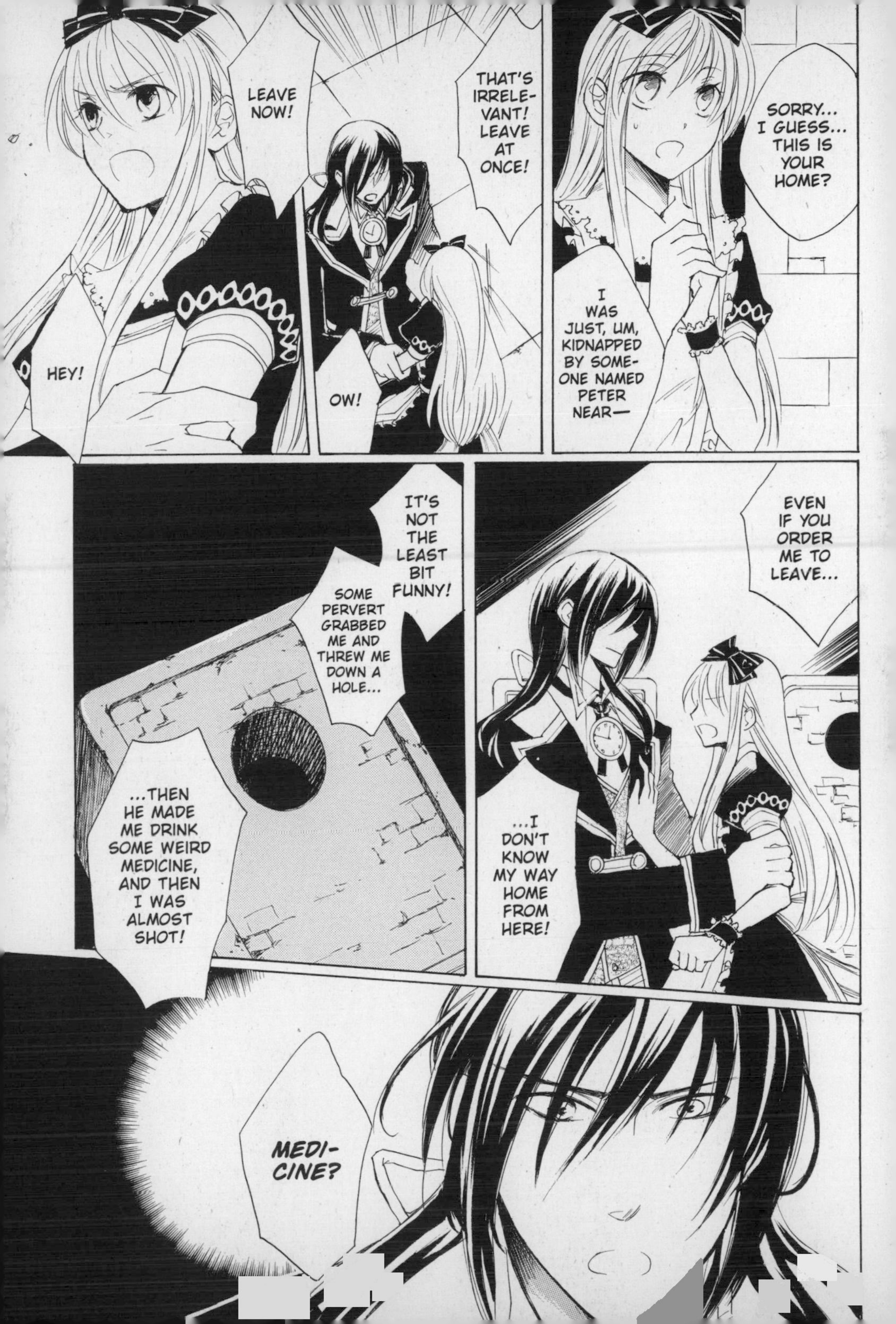
SORRY... I GUESS... THIS IS YOUR HOME?
I WAS JUST, UM, KIDNAPPED BY SOME-ONE NAMED PETER NEAR—
THAT'S IRRELE-VANT! LEAVE AT ONCE!
OW!
LEAVE NOW!
HEY!
EVEN IF YOU ORDER ME TO LEAVE...
...I DON'T KNOW MY WAY HOME FROM HERE!
IT'S NOT THE LEAST BIT FUNNY!
SOME PERVERT GRABBED ME AND THREW ME DOWN A HOLE...
...THEN HE MADE ME DRINK SOME WEIRD MEDICINE, AND THEN I WAS ALMOST SHOT!
MEDI-CINE?

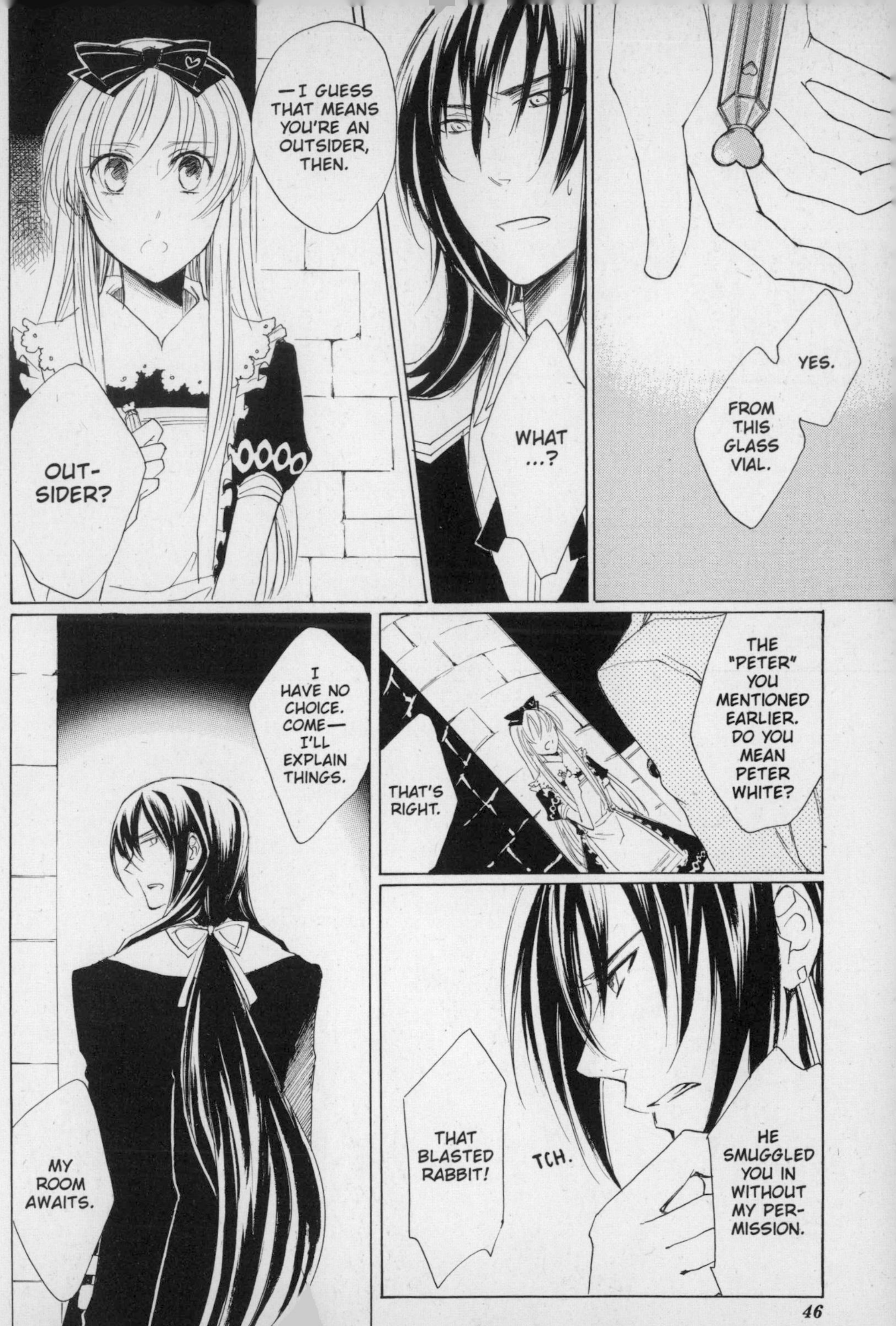
YES.
FROM THIS GLASS VIAL.
WHAT ...?
—I GUESS THAT MEANS YOU'RE AN OUTSIDER, THEN.
OUT-SIDER?
THE "PETER" YOU MENTIONED EARLIER. DO YOU MEAN PETER WHITE?
THAT'S RIGHT.
HE SMUGGLED YOU IN WITHOUT MY PER-MISSION.
TCH.
THAT BLASTED RABBIT!
I HAVE NO CHOICE. COME— I'LL EXPLAIN THINGS.
MY ROOM AWAITS.

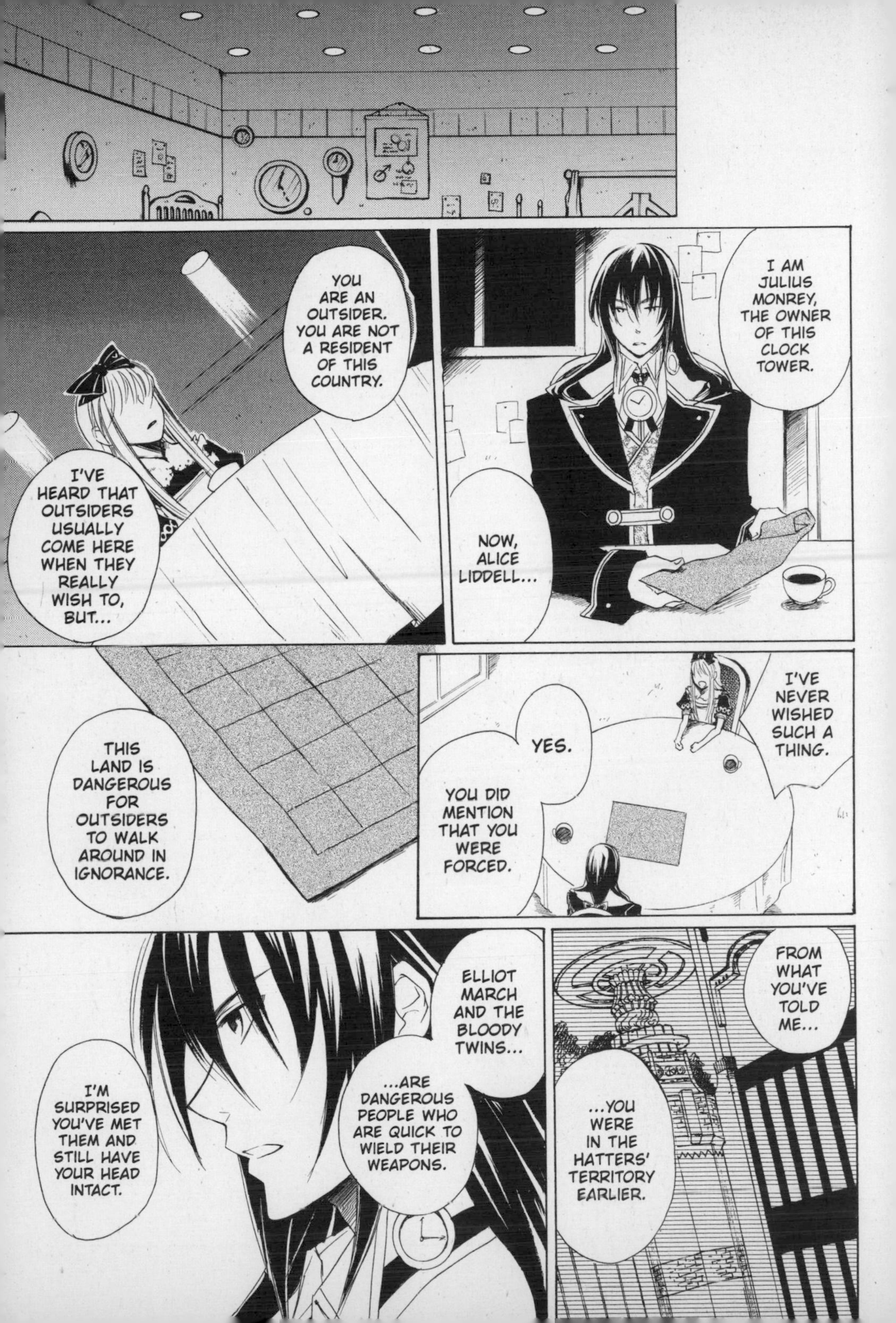
I AM JULIUS MONREY, THE OWNER OF THIS CLOCK TOWER.
NOW, ALICE LIDDELL...
YOU ARE AN OUTSIDER. YOU ARE NOT A RESIDENT OF THIS COUNTRY.
I'VE HEARD THAT OUTSIDERS USUALLY COME HERE WHEN THEY REALLY WISH TO, BUT...
I'VE NEVER WISHED SUCH A THING.
YES.
YOU DID MENTION THAT YOU WERE FORCED.
THIS LAND IS DANGEROUS FOR OUTSIDERS TO WALK AROUND IN IGNORANCE.
FROM WHAT YOU'VE TOLD ME...
...YOU WERE IN THE HATTERS' TERRITORY EARLIER.
ELLIOT MARCH AND THE BLOODY TWINS...
...ARE DANGEROUS PEOPLE WHO ARE QUICK TO WIELD THEIR WEAPONS.
I'M SURPRISED YOU'VE MET THEM AND STILL HAVE YOUR HEAD INTACT.

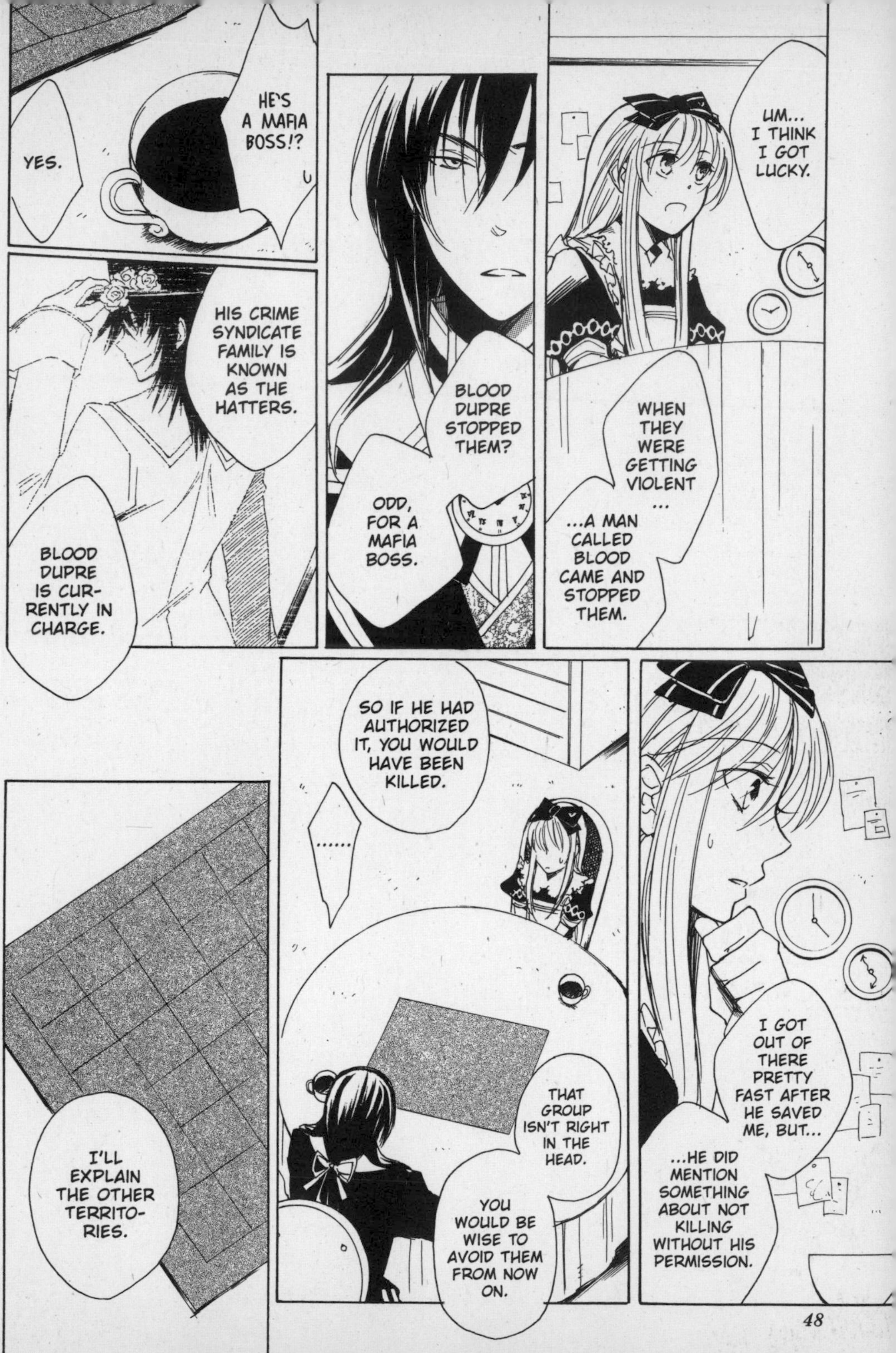
UM... I THINK I GOT LUCKY.
WHEN THEY WERE GETTING VIOLENT ...
...A MAN CALLED BLOOD CAME AND STOPPED THEM.
BLOOD DUPRE STOPPED THEM?
ODD, FOR A MAFIA BOSS.
HE'S A MAFIA BOSS!?
YES.
HIS CRIME SYNDICATE FAMILY IS KNOWN AS THE HATTERS.
BLOOD DUPRE IS CUR-RENTLY IN CHARGE.
I GOT OUT OF THERE PRETTY FAST AFTER HE SAVED ME, BUT...
...HE DID MENTION SOMETHING ABOUT NOT KILLING WITHOUT HIS PERMISSION.
SO IF HE HAD AUTHORIZED IT, YOU WOULD HAVE BEEN KILLED.
......
THAT GROUP ISN'T RIGHT IN THE HEAD.
YOU WOULD BE WISE TO AVOID THEM FROM NOW ON.
I'LL EXPLAIN THE OTHER TERRITO-RIES.

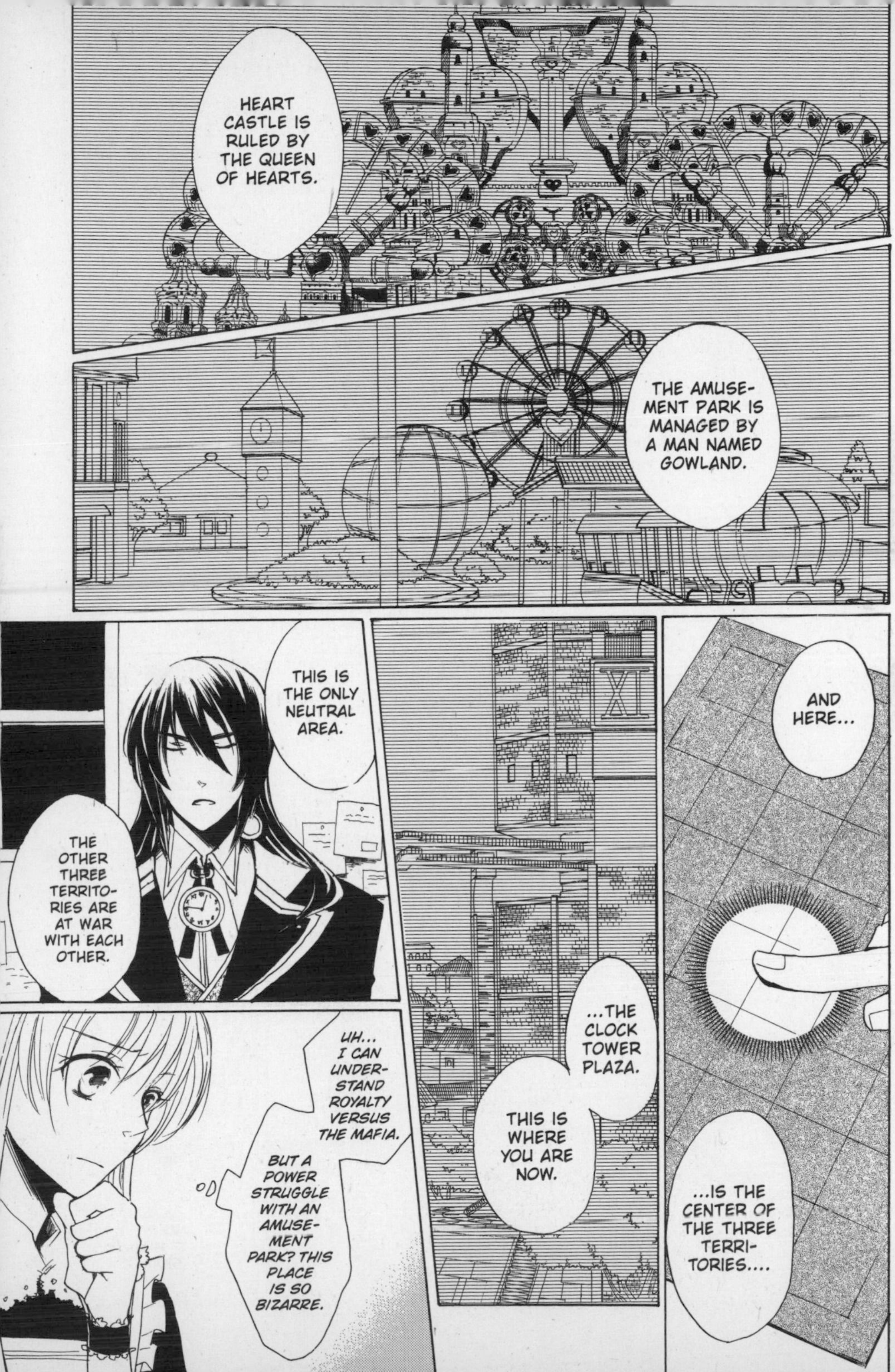
HEART CASTLE IS RULED BY THE QUEEN OF HEARTS.
THE AMUSEMENT PARK IS MANAGED BY A MAN NAMED GOWLAND.
AND HERE...
...IS THE CENTER OF THE THREE TERRITORIES....
...THE CLOCK TOWER PLAZA.
THIS IS WHERE YOU ARE NOW.
XI
THIS IS THE ONLY NEUTRAL AREA.
THE OTHER THREE TERRITORIES ARE AT WAR WITH EACH OTHER.
UH... I CAN UNDERSTAND ROYALTY VERSUS THE MAFIA.
BUT A POWER STRUGGLE WITH AN AMUSEMENT PARK? THIS PLACE IS SO BIZARRE.

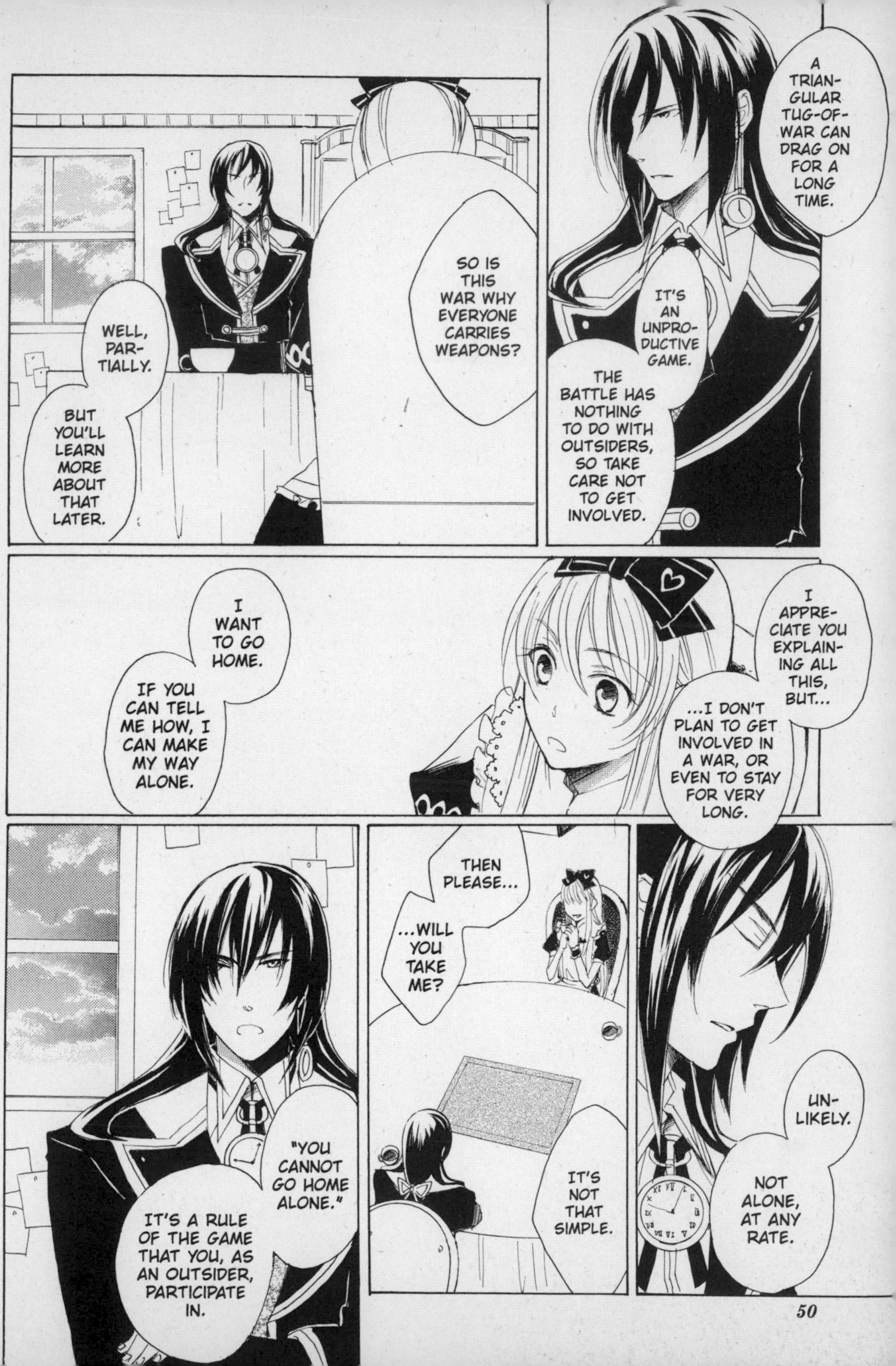
A TRIANGULAR TUG-OF-WAR CAN DRAG ON FOR A LONG TIME.
IT'S AN UNPRODUCTIVE GAME.
THE BATTLE HAS NOTHING TO DO WITH OUTSIDERS, SO TAKE CARE NOT TO GET INVOLVED.
SO IS THIS WAR WHY EVERYONE CARRIES WEAPONS?
WELL, PARTIALLY.
BUT YOU'LL LEARN MORE ABOUT THAT LATER.
I APPRECIATE YOU EXPLAINING ALL THIS, BUT...
...I DON'T PLAN TO GET INVOLVED IN A WAR, OR EVEN TO STAY FOR VERY LONG.
I WANT TO GO HOME.
IF YOU CAN TELL ME HOW, I CAN MAKE MY WAY ALONE.
UNLIKELY.
NOT ALONE, AT ANY RATE.
THEN PLEASE...
...WILL YOU TAKE ME?
IT'S NOT THAT SIMPLE.
"YOU CANNOT GO HOME ALONE."
IT'S A RULE OF THE GAME THAT YOU, AS AN OUTSIDER, PARTICIPATE IN.

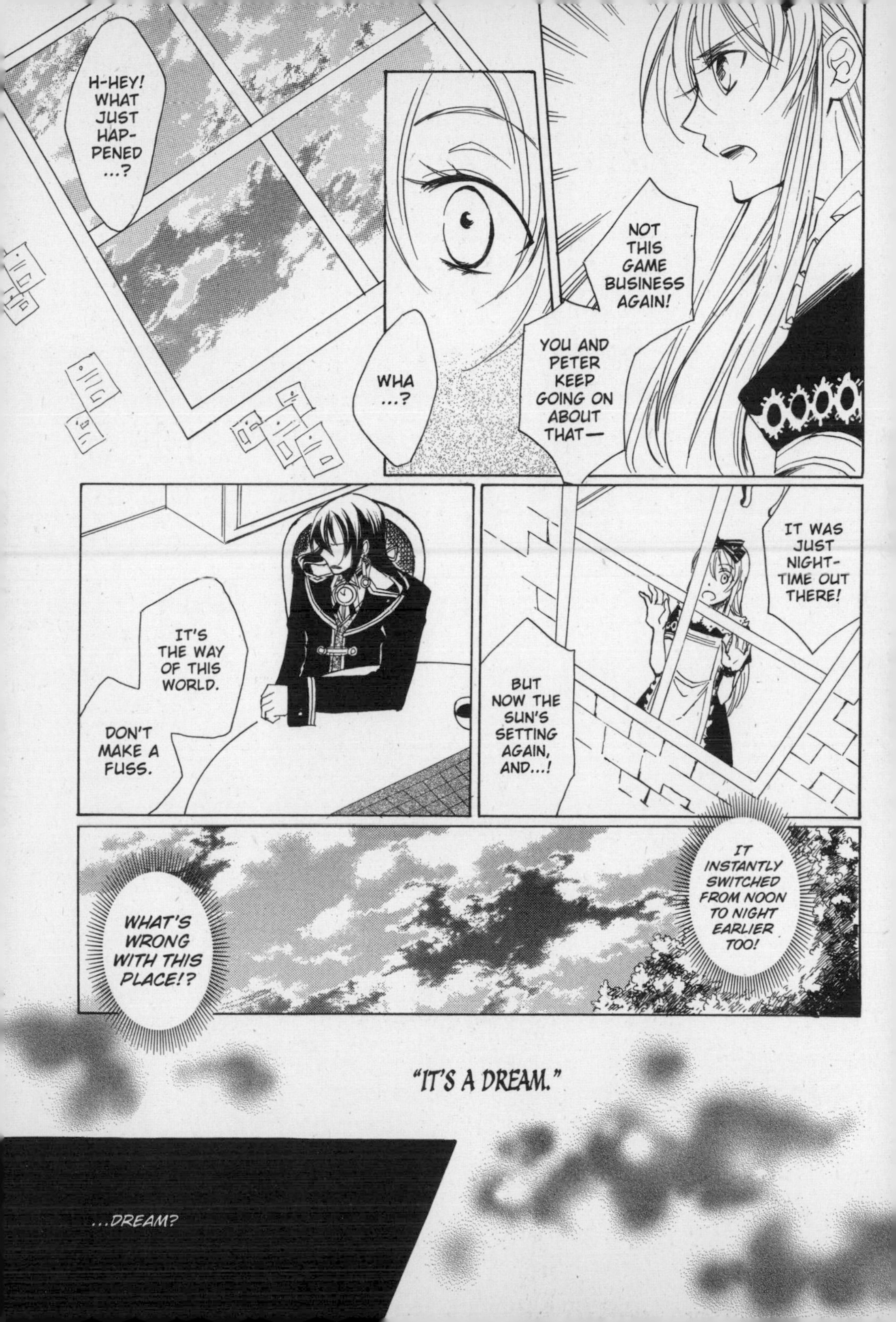
NOT THIS GAME BUSINESS AGAIN!
YOU AND PETER KEEP GOING ON ABOUT THAT—
WHA...?
H-HEY! WHAT JUST HAP-PENED ...?
IT WAS JUST NIGHT-TIME OUT THERE!
BUT NOW THE SUN'S SETTING AGAIN, AND...!
IT'S THE WAY OF THIS WORLD.
DON'T MAKE A FUSS.
IT INSTANTLY SWITCHED FROM NOON TO NIGHT EARLIER TOO!
WHAT'S WRONG WITH THIS PLACE!?
"IT'S A DREAM."
...DREAM?

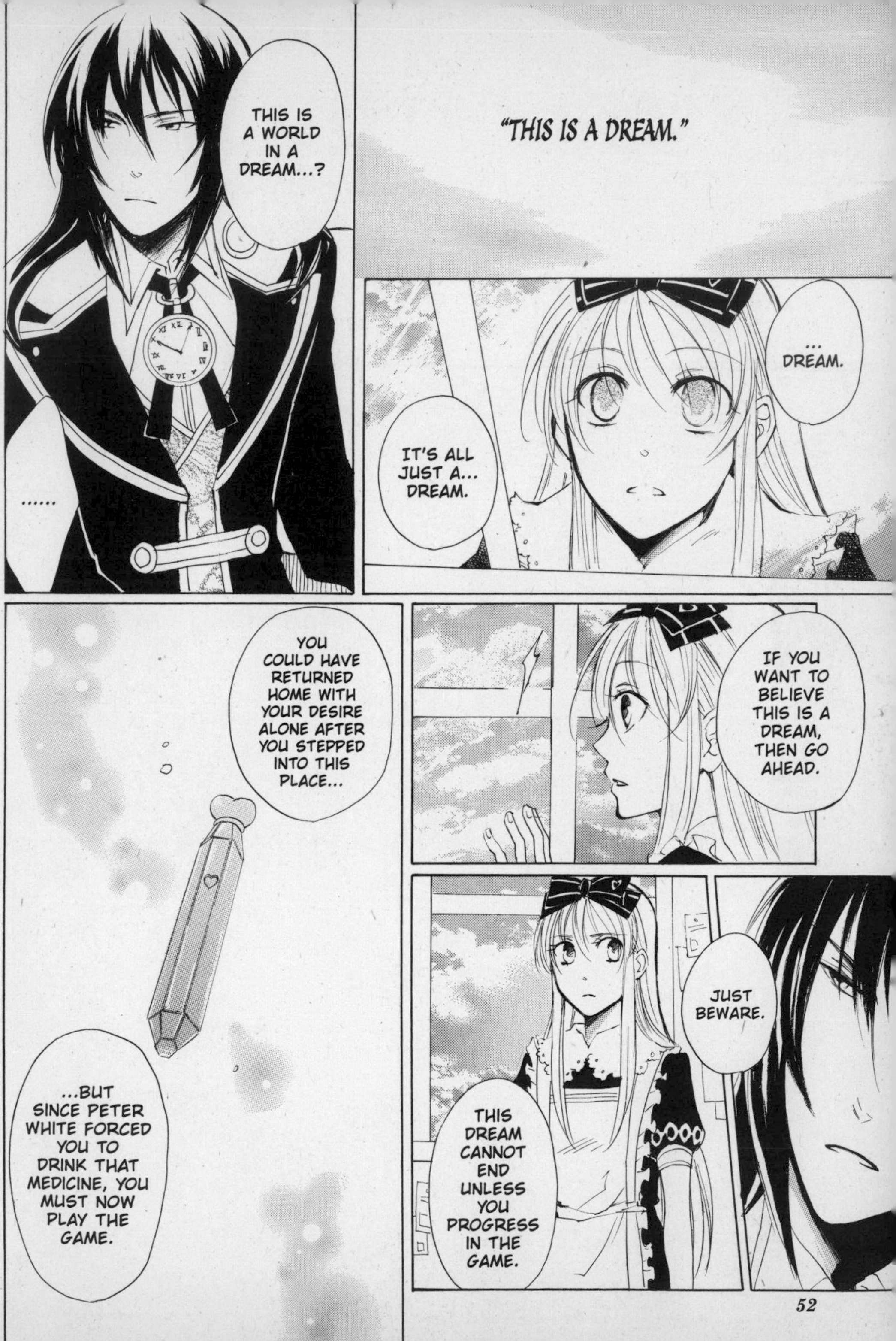
"THIS IS A DREAM."
... DREAM.
IT'S ALL JUST A... DREAM.
THIS IS A WORLD IN A DREAM...?
......
IF YOU WANT TO BELIEVE THIS IS A DREAM, THEN GO AHEAD.
JUST BEWARE.
THIS DREAM CANNOT END UNLESS YOU PROGRESS IN THE GAME.
YOU COULD HAVE RETURNED HOME WITH YOUR DESIRE ALONE AFTER YOU STEPPED INTO THIS PLACE...
...BUT SINCE PETER WHITE FORCED YOU TO DRINK THAT MEDICINE, YOU MUST NOW PLAY THE GAME.

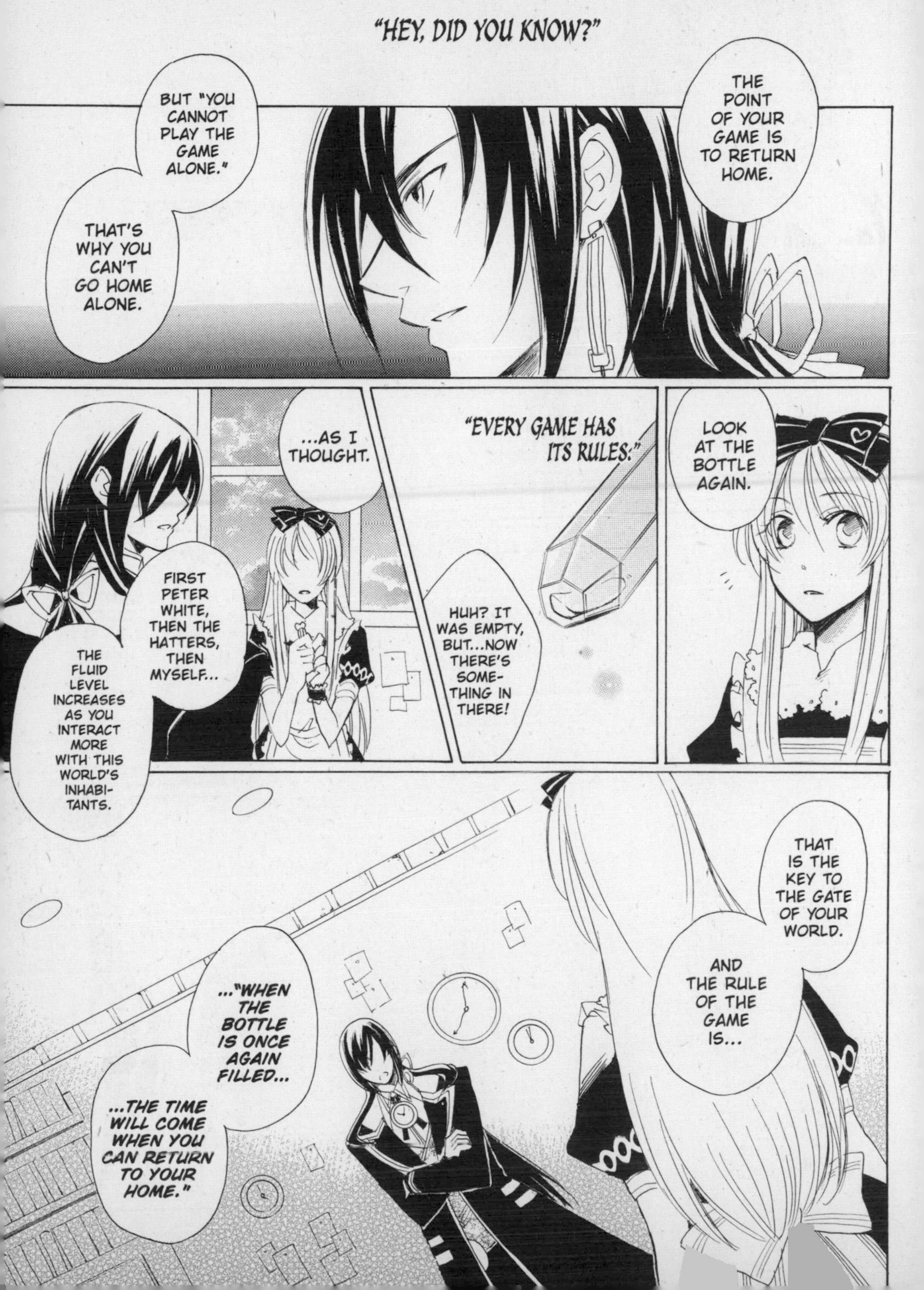
"HEY, DID YOU KNOW?"
THE POINT OF YOUR GAME IS TO RETURN HOME.
BUT "YOU CANNOT PLAY THE GAME ALONE."
THAT'S WHY YOU CAN'T GO HOME ALONE.
LOOK AT THE BOTTLE AGAIN.
"EVERY GAME HAS ITS RULES."
HUH? IT WAS EMPTY, BUT...NOW THERE'S SOME-THING IN THERE!
...AS I THOUGHT.
FIRST PETER WHITE, THEN THE HATTERS, THEN MYSELF...
THE FLUID LEVEL INCREASES AS YOU INTERACT MORE WITH THIS WORLD'S INHABI-TANTS.
THAT IS THE KEY TO THE GATE OF YOUR WORLD.
AND THE RULE OF THE GAME IS...
..."WHEN THE BOTTLE IS ONCE AGAIN FILLED...
...THE TIME WILL COME WHEN YOU CAN RETURN TO YOUR HOME."

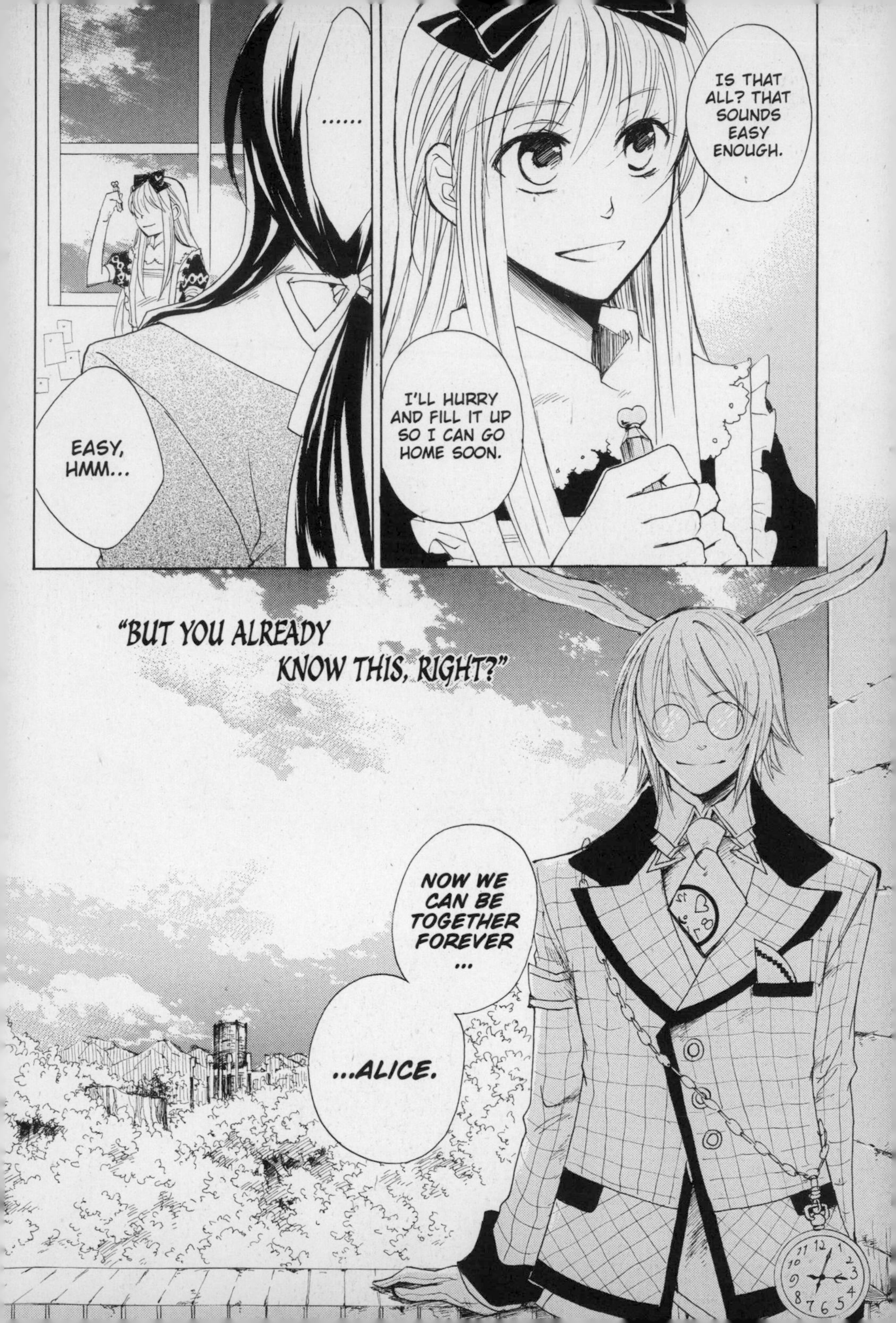
IS THAT ALL? THAT SOUNDS EASY ENOUGH.
I'LL HURRY AND FILL IT UP SO I CAN GO HOME SOON.
......
EASY, HMM...
"BUT YOU ALREADY KNOW THIS, RIGHT?"
NOW WE CAN BE TOGETHER FOREVER ...
...ALICE.

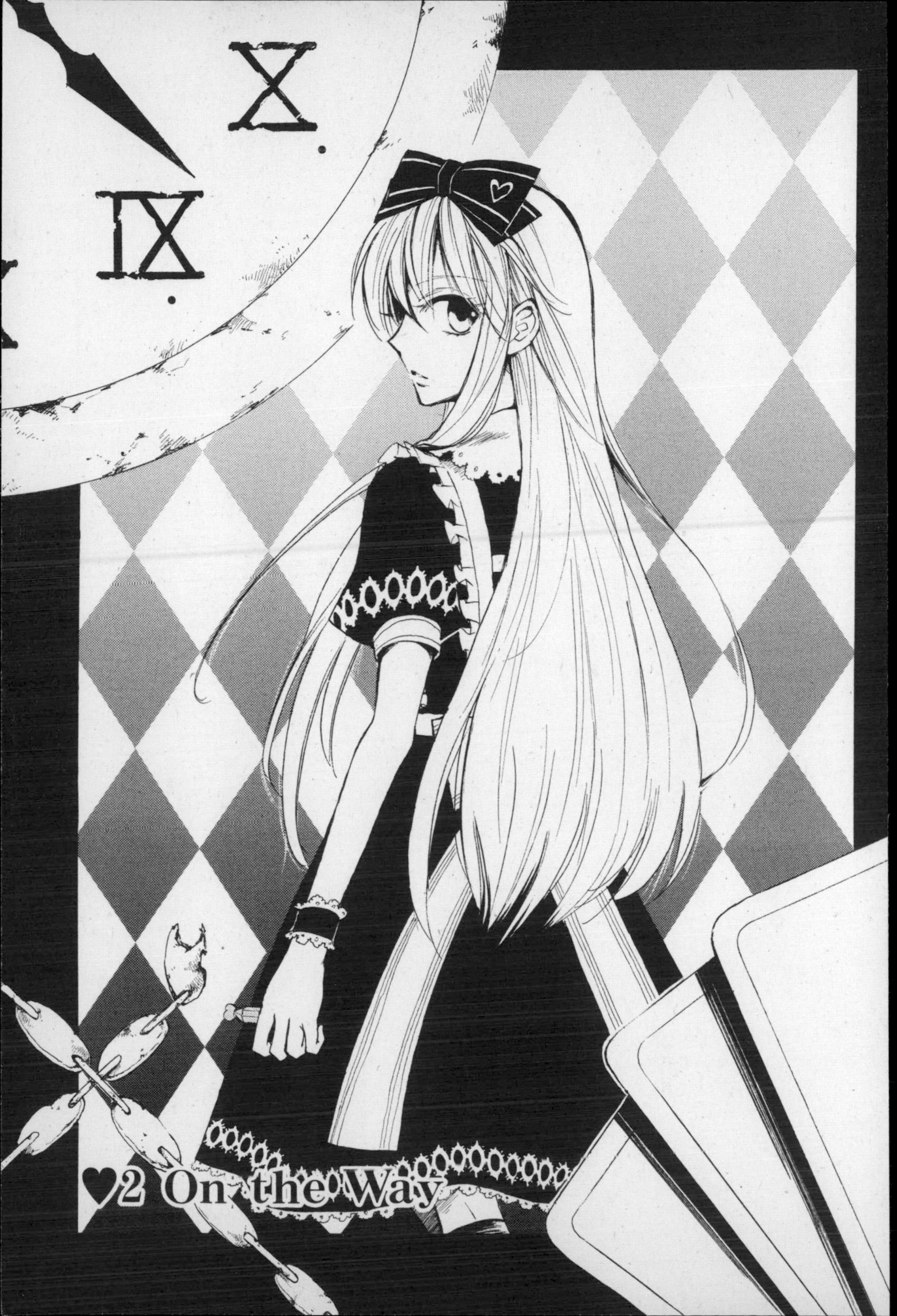

♥2 On the Way

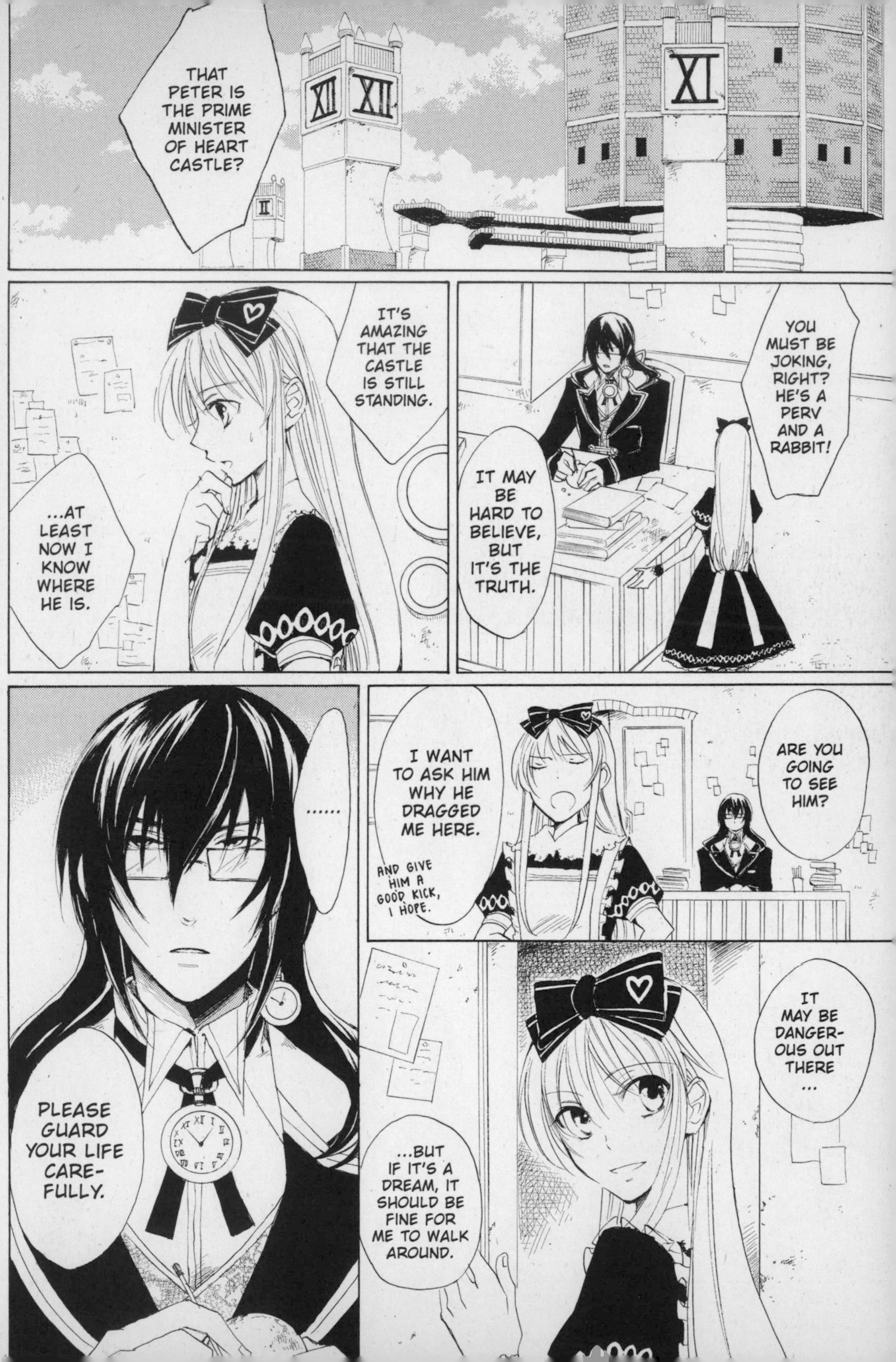
THAT PETER IS THE PRIME MINISTER OF HEART CASTLE?
YOU MUST BE JOKING, RIGHT? HE'S A PERV AND A RABBIT!
IT MAY BE HARD TO BELIEVE, BUT IT'S THE TRUTH.
IT'S AMAZING THAT THE CASTLE IS STILL STANDING.
...AT LEAST NOW I KNOW WHERE HE IS.
ARE YOU GOING TO SEE HIM?
I WANT TO ASK HIM WHY HE DRAGGED ME HERE.
AND GIVE HIM A GOOD KICK, I HOPE.
IT MAY BE DANGEROUS OUT THERE...
...BUT IF IT'S A DREAM, IT SHOULD BE FINE FOR ME TO WALK AROUND.
......
PLEASE GUARD YOUR LIFE CAREFULLY.

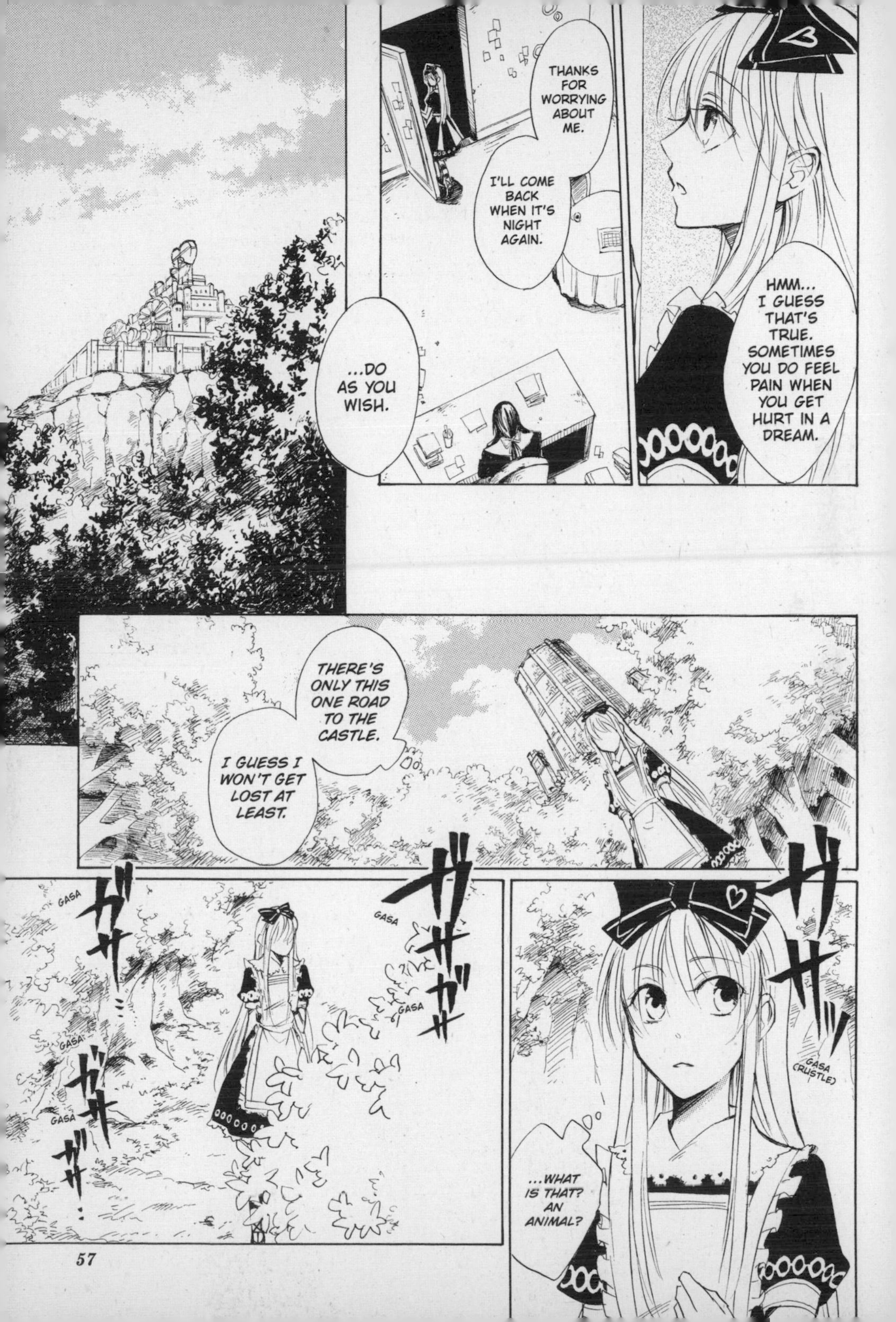
HMM... I GUESS THAT'S TRUE. SOMETIMES YOU DO FEEL PAIN WHEN YOU GET HURT IN A DREAM.
THANKS FOR WORRYING ABOUT ME.
I'LL COME BACK WHEN IT'S NIGHT AGAIN.
...DO AS YOU WISH.
THERE'S ONLY THIS ONE ROAD TO THE CASTLE.
I GUESS I WON'T GET LOST AT LEAST.
GASA (RUSTLE)
...WHAT IS THAT? AN ANIMAL?
GASA
GASA
GASA
GASA
GASA

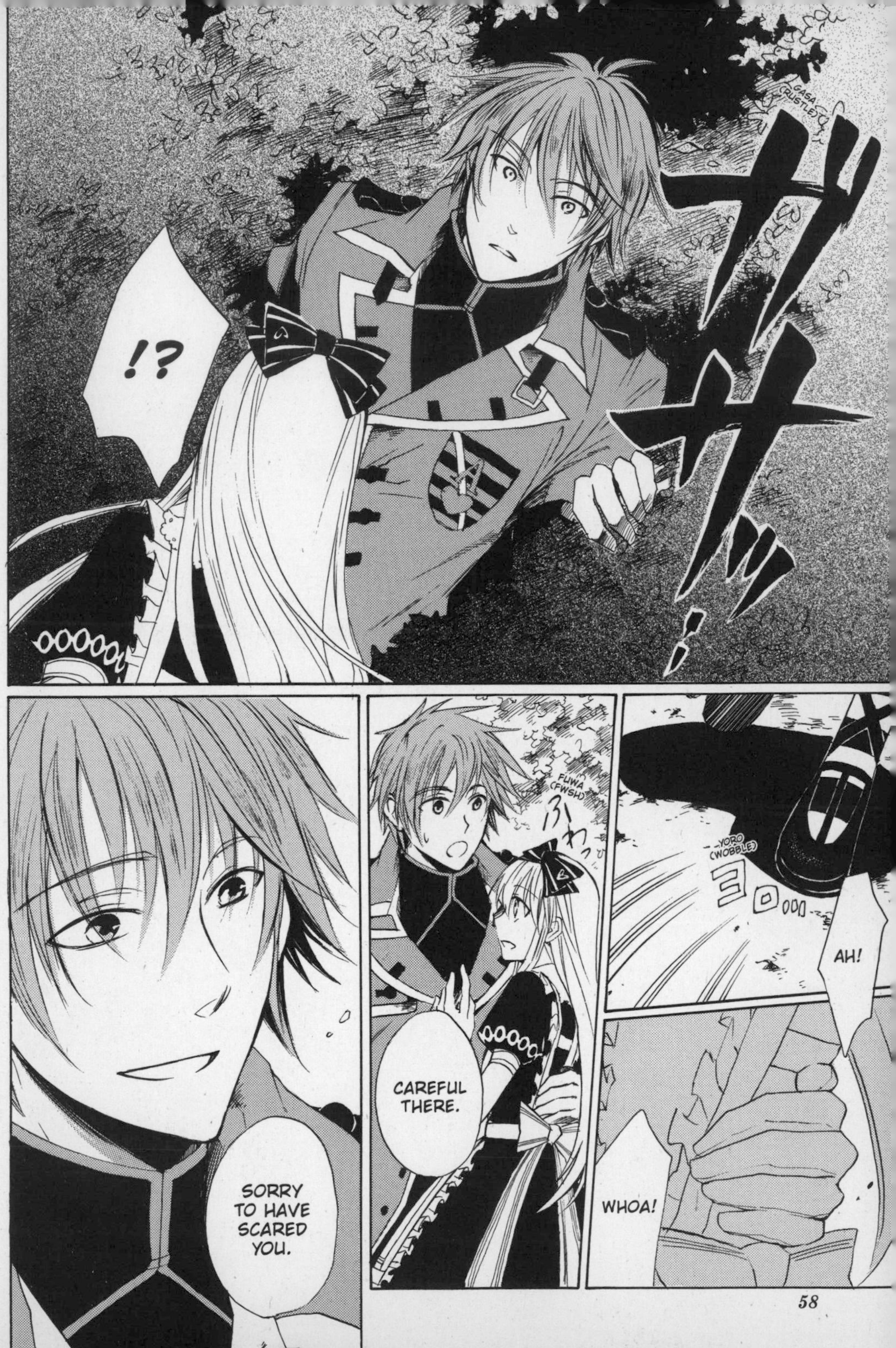
GASA (RUSTLE)
!?
YORO (WOBBLE)
AH!
WHOA!
FUWA (FWSH)
CAREFUL THERE.
SORRY TO HAVE SCARED YOU.

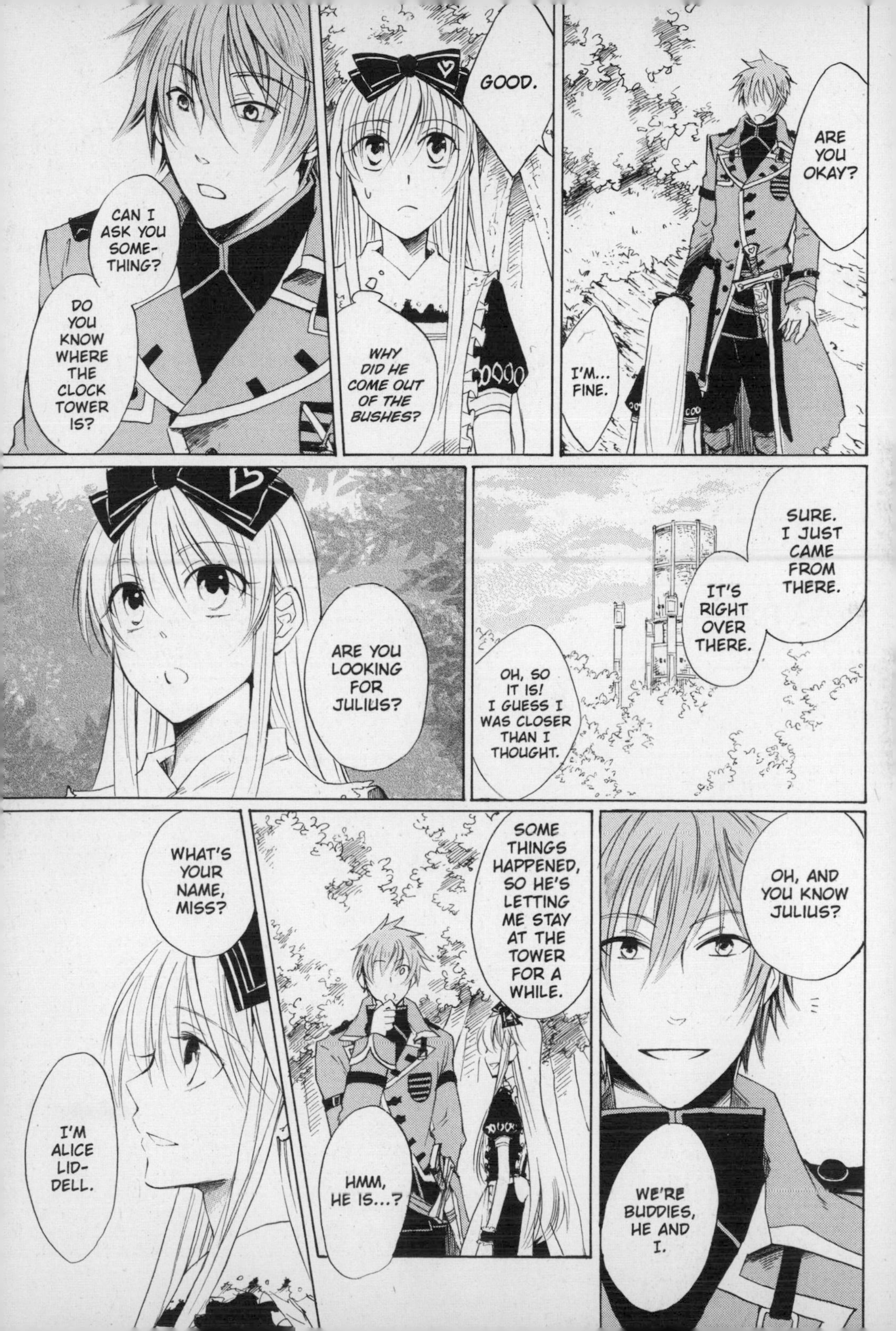
ARE YOU OKAY?
I'M... FINE.
GOOD.
WHY DID HE COME OUT OF THE BUSHES?
CAN I ASK YOU SOME-THING?
DO YOU KNOW WHERE THE CLOCK TOWER IS?
SURE. I JUST CAME FROM THERE.
IT'S RIGHT OVER THERE.
OH, SO IT IS! I GUESS I WAS CLOSER THAN I THOUGHT.
ARE YOU LOOKING FOR JULIUS?
OH, AND YOU KNOW JULIUS?
WE'RE BUDDIES, HE AND I.
SOME THINGS HAPPENED, SO HE'S LETTING ME STAY AT THE TOWER FOR A WHILE.
HMM, HE IS...?
WHAT'S YOUR NAME, MISS?
I'M ALICE LID-DELL.

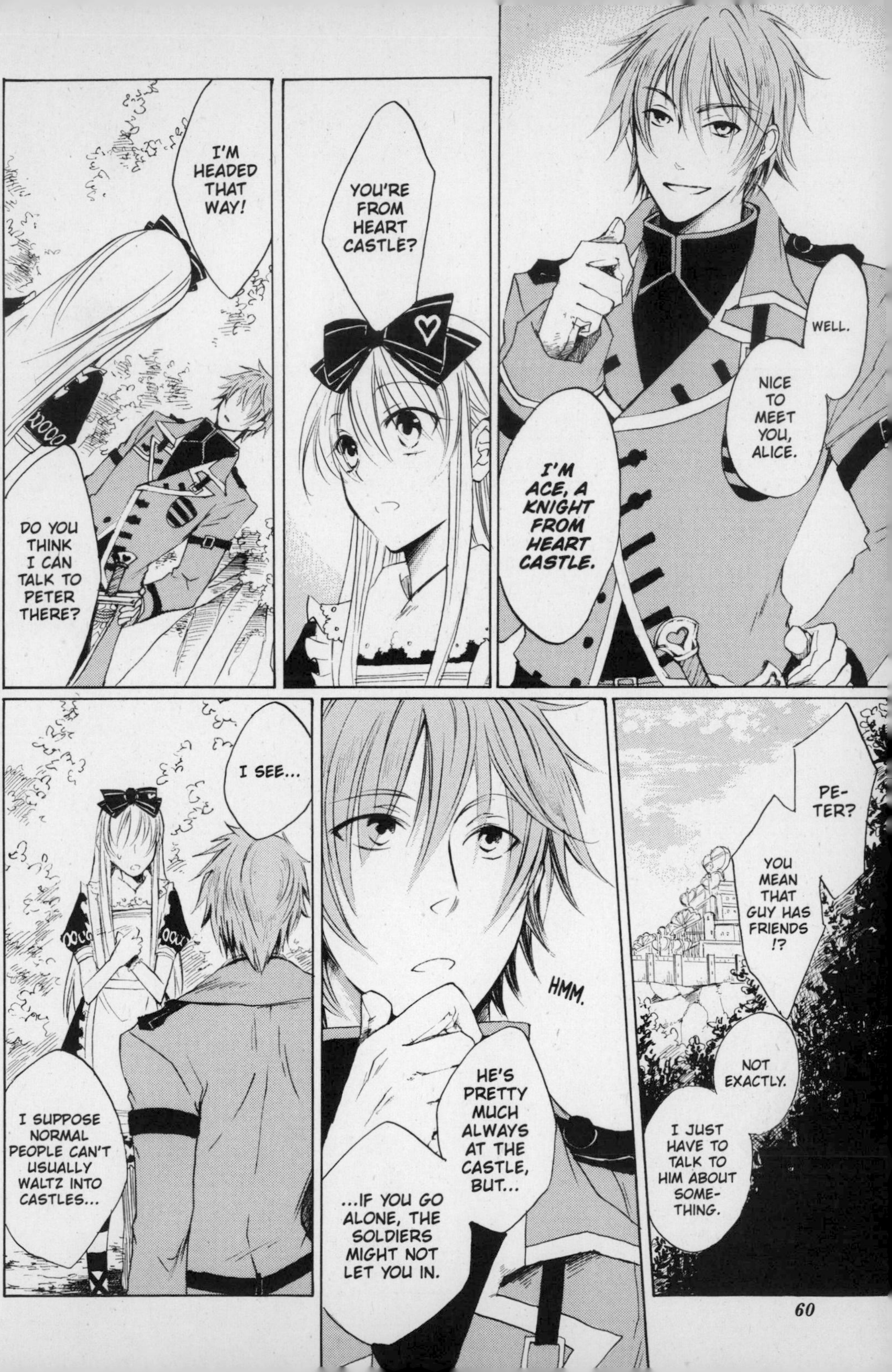
WELL.
NICE TO MEET YOU, ALICE.
I'M ACE, A KNIGHT FROM HEART CASTLE.
YOU'RE FROM HEART CASTLE?
I'M HEADED THAT WAY!
DO YOU THINK I CAN TALK TO PETER THERE?
PE-TER?
YOU MEAN THAT GUY HAS FRIENDS !?
NOT EXACTLY.
I JUST HAVE TO TALK TO HIM ABOUT SOME-THING.
HMM.
HE'S PRETTY MUCH ALWAYS AT THE CASTLE, BUT...
...IF YOU GO ALONE, THE SOLDIERS MIGHT NOT LET YOU IN.
I SEE...
I SUPPOSE NORMAL PEOPLE CAN'T USUALLY WALTZ INTO CASTLES...

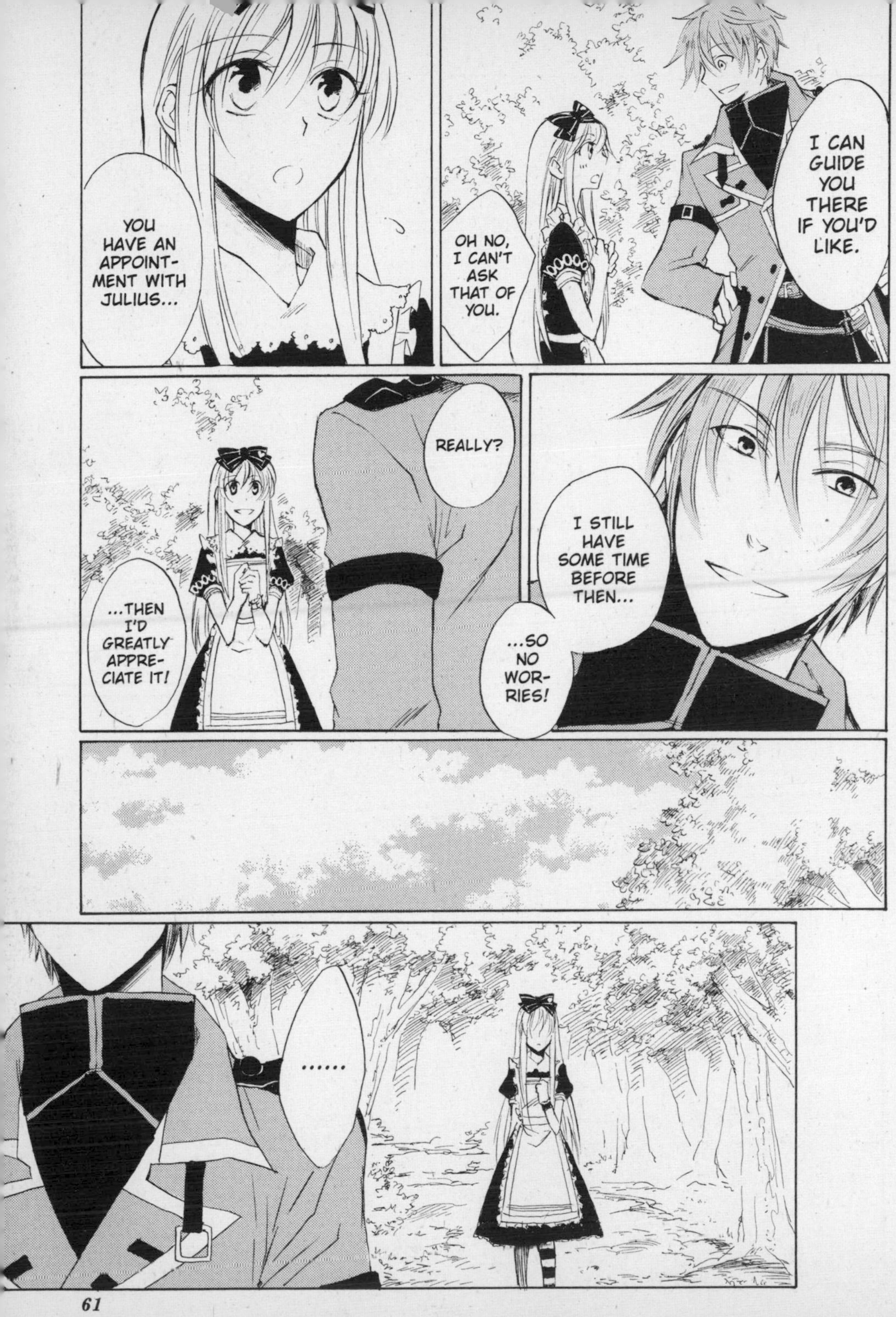
I CAN GUIDE YOU THERE IF YOU'D LIKE.
OH NO, I CAN'T ASK THAT OF YOU.
YOU HAVE AN APPOINTMENT WITH JULIUS...
I STILL HAVE SOME TIME BEFORE THEN...
...SO NO WORRIES!
REALLY?
...THEN I'D GREATLY APPRECIATE IT!
......

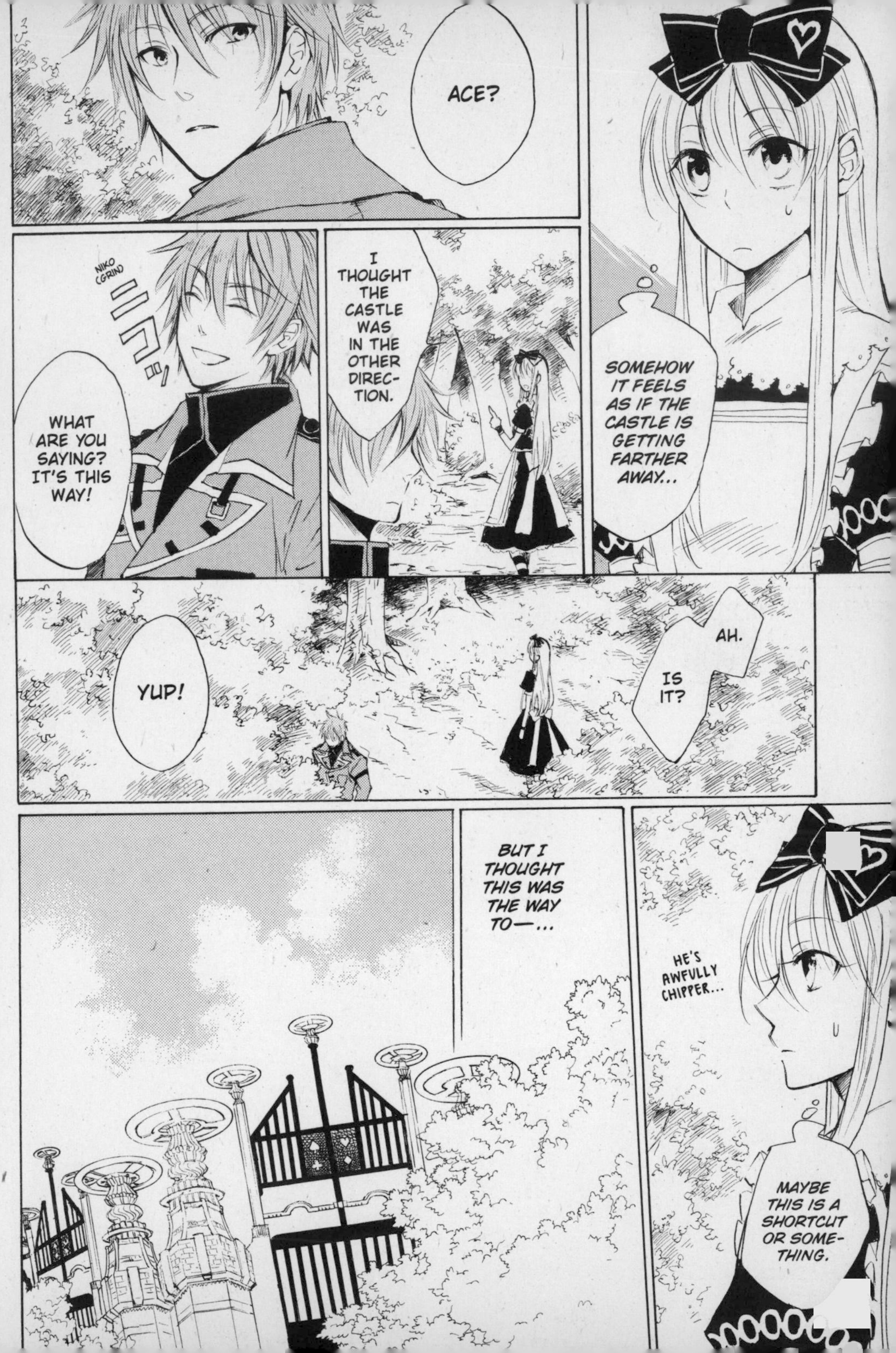
SOMEHOW IT FEELS AS IF THE CASTLE IS GETTING FARTHER AWAY...
ACE?
I THOUGHT THE CASTLE WAS IN THE OTHER DIRECTION.
NIKO (GRIN)
WHAT ARE YOU SAYING? IT'S THIS WAY!
AH.
IS IT?
YUP!
HE'S AWFULLY CHIPPER...
MAYBE THIS IS A SHORTCUT OR SOMETHING.
BUT I THOUGHT THIS WAS THE WAY TO—...

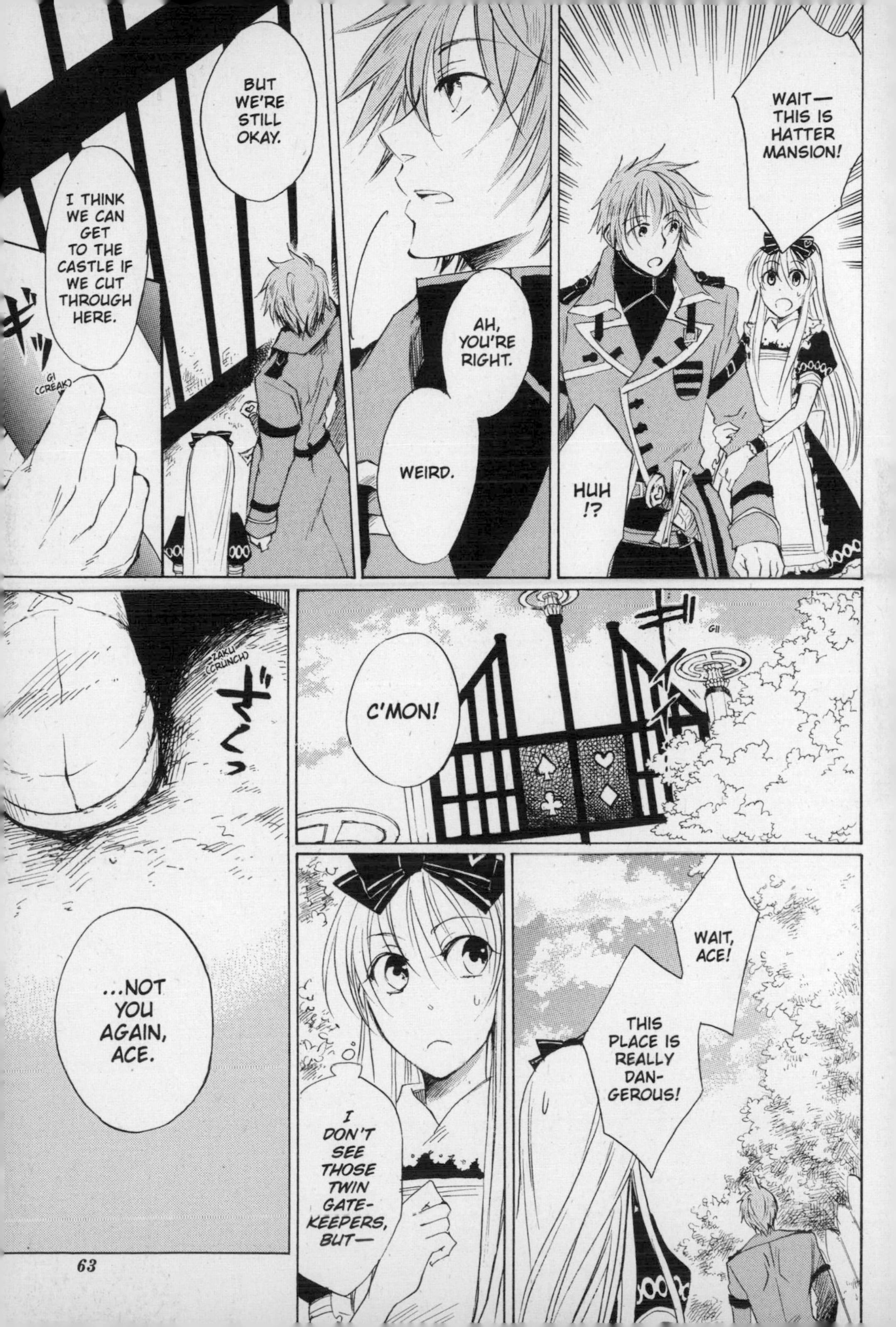

WAIT— THIS IS HATTER MANSION!
HUH!?
AH, YOU'RE RIGHT.
WEIRD.
BUT WE'RE STILL OKAY.
I THINK WE CAN GET TO THE CASTLE IF WE CUT THROUGH HERE.
GI (CREAK)
GII
C'MON!
WAIT, ACE!
THIS PLACE IS REALLY DAN-GEROUS!
I DON'T SEE THOSE TWIN GATE-KEEPERS, BUT—
ZAKU (CRUNCH)
...NOT YOU AGAIN, ACE.

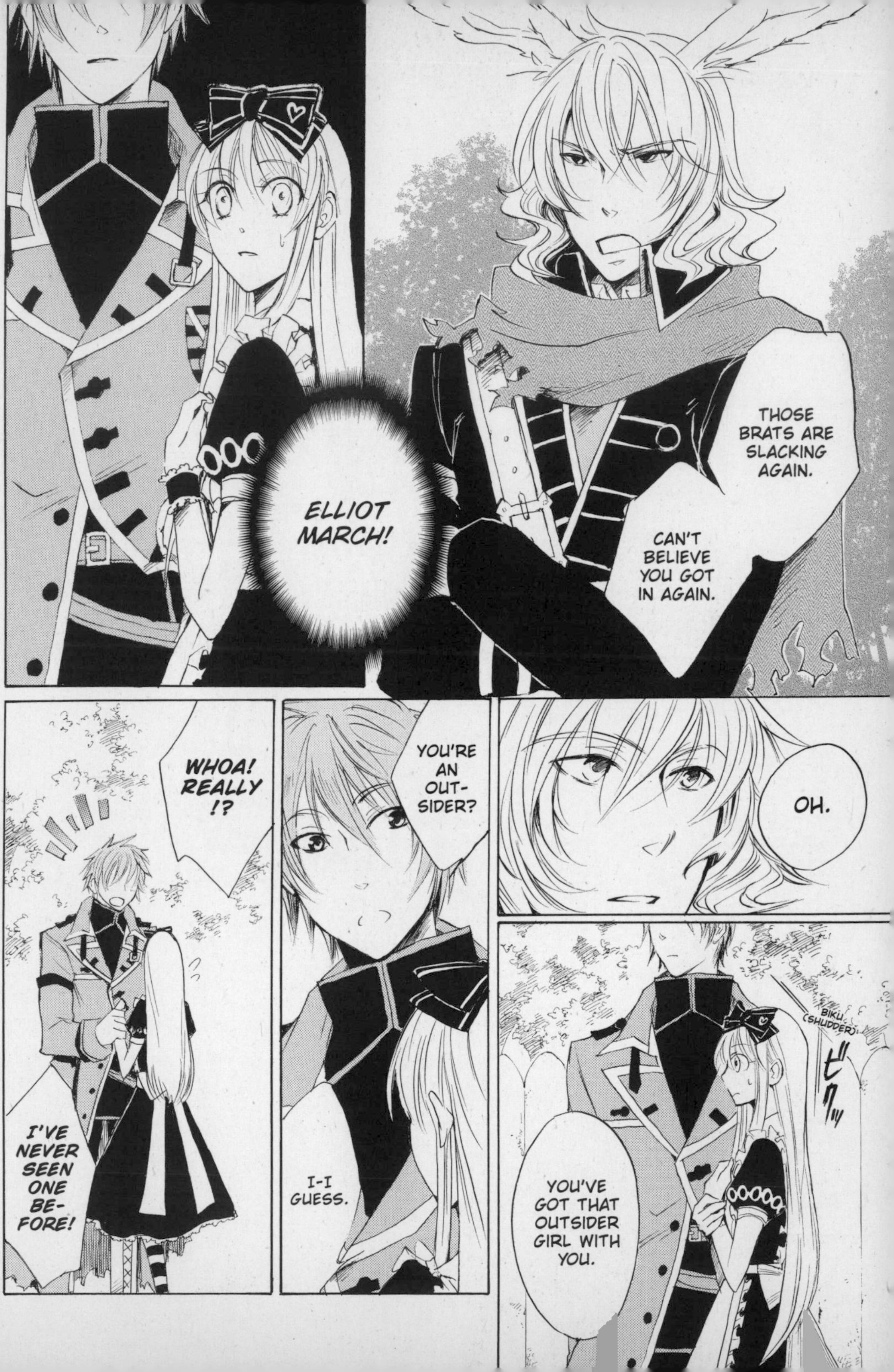
THOSE BRATS ARE SLACKING AGAIN.
CAN'T BELIEVE YOU GOT IN AGAIN.
ELLIOT MARCH!
OH.
BIKU (SHUDDER)
YOU'VE GOT THAT OUTSIDER GIRL WITH YOU.
YOU'RE AN OUT-SIDER?
I-I GUESS.
WHOA! REALLY!?
I'VE NEVER SEEN ONE BE-FORE!

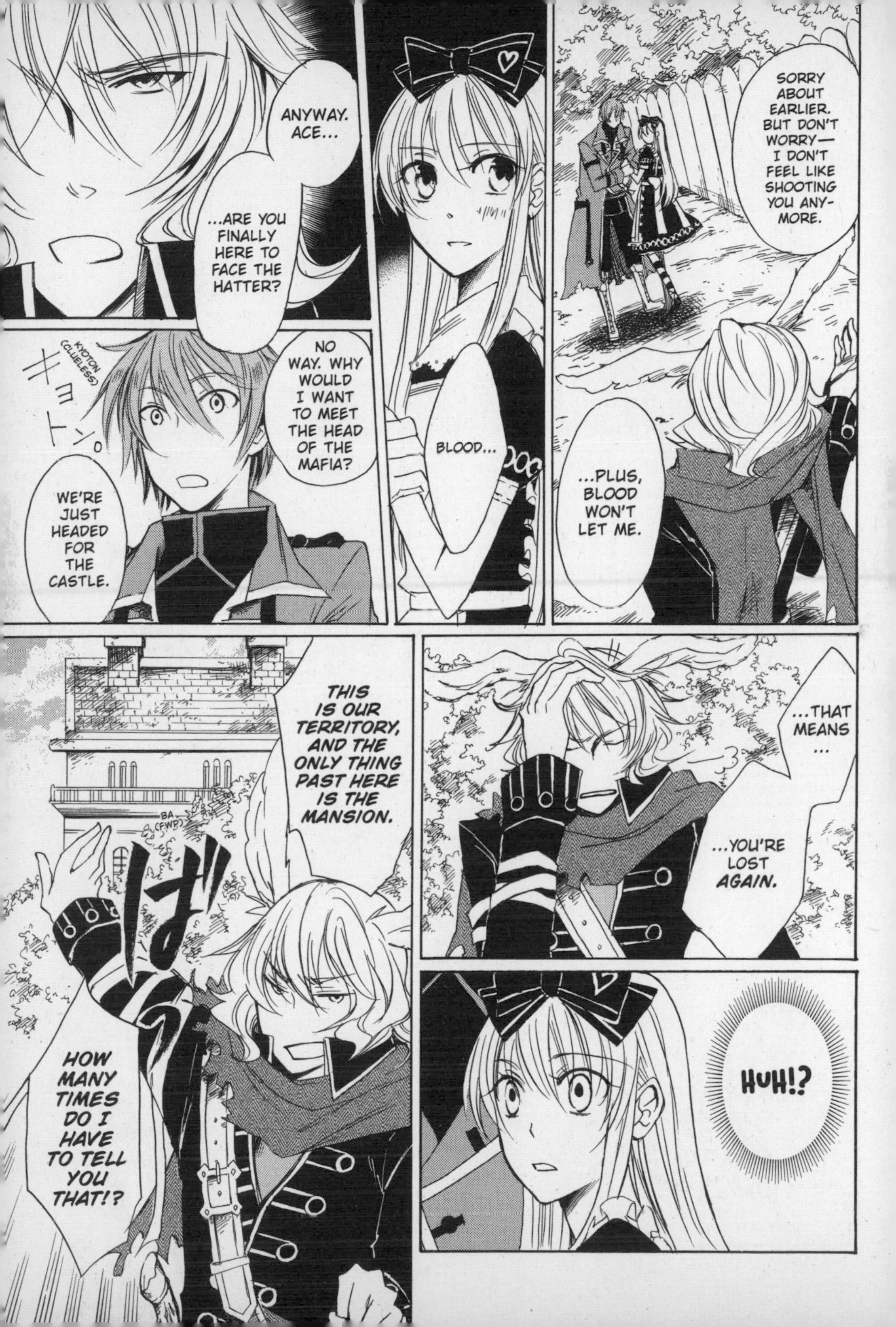
SORRY ABOUT EARLIER. BUT DON'T WORRY—I DON'T FEEL LIKE SHOOTING YOU ANYMORE.
...PLUS, BLOOD WON'T LET ME.
BLOOD...
ANYWAY. ACE...
...ARE YOU FINALLY HERE TO FACE THE HATTER?
NO WAY. WHY WOULD I WANT TO MEET THE HEAD OF THE MAFIA?
KYOTON (CLUELESS)
WE'RE JUST HEADED FOR THE CASTLE.
...THAT MEANS ...
...YOU'RE LOST AGAIN.
HUH!?
THIS IS OUR TERRITORY, AND THE ONLY THING PAST HERE IS THE MANSION.
BA (FWP)
HOW MANY TIMES DO I HAVE TO TELL YOU THAT!?

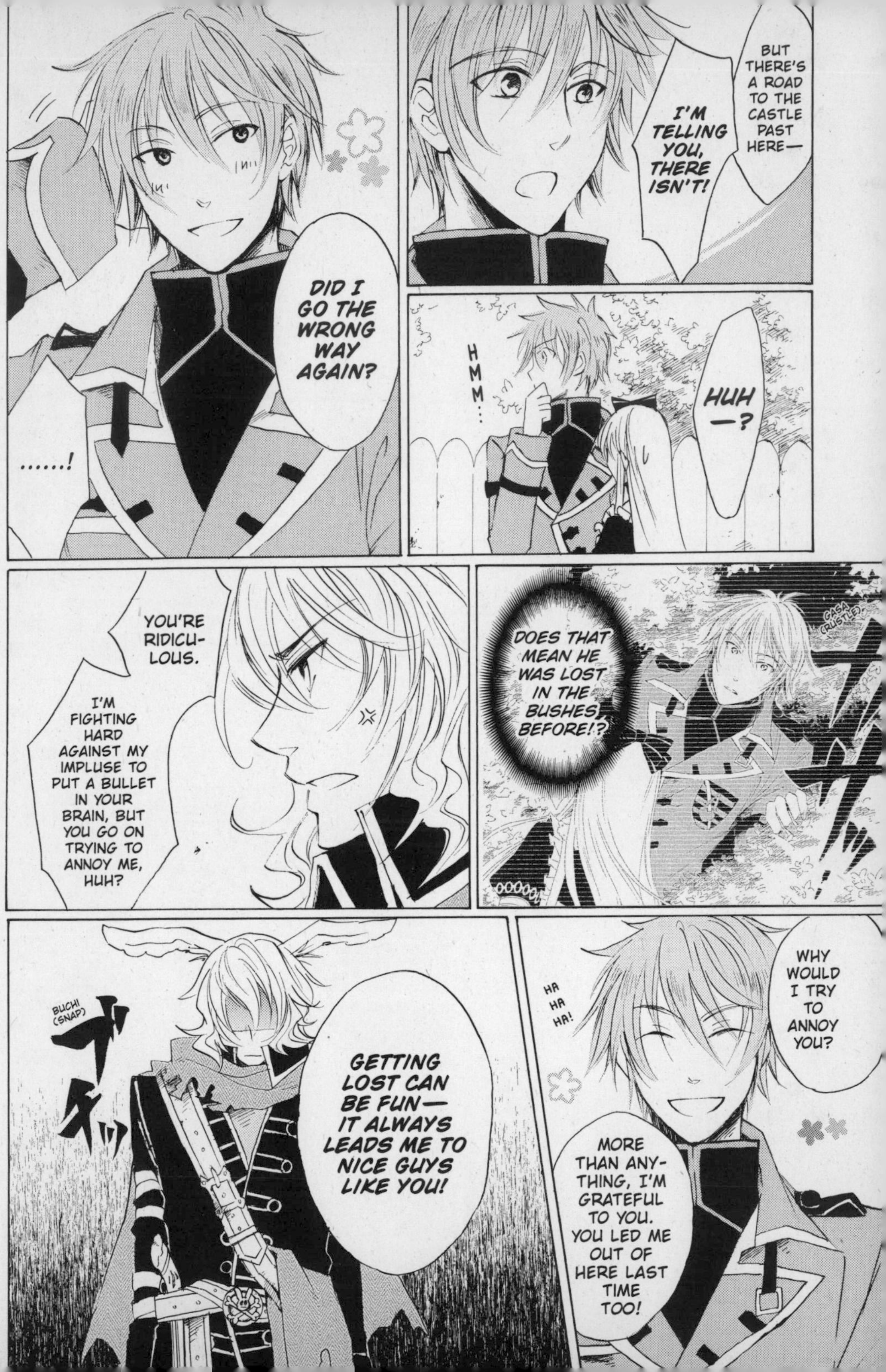
BUT THERE'S A ROAD TO THE CASTLE PAST HERE—
I'M TELLING YOU, THERE ISN'T!
HUH—?
HMM...
DID I GO THE WRONG WAY AGAIN?
......!
GASA (RUSTLE)
DOES THAT MEAN HE WAS LOST IN THE BUSHES BEFORE!?
YOU'RE RIDICULOUS.
I'M FIGHTING HARD AGAINST MY IMPLUSE TO PUT A BULLET IN YOUR BRAIN, BUT YOU GO ON TRYING TO ANNOY ME, HUH?
WHY WOULD I TRY TO ANNOY YOU?
HA HA HA!
MORE THAN ANY-THING, I'M GRATEFUL TO YOU. YOU LED ME OUT OF HERE LAST TIME TOO!
GETTING LOST CAN BE FUN—IT ALWAYS LEADS ME TO NICE GUYS LIKE YOU!
BUCHI (SNAP)

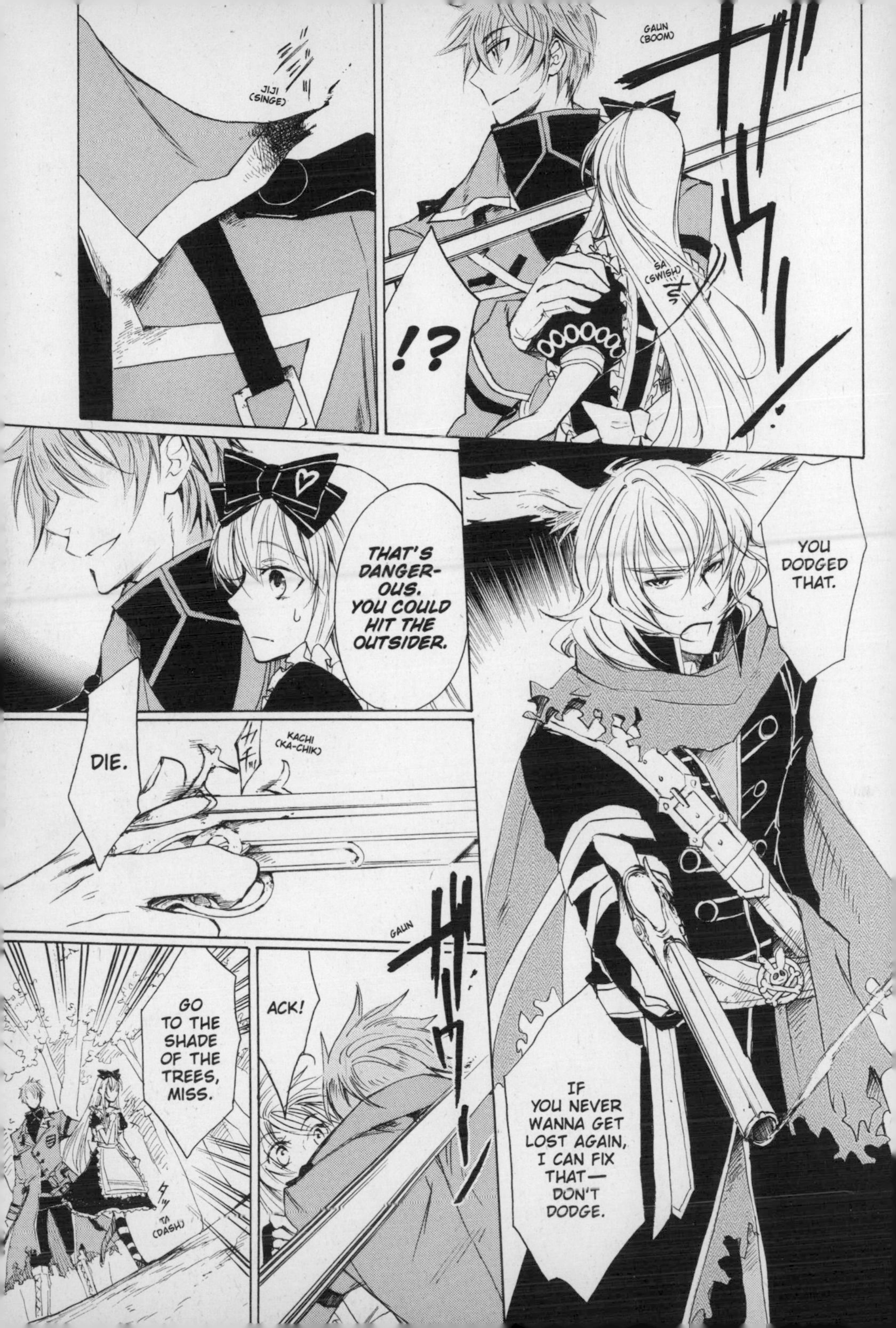
GAUN (BOOM)
SA (SWISH)
!?
JIJI (SINGE)
YOU DODGED THAT.
IF YOU NEVER WANNA GET LOST AGAIN, I CAN FIX THAT—DON'T DODGE.
THAT'S DANGER-OUS. YOU COULD HIT THE OUTSIDER.
DIE.
KACHI (KA-CHIK)
GAUN
ACK!
GO TO THE SHADE OF THE TREES, MISS.
TA (DASH)

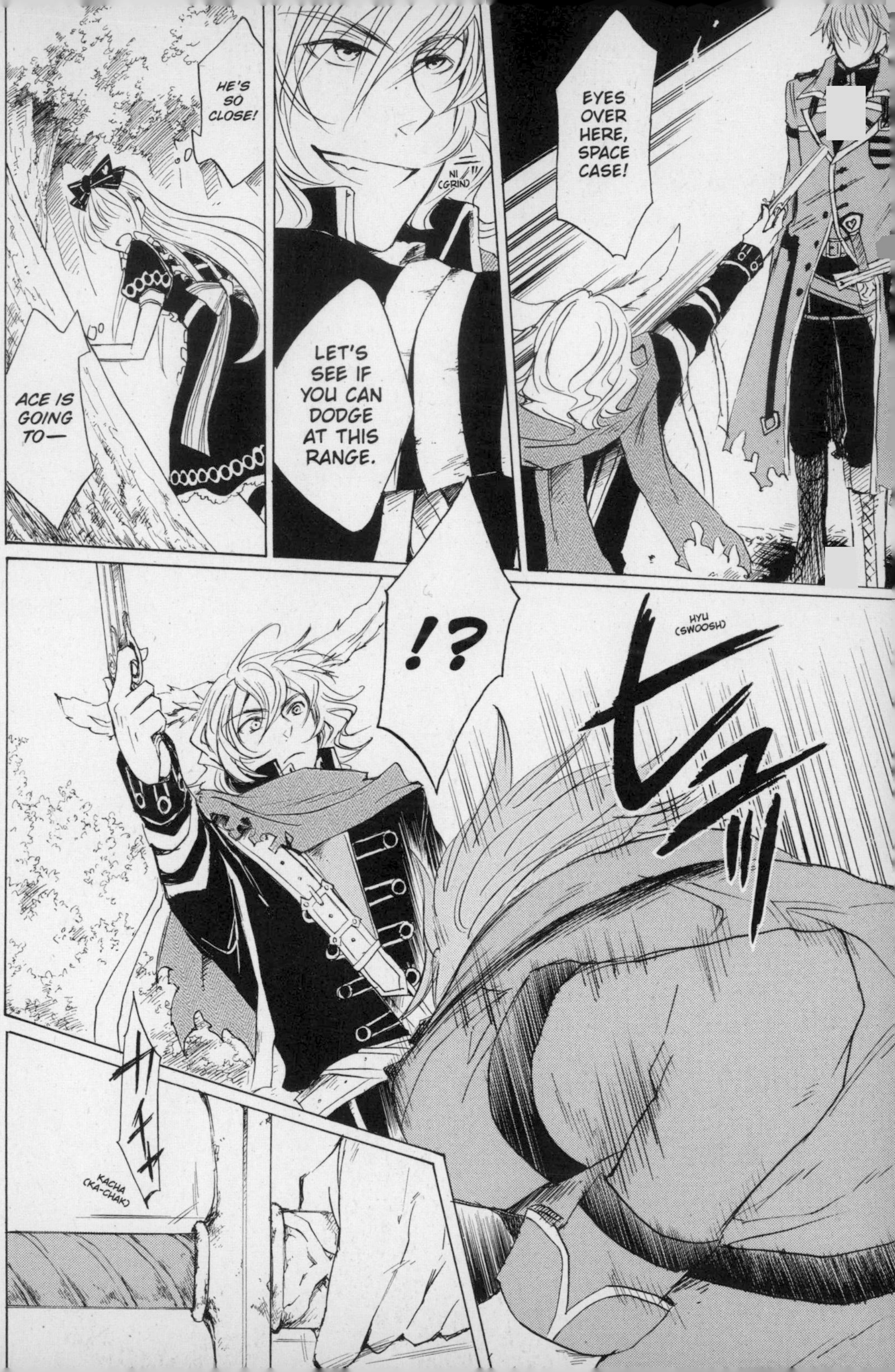
EYES OVER HERE, SPACE CASE!
NI (GRIN)
LET'S SEE IF YOU CAN DODGE AT THIS RANGE.
HE'S SO CLOSE!
ACE IS GOING TO—
HYU (SWOOSH)
!?
KACHA (KA-CHAK)

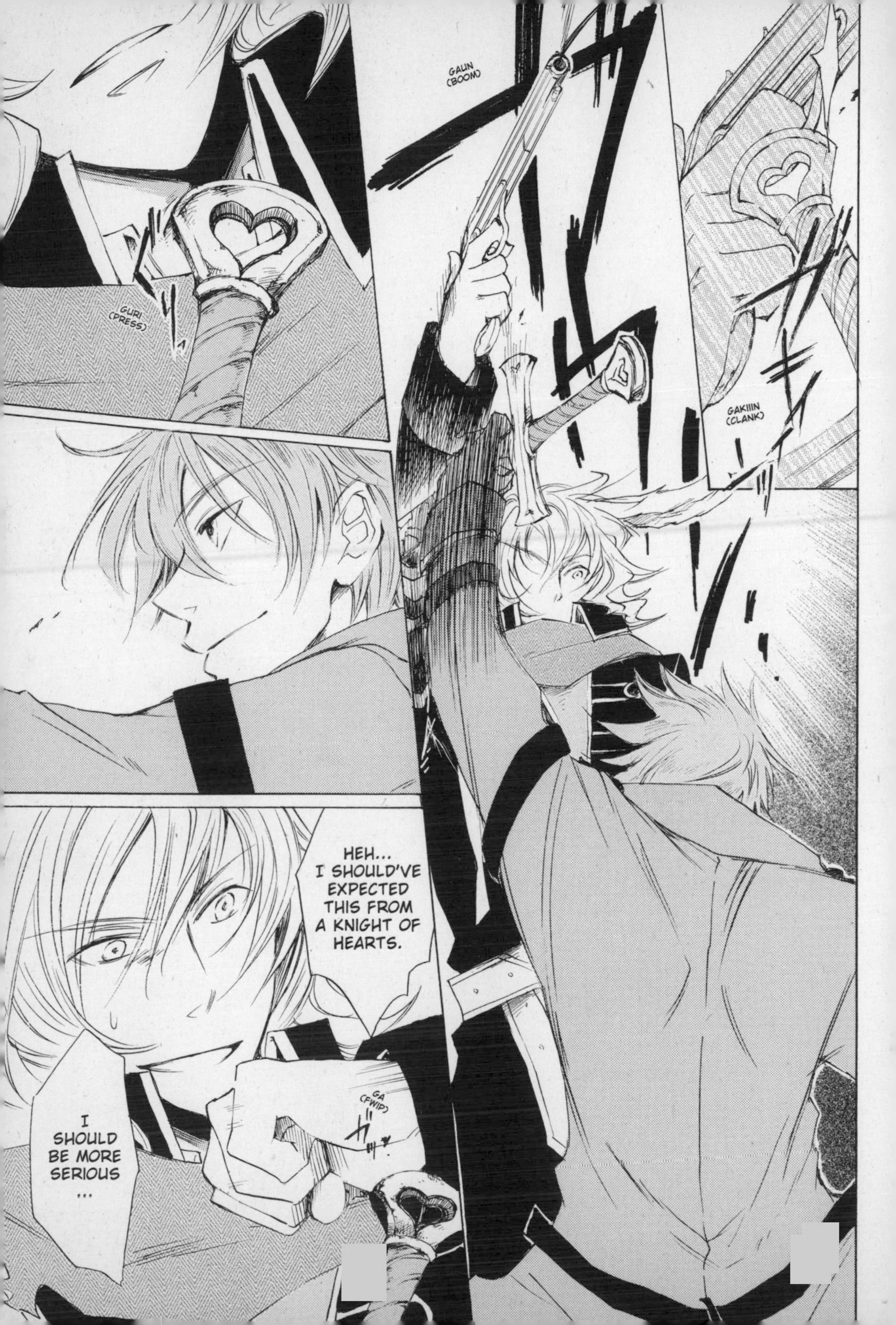
GAKIIN (CLANK)
GAUN (BOOM)
GURI (PRESS)
HEH... I SHOULD'VE EXPECTED THIS FROM A KNIGHT OF HEARTS.
GA (FWIP)
I SHOULD BE MORE SERIOUS ...

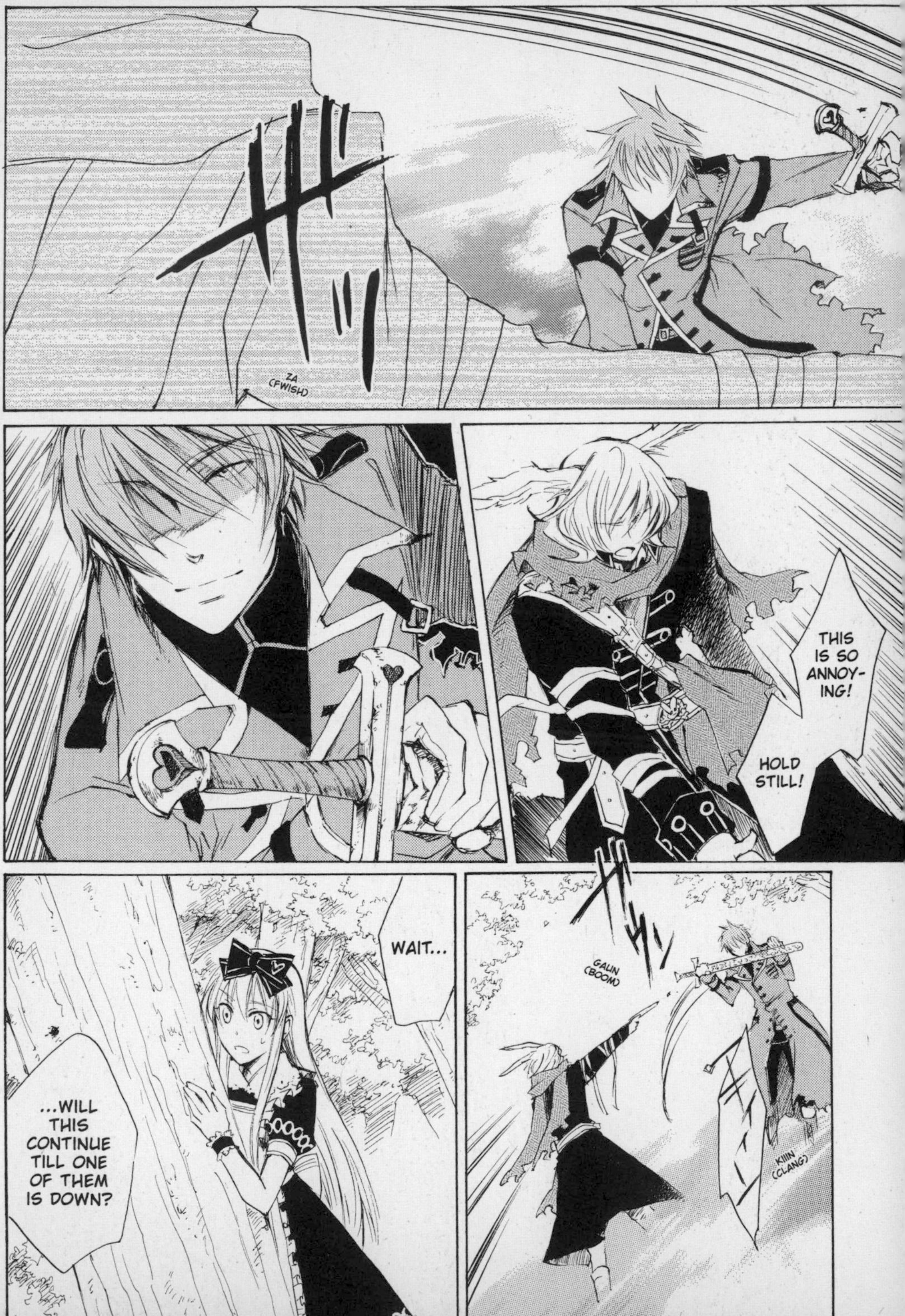
ZA
(FWISH)
THIS IS SO ANNOY-ING!
HOLD STILL!
GALIN
(BOOM)
KIIIN
(CLANG)
WAIT...
...WILL THIS CONTINUE TILL ONE OF THEM IS DOWN?

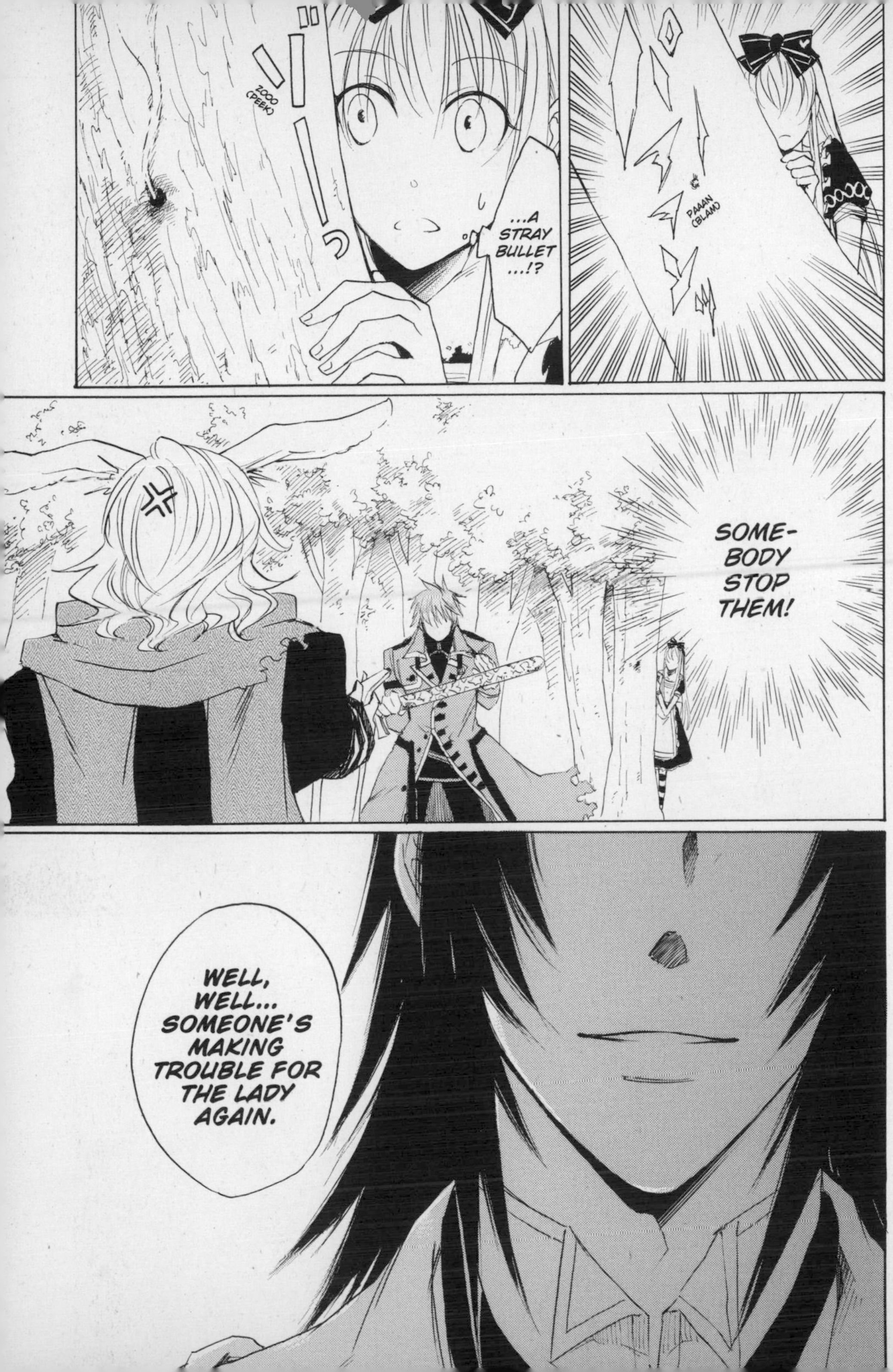
PAAAN (BLAM)
ZOOO (PEEK)
...A STRAY BULLET ...!?
SOME-BODY STOP THEM!
WELL, WELL... SOMEONE'S MAKING TROUBLE FOR THE LADY AGAIN.

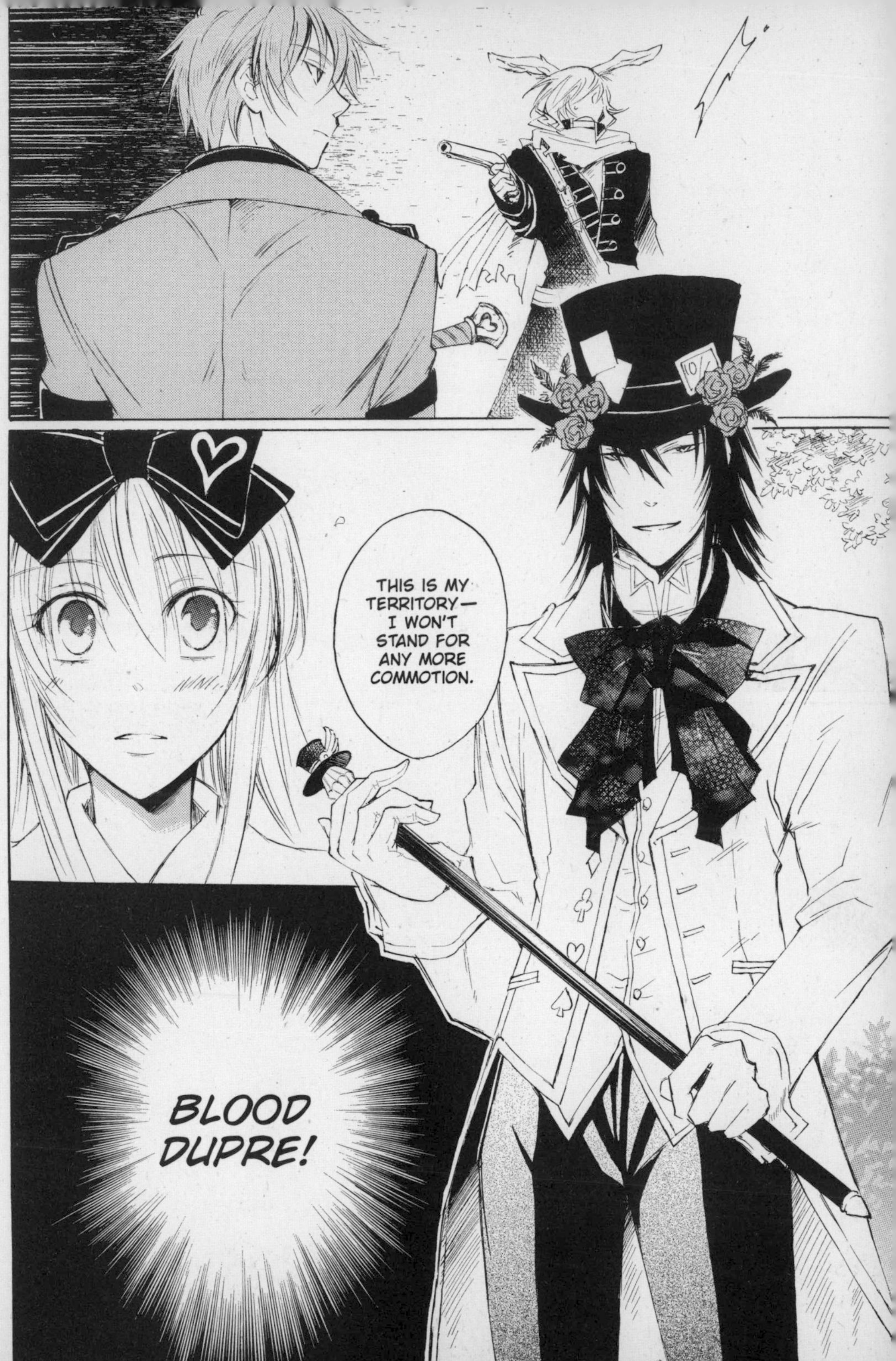
THIS IS MY TERRITORY—I WON'T STAND FOR ANY MORE COMMOTION.
BLOOD DUPRE!

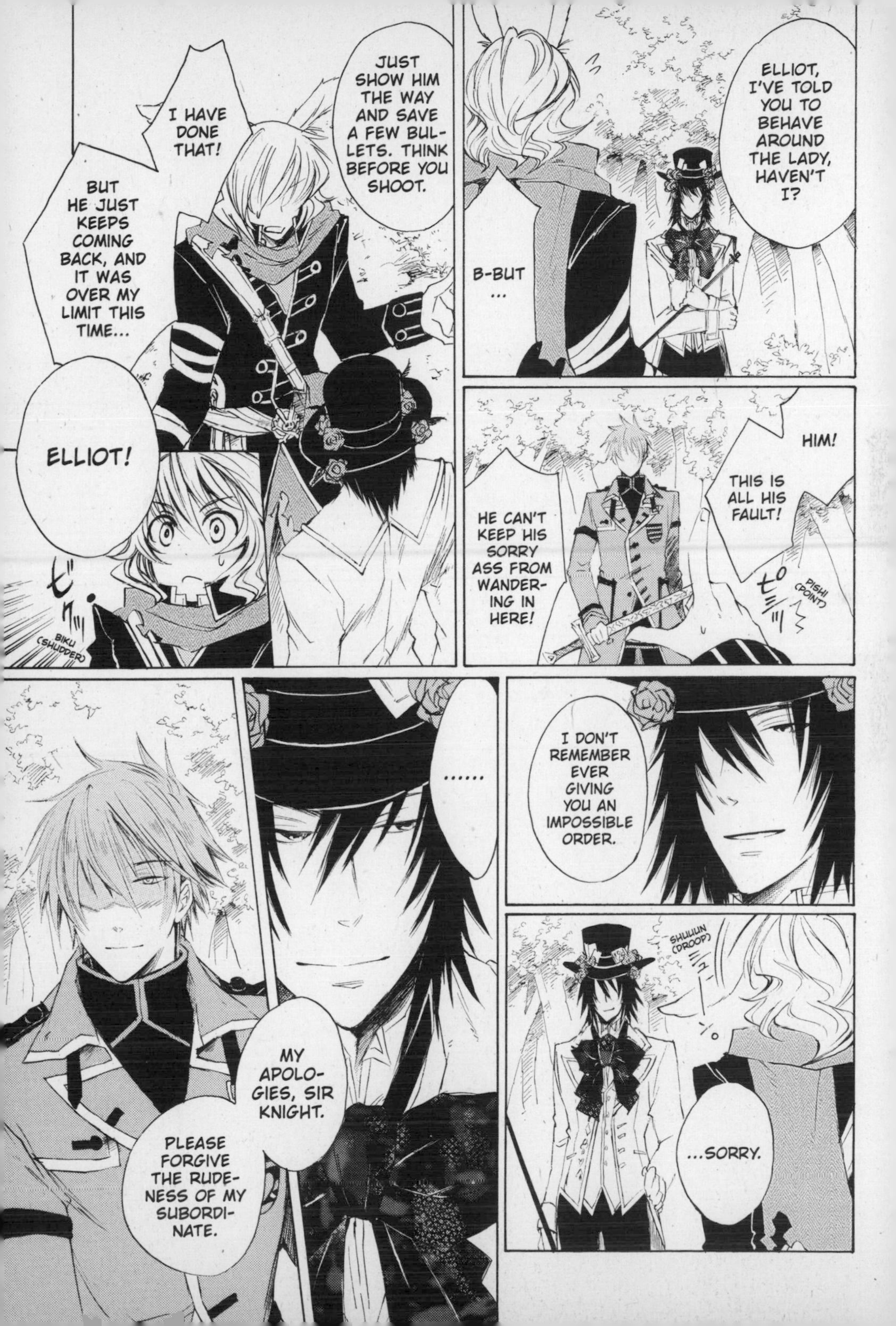
ELLIOT, I'VE TOLD YOU TO BEHAVE AROUND THE LADY, HAVEN'T I?
B-BUT ...
HIM!
THIS IS ALL HIS FAULT!
PISHI (POINT)
HE CAN'T KEEP HIS SORRY ASS FROM WANDERING IN HERE!
JUST SHOW HIM THE WAY AND SAVE A FEW BULLETS. THINK BEFORE YOU SHOOT.
I HAVE DONE THAT!
BUT HE JUST KEEPS COMING BACK, AND IT WAS OVER MY LIMIT THIS TIME...
ELLIOT!
BIKU (SHUDDER)
I DON'T REMEMBER EVER GIVING YOU AN IMPOSSIBLE ORDER.
SHUUUN (DROOP)
...SORRY.
......
MY APOLOGIES, SIR KNIGHT.
PLEASE FORGIVE THE RUDENESS OF MY SUBORDINATE.

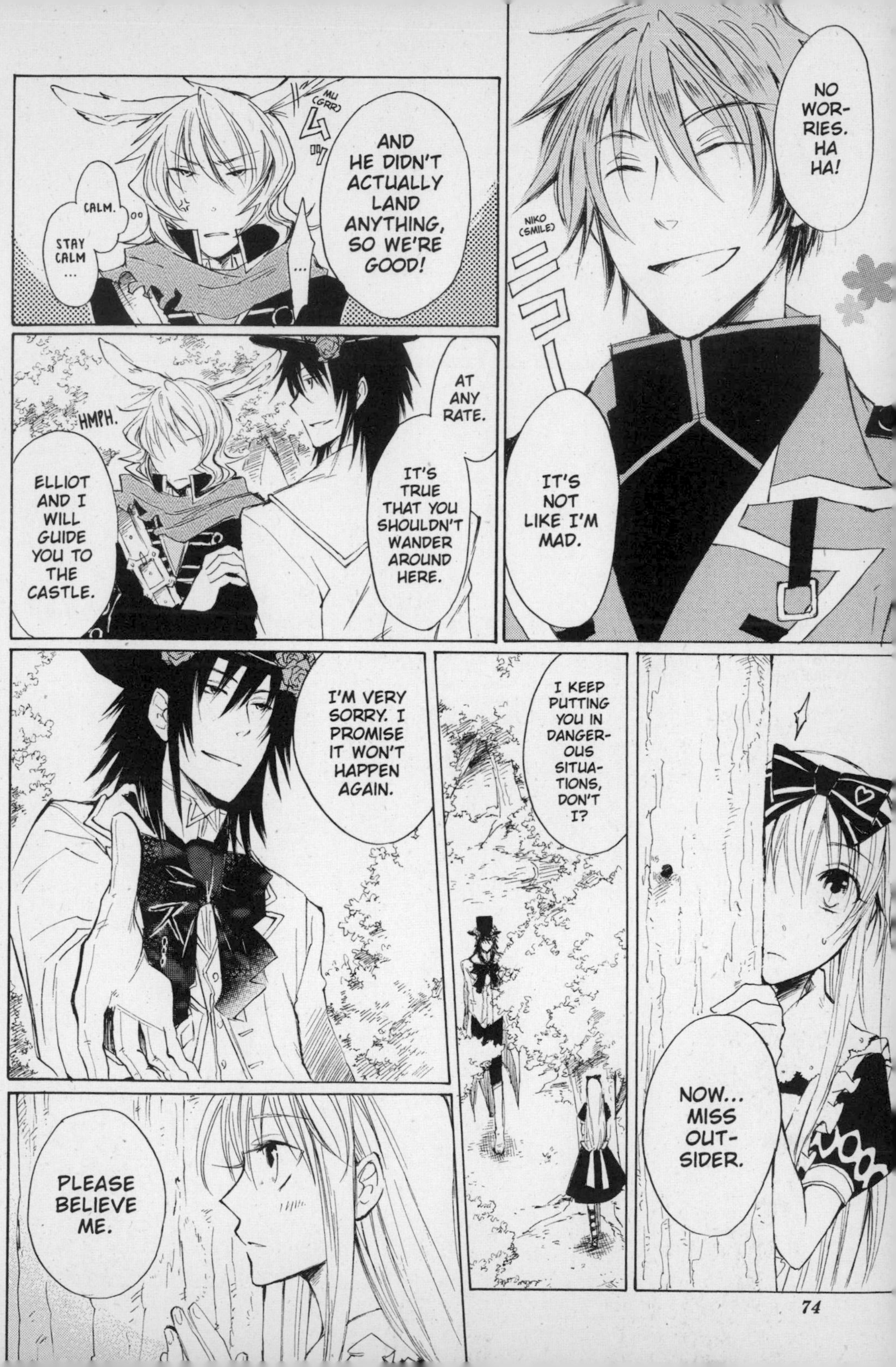
NO WORRIES. HA HA!
NIKO (SMILE)
IT'S NOT LIKE I'M MAD.
AND HE DIDN'T ACTUALLY LAND ANYTHING, SO WE'RE GOOD!
MU (GRR)
...
CALM.
STAY CALM ...
AT ANY RATE.
IT'S TRUE THAT YOU SHOULDN'T WANDER AROUND HERE.
HMPH.
ELLIOT AND I WILL GUIDE YOU TO THE CASTLE.
NOW... MISS OUTSIDER.
I KEEP PUTTING YOU IN DANGEROUS SITUATIONS, DON'T I?
I'M VERY SORRY. I PROMISE IT WON'T HAPPEN AGAIN.
PLEASE BELIEVE ME.

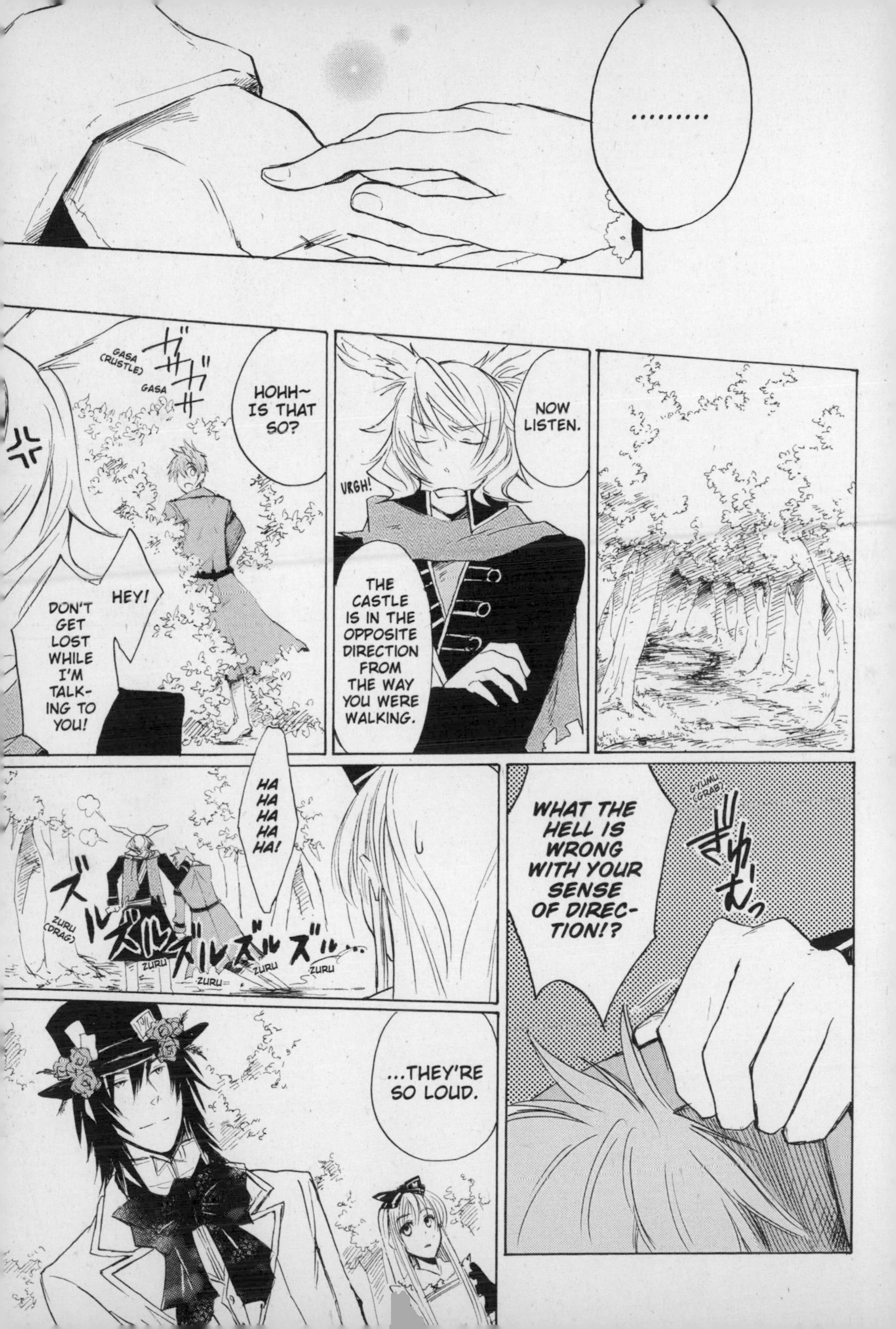
....
NOW LISTEN.
URGH!
THE CASTLE IS IN THE OPPOSITE DIRECTION FROM THE WAY YOU WERE WALKING.
HOHH~ IS THAT SO?
ガサガサ
GASA (RUSTLE) GASA
HEY!
DON'T GET LOST WHILE I'M TALKING TO YOU!
ぎゅむっ
GYUMU (GRAB)
WHAT THE HELL IS WRONG WITH YOUR SENSE OF DIREC-TION!?
HA HA HA HA HA!
ズルズルズルズルズル…
ZURU (DRAG)
ZURU
ZURU
ZURU
ZURU
...THEY'RE SO LOUD.

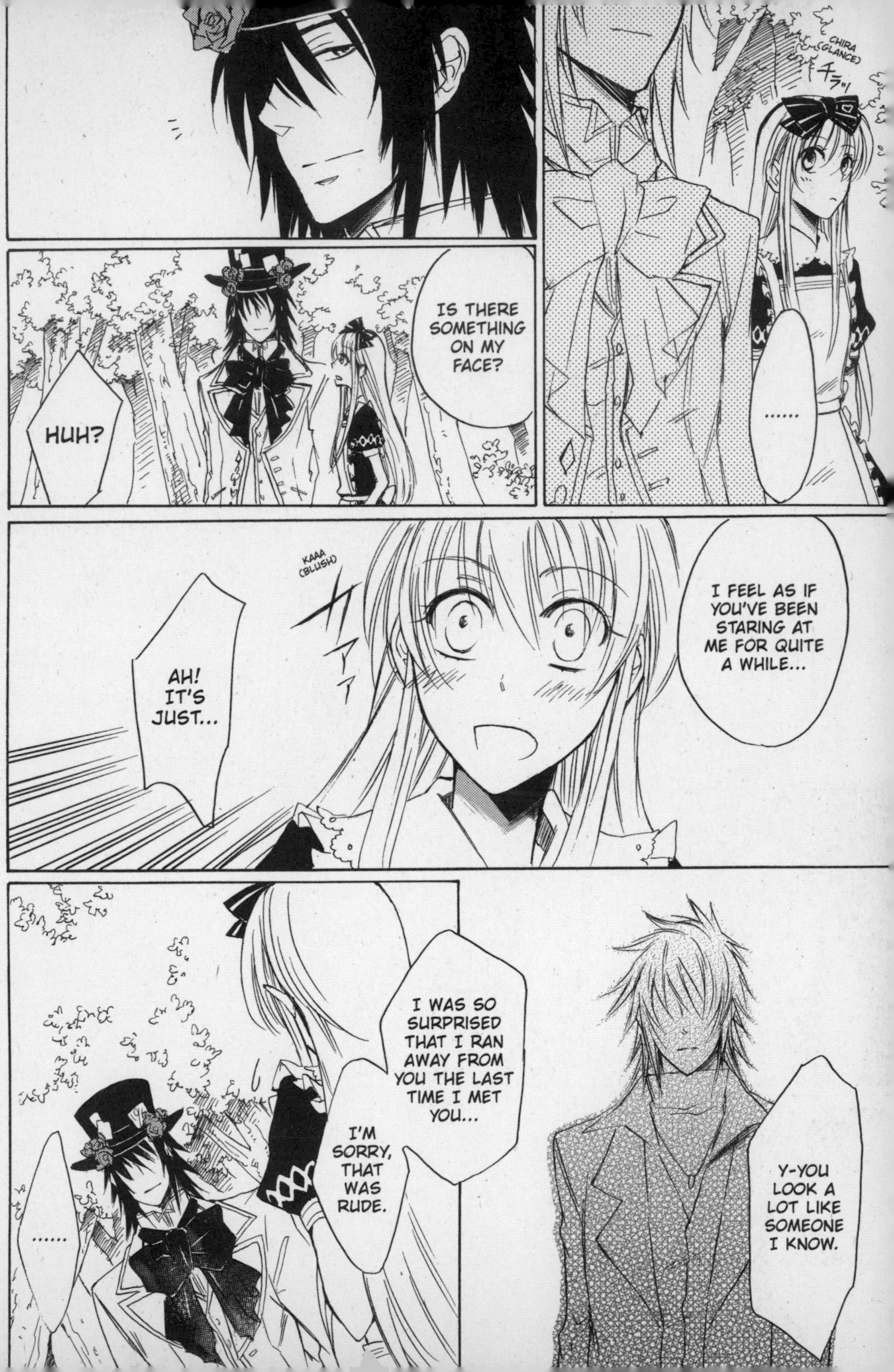
CHIRA (GLANCE)
......
IS THERE SOMETHING ON MY FACE?
HUH?
I FEEL AS IF YOU'VE BEEN STARING AT ME FOR QUITE A WHILE...
KAAA (BLUSH)
AH! IT'S JUST...
Y-YOU LOOK A LOT LIKE SOMEONE I KNOW.
I WAS SO SURPRISED THAT I RAN AWAY FROM YOU THE LAST TIME I MET YOU...
I'M SORRY, THAT WAS RUDE.
......

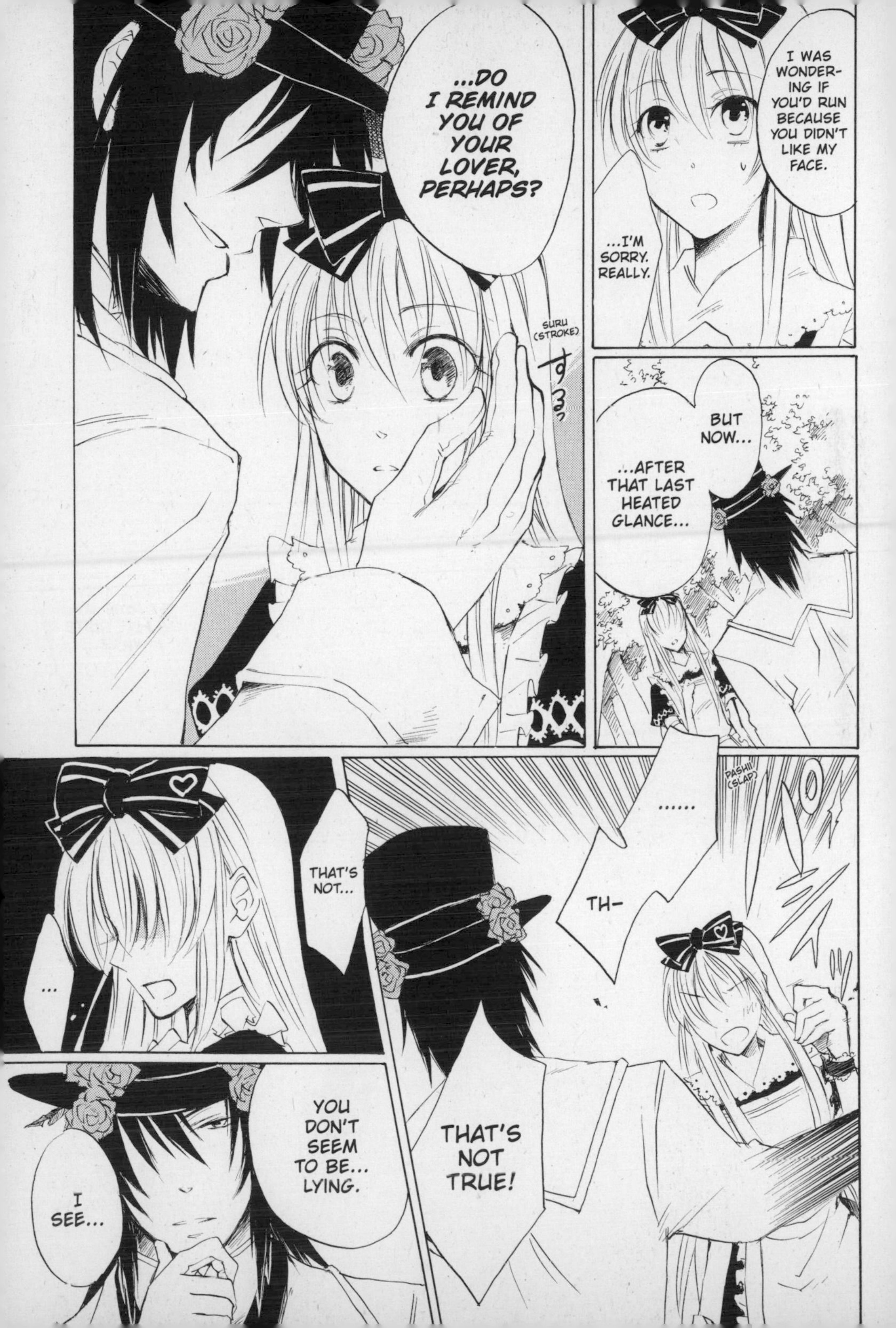
I WAS WONDERING IF YOU'D RUN BECAUSE YOU DIDN'T LIKE MY FACE.
...I'M SORRY. REALLY.
BUT NOW...
...AFTER THAT LAST HEATED GLANCE...
...DO I REMIND YOU OF YOUR LOVER, PERHAPS?
SURU (STROKE)
すぅ
PASHI! (SLAP)
......
TH-
THAT'S NOT TRUE!
THAT'S NOT...
...
YOU DON'T SEEM TO BE... LYING.
I SEE...

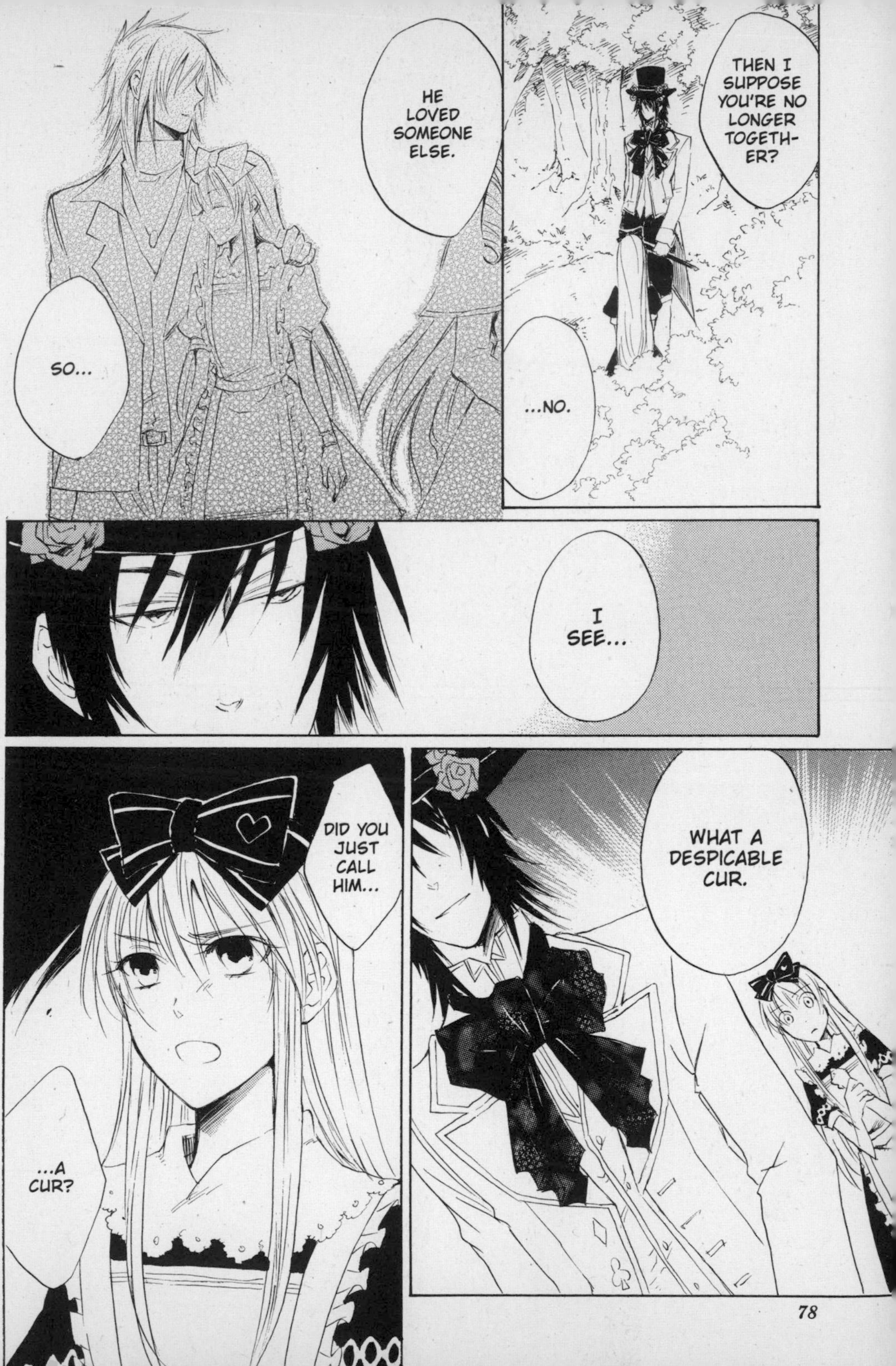
THEN I SUPPOSE YOU'RE NO LONGER TOGETHER?
...NO.
HE LOVED SOMEONE ELSE.
SO...
I SEE...
WHAT A DESPICABLE CUR.
DID YOU JUST CALL HIM...
...A CUR?

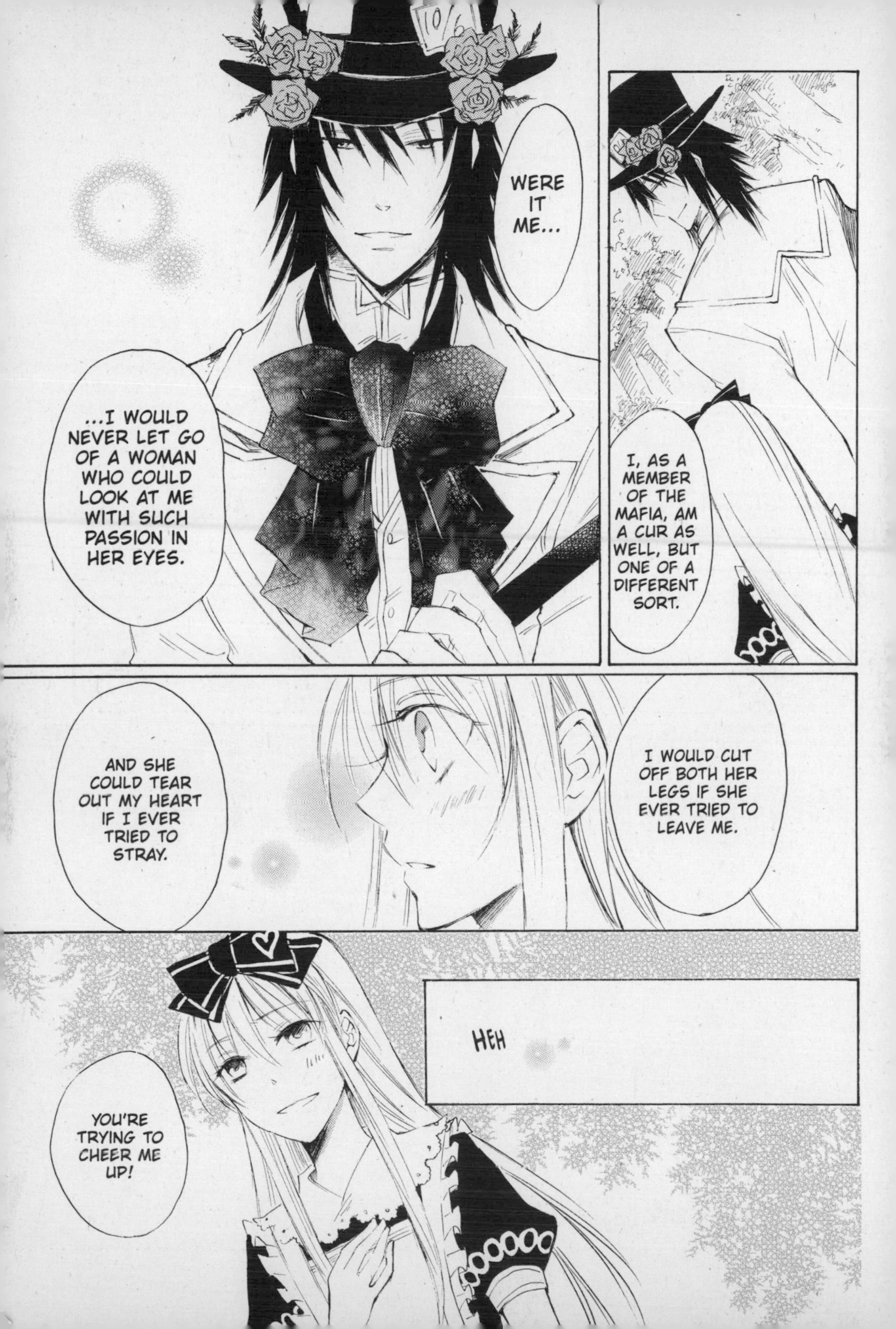
I, AS A MEMBER OF THE MAFIA, AM A CUR AS WELL, BUT ONE OF A DIFFERENT SORT.
WERE IT ME...
...I WOULD NEVER LET GO OF A WOMAN WHO COULD LOOK AT ME WITH SUCH PASSION IN HER EYES.
I WOULD CUT OFF BOTH HER LEGS IF SHE EVER TRIED TO LEAVE ME.
AND SHE COULD TEAR OUT MY HEART IF I EVER TRIED TO STRAY.
HEH
YOU'RE TRYING TO CHEER ME UP!

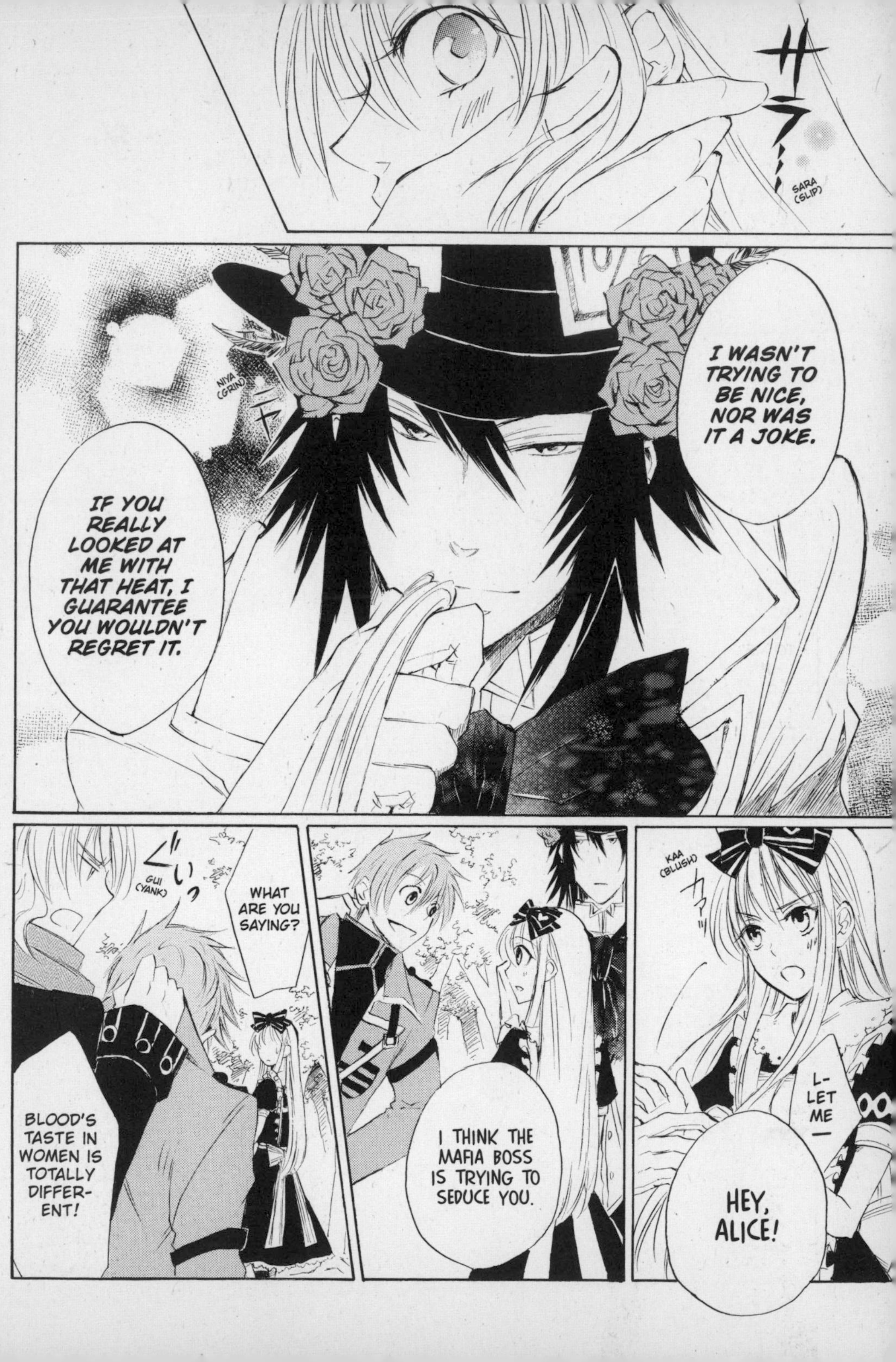
SARA (SLIP)
I WASN'T TRYING TO BE NICE, NOR WAS IT A JOKE.
NIYA (GRIN)
IF YOU REALLY LOOKED AT ME WITH THAT HEAT, I GUARANTEE YOU WOULDN'T REGRET IT.
KAA (BLUSH)
L-LET ME —
HEY, ALICE!
I THINK THE MAFIA BOSS IS TRYING TO SEDUCE YOU.
WHAT ARE YOU SAYING?
GUI (YANK)
BLOOD'S TASTE IN WOMEN IS TOTALLY DIFFER-ENT!

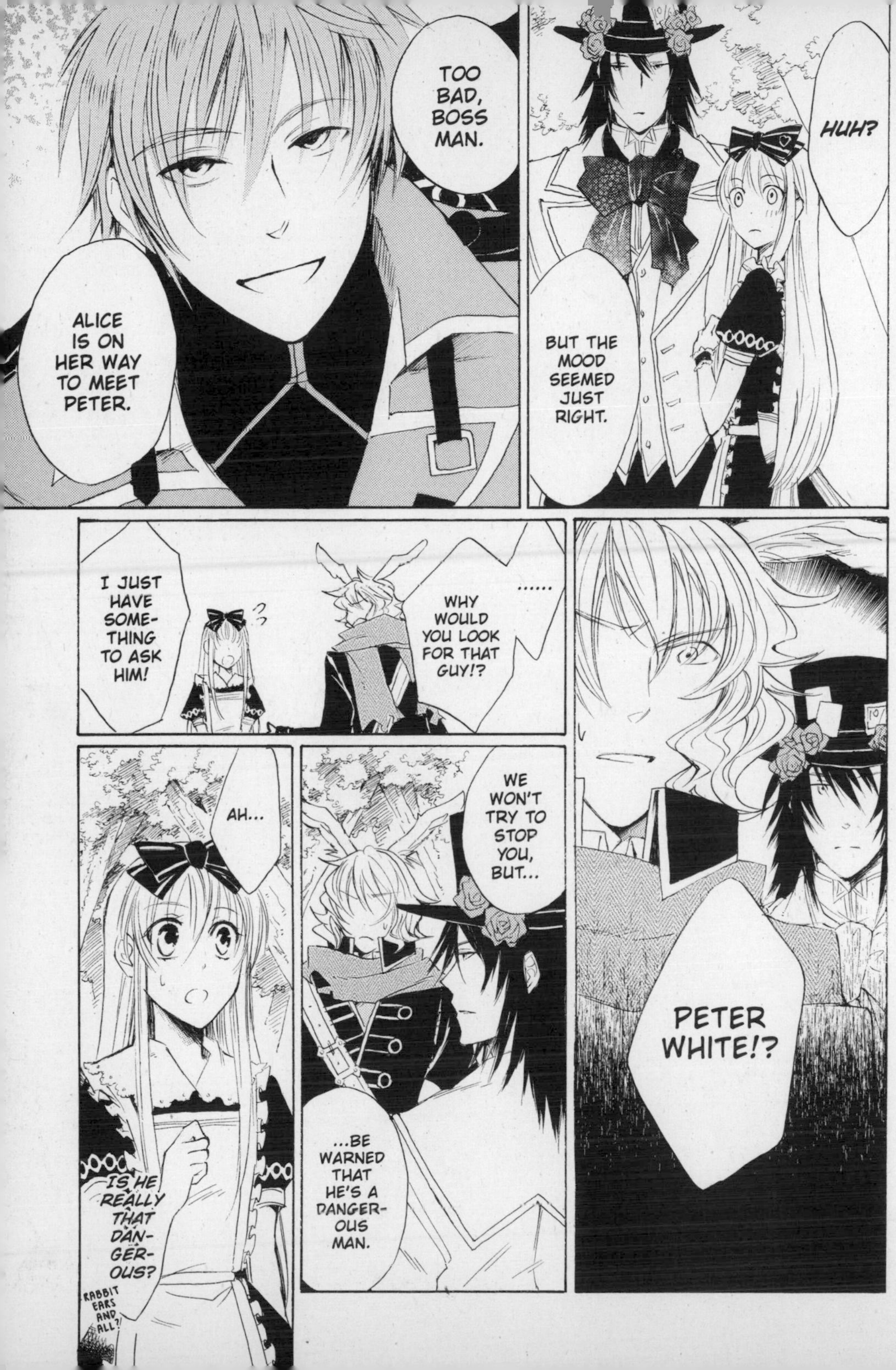
HUH?
BUT THE MOOD SEEMED JUST RIGHT.
TOO BAD, BOSS MAN.
ALICE IS ON HER WAY TO MEET PETER.
PETER WHITE!?
......
WHY WOULD YOU LOOK FOR THAT GUY!?
I JUST HAVE SOME-THING TO ASK HIM!
WE WON'T TRY TO STOP YOU, BUT...
...BE WARNED THAT HE'S A DANGER-OUS MAN.
AH...
IS HE REALLY THAT DAN-GER-OUS?
RABBIT EARS AND ALL!?

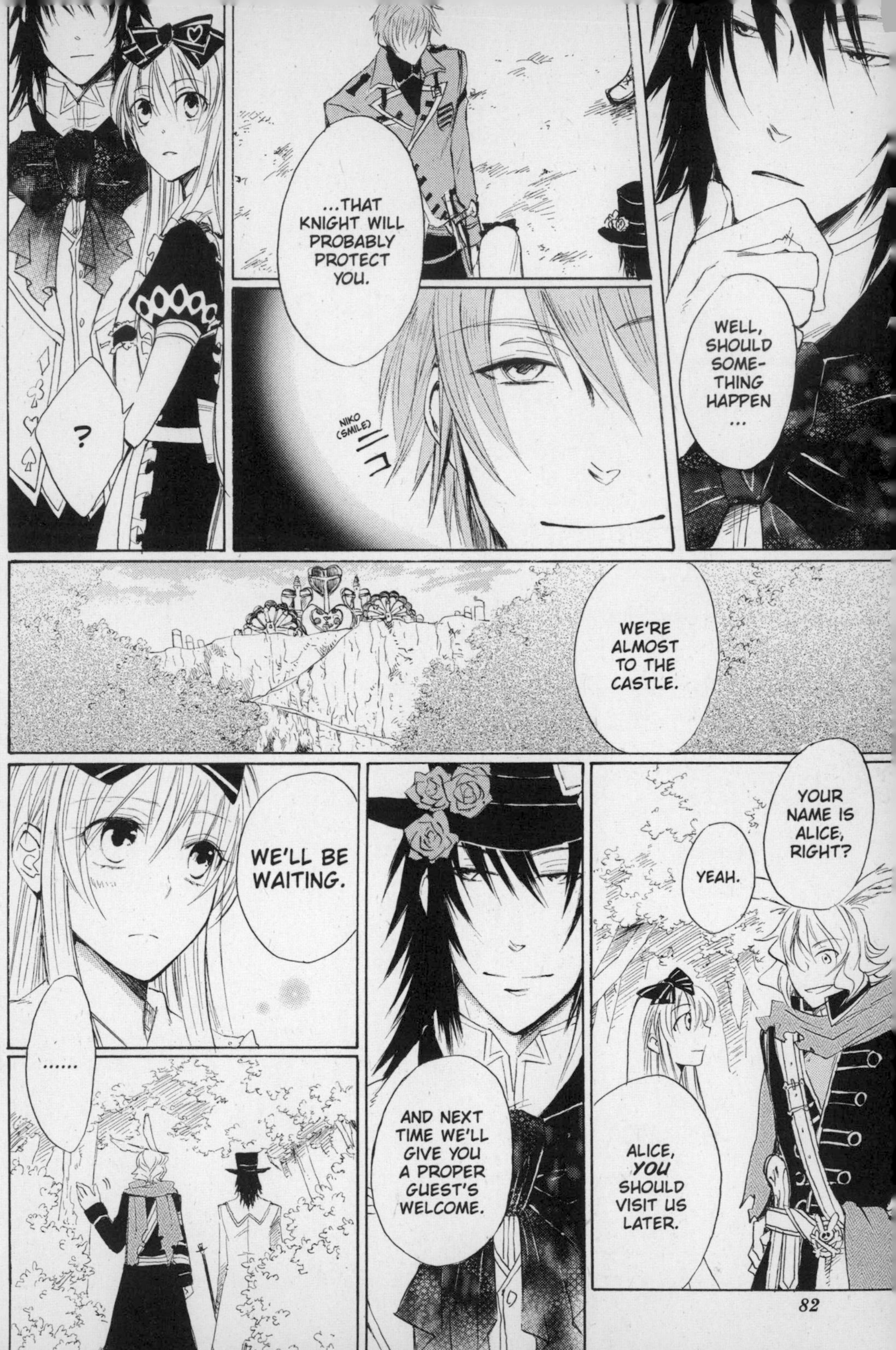
WELL, SHOULD SOME-THING HAPPEN ...
...THAT KNIGHT WILL PROBABLY PROTECT YOU.
NIKO (SMILE)
?
WE'RE ALMOST TO THE CASTLE.
YOUR NAME IS ALICE, RIGHT?
YEAH.
ALICE, *YOU* SHOULD VISIT US LATER.
AND NEXT TIME WE'LL GIVE YOU A PROPER GUEST'S WELCOME.
WE'LL BE WAITING.
......

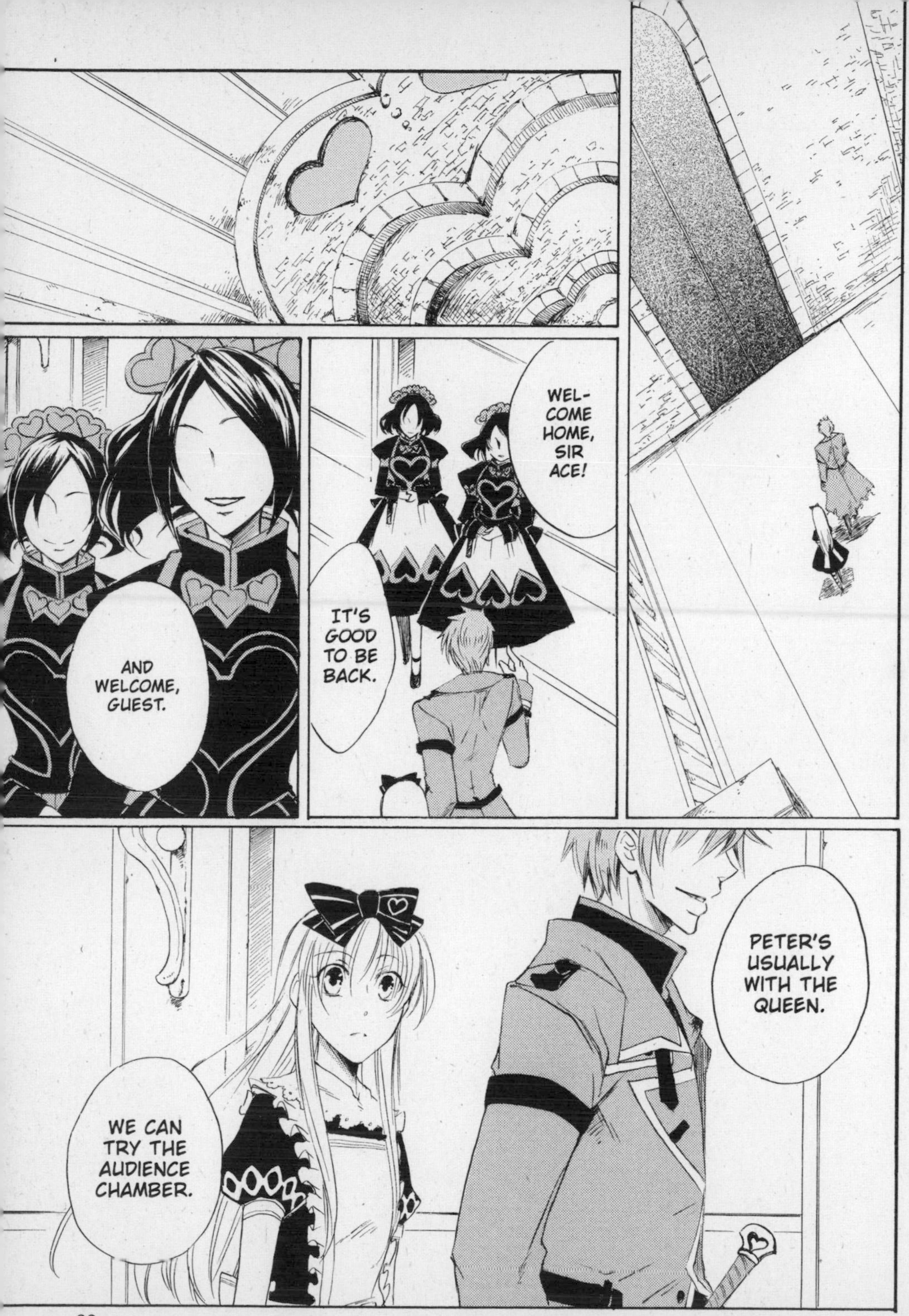
WEL-COME HOME, SIR ACE!
IT'S GOOD TO BE BACK.
AND WELCOME, GUEST.
PETER'S USUALLY WITH THE QUEEN.
WE CAN TRY THE AUDIENCE CHAMBER.

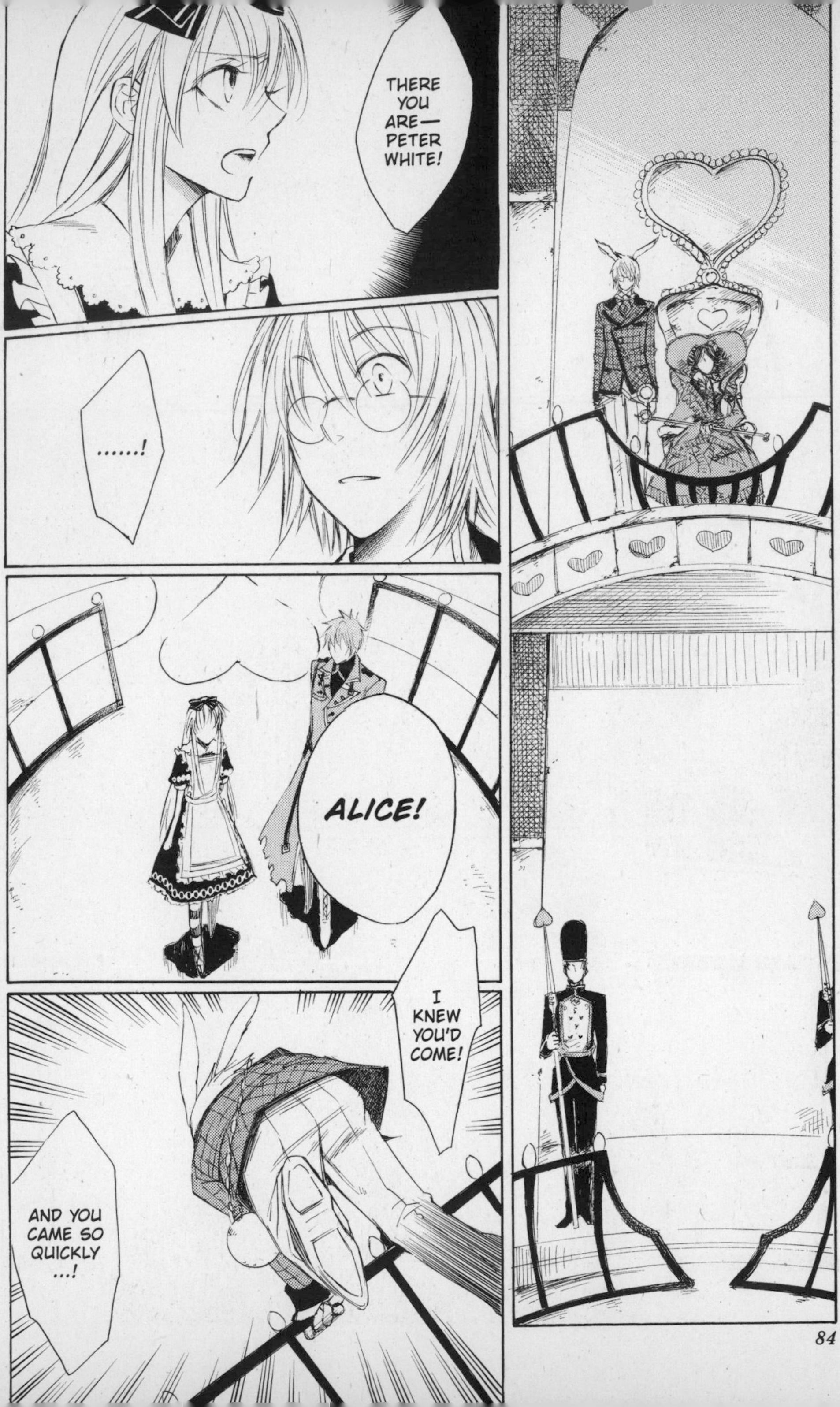
THERE YOU ARE— PETER WHITE!
......!
ALICE!
I KNEW YOU'D COME!
AND YOU CAME SO QUICKLY ...!

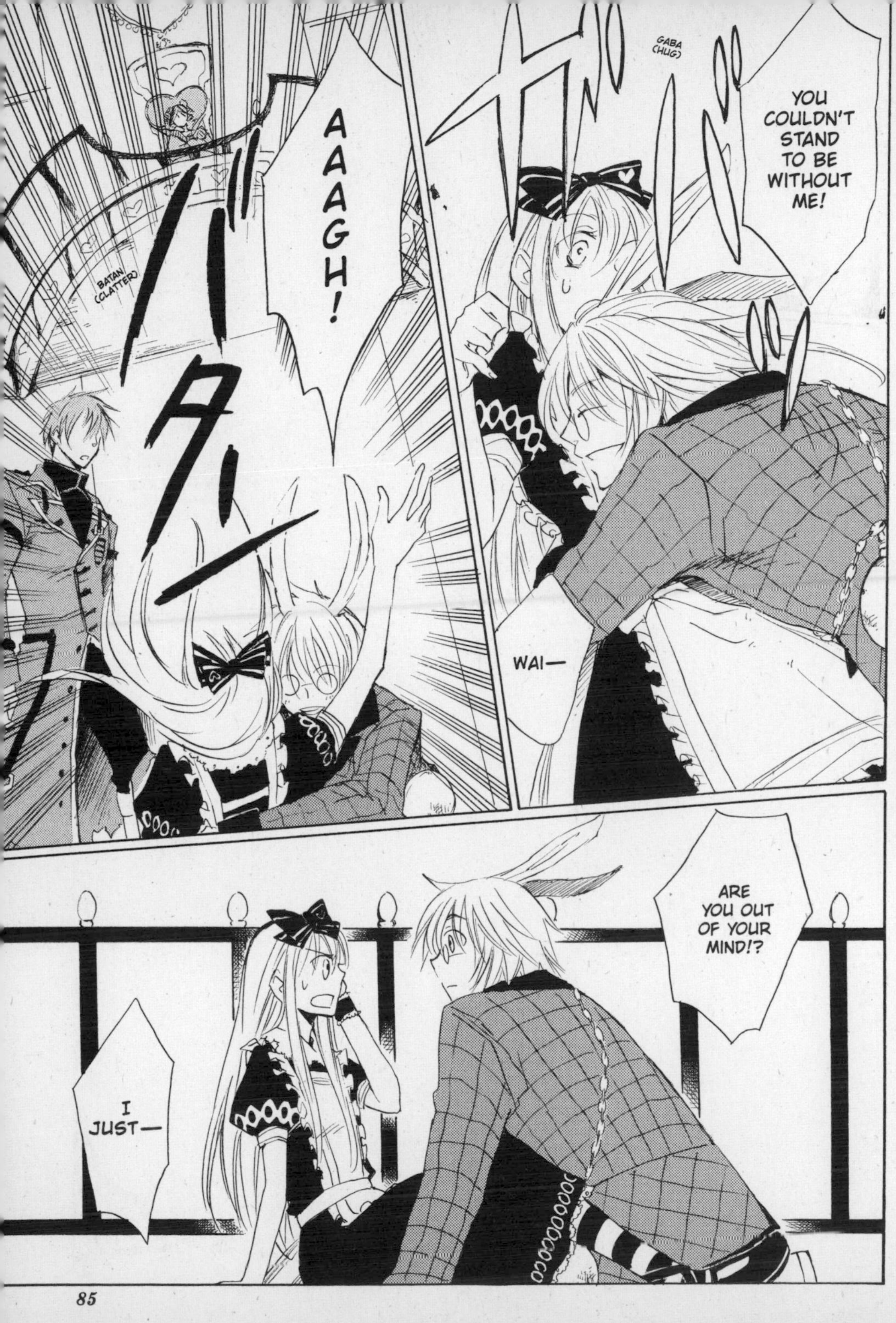
GABA (HUG)
YOU COULDN'T STAND TO BE WITHOUT ME!
WAI—
AAAAGH!
BATAN (CLATTER)
ARE YOU OUT OF YOUR MIND!?
I JUST—

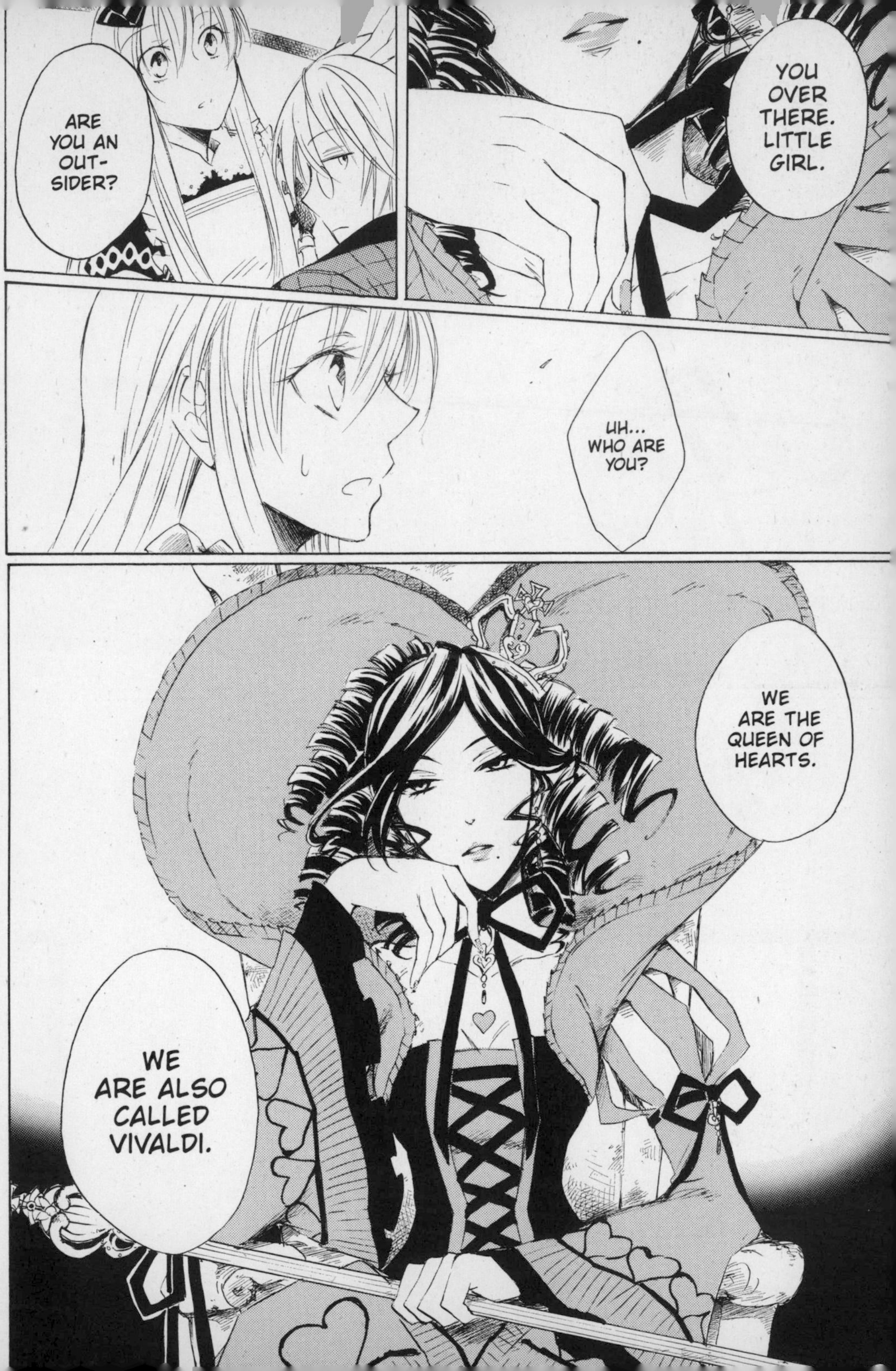
YOU OVER THERE. LITTLE GIRL.
ARE YOU AN OUT-SIDER?
UH... WHO ARE YOU?
WE ARE THE QUEEN OF HEARTS.
WE ARE ALSO CALLED VIVALDI.

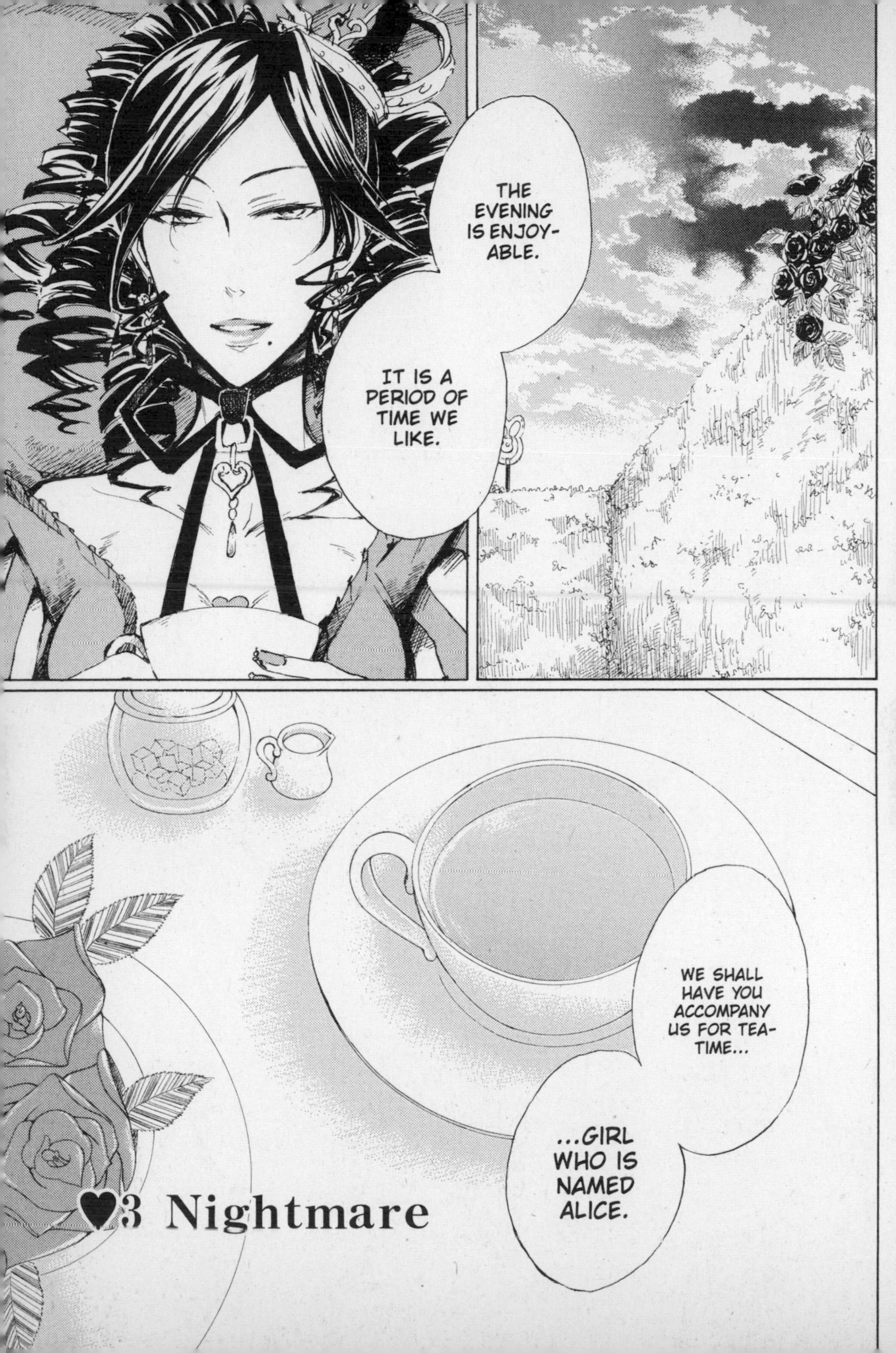
THE EVENING IS ENJOY-ABLE.
IT IS A PERIOD OF TIME WE LIKE.
WE SHALL HAVE YOU ACCOMPANY US FOR TEA-TIME...
...GIRL WHO IS NAMED ALICE.
♥3 Nightmare

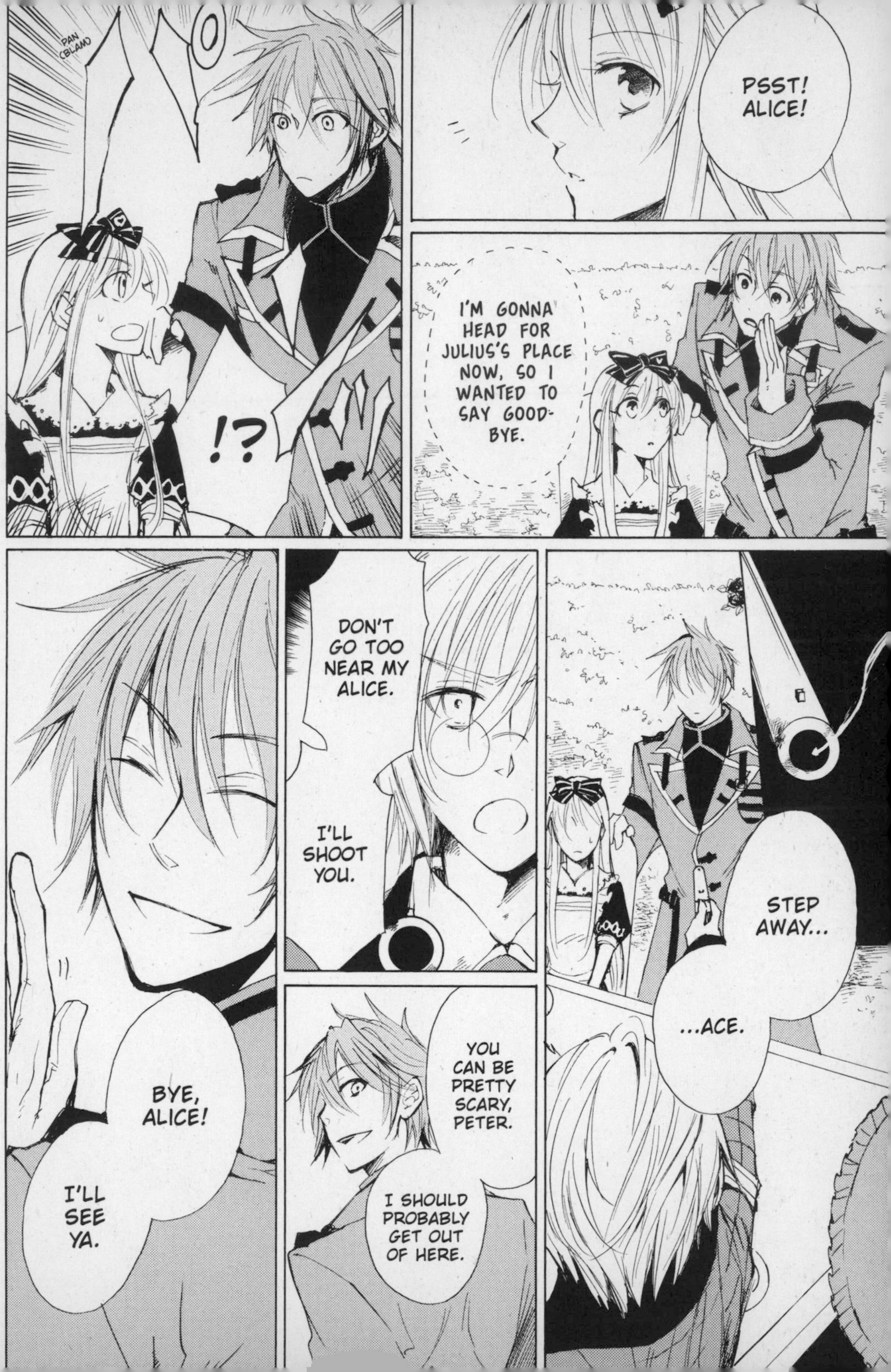
PSST! ALICE!
I'M GONNA HEAD FOR JULIUS'S PLACE NOW, SO I WANTED TO SAY GOOD-BYE.
PAN (BLAM)
!?
STEP AWAY...
...ACE.
DON'T GO TOO NEAR MY ALICE.
I'LL SHOOT YOU.
YOU CAN BE PRETTY SCARY, PETER.
I SHOULD PROBABLY GET OUT OF HERE.
BYE, ALICE!
I'LL SEE YA.

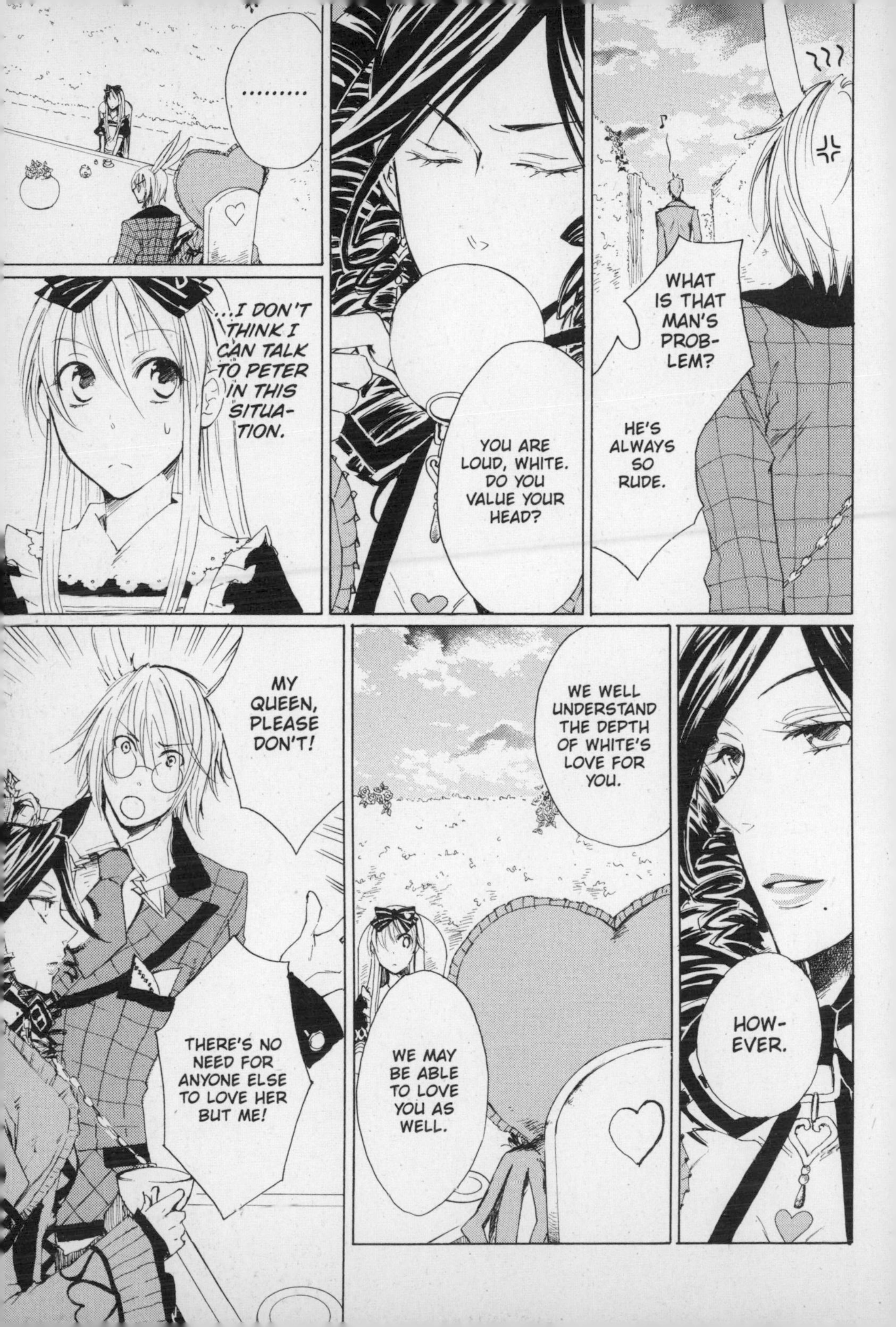
WHAT IS THAT MAN'S PROBLEM?
HE'S ALWAYS SO RUDE.
YOU ARE LOUD, WHITE. DO YOU VALUE YOUR HEAD?
....
...I DON'T THINK I CAN TALK TO PETER IN THIS SITUATION.
HOW-EVER.
WE WELL UNDERSTAND THE DEPTH OF WHITE'S LOVE FOR YOU.
WE MAY BE ABLE TO LOVE YOU AS WELL.
MY QUEEN, PLEASE DON'T!
THERE'S NO NEED FOR ANYONE ELSE TO LOVE HER BUT ME!

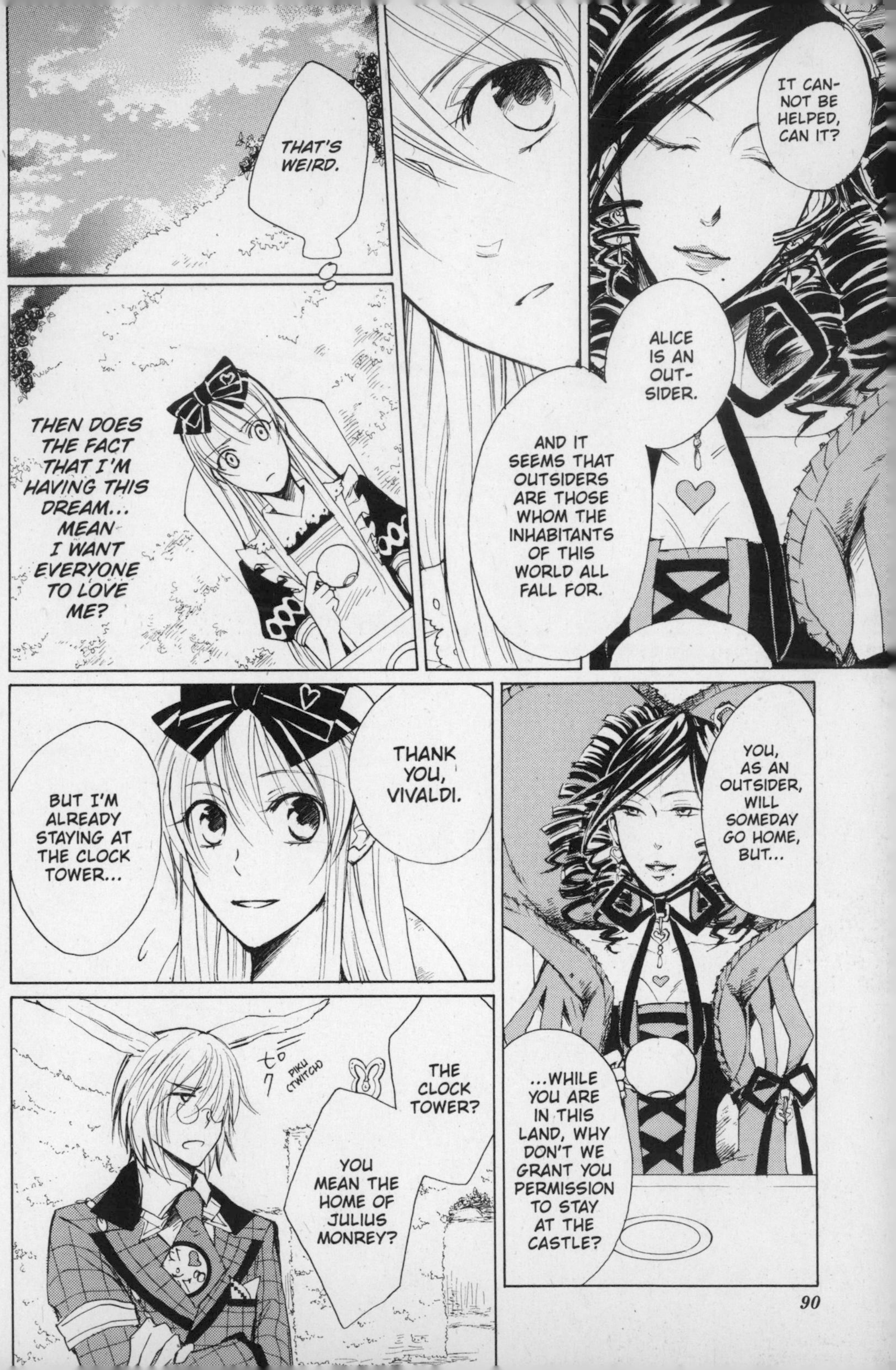
IT CAN-NOT BE HELPED, CAN IT?
ALICE IS AN OUT-SIDER.
AND IT SEEMS THAT OUTSIDERS ARE THOSE WHOM THE INHABITANTS OF THIS WORLD ALL FALL FOR.
THAT'S WEIRD.
THEN DOES THE FACT THAT I'M HAVING THIS DREAM... MEAN I WANT EVERYONE TO LOVE ME?
YOU, AS AN OUTSIDER, WILL SOMEDAY GO HOME, BUT...
...WHILE YOU ARE IN THIS LAND, WHY DON'T WE GRANT YOU PERMISSION TO STAY AT THE CASTLE?
THANK YOU, VIVALDI.
BUT I'M ALREADY STAYING AT THE CLOCK TOWER...
PIKU (TWITCH)
THE CLOCK TOWER?
YOU MEAN THE HOME OF JULIUS MONREY?

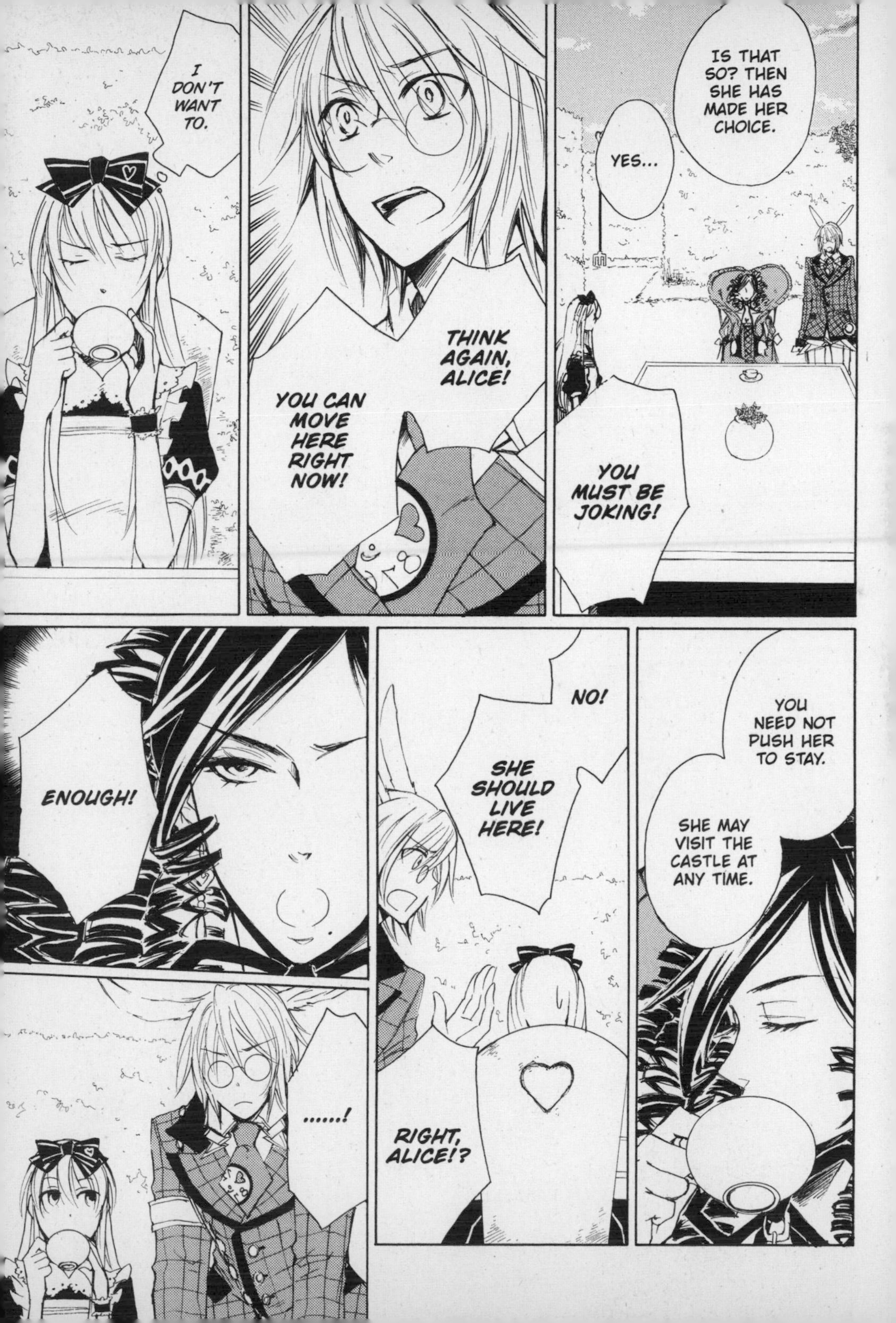
IS THAT SO? THEN SHE HAS MADE HER CHOICE.
YES...
YOU MUST BE JOKING!
THINK AGAIN, ALICE!
YOU CAN MOVE HERE RIGHT NOW!
I DON'T WANT TO.
YOU NEED NOT PUSH HER TO STAY.
SHE MAY VISIT THE CASTLE AT ANY TIME.
NO!
SHE SHOULD LIVE HERE!
RIGHT, ALICE!?
ENOUGH!
......!

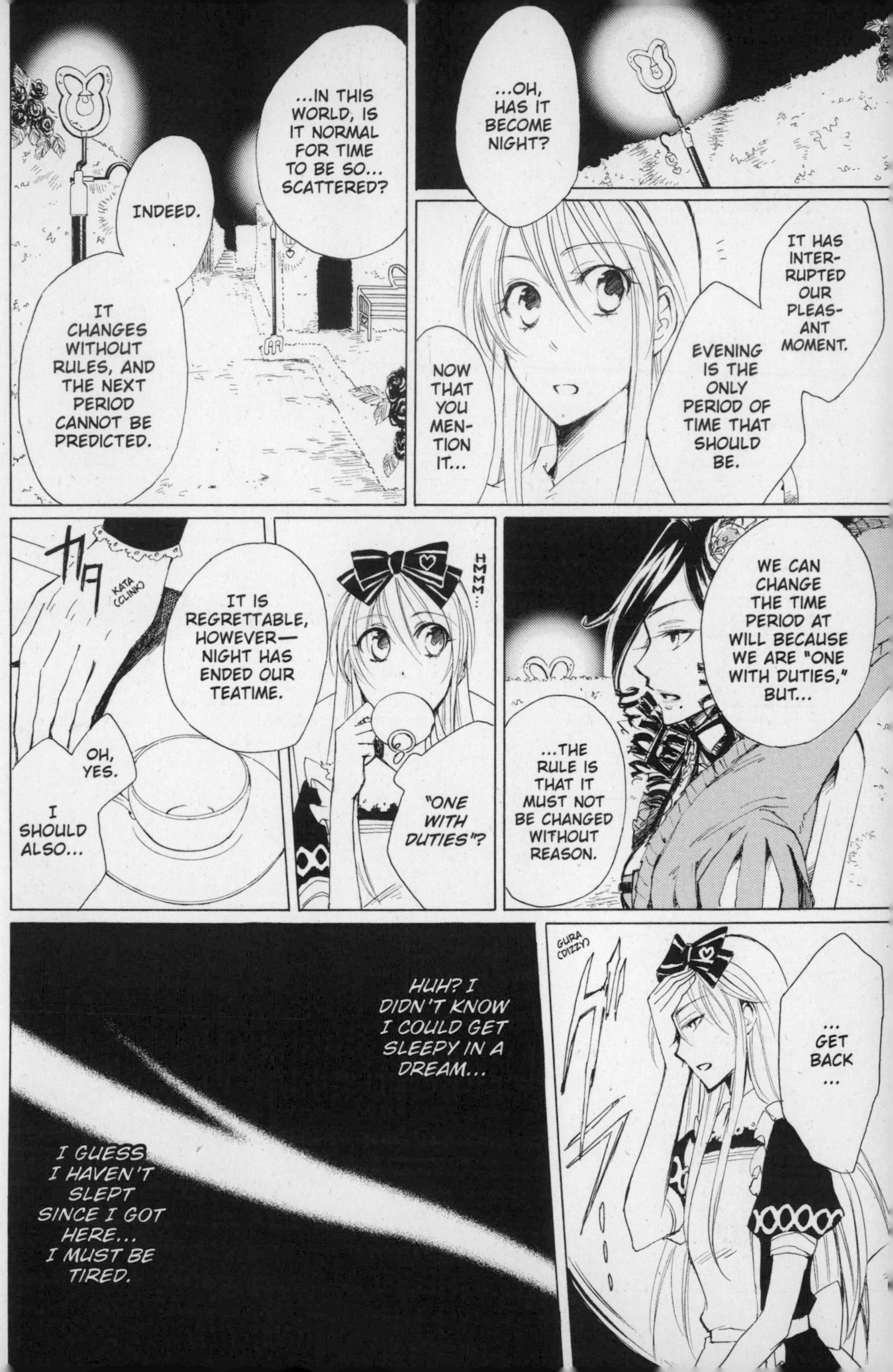
...OH, HAS IT BECOME NIGHT?
IT HAS INTERRUPTED OUR PLEASANT MOMENT.
EVENING IS THE ONLY PERIOD OF TIME THAT SHOULD BE.
NOW THAT YOU MENTION IT...
...IN THIS WORLD, IS IT NORMAL FOR TIME TO BE SO... SCATTERED?
INDEED.
IT CHANGES WITHOUT RULES, AND THE NEXT PERIOD CANNOT BE PREDICTED.
WE CAN CHANGE THE TIME PERIOD AT WILL BECAUSE WE ARE "ONE WITH DUTIES," BUT...
...THE RULE IS THAT IT MUST NOT BE CHANGED WITHOUT REASON.
HMMM...
"ONE WITH DUTIES"?
IT IS REGRETTABLE, HOWEVER—NIGHT HAS ENDED OUR TEATIME.
KATA (CLINK)
OH, YES.
I SHOULD ALSO...
GURA (DIZZY)
...GET BACK...
HUH? I DIDN'T KNOW I COULD GET SLEEPY IN A DREAM...
I GUESS I HAVEN'T SLEPT SINCE I GOT HERE... I MUST BE TIRED.

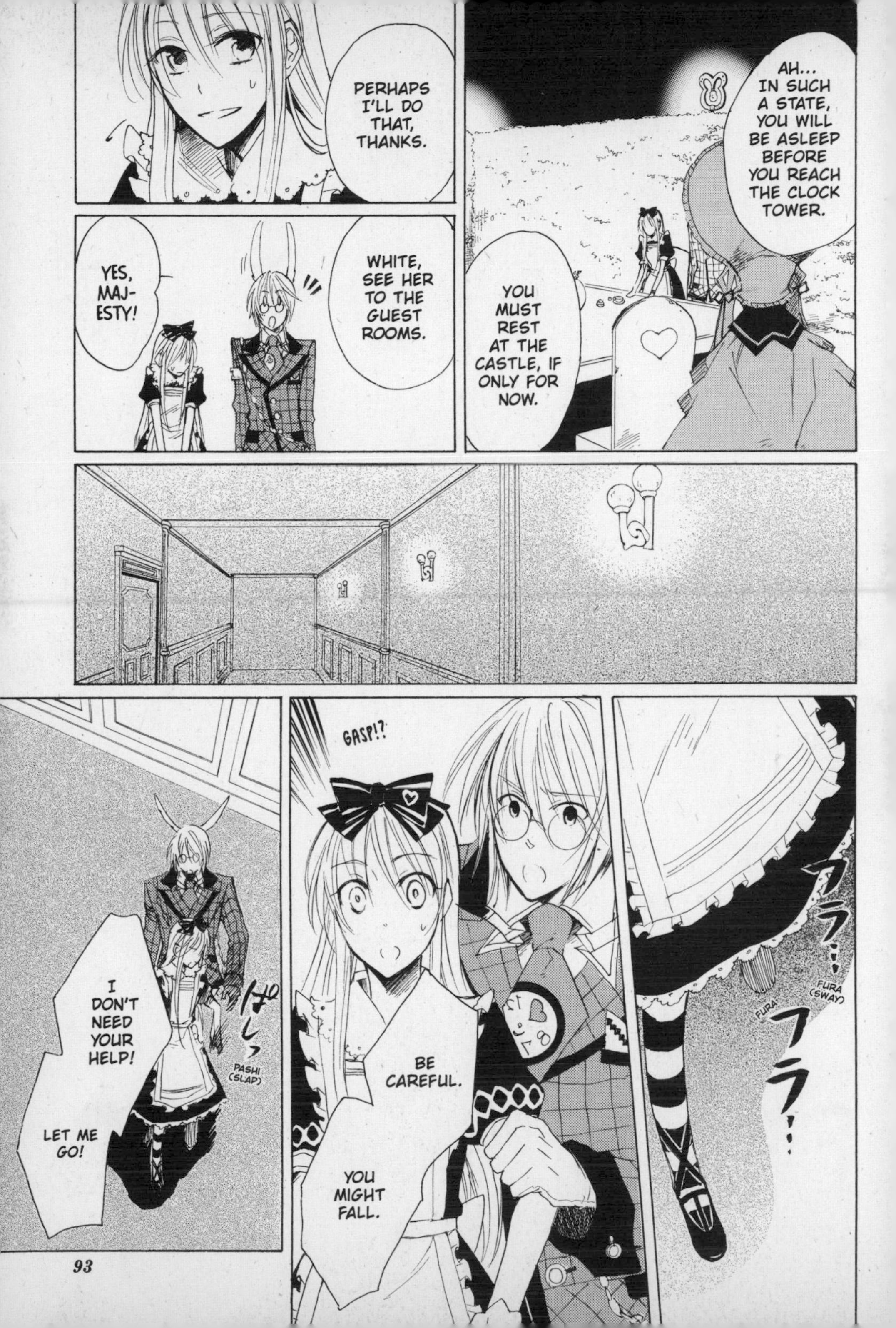
AH... IN SUCH A STATE, YOU WILL BE ASLEEP BEFORE YOU REACH THE CLOCK TOWER.
YOU MUST REST AT THE CASTLE, IF ONLY FOR NOW.
PERHAPS I'LL DO THAT, THANKS.
WHITE, SEE HER TO THE GUEST ROOMS.
YES, MAJ-ESTY!
FURA (SWAY)
FURA
GASP!?
BE CAREFUL.
YOU MIGHT FALL.
I DON'T NEED YOUR HELP!
PASHI (SLAP)
LET ME GO!

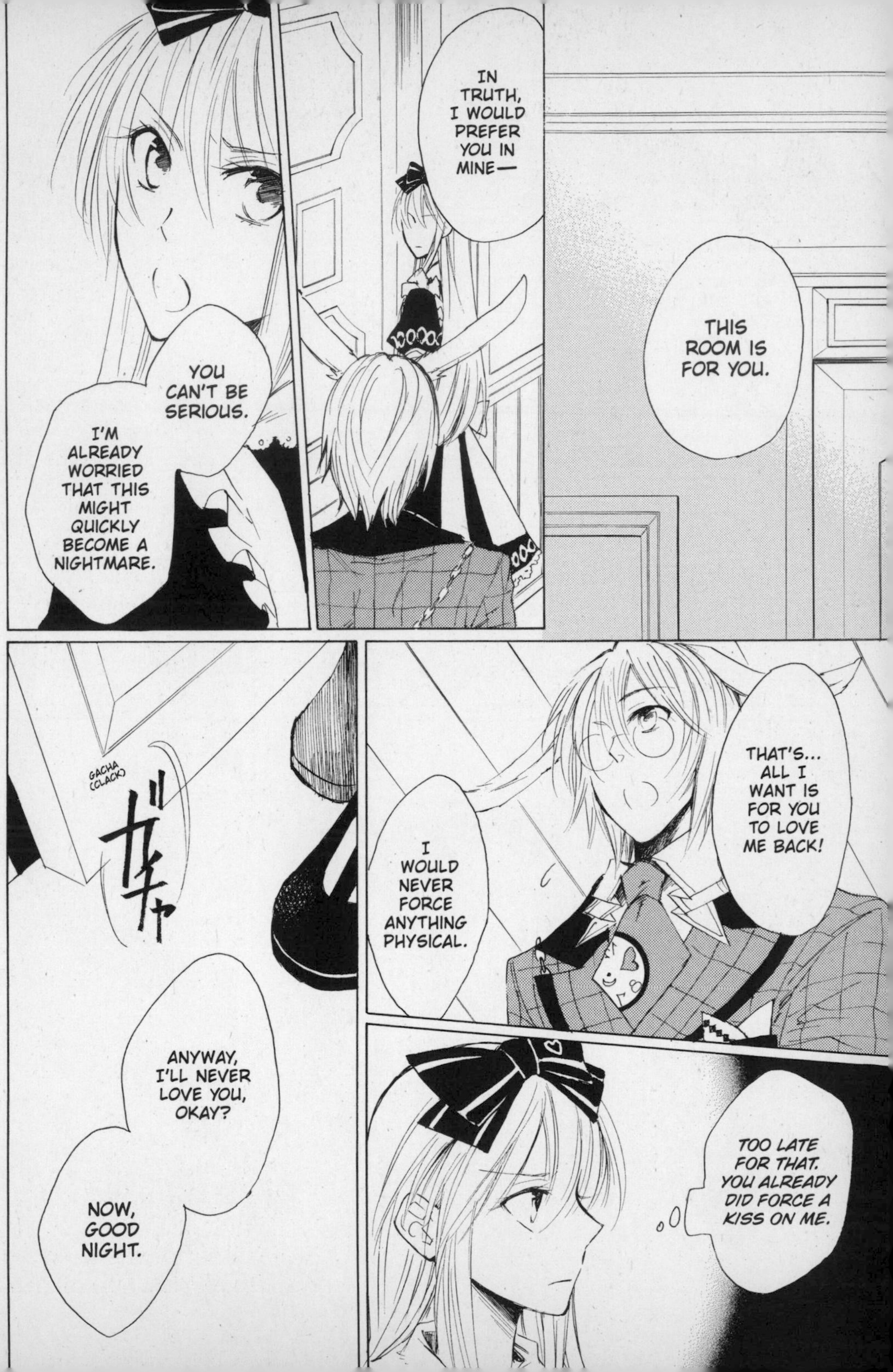
THIS ROOM IS FOR YOU.
IN TRUTH, I WOULD PREFER YOU IN MINE—
YOU CAN'T BE SERIOUS.
I'M ALREADY WORRIED THAT THIS MIGHT QUICKLY BECOME A NIGHTMARE.
THAT'S... ALL I WANT IS FOR YOU TO LOVE ME BACK!
I WOULD NEVER FORCE ANYTHING PHYSICAL.
TOO LATE FOR THAT. YOU ALREADY DID FORCE A KISS ON ME.
ガチャ
GACHA (CLACK)
ANYWAY, I'LL NEVER LOVE YOU, OKAY?
NOW, GOOD NIGHT.

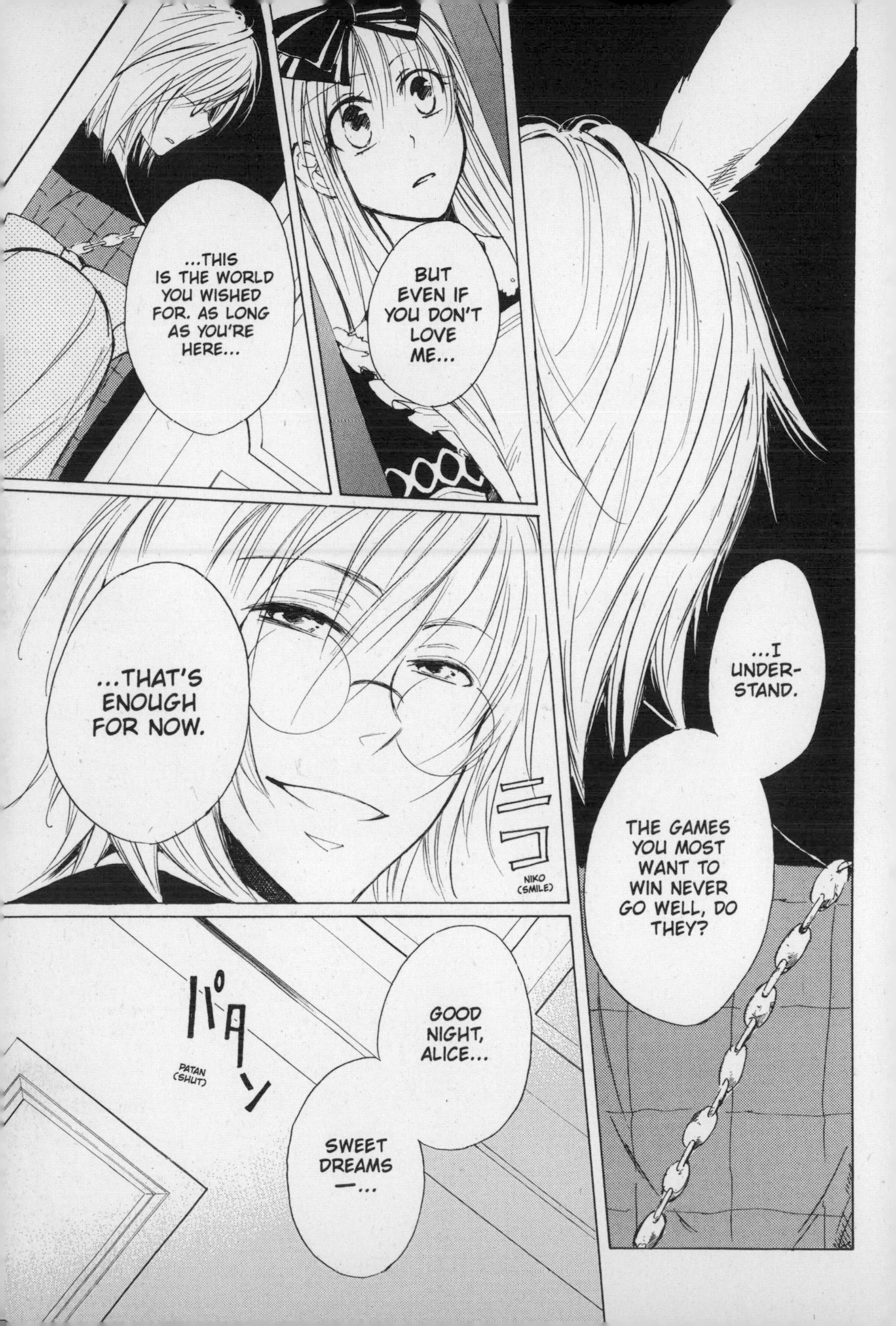

...I UNDER-STAND.
THE GAMES YOU MOST WANT TO WIN NEVER GO WELL, DO THEY?
BUT EVEN IF YOU DON'T LOVE ME...
...THIS IS THE WORLD YOU WISHED FOR. AS LONG AS YOU'RE HERE...
...THAT'S ENOUGH FOR NOW.
ニコ
NIKO (SMILE)
GOOD NIGHT, ALICE...
SWEET DREAMS—...
パタン
PATAN (SHUT)

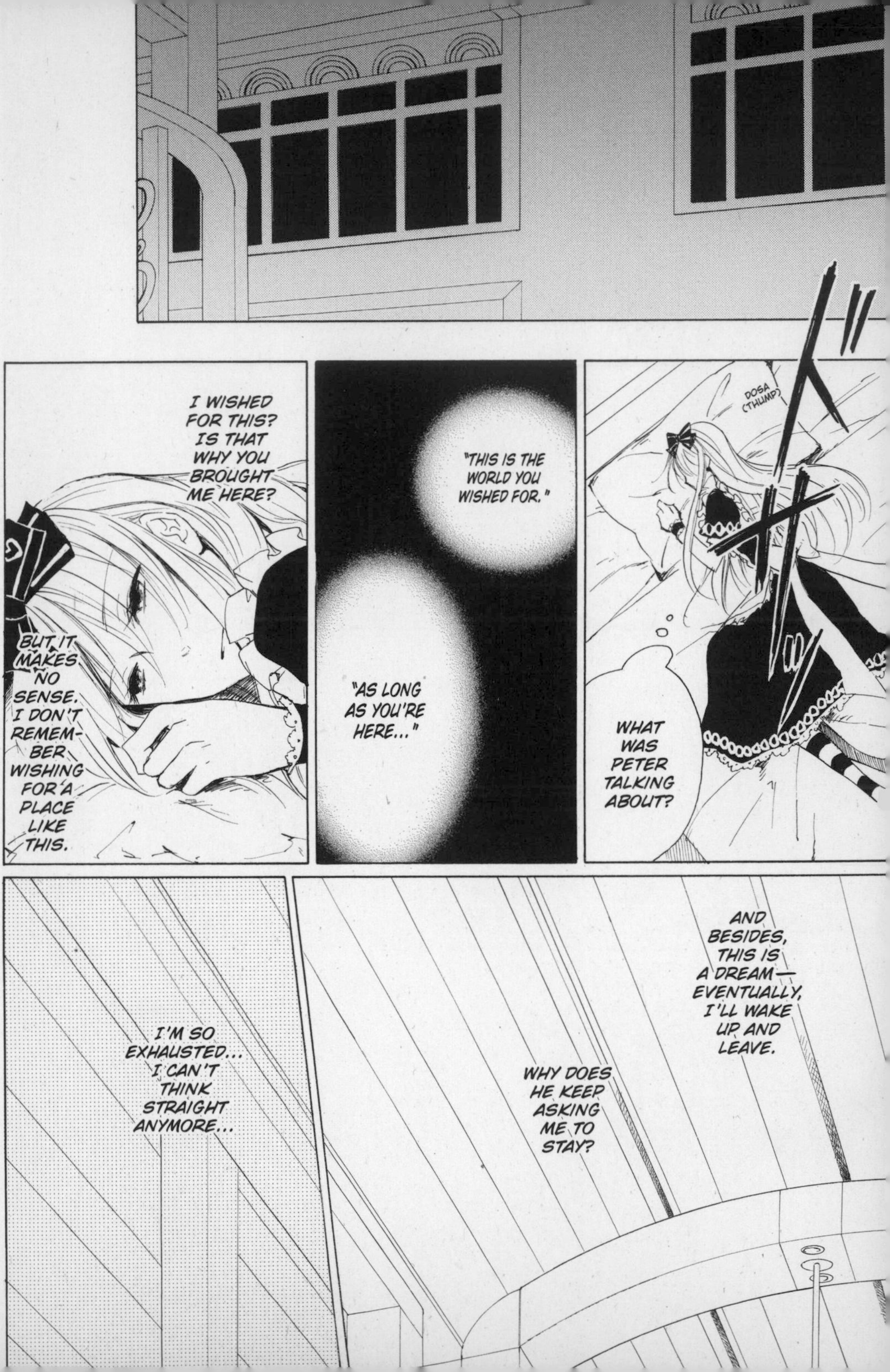
DOSA (THUMP)
WHAT WAS PETER TALKING ABOUT?
"THIS IS THE WORLD YOU WISHED FOR."
"AS LONG AS YOU'RE HERE..."
I WISHED FOR THIS? IS THAT WHY YOU BROUGHT ME HERE?
BUT IT MAKES NO SENSE. I DON'T REMEMBER WISHING FOR A PLACE LIKE THIS.
AND BESIDES, THIS IS A DREAM— EVENTUALLY, I'LL WAKE UP AND LEAVE.
WHY DOES HE KEEP ASKING ME TO STAY?
I'M SO EXHAUSTED... I CAN'T THINK STRAIGHT ANYMORE...

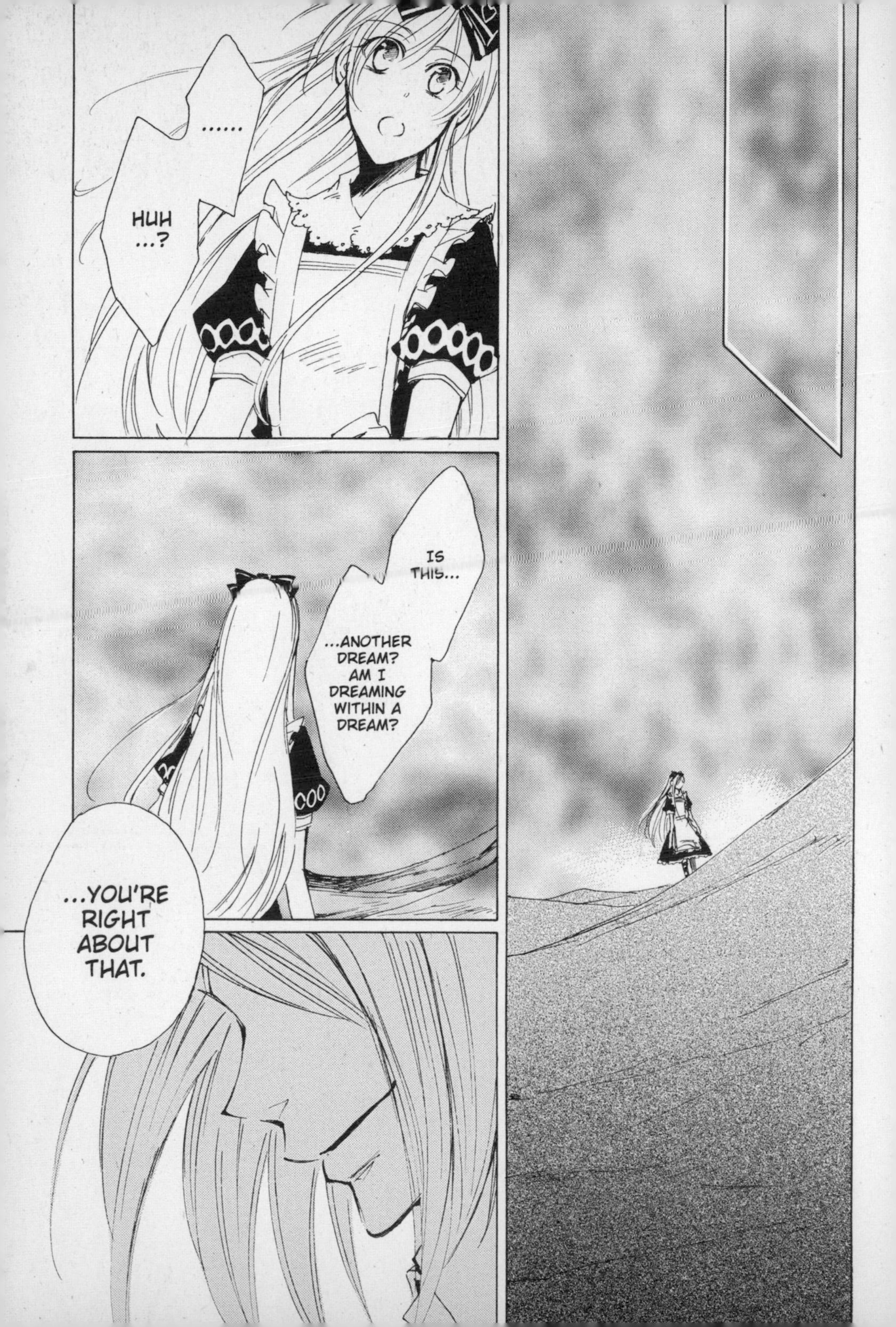
......
HUH ...?
IS THIS...
...ANOTHER DREAM? AM I DREAMING WITHIN A DREAM?
...YOU'RE RIGHT ABOUT THAT.

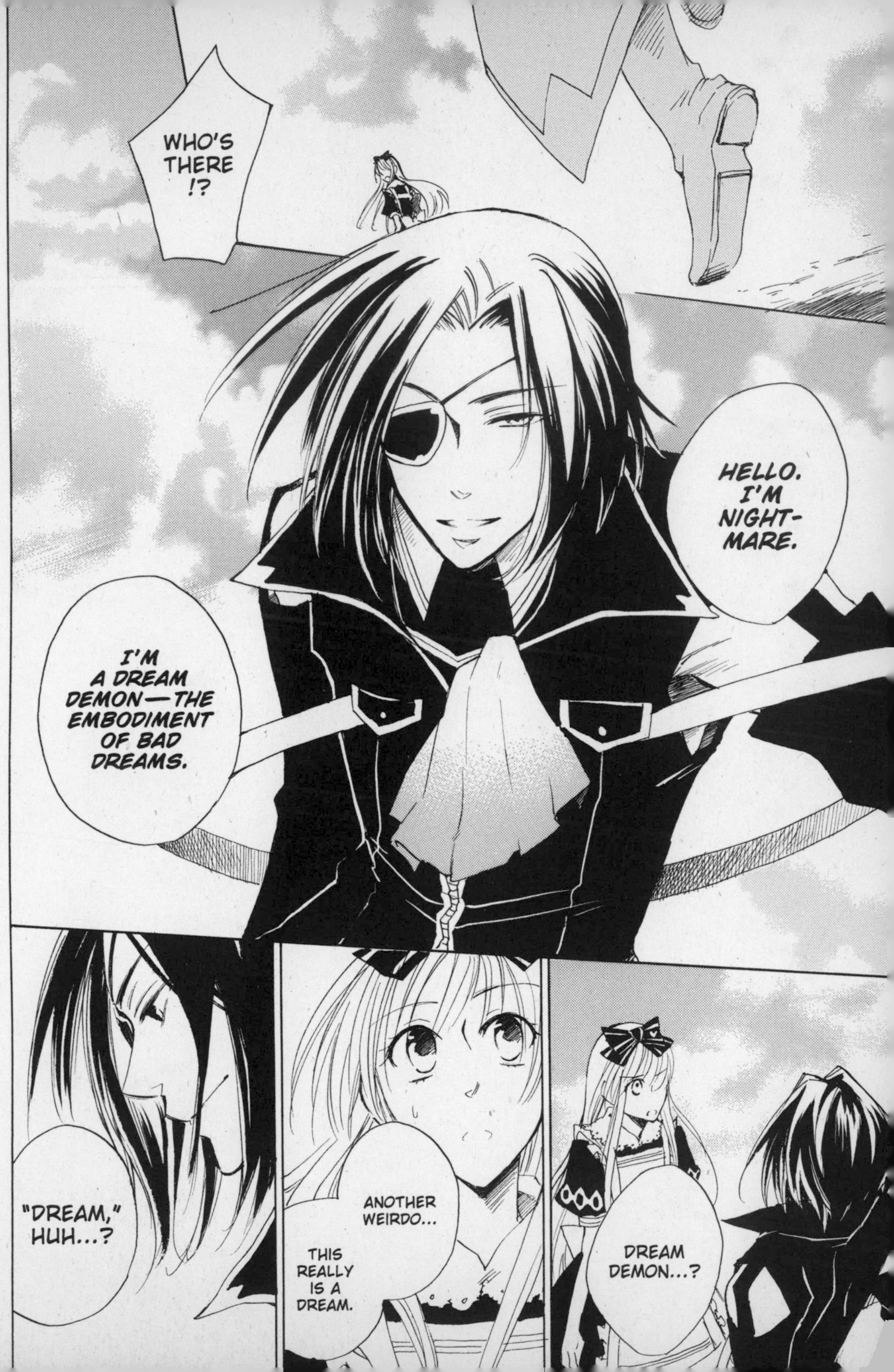
WHO'S THERE!?
HELLO. I'M NIGHT-MARE.
I'M A DREAM DEMON—THE EMBODIMENT OF BAD DREAMS.
DREAM DEMON...?
ANOTHER WEIRDO...
THIS REALLY IS A DREAM.
"DREAM," HUH...?

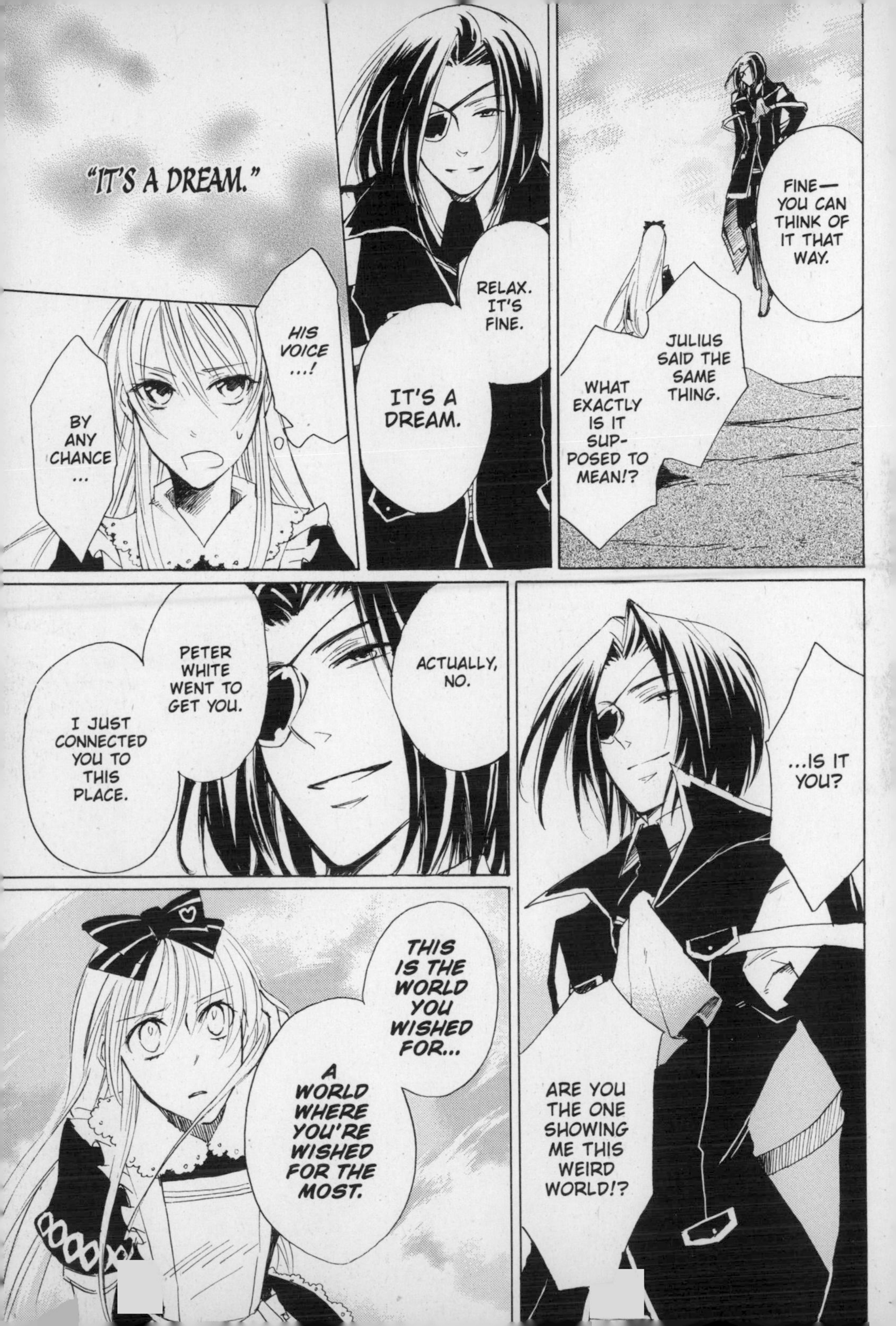
FINE— YOU CAN THINK OF IT THAT WAY.
JULIUS SAID THE SAME THING.
WHAT EXACTLY IS IT SUP-POSED TO MEAN!?
RELAX. IT'S FINE.
IT'S A DREAM.
"IT'S A DREAM."
HIS VOICE ...!
BY ANY CHANCE ...
...IS IT YOU?
ARE YOU THE ONE SHOWING ME THIS WEIRD WORLD!?
ACTUALLY, NO.
PETER WHITE WENT TO GET YOU.
I JUST CONNECTED YOU TO THIS PLACE.
THIS IS THE WORLD YOU WISHED FOR...
A WORLD WHERE YOU'RE WISHED FOR THE MOST.

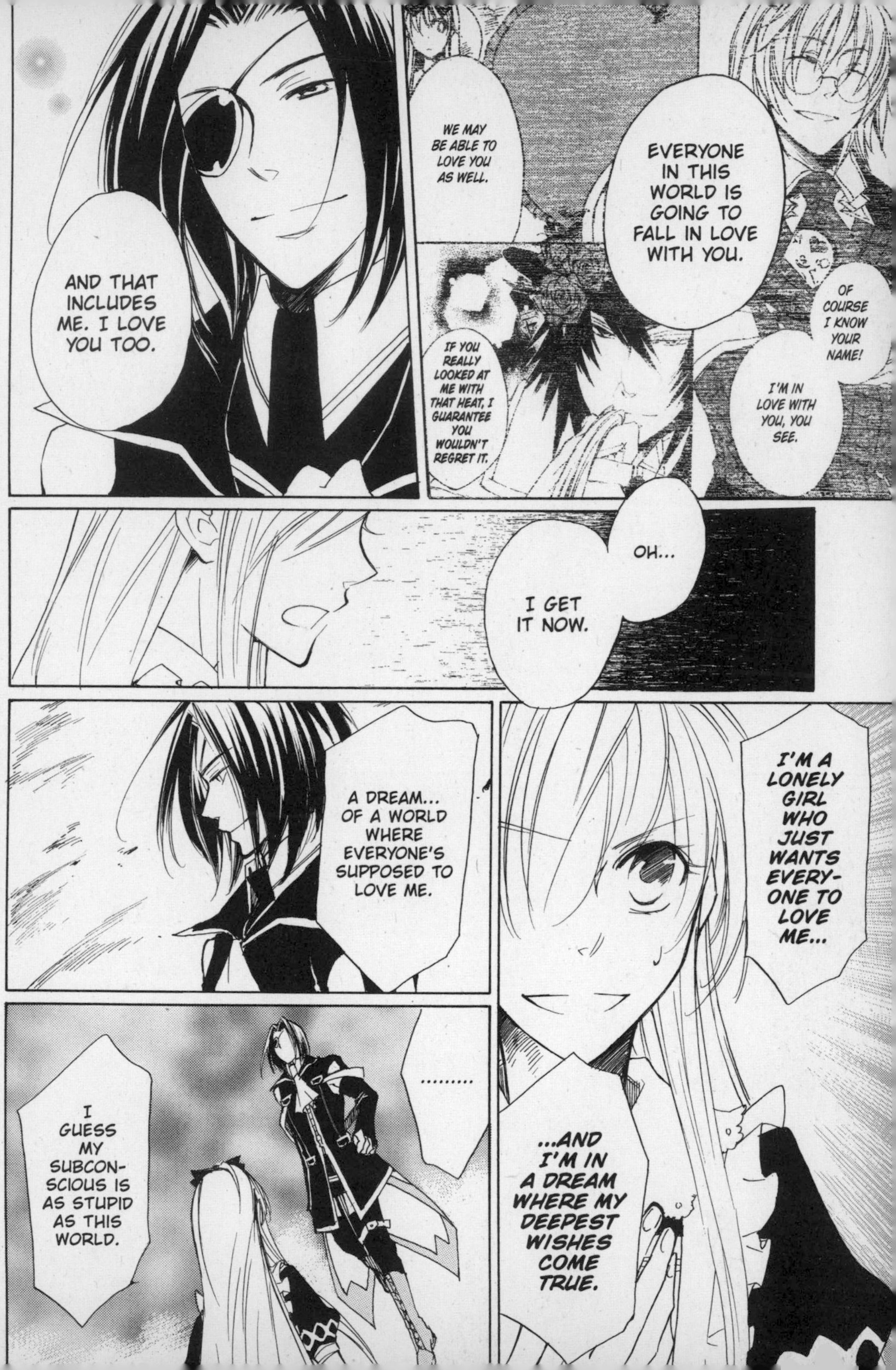
EVERYONE IN THIS WORLD IS GOING TO FALL IN LOVE WITH YOU.
WE MAY BE ABLE TO LOVE YOU AS WELL.
OF COURSE I KNOW YOUR NAME!
I'M IN LOVE WITH YOU, YOU SEE.
IF YOU REALLY LOOKED AT ME WITH THAT HEAT, I GUARANTEE YOU WOULDN'T REGRET IT.
AND THAT INCLUDES ME. I LOVE YOU TOO.
OH...
I GET IT NOW.
I'M A LONELY GIRL WHO JUST WANTS EVERY-ONE TO LOVE ME...
...AND I'M IN A DREAM WHERE MY DEEPEST WISHES COME TRUE.
A DREAM... OF A WORLD WHERE EVERYONE'S SUPPOSED TO LOVE ME.
....
I GUESS MY SUBCON-SCIOUS IS AS STUPID AS THIS WORLD.

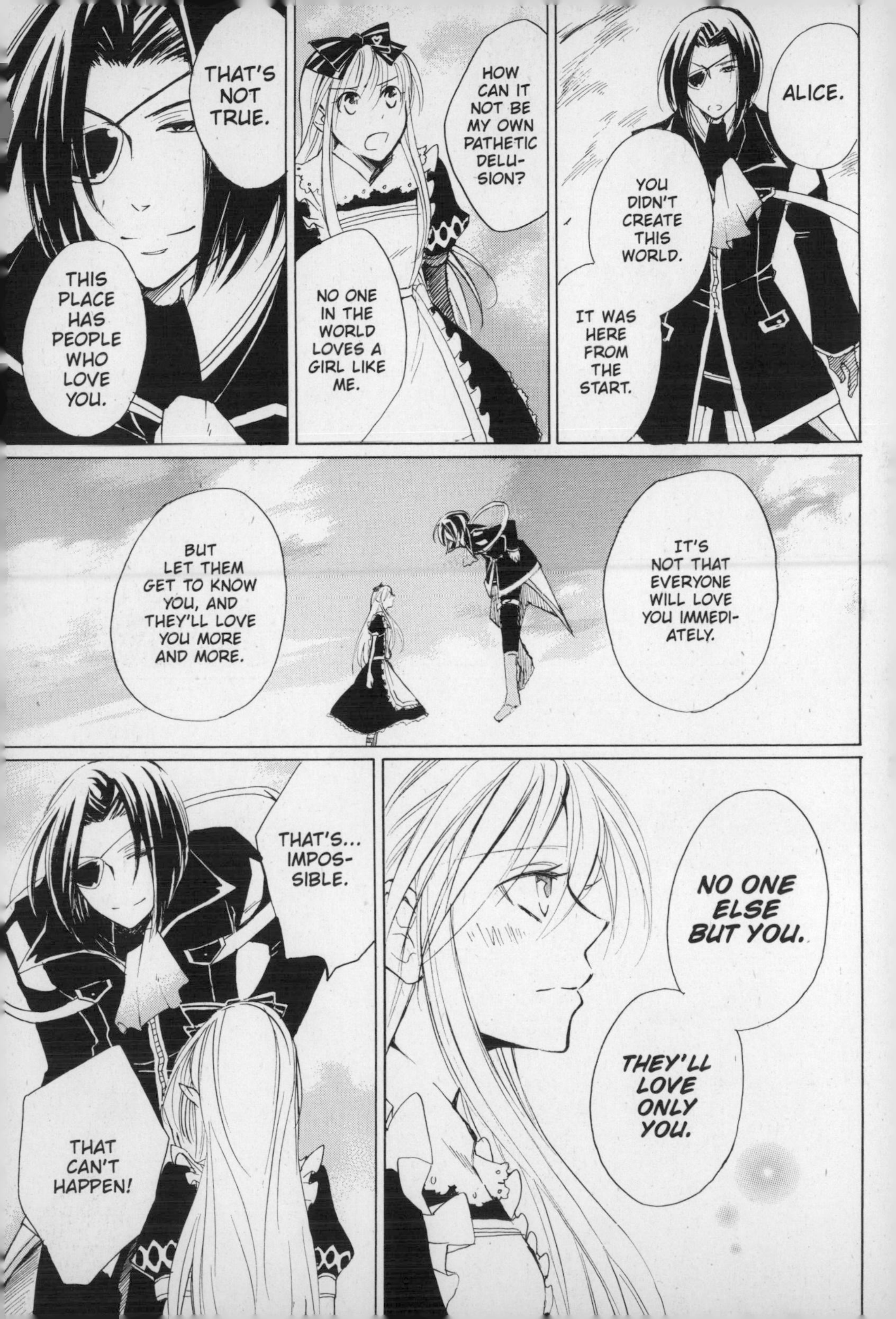
ALICE.
YOU DIDN'T CREATE THIS WORLD.
IT WAS HERE FROM THE START.
HOW CAN IT NOT BE MY OWN PATHETIC DELUSION?
NO ONE IN THE WORLD LOVES A GIRL LIKE ME.
THAT'S NOT TRUE.
THIS PLACE HAS PEOPLE WHO LOVE YOU.
IT'S NOT THAT EVERYONE WILL LOVE YOU IMMEDIATELY.
BUT LET THEM GET TO KNOW YOU, AND THEY'LL LOVE YOU MORE AND MORE.
NO ONE ELSE BUT YOU.
THEY'LL LOVE ONLY YOU.
THAT'S... IMPOSSIBLE.
THAT CAN'T HAPPEN!

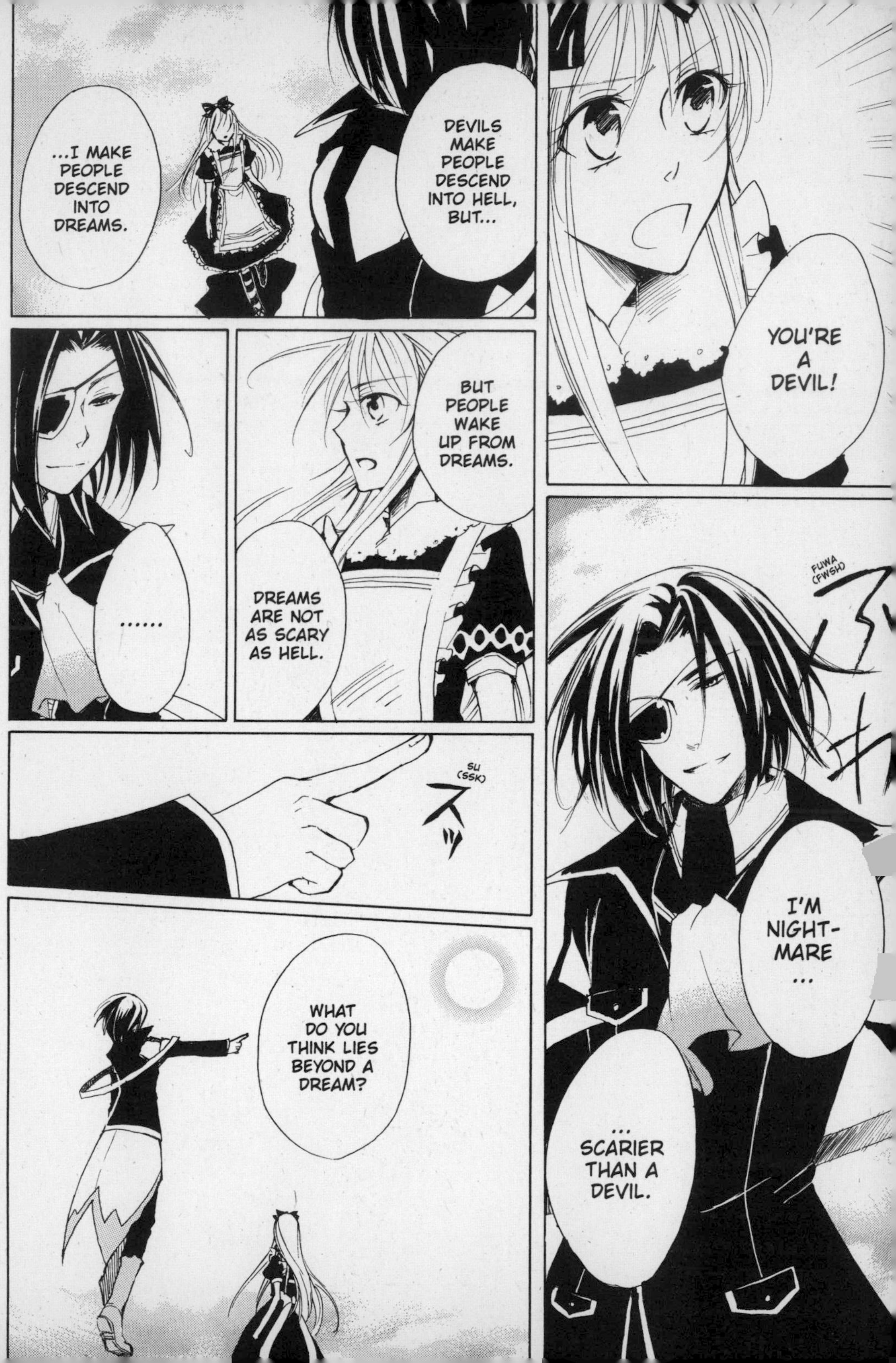
YOU'RE A DEVIL!
DEVILS MAKE PEOPLE DESCEND INTO HELL, BUT...
...I MAKE PEOPLE DESCEND INTO DREAMS.
BUT PEOPLE WAKE UP FROM DREAMS.
DREAMS ARE NOT AS SCARY AS HELL.
......
FUWA (FWSH)
I'M NIGHT-MARE...
...SCARIER THAN A DEVIL.
SU (SSK)
WHAT DO YOU THINK LIES BEYOND A DREAM?

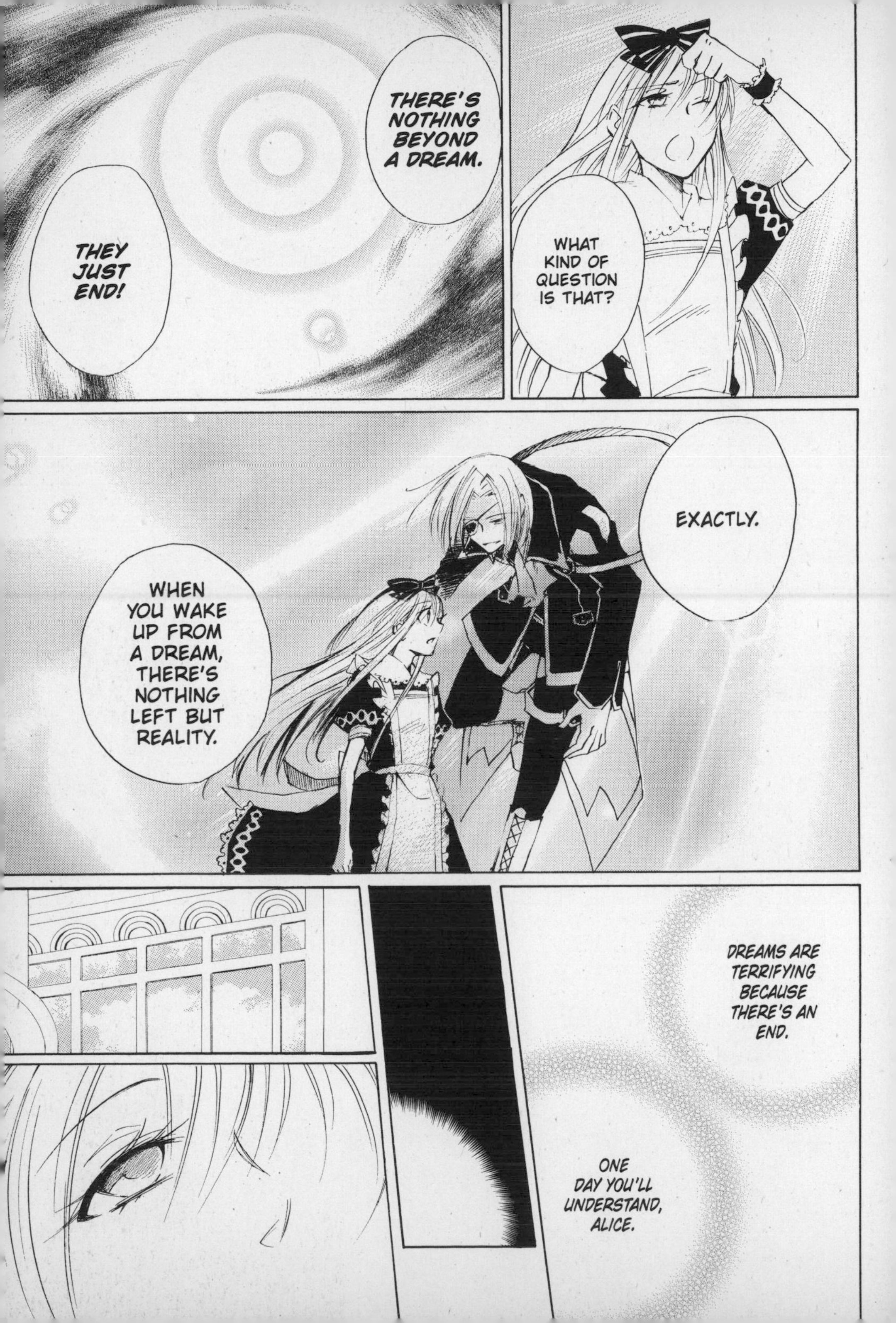
WHAT KIND OF QUESTION IS THAT?
THERE'S NOTHING BEYOND A DREAM.
THEY JUST END!
EXACTLY.
WHEN YOU WAKE UP FROM A DREAM, THERE'S NOTHING LEFT BUT REALITY.
DREAMS ARE TERRIFYING BECAUSE THERE'S AN END.
ONE DAY YOU'LL UNDERSTAND, ALICE.

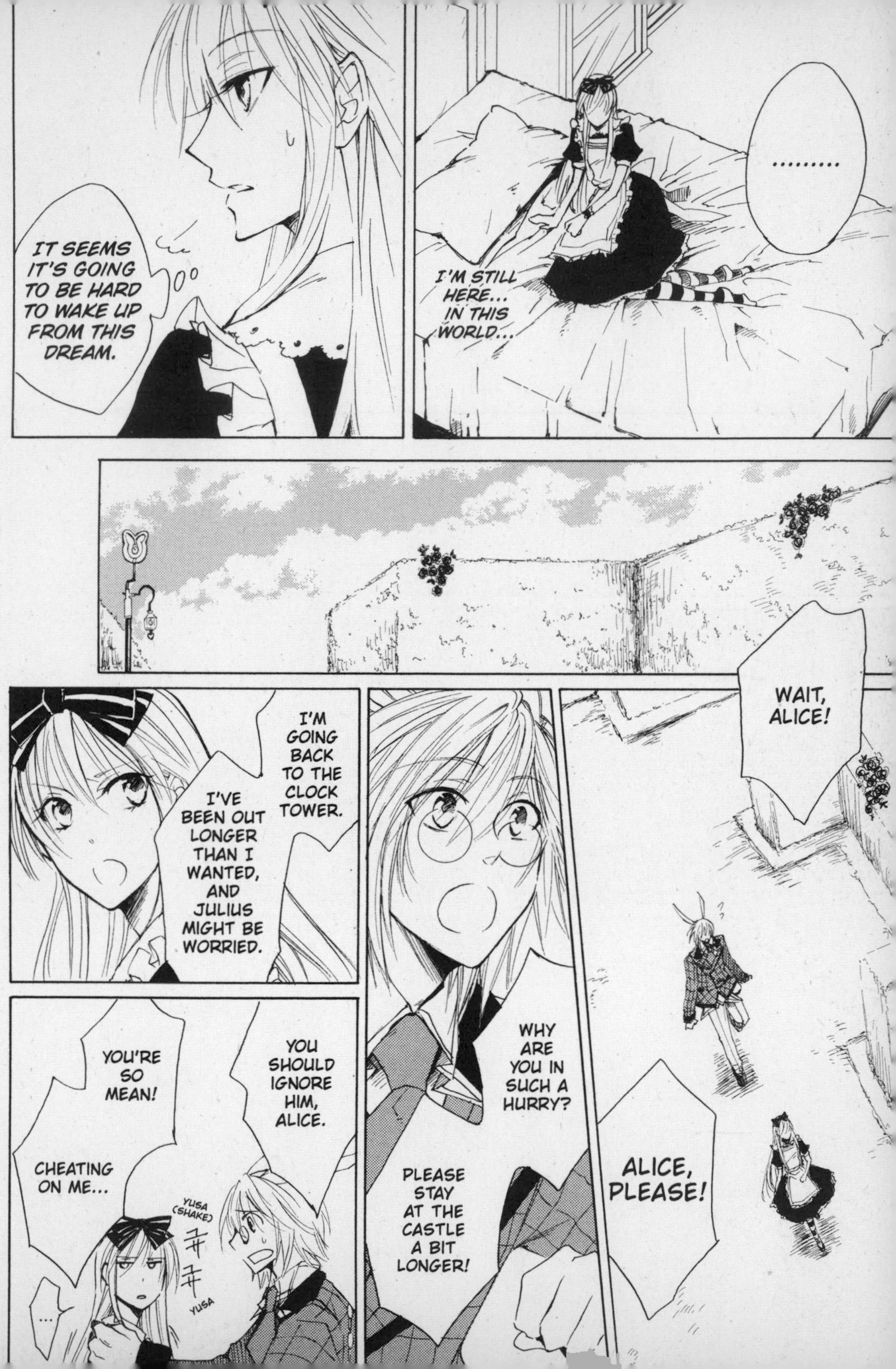
....
I'M STILL HERE... IN THIS WORLD...
IT SEEMS IT'S GOING TO BE HARD TO WAKE UP FROM THIS DREAM.
WAIT, ALICE!
ALICE, PLEASE!
WHY ARE YOU IN SUCH A HURRY?
PLEASE STAY AT THE CASTLE A BIT LONGER!
I'M GOING BACK TO THE CLOCK TOWER.
I'VE BEEN OUT LONGER THAN I WANTED, AND JULIUS MIGHT BE WORRIED.
YOU SHOULD IGNORE HIM, ALICE.
YOU'RE SO MEAN!
CHEATING ON ME...
YUSA (SHAKE)
YUSA
...

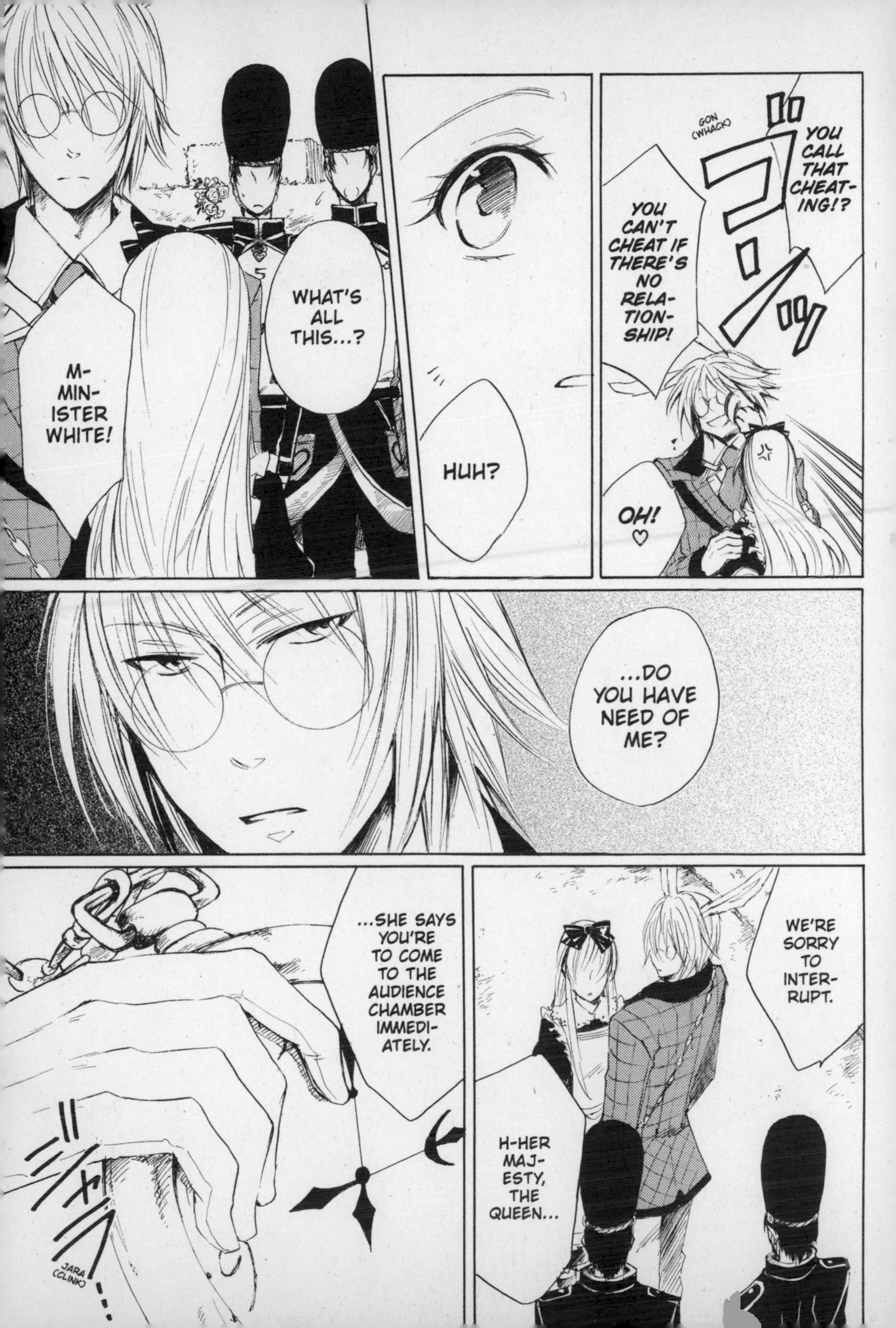
YOU CALL THAT CHEAT-ING!?
GON (WHACK)
YOU CAN'T CHEAT IF THERE'S NO RELA-TION-SHIP!
OH! ♡
HUH?
WHAT'S ALL THIS...?
M-MIN-ISTER WHITE!
...DO YOU HAVE NEED OF ME?
WE'RE SORRY TO INTER-RUPT.
H-HER MAJ-ESTY, THE QUEEN...
...SHE SAYS YOU'RE TO COME TO THE AUDIENCE CHAMBER IMMEDI-ATELY.
JARA (CLINK)

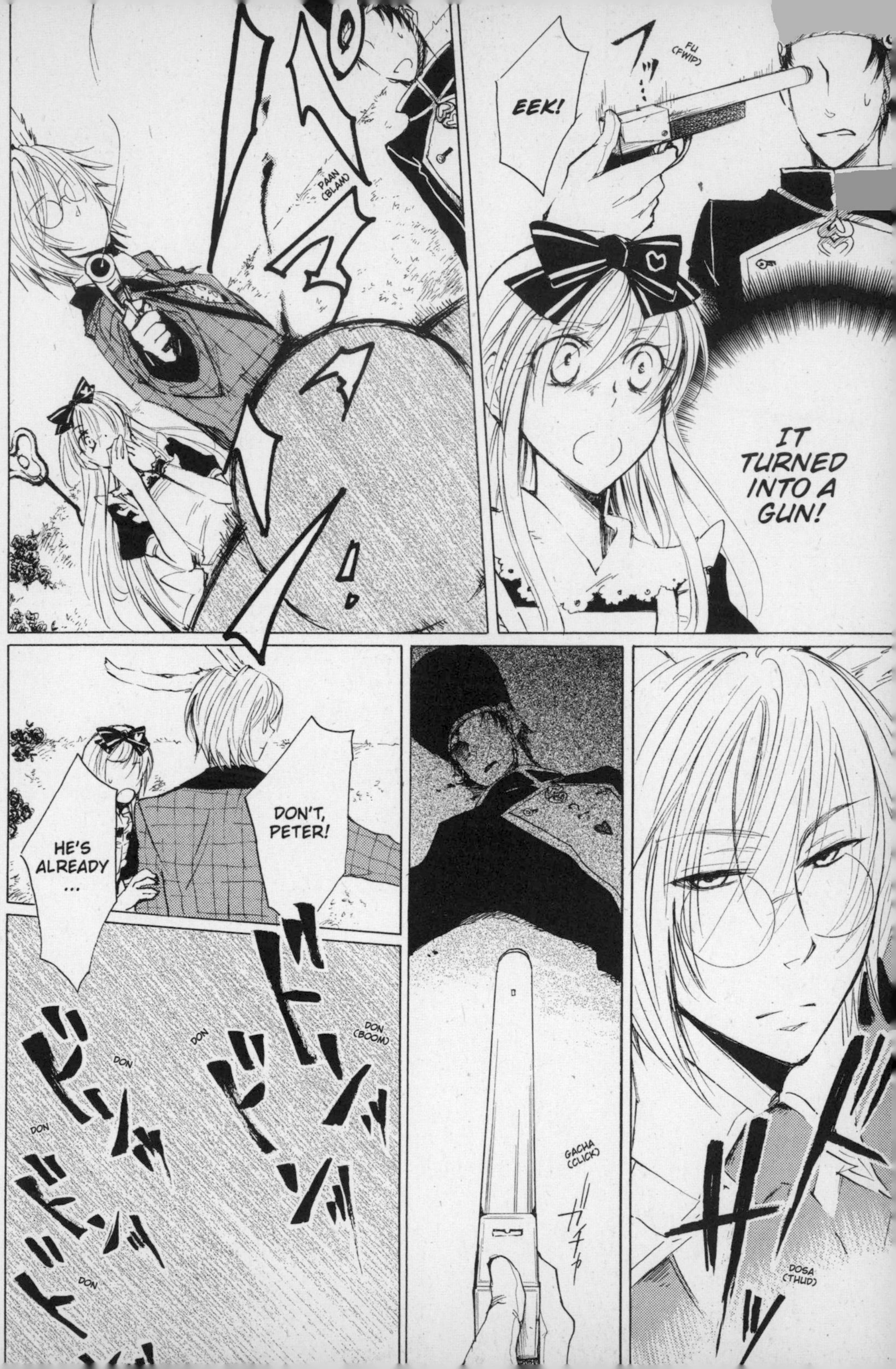
FU (FWIP)
EEK!
IT TURNED INTO A GUN!
PAAN (BLAM)
DOSA (THUD)
GACHA (CLICK)
DON'T, PETER!
HE'S ALREADY ...
DON (BOOM)
DON
DON
DON
DON

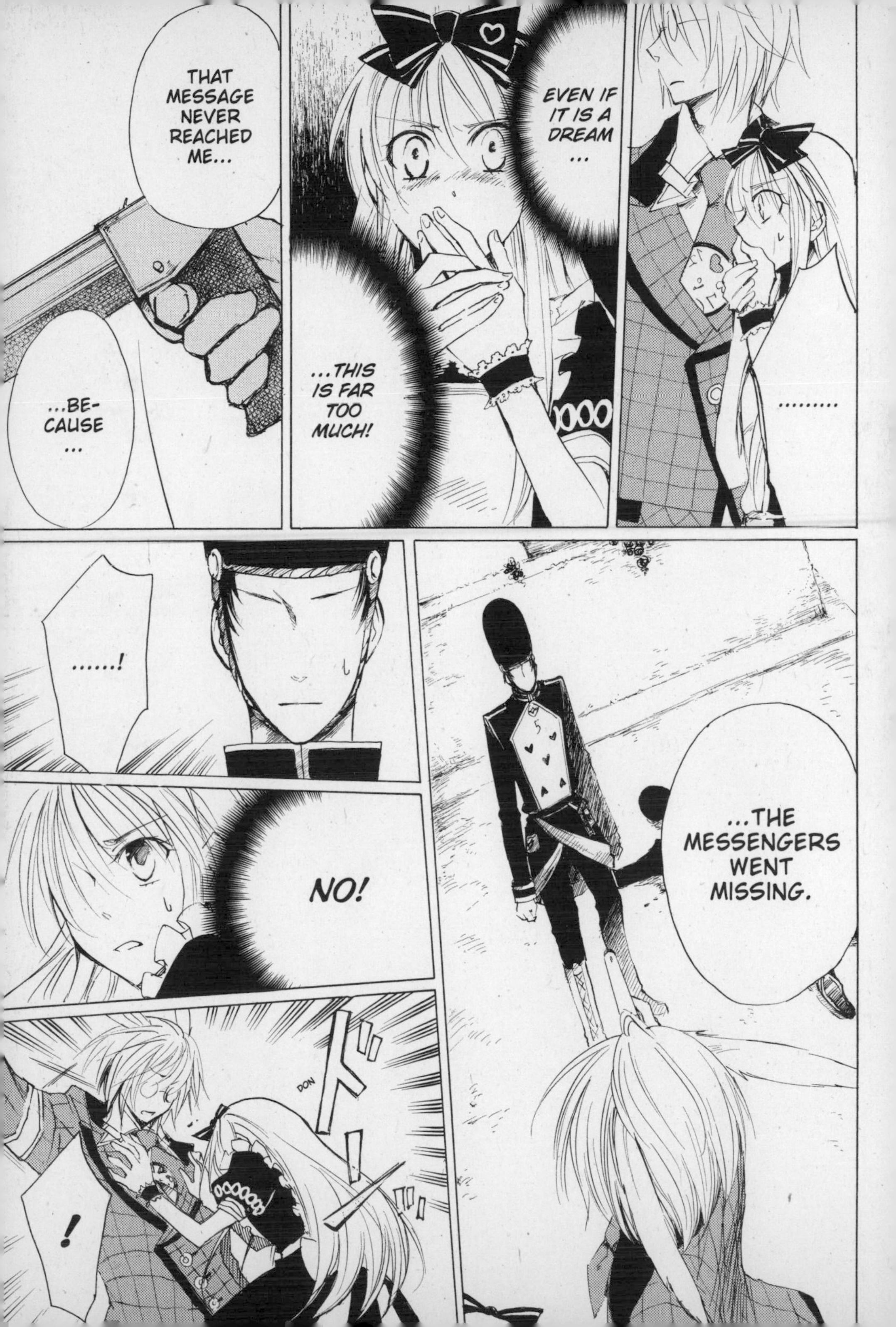
....
EVEN IF IT IS A DREAM ...
...THIS IS FAR TOO MUCH!
THAT MESSAGE NEVER REACHED ME...
...BE-CAUSE ...
...THE MESSENGERS WENT MISSING.
......!
NO!
DON
!

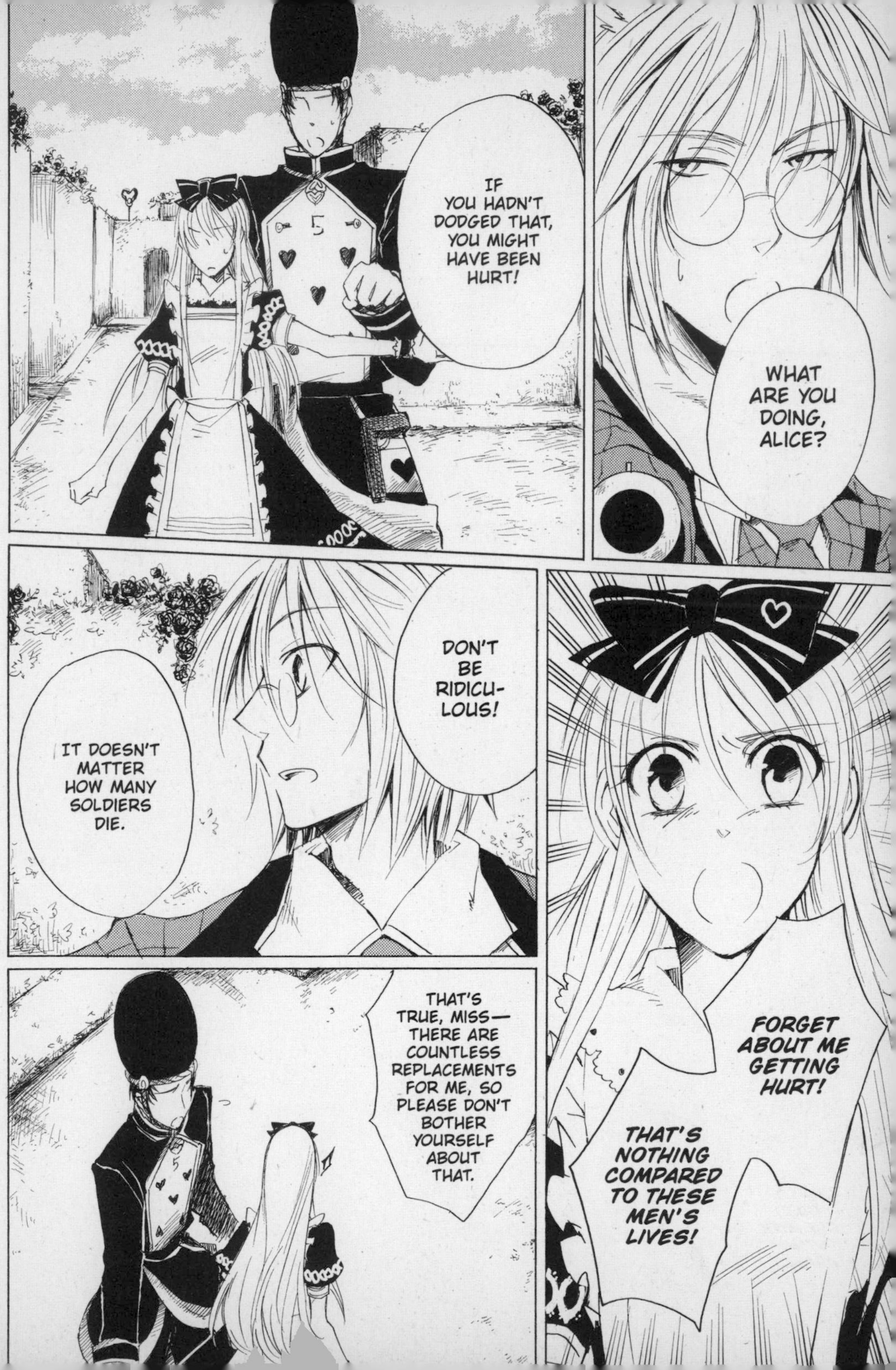
WHAT ARE YOU DOING, ALICE?
IF YOU HADN'T DODGED THAT, YOU MIGHT HAVE BEEN HURT!
FORGET ABOUT ME GETTING HURT!
THAT'S NOTHING COMPARED TO THESE MEN'S LIVES!
DON'T BE RIDICULOUS!
IT DOESN'T MATTER HOW MANY SOLDIERS DIE.
THAT'S TRUE, MISS—THERE ARE COUNTLESS REPLACEMENTS FOR ME, SO PLEASE DON'T BOTHER YOURSELF ABOUT THAT.

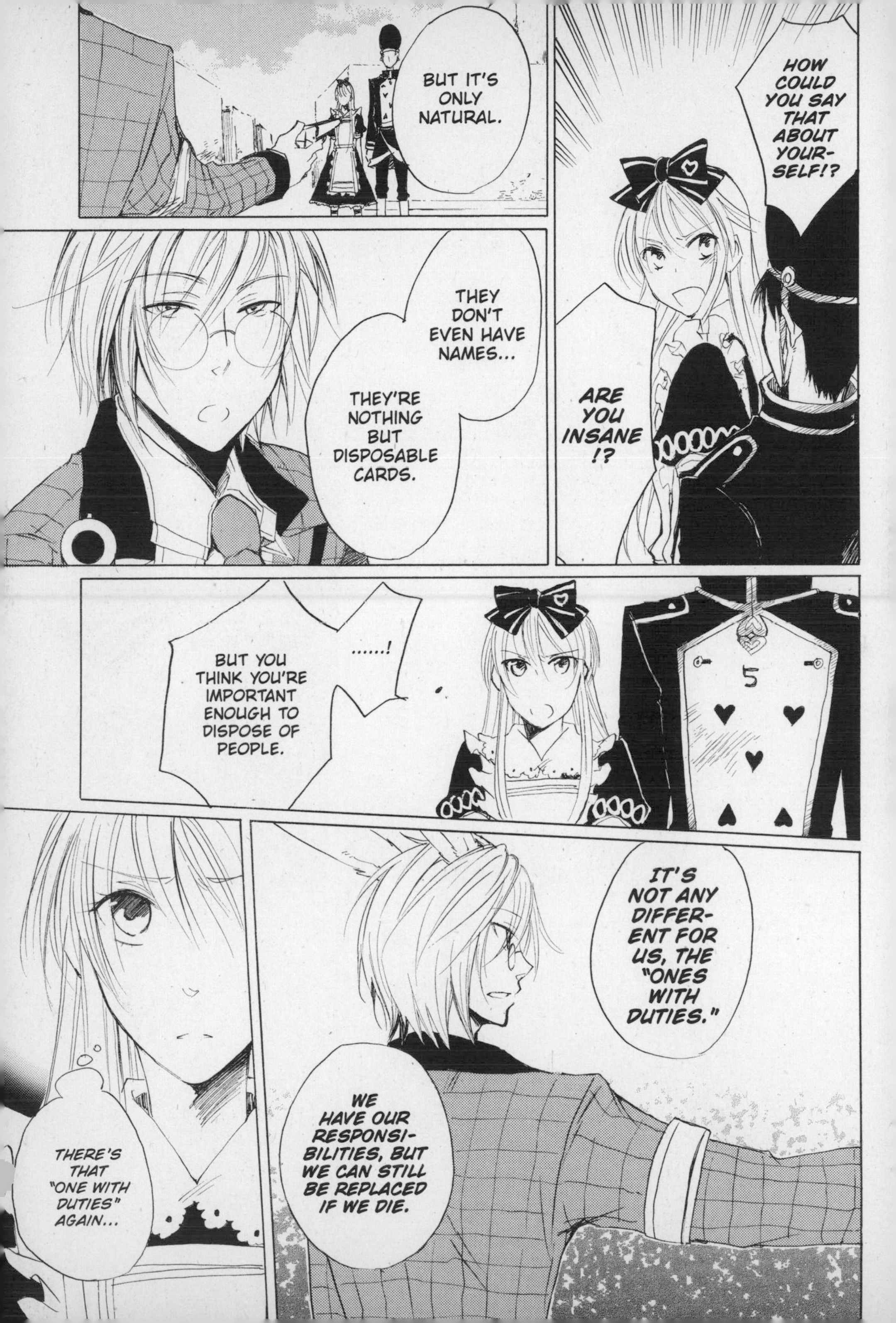
HOW COULD YOU SAY THAT ABOUT YOURSELF!?
ARE YOU INSANE!?
BUT IT'S ONLY NATURAL.
THEY DON'T EVEN HAVE NAMES...
THEY'RE NOTHING BUT DISPOSABLE CARDS.
......!
BUT YOU THINK YOU'RE IMPORTANT ENOUGH TO DISPOSE OF PEOPLE.
IT'S NOT ANY DIFFERENT FOR US, THE "ONES WITH DUTIES."
WE HAVE OUR RESPONSIBILITIES, BUT WE CAN STILL BE REPLACED IF WE DIE.
THERE'S THAT "ONE WITH DUTIES" AGAIN...

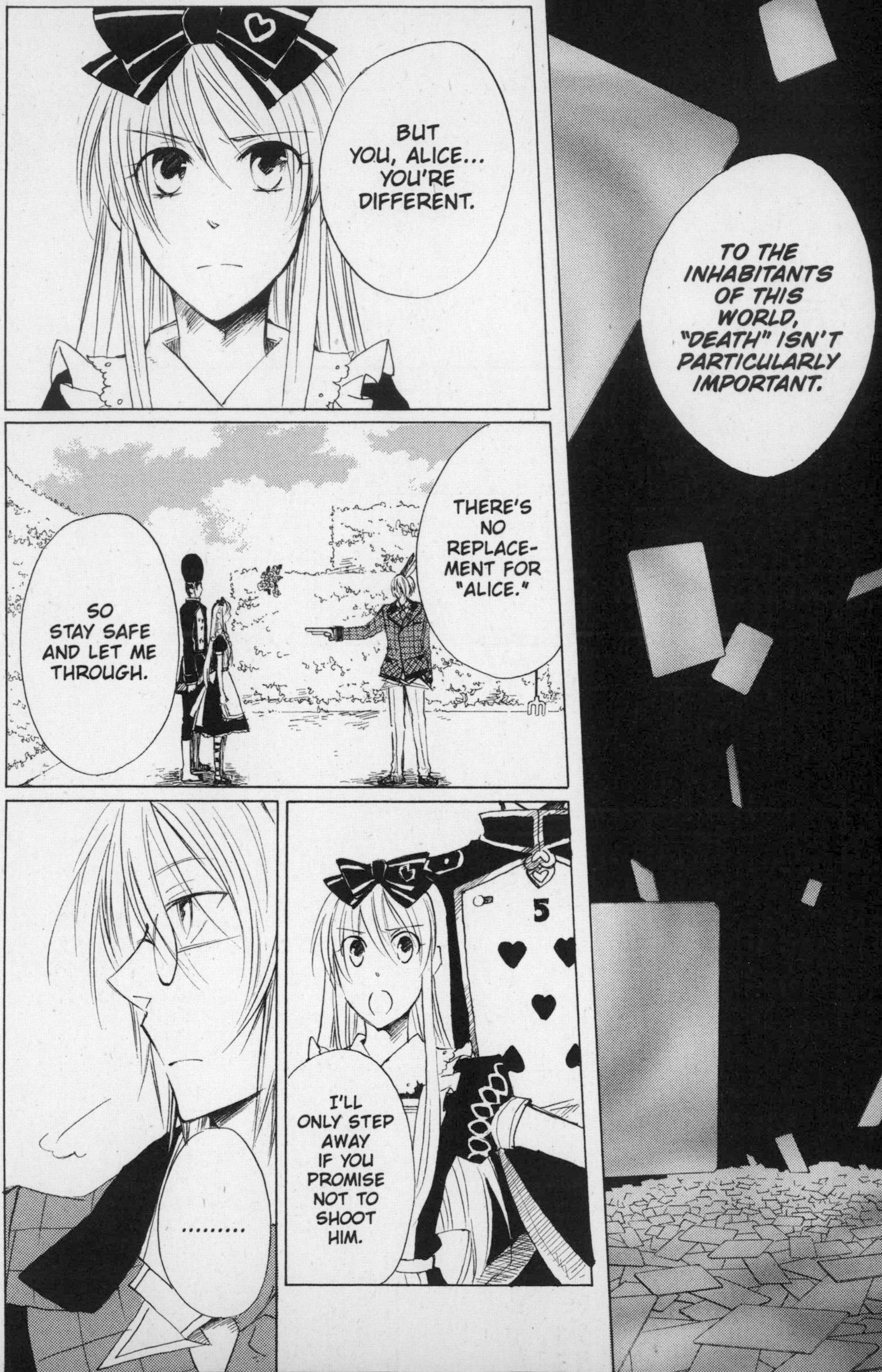
TO THE INHABITANTS OF THIS WORLD, "DEATH" ISN'T PARTICULARLY IMPORTANT.
BUT YOU, ALICE... YOU'RE DIFFERENT.
THERE'S NO REPLACEMENT FOR "ALICE."
SO STAY SAFE AND LET ME THROUGH.
I'LL ONLY STEP AWAY IF YOU PROMISE NOT TO SHOOT HIM.
....

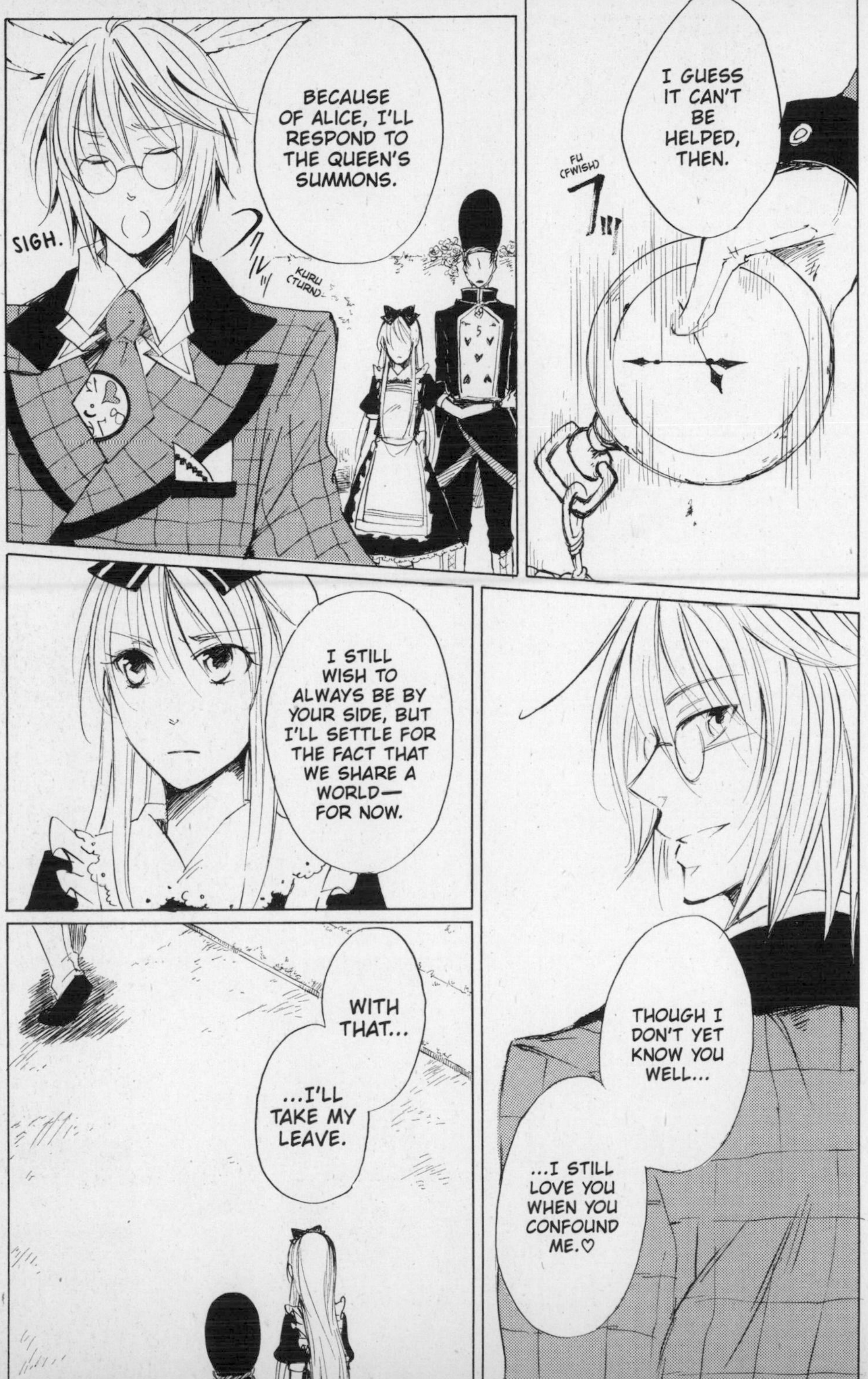
I GUESS IT CAN'T BE HELPED, THEN.
FU (FWISH)
BECAUSE OF ALICE, I'LL RESPOND TO THE QUEEN'S SUMMONS.
KURU (TURN)
SIGH.
THOUGH I DON'T YET KNOW YOU WELL...
...I STILL LOVE YOU WHEN YOU CONFOUND ME.♡
I STILL WISH TO ALWAYS BE BY YOUR SIDE, BUT I'LL SETTLE FOR THE FACT THAT WE SHARE A WORLD— FOR NOW.
WITH THAT...
...I'LL TAKE MY LEAVE.

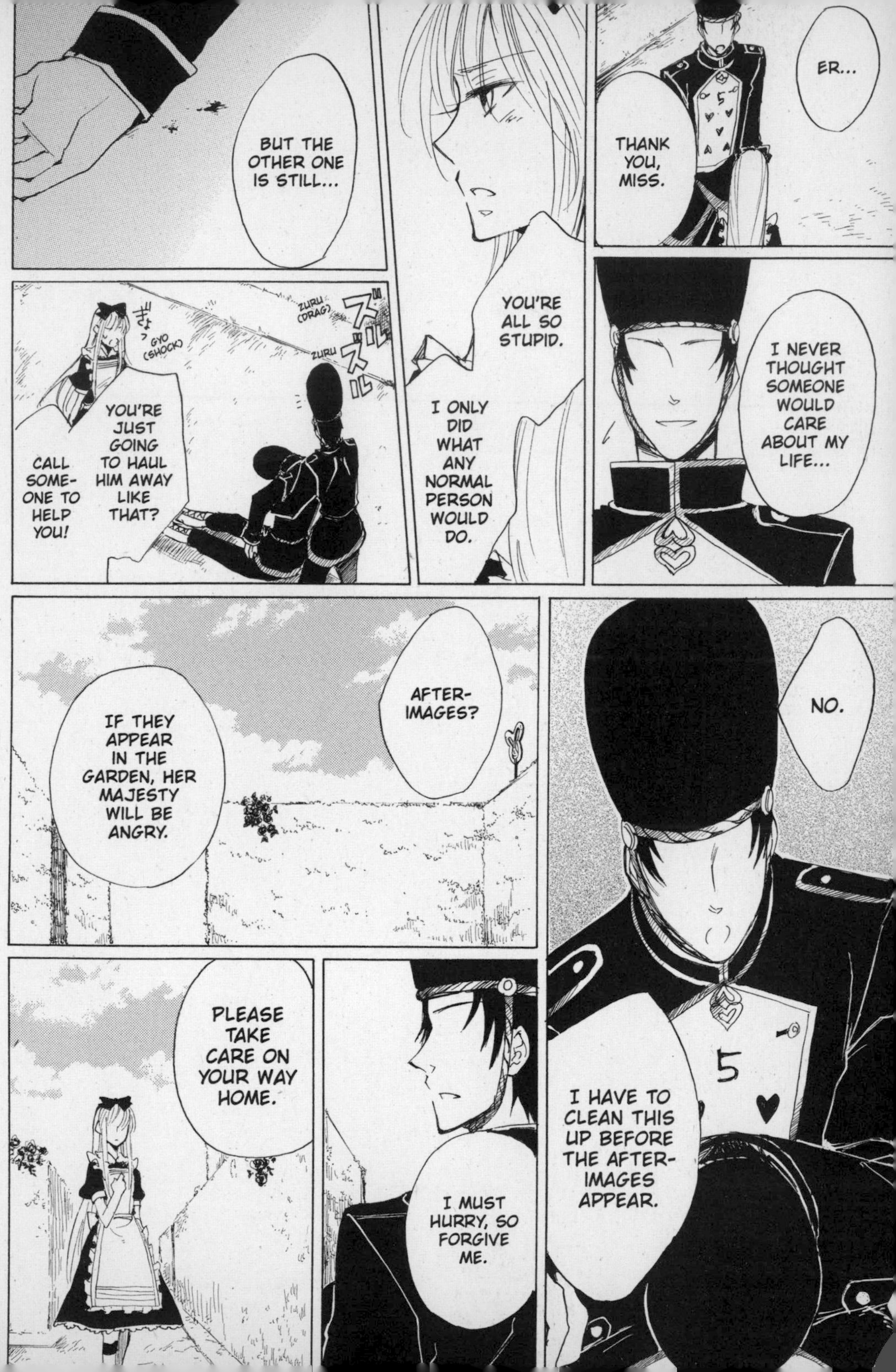
ER...
THANK YOU, MISS.
I NEVER THOUGHT SOMEONE WOULD CARE ABOUT MY LIFE...
YOU'RE ALL SO STUPID.
I ONLY DID WHAT ANY NORMAL PERSON WOULD DO.
BUT THE OTHER ONE IS STILL...
ズル
ZURU (DRAG)
ズル
ZURU
ぎょっ
GYO (SHOCK)
YOU'RE JUST GOING TO HAUL HIM AWAY LIKE THAT?
CALL SOME-ONE TO HELP YOU!
NO.
I HAVE TO CLEAN THIS UP BEFORE THE AFTER-IMAGES APPEAR.
AFTER-IMAGES?
IF THEY APPEAR IN THE GARDEN, HER MAJESTY WILL BE ANGRY.
I MUST HURRY, SO FORGIVE ME.
PLEASE TAKE CARE ON YOUR WAY HOME.

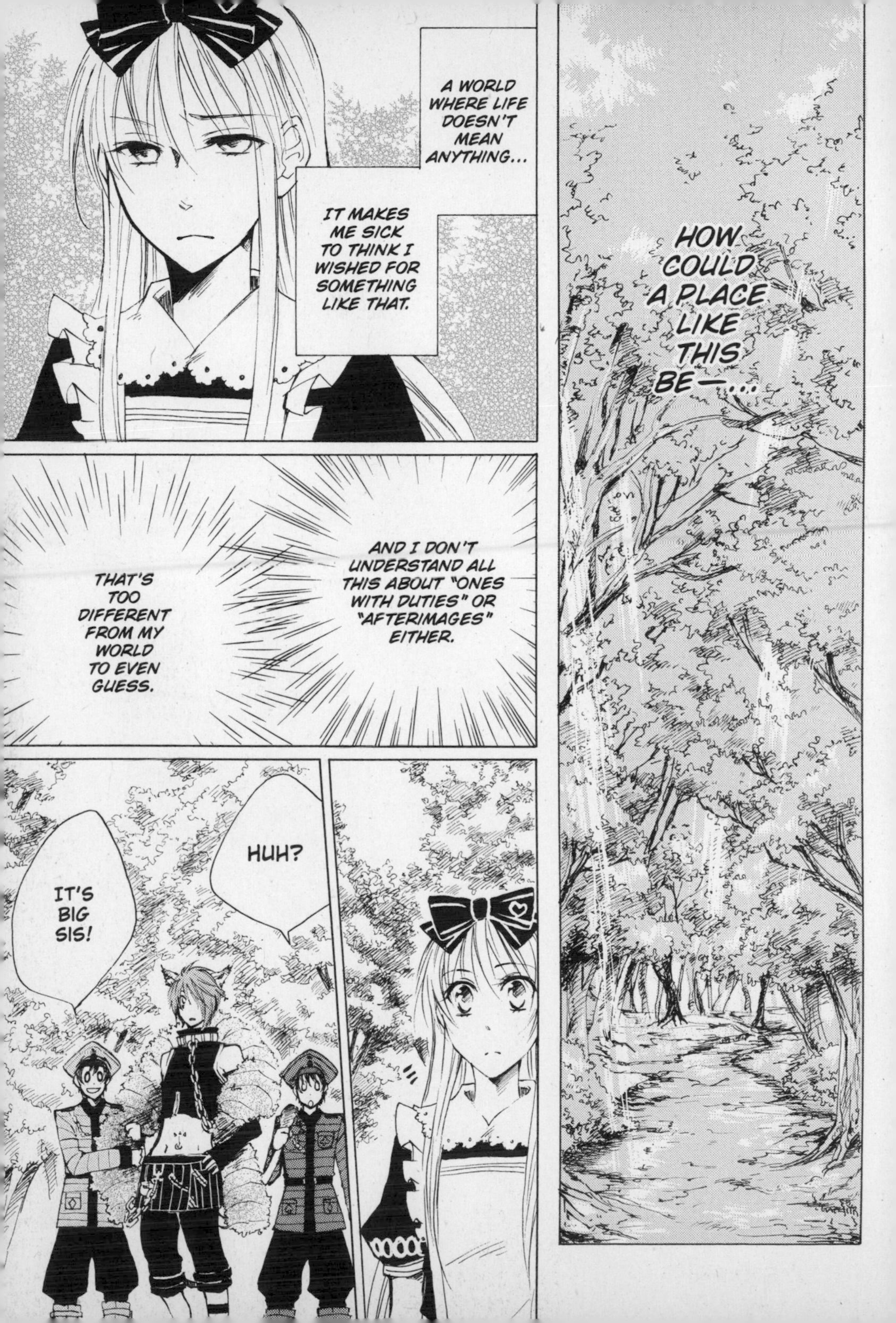

HOW COULD A PLACE LIKE THIS BE—...
A WORLD WHERE LIFE DOESN'T MEAN ANYTHING...
IT MAKES ME SICK TO THINK I WISHED FOR SOMETHING LIKE THAT.
AND I DON'T UNDERSTAND ALL THIS ABOUT "ONES WITH DUTIES" OR "AFTERIMAGES" EITHER.
THAT'S TOO DIFFERENT FROM MY WORLD TO EVEN GUESS.
HUH?
IT'S BIG SIS!

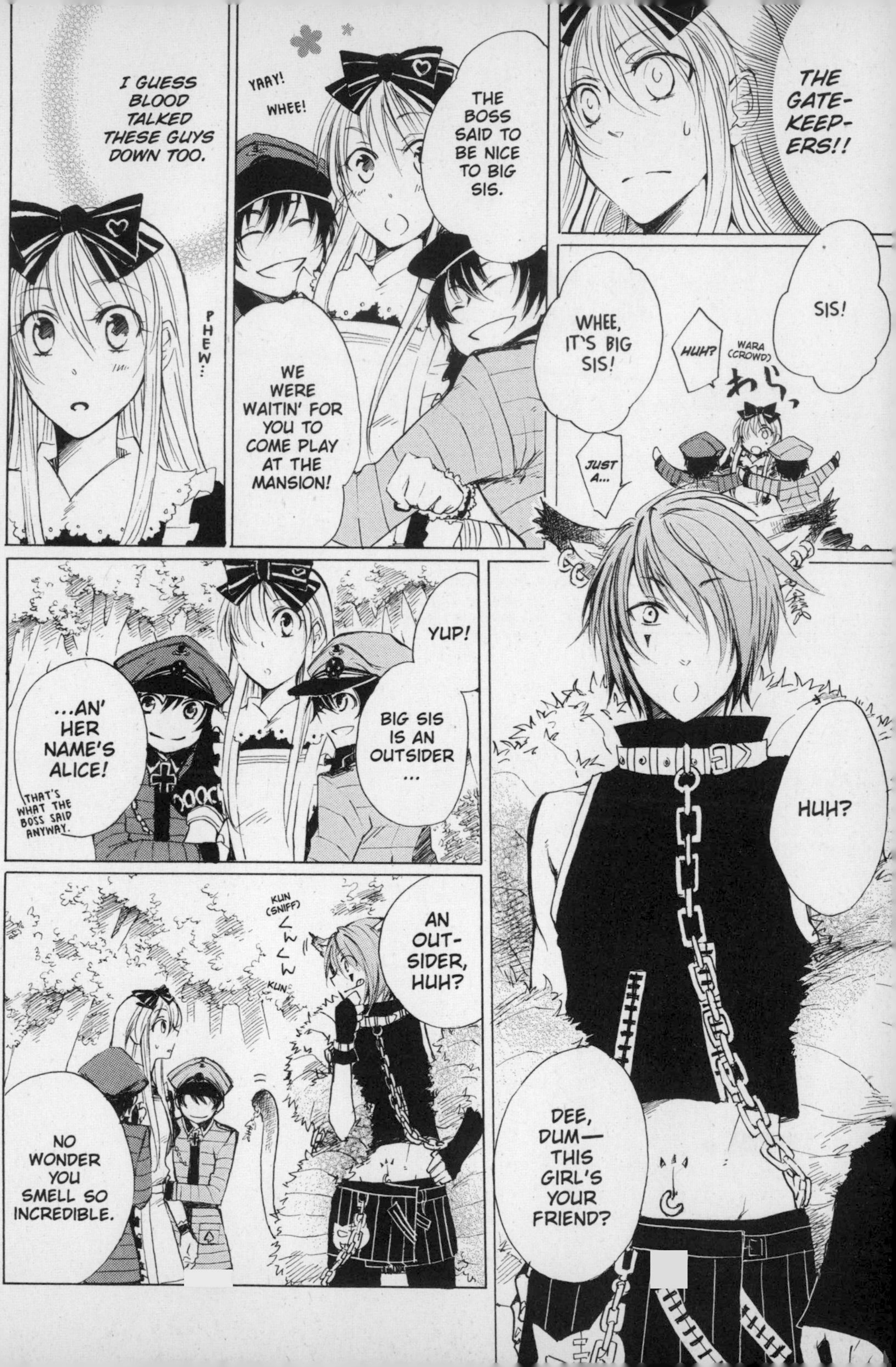
THE GATE-KEEPERS!!
SIS!
WARA (CROWD)
わら
HUH?
WHEE, IT'S BIG SIS!
JUST A...
YAAY!
WHEE!
THE BOSS SAID TO BE NICE TO BIG SIS.
WE WERE WAITIN' FOR YOU TO COME PLAY AT THE MANSION!
I GUESS BLOOD TALKED THESE GUYS DOWN TOO.
PHEW...
HUH?
DEE, DUM— THIS GIRL'S YOUR FRIEND?
YUP!
BIG SIS IS AN OUTSIDER...
...AN' HER NAME'S ALICE!
THAT'S WHAT THE BOSS SAID ANYWAY.
AN OUT-SIDER, HUH?
KUN (SNIFF)
くんくん
KUN
NO WONDER YOU SMELL SO INCREDIBLE.

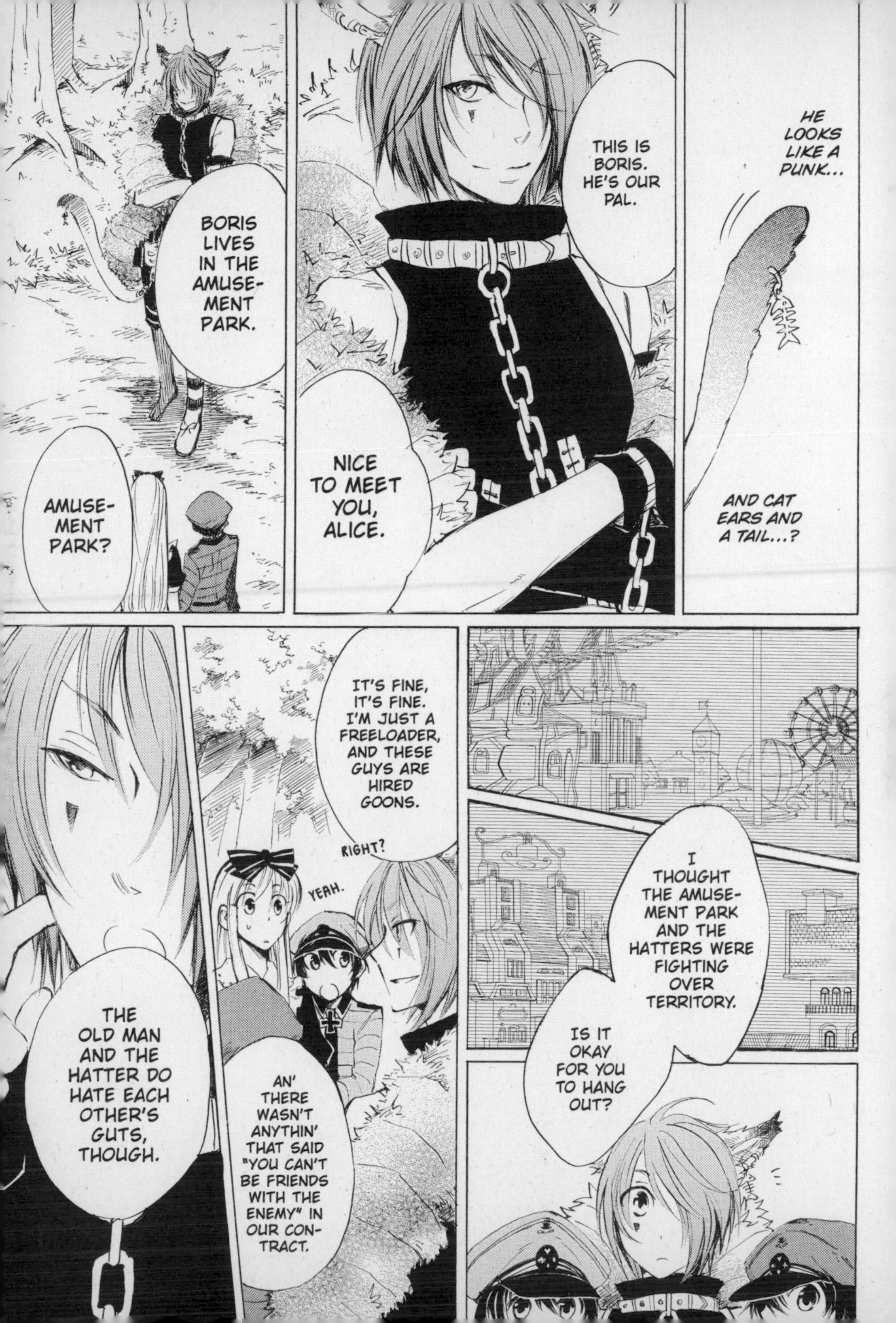
HE LOOKS LIKE A PUNK...
AND CAT EARS AND A TAIL...?
THIS IS BORIS. HE'S OUR PAL.
NICE TO MEET YOU, ALICE.
BORIS LIVES IN THE AMUSEMENT PARK.
AMUSEMENT PARK?
I THOUGHT THE AMUSEMENT PARK AND THE HATTERS WERE FIGHTING OVER TERRITORY.
IS IT OKAY FOR YOU TO HANG OUT?
IT'S FINE, IT'S FINE. I'M JUST A FREELOADER, AND THESE GUYS ARE HIRED GOONS.
RIGHT?
YEAH.
AN' THERE WASN'T ANYTHIN' THAT SAID "YOU CAN'T BE FRIENDS WITH THE ENEMY" IN OUR CONTRACT.
THE OLD MAN AND THE HATTER DO HATE EACH OTHER'S GUTS, THOUGH.

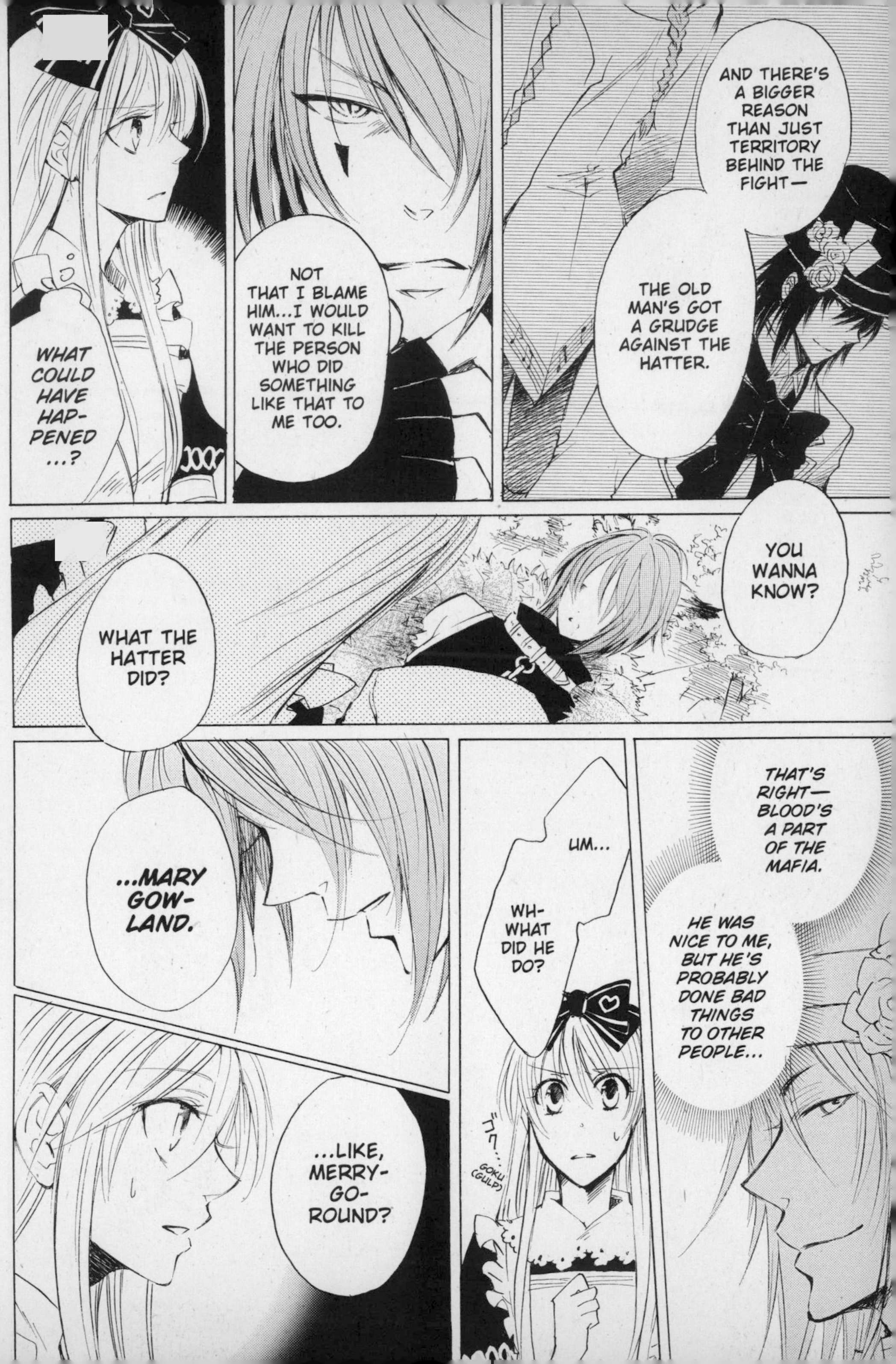
AND THERE'S A BIGGER REASON THAN JUST TERRITORY BEHIND THE FIGHT—
THE OLD MAN'S GOT A GRUDGE AGAINST THE HATTER.
NOT THAT I BLAME HIM...I WOULD WANT TO KILL THE PERSON WHO DID SOMETHING LIKE THAT TO ME TOO.
WHAT COULD HAVE HAP-PENED...?
YOU WANNA KNOW?
WHAT THE HATTER DID?
THAT'S RIGHT—BLOOD'S A PART OF THE MAFIA.
HE WAS NICE TO ME, BUT HE'S PROBABLY DONE BAD THINGS TO OTHER PEOPLE...
UM...
WH-WHAT DID HE DO?
GOKU (GULP)
...MARY GOW-LAND.
...LIKE, MERRY-GO-ROUND?

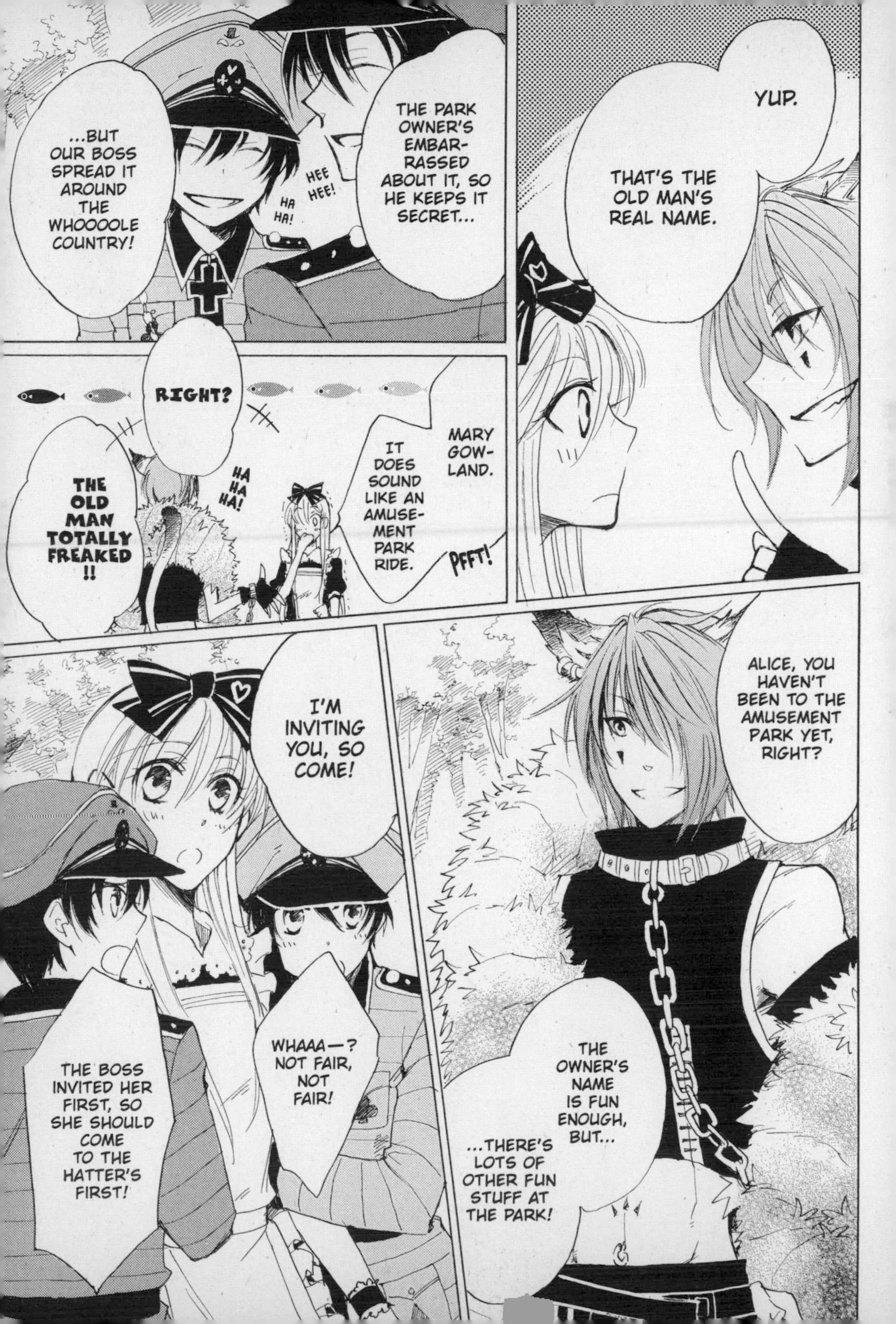
YUP.
THAT'S THE OLD MAN'S REAL NAME.
THE PARK OWNER'S EMBAR-RASSED ABOUT IT, SO HE KEEPS IT SECRET...
HEE HEE!
HA HA!
...BUT OUR BOSS SPREAD IT AROUND THE WHOOOOLE COUNTRY!
MARY GOW-LAND.
PFFT!
IT DOES SOUND LIKE AN AMUSE-MENT PARK RIDE.
RIGHT?
HA HA HA!
THE OLD MAN TOTALLY FREAKED!!
ALICE, YOU HAVEN'T BEEN TO THE AMUSEMENT PARK YET, RIGHT?
THE OWNER'S NAME IS FUN ENOUGH, BUT...
...THERE'S LOTS OF OTHER FUN STUFF AT THE PARK!
I'M INVITING YOU, SO COME!
WHAAA—? NOT FAIR, NOT FAIR!
THE BOSS INVITED HER FIRST, SO SHE SHOULD COME TO THE HATTER'S FIRST!

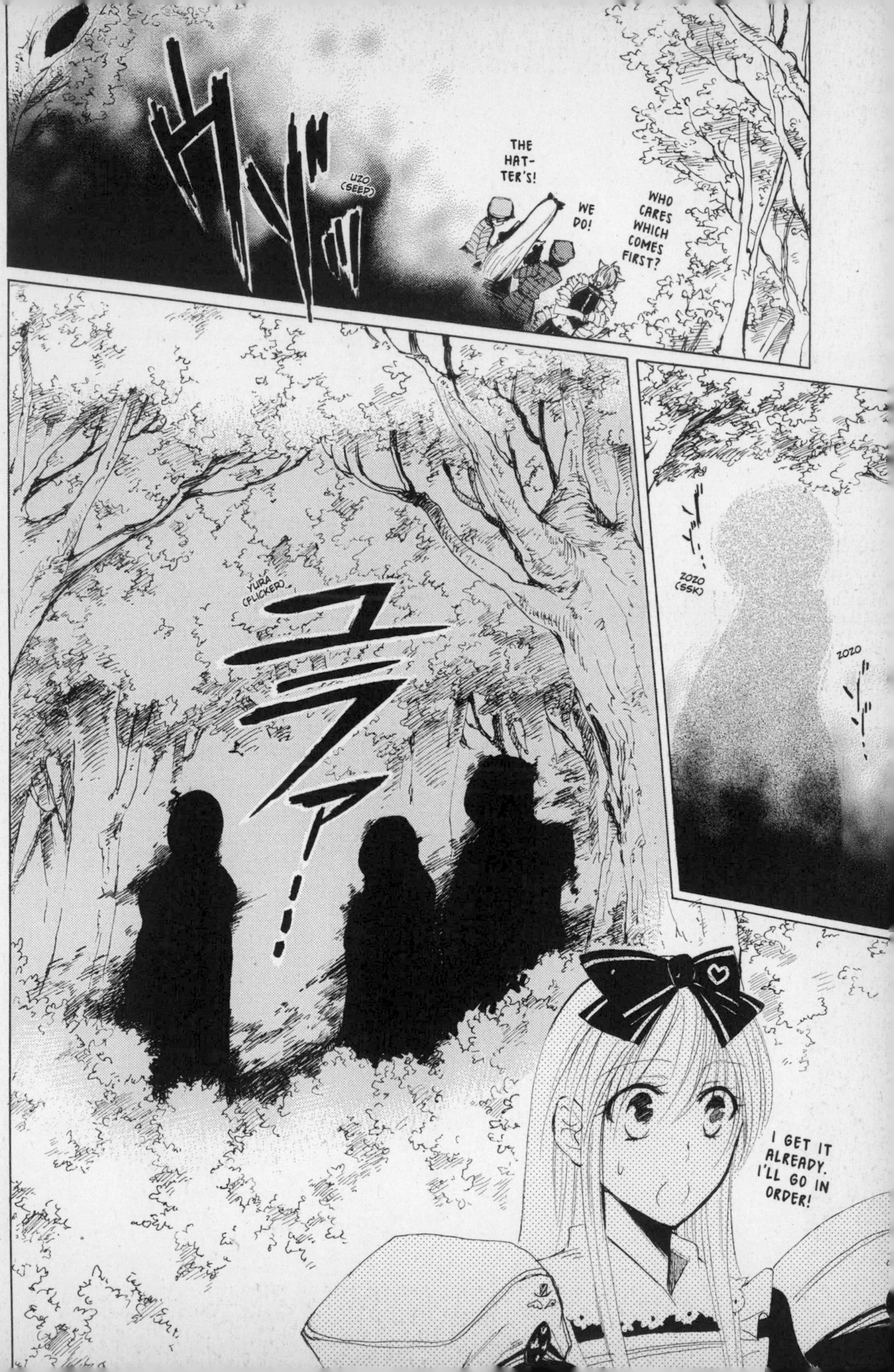
WHO CARES WHICH COMES FIRST?
WE DO!
THE HAT-TER'S!
UZO (SEEP)
ZOZO
ZOZO (SSK)
YURA (FLICKER)
I GET IT ALREADY. I'LL GO IN ORDER!

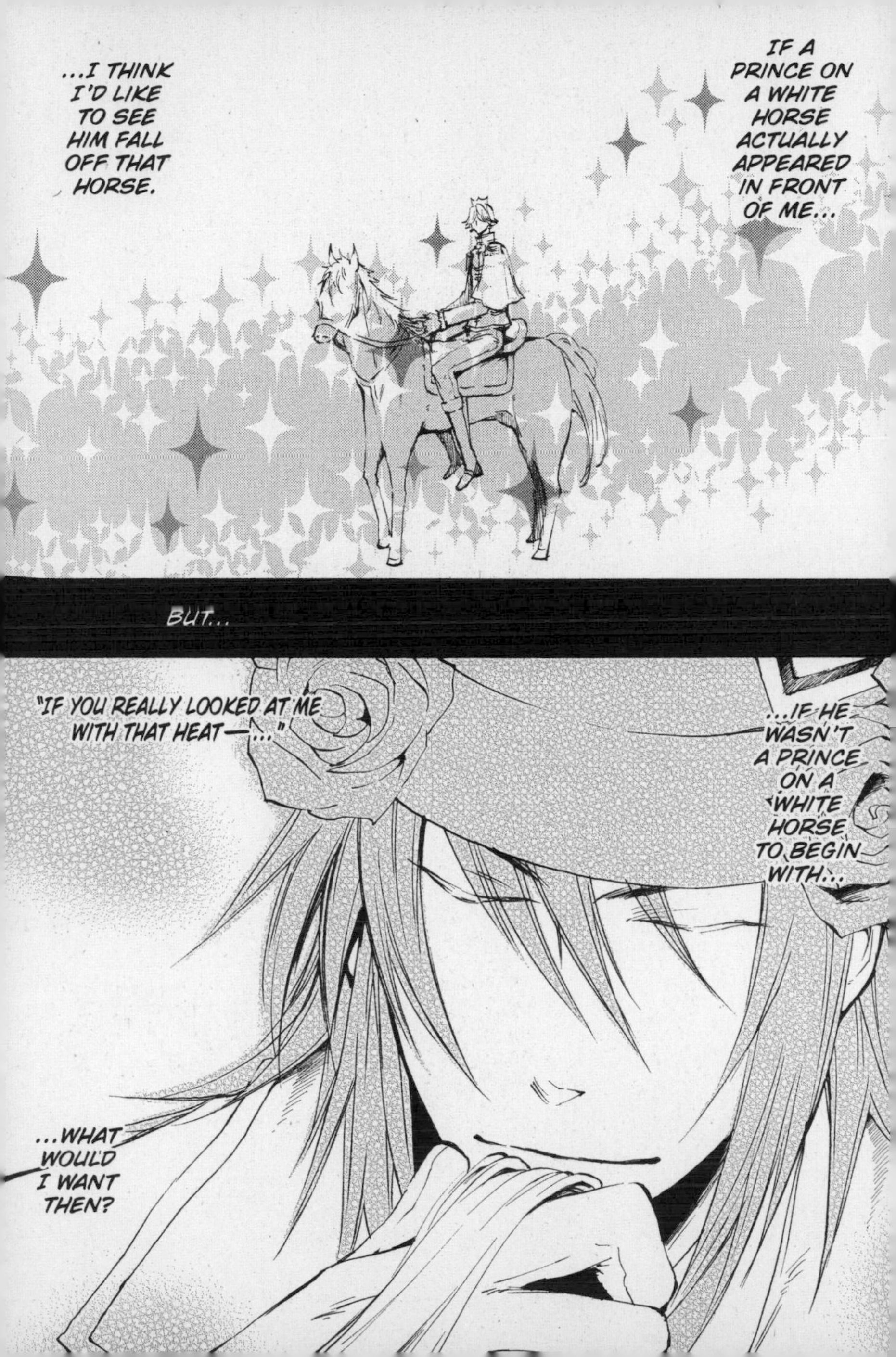
IF A PRINCE ON A WHITE HORSE ACTUALLY APPEARED IN FRONT OF ME...
...I THINK I'D LIKE TO SEE HIM FALL OFF THAT HORSE.
BUT...
...IF HE WASN'T A PRINCE ON A WHITE HORSE TO BEGIN WITH...
"IF YOU REALLY LOOKED AT ME WITH THAT HEAT—...."
...WHAT WOULD I WANT THEN?

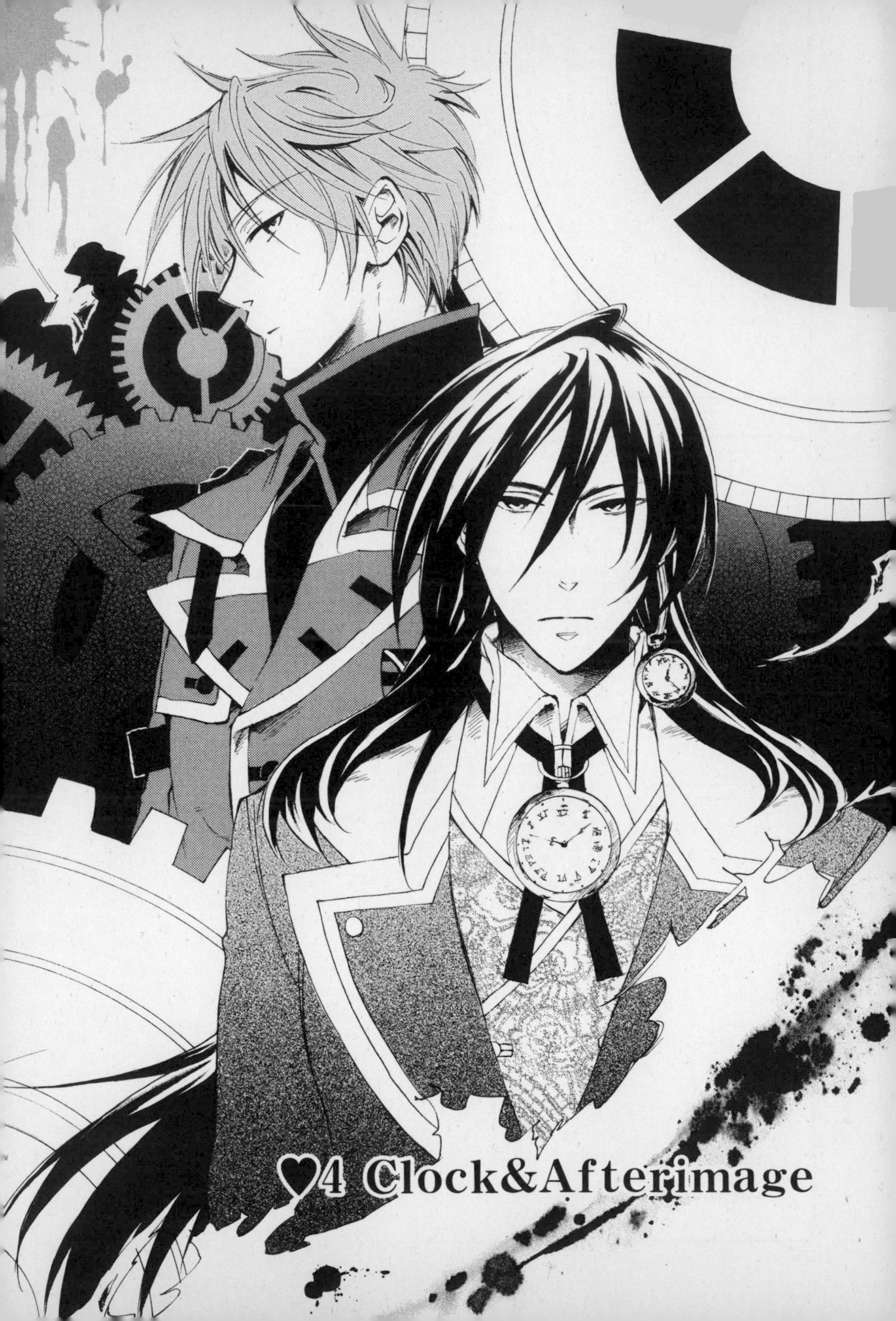
♥4 Clock&Afterimage

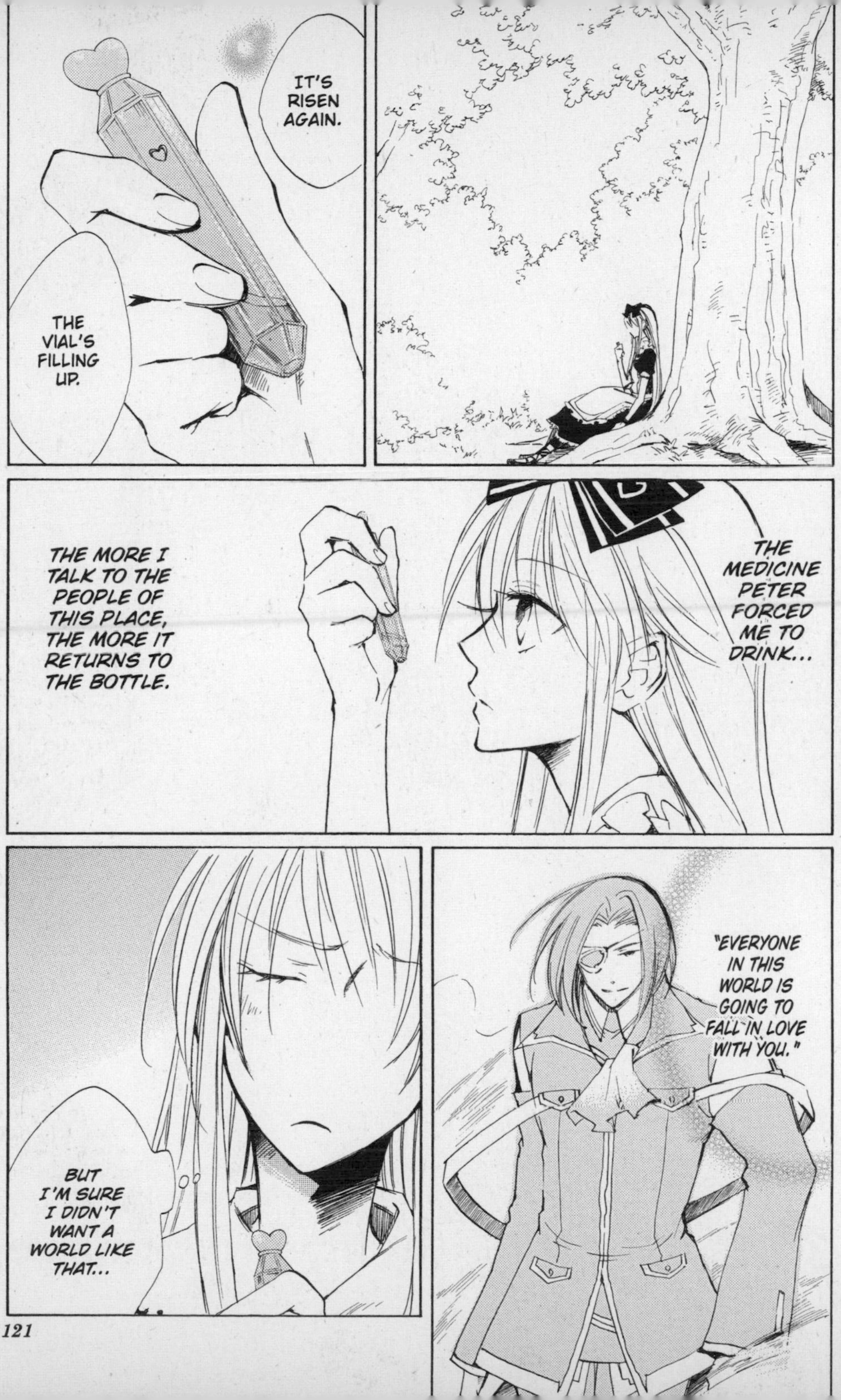
IT'S RISEN AGAIN.
THE VIAL'S FILLING UP.
THE MEDICINE PETER FORCED ME TO DRINK...
THE MORE I TALK TO THE PEOPLE OF THIS PLACE, THE MORE IT RETURNS TO THE BOTTLE.
"EVERYONE IN THIS WORLD IS GOING TO FALL IN LOVE WITH YOU."
BUT I'M SURE I DIDN'T WANT A WORLD LIKE THAT...

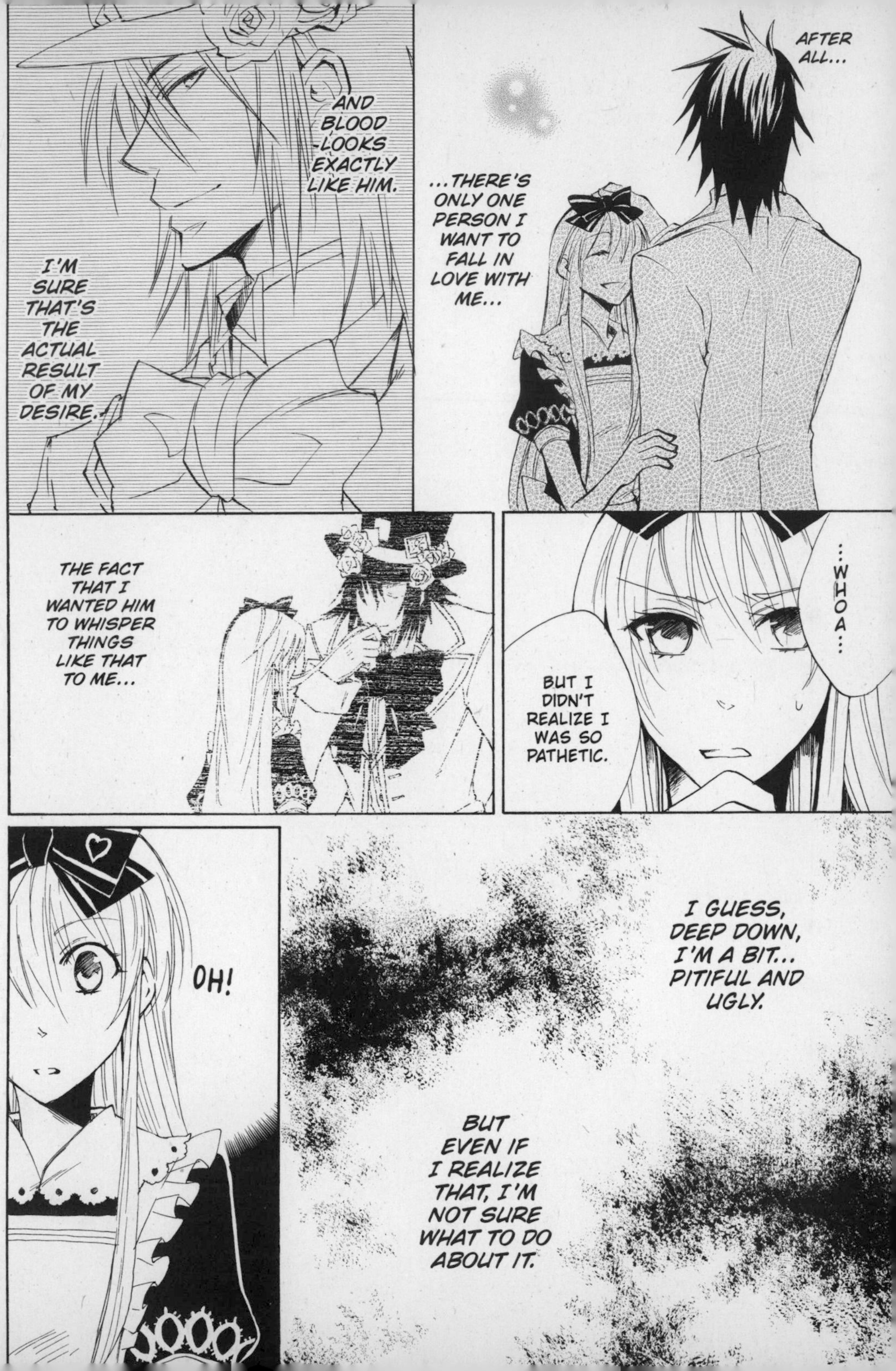
AFTER ALL...
...THERE'S ONLY ONE PERSON I WANT TO FALL IN LOVE WITH ME...
AND BLOOD LOOKS EXACTLY LIKE HIM.
I'M SURE THAT'S THE ACTUAL RESULT OF MY DESIRE.
...WHOA...
BUT I DIDN'T REALIZE I WAS SO PATHETIC.
THE FACT THAT I WANTED HIM TO WHISPER THINGS LIKE THAT TO ME...
I GUESS, DEEP DOWN, I'M A BIT... PITIFUL AND UGLY.
BUT EVEN IF I REALIZE THAT, I'M NOT SURE WHAT TO DO ABOUT IT.
OH!

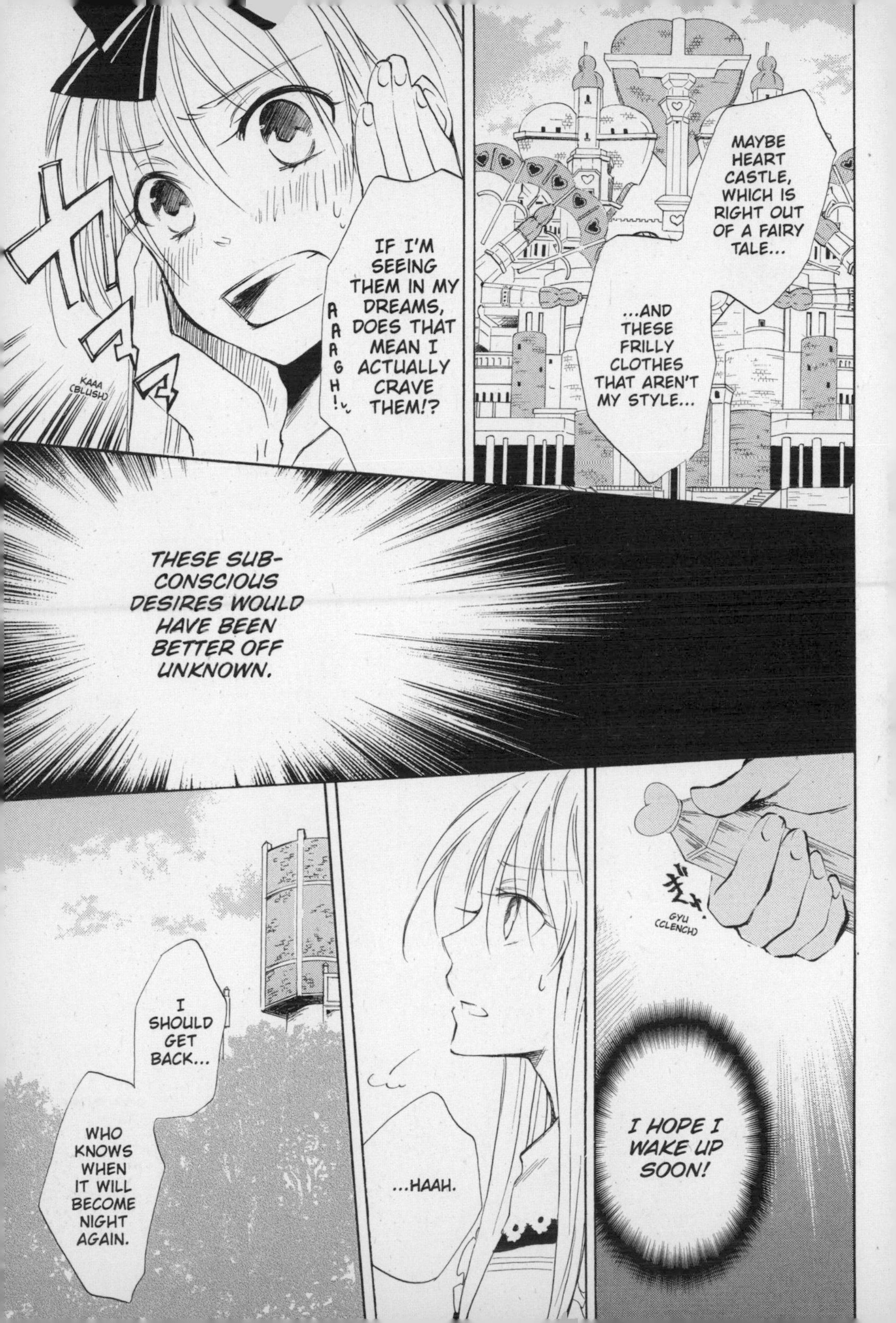
MAYBE HEART CASTLE, WHICH IS RIGHT OUT OF A FAIRY TALE...
...AND THESE FRILLY CLOTHES THAT AREN'T MY STYLE...
IF I'M SEEING THEM IN MY DREAMS, DOES THAT MEAN I ACTUALLY CRAVE THEM!?
AAAGH!
KAAA (BLUSH)
THESE SUB-CONSCIOUS DESIRES WOULD HAVE BEEN BETTER OFF UNKNOWN.
GYU (CLENCH)
I HOPE I WAKE UP SOON!
...HAAH.
I SHOULD GET BACK...
WHO KNOWS WHEN IT WILL BECOME NIGHT AGAIN.

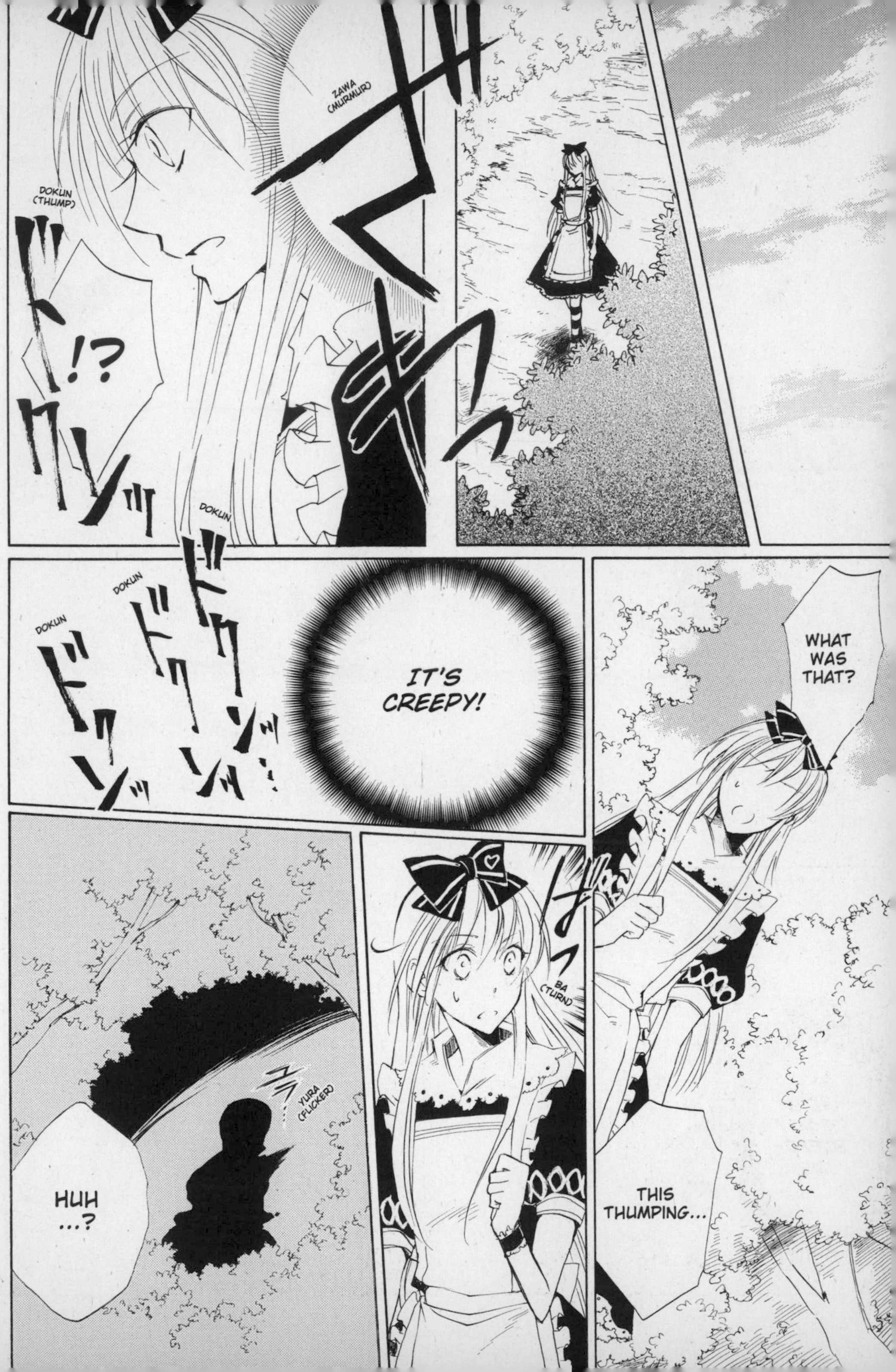

ZAWA (MURMUR)
DOKUN (THUMP)
!?
DOKUN
WHAT WAS THAT?
THIS THUMPING...
IT'S CREEPY!
DOKUN
DOKUN
BA (TURN)
YURA (FLICKER)
HUH ...?

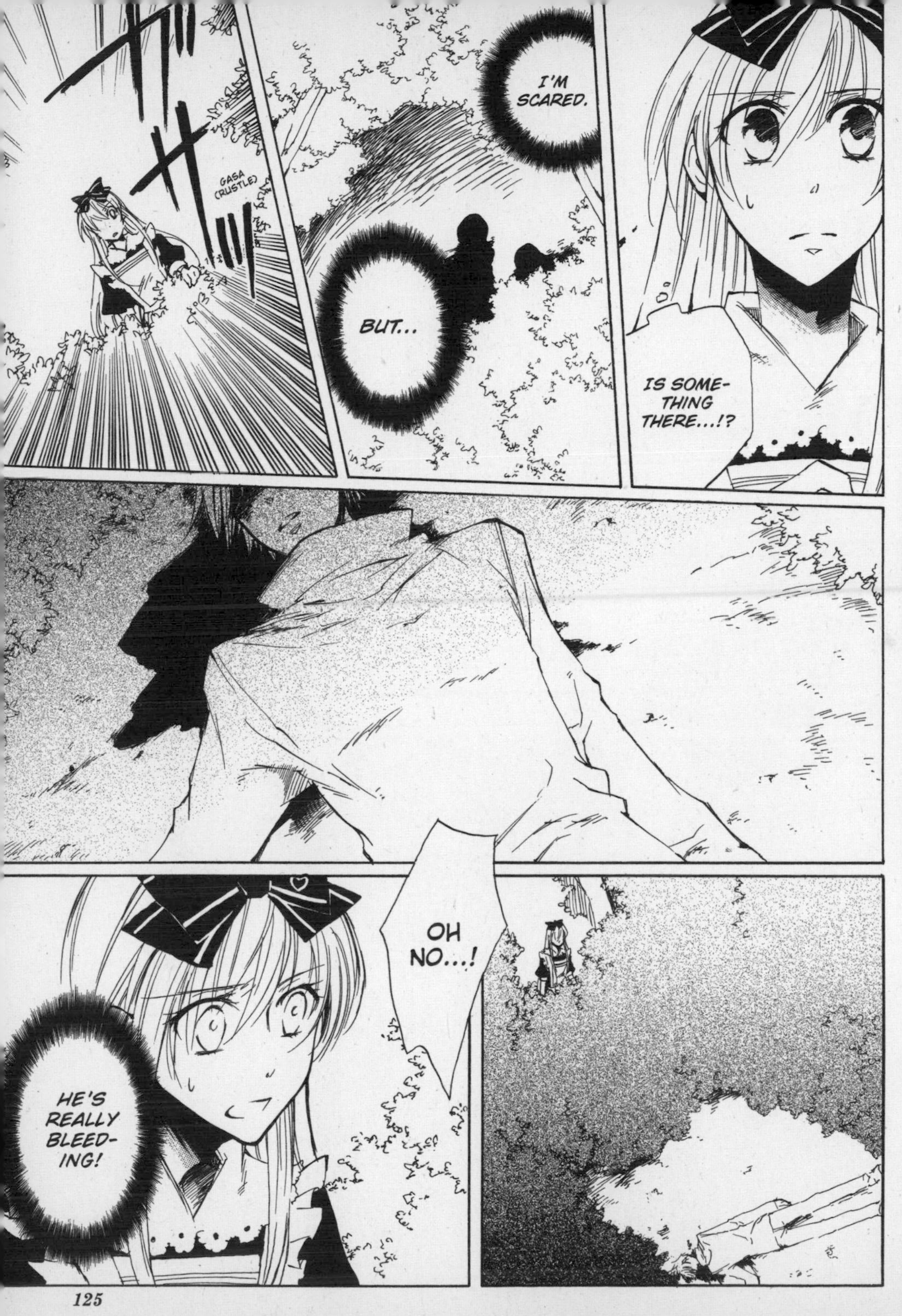
IS SOME-
THING
THERE...!?
I'M
SCARED.
BUT...
GASA
(RUSTLE)
OH
NO...!
HE'S
REALLY
BLEED-
ING!

HEY, ARE YOU ALL RIGHT!?

ARE YOU HURT!?

HANG ON—I'M GOING FOR HELP!

HE'S NOT ANSWERING.

IS HE ALREADY DEAD...?

ZOZO (SSSSK)

ZO

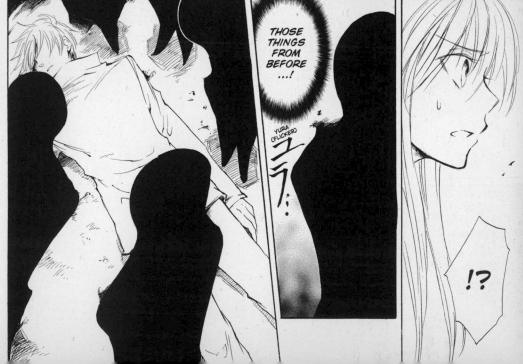

THOSE THINGS FROM BEFORE ...!

YURA (FLICKER)

!?

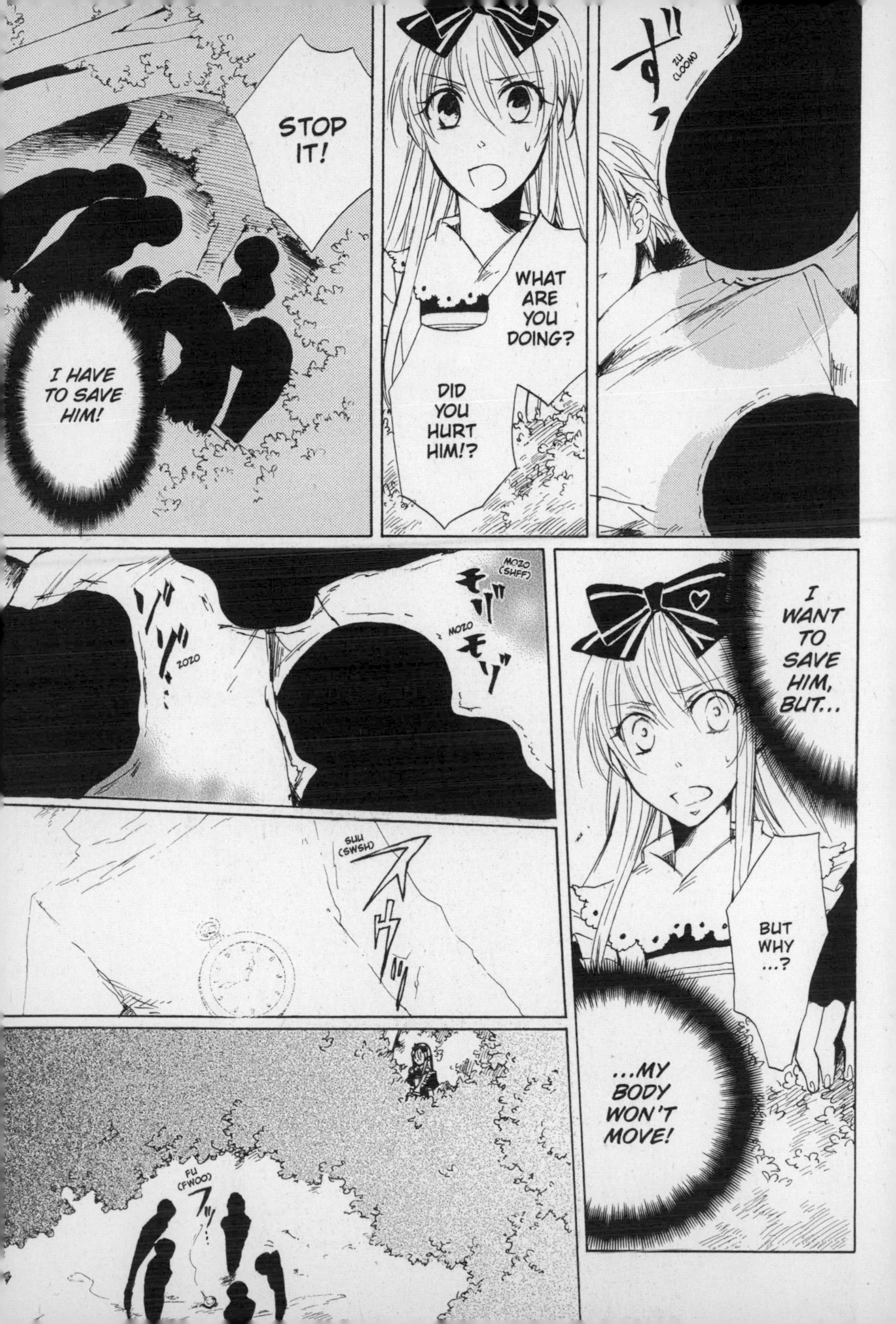
ZU (LOOOM)
WHAT ARE YOU DOING?
DID YOU HURT HIM!?
STOP IT!
I HAVE TO SAVE HIM!
I WANT TO SAVE HIM, BUT...
BUT WHY ...?
...MY BODY WON'T MOVE!
MOZO (SHFF)
MOZO
ZOZO
SUU (SWSH)
FU (FWOO)

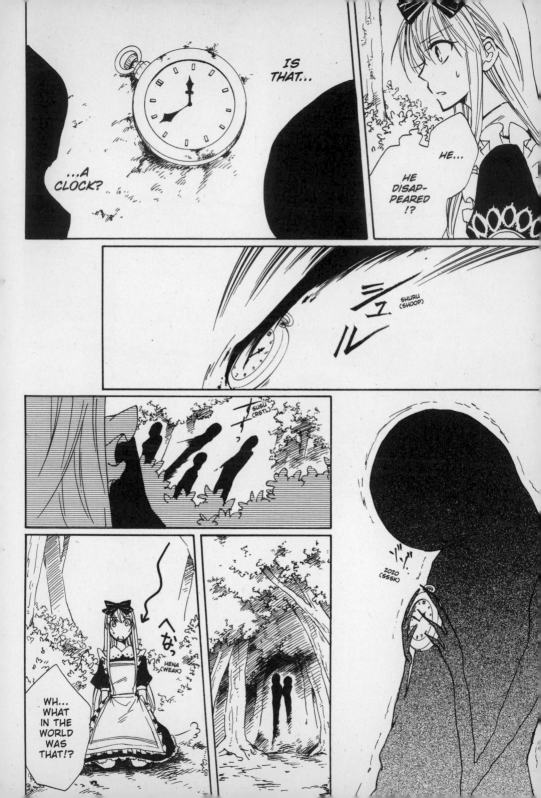

IS THAT...

...A CLOCK?

HE...

HE DISAPPEARED!?

シュル SHURU (SHOOP)

スッ SUGU (RSTL)

ゾゾ ZOZO (SSSK)

へなっ HENA (WEAK)

WH... WHAT IN THE WORLD WAS THAT!?

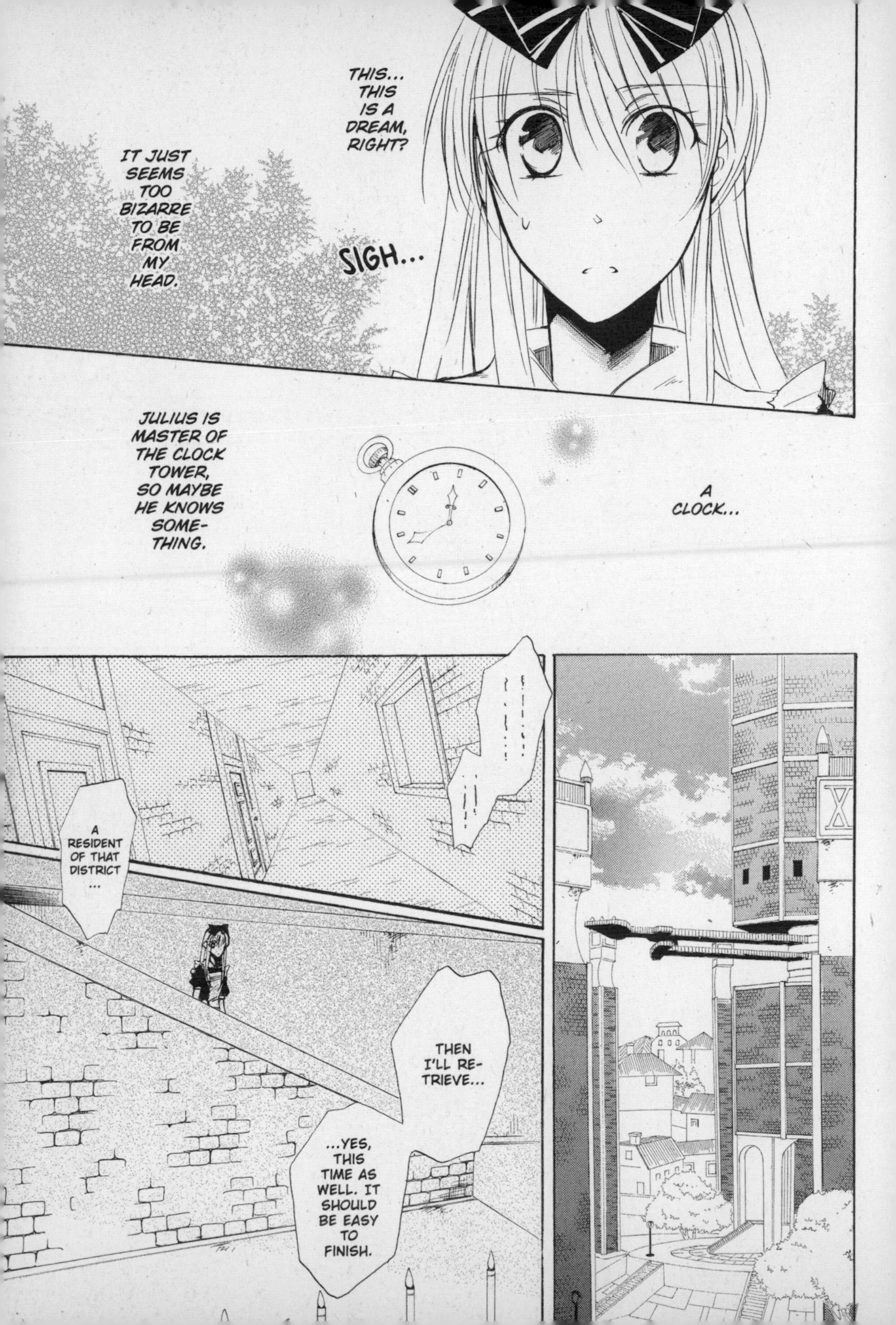
THIS... THIS IS A DREAM, RIGHT?
SIGH...
IT JUST SEEMS TOO BIZARRE TO BE FROM MY HEAD.
A CLOCK...
JULIUS IS MASTER OF THE CLOCK TOWER, SO MAYBE HE KNOWS SOME-THING.
A RESIDENT OF THAT DISTRICT...
THEN I'LL RE-TRIEVE...
...YES, THIS TIME AS WELL. IT SHOULD BE EASY TO FINISH.

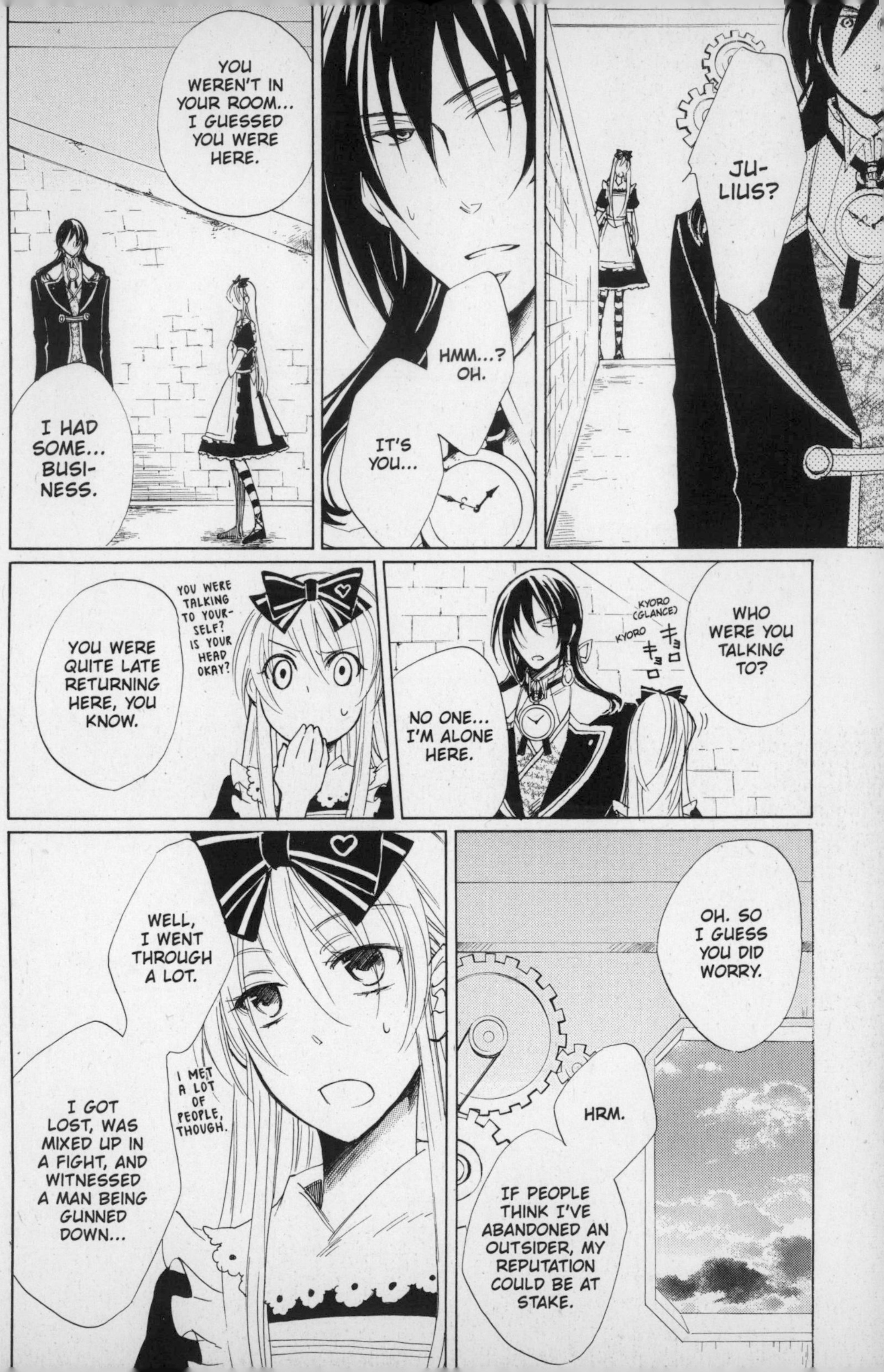
JULIUS?
HMM...? OH.
IT'S YOU...
YOU WEREN'T IN YOUR ROOM... I GUESSED YOU WERE HERE.
I HAD SOME... BUSINESS.
WHO WERE YOU TALKING TO?
KYORO (GLANCE) KYORO
NO ONE... I'M ALONE HERE.
YOU WERE TALKING TO YOURSELF? IS YOUR HEAD OKAY?
YOU WERE QUITE LATE RETURNING HERE, YOU KNOW.
OH. SO I GUESS YOU DID WORRY.
HRM.
IF PEOPLE THINK I'VE ABANDONED AN OUTSIDER, MY REPUTATION COULD BE AT STAKE.
WELL, I WENT THROUGH A LOT.
I MET A LOT OF PEOPLE, THOUGH.
I GOT LOST, WAS MIXED UP IN A FIGHT, AND WITNESSED A MAN BEING GUNNED DOWN...

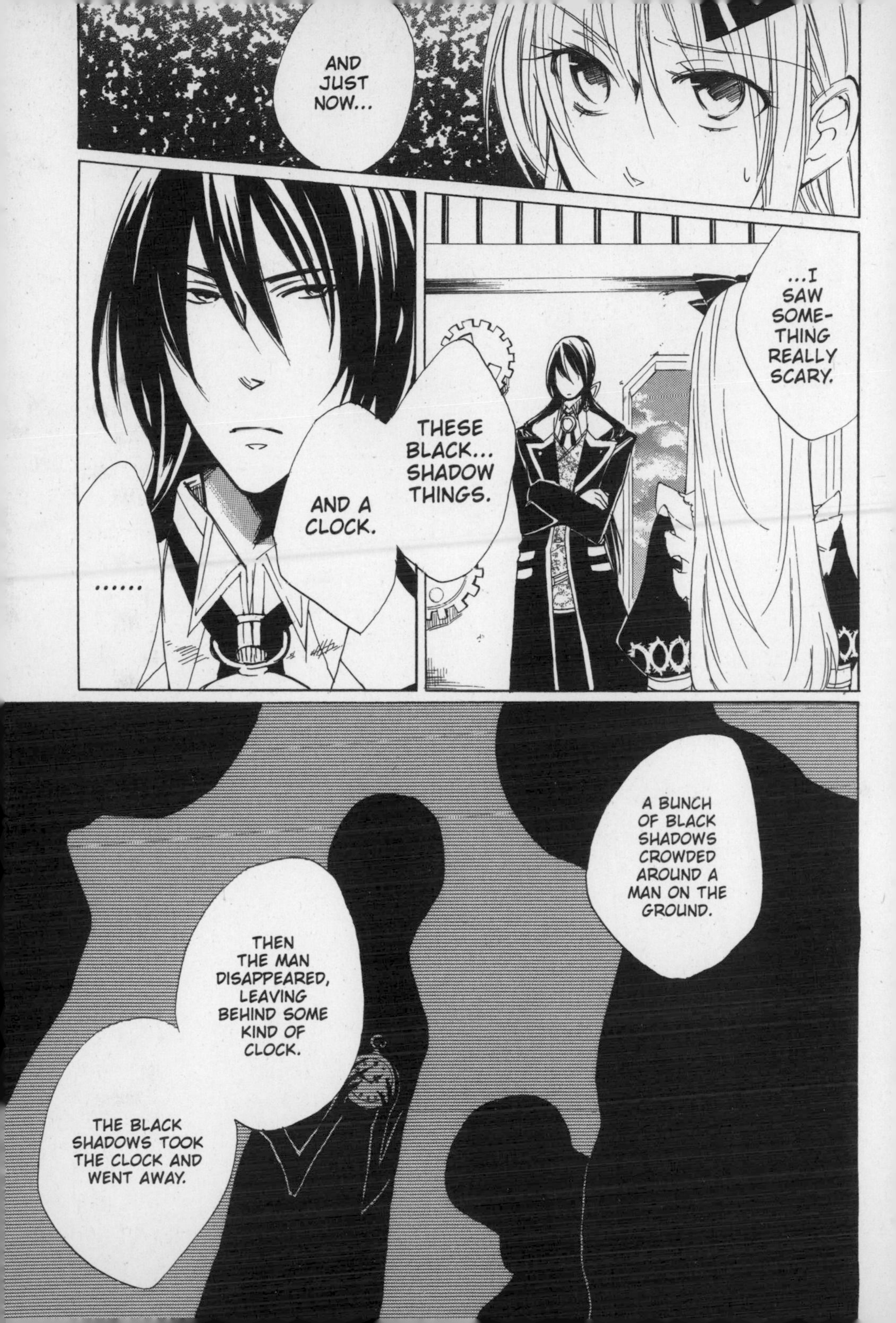
AND JUST NOW...
...I SAW SOME-THING REALLY SCARY.
THESE BLACK... SHADOW THINGS.
AND A CLOCK.
......
A BUNCH OF BLACK SHADOWS CROWDED AROUND A MAN ON THE GROUND.
THEN THE MAN DISAPPEARED, LEAVING BEHIND SOME KIND OF CLOCK.
THE BLACK SHADOWS TOOK THE CLOCK AND WENT AWAY.

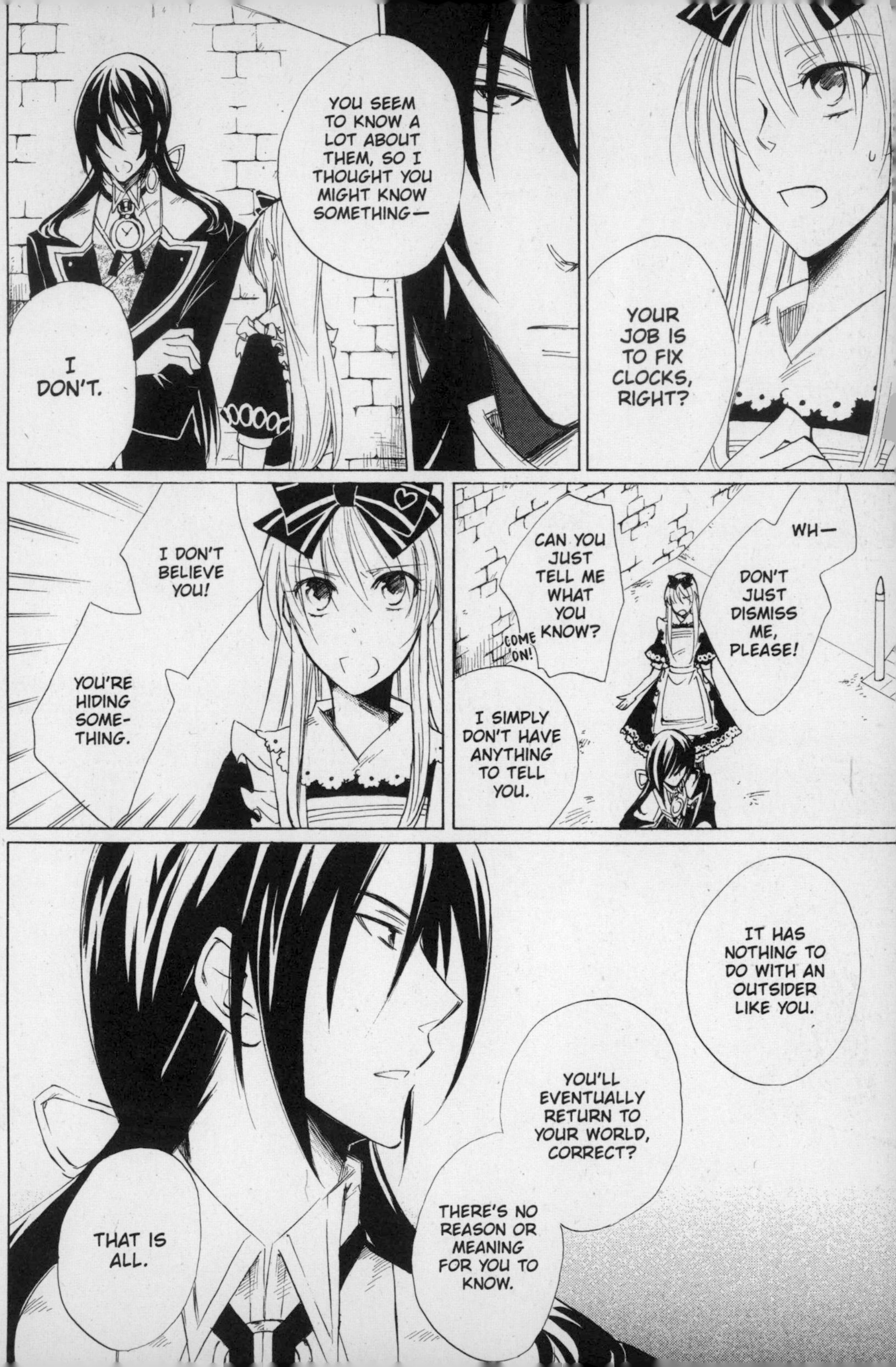
YOUR JOB IS TO FIX CLOCKS, RIGHT?
YOU SEEM TO KNOW A LOT ABOUT THEM, SO I THOUGHT YOU MIGHT KNOW SOMETHING—
I DON'T.
WH—
DON'T JUST DISMISS ME, PLEASE!
CAN YOU JUST TELL ME WHAT YOU KNOW?
COME ON!
I SIMPLY DON'T HAVE ANYTHING TO TELL YOU.
I DON'T BELIEVE YOU!
YOU'RE HIDING SOME-THING.
IT HAS NOTHING TO DO WITH AN OUTSIDER LIKE YOU.
YOU'LL EVENTUALLY RETURN TO YOUR WORLD, CORRECT?
THERE'S NO REASON OR MEANING FOR YOU TO KNOW.
THAT IS ALL.

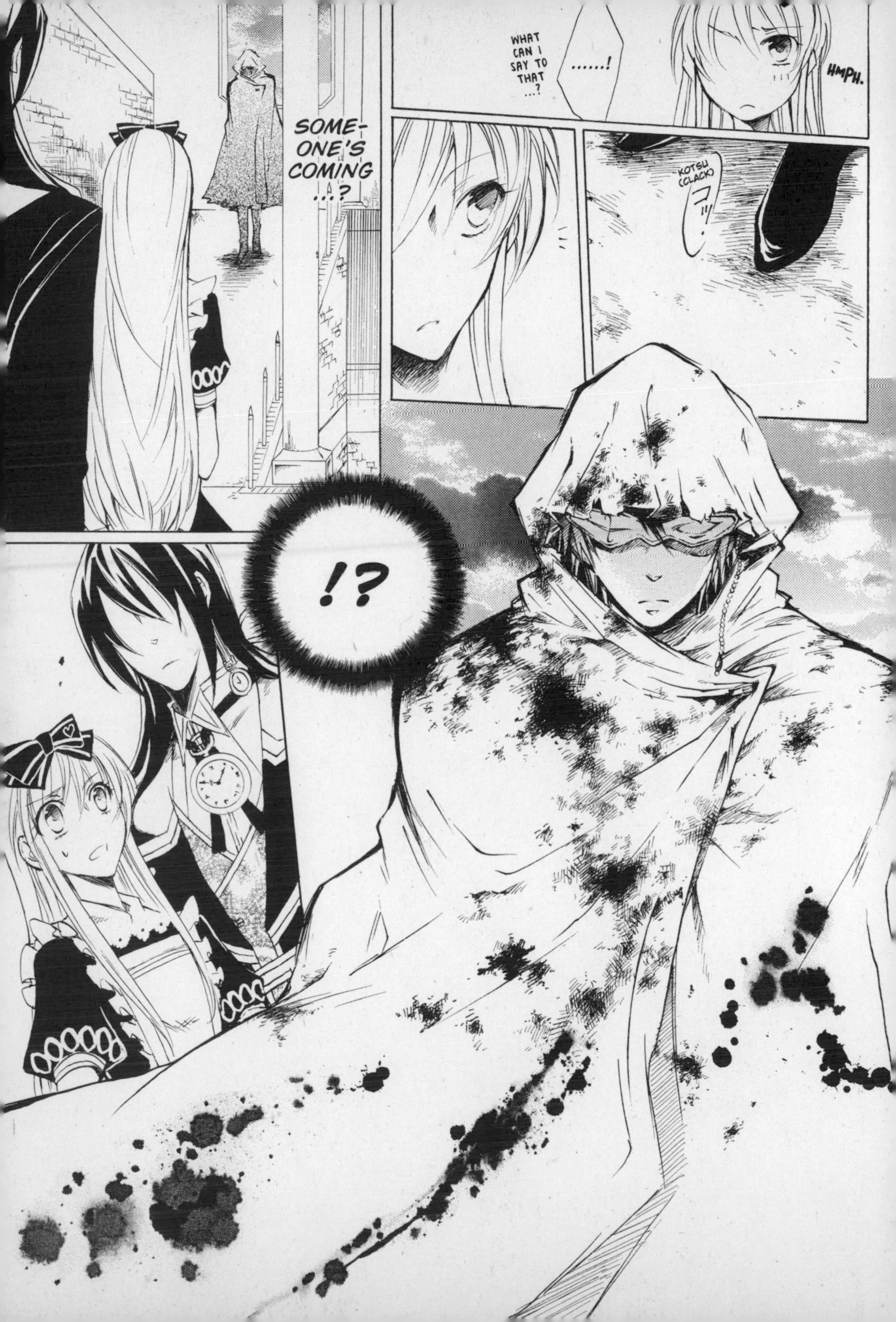
HMPH.
......!
WHAT CAN I SAY TO THAT ...?
KOTSU (CLACK)
?!
SOME-ONE'S COMING ...?
!?

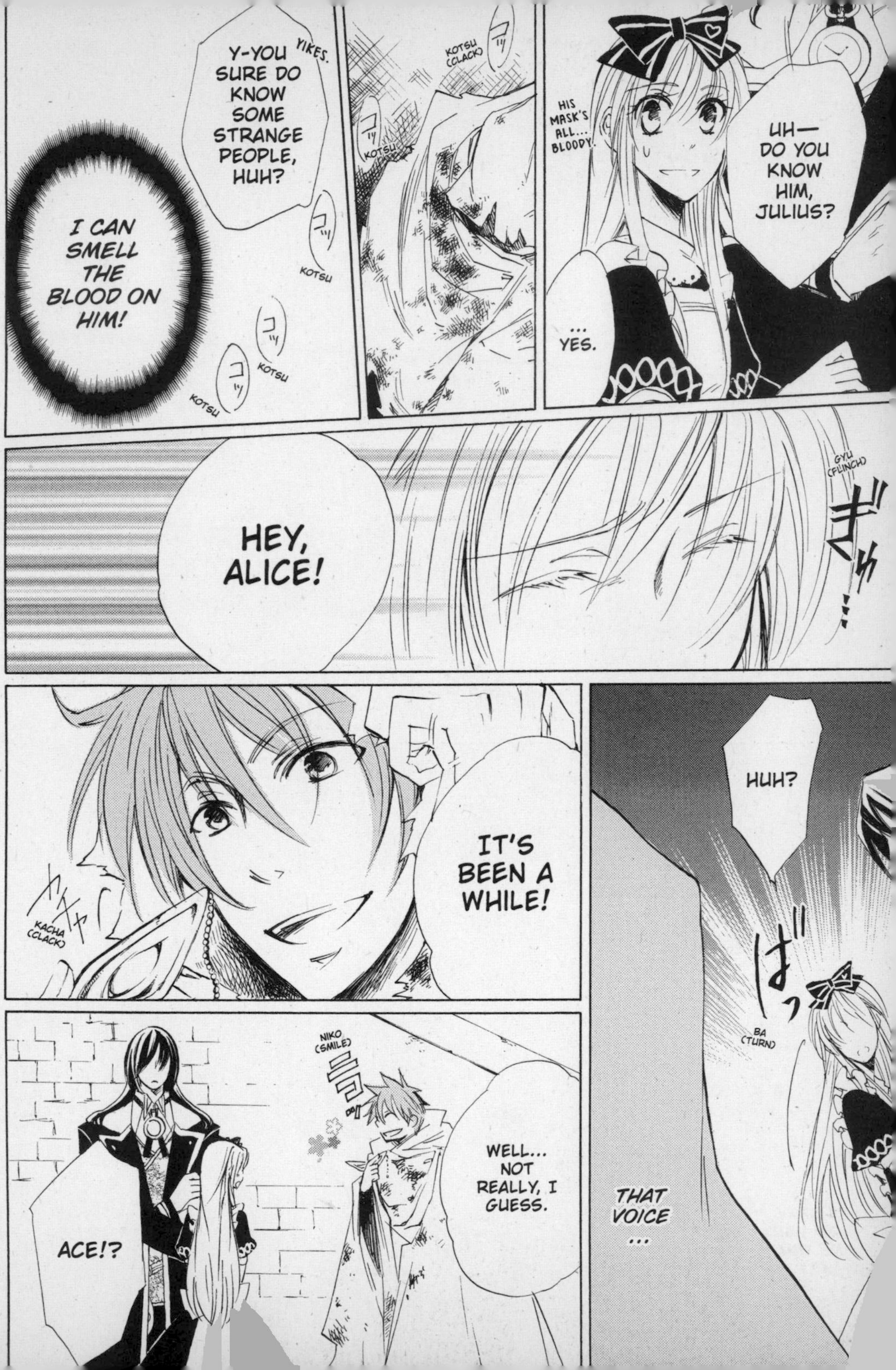
UH— DO YOU KNOW HIM, JULIUS?
HIS MASK'S ALL... BLOODY.
...YES.
KOTSU (CLACK)
KOTSU
KOTSU
YIKES.
Y-YOU SURE DO KNOW SOME STRANGE PEOPLE, HUH?
I CAN SMELL THE BLOOD ON HIM!
KOTSU
KOTSU
GYU (FLINCH)
HEY, ALICE!
HUH?
BA (TURN)
THAT VOICE...
IT'S BEEN A WHILE!
KACHA (CLACK)
NIKO (SMILE)
WELL... NOT REALLY, I GUESS.
ACE!?

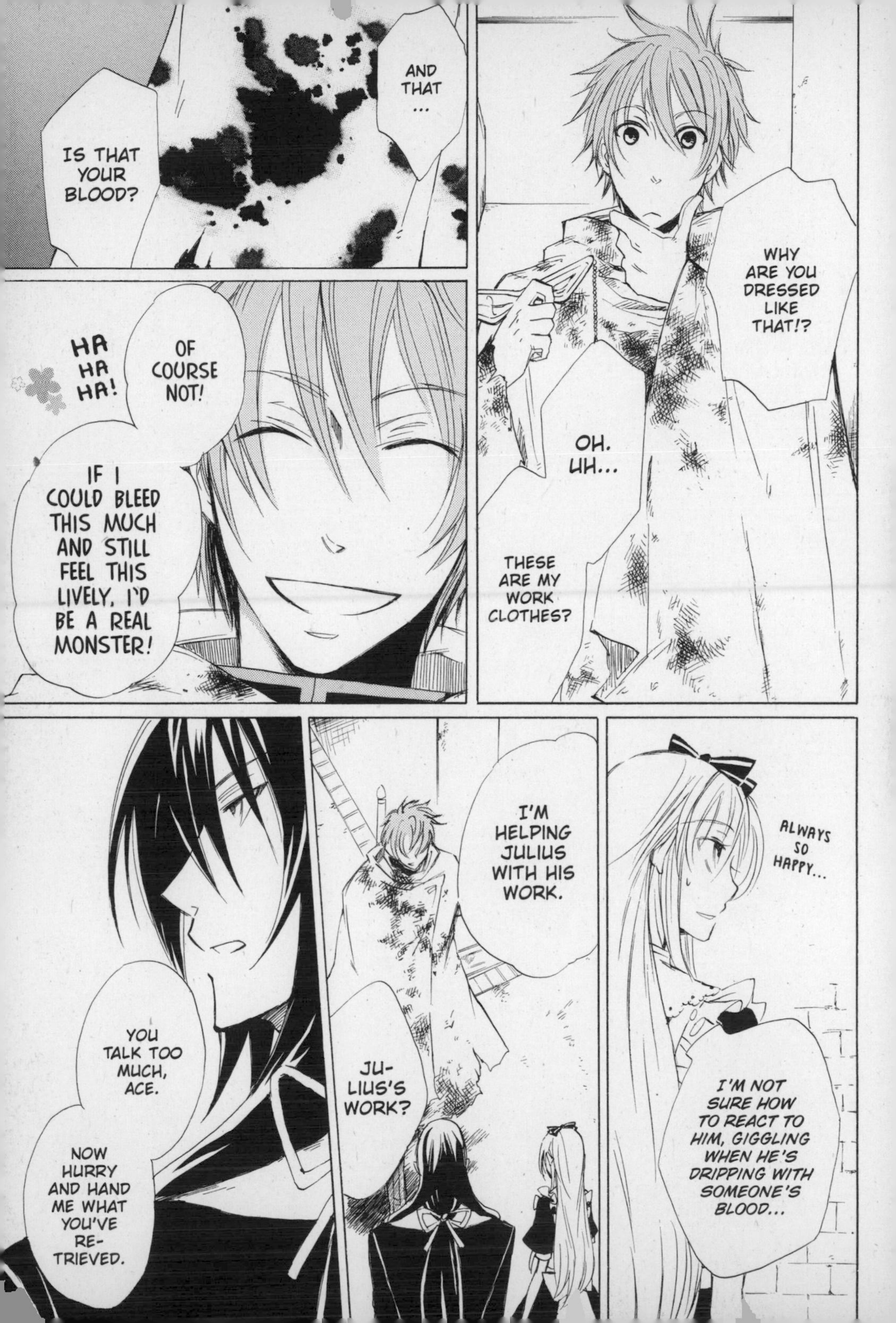
WHY ARE YOU DRESSED LIKE THAT!?
OH. UH...
THESE ARE MY WORK CLOTHES?
AND THAT...
IS THAT YOUR BLOOD?
OF COURSE NOT!
HA HA HA!
IF I COULD BLEED THIS MUCH AND STILL FEEL THIS LIVELY, I'D BE A REAL MONSTER!
ALWAYS SO HAPPY...
I'M NOT SURE HOW TO REACT TO HIM, GIGGLING WHEN HE'S DRIPPING WITH SOMEONE'S BLOOD...
I'M HELPING JULIUS WITH HIS WORK.
JU-LIUS'S WORK?
YOU TALK TOO MUCH, ACE.
NOW HURRY AND HAND ME WHAT YOU'VE RE-TRIEVED.

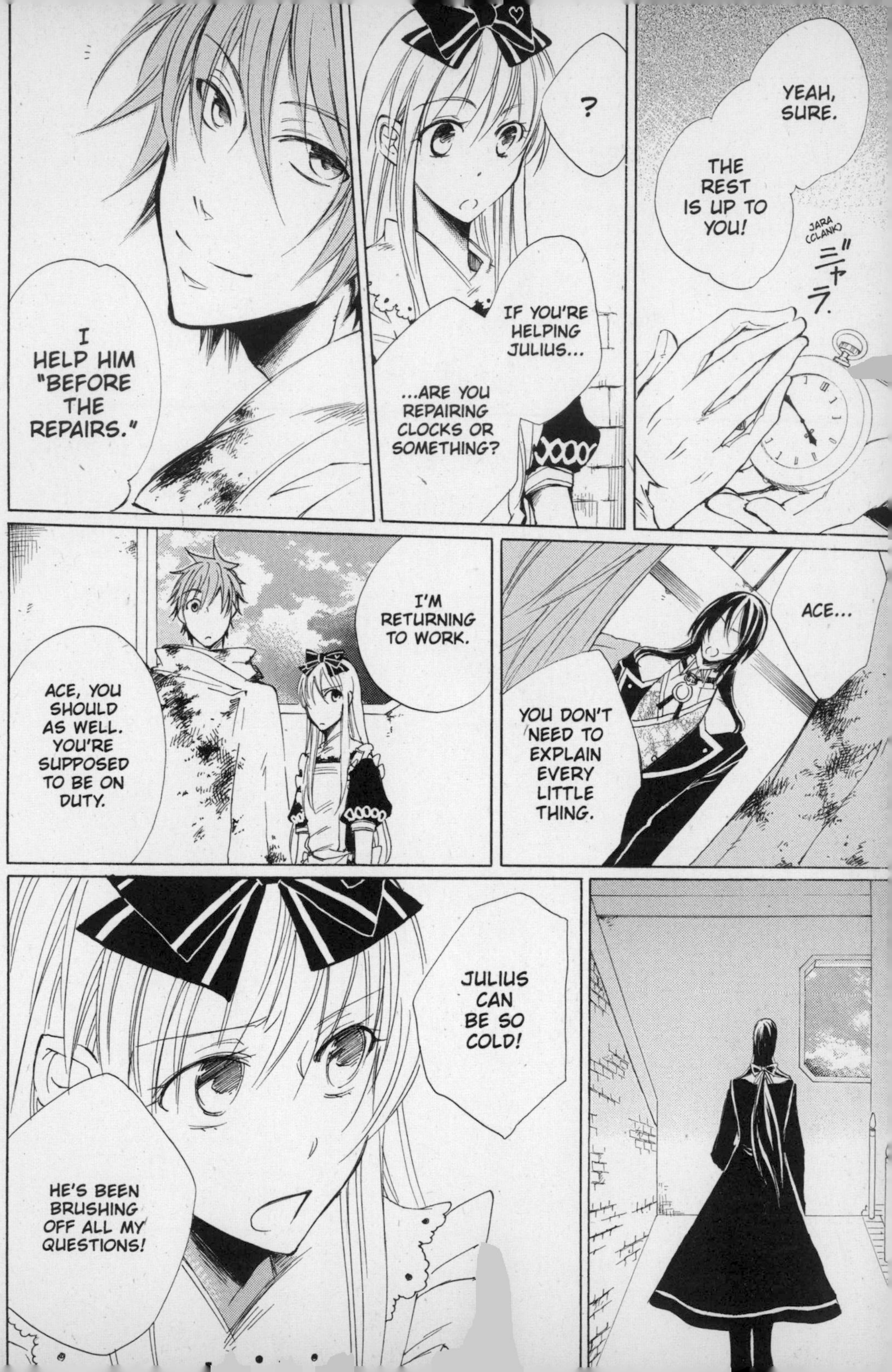
YEAH, SURE.
THE REST IS UP TO YOU!
JARA (CLANK)
ジャラ
?
IF YOU'RE HELPING JULIUS...
...ARE YOU REPAIRING CLOCKS OR SOMETHING?
I HELP HIM "BEFORE THE REPAIRS."
ACE...
YOU DON'T NEED TO EXPLAIN EVERY LITTLE THING.
I'M RETURNING TO WORK.
ACE, YOU SHOULD AS WELL. YOU'RE SUPPOSED TO BE ON DUTY.
JULIUS CAN BE SO COLD!
HE'S BEEN BRUSHING OFF ALL MY QUESTIONS!

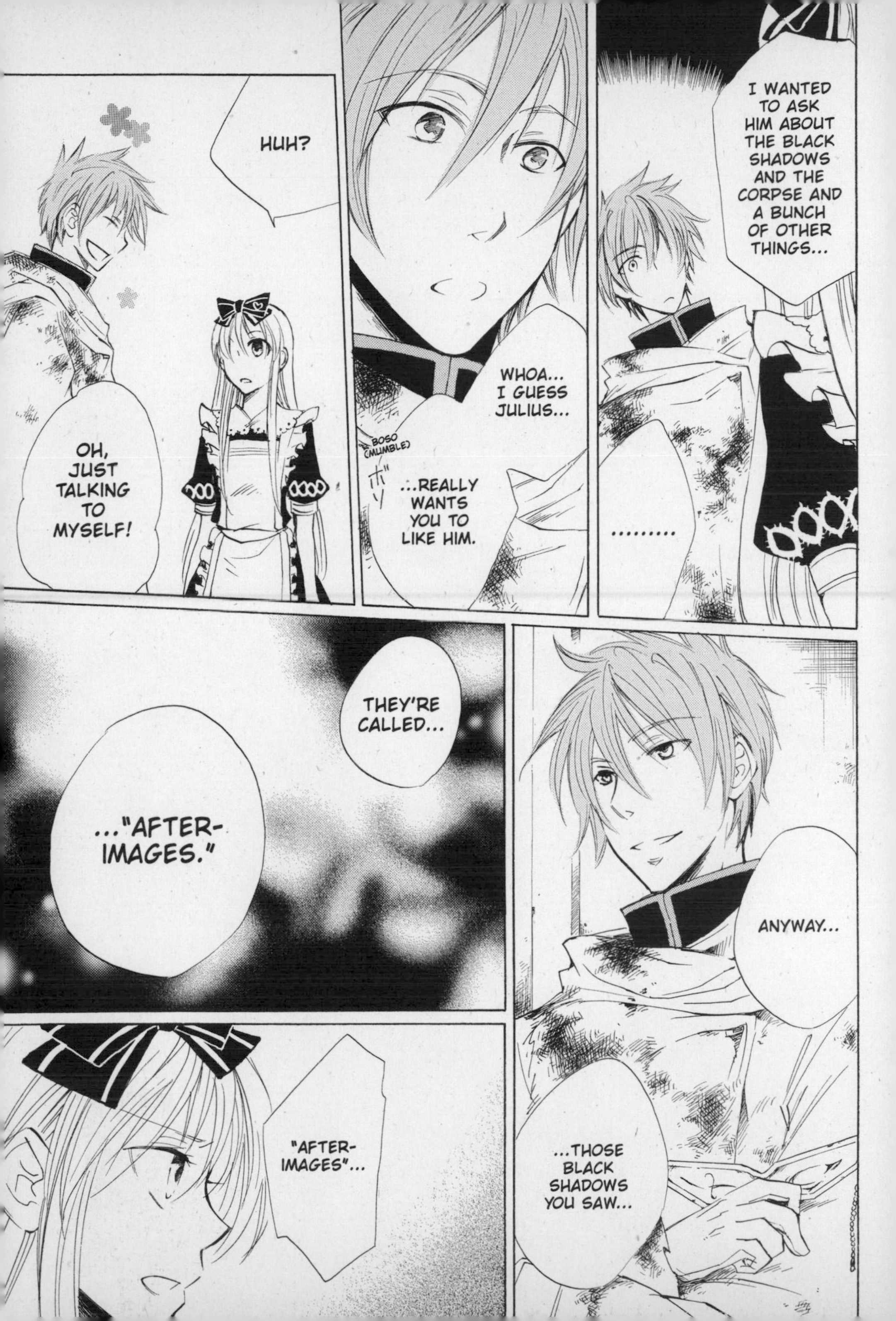
I WANTED TO ASK HIM ABOUT THE BLACK SHADOWS AND THE CORPSE AND A BUNCH OF OTHER THINGS...
....
WHOA... I GUESS JULIUS...
BOSO (MUMBLE)
...REALLY WANTS YOU TO LIKE HIM.
HUH?
OH, JUST TALKING TO MYSELF!
ANYWAY...
...THOSE BLACK SHADOWS YOU SAW...
THEY'RE CALLED...
..."AFTER-IMAGES."
"AFTER-IMAGES"...

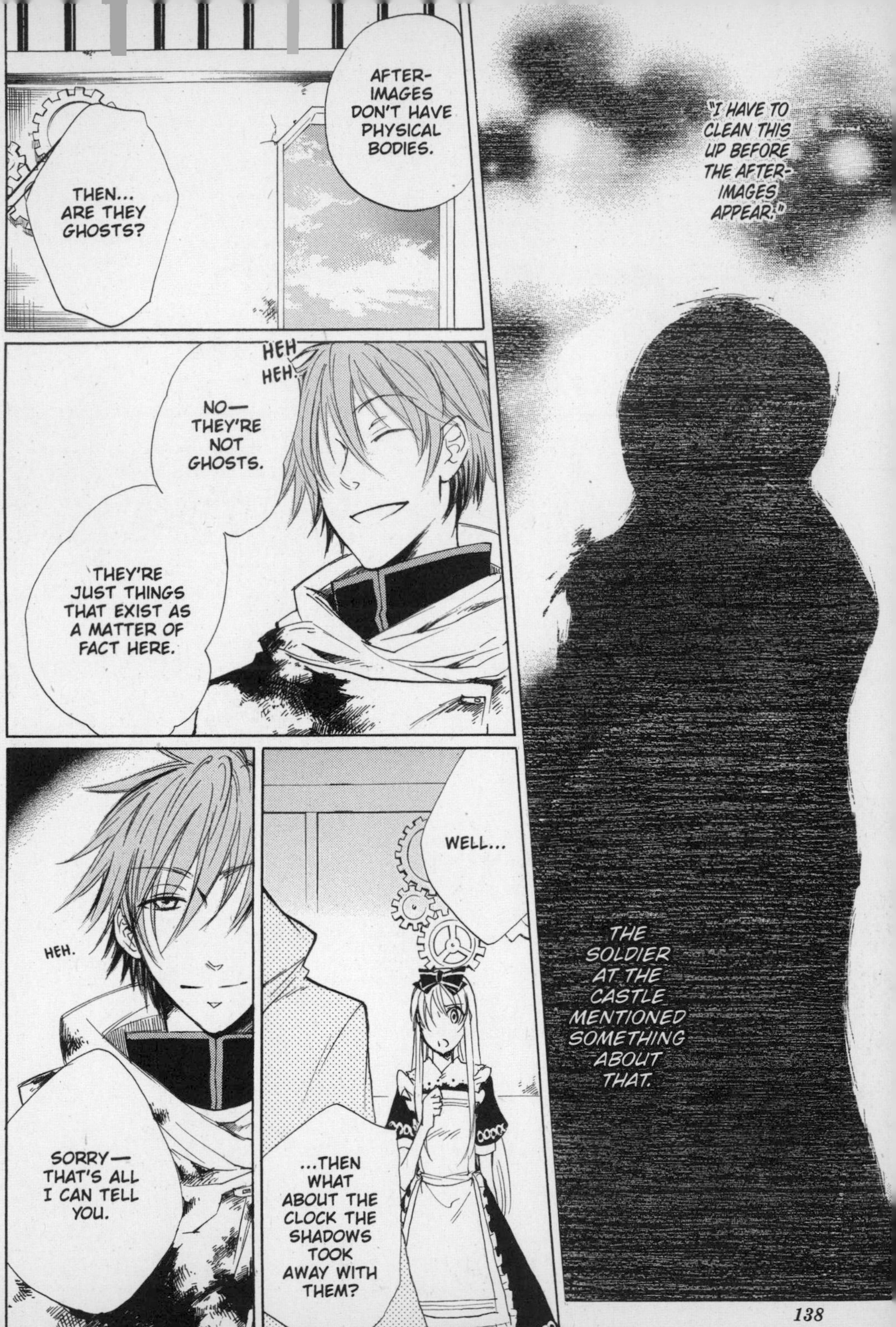
"I HAVE TO CLEAN THIS UP BEFORE THE AFTER-IMAGES APPEAR."
THE SOLDIER AT THE CASTLE MENTIONED SOMETHING ABOUT THAT.
AFTER-IMAGES DON'T HAVE PHYSICAL BODIES.
THEN... ARE THEY GHOSTS?
HEH HEH
NO— THEY'RE NOT GHOSTS.
THEY'RE JUST THINGS THAT EXIST AS A MATTER OF FACT HERE.
WELL...
...THEN WHAT ABOUT THE CLOCK THE SHADOWS TOOK AWAY WITH THEM?
HEH.
SORRY— THAT'S ALL I CAN TELL YOU.

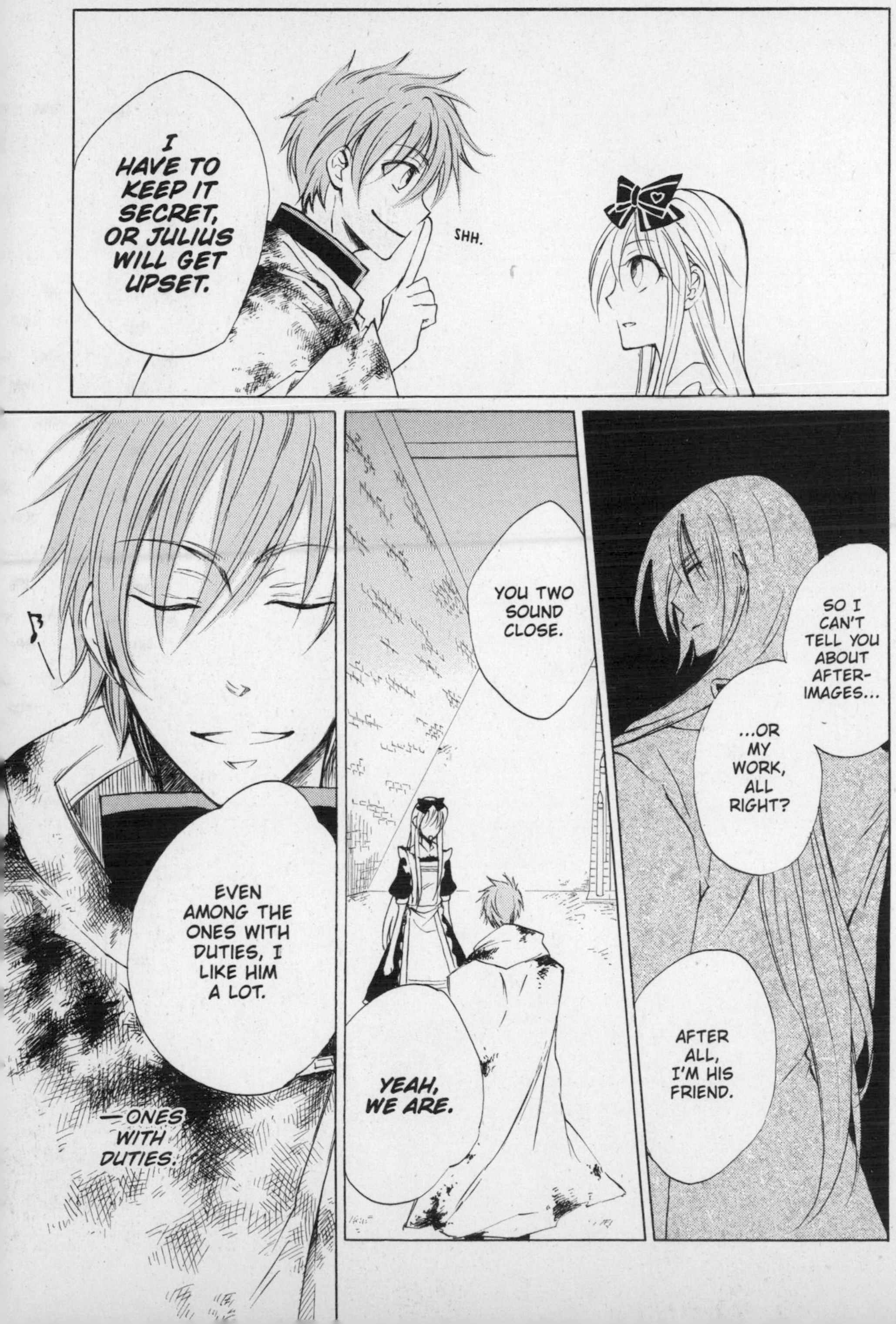
SHH.
I HAVE TO KEEP IT SECRET, OR JULIUS WILL GET UPSET.
SO I CAN'T TELL YOU ABOUT AFTER-IMAGES...
...OR MY WORK, ALL RIGHT?
AFTER ALL, I'M HIS FRIEND.
YOU TWO SOUND CLOSE.
YEAH, WE ARE.
EVEN AMONG THE ONES WITH DUTIES, I LIKE HIM A LOT.
—ONES WITH DUTIES.

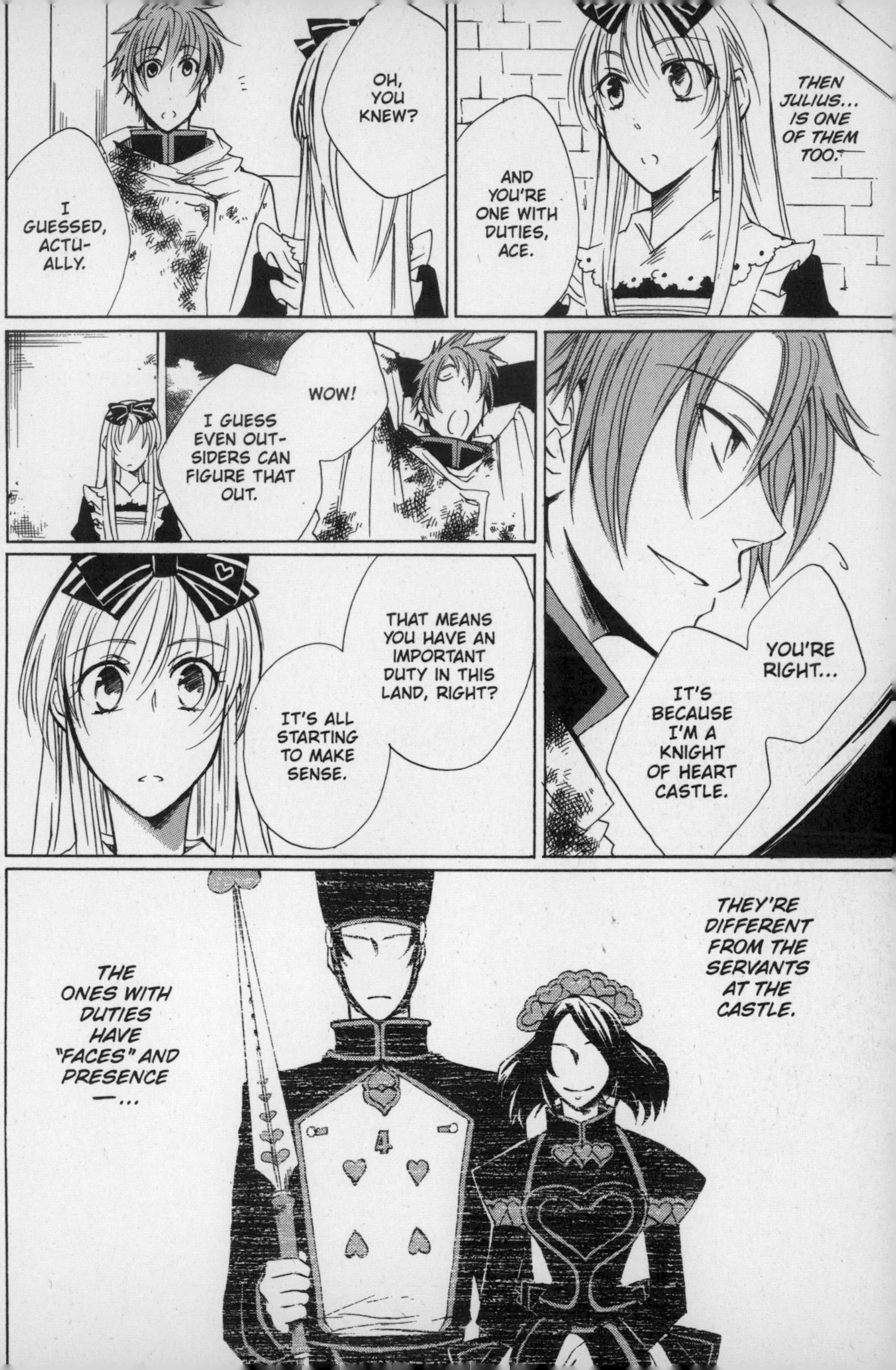
THEN JULIUS... IS ONE OF THEM TOO.
AND YOU'RE ONE WITH DUTIES, ACE.
OH, YOU KNEW?
I GUESSED, ACTUALLY.
YOU'RE RIGHT...
IT'S BECAUSE I'M A KNIGHT OF HEART CASTLE.
WOW!
I GUESS EVEN OUTSIDERS CAN FIGURE THAT OUT.
THAT MEANS YOU HAVE AN IMPORTANT DUTY IN THIS LAND, RIGHT?
IT'S ALL STARTING TO MAKE SENSE.
THEY'RE DIFFERENT FROM THE SERVANTS AT THE CASTLE.
THE ONES WITH DUTIES HAVE "FACES" AND PRESENCE—...

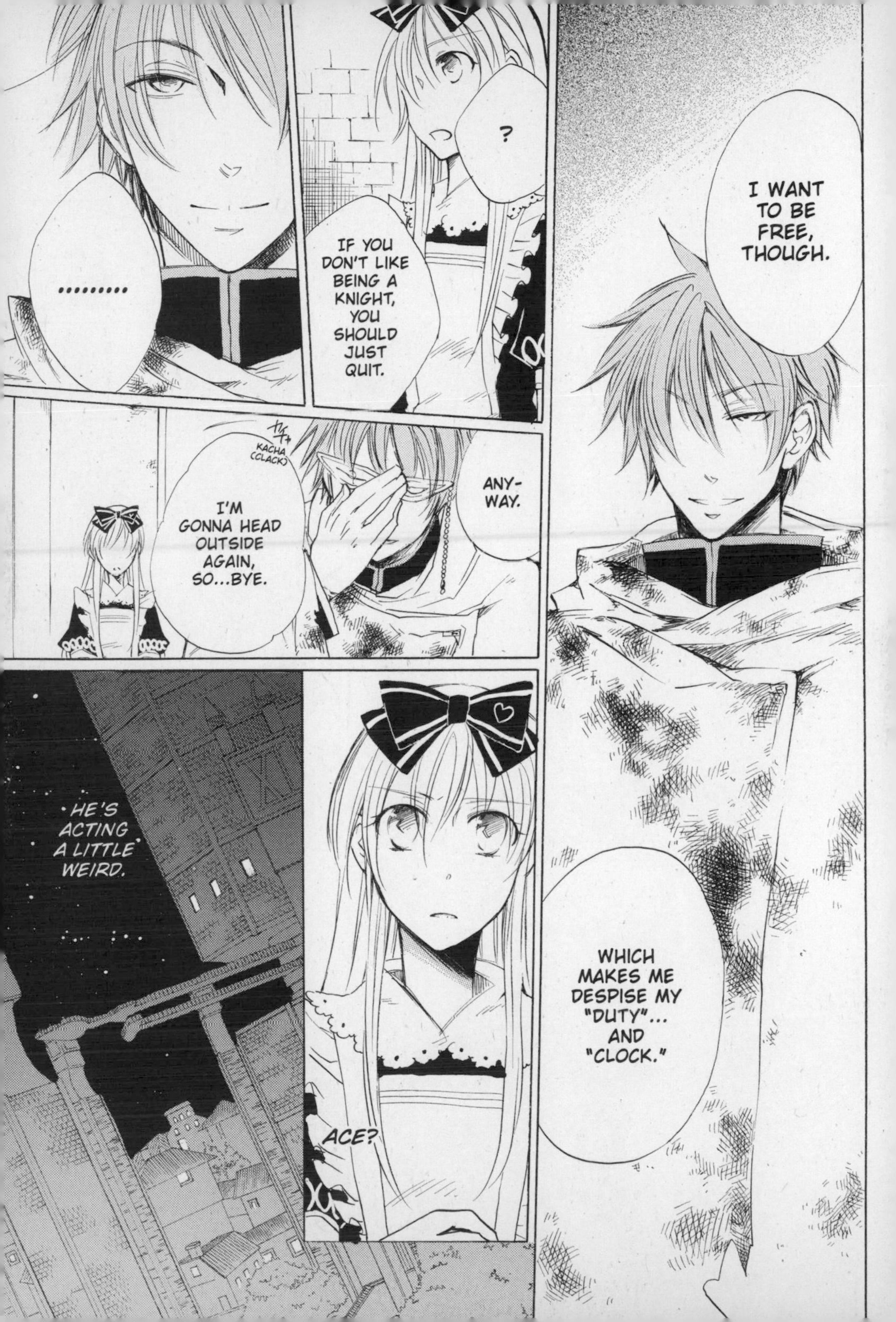
I WANT TO BE FREE, THOUGH.
WHICH MAKES ME DESPISE MY "DUTY"... AND "CLOCK."
?
IF YOU DON'T LIKE BEING A KNIGHT, YOU SHOULD JUST QUIT.
....
ANY-WAY.
KACHA (CLACK)
I'M GONNA HEAD OUTSIDE AGAIN, SO...BYE.
ACE?
HE'S ACTING A LITTLE WEIRD.

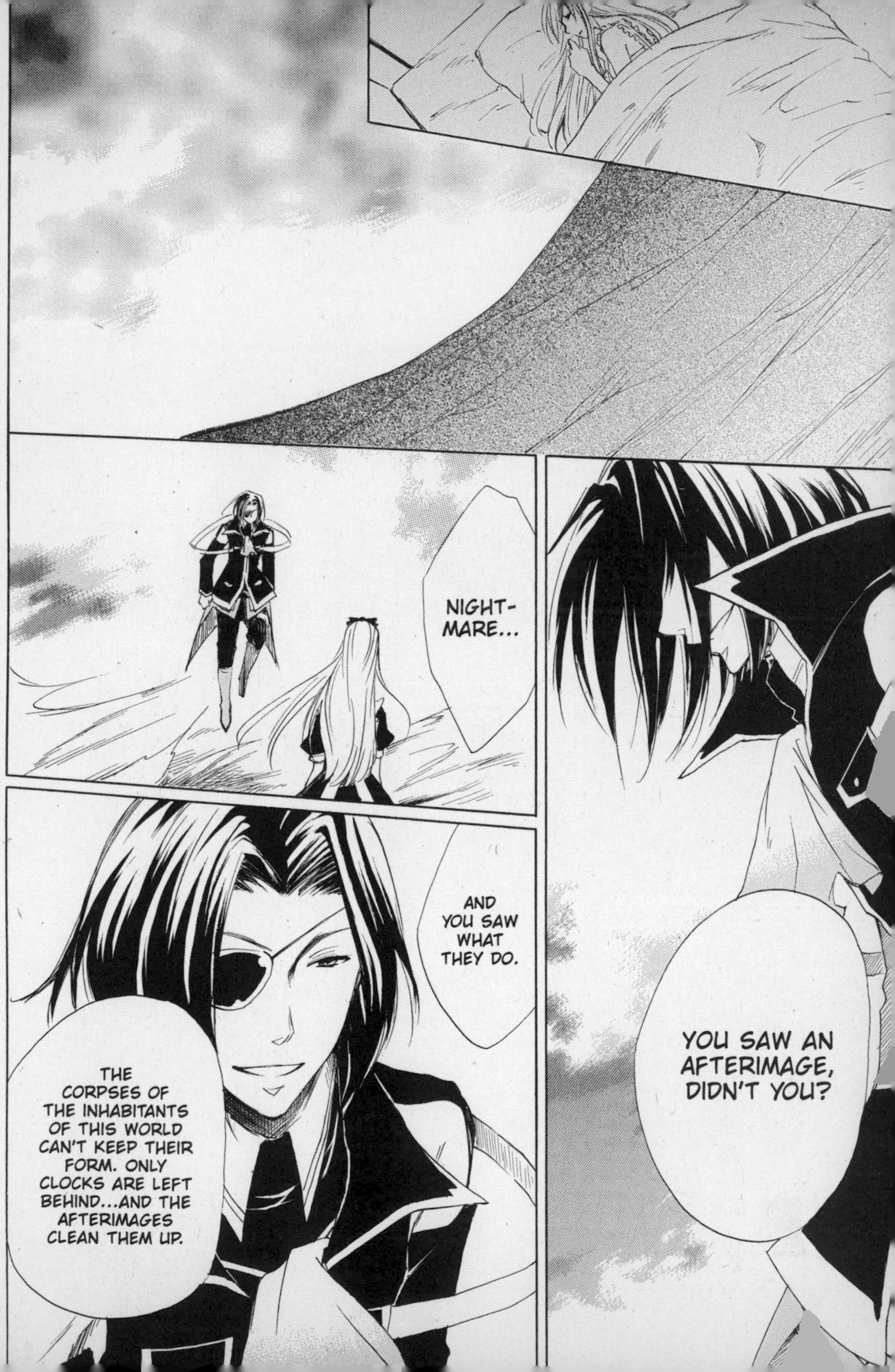
YOU SAW AN AFTERIMAGE, DIDN'T YOU?
NIGHT-MARE...
AND YOU SAW WHAT THEY DO.
THE CORPSES OF THE INHABITANTS OF THIS WORLD CAN'T KEEP THEIR FORM. ONLY CLOCKS ARE LEFT BEHIND...AND THE AFTERIMAGES CLEAN THEM UP.

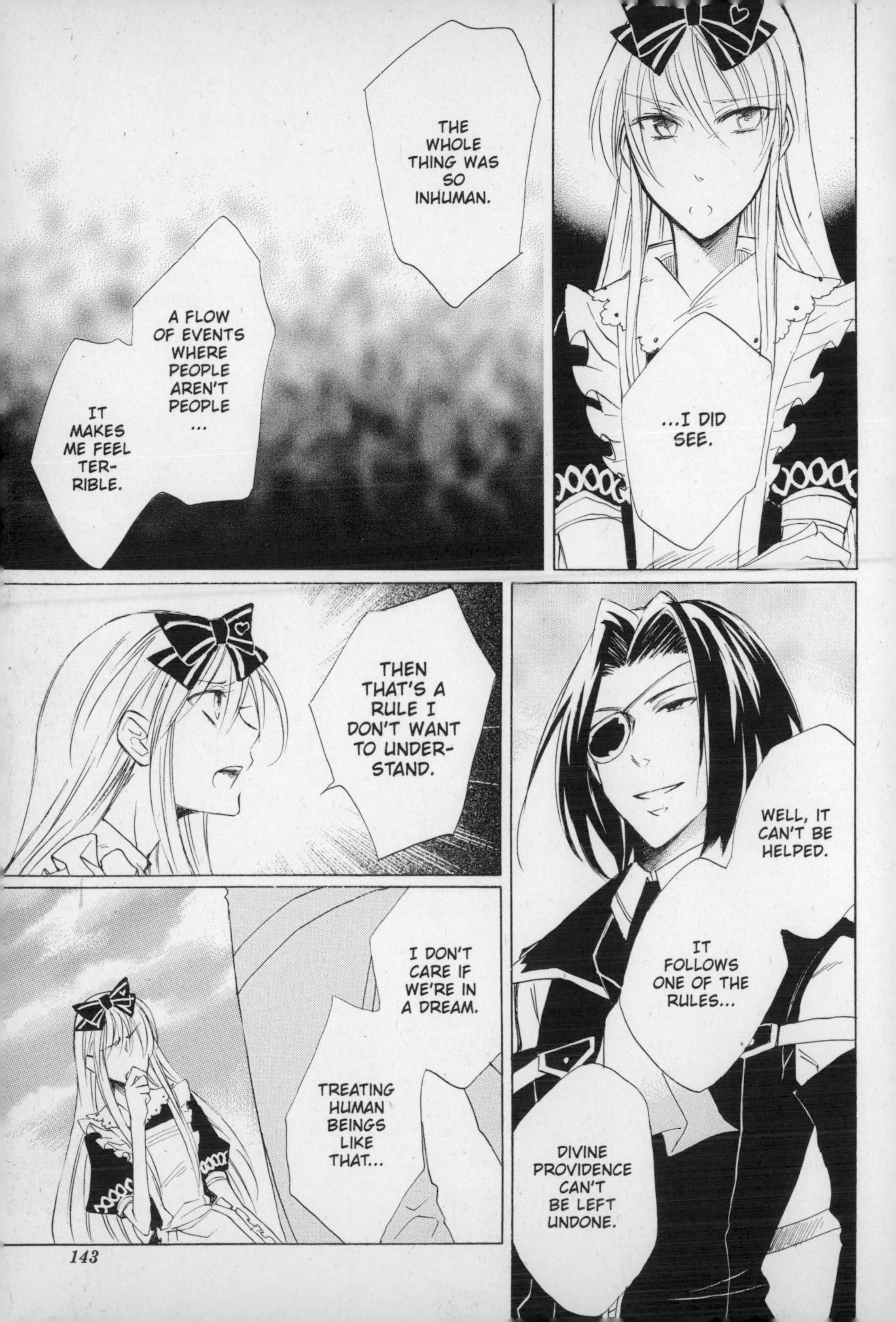
...I DID SEE.
THE WHOLE THING WAS SO INHUMAN.
A FLOW OF EVENTS WHERE PEOPLE AREN'T PEOPLE ...
IT MAKES ME FEEL TER-RIBLE.
WELL, IT CAN'T BE HELPED.
IT FOLLOWS ONE OF THE RULES...
DIVINE PROVIDENCE CAN'T BE LEFT UNDONE.
THEN THAT'S A RULE I DON'T WANT TO UNDER-STAND.
I DON'T CARE IF WE'RE IN A DREAM.
TREATING HUMAN BEINGS LIKE THAT...

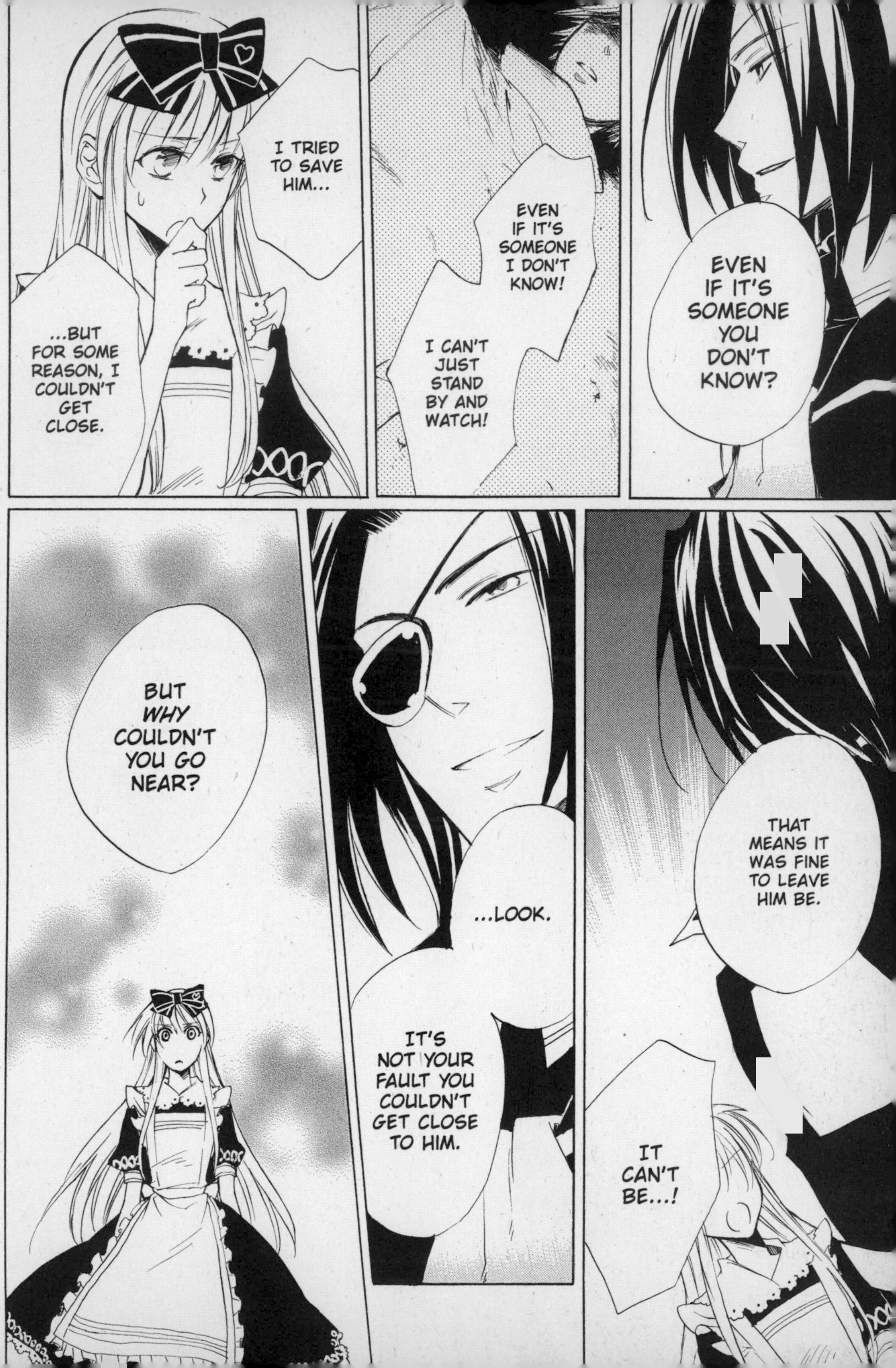
EVEN IF IT'S SOMEONE YOU DON'T KNOW?
EVEN IF IT'S SOMEONE I DON'T KNOW!
I CAN'T JUST STAND BY AND WATCH!
I TRIED TO SAVE HIM...
...BUT FOR SOME REASON, I COULDN'T GET CLOSE.
THAT MEANS IT WAS FINE TO LEAVE HIM BE.
IT CAN'T BE...!
...LOOK.
IT'S NOT YOUR FAULT YOU COULDN'T GET CLOSE TO HIM.
BUT *WHY* COULDN'T YOU GO NEAR?

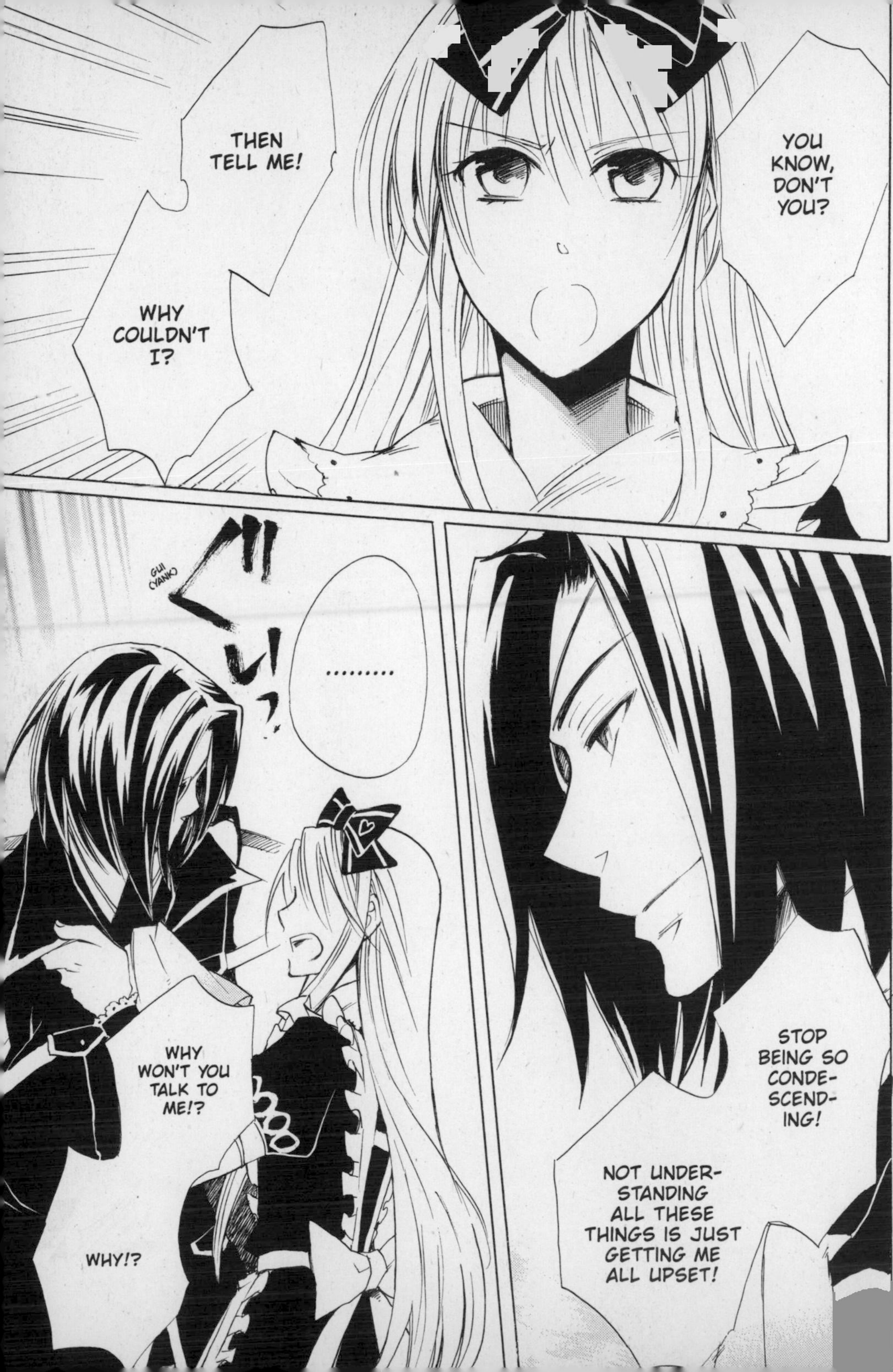
YOU KNOW, DON'T YOU?
THEN TELL ME!
WHY COULDN'T I?
STOP BEING SO CONDE-SCEND-ING!
NOT UNDER-STANDING ALL THESE THINGS IS JUST GETTING ME ALL UPSET!
....
GUI (YANK)
WHY WON'T YOU TALK TO ME!?
WHY!?

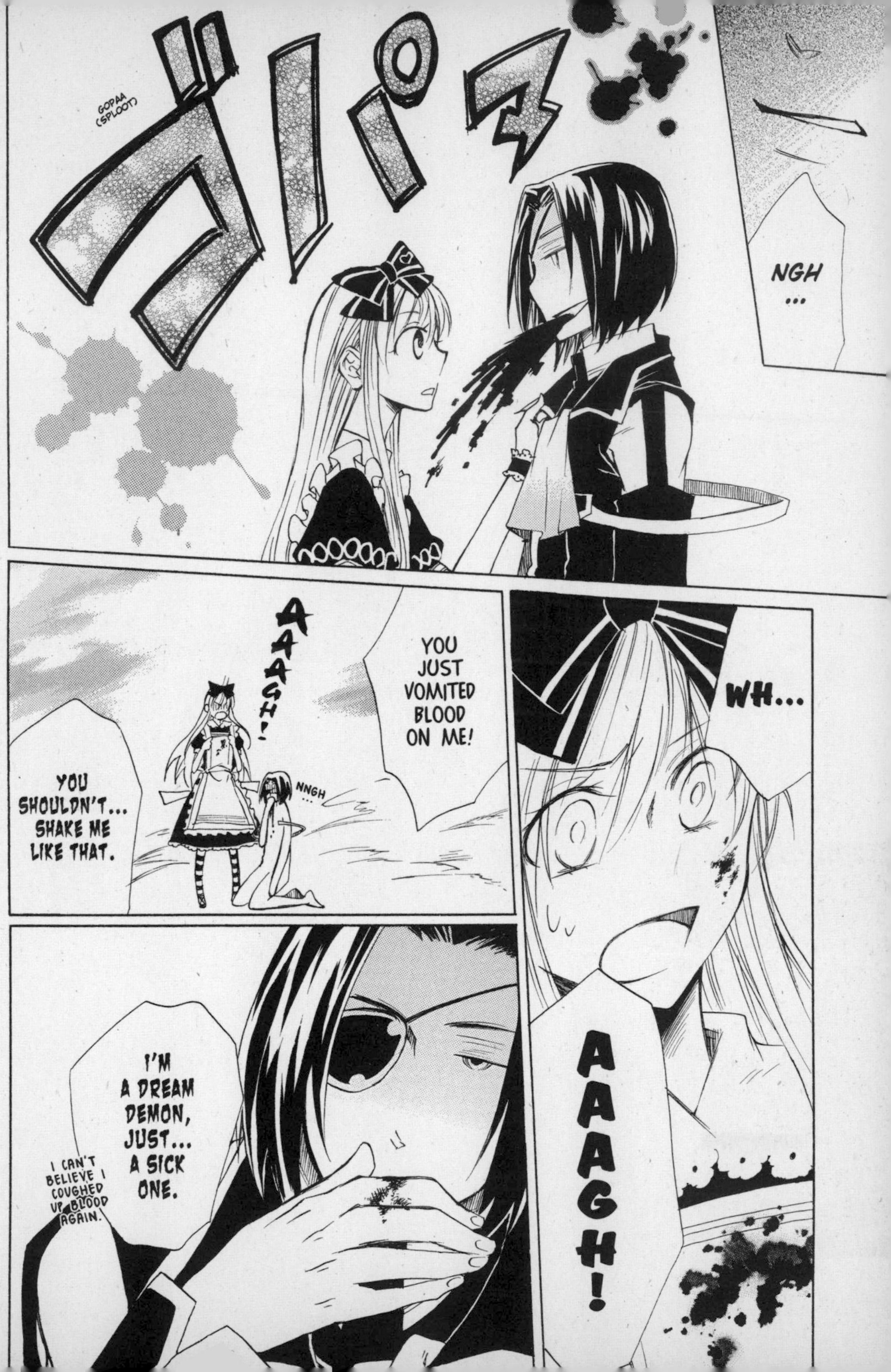
NGH ...
GOPAA (SPLOOT)
WH...
AAAGH!
YOU JUST VOMITED BLOOD ON ME!
AAAGH!
NNGH ...
YOU SHOULDN'T... SHAKE ME LIKE THAT.
I'M A DREAM DEMON, JUST... A SICK ONE.
I CAN'T BELIEVE I COUGHED UP BLOOD AGAIN.

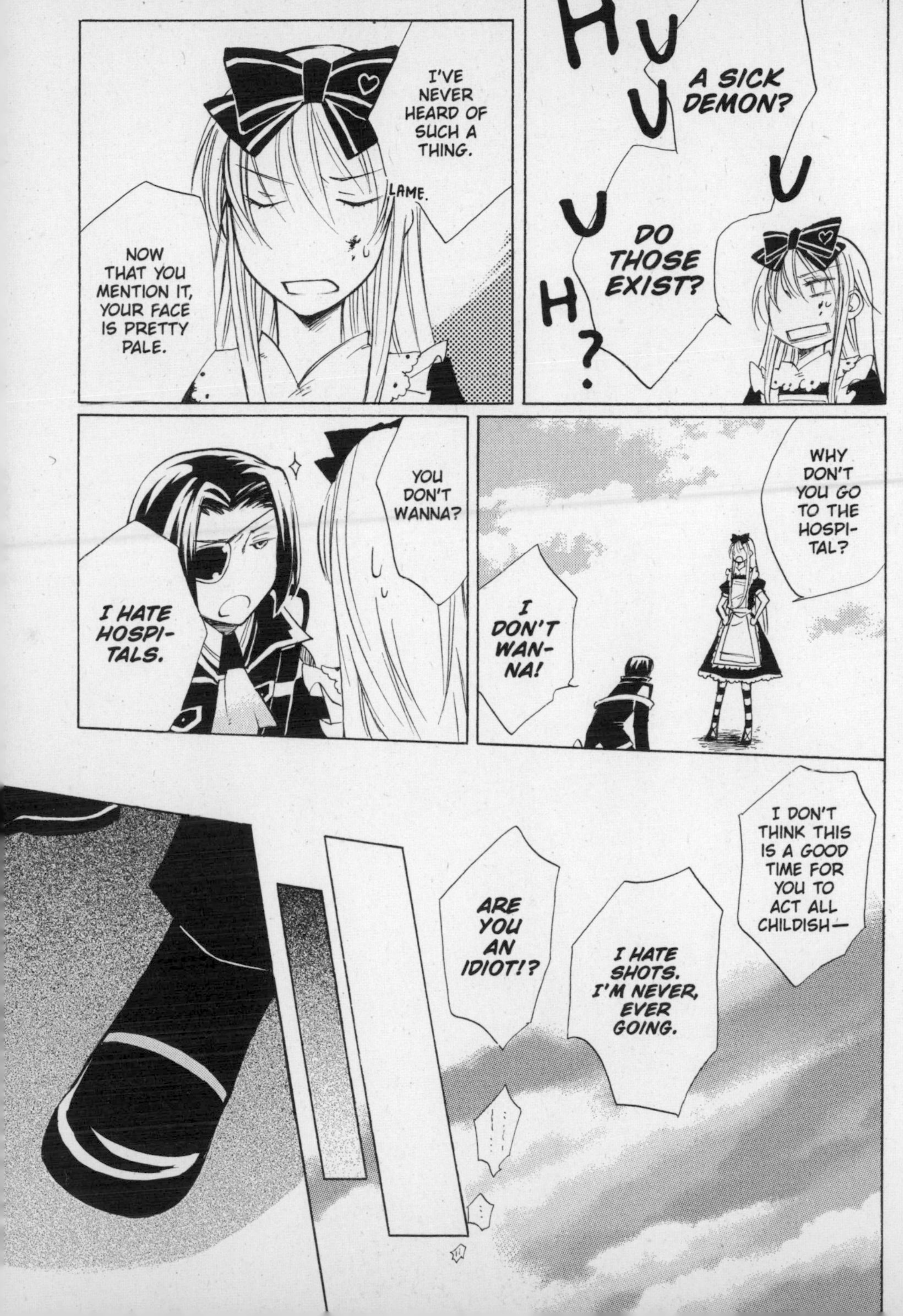
HUUUUUH?
A SICK DEMON?
DO THOSE EXIST?
I'VE NEVER HEARD OF SUCH A THING.
LAME.
NOW THAT YOU MENTION IT, YOUR FACE IS PRETTY PALE.
WHY DON'T YOU GO TO THE HOSPITAL?
I DON'T WANNA!
YOU DON'T WANNA?
I HATE HOSPITALS.
I DON'T THINK THIS IS A GOOD TIME FOR YOU TO ACT ALL CHILDISH—
I HATE SHOTS. I'M NEVER, EVER GOING.
ARE YOU AN IDIOT!?

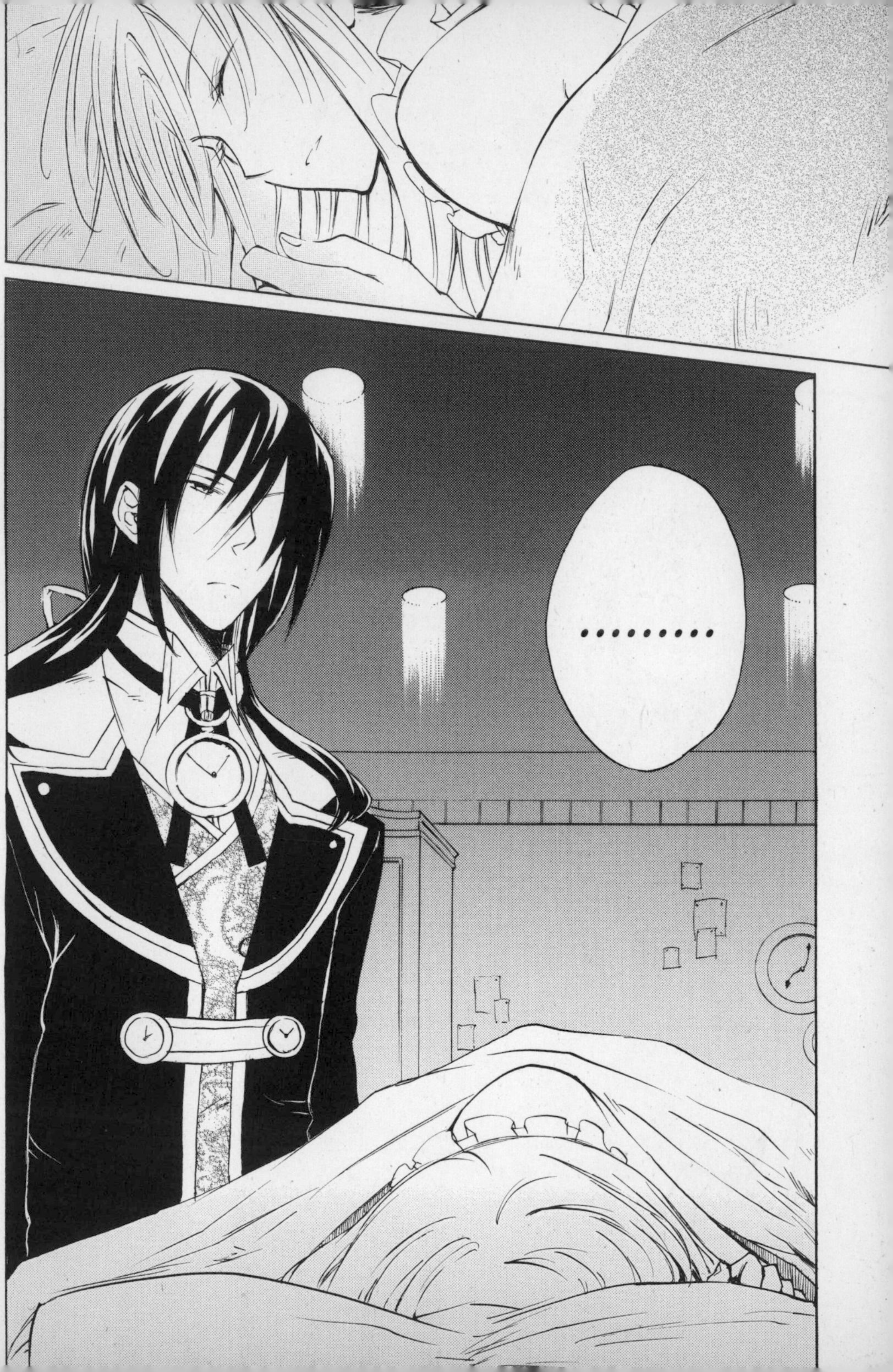
....

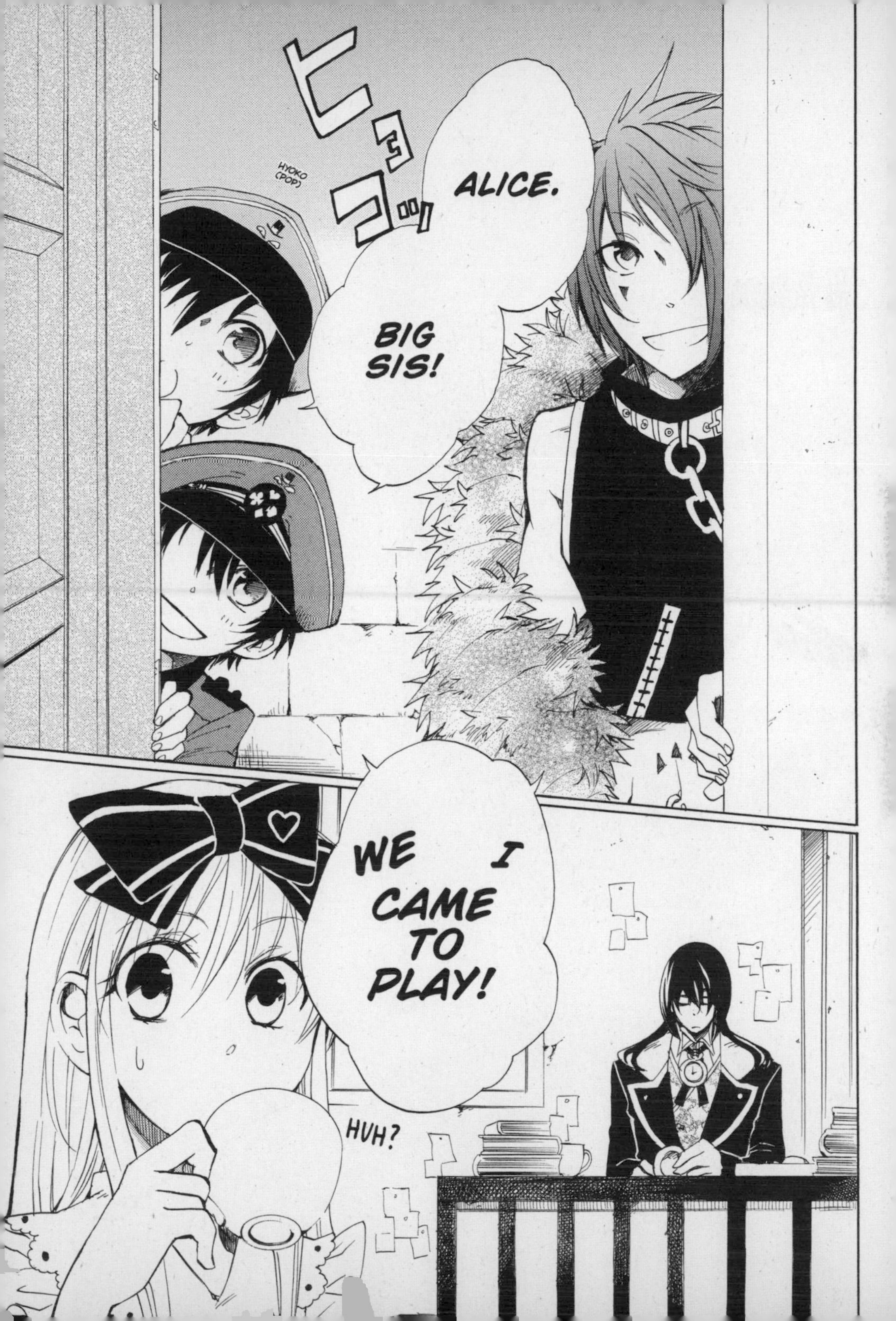
ALICE.
BIG SIS!
HYOKO (POP)
WE I CAME TO PLAY!
HUH?

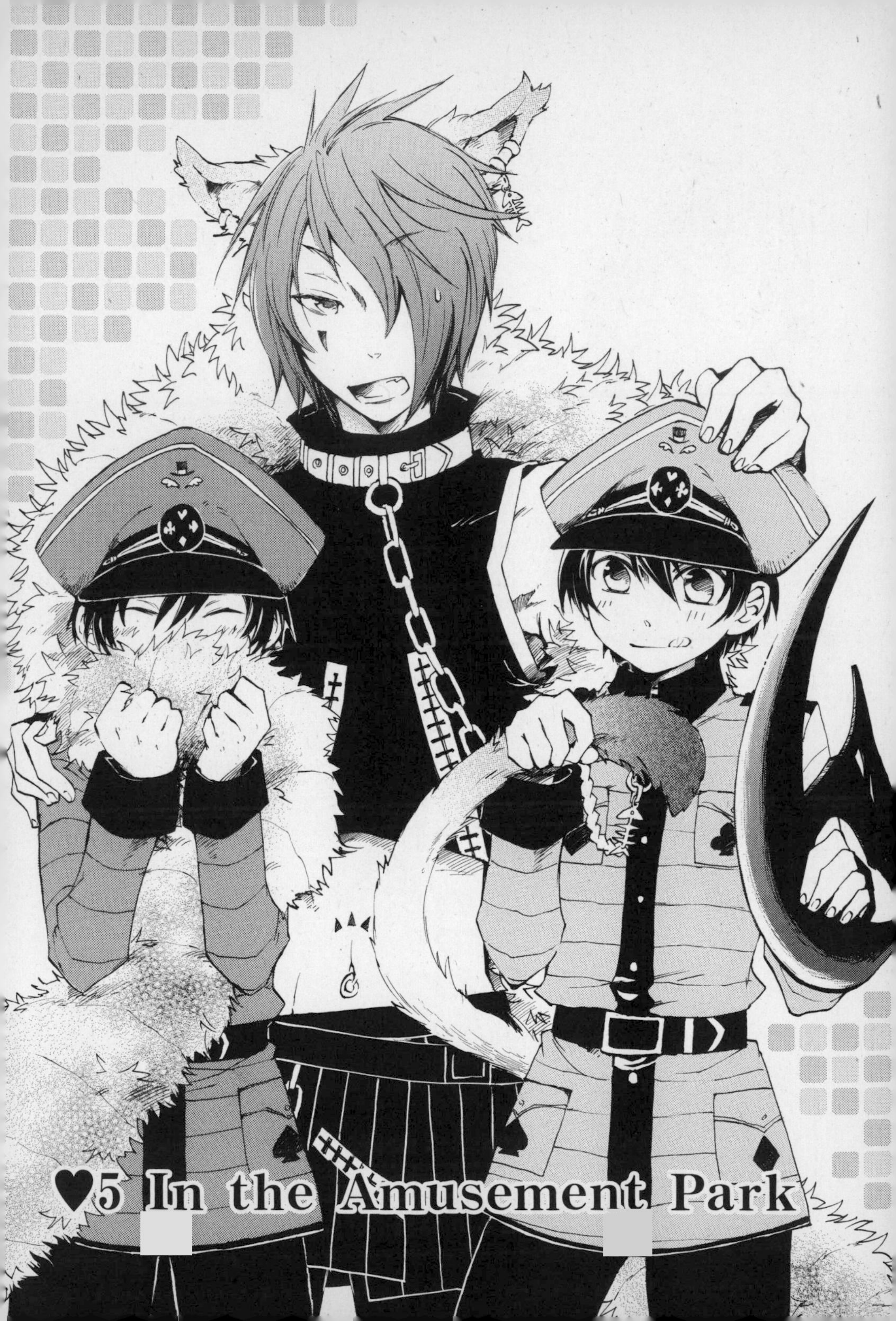
♥5 In the Amusement Park

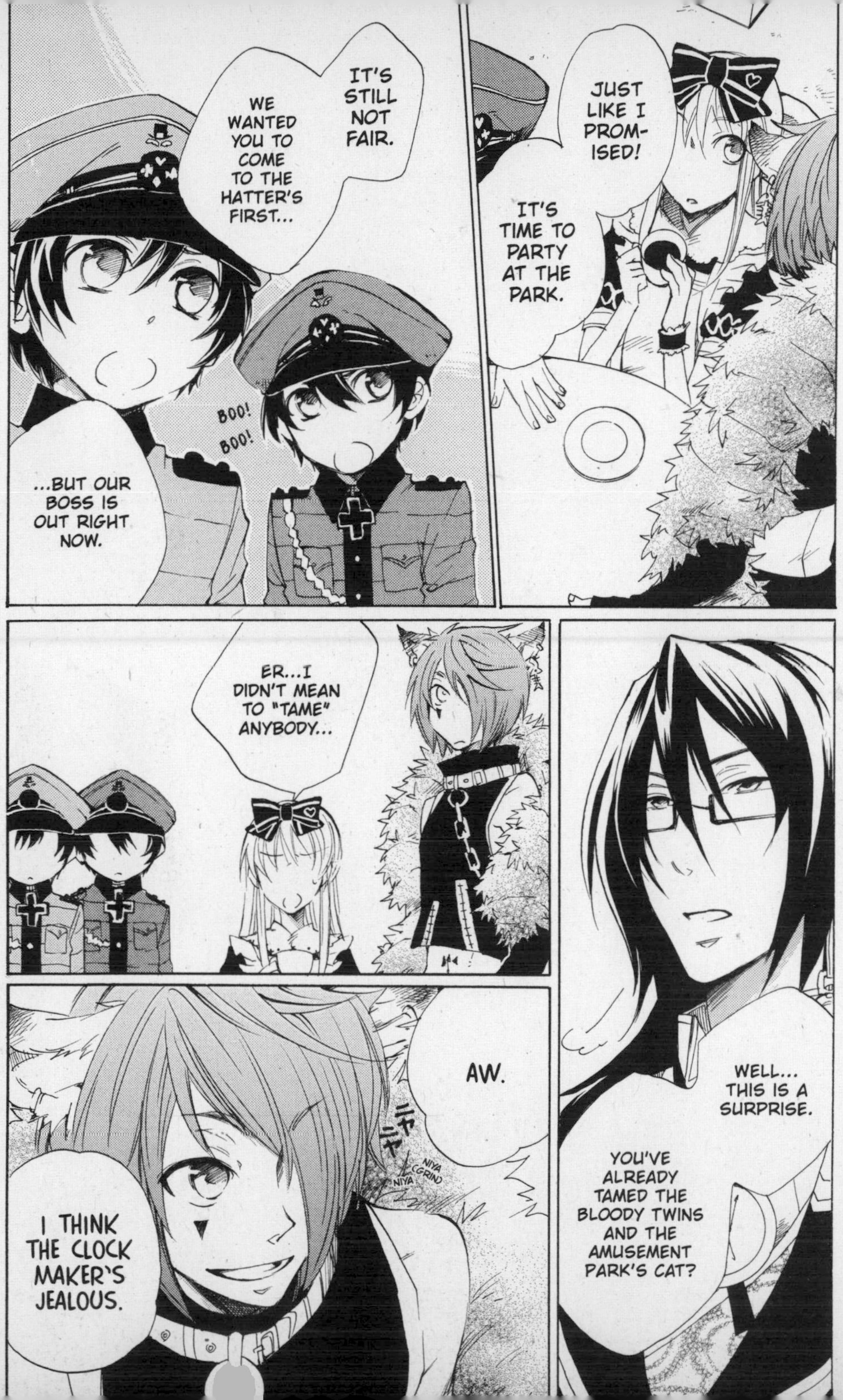
JUST LIKE I PROMISED!
IT'S TIME TO PARTY AT THE PARK.
IT'S STILL NOT FAIR.
WE WANTED YOU TO COME TO THE HATTER'S FIRST...
BOO! BOO!
...BUT OUR BOSS IS OUT RIGHT NOW.
WELL... THIS IS A SURPRISE.
YOU'VE ALREADY TAMED THE BLOODY TWINS AND THE AMUSEMENT PARK'S CAT?
ER...I DIDN'T MEAN TO "TAME" ANYBODY...
AW.
ニヤ
NIYA NIYA (GRIN)
I THINK THE CLOCK MAKER'S JEALOUS.

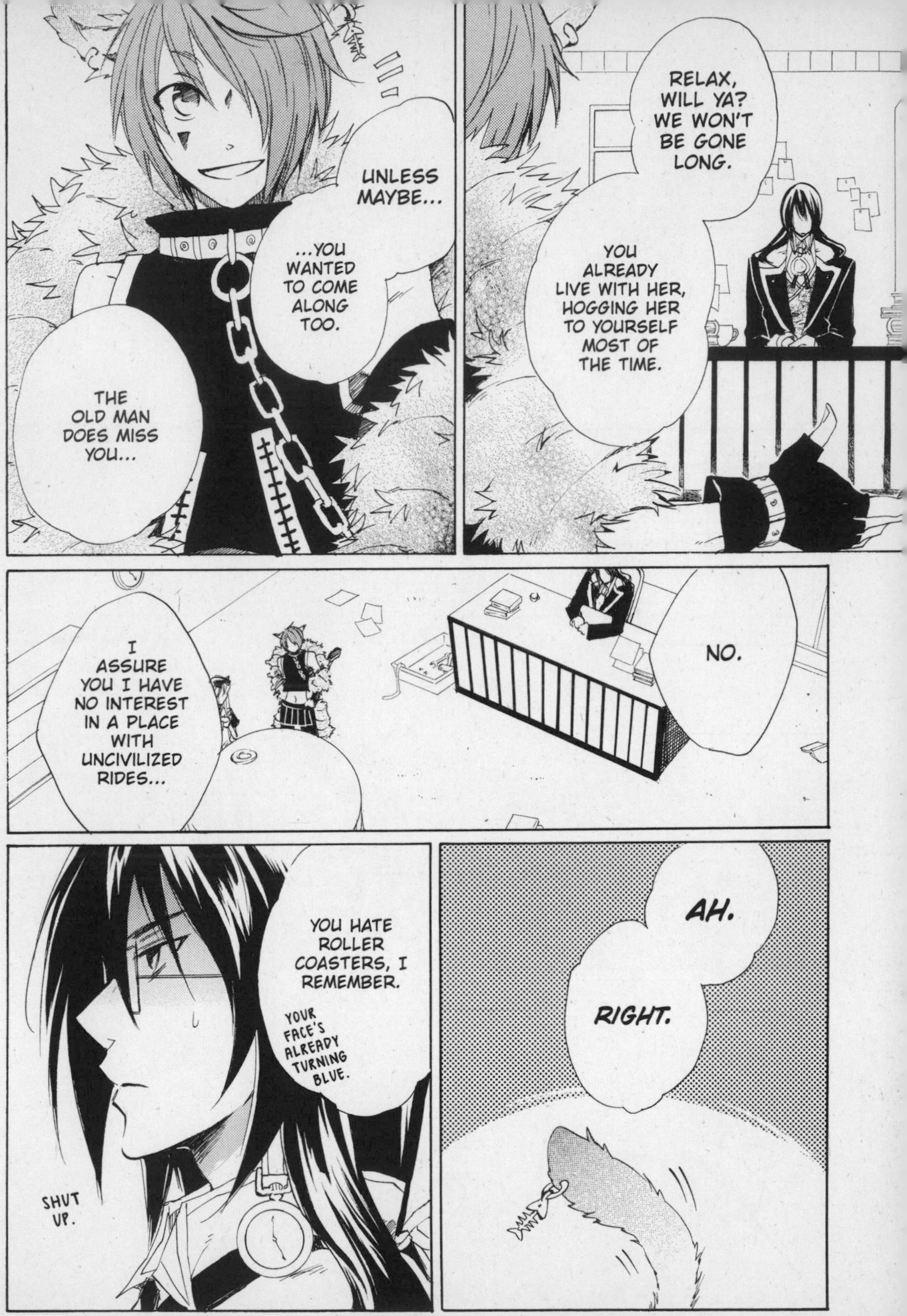
RELAX, WILL YA? WE WON'T BE GONE LONG.
YOU ALREADY LIVE WITH HER, HOGGING HER TO YOURSELF MOST OF THE TIME.
UNLESS MAYBE...
...YOU WANTED TO COME ALONG TOO.
THE OLD MAN DOES MISS YOU...
NO.
I ASSURE YOU I HAVE NO INTEREST IN A PLACE WITH UNCIVILIZED RIDES...
AH.
RIGHT.
YOU HATE ROLLER COASTERS, I REMEMBER.
YOUR FACE'S ALREADY TURNING BLUE.
SHUT UP.

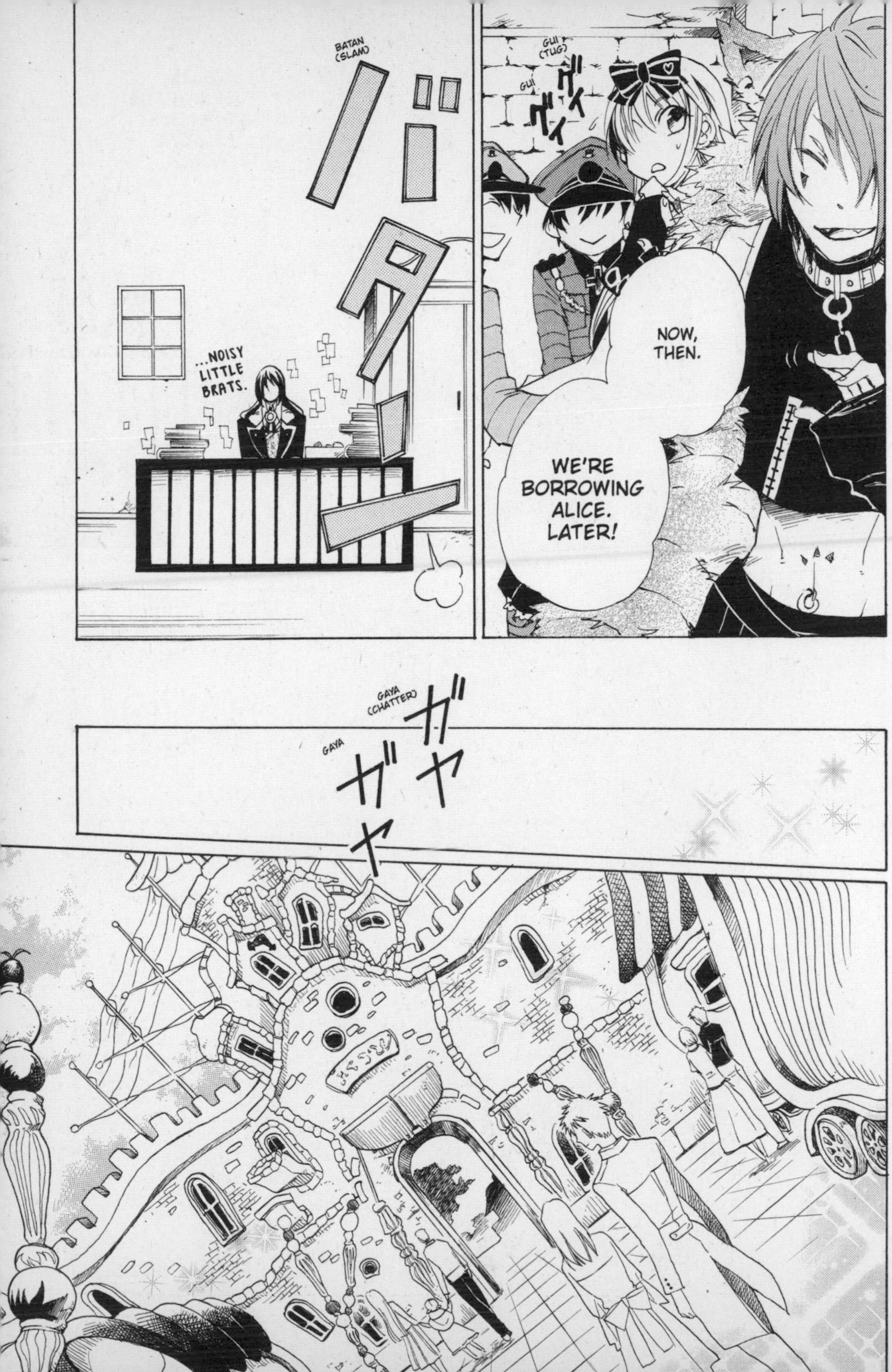
GUI (TUG)
GUI
グイ グイ
NOW, THEN.
WE'RE BORROWING ALICE. LATER!
BATAN (SLAM)
バタン
...NOISY LITTLE BRATS.
GAYA (CHATTER)
GAYA
ガヤ ガヤ

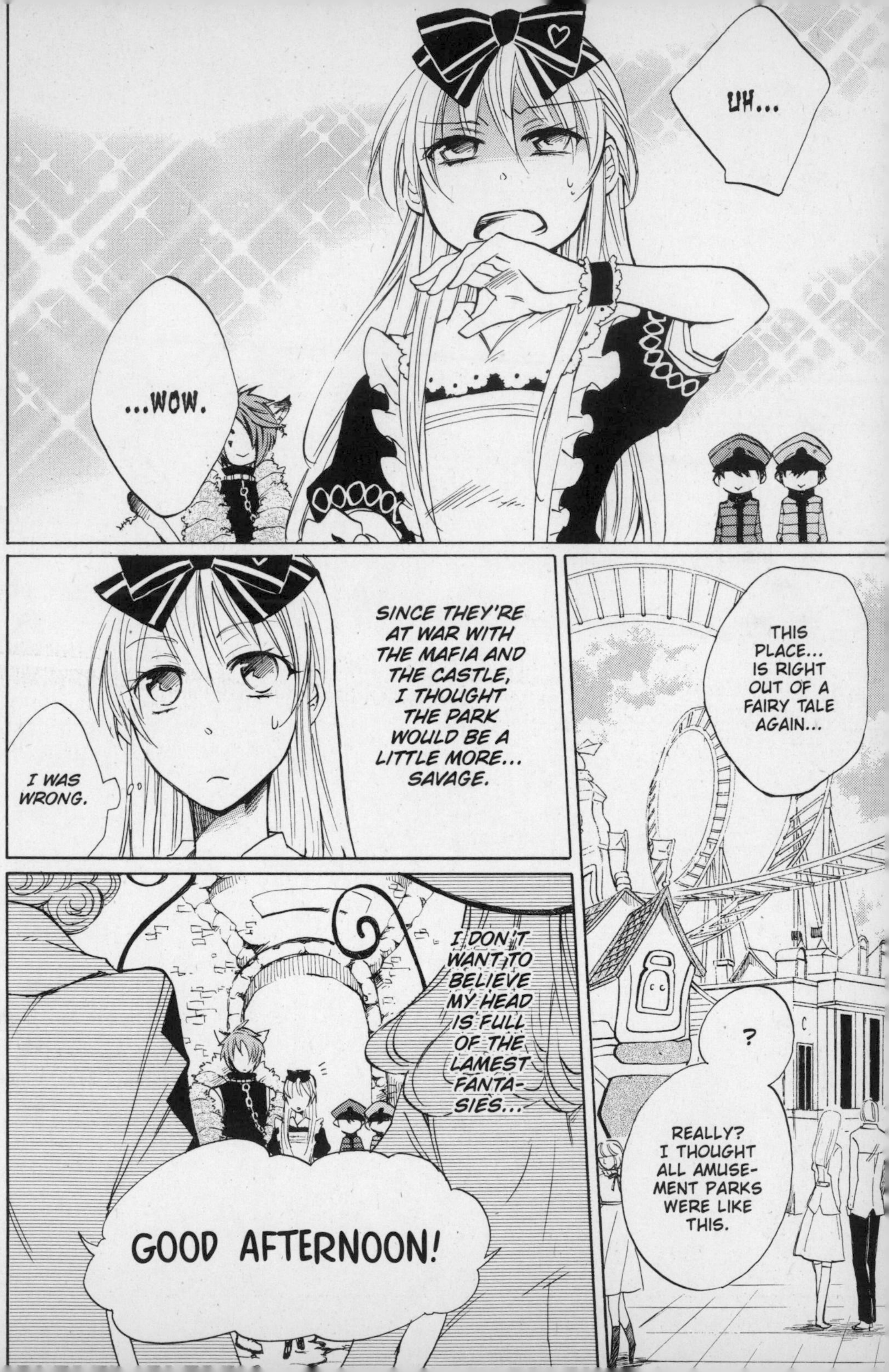
UH...
...WOW.
THIS PLACE... IS RIGHT OUT OF A FAIRY TALE AGAIN...
?
REALLY? I THOUGHT ALL AMUSEMENT PARKS WERE LIKE THIS.
SINCE THEY'RE AT WAR WITH THE MAFIA AND THE CASTLE, I THOUGHT THE PARK WOULD BE A LITTLE MORE... SAVAGE.
I WAS WRONG.
I DON'T WANT TO BELIEVE MY HEAD IS FULL OF THE LAMEST FANTASIES...
GOOD AFTERNOON!

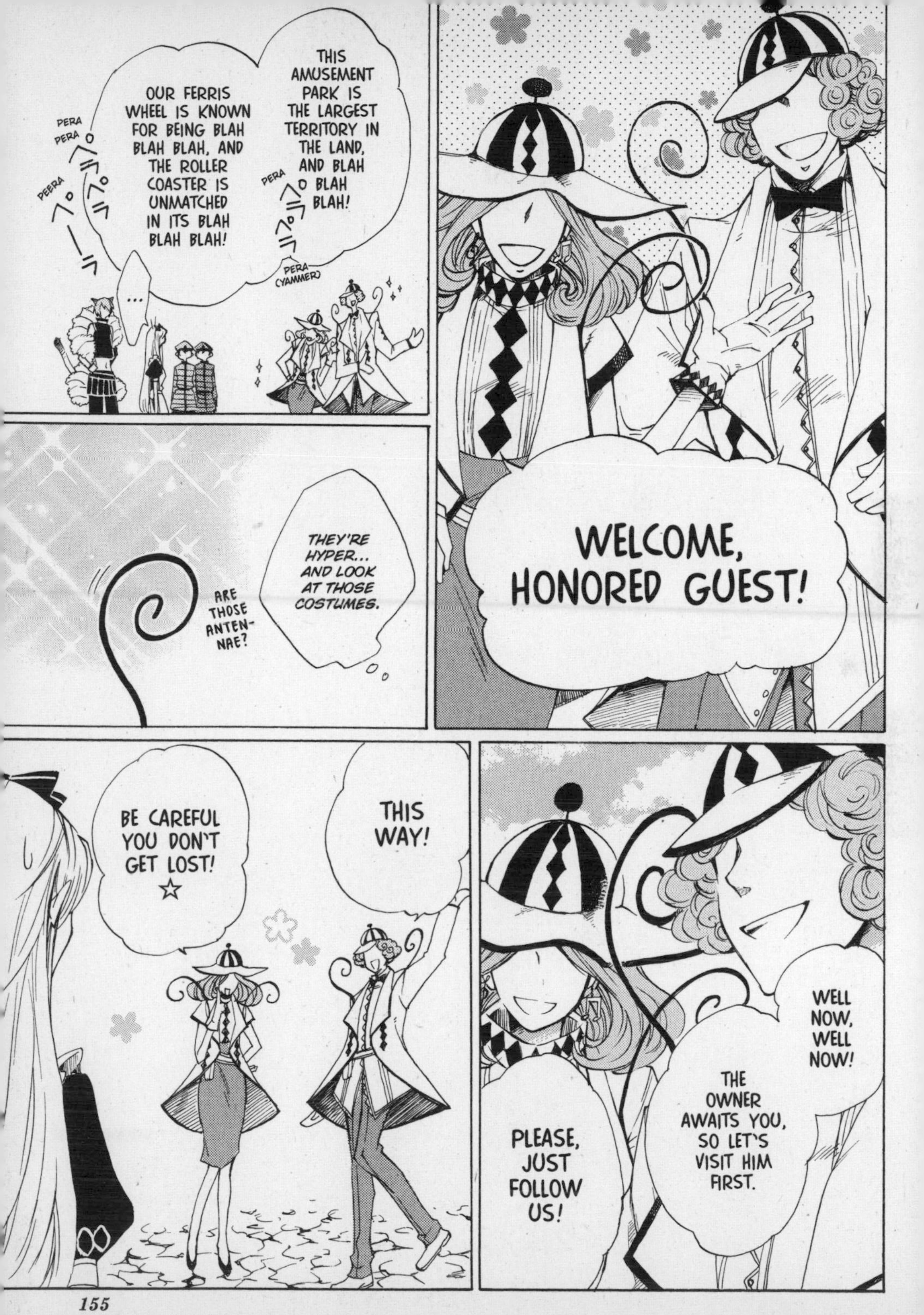
WELCOME, HONORED GUEST!
THIS AMUSEMENT PARK IS THE LARGEST TERRITORY IN THE LAND, AND BLAH BLAH BLAH!
PERA
PERA (YAMMER)
OUR FERRIS WHEEL IS KNOWN FOR BEING BLAH BLAH BLAH, AND THE ROLLER COASTER IS UNMATCHED IN ITS BLAH BLAH BLAH!
PERA PERA
PEERA
...
THEY'RE HYPER... AND LOOK AT THOSE COSTUMES.
ARE THOSE ANTEN-NAE?
WELL NOW, WELL NOW!
THE OWNER AWAITS YOU, SO LET'S VISIT HIM FIRST.
PLEASE, JUST FOLLOW US!
THIS WAY!
BE CAREFUL YOU DON'T GET LOST! ☆

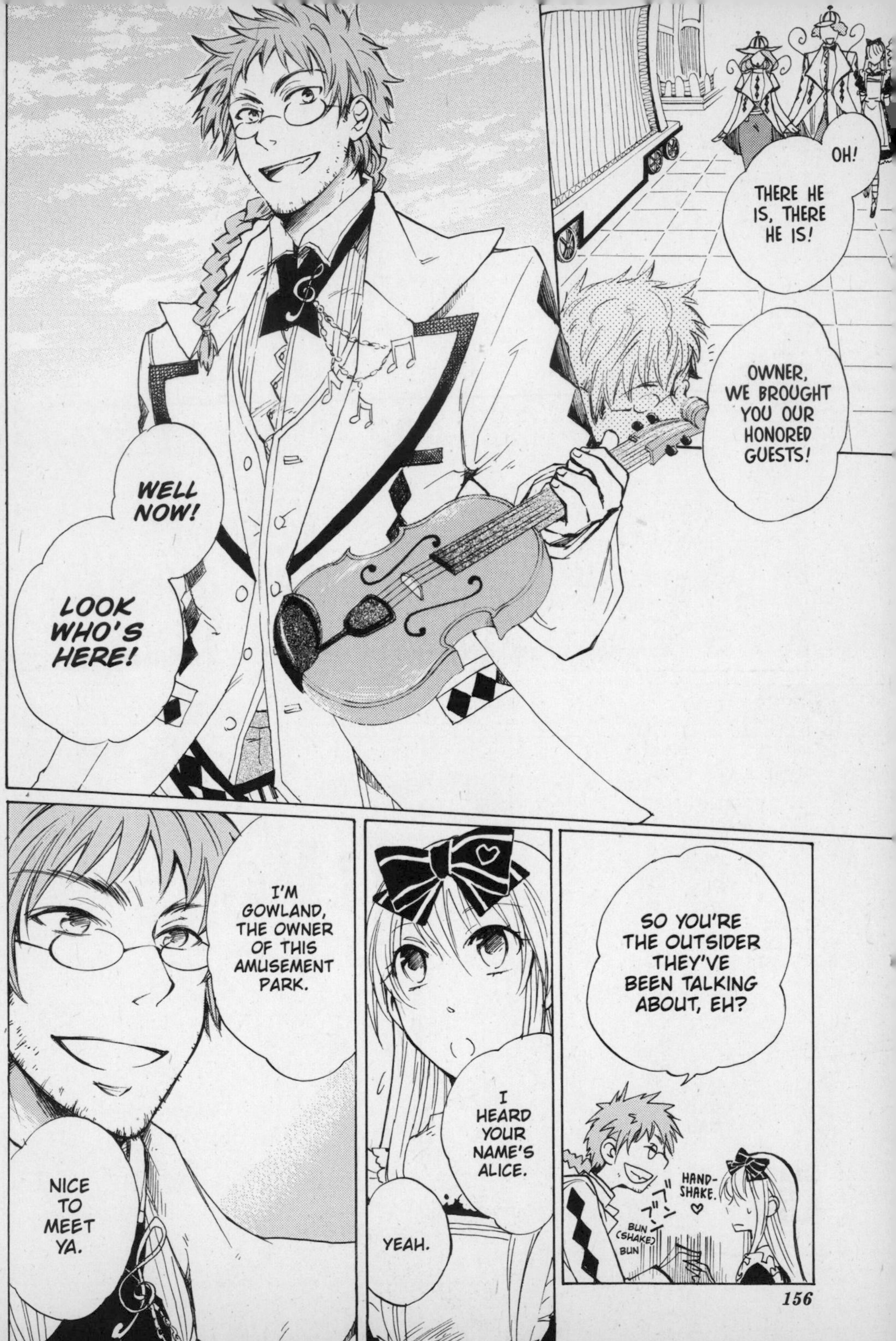
OH!
THERE HE IS, THERE HE IS!
OWNER, WE BROUGHT YOU OUR HONORED GUESTS!
WELL NOW!
LOOK WHO'S HERE!
SO YOU'RE THE OUTSIDER THEY'VE BEEN TALKING ABOUT, EH?
HAND-SHAKE.
BUN (SHAKE) BUN
I HEARD YOUR NAME'S ALICE.
YEAH.
I'M GOWLAND, THE OWNER OF THIS AMUSEMENT PARK.
NICE TO MEET YA.

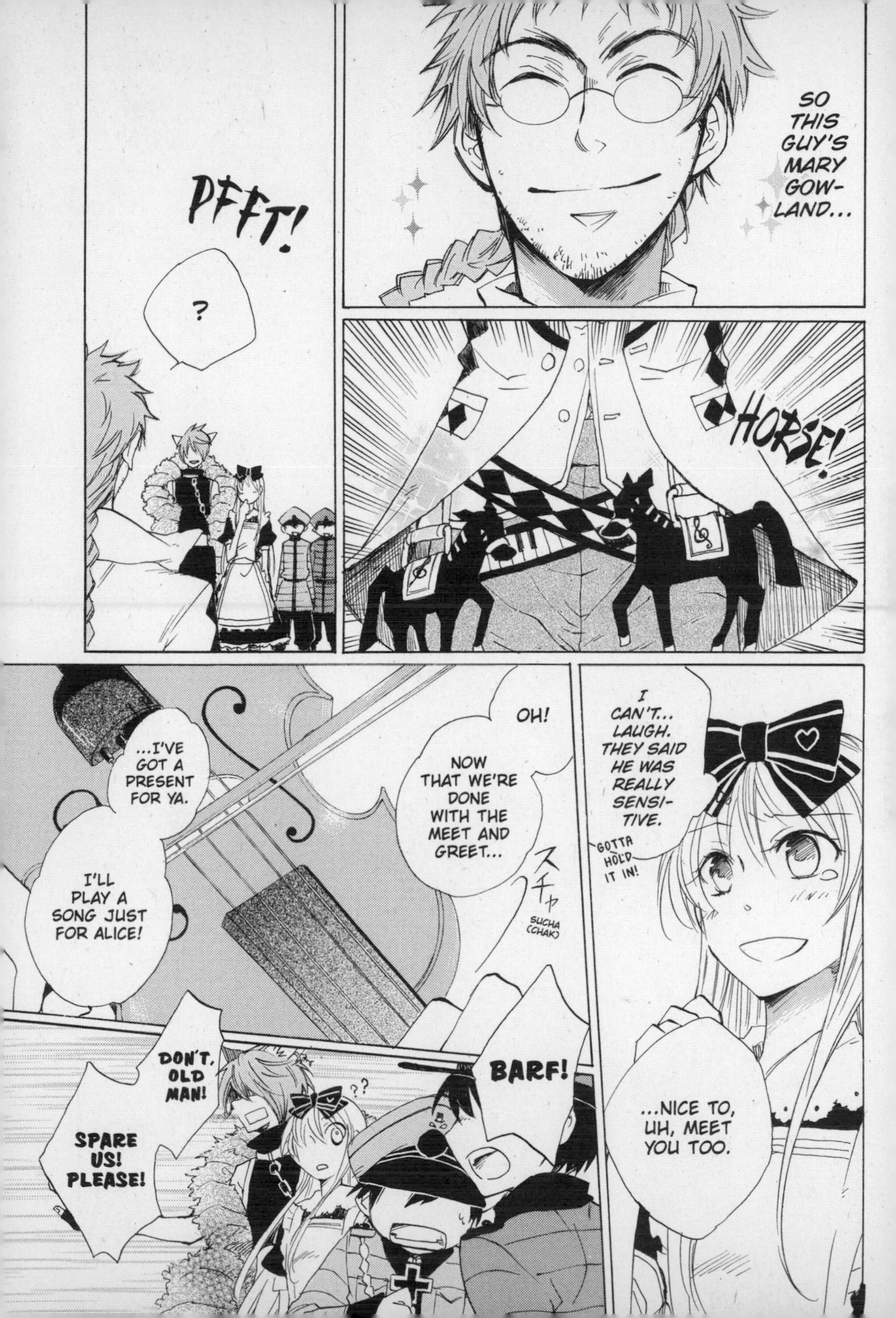
SO THIS GUY'S MARY GOW-LAND...
HORSE!
PFFT!
?
I CAN'T... LAUGH. THEY SAID HE WAS REALLY SENSI-TIVE.
GOTTA HOLD IT IN!
...NICE TO, UH, MEET YOU TOO.
OH!
NOW THAT WE'RE DONE WITH THE MEET AND GREET...
スチャ
SUCHA (CHAK)
...I'VE GOT A PRESENT FOR YA.
I'LL PLAY A SONG JUST FOR ALICE!
BARF!
DON'T, OLD MAN!
SPARE US! PLEASE!

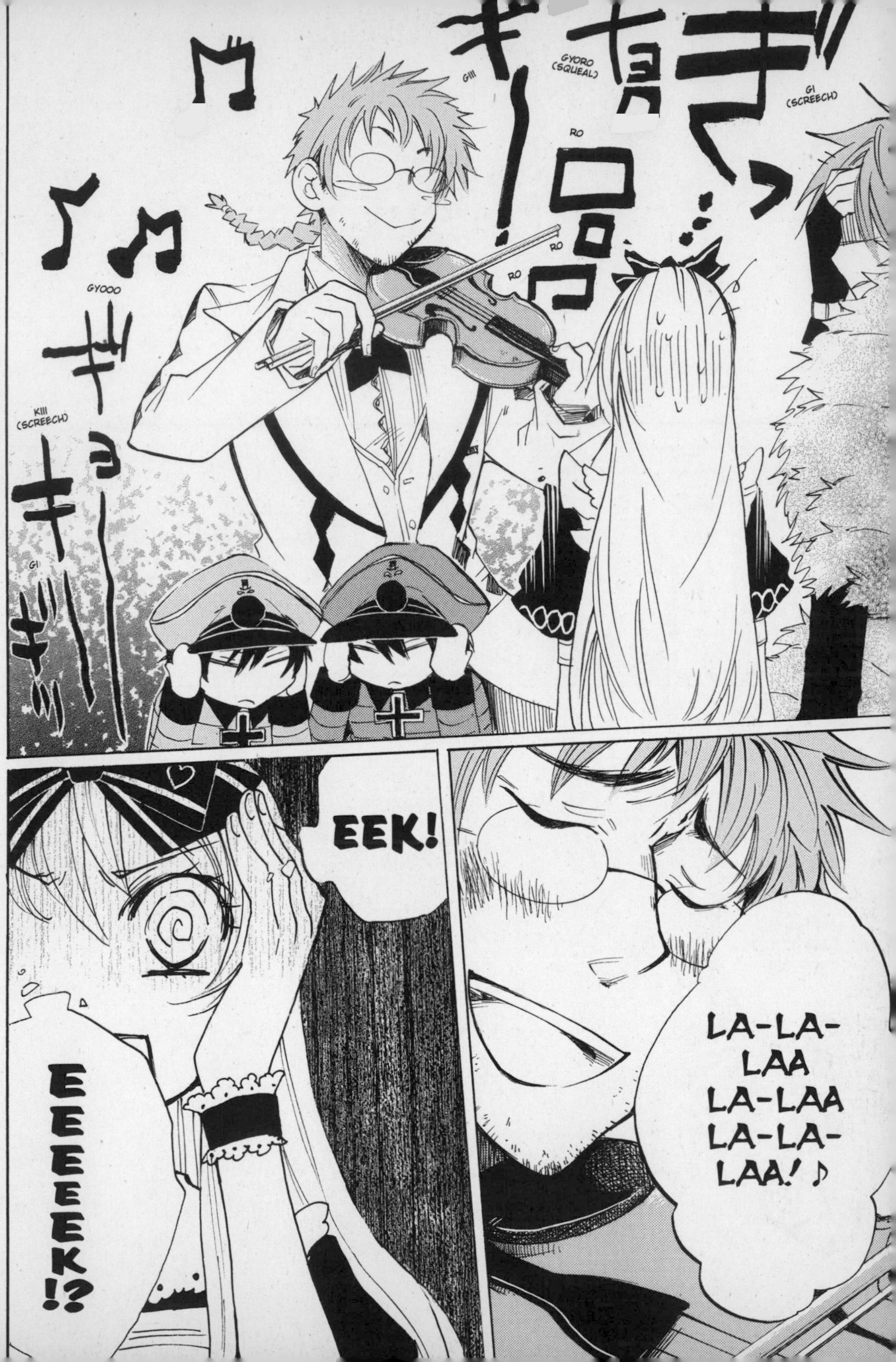
GI (SCREECH)
GYORO (SQUEAL)
GIII
RO
RO
RO
RO
GYOOO
KIII (SCREECH)
GI
LA-LA-LAA LA-LAA LA-LA-LAA! ♪
EEK!
EEEEEEK!?

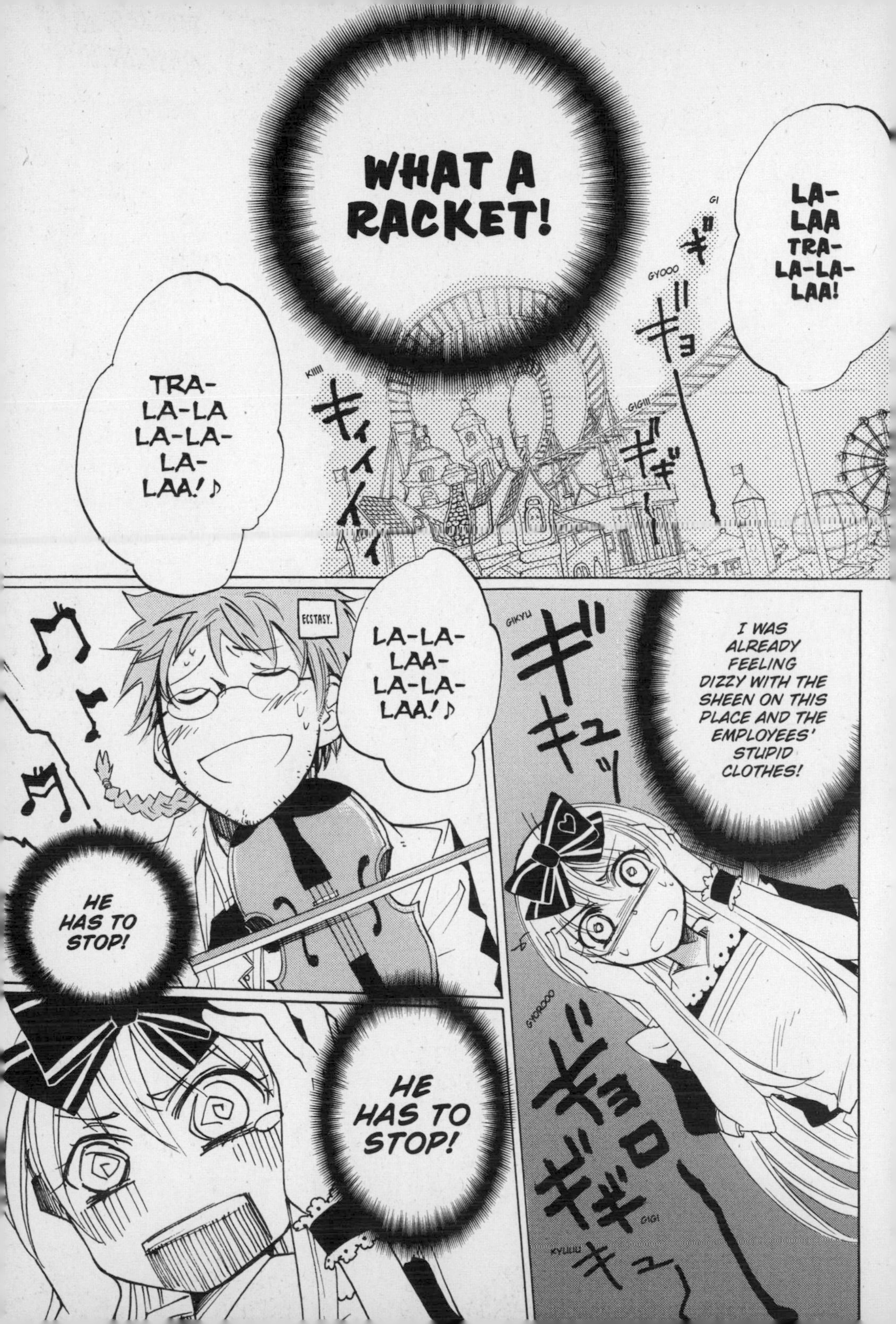
WHAT A RACKET!
LA-LAA TRA-LA-LA-LAA!
GI
GYOOO
GIGIII
KIIIII
TRA-LA-LA LA-LA-LA-LA-LAA!♪
GIKYU
I WAS ALREADY FEELING DIZZY WITH THE SHEEN ON THIS PLACE AND THE EMPLOYEES' STUPID CLOTHES!
GYOROOO
GIGI
KYUUU
ECSTASY.
LA-LA-LAA-LA-LA-LAA!♪
HE HAS TO STOP!
HE HAS TO STOP!

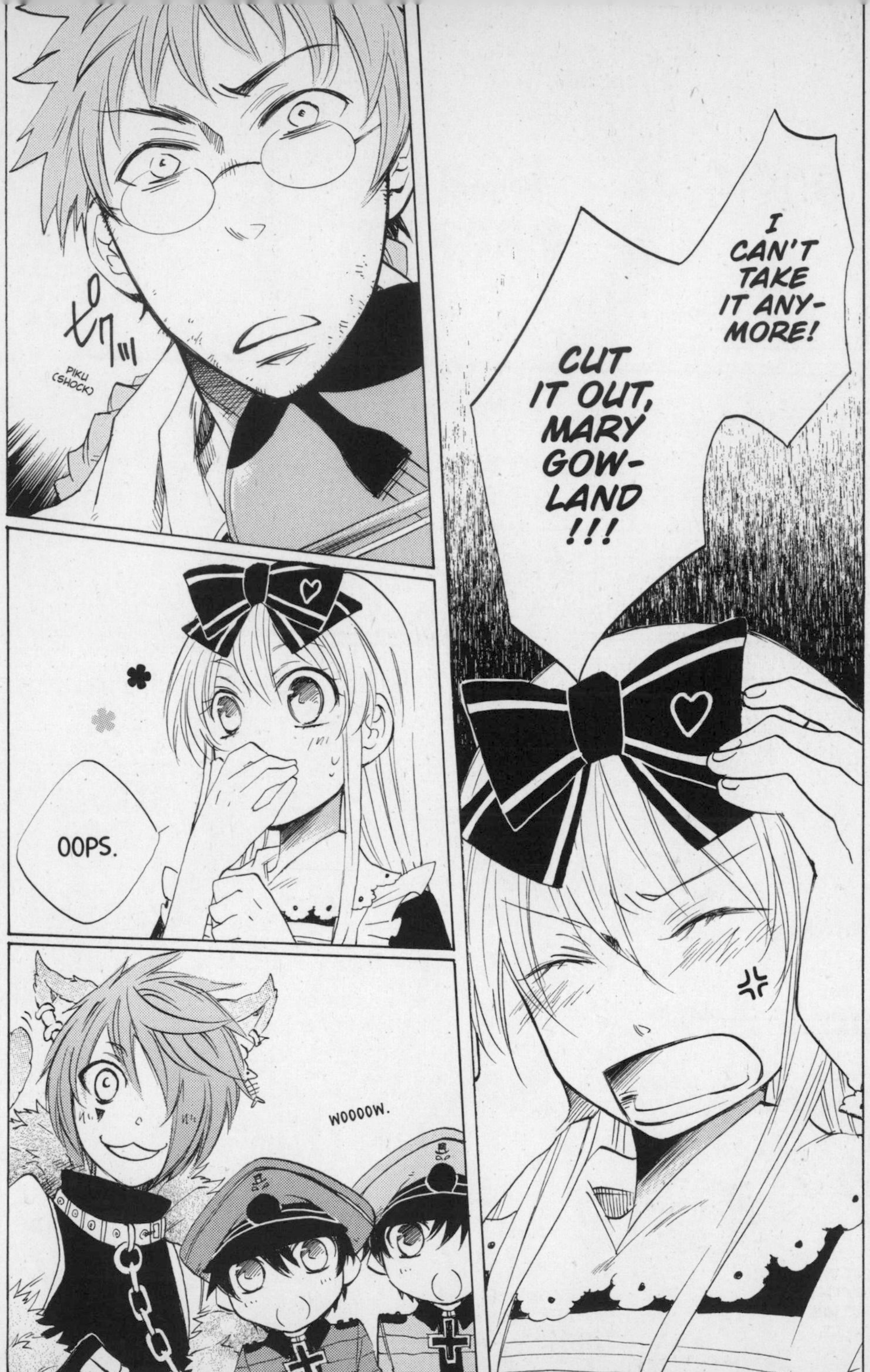
I CAN'T TAKE IT ANY-MORE!
CUT IT OUT, MARY GOW-LAND!!!
ピク
PIKU (SHOCK)
OOPS.
WOOOOW.

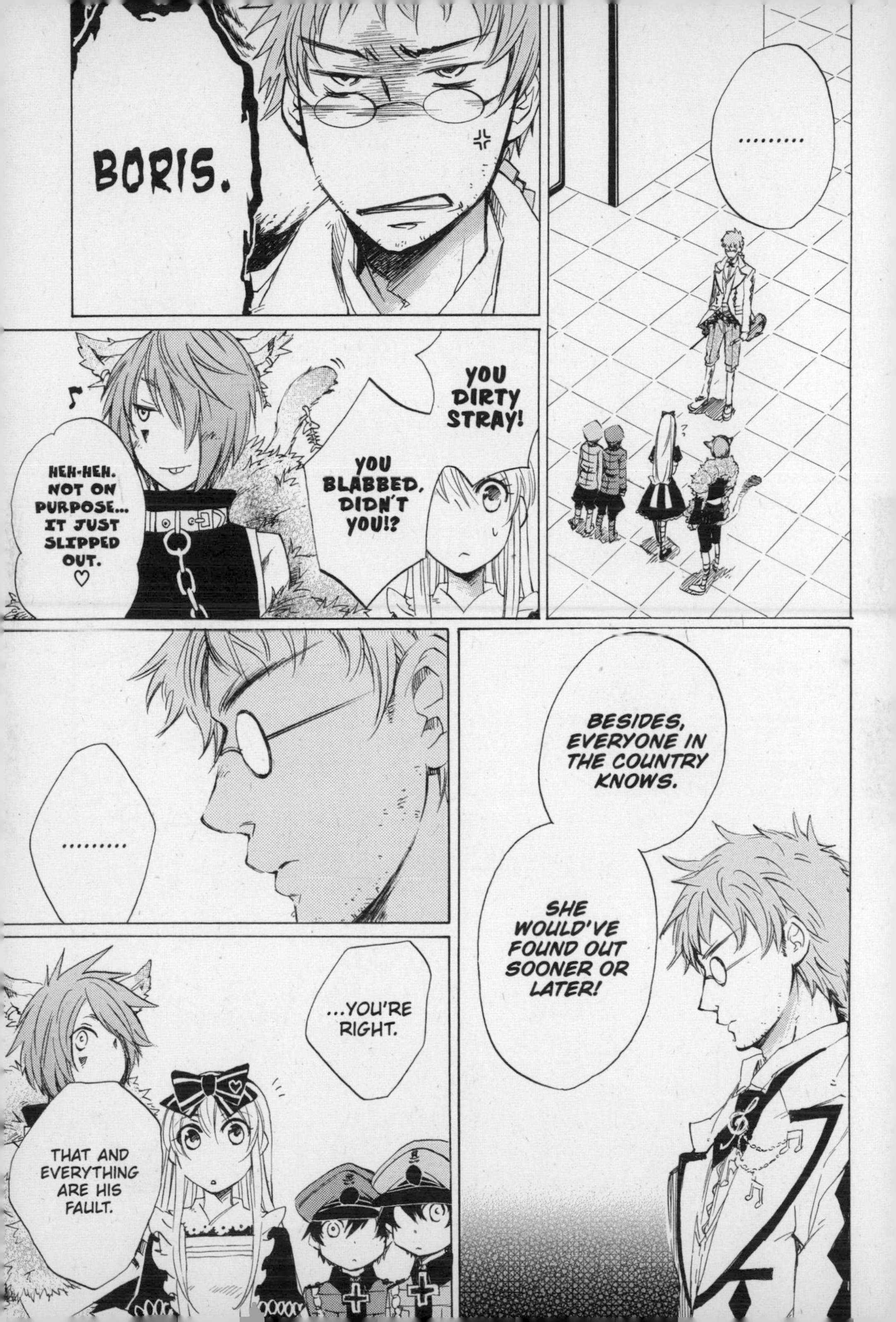

....
BORIS.
YOU DIRTY STRAY!
YOU BLABBED, DIDN'T YOU!?
HEH-HEH. NOT ON PURPOSE... IT JUST SLIPPED OUT. ♡
BESIDES, EVERYONE IN THE COUNTRY KNOWS.
SHE WOULD'VE FOUND OUT SOONER OR LATER!
....
...YOU'RE RIGHT.
THAT AND EVERYTHING ARE HIS FAULT.

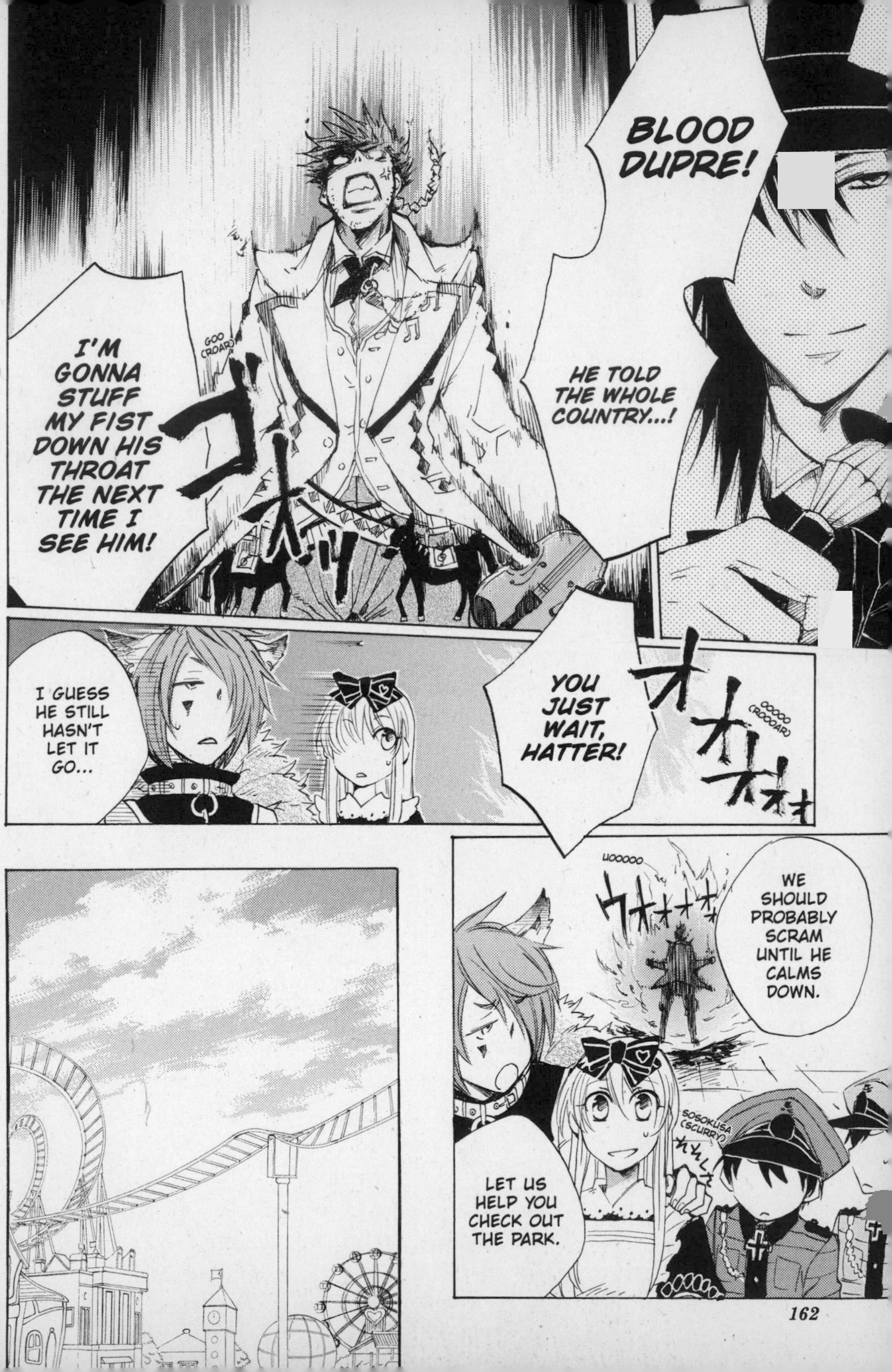
BLOOD DUPRE!
HE TOLD THE WHOLE COUNTRY...!
GOO (ROAR)
I'M GONNA STUFF MY FIST DOWN HIS THROAT THE NEXT TIME I SEE HIM!
YOU JUST WAIT, HATTER!
OOOOO (ROOOAR)
I GUESS HE STILL HASN'T LET IT GO...
UOOOOO
WE SHOULD PROBABLY SCRAM UNTIL HE CALMS DOWN.
SOSOKUSA (SCURRY)
LET US HELP YOU CHECK OUT THE PARK.

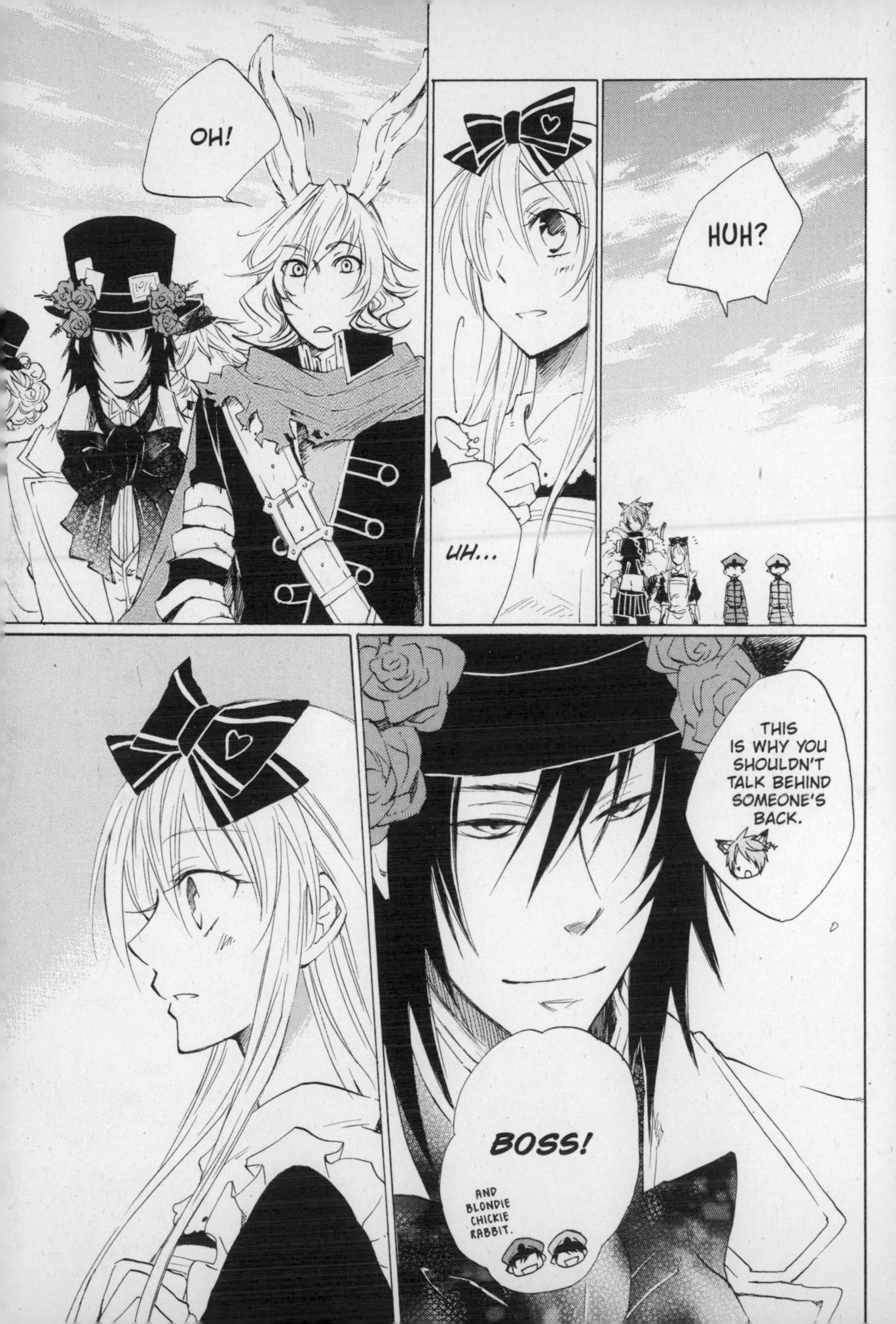
HUH?
UH...
OH!
THIS IS WHY YOU SHOULDN'T TALK BEHIND SOMEONE'S BACK.
BOSS!
AND BLONDIE CHICKIE RABBIT.

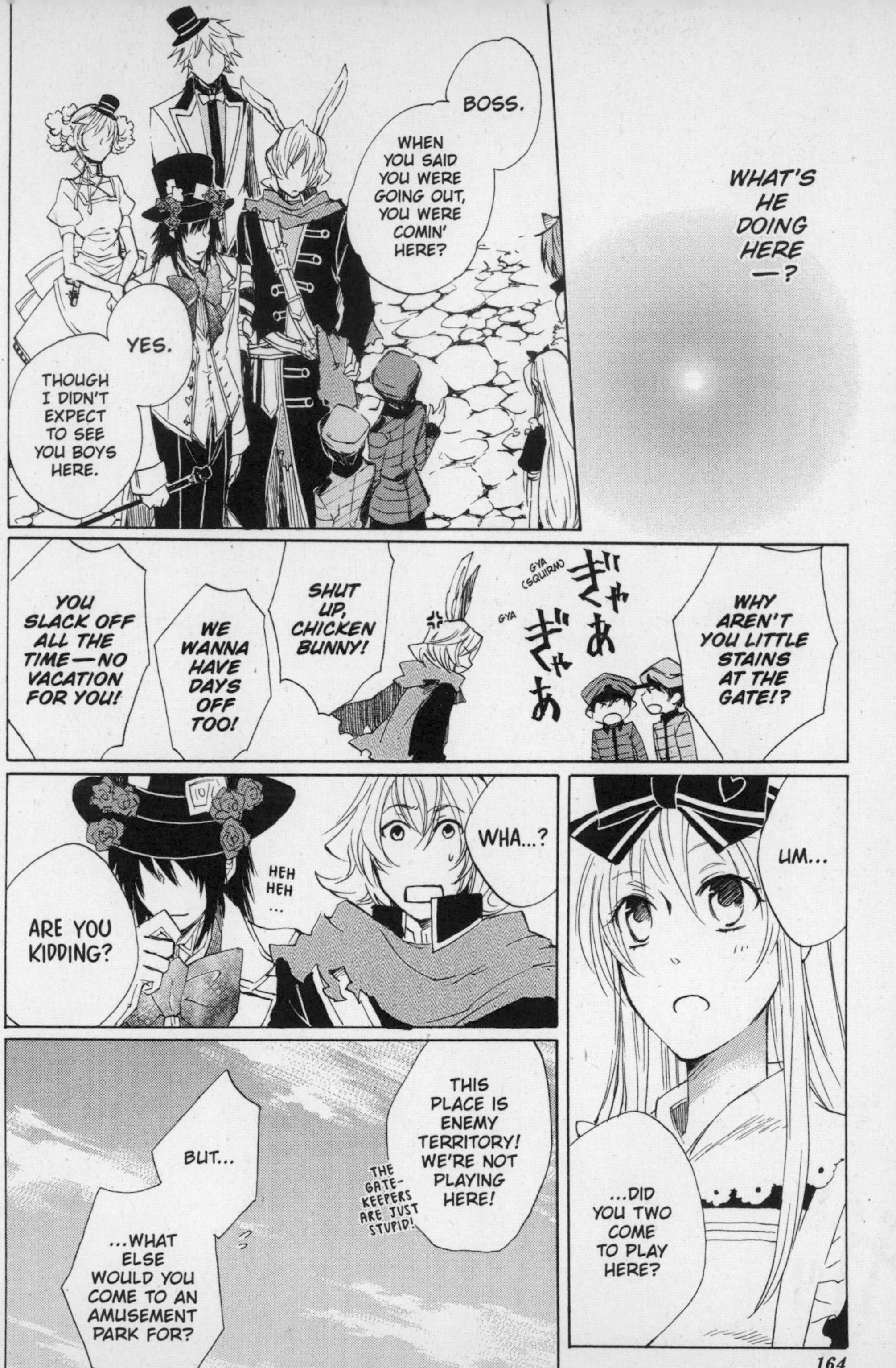
WHAT'S HE DOING HERE—?
BOSS.
WHEN YOU SAID YOU WERE GOING OUT, YOU WERE COMIN' HERE?
YES.
THOUGH I DIDN'T EXPECT TO SEE YOU BOYS HERE.
WHY AREN'T YOU LITTLE STAINS AT THE GATE!?
GYA (SQUIRM)
GYA
SHUT UP, CHICKEN BUNNY!
WE WANNA HAVE DAYS OFF TOO!
YOU SLACK OFF ALL THE TIME—NO VACATION FOR YOU!
UM...
...DID YOU TWO COME TO PLAY HERE?
WHA...?
HEH HEH ...
ARE YOU KIDDING?
THIS PLACE IS ENEMY TERRITORY! WE'RE NOT PLAYING HERE!
THE GATE-KEEPERS ARE JUST STUPID!
BUT...
...WHAT ELSE WOULD YOU COME TO AN AMUSEMENT PARK FOR?

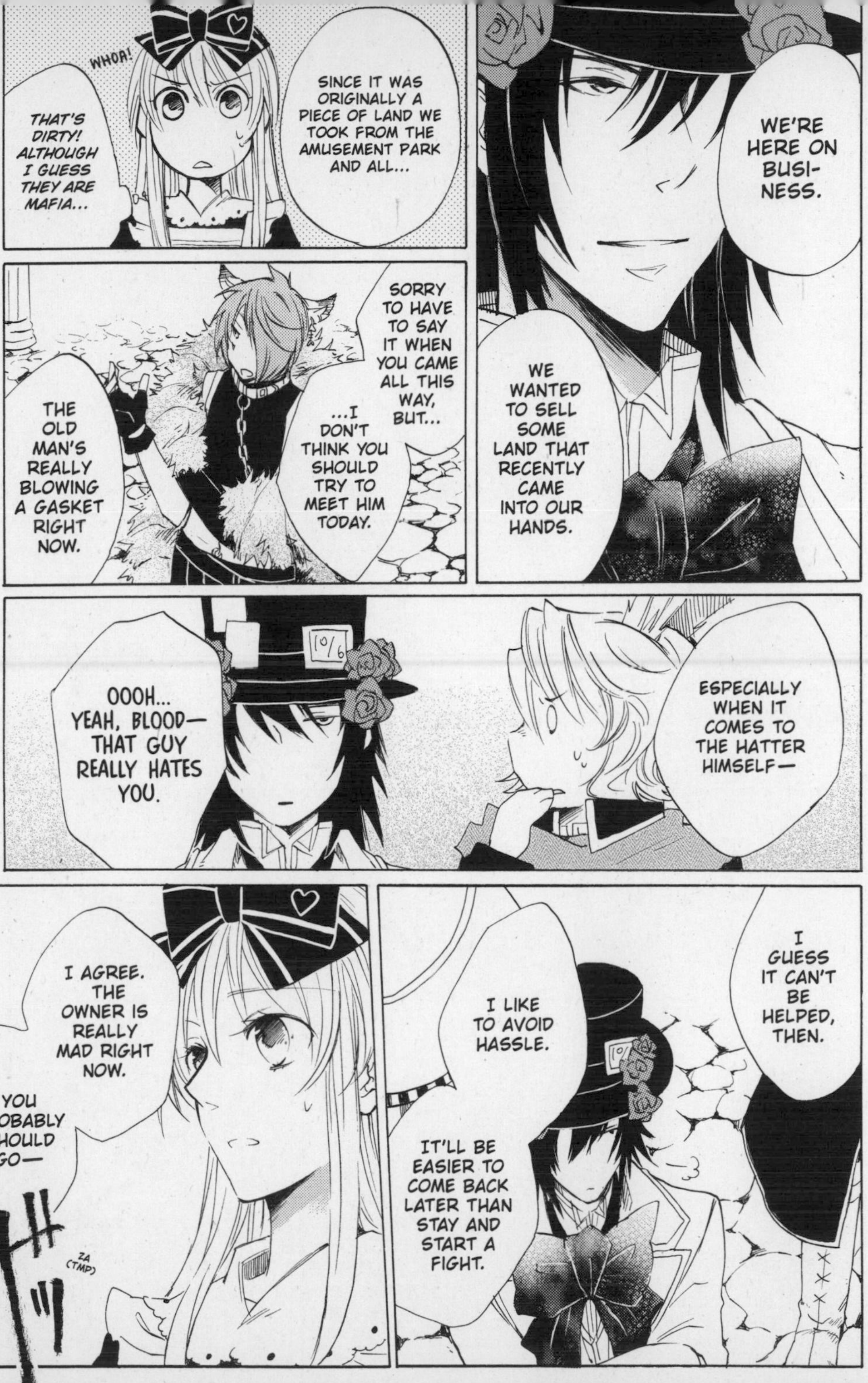
WE'RE HERE ON BUSI-NESS.
WE WANTED TO SELL SOME LAND THAT RECENTLY CAME INTO OUR HANDS.
SINCE IT WAS ORIGINALLY A PIECE OF LAND WE TOOK FROM THE AMUSEMENT PARK AND ALL...
WHOA!
THAT'S DIRTY! ALTHOUGH I GUESS THEY ARE MAFIA...
SORRY TO HAVE TO SAY IT WHEN YOU CAME ALL THIS WAY, BUT...
...I DON'T THINK YOU SHOULD TRY TO MEET HIM TODAY.
THE OLD MAN'S REALLY BLOWING A GASKET RIGHT NOW.
ESPECIALLY WHEN IT COMES TO THE HATTER HIMSELF—
OOOH... YEAH, BLOOD— THAT GUY REALLY HATES YOU.
I GUESS IT CAN'T BE HELPED, THEN.
I LIKE TO AVOID HASSLE.
IT'LL BE EASIER TO COME BACK LATER THAN STAY AND START A FIGHT.
I AGREE. THE OWNER IS REALLY MAD RIGHT NOW.
YOU PROBABLY SHOULD GO—
ZA (TMP)

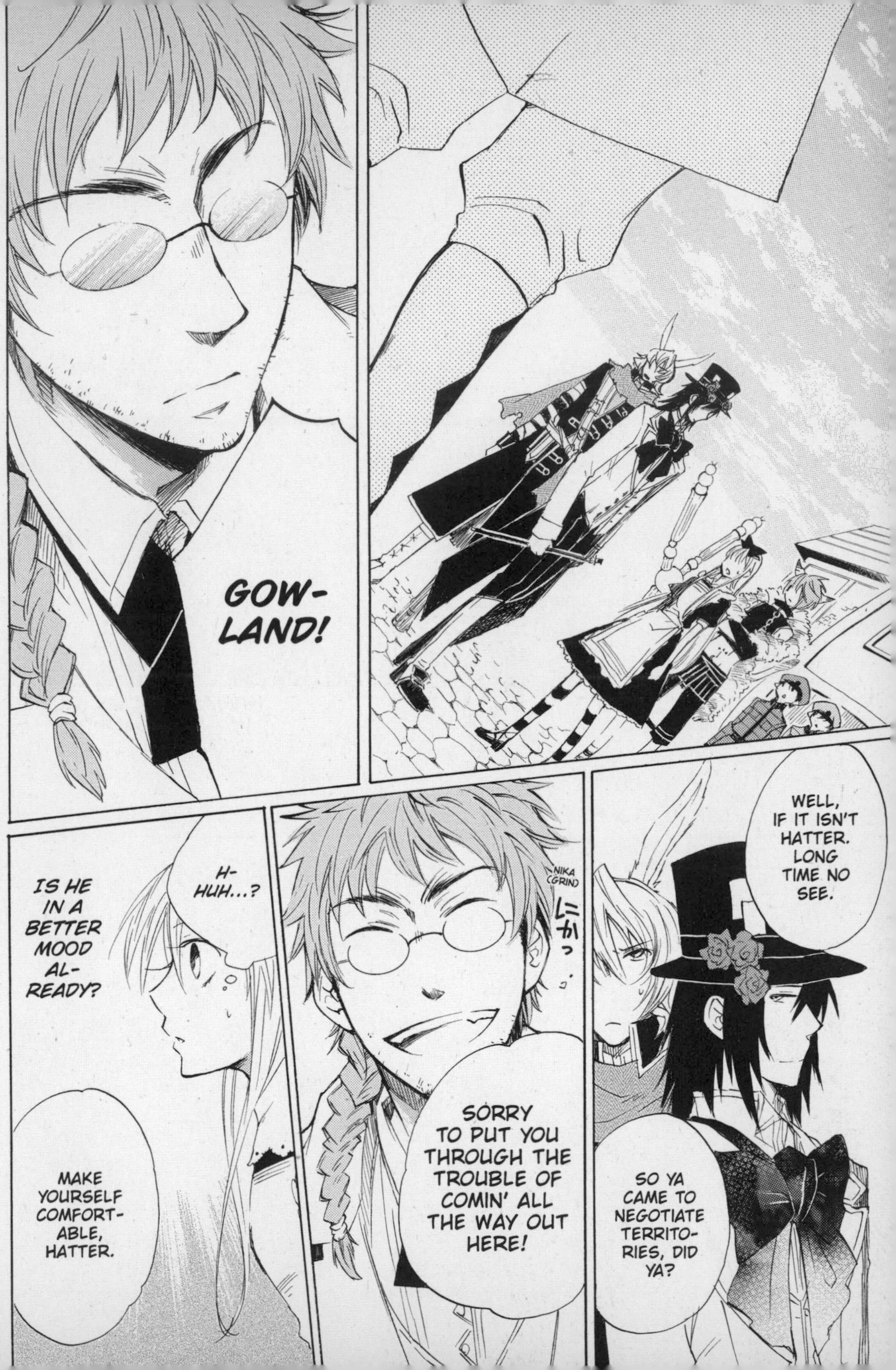
GOW-
LAND!
WELL, IF IT ISN'T HATTER. LONG TIME NO SEE.
SO YA CAME TO NEGOTIATE TERRITO-RIES, DID YA?
NIKA (GRIN)
SORRY TO PUT YOU THROUGH THE TROUBLE OF COMIN' ALL THE WAY OUT HERE!
H-HUH...?
IS HE IN A BETTER MOOD AL-READY?
MAKE YOURSELF COMFORT-ABLE, HATTER.

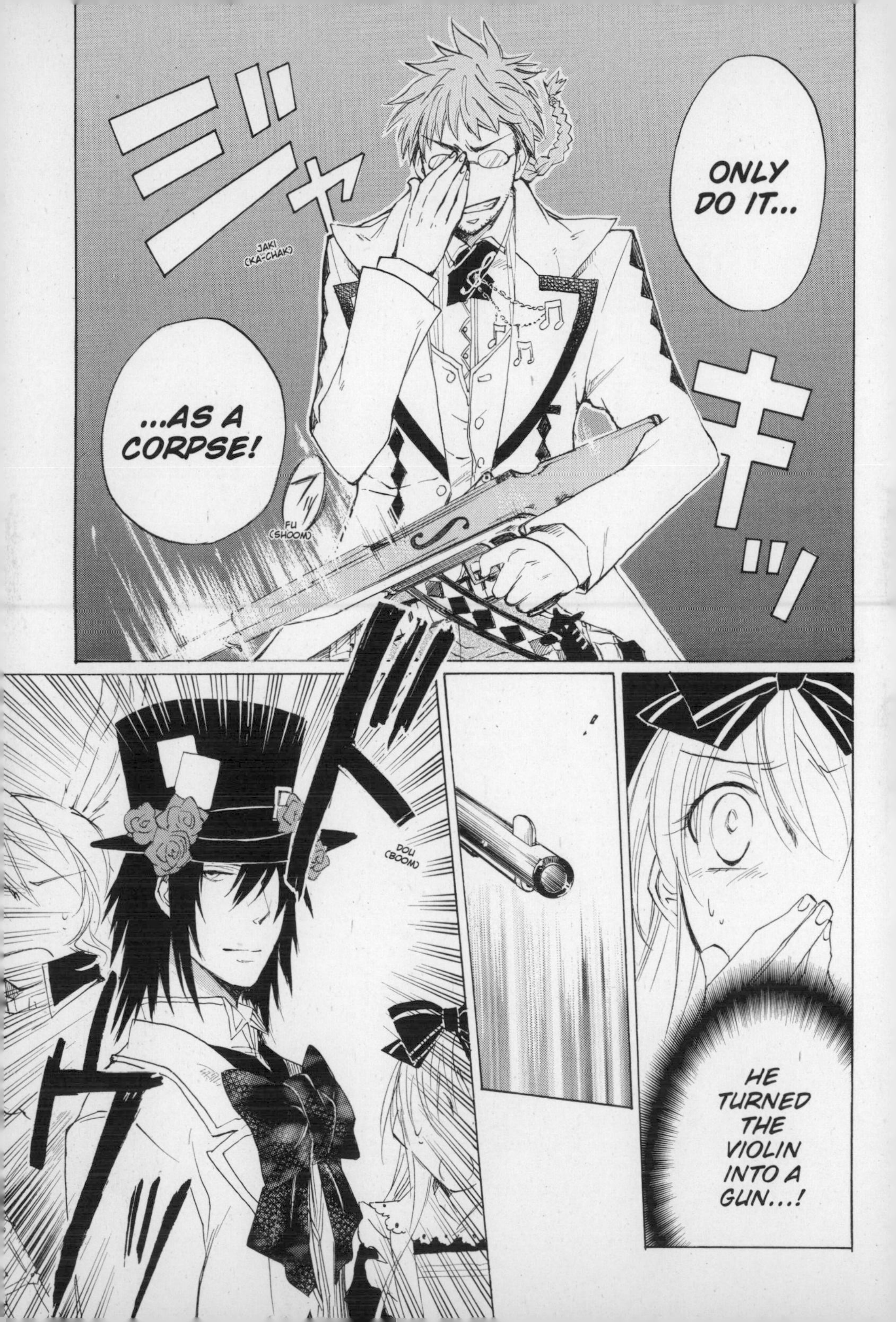
ONLY DO IT...
JAKI (KA-CHAK)
...AS A CORPSE!
FU (SHOOM)
HE TURNED THE VIOLIN INTO A GUN...!
!
DOU (BOOM)

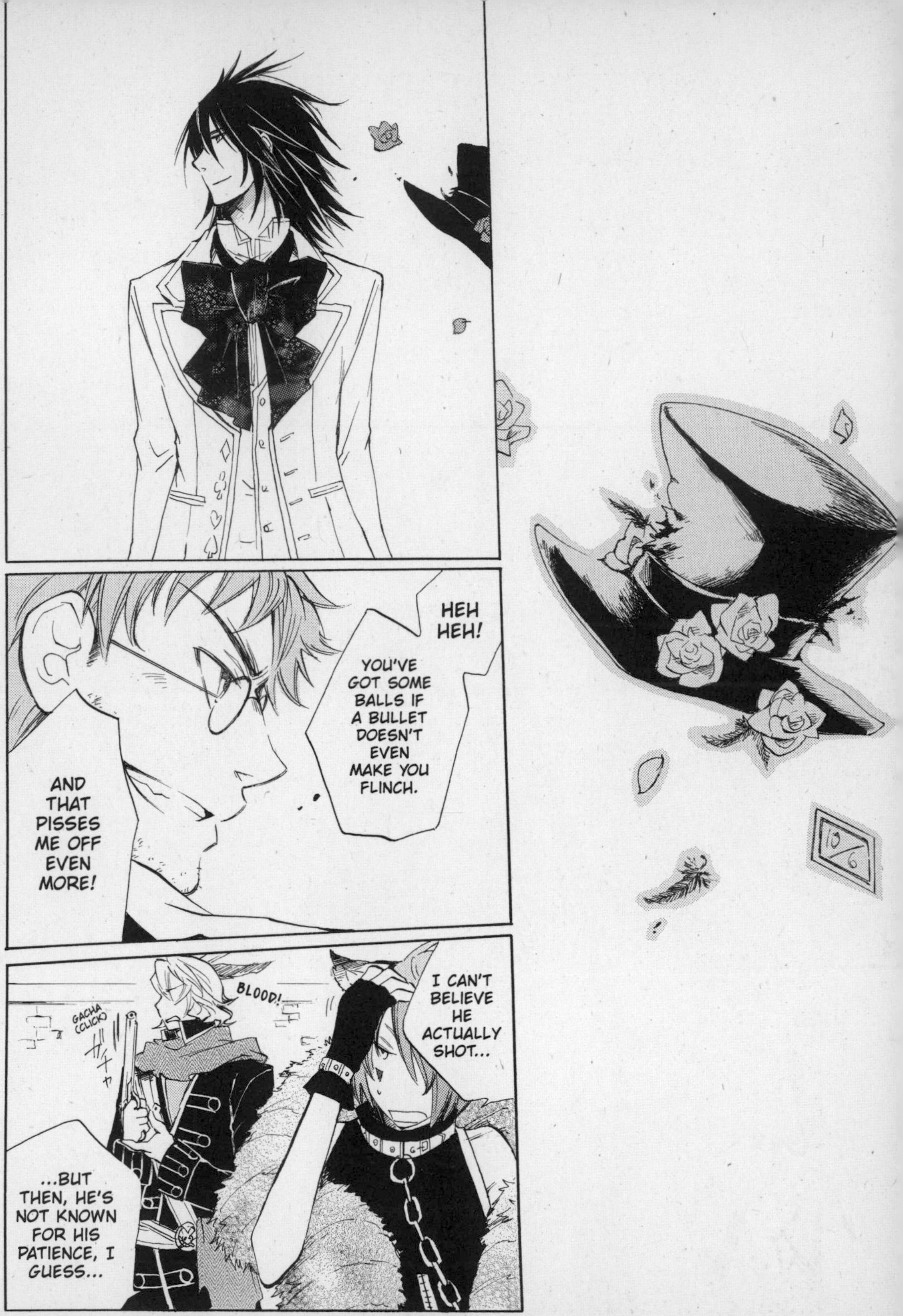
10/6
HEH HEH!
YOU'VE GOT SOME BALLS IF A BULLET DOESN'T EVEN MAKE YOU FLINCH.
AND THAT PISSES ME OFF EVEN MORE!
I CAN'T BELIEVE HE ACTUALLY SHOT...
BLOOD!
GACHA (CLICK)
ガチャ
...BUT THEN, HE'S NOT KNOWN FOR HIS PATIENCE, I GUESS...

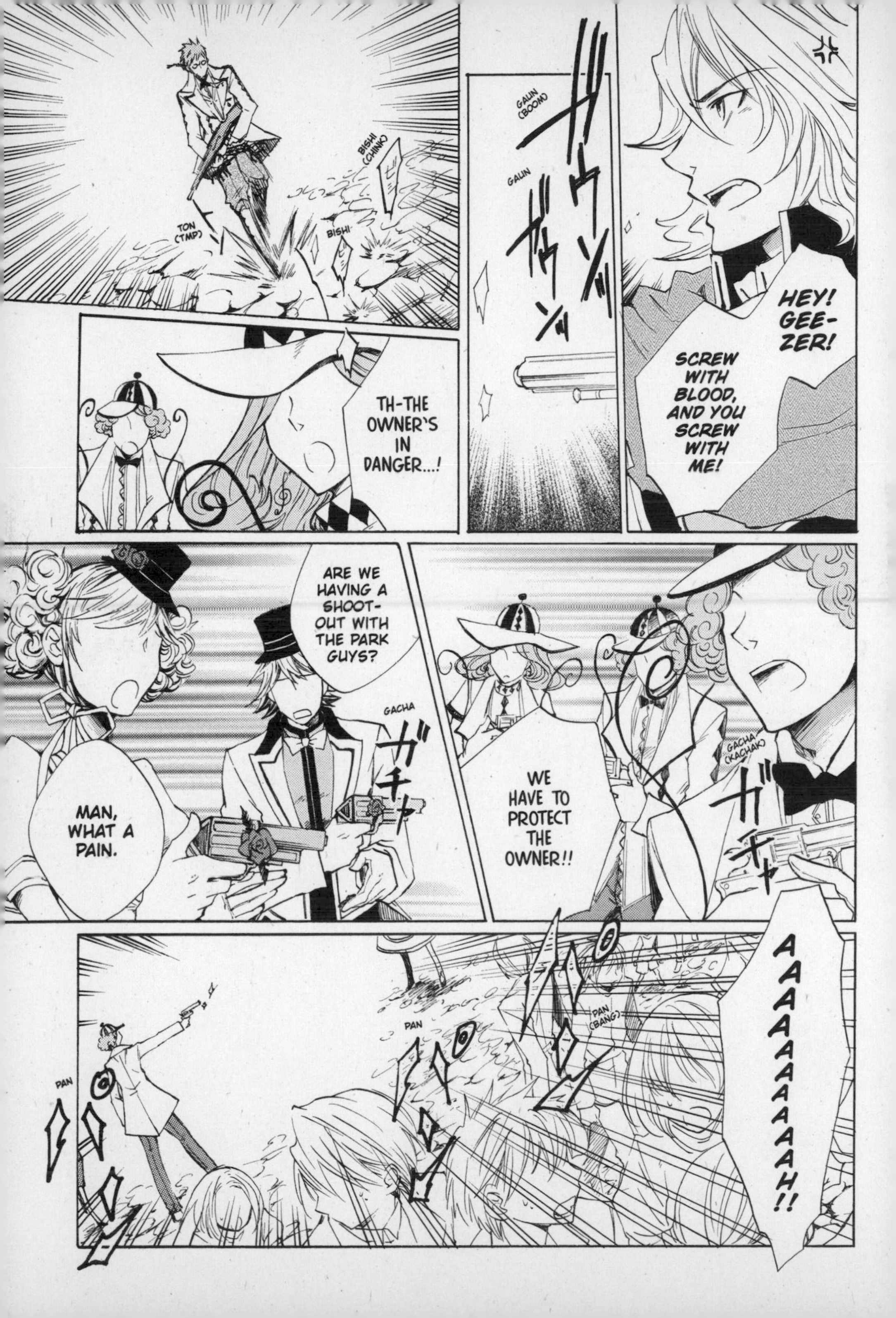
HEY! GEEZER!
SCREW WITH BLOOD, AND YOU SCREW WITH ME!
GAUN (BOOM)
GAUN
BISHI (CHINK)
TON (TMP)
BISHI
TH-THE OWNER'S IN DANGER...!
GACHA (KACHAK)
WE HAVE TO PROTECT THE OWNER!!
ARE WE HAVING A SHOOT-OUT WITH THE PARK GUYS?
GACHA
MAN, WHAT A PAIN.
AAAAAAAAAAH!!
PAN (BANG)
PAN
PAN

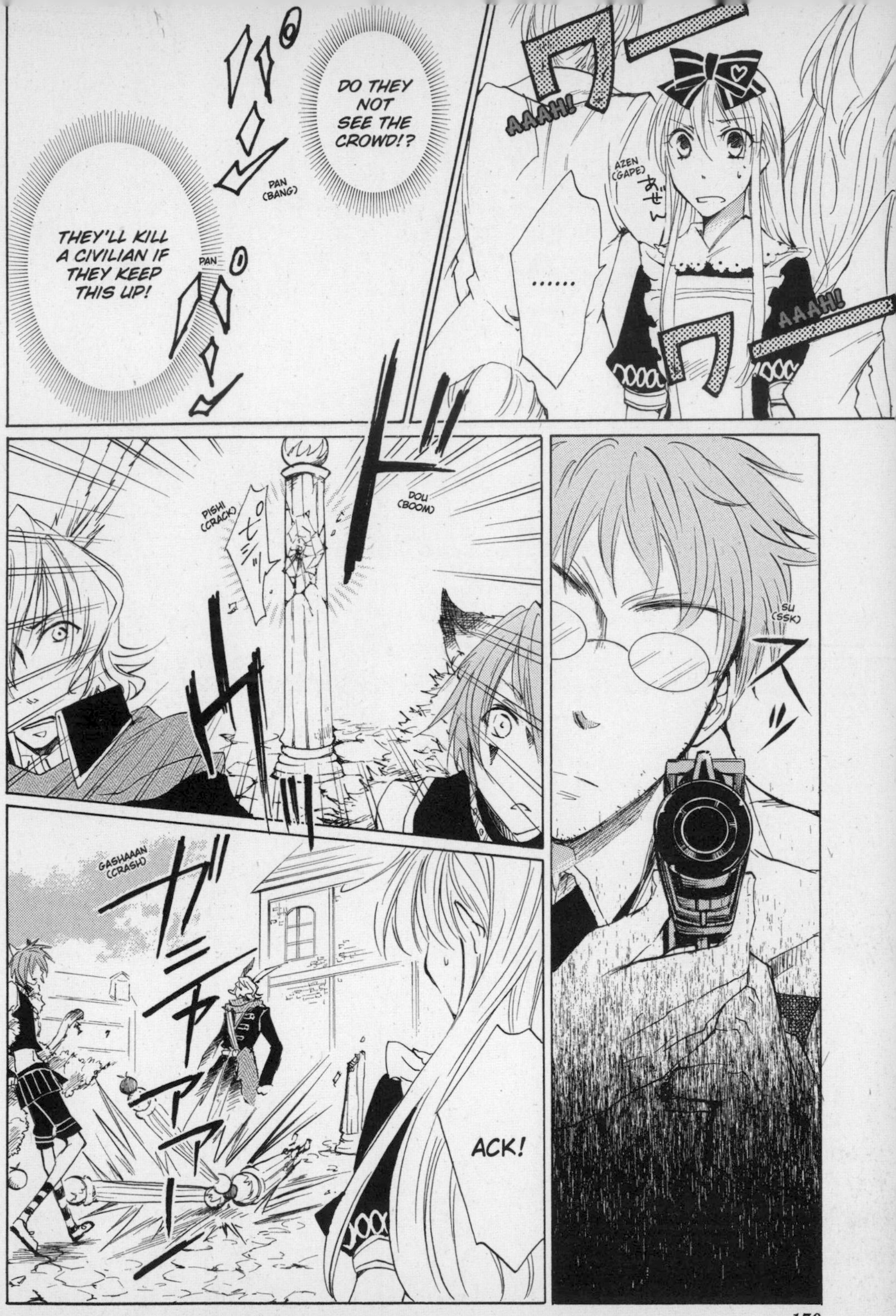
AAAH!
AZEN (GAPE)
あぜん
......
AAAH!
DO THEY NOT SEE THE CROWD!?
PAN (BANG)
PAN
THEY'LL KILL A CIVILIAN IF THEY KEEP THIS UP!
SU (SSK)
DOU (BOOM)
PISHI (CRACK)
GASHAAAN (CRASH)
ACK!

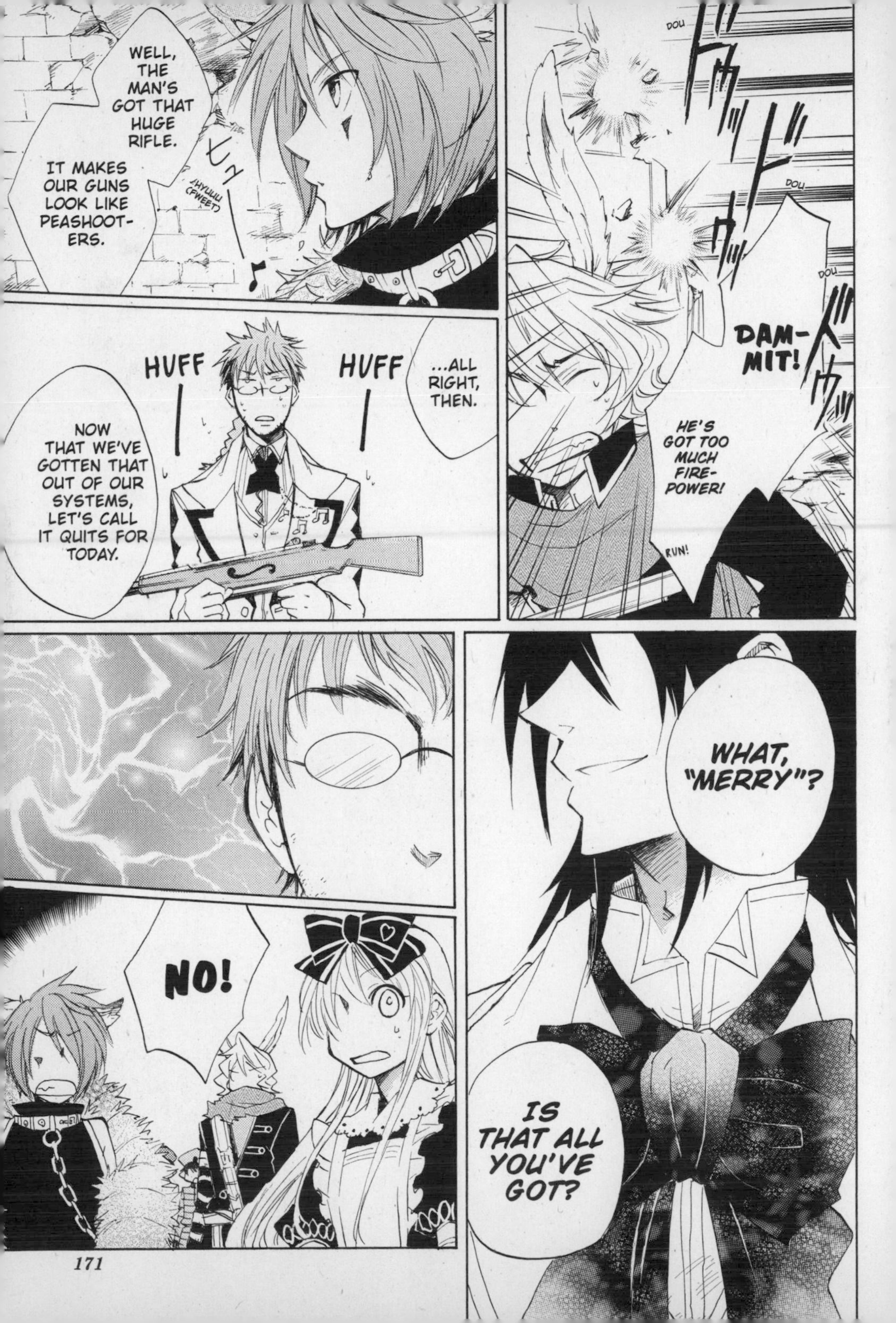
DOU
DOU
DOU
DAM-MIT!
HE'S GOT TOO MUCH FIRE-POWER!
RUN!
WELL, THE MAN'S GOT THAT HUGE RIFLE.
IT MAKES OUR GUNS LOOK LIKE PEASHOOTERS.
HYUUU (FWEET)
...ALL RIGHT, THEN.
HUFF
HUFF
NOW THAT WE'VE GOTTEN THAT OUT OF OUR SYSTEMS, LET'S CALL IT QUITS FOR TODAY.
WHAT, "MERRY"?
IS THAT ALL YOU'VE GOT?
NO!

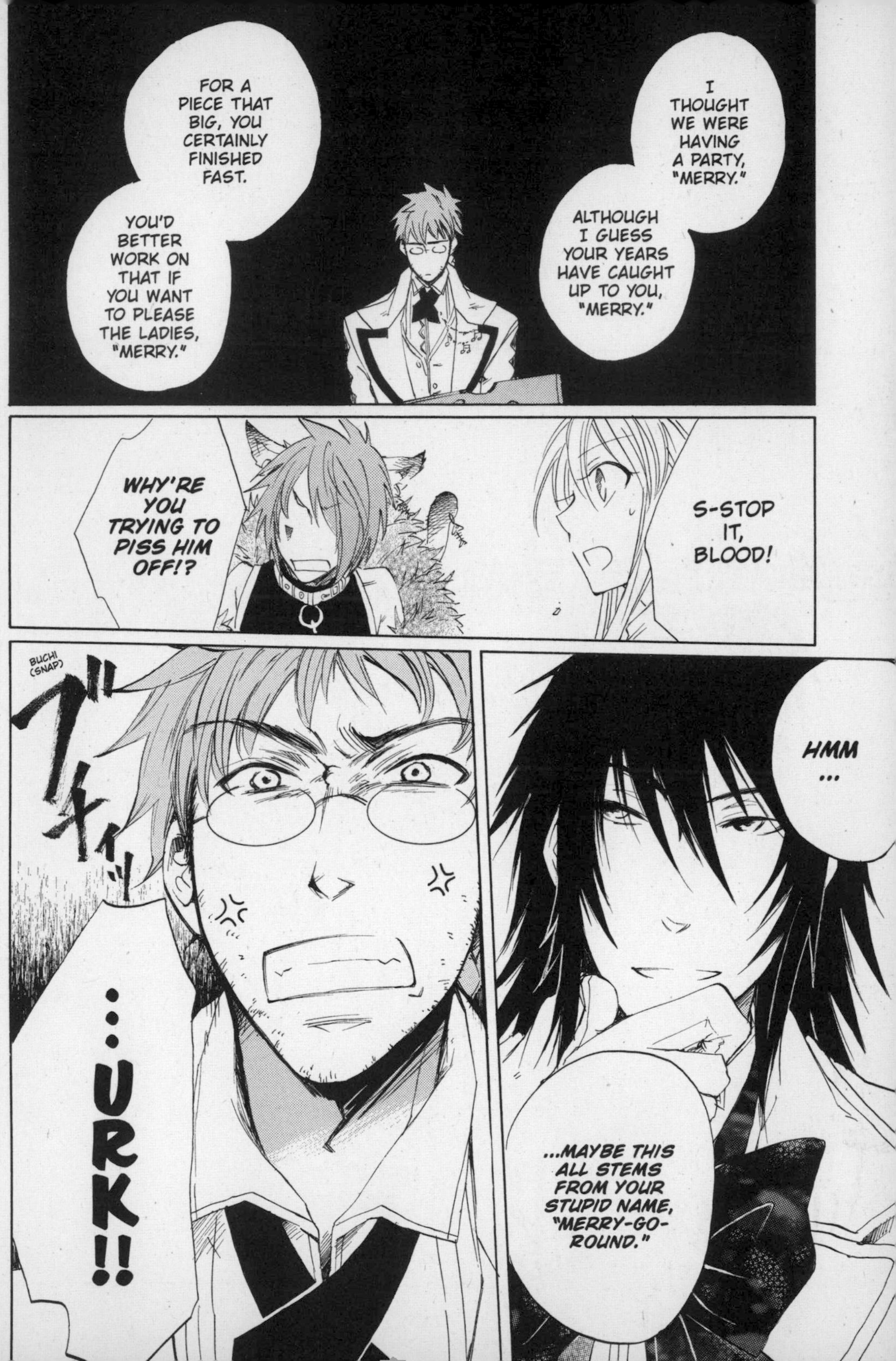
I THOUGHT WE WERE HAVING A PARTY, "MERRY."
ALTHOUGH I GUESS YOUR YEARS HAVE CAUGHT UP TO YOU, "MERRY."
FOR A PIECE THAT BIG, YOU CERTAINLY FINISHED FAST.
YOU'D BETTER WORK ON THAT IF YOU WANT TO PLEASE THE LADIES, "MERRY."
S-STOP IT, BLOOD!
WHY'RE YOU TRYING TO PISS HIM OFF!?
HMM ...
...MAYBE THIS ALL STEMS FROM YOUR STUPID NAME, "MERRY-GO-ROUND."
BUCHI (SNAP)
ブチイッ
...URK!!

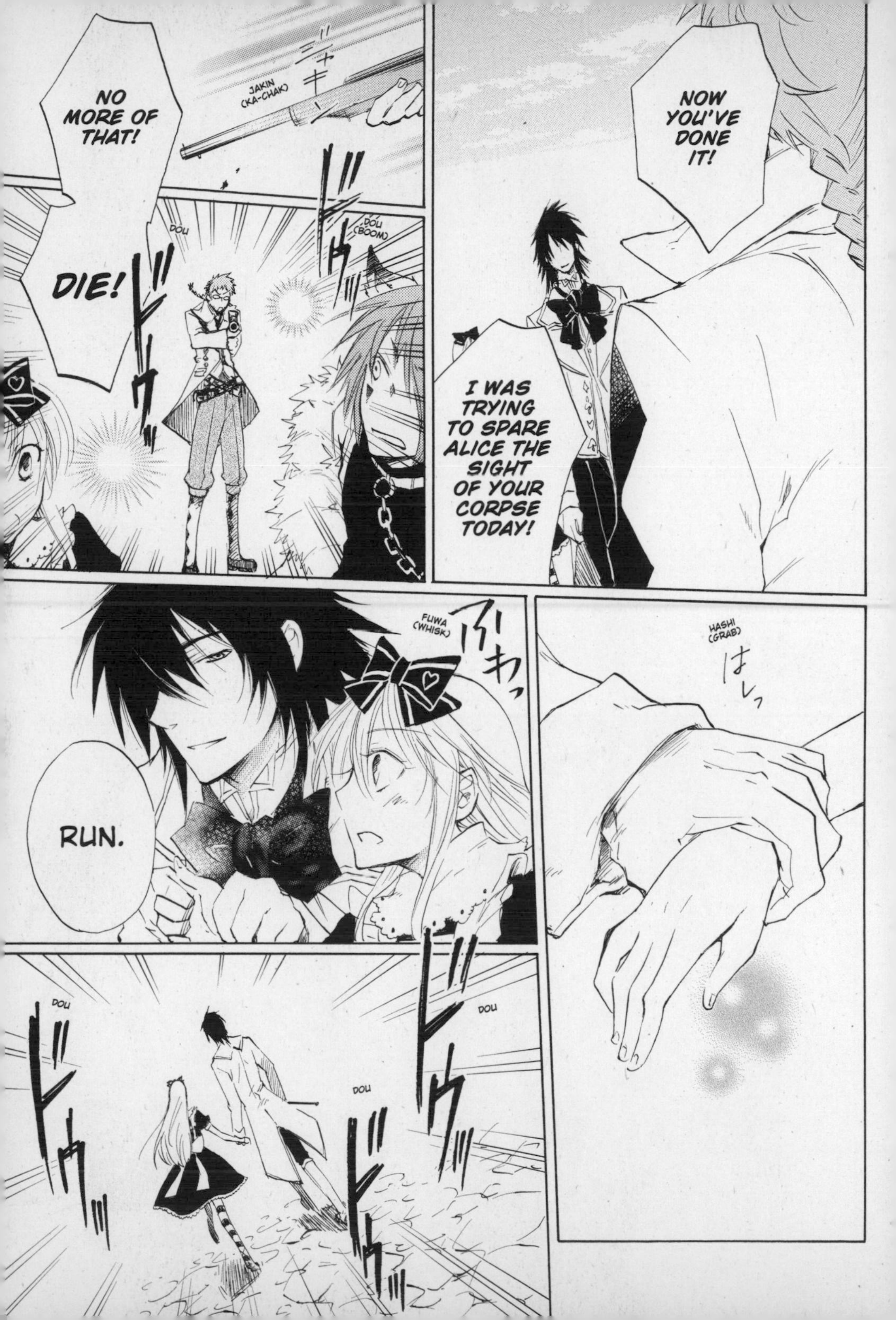
NOW YOU'VE DONE IT!
I WAS TRYING TO SPARE ALICE THE SIGHT OF YOUR CORPSE TODAY!
JAKIN (KA-CHAK)
NO MORE OF THAT!
DOU (BOOM)
DOU
DIE!
HASHI (GRAB)
FUWA (WHISK)
RUN.
DOU
DOU
DOU

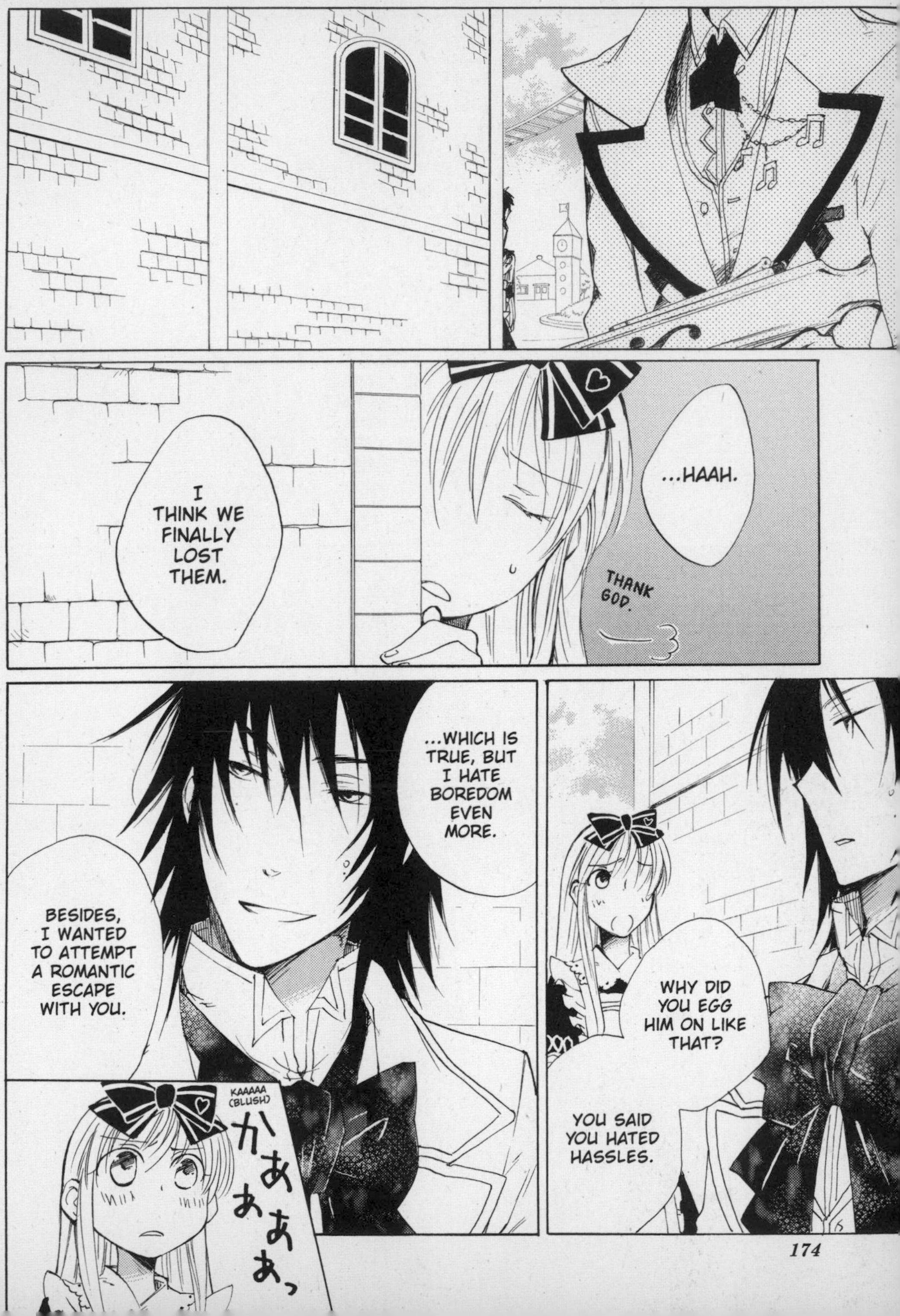
...HAAH.
THANK GOD.
I THINK WE FINALLY LOST THEM.
WHY DID YOU EGG HIM ON LIKE THAT?
YOU SAID YOU HATED HASSLES.
...WHICH IS TRUE, BUT I HATE BOREDOM EVEN MORE.
BESIDES, I WANTED TO ATTEMPT A ROMANTIC ESCAPE WITH YOU.
KAAAAA (BLUSH)
かあぁあぁっ

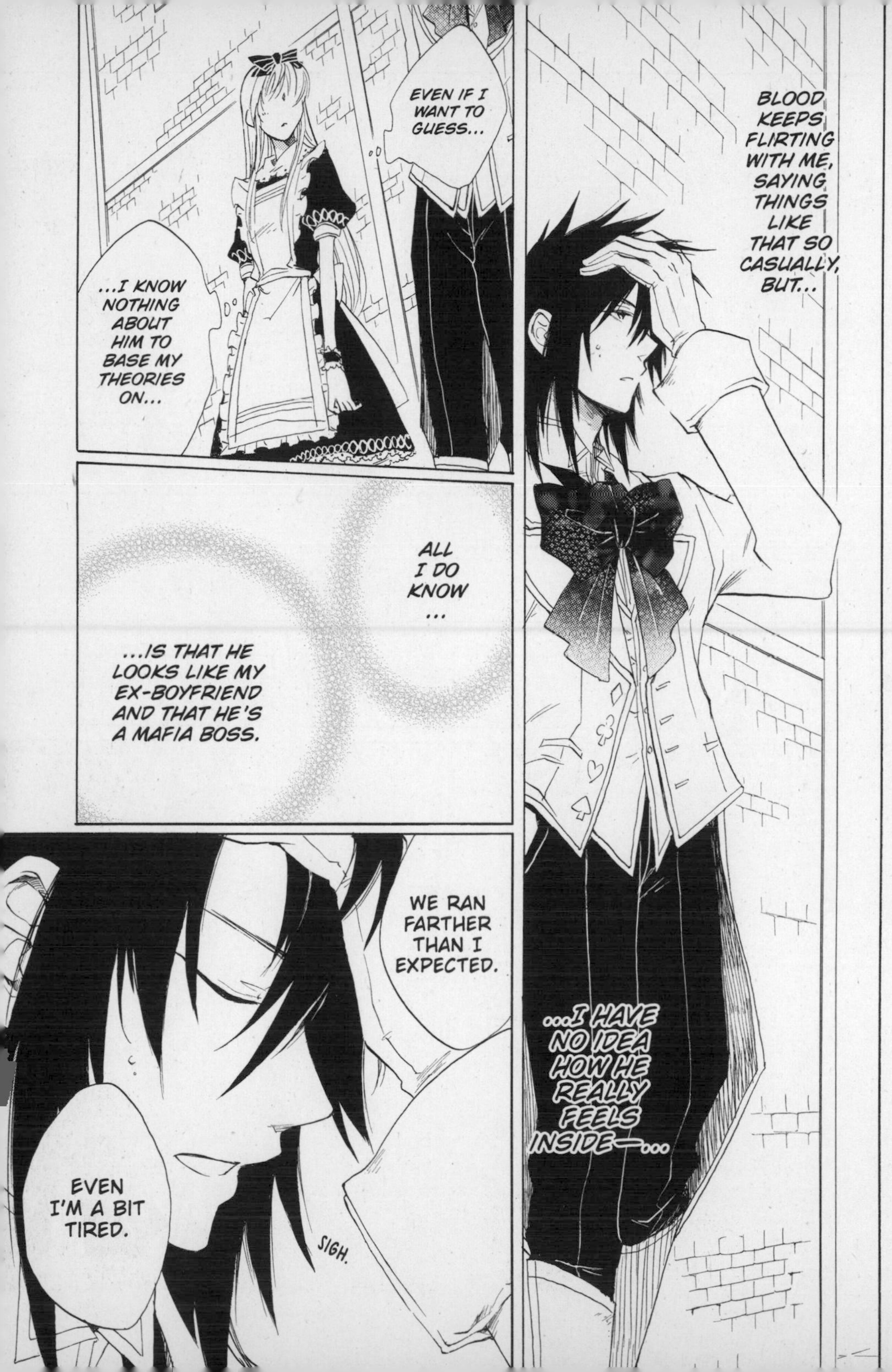
BLOOD KEEPS FLIRTING WITH ME, SAYING THINGS LIKE THAT SO CASUALLY, BUT...
...I HAVE NO IDEA HOW HE REALLY FEELS INSIDE—...
EVEN IF I WANT TO GUESS...
...I KNOW NOTHING ABOUT HIM TO BASE MY THEORIES ON...
ALL I DO KNOW...
...IS THAT HE LOOKS LIKE MY EX-BOYFRIEND AND THAT HE'S A MAFIA BOSS.
WE RAN FARTHER THAN I EXPECTED.
EVEN I'M A BIT TIRED.
SIGH.

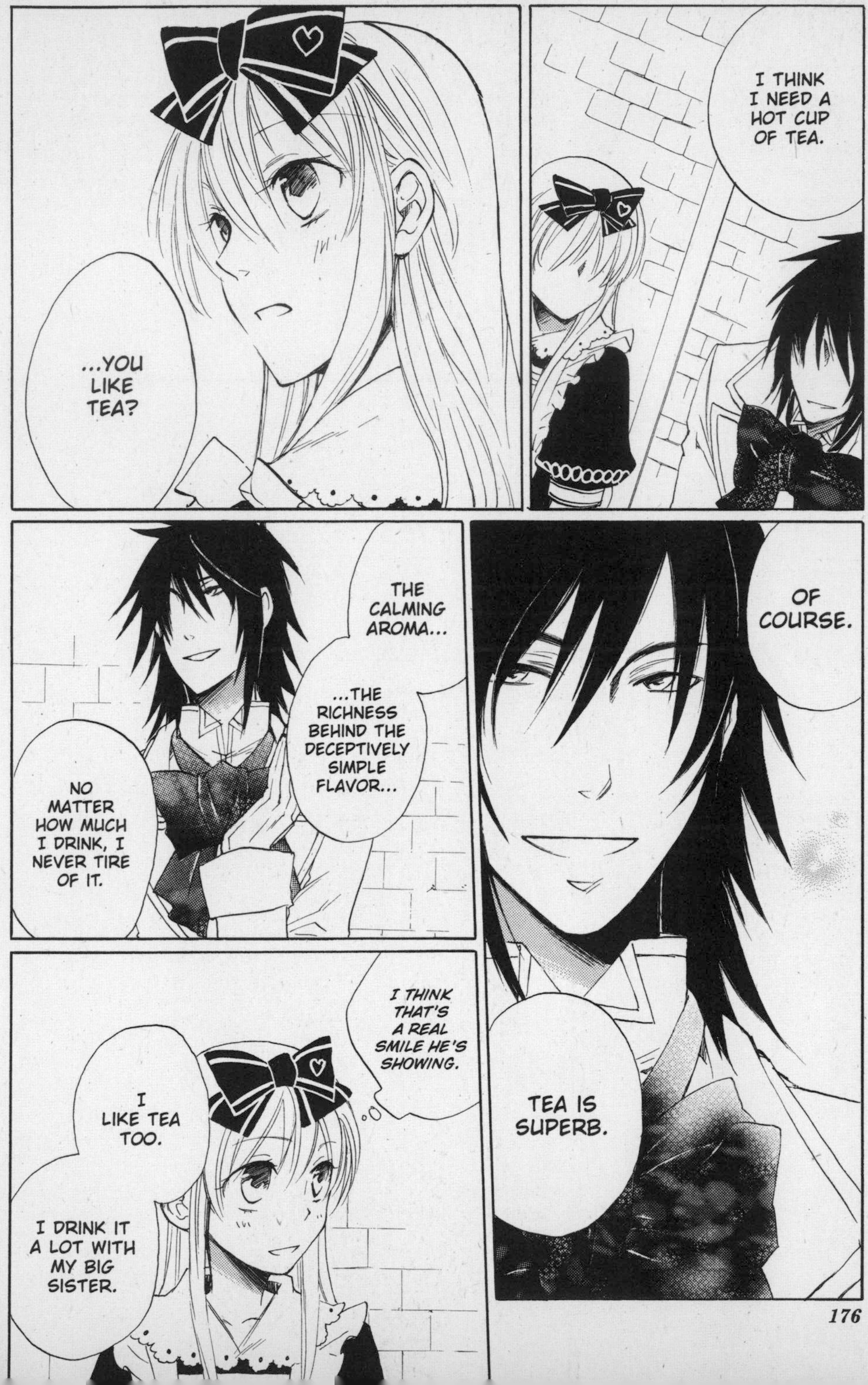
I THINK I NEED A HOT CUP OF TEA.
...YOU LIKE TEA?
OF COURSE.
TEA IS SUPERB.
THE CALMING AROMA...
...THE RICHNESS BEHIND THE DECEPTIVELY SIMPLE FLAVOR...
NO MATTER HOW MUCH I DRINK, I NEVER TIRE OF IT.
I THINK THAT'S A REAL SMILE HE'S SHOWING.
I LIKE TEA TOO.
I DRINK IT A LOT WITH MY BIG SISTER.

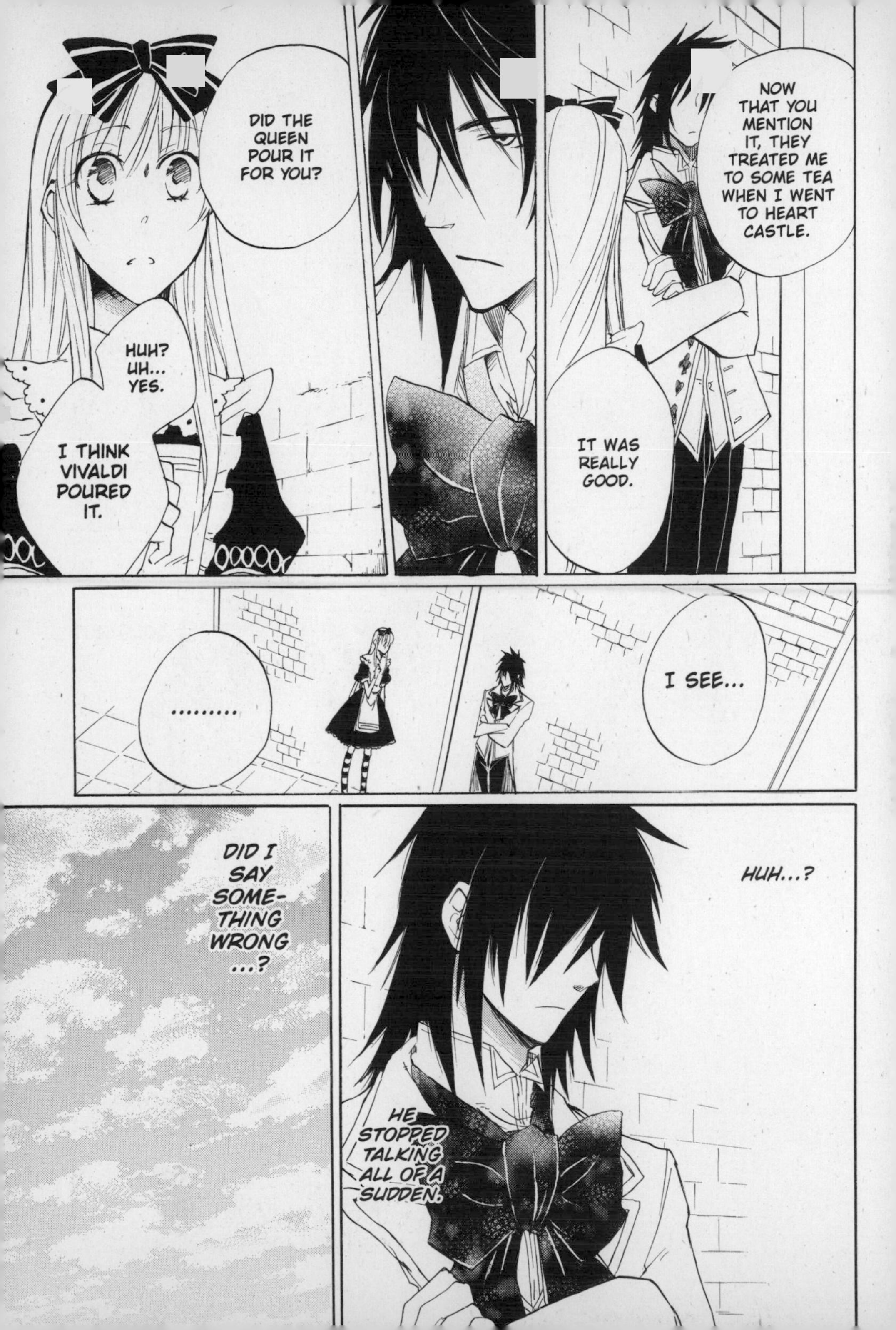
NOW THAT YOU MENTION IT, THEY TREATED ME TO SOME TEA WHEN I WENT TO HEART CASTLE.
IT WAS REALLY GOOD.
DID THE QUEEN POUR IT FOR YOU?
HUH? UH... YES.
I THINK VIVALDI POURED IT.
I SEE...
....
HUH...?
HE STOPPED TALKING ALL OF A SUDDEN.
DID I SAY SOME-THING WRONG ...?

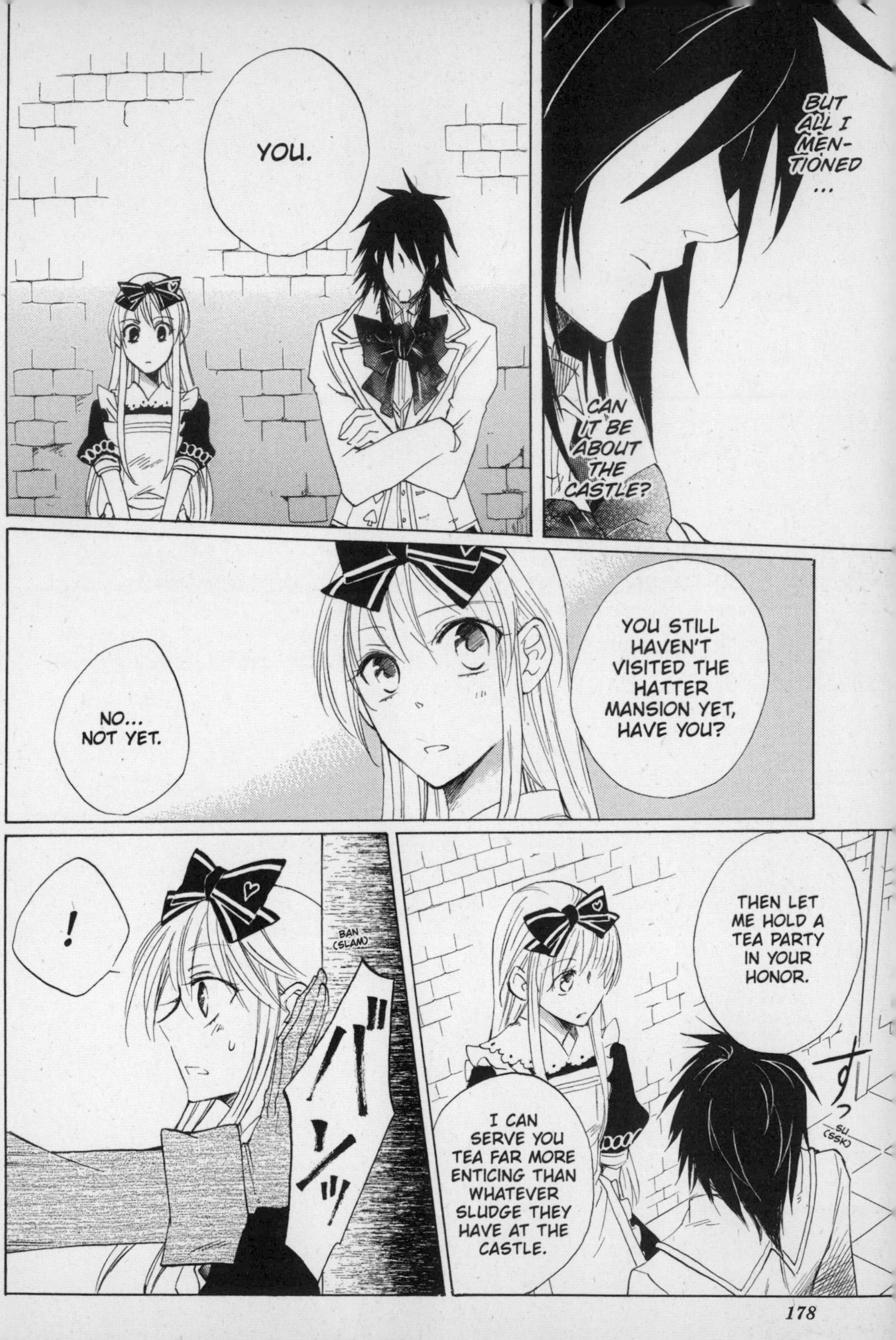
BUT ALL I MEN-TIONED ...
CAN IT BE ABOUT THE CASTLE?
YOU.
YOU STILL HAVEN'T VISITED THE HATTER MANSION YET, HAVE YOU?
NO... NOT YET.
THEN LET ME HOLD A TEA PARTY IN YOUR HONOR.
SU (SSK)
I CAN SERVE YOU TEA FAR MORE ENTICING THAN WHATEVER SLUDGE THEY HAVE AT THE CASTLE.
!
BAN (SLAM)

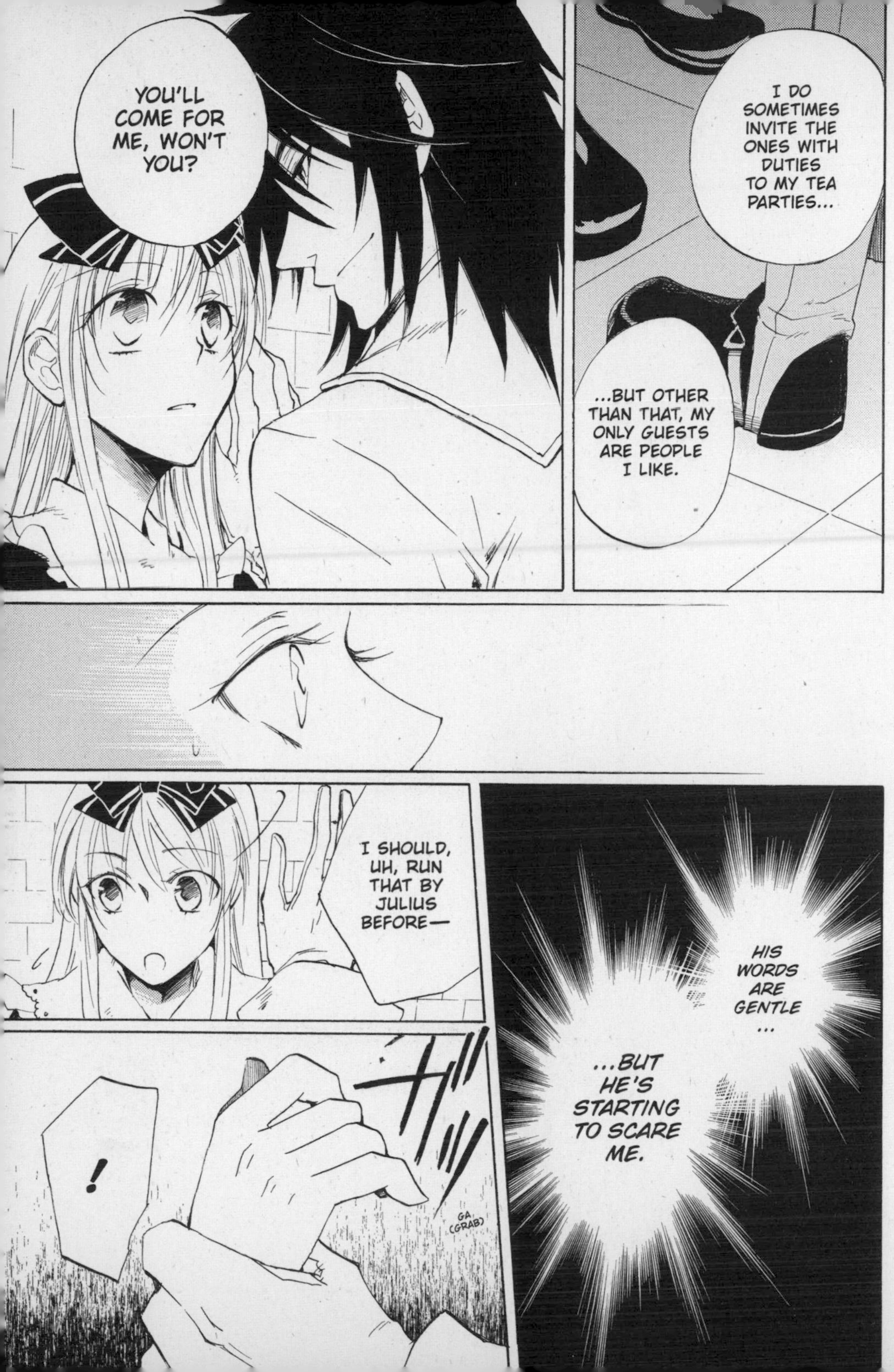
I DO SOMETIMES INVITE THE ONES WITH DUTIES TO MY TEA PARTIES...
...BUT OTHER THAN THAT, MY ONLY GUESTS ARE PEOPLE I LIKE.
YOU'LL COME FOR ME, WON'T YOU?
HIS WORDS ARE GENTLE...
...BUT HE'S STARTING TO SCARE ME.
I SHOULD, UH, RUN THAT BY JULIUS BEFORE—
!
GA (GRAB)

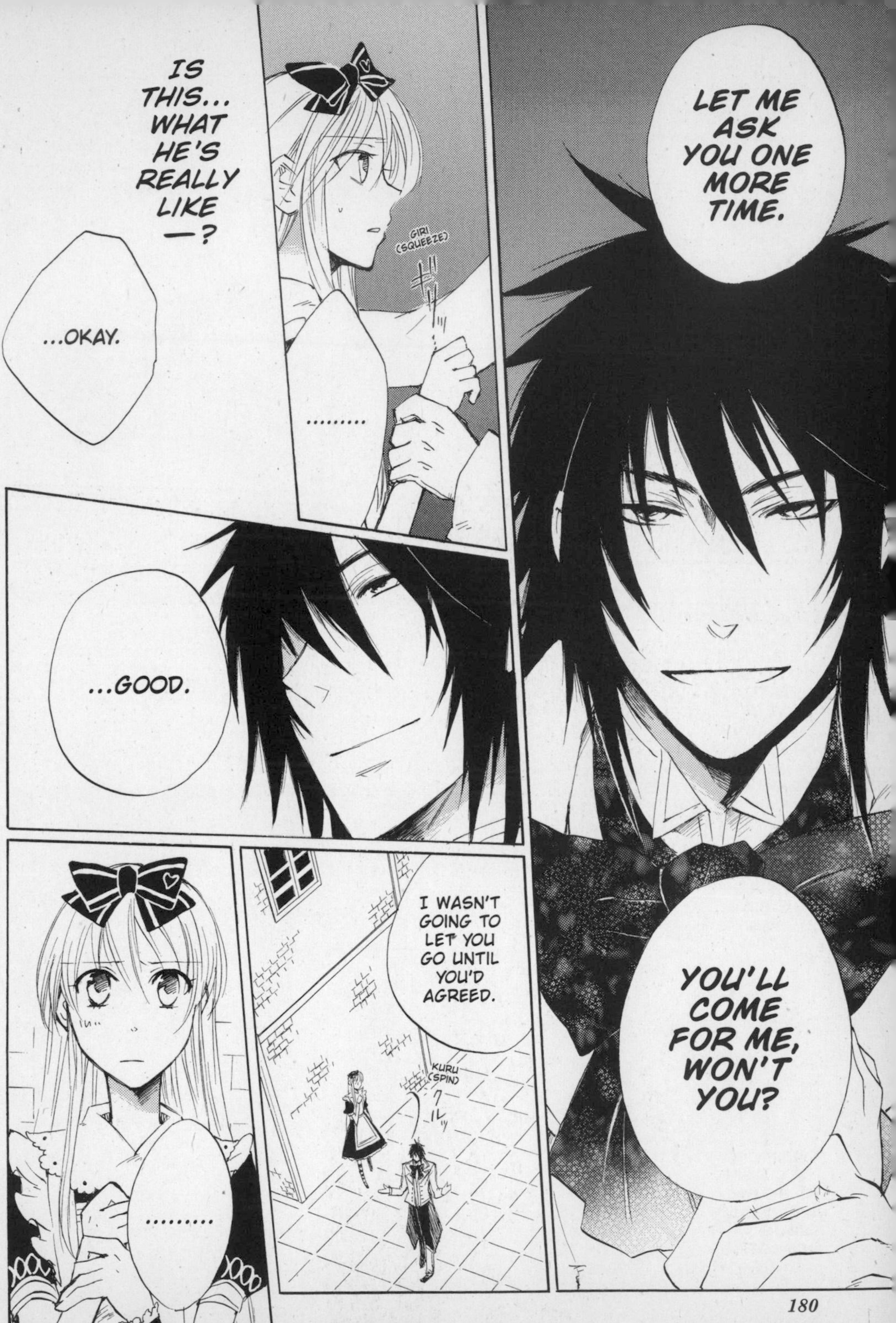
LET ME ASK YOU ONE MORE TIME.
YOU'LL COME FOR ME, WON'T YOU?
GIRI (SQUEEZE)
IS THIS... WHAT HE'S REALLY LIKE—?
....
...OKAY.
...GOOD.
I WASN'T GOING TO LET YOU GO UNTIL YOU'D AGREED.
KURU (SPIN)
....

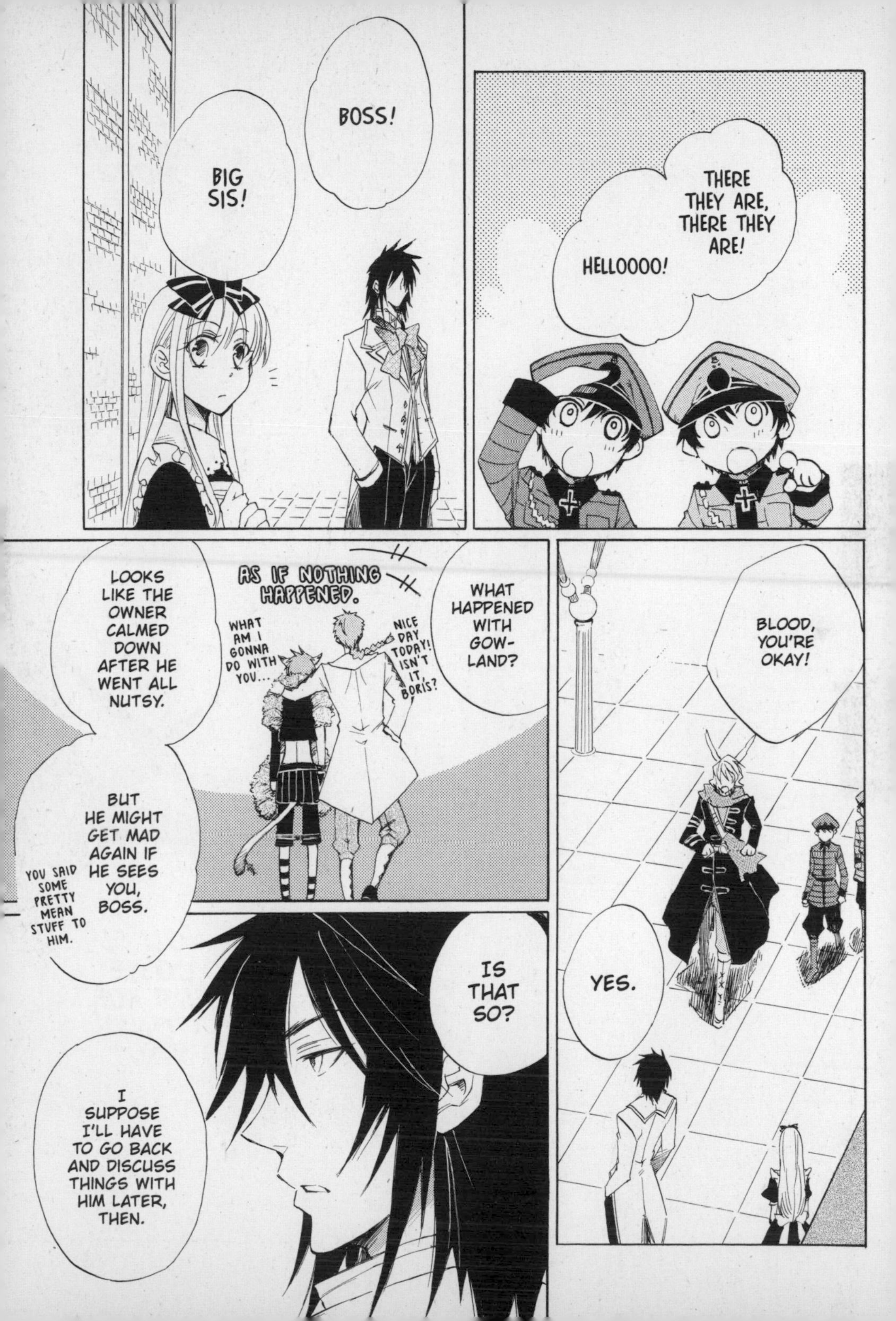
THERE THEY ARE, THERE THEY ARE!
HELLOOOO!
BOSS!
BIG SIS!
BLOOD, YOU'RE OKAY!
YES.
WHAT HAPPENED WITH GOW-LAND?
NICE DAY TODAY! ISN'T IT, BORIS?
AS IF NOTHING HAPPENED.
WHAT AM I GONNA DO WITH YOU...
LOOKS LIKE THE OWNER CALMED DOWN AFTER HE WENT ALL NUTSY.
BUT HE MIGHT GET MAD AGAIN IF HE SEES YOU, BOSS.
YOU SAID SOME PRETTY MEAN STUFF TO HIM.
IS THAT SO?
I SUPPOSE I'LL HAVE TO GO BACK AND DISCUSS THINGS WITH HIM LATER, THEN.

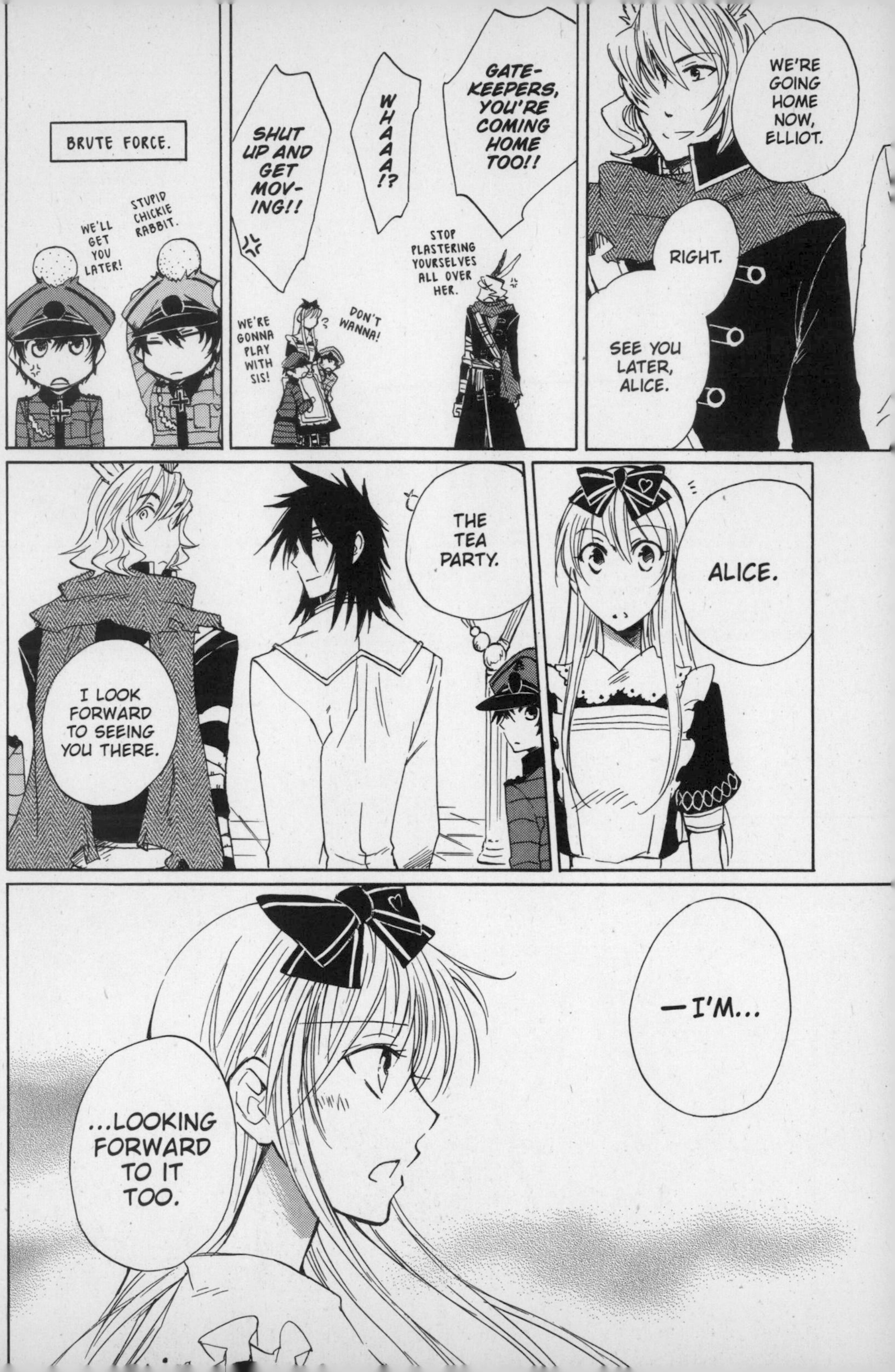
WE'RE GOING HOME NOW, ELLIOT.
RIGHT.
SEE YOU LATER, ALICE.
GATE-KEEPERS, YOU'RE COMING HOME TOO!!
WHAAAA!?
SHUT UP AND GET MOVING!!
STOP PLASTERING YOURSELVES ALL OVER HER.
DON'T WANNA!
WE'RE GONNA PLAY WITH SIS!
BRUTE FORCE.
STUPID CHICKIE RABBIT.
WE'LL GET YOU LATER!
ALICE.
THE TEA PARTY.
I LOOK FORWARD TO SEEING YOU THERE.
—I'M...
...LOOKING FORWARD TO IT TOO.

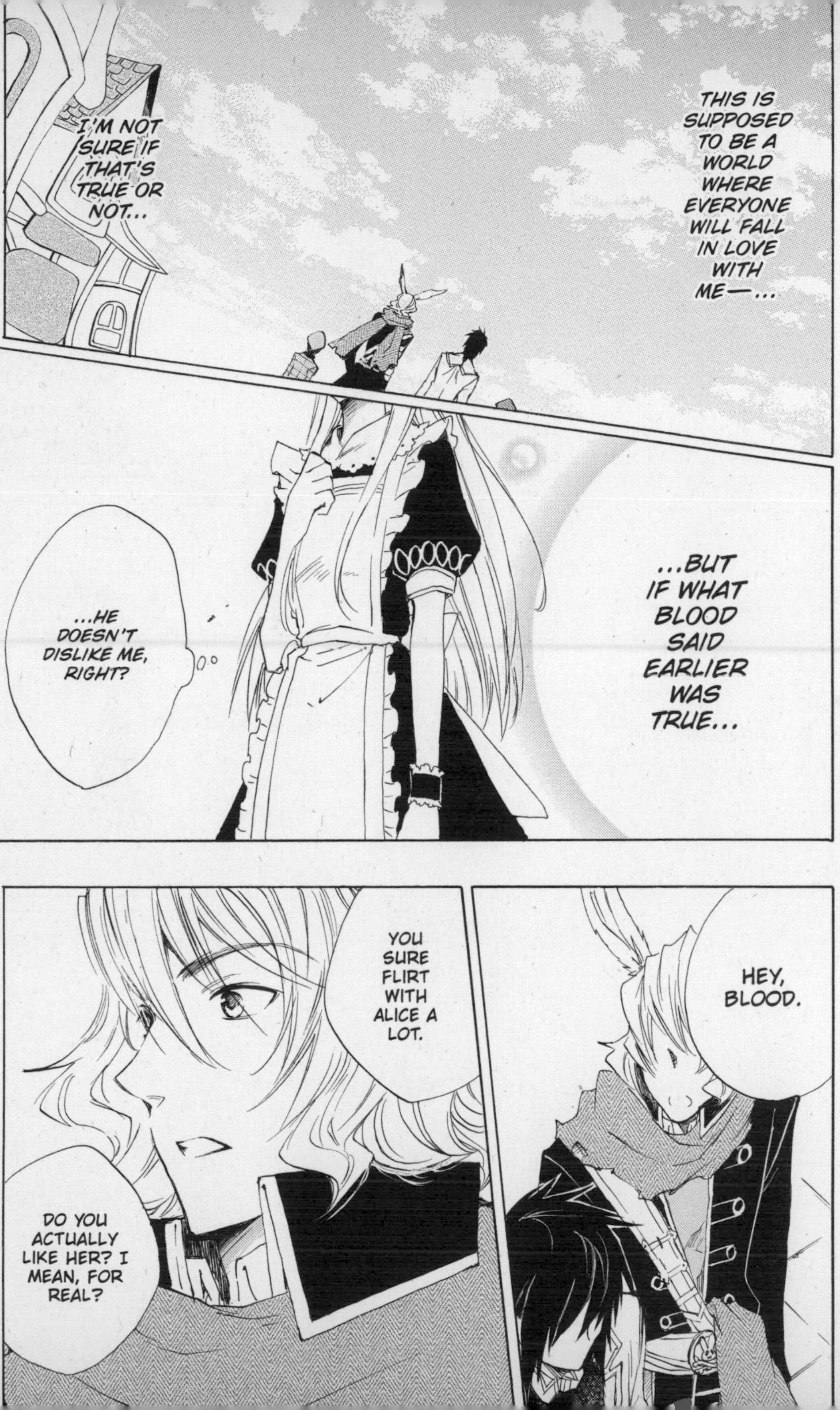
THIS IS SUPPOSED TO BE A WORLD WHERE EVERYONE WILL FALL IN LOVE WITH ME—...
I'M NOT SURE IF THAT'S TRUE OR NOT...
...BUT IF WHAT BLOOD SAID EARLIER WAS TRUE...
...HE DOESN'T DISLIKE ME, RIGHT?
HEY, BLOOD.
YOU SURE FLIRT WITH ALICE A LOT.
DO YOU ACTUALLY LIKE HER? I MEAN, FOR REAL?

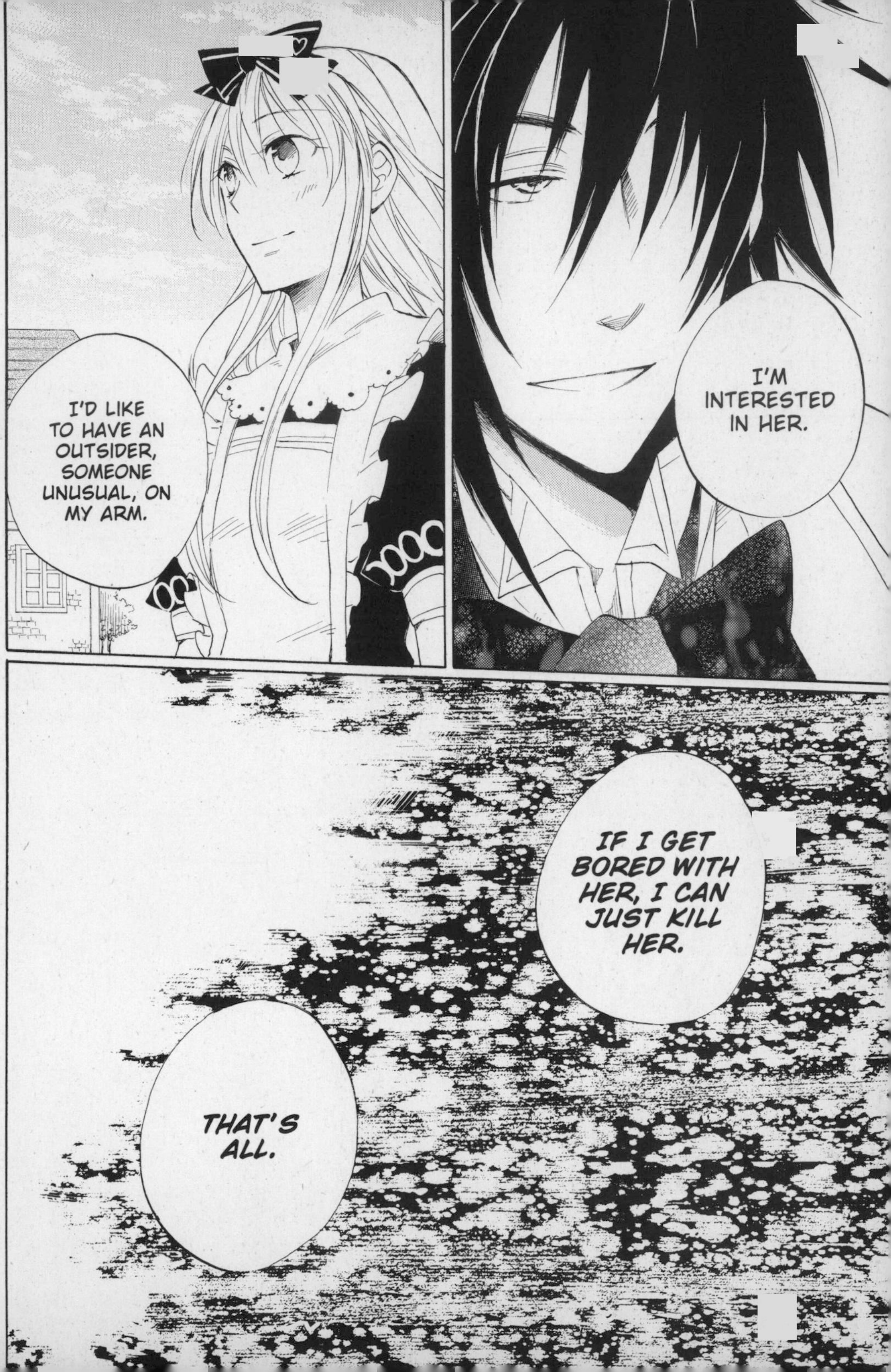

I'M INTERESTED IN HER.
I'D LIKE TO HAVE AN OUTSIDER, SOMEONE UNUSUAL, ON MY ARM.
IF I GET BORED WITH HER, I CAN JUST KILL HER.
THAT'S ALL.

ALICE IN THE COUNTRY OF HEARTS

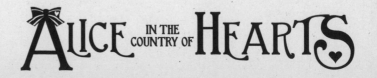

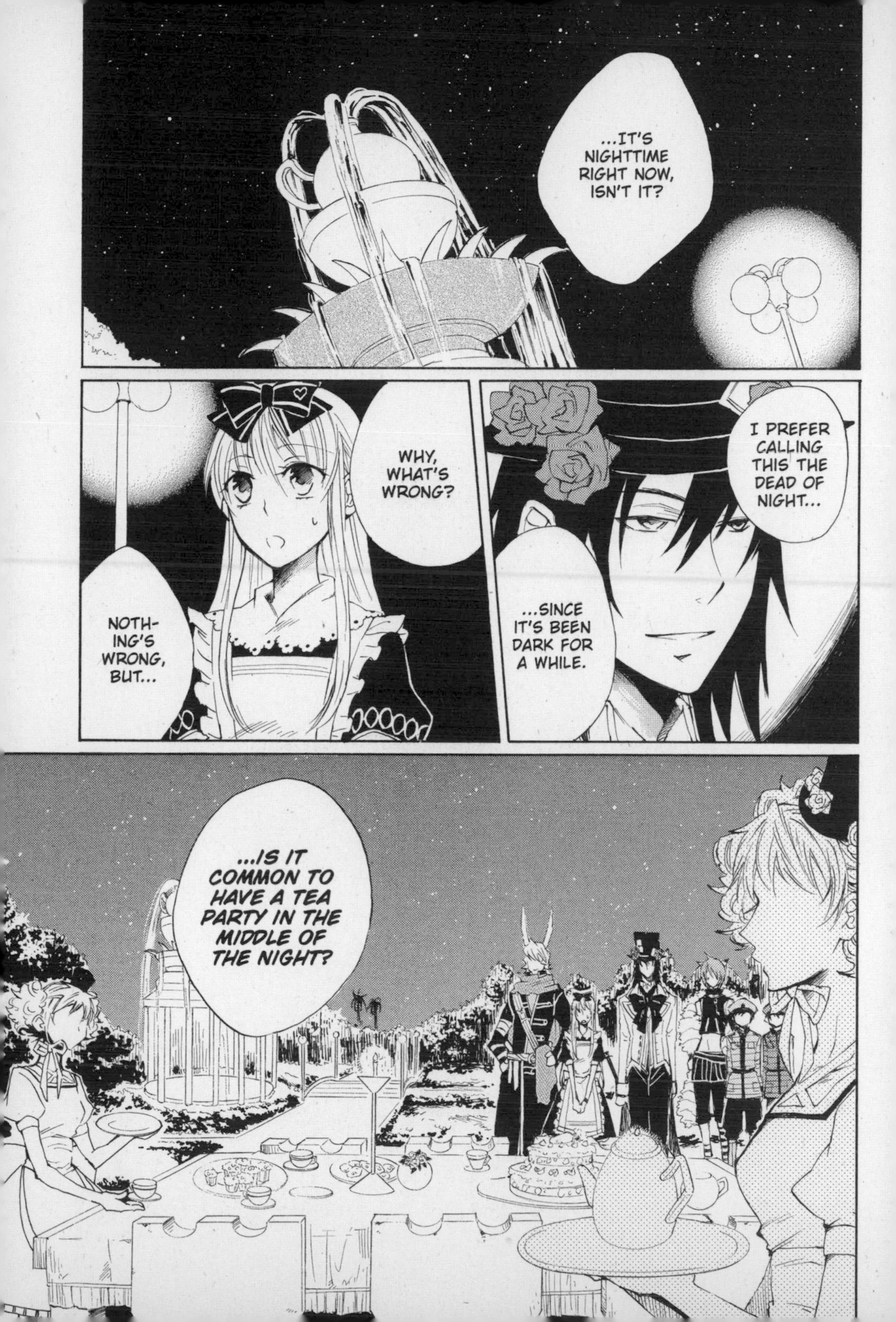
...IT'S NIGHTTIME RIGHT NOW, ISN'T IT?
I PREFER CALLING THIS THE DEAD OF NIGHT...
...SINCE IT'S BEEN DARK FOR A WHILE.
WHY, WHAT'S WRONG?
NOTH-ING'S WRONG, BUT...
...IS IT COMMON TO HAVE A TEA PARTY IN THE MIDDLE OF THE NIGHT?

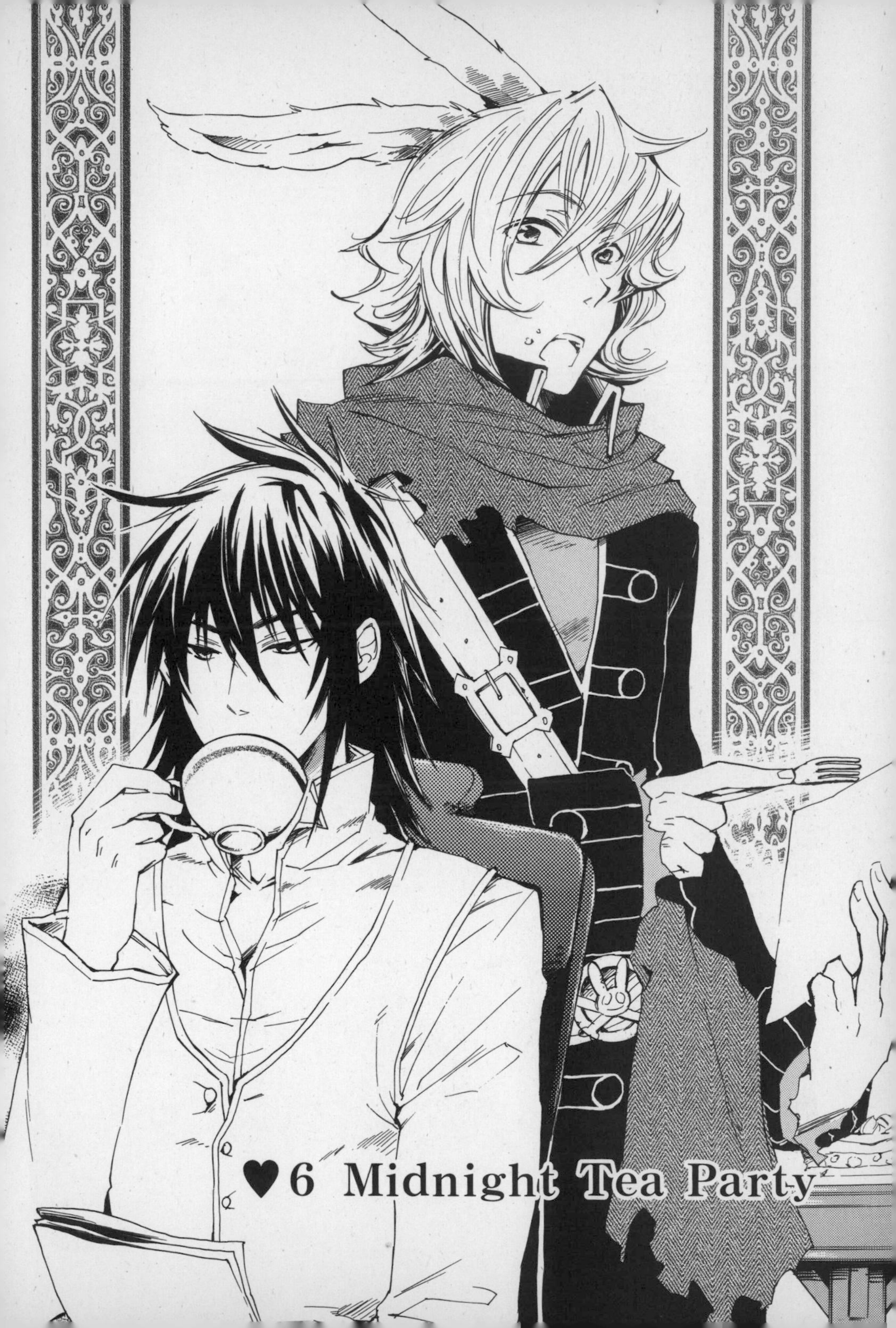
♥6 Midnight Tea Party

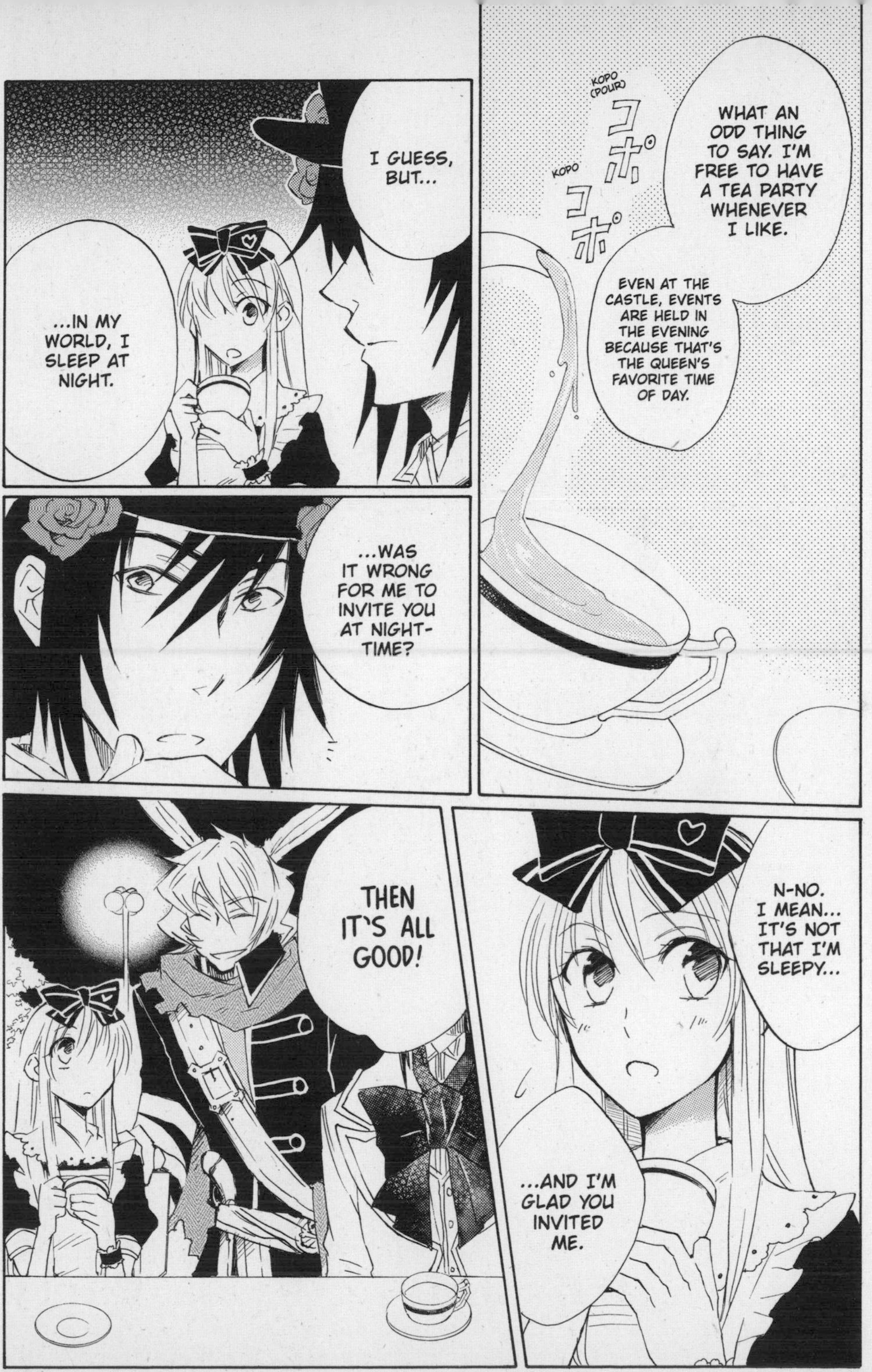
KOPO (POUR)
コポ
KOPO
コポ
WHAT AN ODD THING TO SAY. I'M FREE TO HAVE A TEA PARTY WHENEVER I LIKE.
EVEN AT THE CASTLE, EVENTS ARE HELD IN THE EVENING BECAUSE THAT'S THE QUEEN'S FAVORITE TIME OF DAY.
I GUESS, BUT...
...IN MY WORLD, I SLEEP AT NIGHT.
...WAS IT WRONG FOR ME TO INVITE YOU AT NIGHT-TIME?
N-NO. I MEAN... IT'S NOT THAT I'M SLEEPY...
...AND I'M GLAD YOU INVITED ME.
THEN IT'S ALL GOOD!

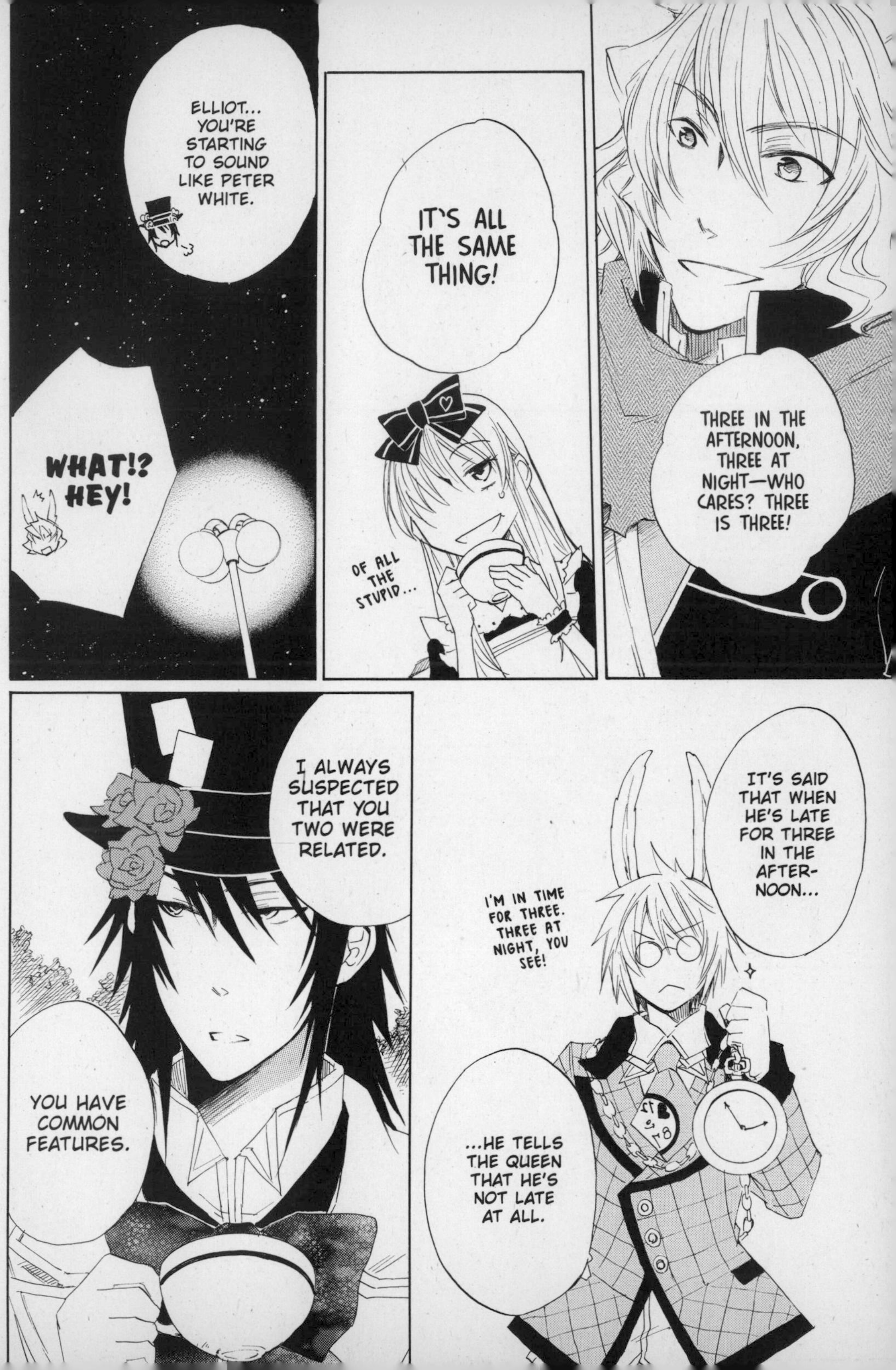
THREE IN THE AFTERNOON, THREE AT NIGHT—WHO CARES? THREE IS THREE!
IT'S ALL THE SAME THING!
OF ALL THE STUPID...
ELLIOT... YOU'RE STARTING TO SOUND LIKE PETER WHITE.
WHAT!? HEY!
IT'S SAID THAT WHEN HE'S LATE FOR THREE IN THE AFTERNOON...
I'M IN TIME FOR THREE. THREE AT NIGHT, YOU SEE!
...HE TELLS THE QUEEN THAT HE'S NOT LATE AT ALL.
I ALWAYS SUSPECTED THAT YOU TWO WERE RELATED.
YOU HAVE COMMON FEATURES.

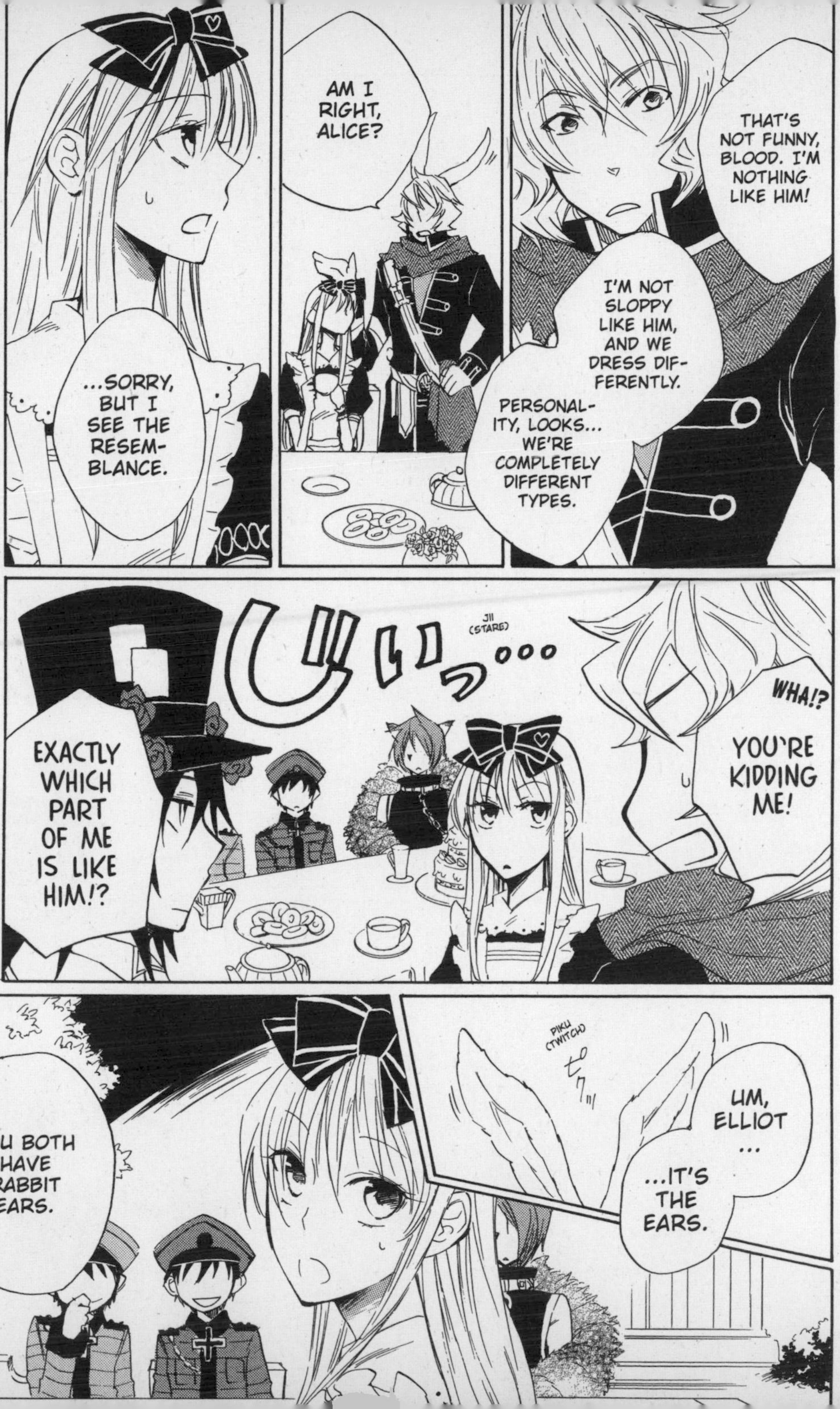
THAT'S NOT FUNNY, BLOOD. I'M NOTHING LIKE HIM!
I'M NOT SLOPPY LIKE HIM, AND WE DRESS DIF-FERENTLY.
PERSONAL-ITY, LOOKS... WE'RE COMPLETELY DIFFERENT TYPES.
AM I RIGHT, ALICE?
...SORRY, BUT I SEE THE RESEM-BLANCE.
WHA!?
YOU'RE KIDDING ME!
JII (STARE)
EXACTLY WHICH PART OF ME IS LIKE HIM!?
PIKU (TWITCH)
UM, ELLIOT ...
...IT'S THE EARS.
YOU BOTH HAVE RABBIT EARS.

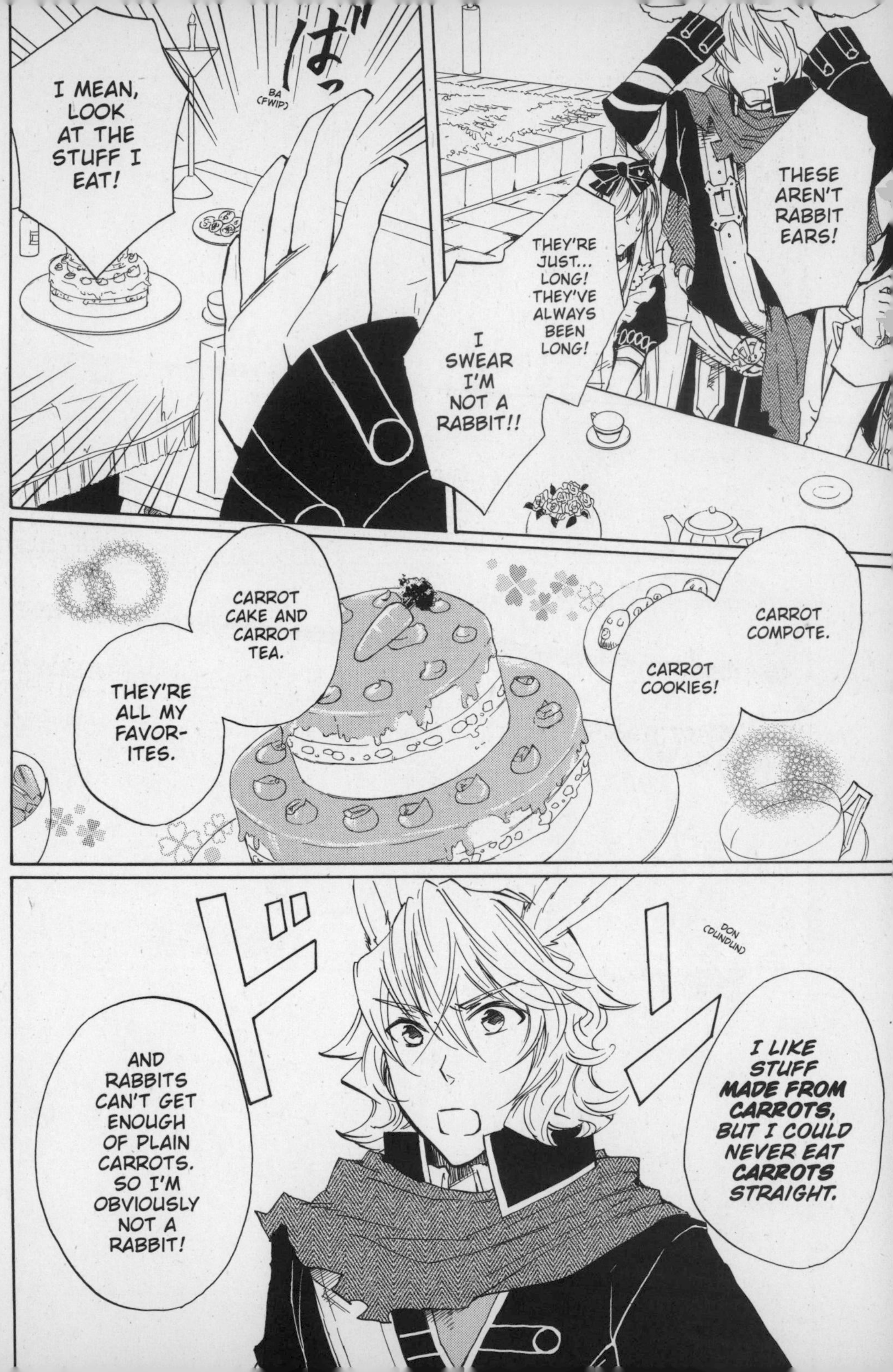

THESE AREN'T RABBIT EARS!
THEY'RE JUST... LONG! THEY'VE ALWAYS BEEN LONG!
I SWEAR I'M NOT A RABBIT!!
ばっ
BA (FWIP)
I MEAN, LOOK AT THE STUFF I EAT!
CARROT COMPOTE.
CARROT COOKIES!
CARROT CAKE AND CARROT TEA.
THEY'RE ALL MY FAVOR-ITES.
ドン
DON (DUNDUN)
I LIKE STUFF **MADE FROM CARROTS,** BUT I COULD NEVER EAT **CARROTS** STRAIGHT.
AND RABBITS CAN'T GET ENOUGH OF PLAIN CARROTS. SO I'M OBVIOUSLY NOT A RABBIT!

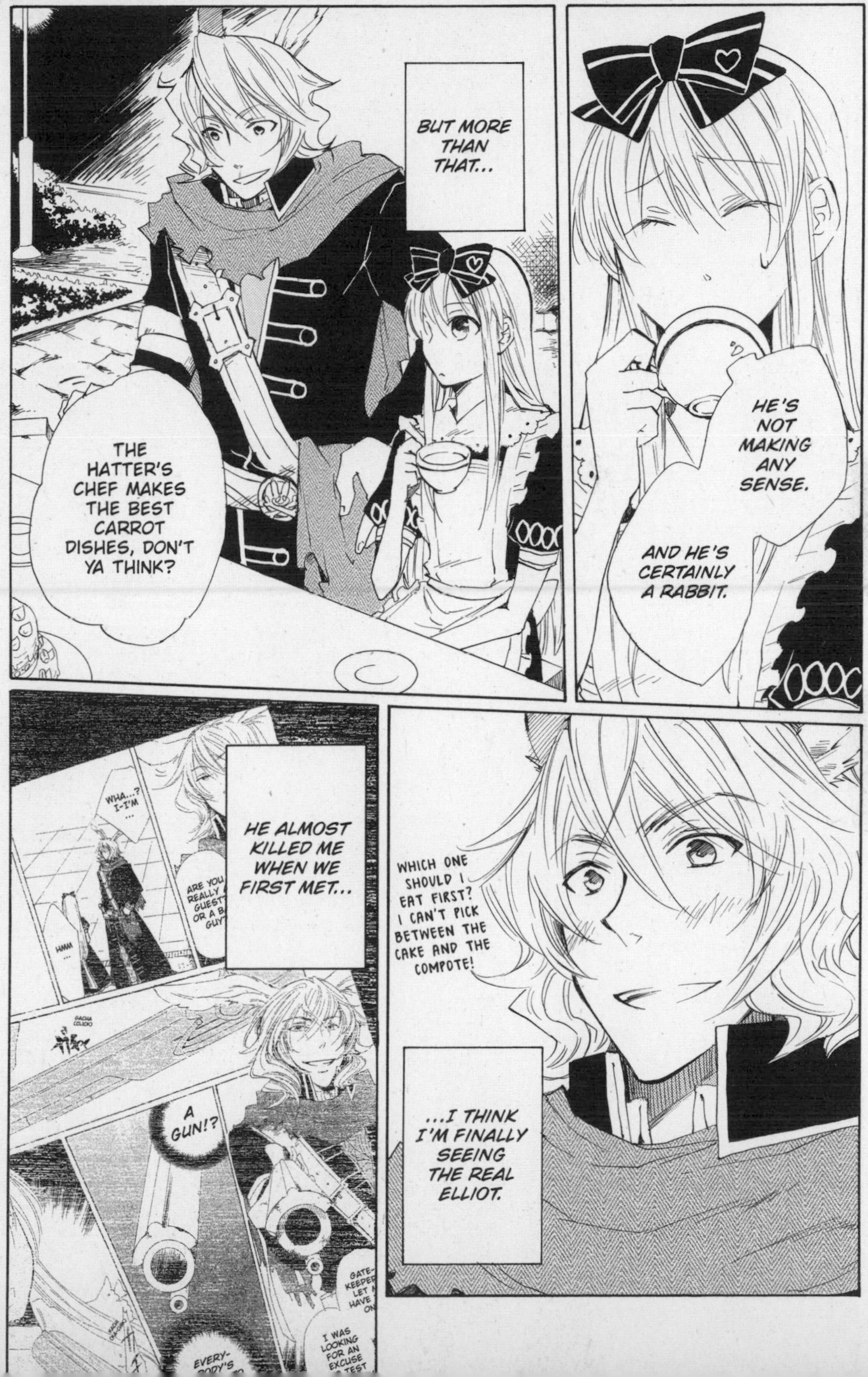
HE'S NOT MAKING ANY SENSE.
AND HE'S CERTAINLY A RABBIT.
BUT MORE THAN THAT...
THE HATTER'S CHEF MAKES THE BEST CARROT DISHES, DON'T YA THINK?
WHICH ONE SHOULD I EAT FIRST? I CAN'T PICK BETWEEN THE CAKE AND THE COMPOTE!
...I THINK I'M FINALLY SEEING THE REAL ELLIOT.
HE ALMOST KILLED ME WHEN WE FIRST MET...
WHA...? I-I'M ...
HMM ...
A GUN!?

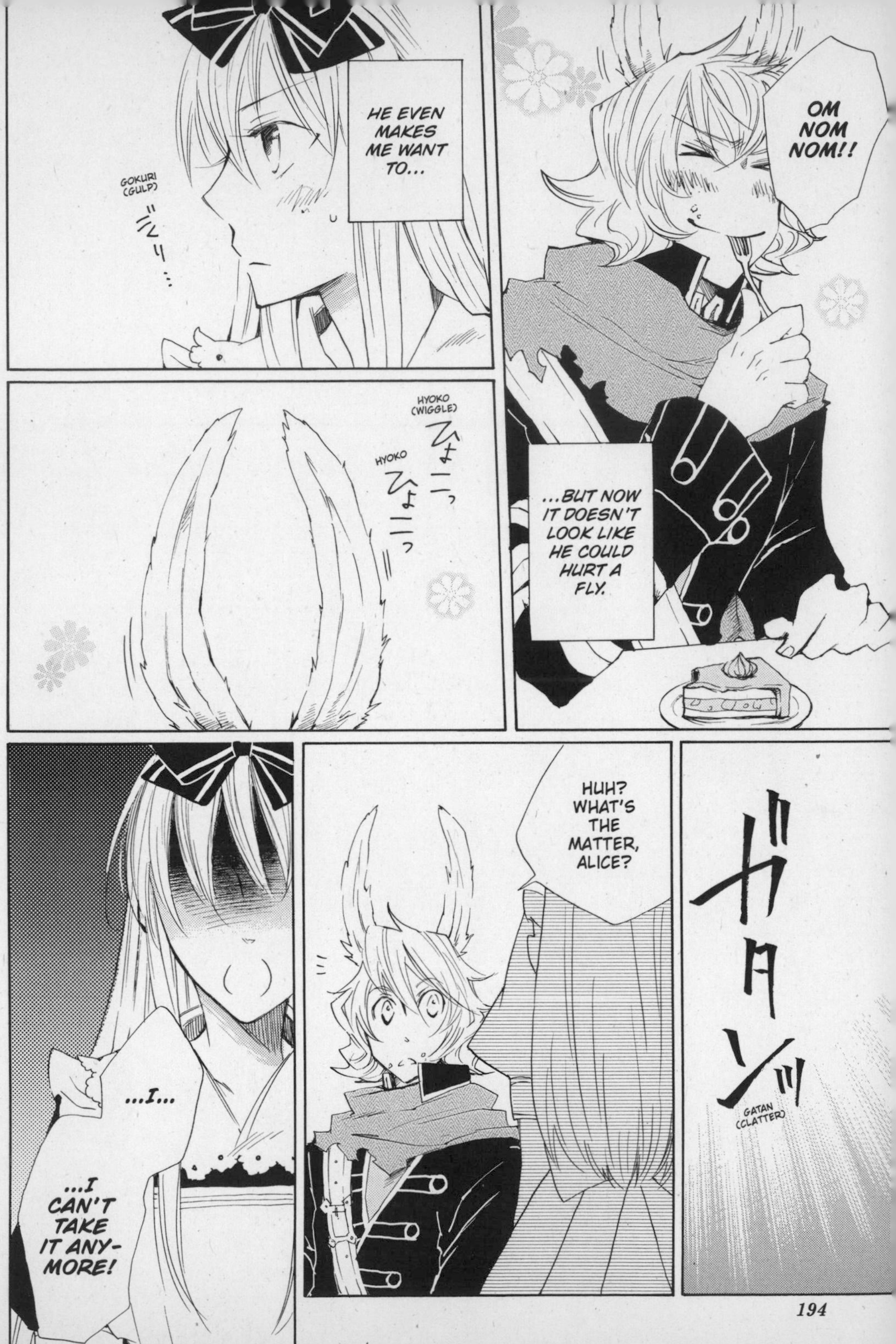
OM NOM NOM!!
...BUT NOW IT DOESN'T LOOK LIKE HE COULD HURT A FLY.
HE EVEN MAKES ME WANT TO...
GOKURI (GULP)
ゴクリ…
HYOKO (WIGGLE)
ぴょこっ
HYOKO
ぴょこっ
ガタンッ
GATAN (CLATTER)
HUH? WHAT'S THE MATTER, ALICE?
...I...
...I CAN'T TAKE IT ANY-MORE!

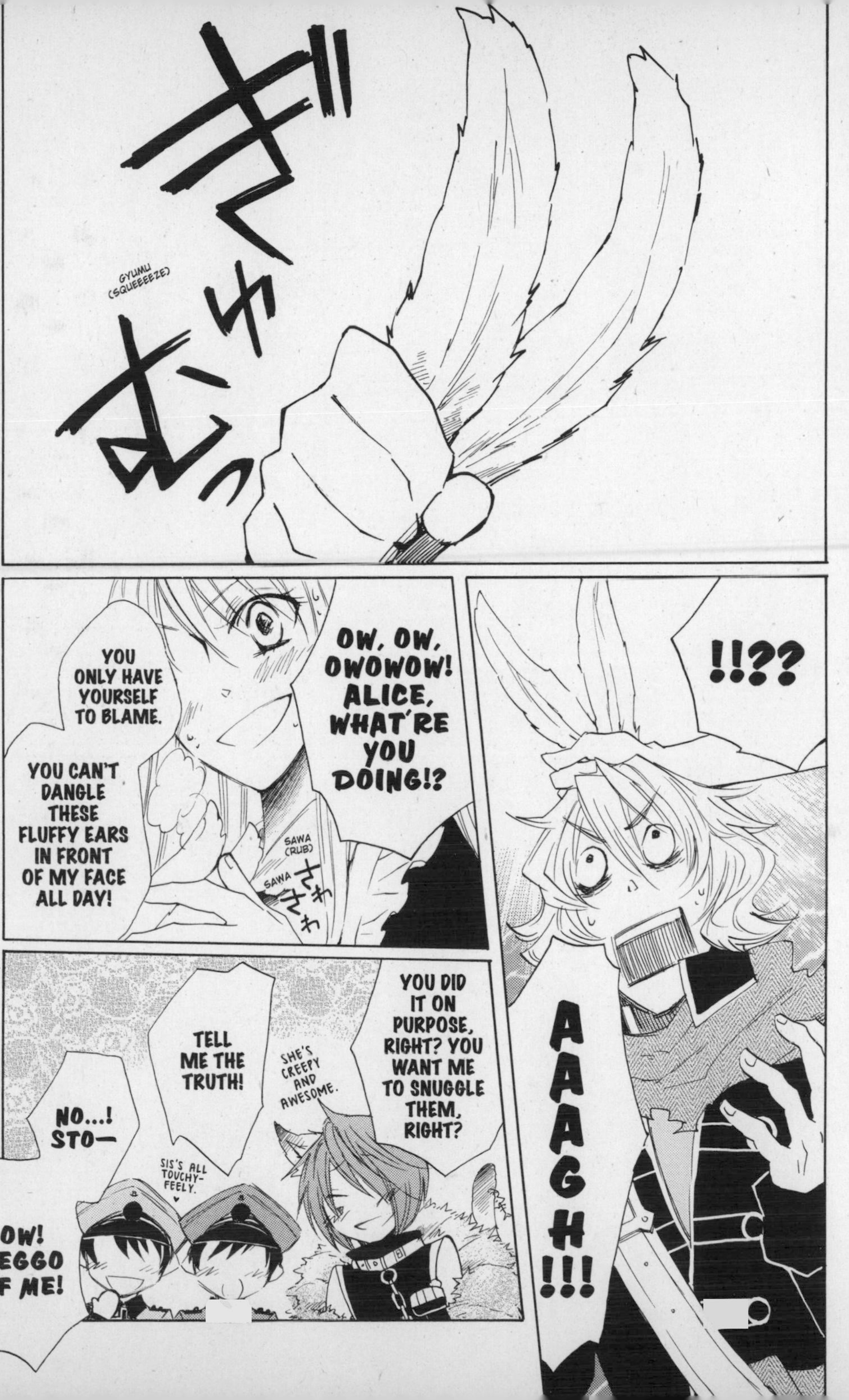
ぎゅむっ
GYUMU (SQUEEEEZE)
!!??
AAAGH!!!
OW, OW, OWOWOW! ALICE, WHAT'RE YOU DOING!?
YOU ONLY HAVE YOURSELF TO BLAME.
YOU CAN'T DANGLE THESE FLUFFY EARS IN FRONT OF MY FACE ALL DAY!
さわさわ
SAWA (RUB) SAWA
YOU DID IT ON PURPOSE, RIGHT? YOU WANT ME TO SNUGGLE THEM, RIGHT?
TELL ME THE TRUTH!
SHE'S CREEPY AND AWESOME.
NO...! STO—
SIS'S ALL TOUCHY-FEELY.
OW! LEGGO OF ME!

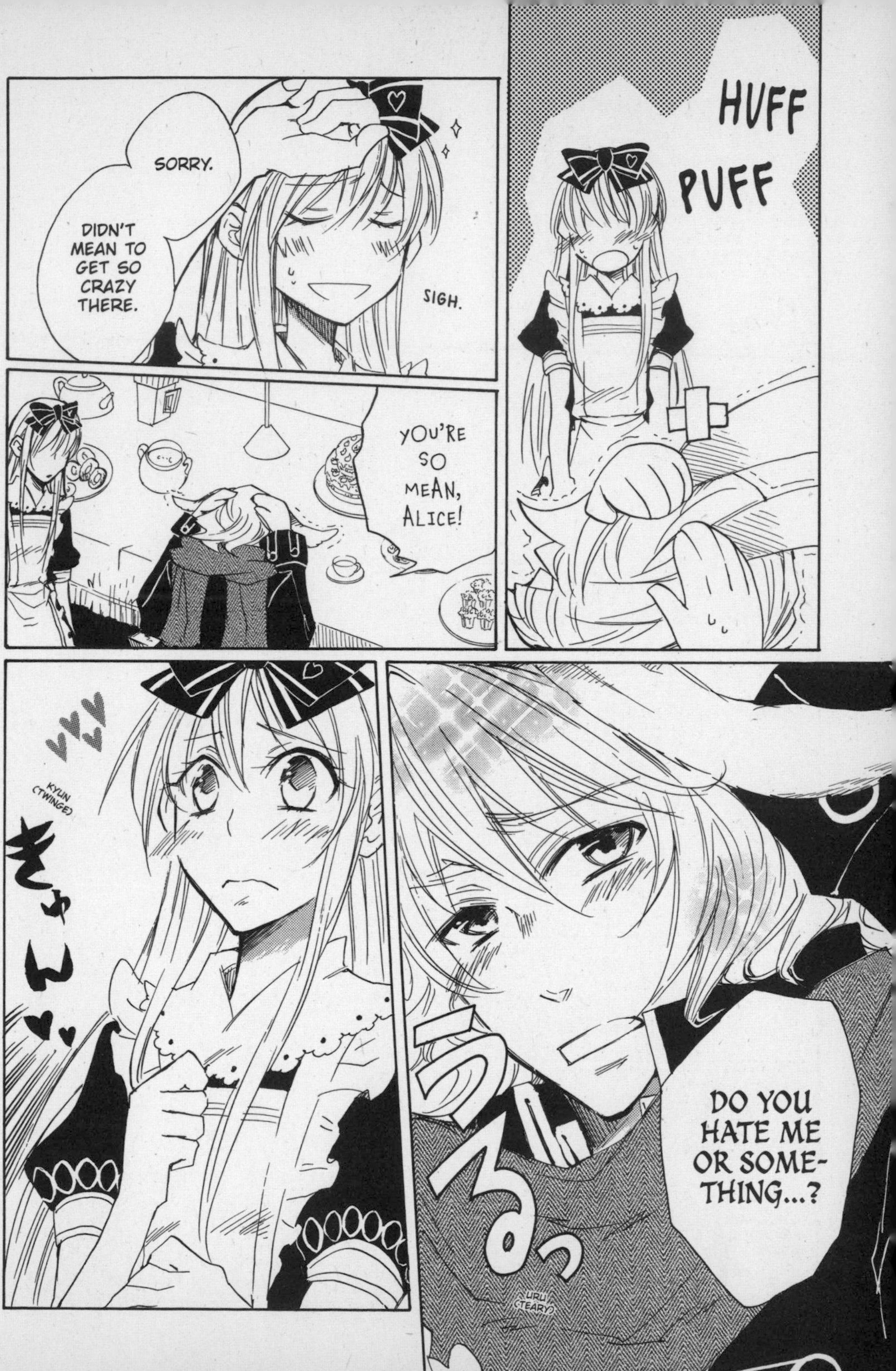
HUFF
PUFF
SORRY.
DIDN'T MEAN TO GET SO CRAZY THERE.
SIGH.
YOU'RE SO MEAN, ALICE!
DO YOU HATE ME OR SOME-THING...?
うるっ
URU (TEARY)
KYUN (TWINGE)
きゅん

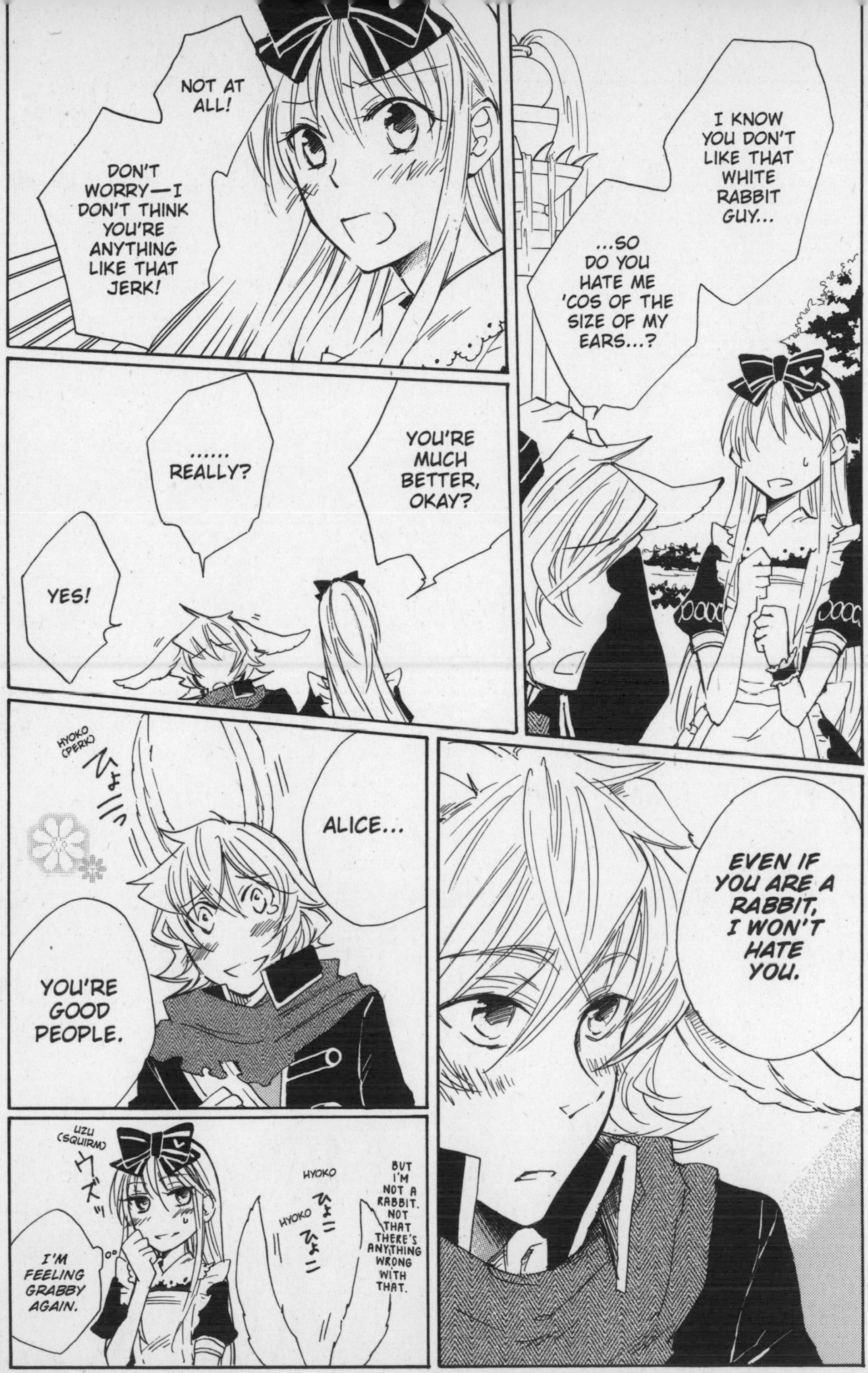
I KNOW YOU DON'T LIKE THAT WHITE RABBIT GUY...
...SO DO YOU HATE ME 'COS OF THE SIZE OF MY EARS...?
NOT AT ALL!
DON'T WORRY—I DON'T THINK YOU'RE ANYTHING LIKE THAT JERK!
YOU'RE MUCH BETTER, OKAY?
......REALLY?
YES!
EVEN IF YOU ARE A RABBIT, I WON'T HATE YOU.
HYOKO (PERK)
ALICE...
YOU'RE GOOD PEOPLE.
BUT I'M NOT A RABBIT. NOT THAT THERE'S ANYTHING WRONG WITH THAT.
HYOKO
HYOKO
UZU (SQUIRM)
I'M FEELING GRABBY AGAIN.

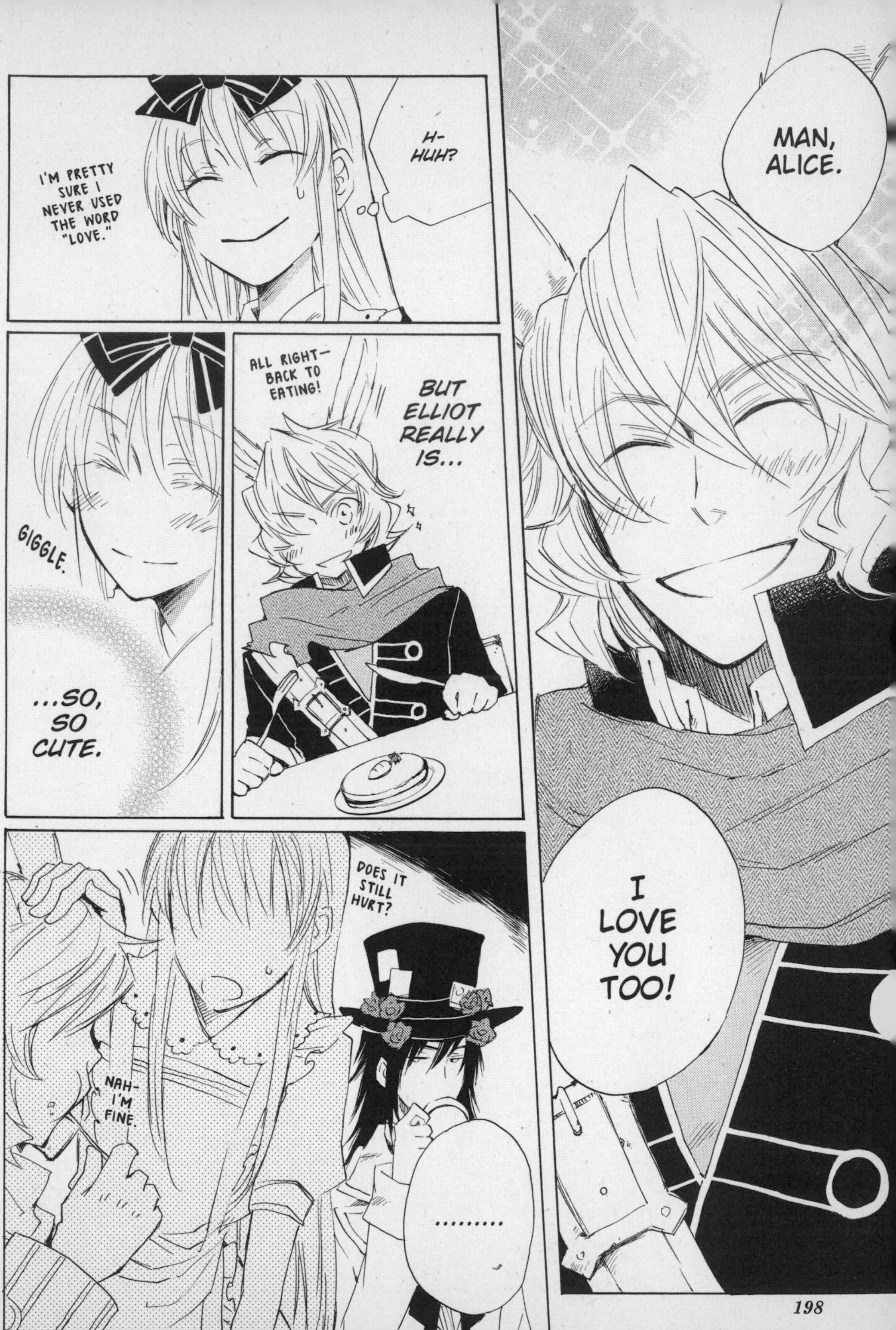
MAN, ALICE.
I LOVE YOU TOO!
H-HUH?
I'M PRETTY SURE I NEVER USED THE WORD "LOVE."
ALL RIGHT—BACK TO EATING!
BUT ELLIOT REALLY IS...
GIGGLE.
...SO, SO CUTE.
DOES IT STILL HURT?
NAH-I'M FINE.
....

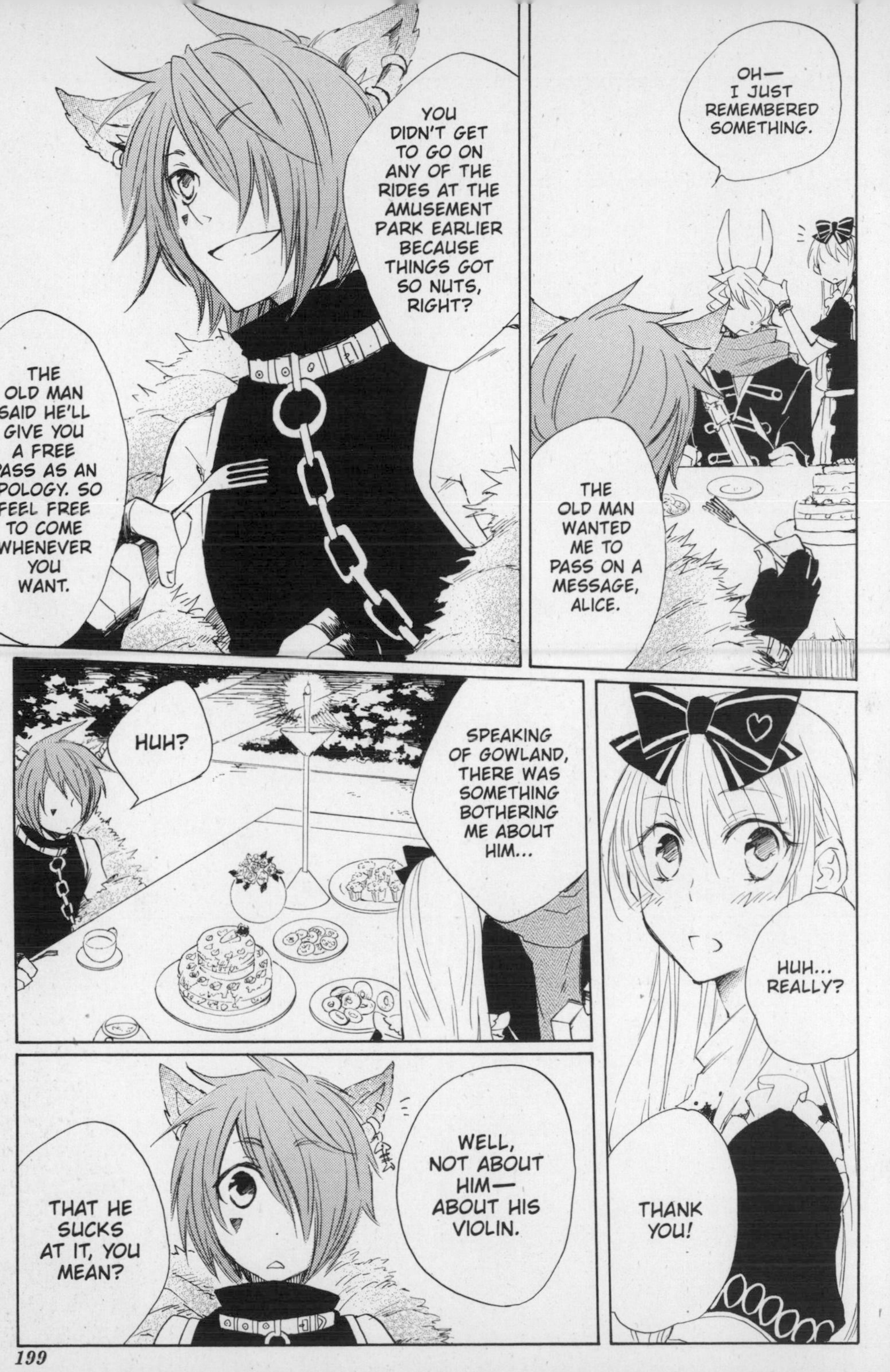
OH— I JUST REMEMBERED SOMETHING.
THE OLD MAN WANTED ME TO PASS ON A MESSAGE, ALICE.
YOU DIDN'T GET TO GO ON ANY OF THE RIDES AT THE AMUSEMENT PARK EARLIER BECAUSE THINGS GOT SO NUTS, RIGHT?
THE OLD MAN SAID HE'LL GIVE YOU A FREE PASS AS AN APOLOGY. SO FEEL FREE TO COME WHENEVER YOU WANT.
HUH... REALLY?
THANK YOU!
SPEAKING OF GOWLAND, THERE WAS SOMETHING BOTHERING ME ABOUT HIM...
HUH?
WELL, NOT ABOUT HIM—ABOUT HIS VIOLIN.
THAT HE SUCKS AT IT, YOU MEAN?

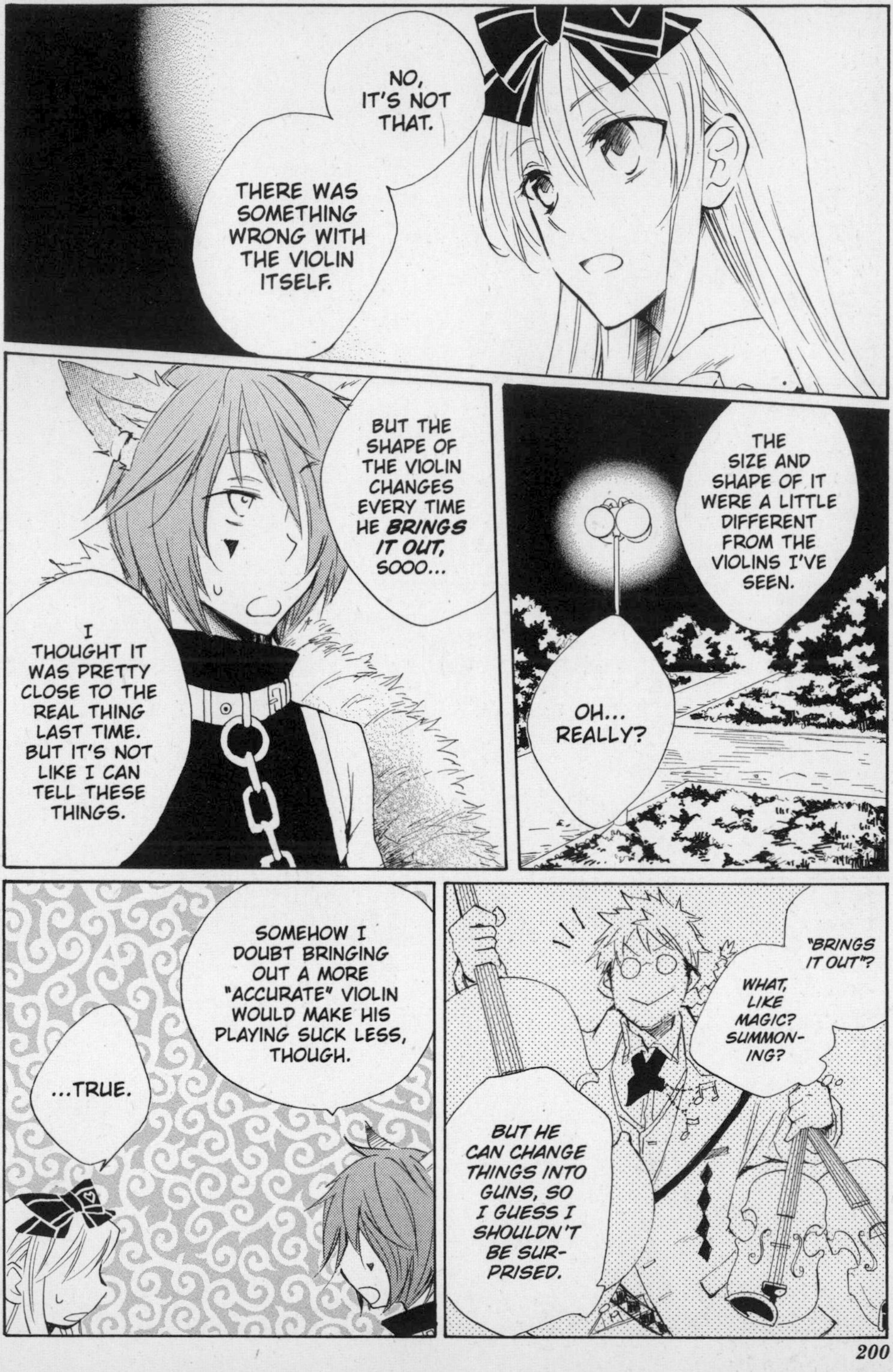
NO, IT'S NOT THAT.
THERE WAS SOMETHING WRONG WITH THE VIOLIN ITSELF.
THE SIZE AND SHAPE OF IT WERE A LITTLE DIFFERENT FROM THE VIOLINS I'VE SEEN.
OH... REALLY?
BUT THE SHAPE OF THE VIOLIN CHANGES EVERY TIME HE *BRINGS IT OUT,* SOOO...
I THOUGHT IT WAS PRETTY CLOSE TO THE REAL THING LAST TIME. BUT IT'S NOT LIKE I CAN TELL THESE THINGS.
"BRINGS IT OUT"?
WHAT, LIKE MAGIC? SUMMONING?
BUT HE CAN CHANGE THINGS INTO GUNS, SO I GUESS I SHOULDN'T BE SURPRISED.
SOMEHOW I DOUBT BRINGING OUT A MORE "ACCURATE" VIOLIN WOULD MAKE HIS PLAYING SUCK LESS, THOUGH.
...TRUE.

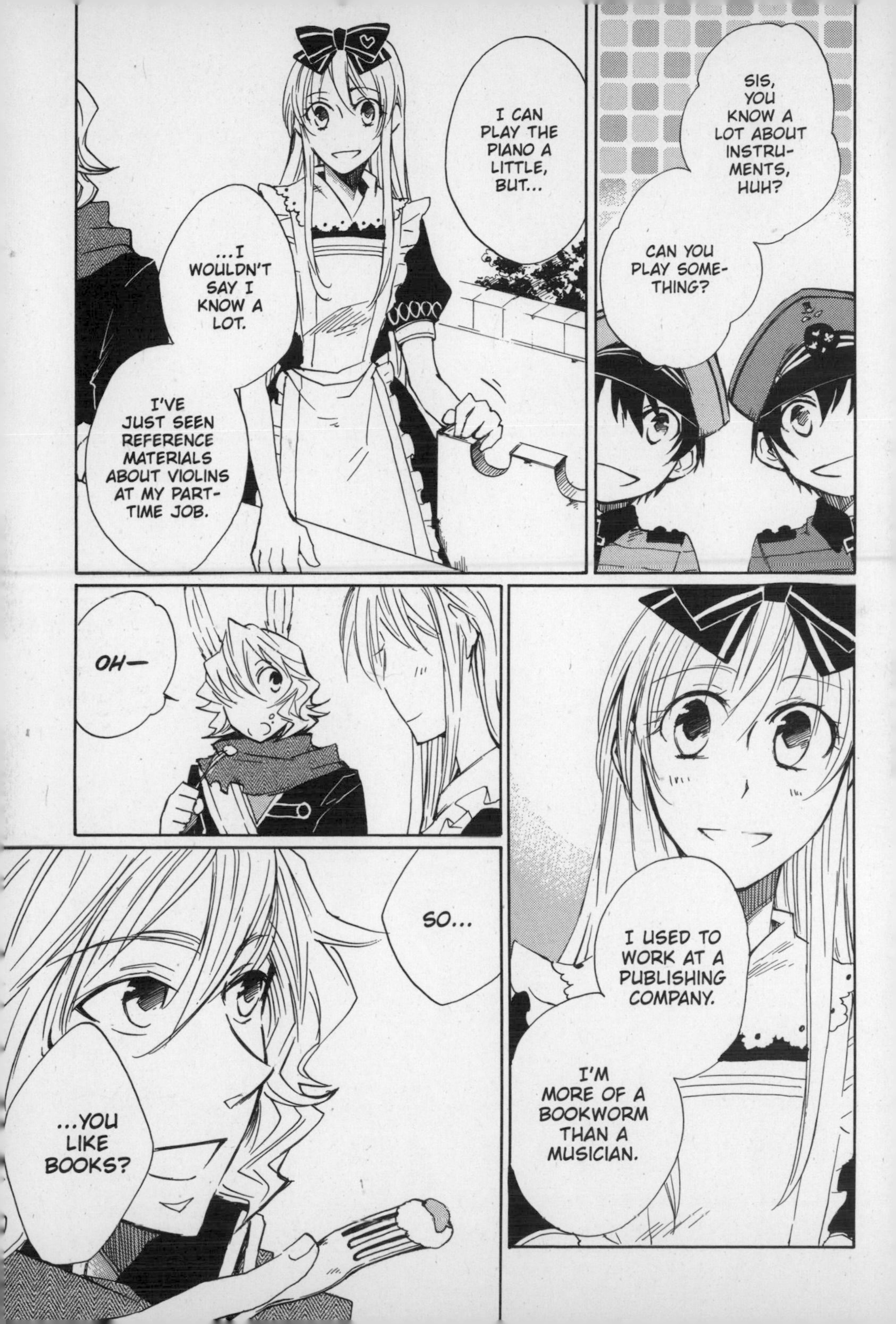
SIS, YOU KNOW A LOT ABOUT INSTRU-MENTS, HUH?
CAN YOU PLAY SOME-THING?
I CAN PLAY THE PIANO A LITTLE, BUT...
...I WOULDN'T SAY I KNOW A LOT.
I'VE JUST SEEN REFERENCE MATERIALS ABOUT VIOLINS AT MY PART-TIME JOB.
I USED TO WORK AT A PUBLISHING COMPANY.
I'M MORE OF A BOOKWORM THAN A MUSICIAN.
OH—
SO...
...YOU LIKE BOOKS?

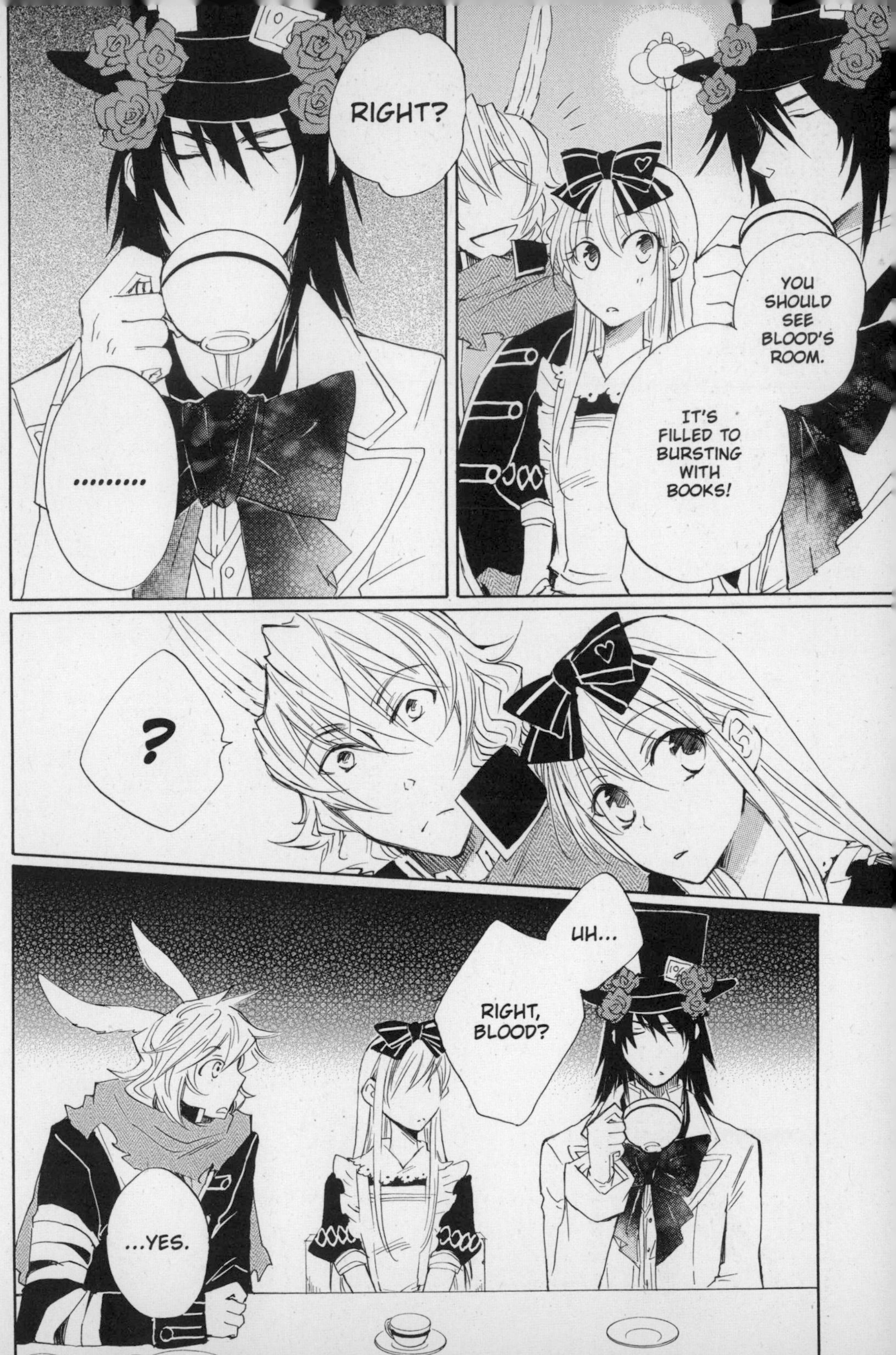
YOU SHOULD SEE BLOOD'S ROOM.
IT'S FILLED TO BURSTING WITH BOOKS!
RIGHT?
....
?
UH...
RIGHT, BLOOD?
...YES.

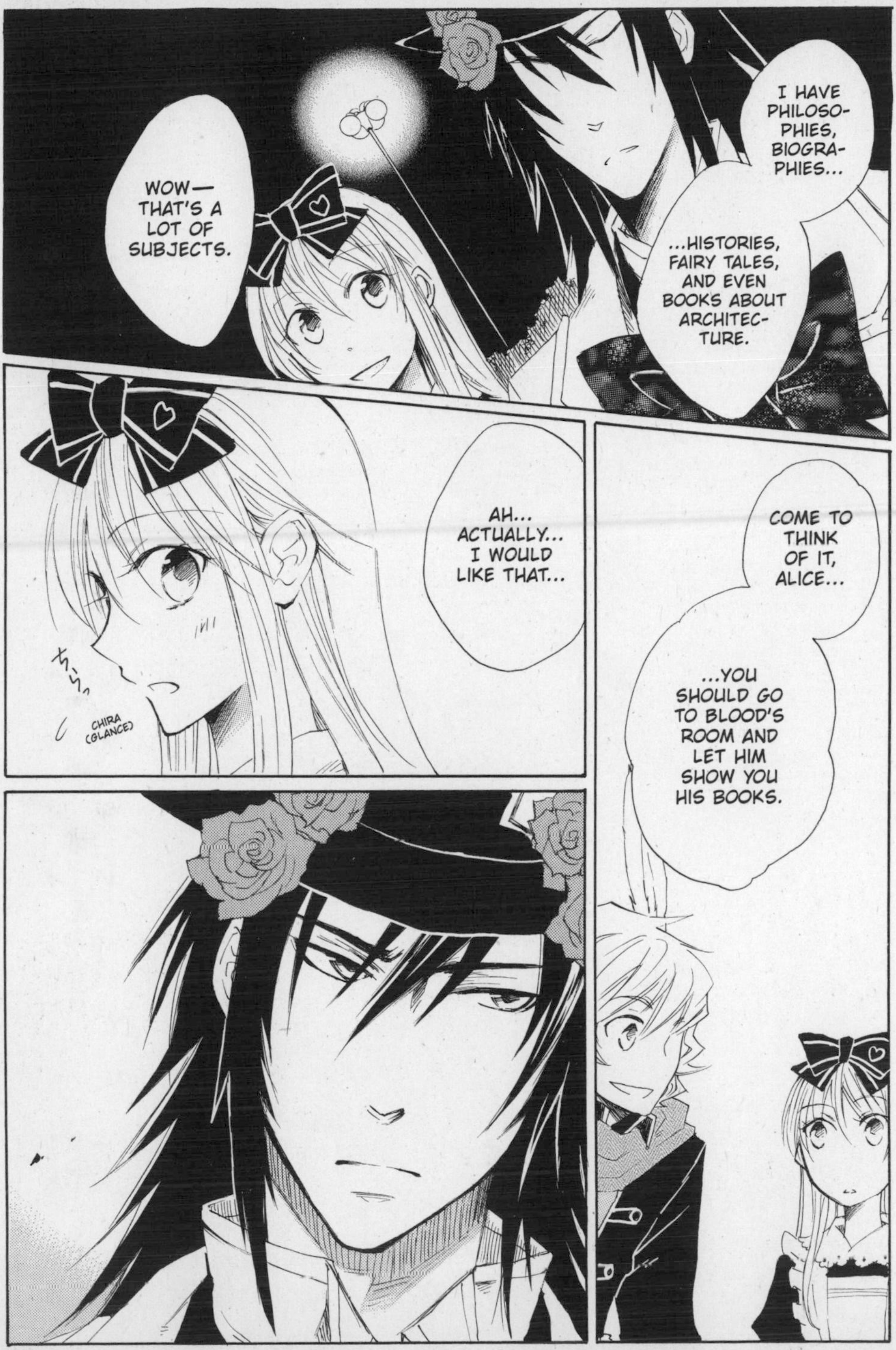
I HAVE PHILOSOPHIES, BIOGRAPHIES...
...HISTORIES, FAIRY TALES, AND EVEN BOOKS ABOUT ARCHITECTURE.
WOW— THAT'S A LOT OF SUBJECTS.
COME TO THINK OF IT, ALICE...
...YOU SHOULD GO TO BLOOD'S ROOM AND LET HIM SHOW YOU HIS BOOKS.
AH... ACTUALLY... I WOULD LIKE THAT...
CHIRA (GLANCE)

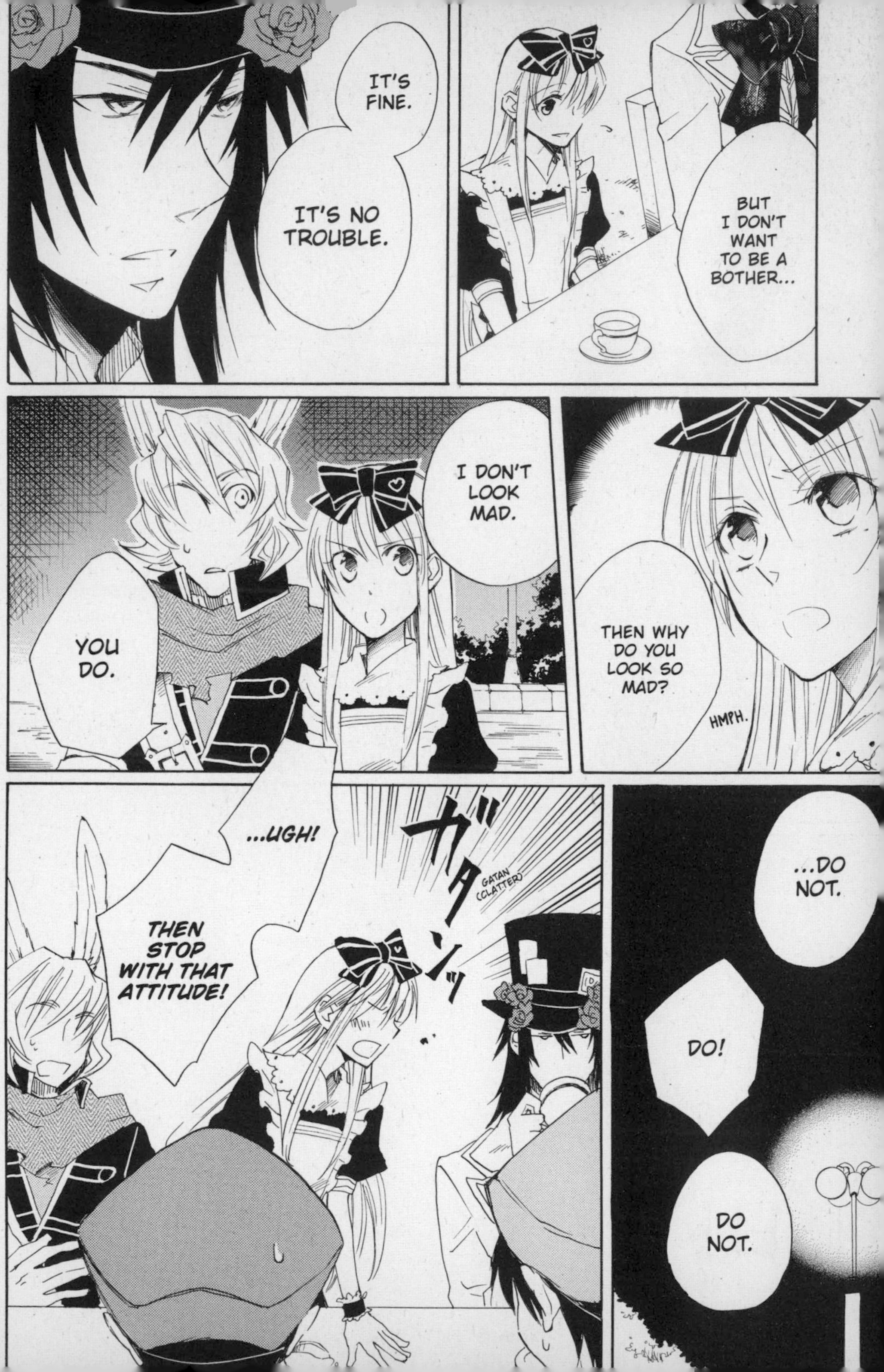
BUT I DON'T WANT TO BE A BOTHER...
IT'S FINE.
IT'S NO TROUBLE.
THEN WHY DO YOU LOOK SO MAD?
HMPH.
I DON'T LOOK MAD.
YOU DO.
...DO NOT.
DO!
DO NOT.
GATAN (CLATTER)
...UGH!
THEN STOP WITH THAT ATTITUDE!

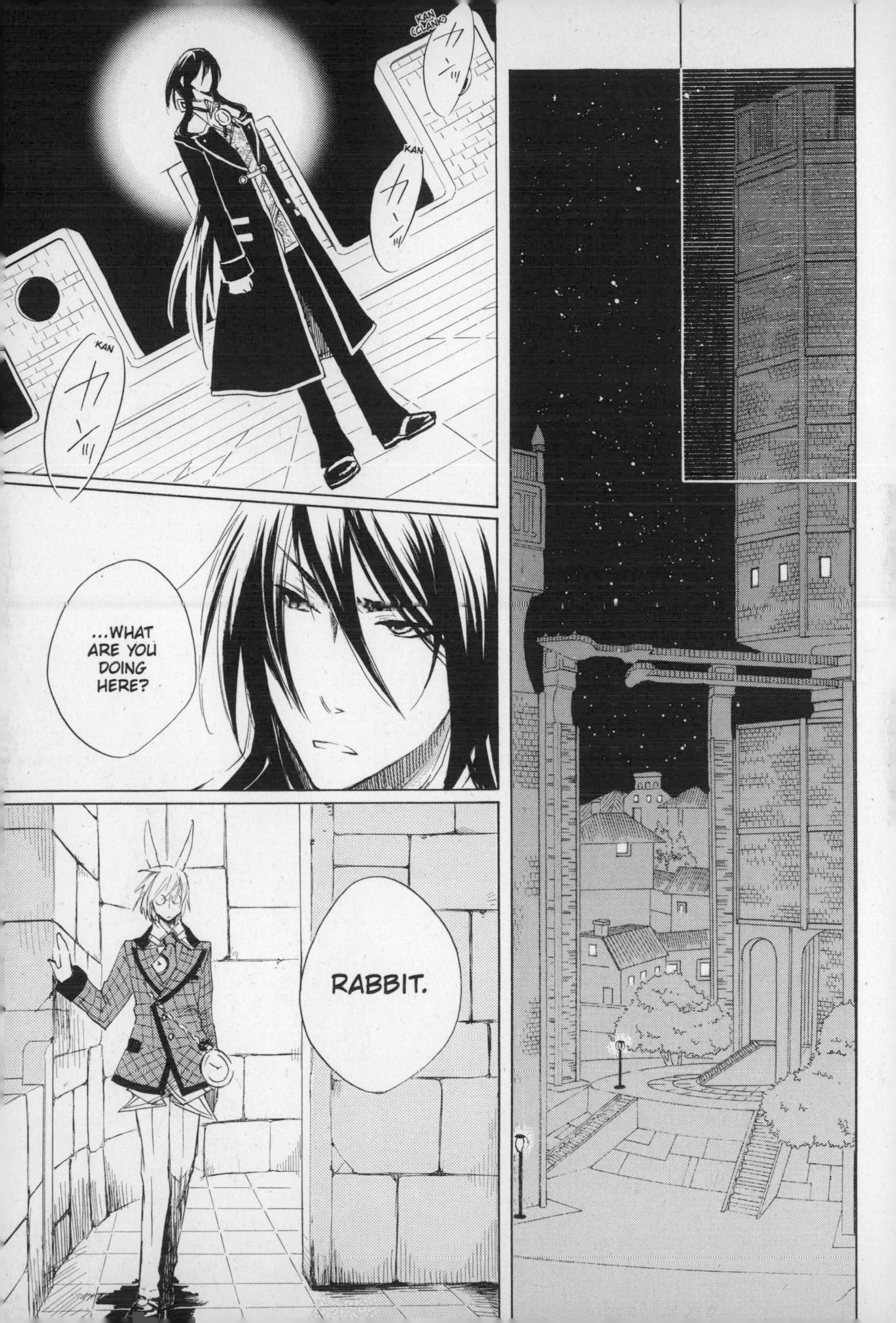
KAN (CLANK)
KAN
KAN
...WHAT ARE YOU DOING HERE?
RABBIT.

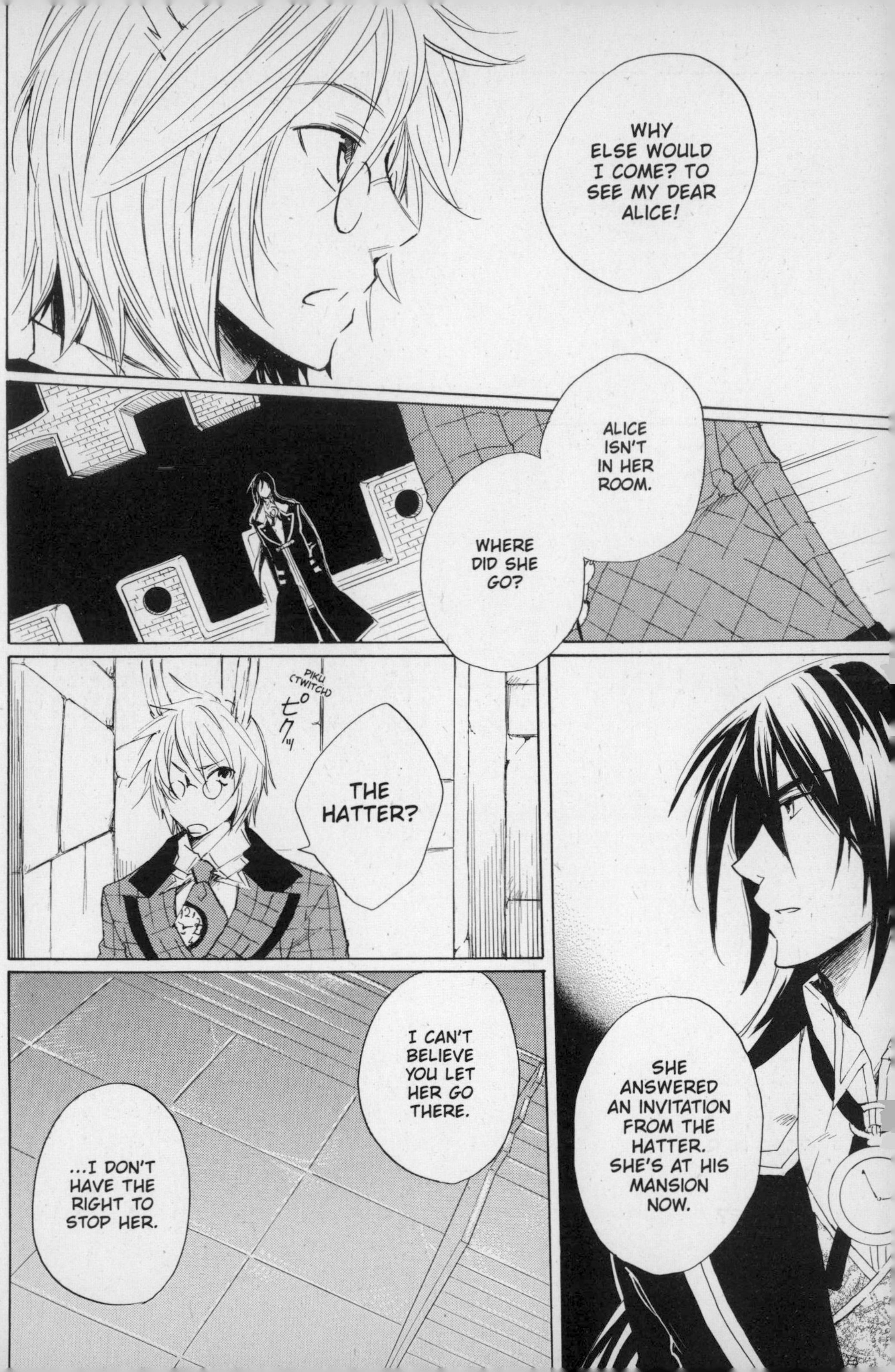
WHY ELSE WOULD I COME? TO SEE MY DEAR ALICE!
ALICE ISN'T IN HER ROOM.
WHERE DID SHE GO?
SHE ANSWERED AN INVITATION FROM THE HATTER. SHE'S AT HIS MANSION NOW.
PIKU (TWITCH)
THE HATTER?
I CAN'T BELIEVE YOU LET HER GO THERE.
...I DON'T HAVE THE RIGHT TO STOP HER.

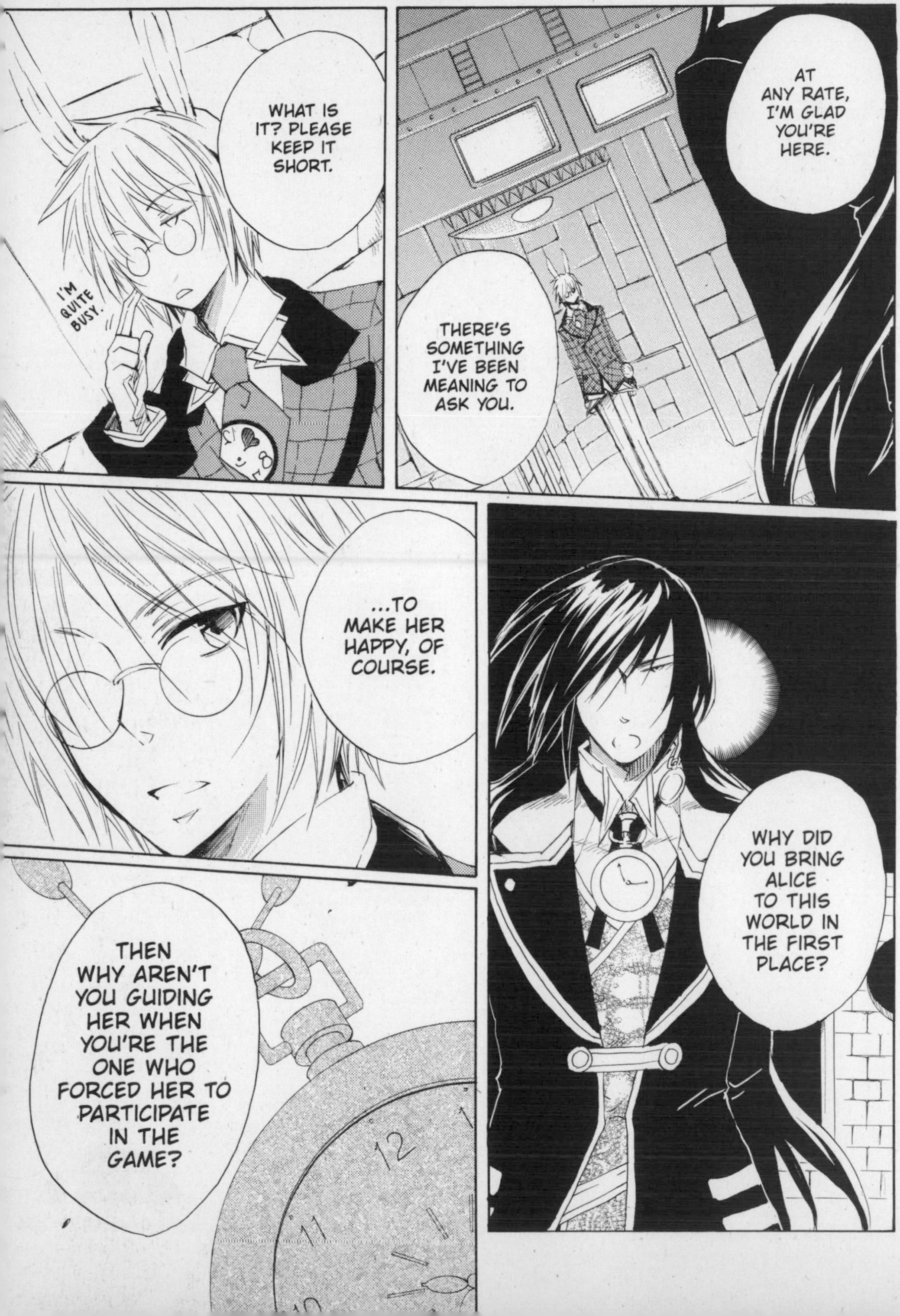
AT ANY RATE, I'M GLAD YOU'RE HERE.
THERE'S SOMETHING I'VE BEEN MEANING TO ASK YOU.
WHAT IS IT? PLEASE KEEP IT SHORT.
I'M QUITE BUSY.
WHY DID YOU BRING ALICE TO THIS WORLD IN THE FIRST PLACE?
...TO MAKE HER HAPPY, OF COURSE.
THEN WHY AREN'T YOU GUIDING HER WHEN YOU'RE THE ONE WHO FORCED HER TO PARTICIPATE IN THE GAME?

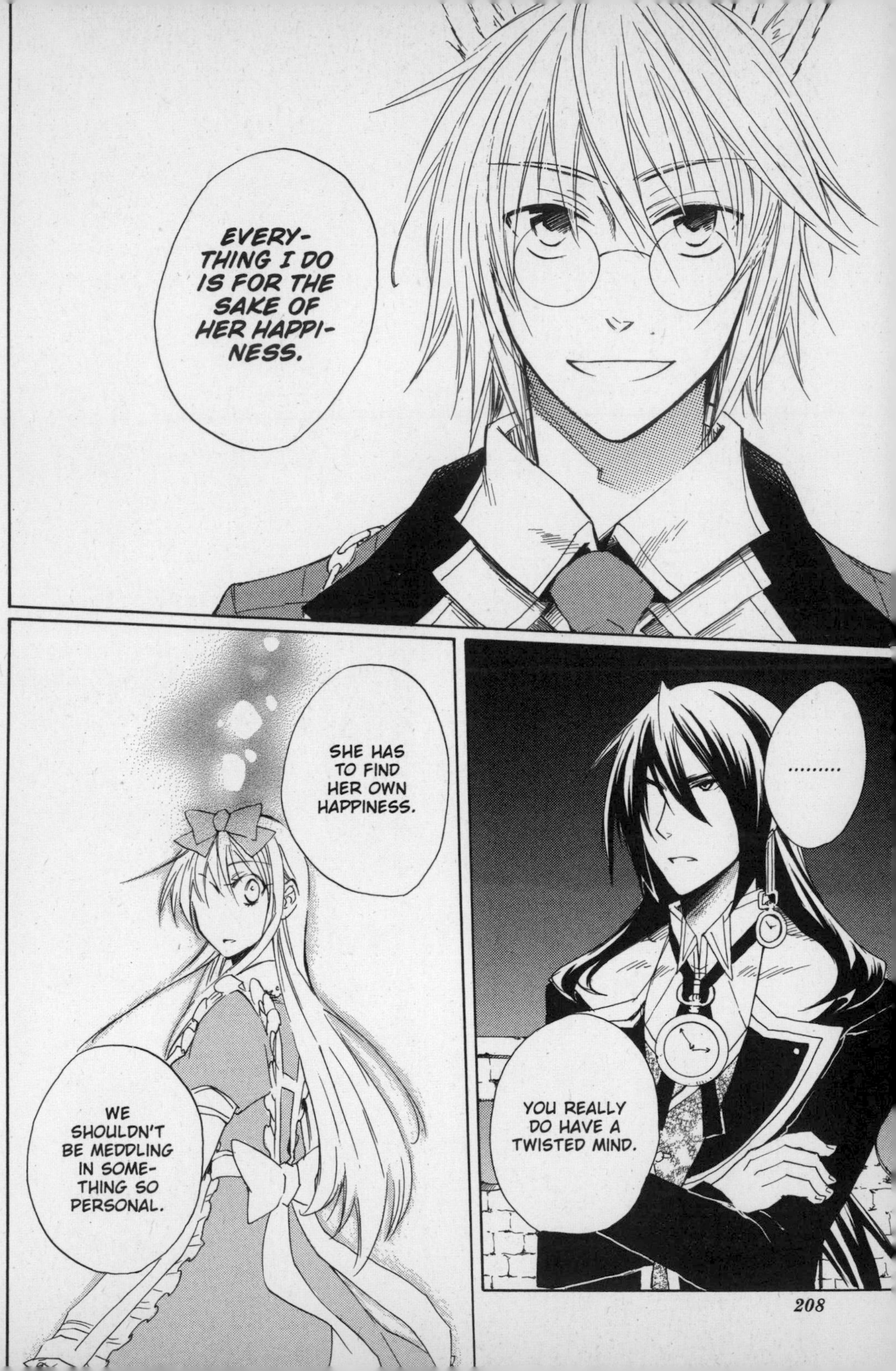
EVERYTHING I DO IS FOR THE SAKE OF HER HAPPINESS.
....
YOU REALLY DO HAVE A TWISTED MIND.
SHE HAS TO FIND HER OWN HAPPINESS.
WE SHOULDN'T BE MEDDLING IN SOMETHING SO PERSONAL.

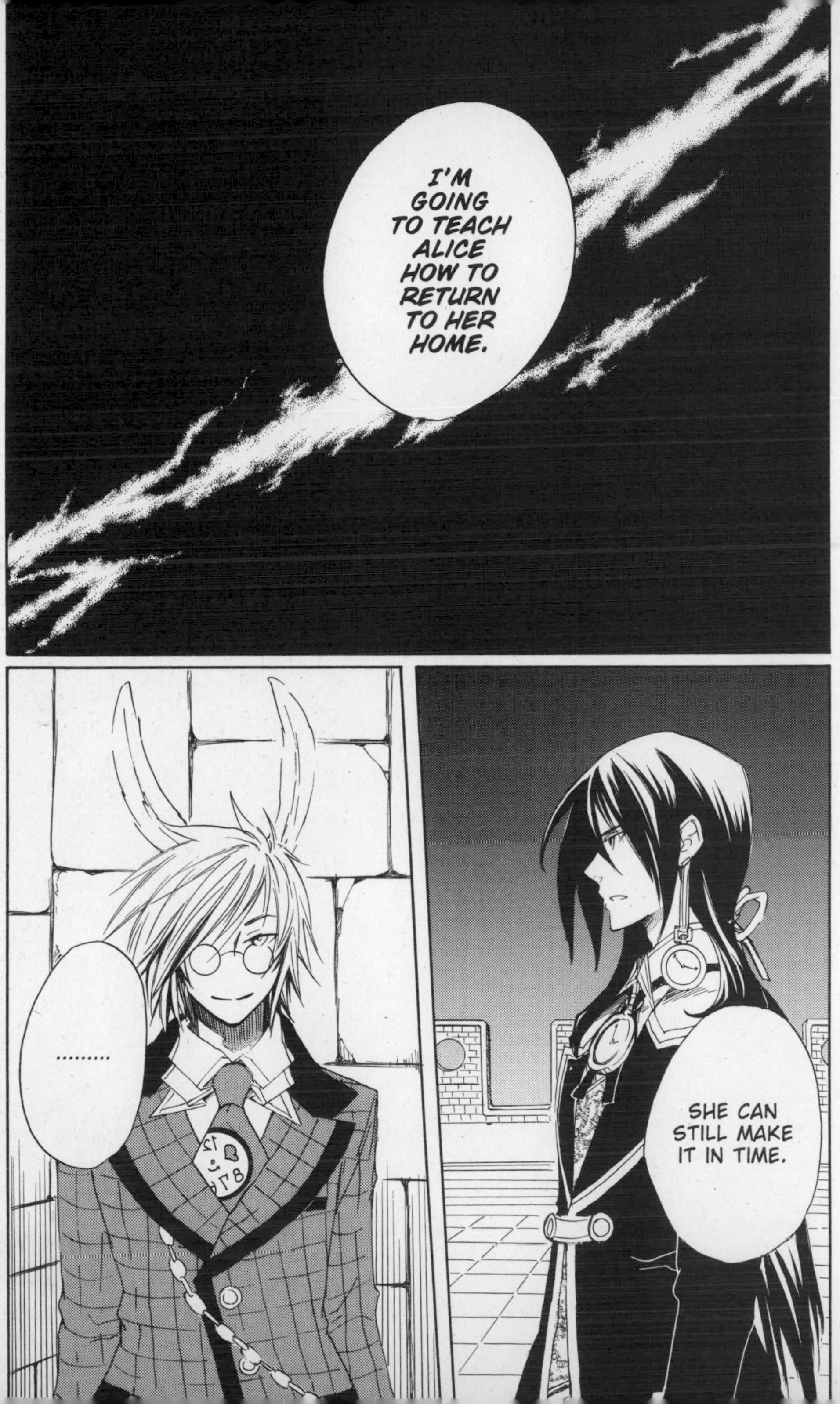
I'M GOING TO TEACH ALICE HOW TO RETURN TO HER HOME.
SHE CAN STILL MAKE IT IN TIME.
....

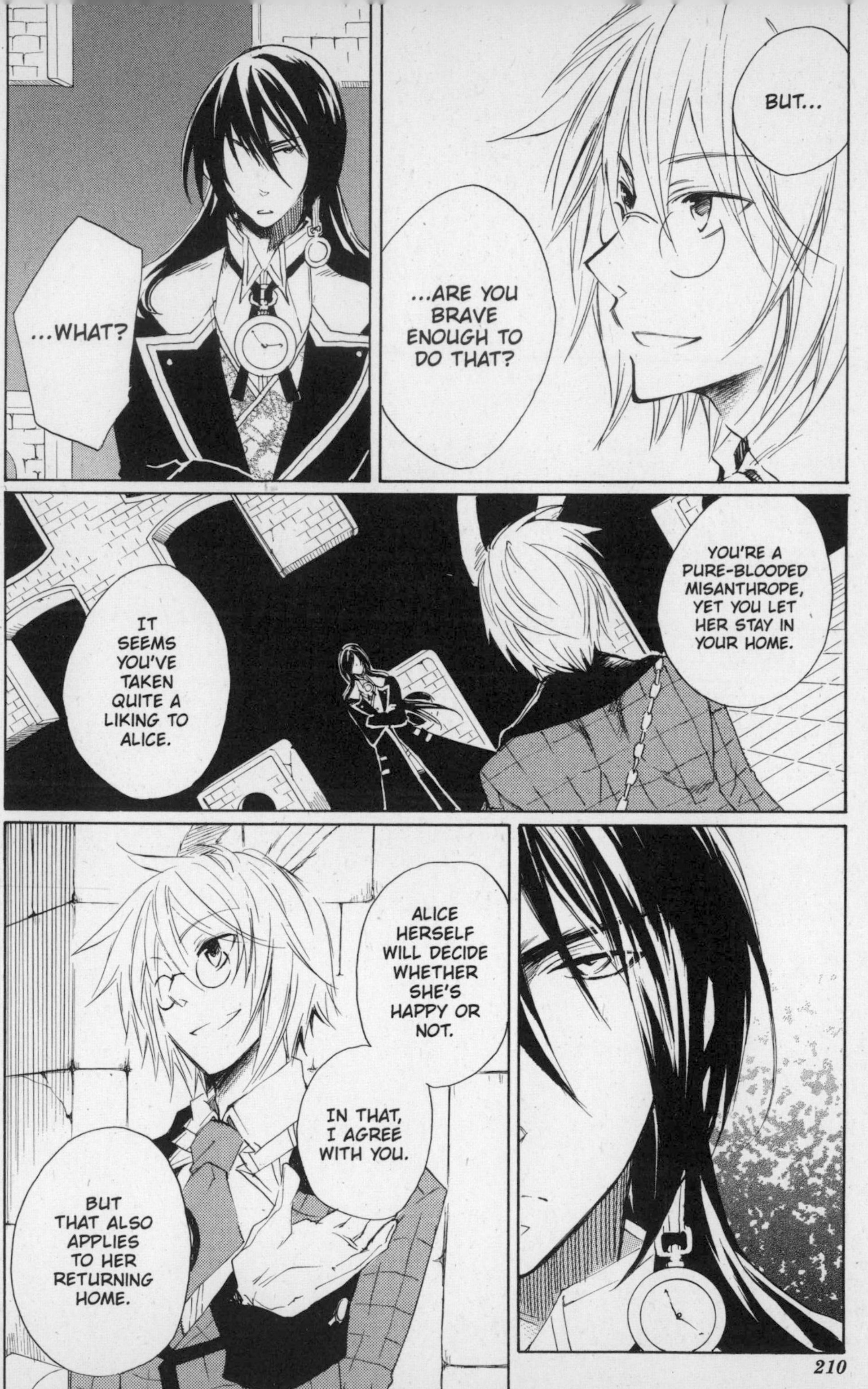
BUT...
...ARE YOU BRAVE ENOUGH TO DO THAT?
...WHAT?
YOU'RE A PURE-BLOODED MISANTHROPE, YET YOU LET HER STAY IN YOUR HOME.
IT SEEMS YOU'VE TAKEN QUITE A LIKING TO ALICE.
ALICE HERSELF WILL DECIDE WHETHER SHE'S HAPPY OR NOT.
IN THAT, I AGREE WITH YOU.
BUT THAT ALSO APPLIES TO HER RETURNING HOME.

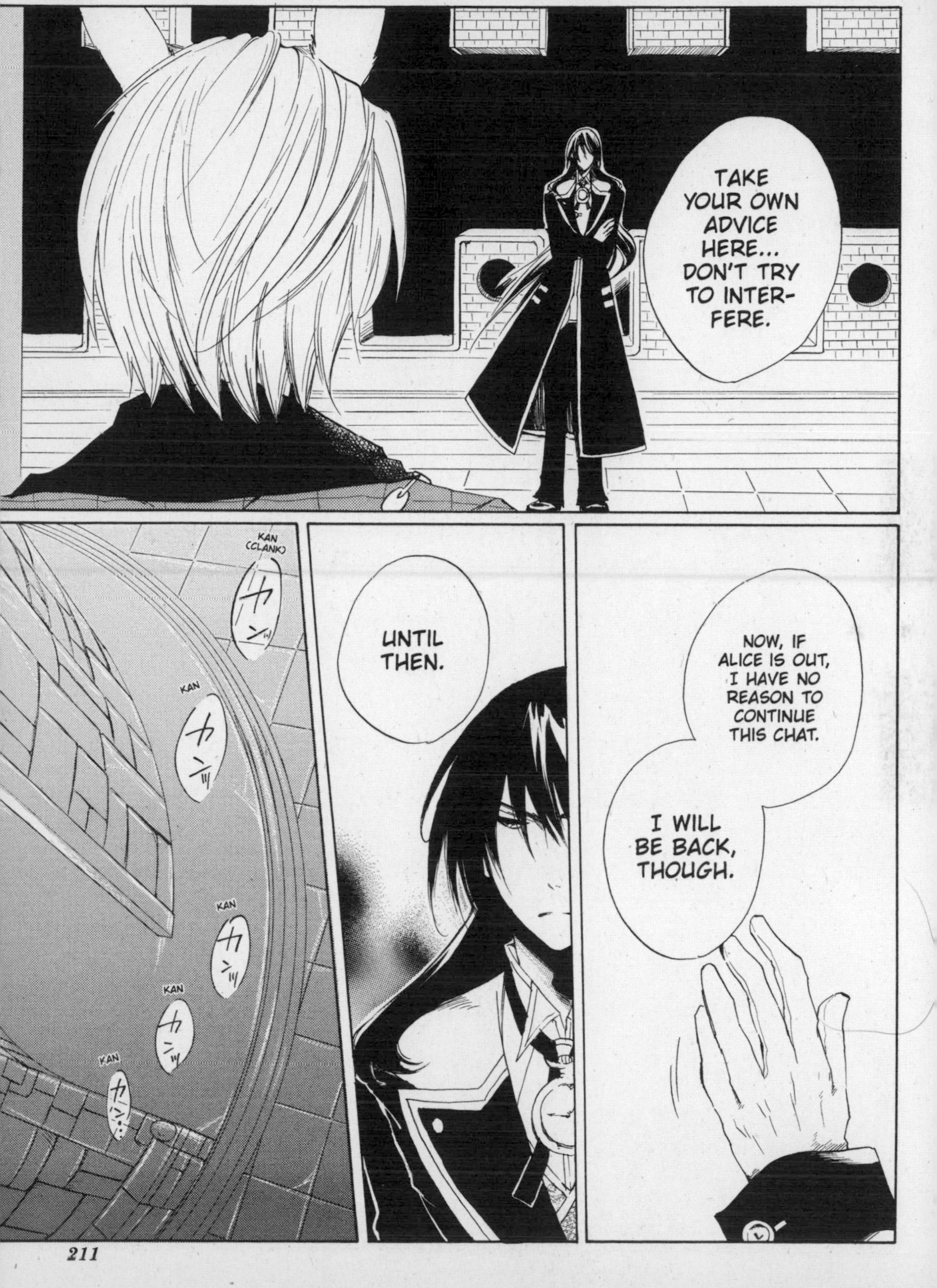
TAKE YOUR OWN ADVICE HERE... DON'T TRY TO INTERFERE.
NOW, IF ALICE IS OUT, I HAVE NO REASON TO CONTINUE THIS CHAT.
I WILL BE BACK, THOUGH.
UNTIL THEN.
KAN (CLANK)
カンッ
KAN
カンッ
KAN
カンッ
KAN
カンッ
KAN
カンッ…

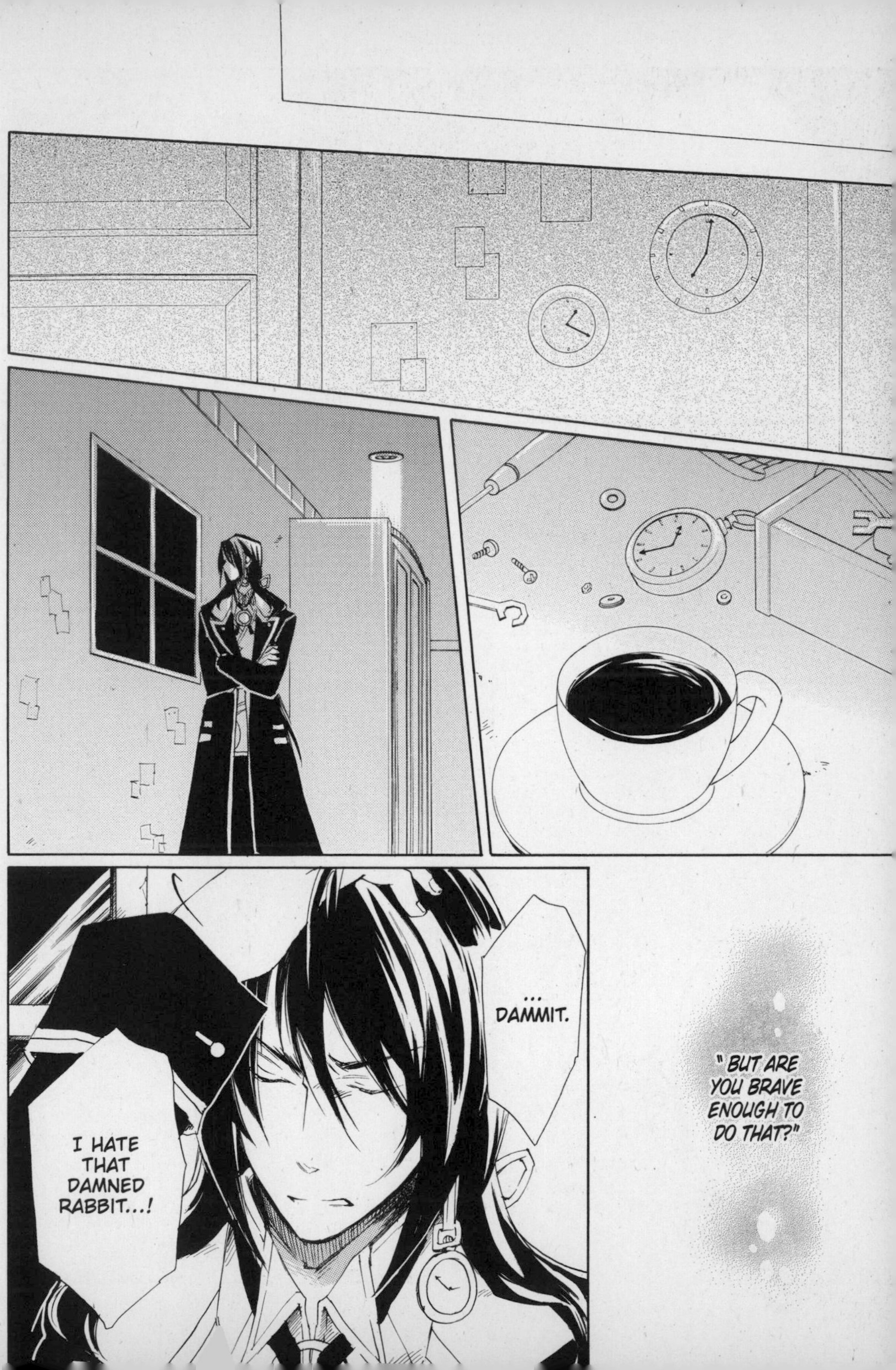
"BUT ARE YOU BRAVE ENOUGH TO DO THAT?"
...DAMMIT.
I HATE THAT DAMNED RABBIT...!

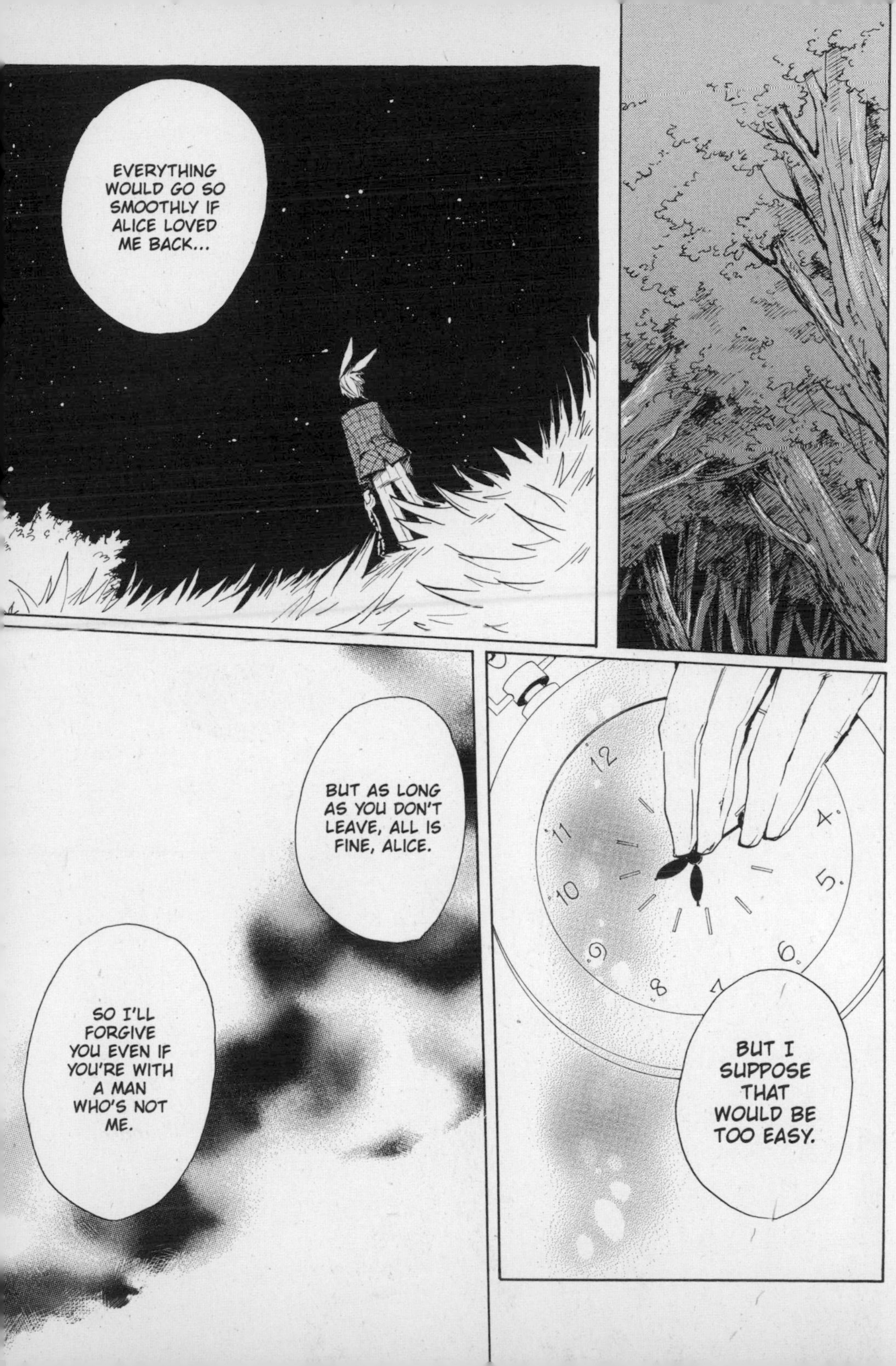
EVERYTHING WOULD GO SO SMOOTHLY IF ALICE LOVED ME BACK...
BUT I SUPPOSE THAT WOULD BE TOO EASY.
BUT AS LONG AS YOU DON'T LEAVE, ALL IS FINE, ALICE.
SO I'LL FORGIVE YOU EVEN IF YOU'RE WITH A MAN WHO'S NOT ME.

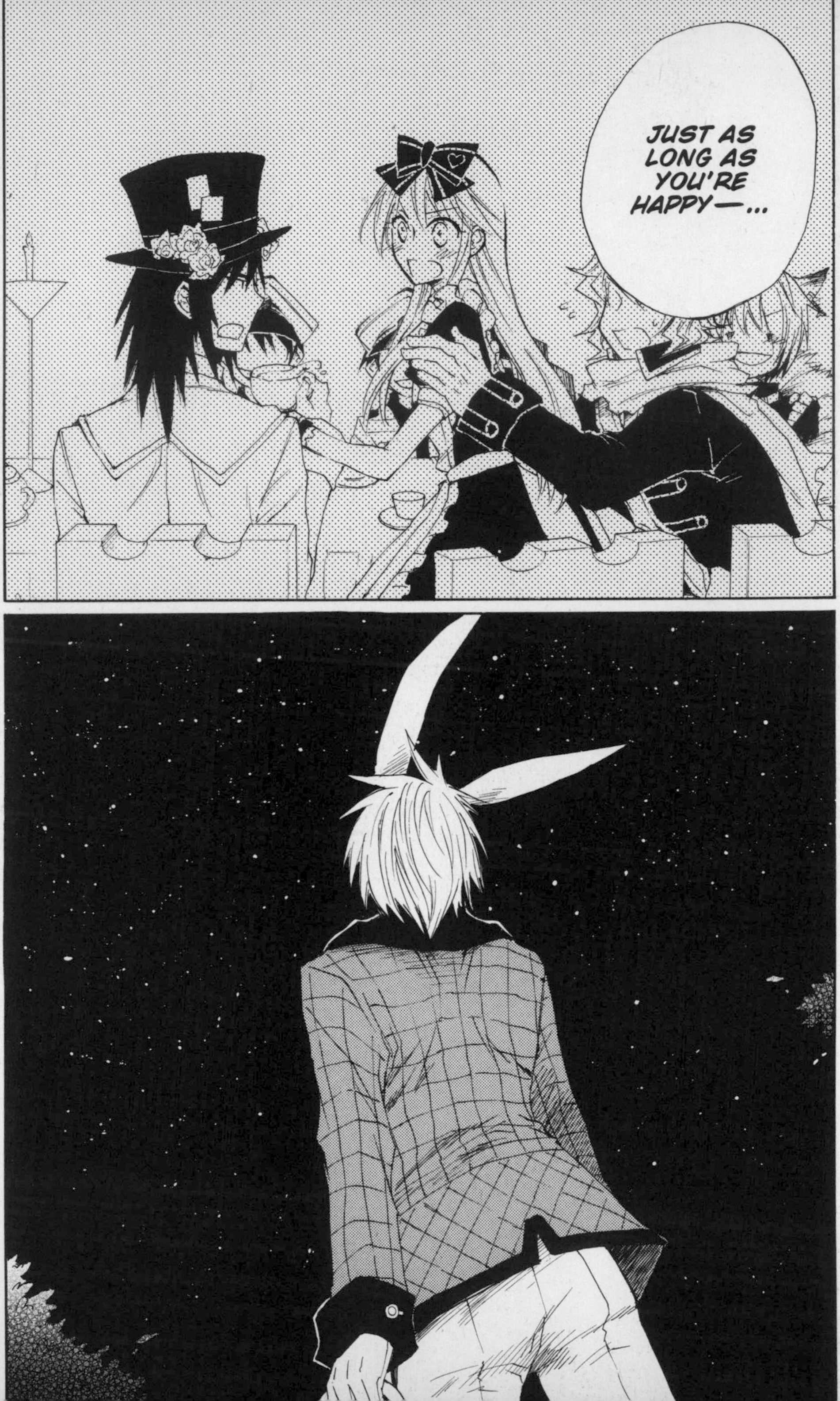
JUST AS LONG AS YOU'RE HAPPY—...

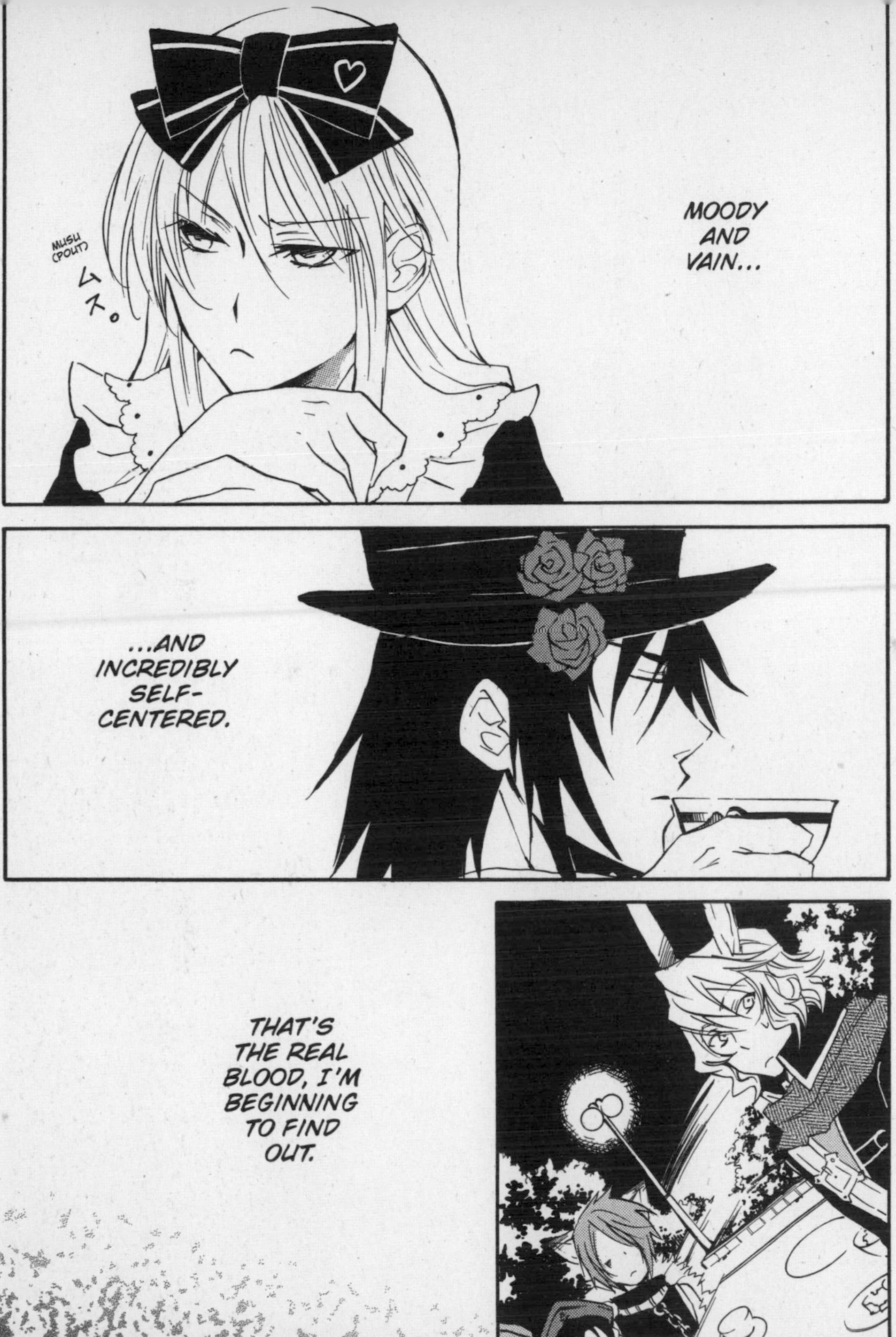
MOODY AND VAIN...
MUSU (POUT)
ムス。
...AND INCREDIBLY SELF-CENTERED.
THAT'S THE REAL BLOOD, I'M BEGINNING TO FIND OUT.

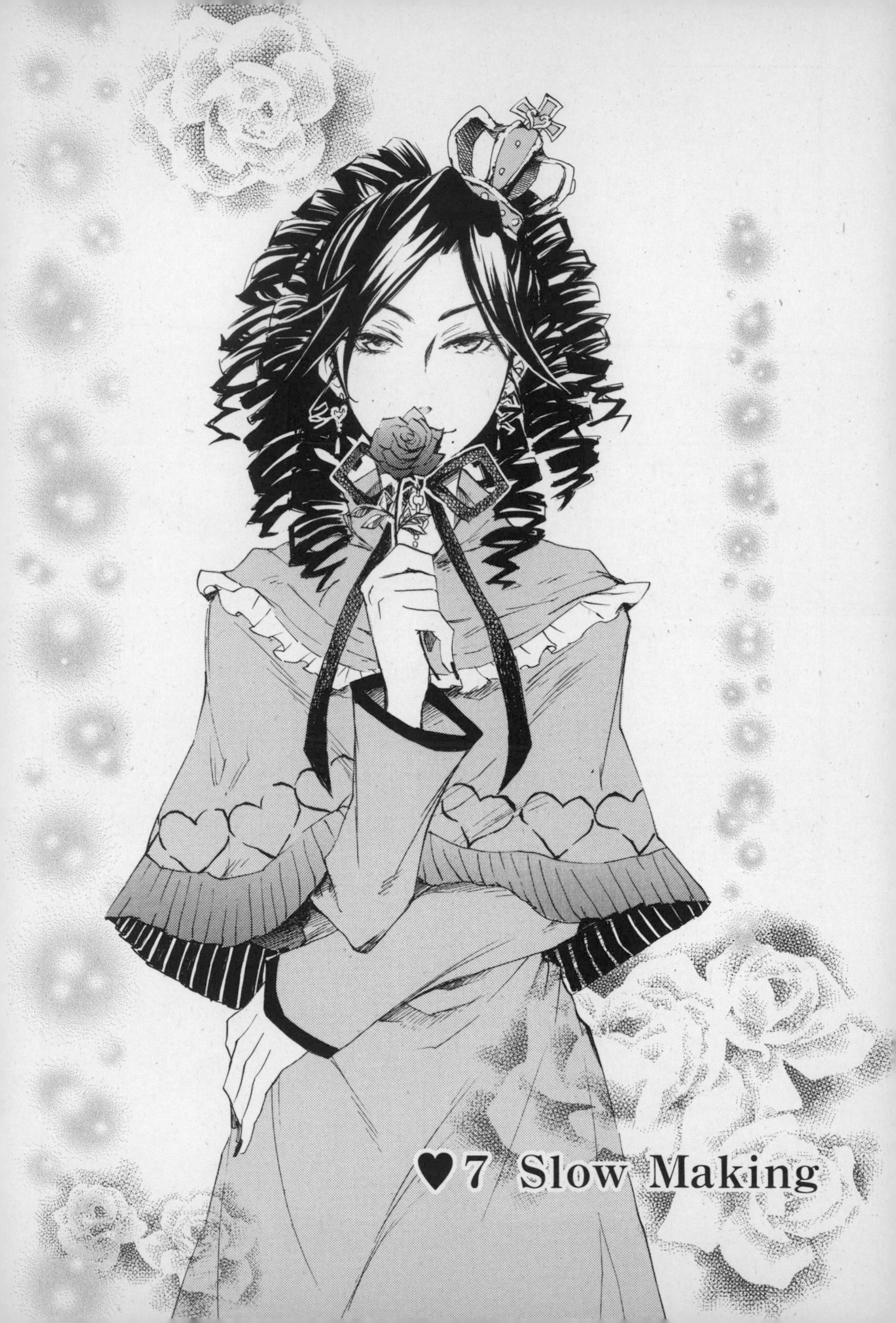
♥7 Slow Making

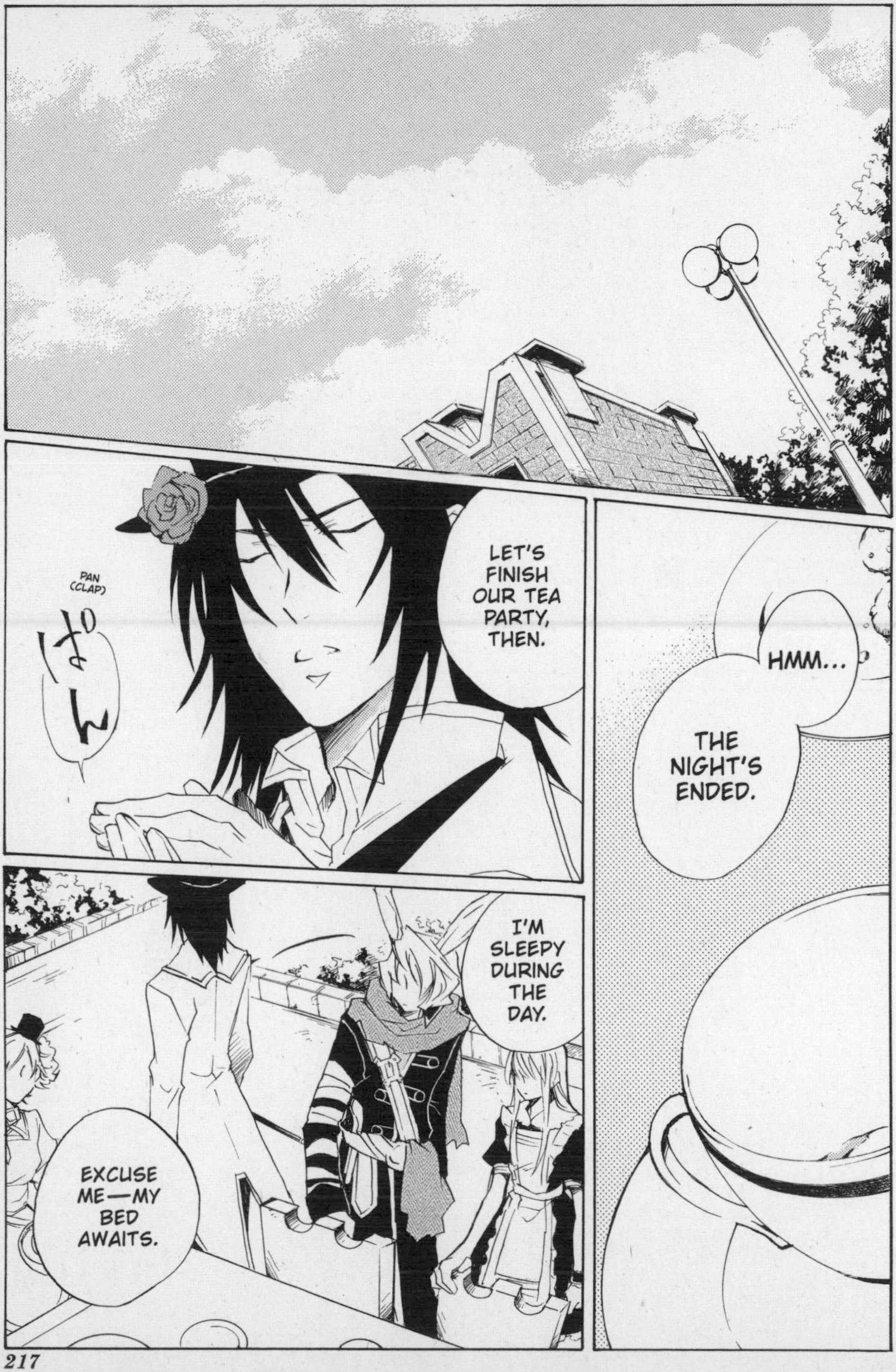
HMM...
THE NIGHT'S ENDED.
LET'S FINISH OUR TEA PARTY, THEN.
PAN (CLAP)
ぱん
I'M SLEEPY DURING THE DAY.
EXCUSE ME—MY BED AWAITS.

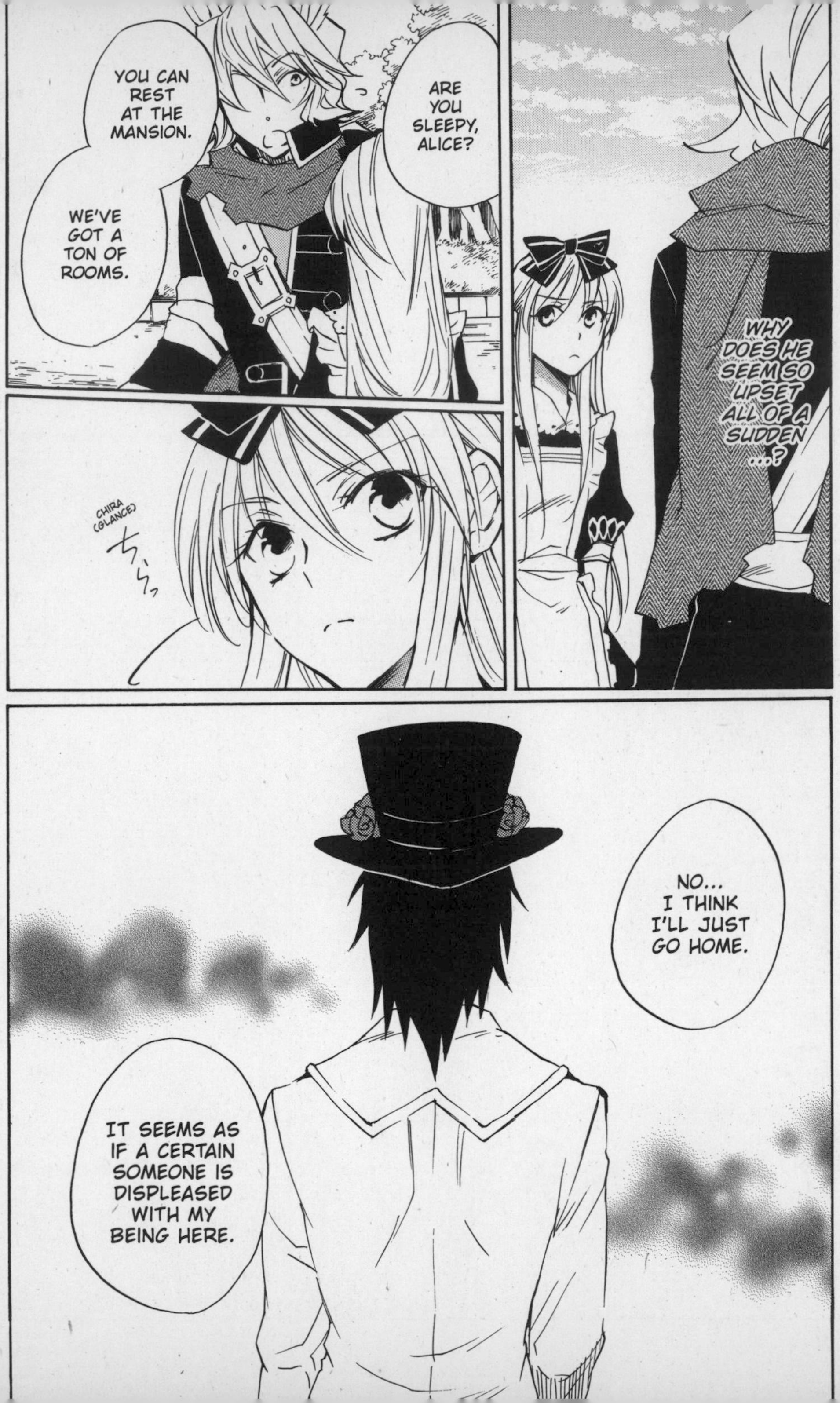
WHY DOES HE SEEM SO UPSET ALL OF A SUDDEN ...?
ARE YOU SLEEPY, ALICE?
YOU CAN REST AT THE MANSION.
WE'VE GOT A TON OF ROOMS.
CHIRA (GLANCE)
ちらっ
NO... I THINK I'LL JUST GO HOME.
IT SEEMS AS IF A CERTAIN SOMEONE IS DISPLEASED WITH MY BEING HERE.

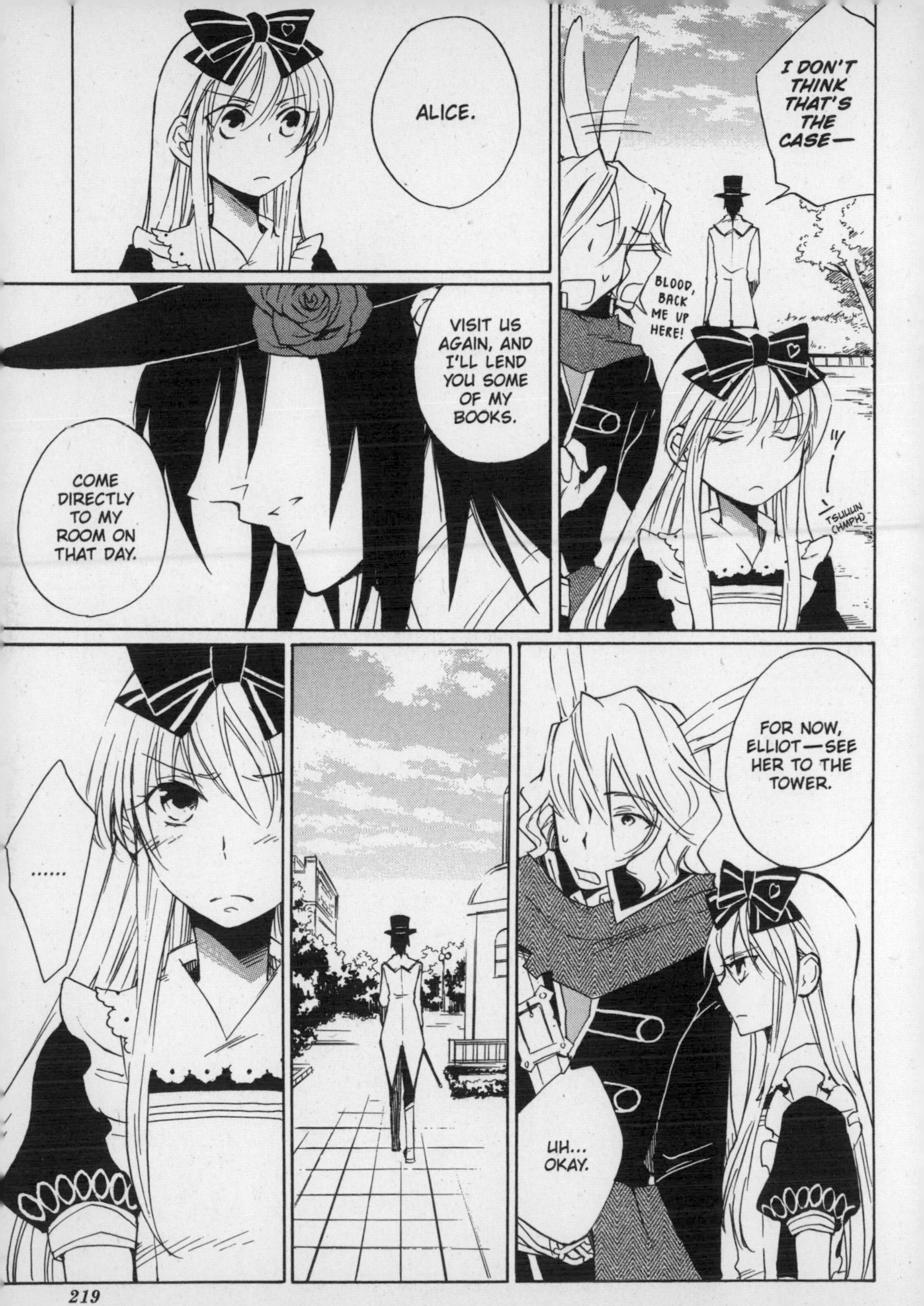
I DON'T THINK THAT'S THE CASE—
BLOOD, BACK ME UP HERE!
TSUUUN (HMPH)
ALICE.
VISIT US AGAIN, AND I'LL LEND YOU SOME OF MY BOOKS.
COME DIRECTLY TO MY ROOM ON THAT DAY.
FOR NOW, ELLIOT—SEE HER TO THE TOWER.
UH... OKAY.
......

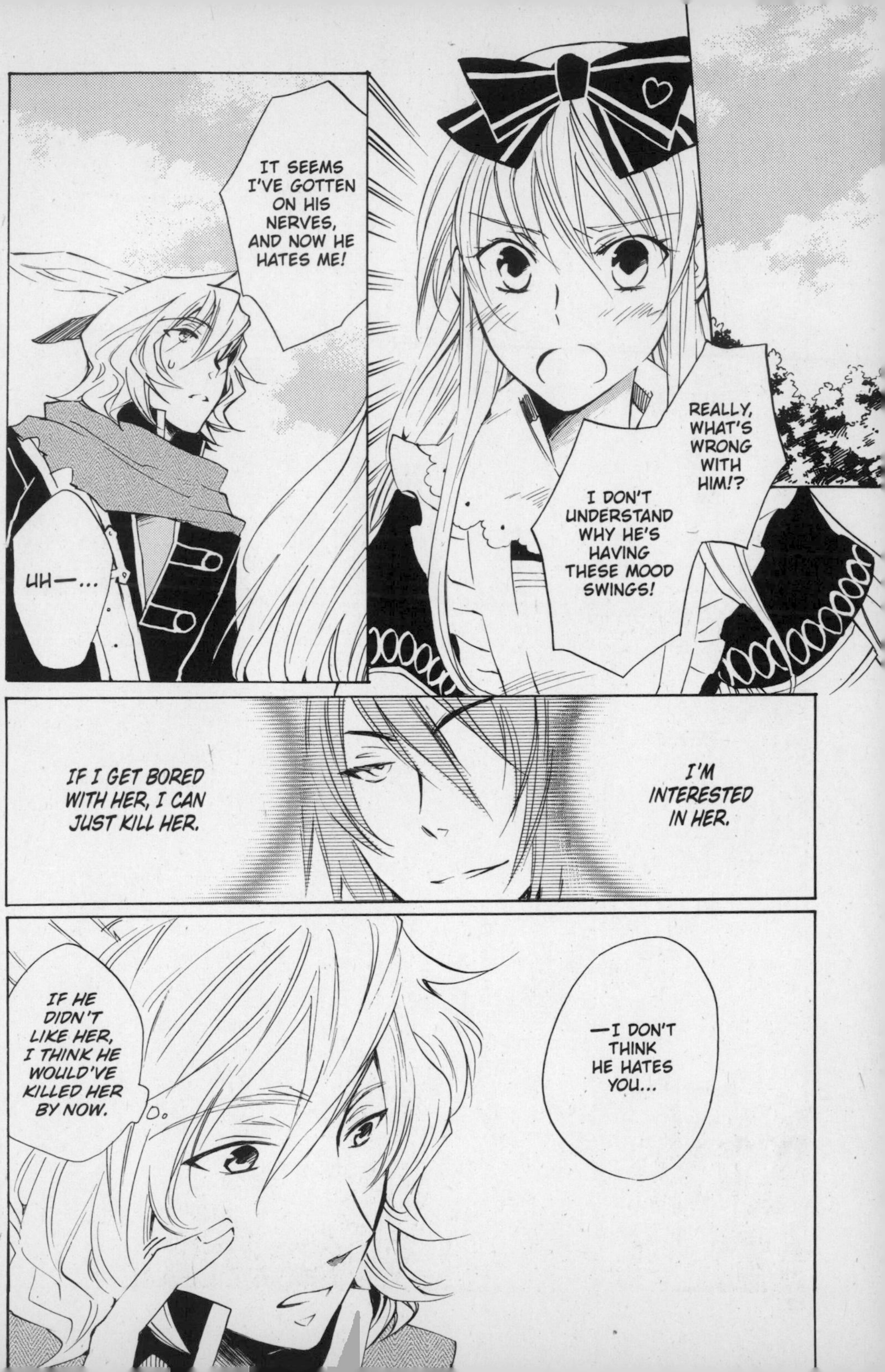
REALLY, WHAT'S WRONG WITH HIM!?
I DON'T UNDERSTAND WHY HE'S HAVING THESE MOOD SWINGS!
IT SEEMS I'VE GOTTEN ON HIS NERVES, AND NOW HE HATES ME!
UH—...
I'M INTERESTED IN HER.
IF I GET BORED WITH HER, I CAN JUST KILL HER.
—I DON'T THINK HE HATES YOU...
IF HE DIDN'T LIKE HER, I THINK HE WOULD'VE KILLED HER BY NOW.

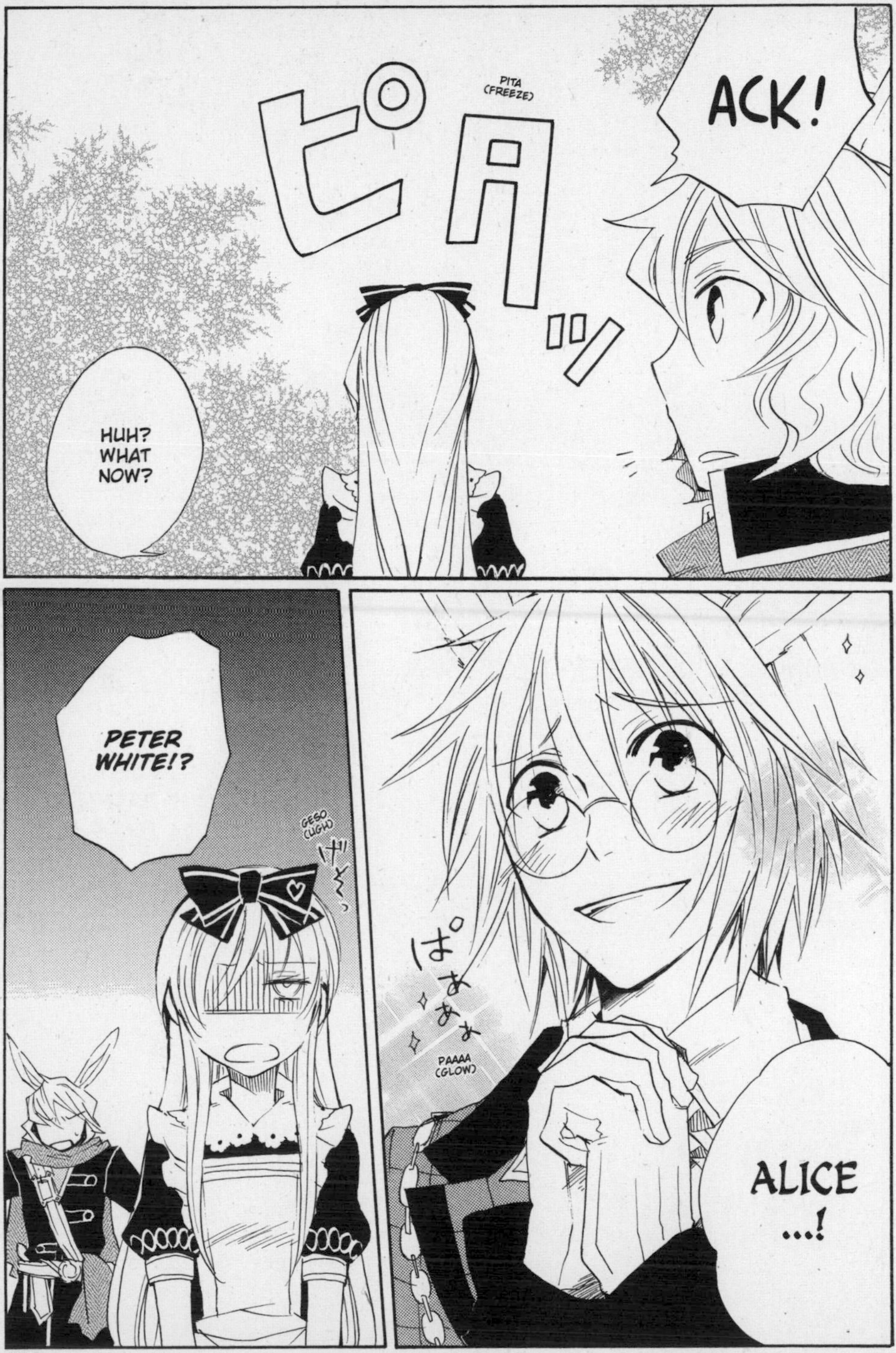
ACK!
ピタッ
PITA (FREEZE)
HUH? WHAT NOW?
PAAAA (GLOW)
ALICE ...!
PETER WHITE!?
GESO (UGH)

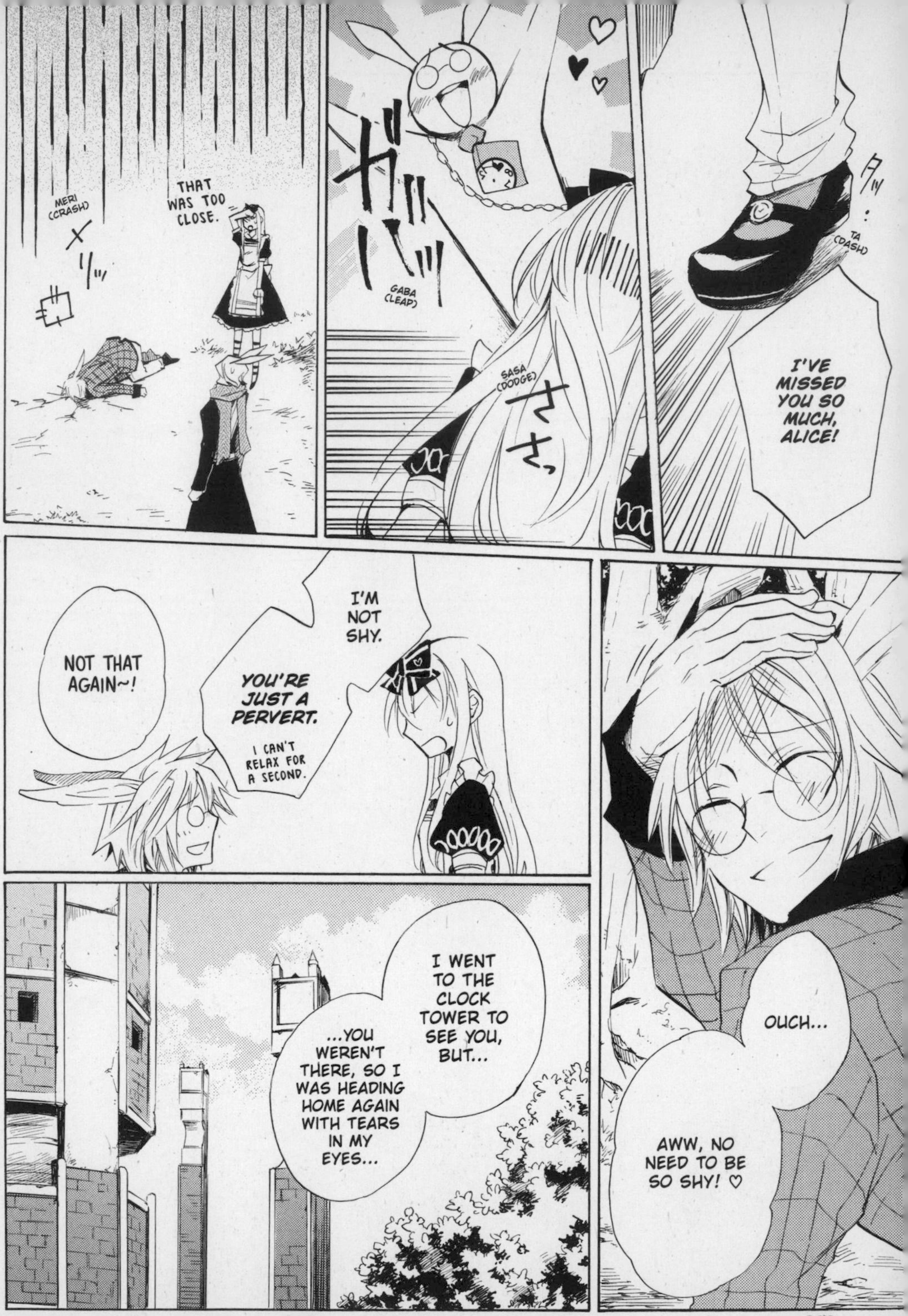
TA (DASH)
I'VE MISSED YOU SO MUCH, ALICE!
GABA (LEAP)
SASA (DODGE)
MERI (CRASH)
THAT WAS TOO CLOSE.
OUCH...
AWW, NO NEED TO BE SO SHY! ♡
I'M NOT SHY.
YOU'RE JUST A PERVERT.
I CAN'T RELAX FOR A SECOND.
NOT THAT AGAIN~!
I WENT TO THE CLOCK TOWER TO SEE YOU, BUT...
...YOU WEREN'T THERE, SO I WAS HEADING HOME AGAIN WITH TEARS IN MY EYES...

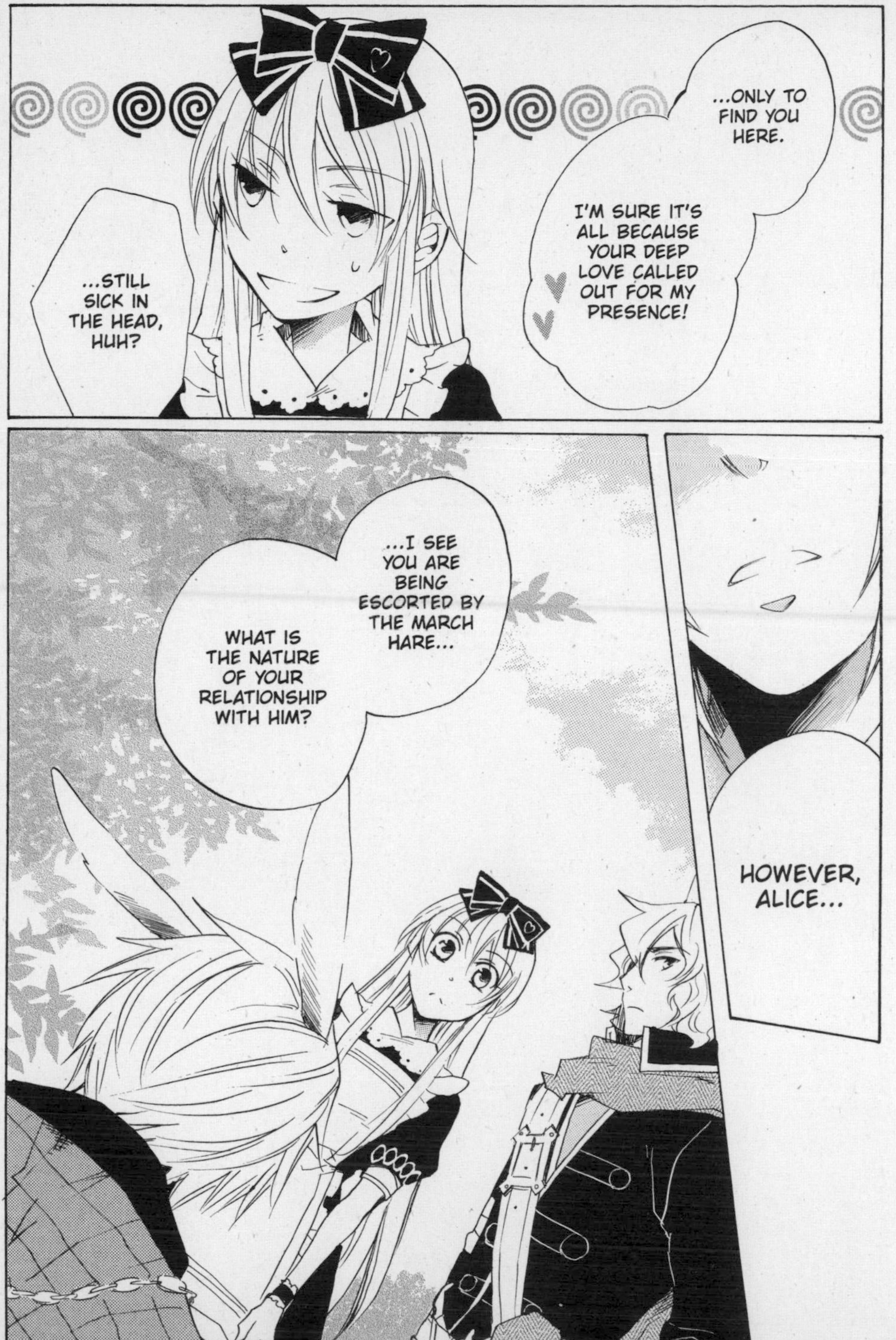
...ONLY TO FIND YOU HERE.
I'M SURE IT'S ALL BECAUSE YOUR DEEP LOVE CALLED OUT FOR MY PRESENCE!
...STILL SICK IN THE HEAD, HUH?
HOWEVER, ALICE...
...I SEE YOU ARE BEING ESCORTED BY THE MARCH HARE...
WHAT IS THE NATURE OF YOUR RELATIONSHIP WITH HIM?

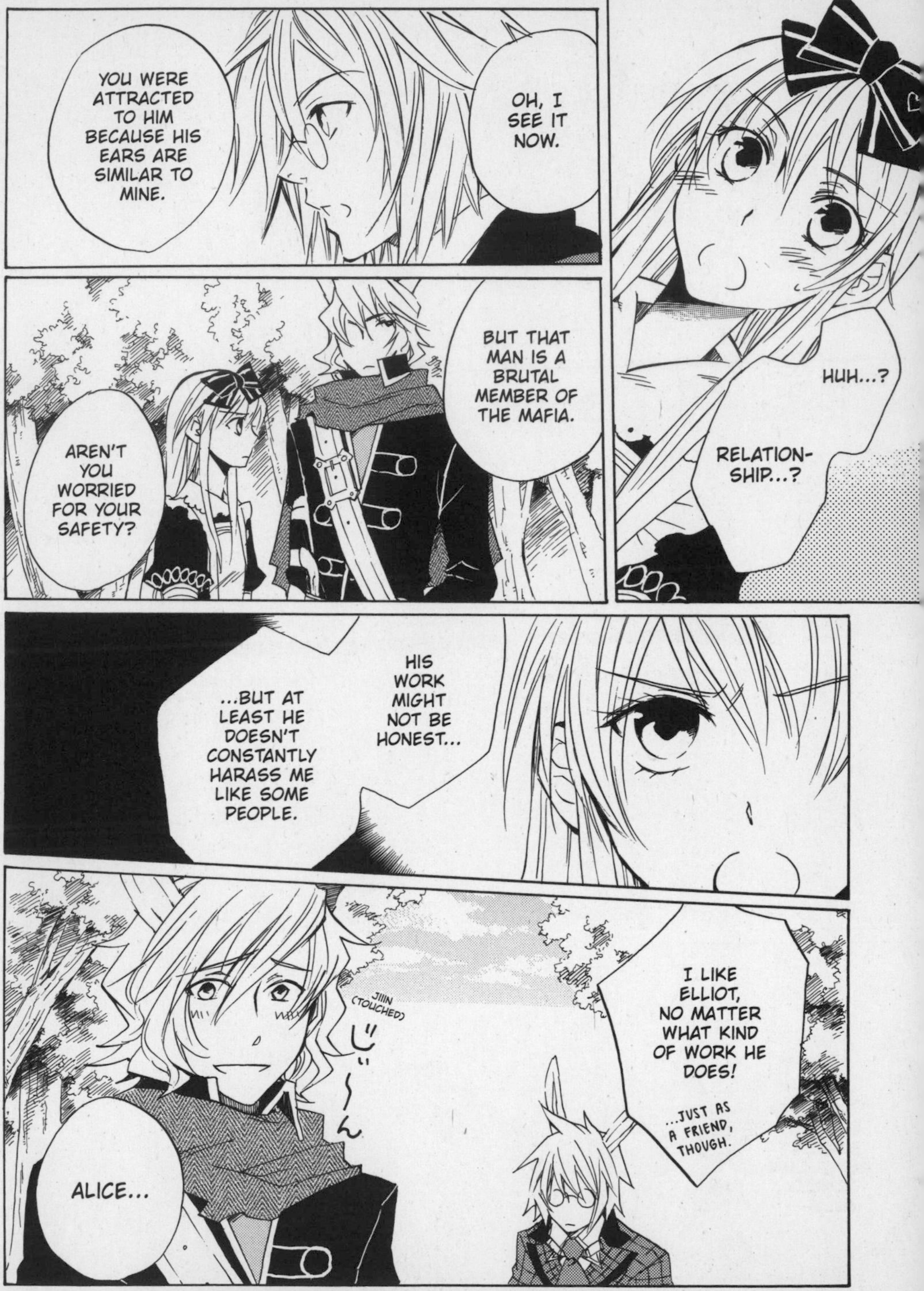
HUH...?
RELATION-SHIP...?
OH, I SEE IT NOW.
YOU WERE ATTRACTED TO HIM BECAUSE HIS EARS ARE SIMILAR TO MINE.
BUT THAT MAN IS A BRUTAL MEMBER OF THE MAFIA.
AREN'T YOU WORRIED FOR YOUR SAFETY?
HIS WORK MIGHT NOT BE HONEST...
...BUT AT LEAST HE DOESN'T CONSTANTLY HARASS ME LIKE SOME PEOPLE.
I LIKE ELLIOT, NO MATTER WHAT KIND OF WORK HE DOES!
...JUST AS A FRIEND, THOUGH.
JIIN (TOUCHED)
じーん
ALICE...

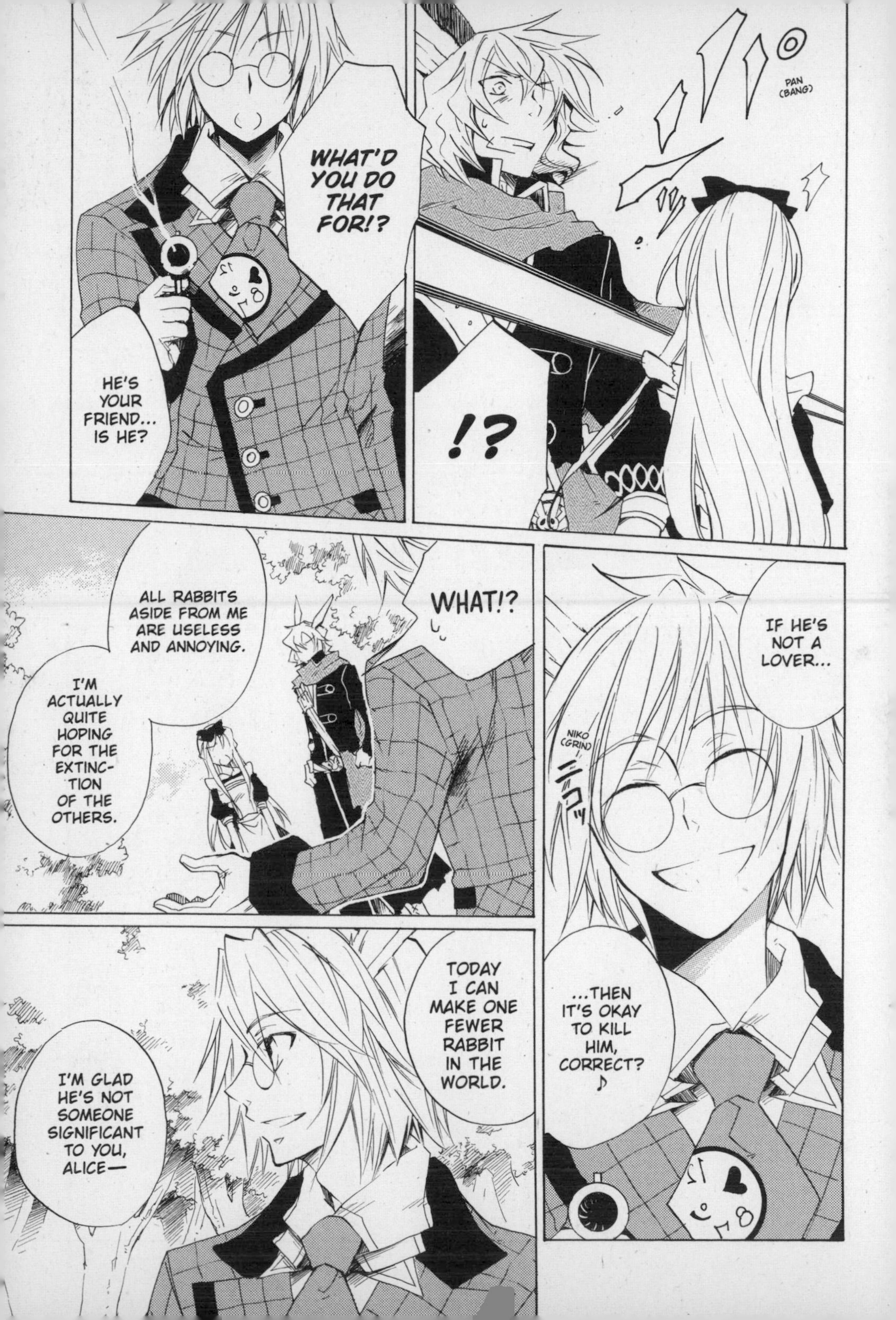
PAN (BANG)
!?
WHAT'D YOU DO THAT FOR!?
HE'S YOUR FRIEND... IS HE?
IF HE'S NOT A LOVER...
NIKO (GRIN)
...THEN IT'S OKAY TO KILL HIM, CORRECT? ♪
WHAT!?
ALL RABBITS ASIDE FROM ME ARE USELESS AND ANNOYING.
I'M ACTUALLY QUITE HOPING FOR THE EXTINCTION OF THE OTHERS.
TODAY I CAN MAKE ONE FEWER RABBIT IN THE WORLD.
I'M GLAD HE'S NOT SOMEONE SIGNIFICANT TO YOU, ALICE—

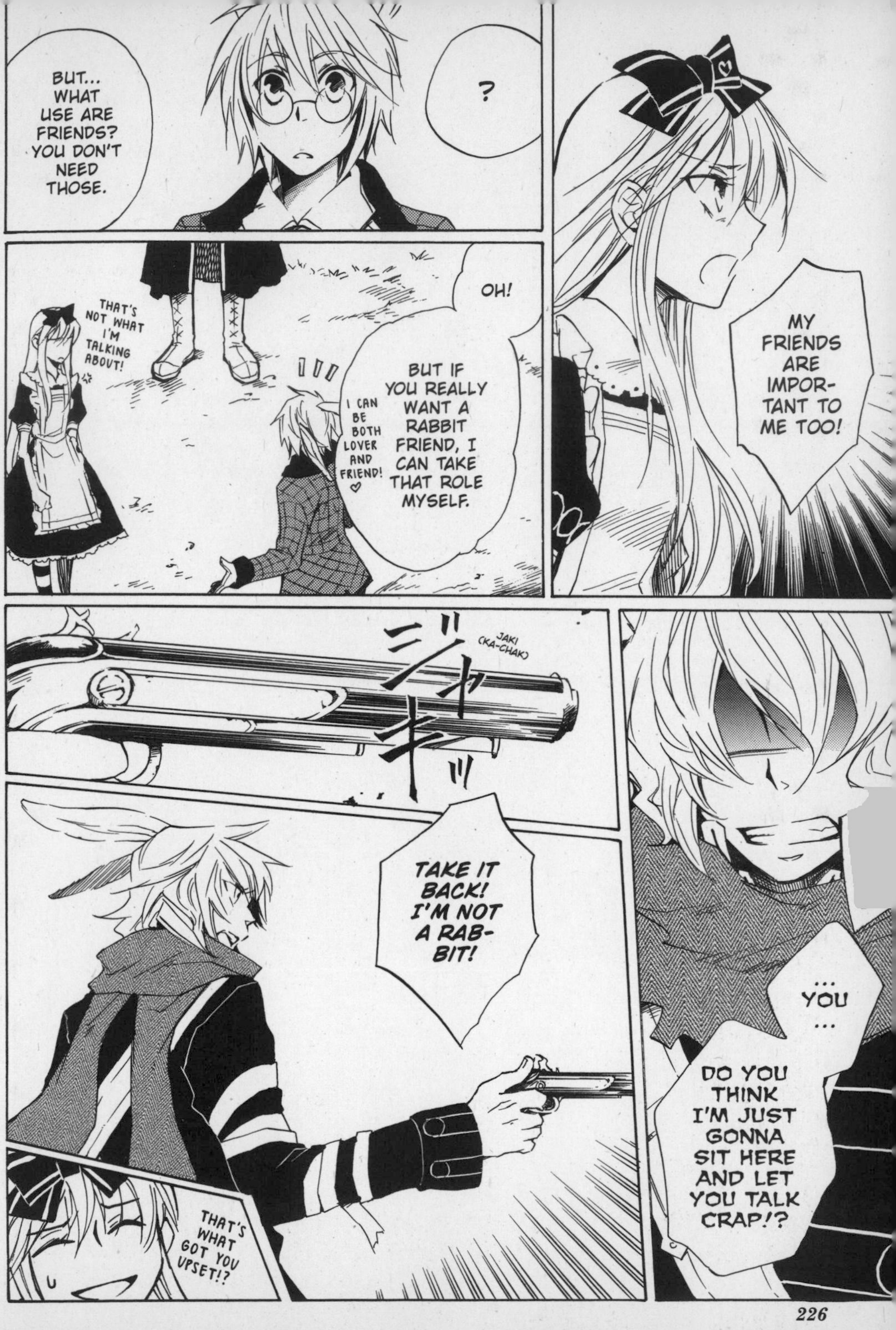
MY FRIENDS ARE IMPORTANT TO ME TOO!
?
BUT... WHAT USE ARE FRIENDS? YOU DON'T NEED THOSE.
OH!
BUT IF YOU REALLY WANT A RABBIT FRIEND, I CAN TAKE THAT ROLE MYSELF.
I CAN BE BOTH LOVER AND FRIEND! ♡
THAT'S NOT WHAT I'M TALKING ABOUT!
... YOU ...
DO YOU THINK I'M JUST GONNA SIT HERE AND LET YOU TALK CRAP!?
ジャキッ
JAKI (KA-CHAK)
TAKE IT BACK! I'M NOT A RAB-BIT!
THAT'S WHAT GOT YOU UPSET!?

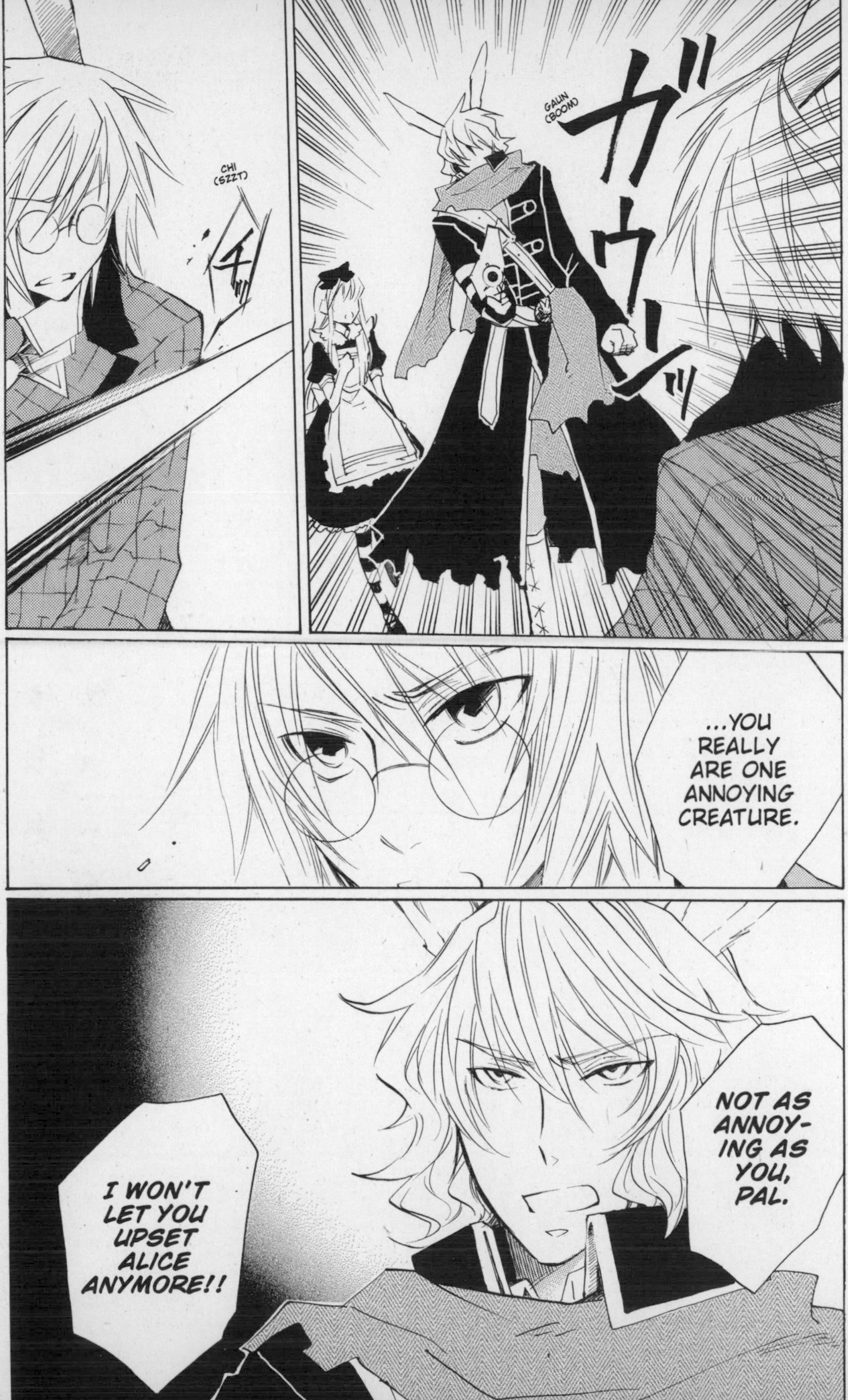
GAUN (BOOM)
ガウーンッ
CHI (SZZT)
チッ
...YOU REALLY ARE ONE ANNOYING CREATURE.
NOT AS ANNOY-ING AS YOU, PAL.
I WON'T LET YOU UPSET ALICE ANYMORE!!

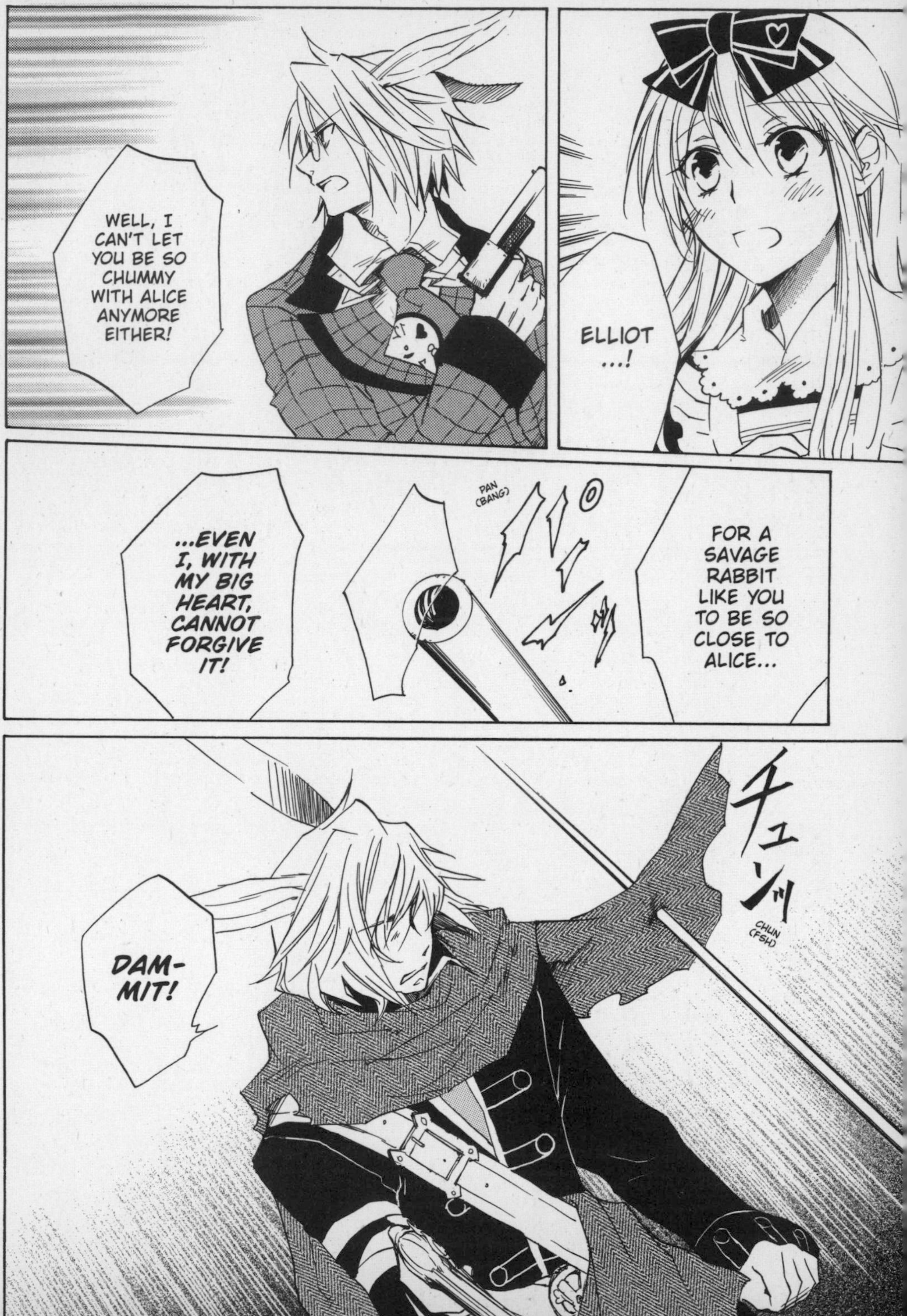
ELLIOT ...!
WELL, I CAN'T LET YOU BE SO CHUMMY WITH ALICE ANYMORE EITHER!
FOR A SAVAGE RABBIT LIKE YOU TO BE SO CLOSE TO ALICE...
PAN (BANG)
...EVEN I, WITH MY BIG HEART, CANNOT FORGIVE IT!
チュン
CHUN (FSH)
DAM-MIT!

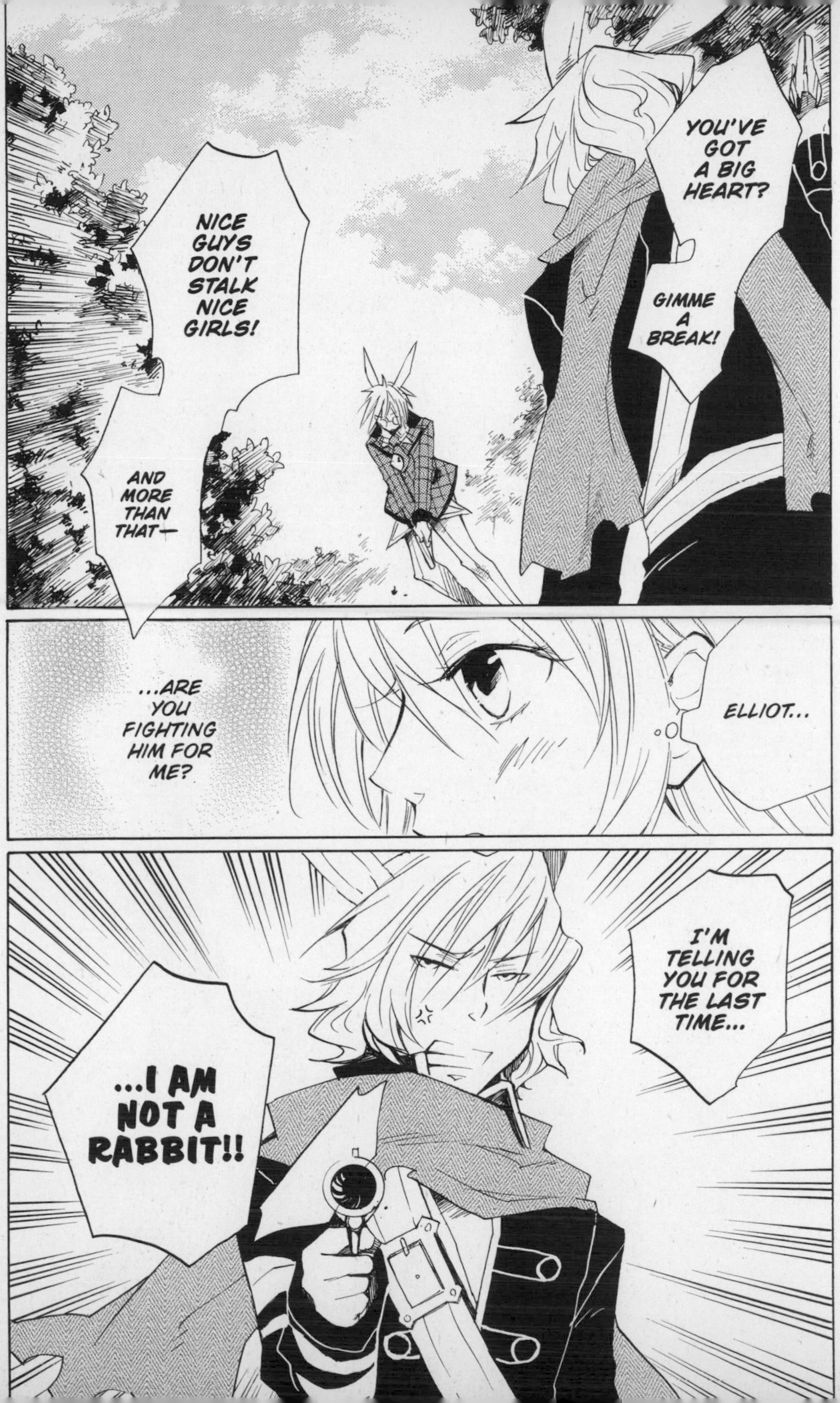
YOU'VE GOT A BIG HEART?
GIMME A BREAK!
NICE GUYS DON'T STALK NICE GIRLS!
AND MORE THAN THAT—
ELLIOT...
...ARE YOU FIGHTING HIM FOR ME?
I'M TELLING YOU FOR THE LAST TIME...
...I AM NOT A RABBIT!!

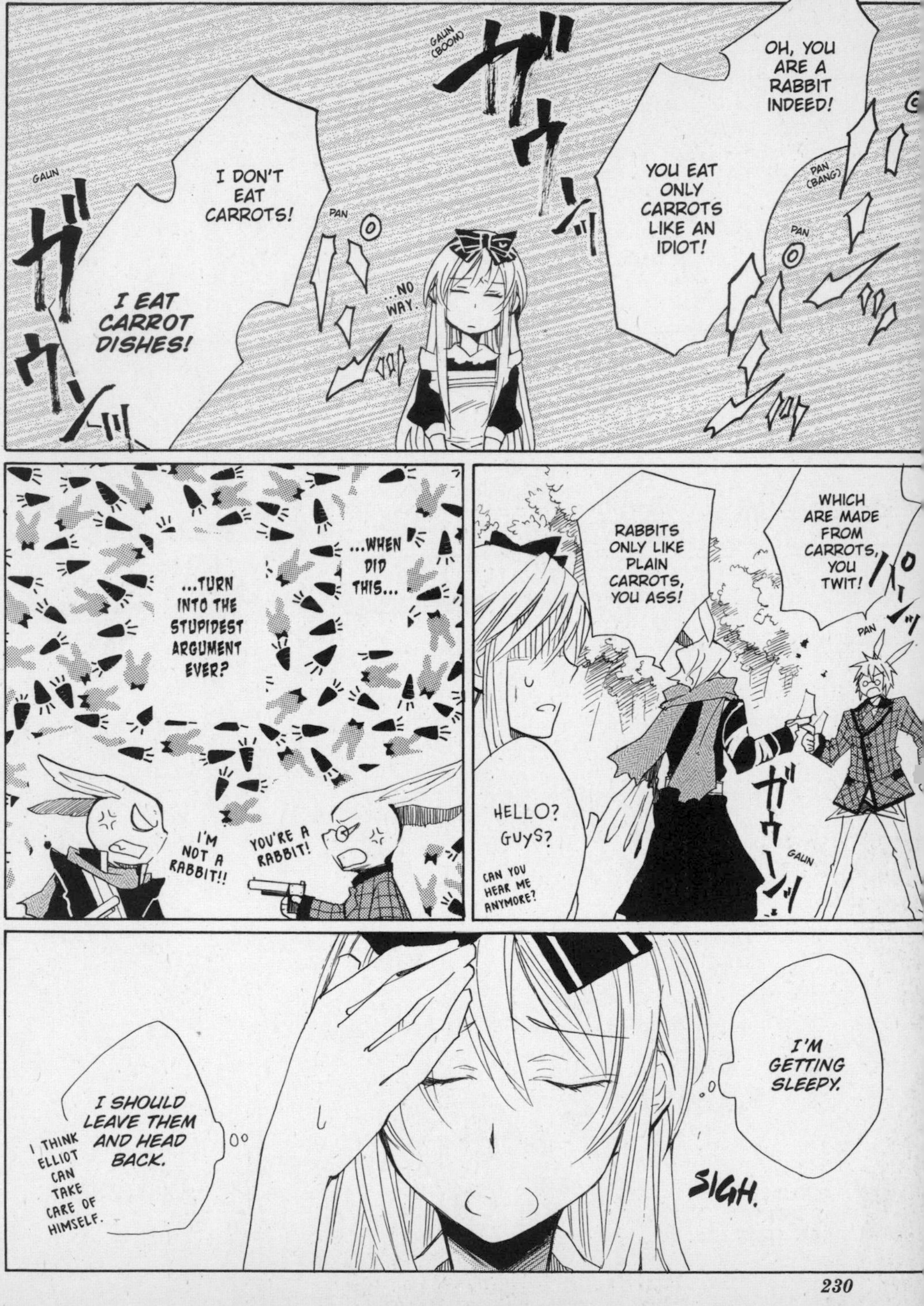

OH, YOU ARE A RABBIT INDEED!
YOU EAT ONLY CARROTS LIKE AN IDIOT!
PAN (BANG)
PAN
GAUN (BOOM)
...NO WAY.
PAN
I DON'T EAT CARROTS!
I EAT CARROT DISHES!
GAUN
WHICH ARE MADE FROM CARROTS, YOU TWIT!
PAN
RABBITS ONLY LIKE PLAIN CARROTS, YOU ASS!
GAUN
HELLO? GUYS?
CAN YOU HEAR ME ANYMORE?
...WHEN DID THIS...
...TURN INTO THE STUPIDEST ARGUMENT EVER?
YOU'RE A RABBIT!
I'M NOT A RABBIT!!
I'M GETTING SLEEPY.
SIGH.
I SHOULD LEAVE THEM AND HEAD BACK.
I THINK ELLIOT CAN TAKE CARE OF HIMSELF.

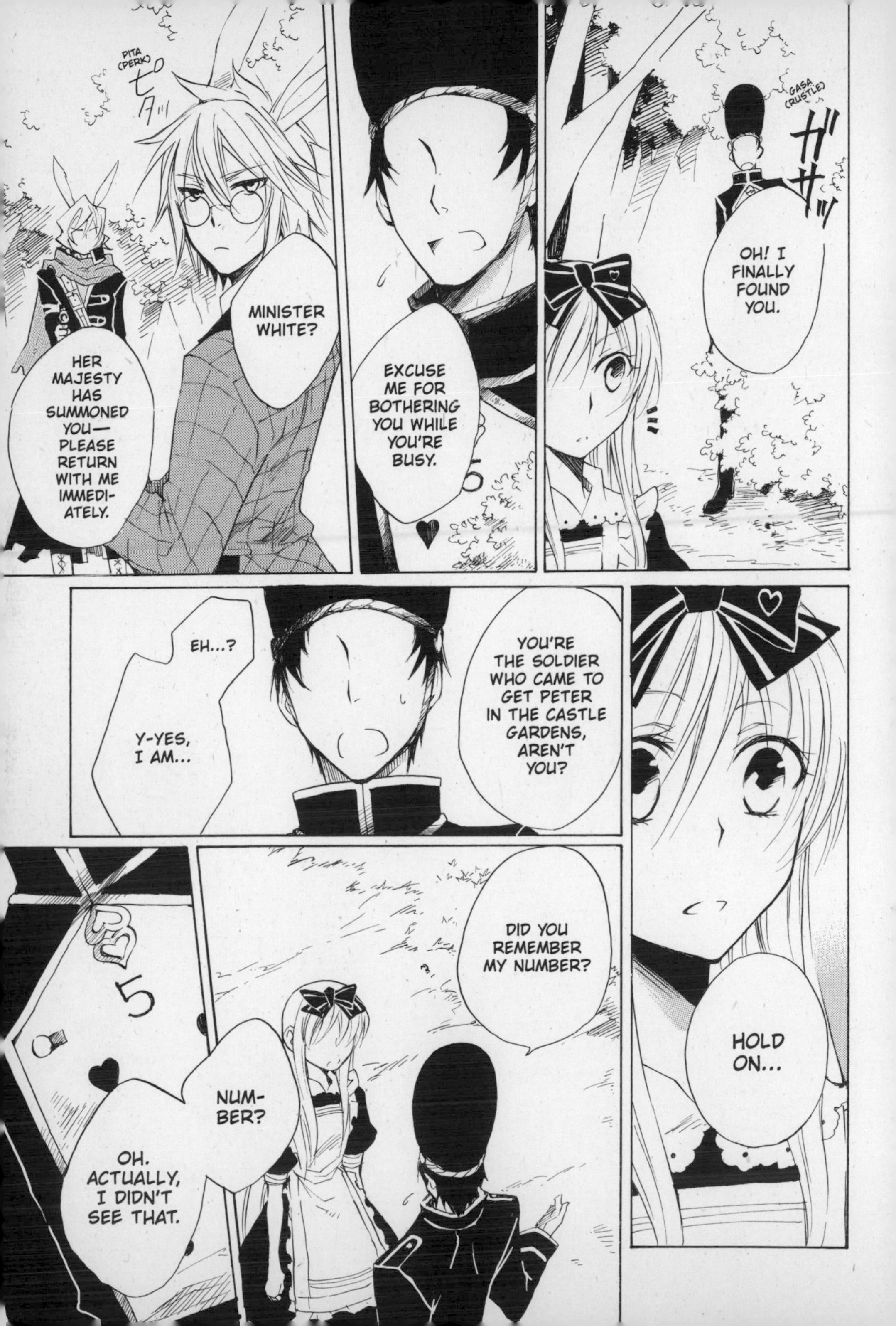
GASA (RUSTLE)
OH! I FINALLY FOUND YOU.
EXCUSE ME FOR BOTHERING YOU WHILE YOU'RE BUSY.
PITA (PERK)
MINISTER WHITE?
HER MAJESTY HAS SUMMONED YOU—PLEASE RETURN WITH ME IMMEDI-ATELY.
HOLD ON...
YOU'RE THE SOLDIER WHO CAME TO GET PETER IN THE CASTLE GARDENS, AREN'T YOU?
EH...?
Y-YES, I AM...
DID YOU REMEMBER MY NUMBER?
NUM-BER?
OH. ACTUALLY, I DIDN'T SEE THAT.

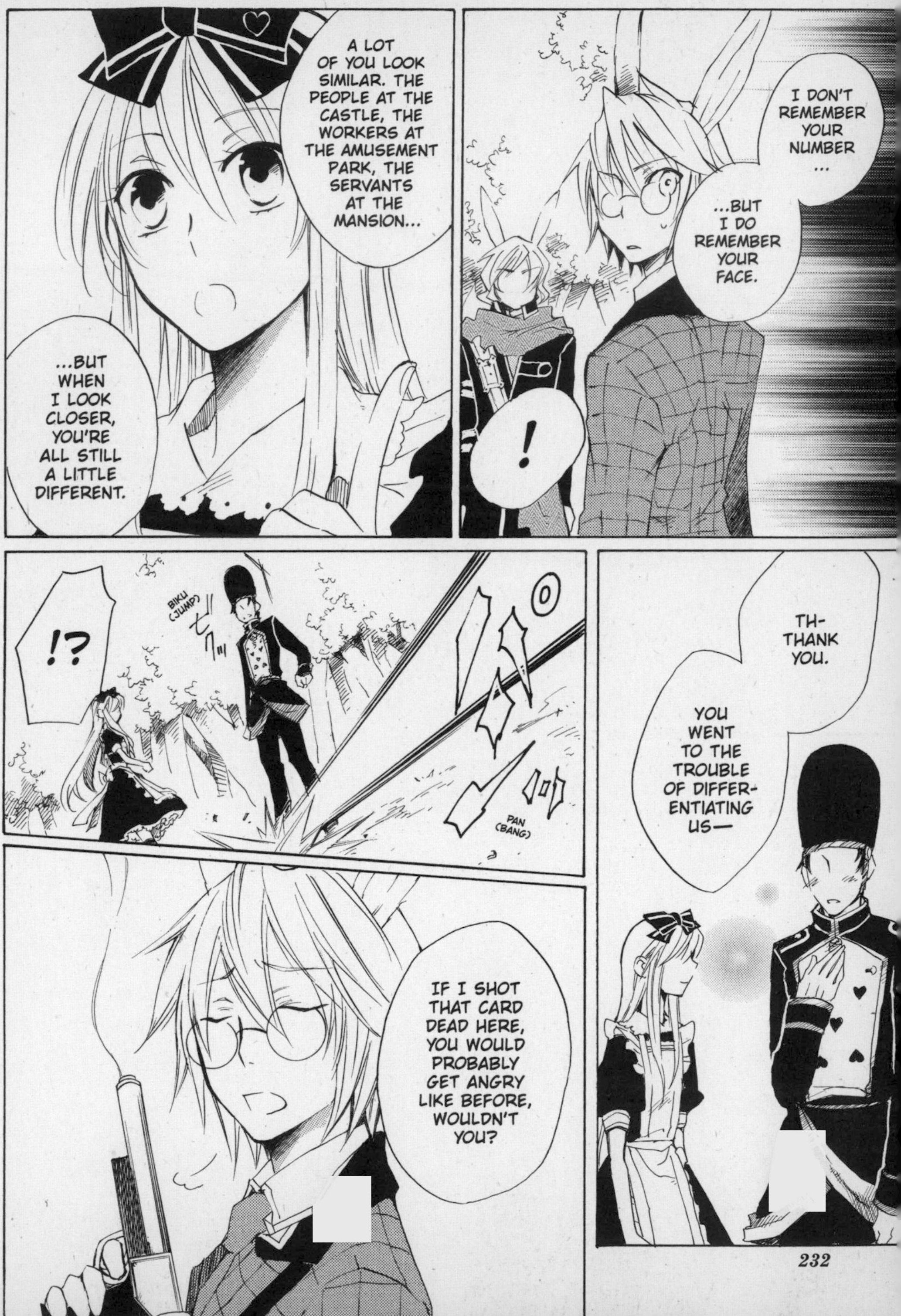
I DON'T REMEMBER YOUR NUMBER ...
...BUT I DO REMEMBER YOUR FACE.
!
A LOT OF YOU LOOK SIMILAR. THE PEOPLE AT THE CASTLE, THE WORKERS AT THE AMUSEMENT PARK, THE SERVANTS AT THE MANSION...
...BUT WHEN I LOOK CLOSER, YOU'RE ALL STILL A LITTLE DIFFERENT.
TH- THANK YOU.
YOU WENT TO THE TROUBLE OF DIFFER- ENTIATING US—
!?
BIKU (JUMP)
PAN (BANG)
IF I SHOT THAT CARD DEAD HERE, YOU WOULD PROBABLY GET ANGRY LIKE BEFORE, WOULDN'T YOU?

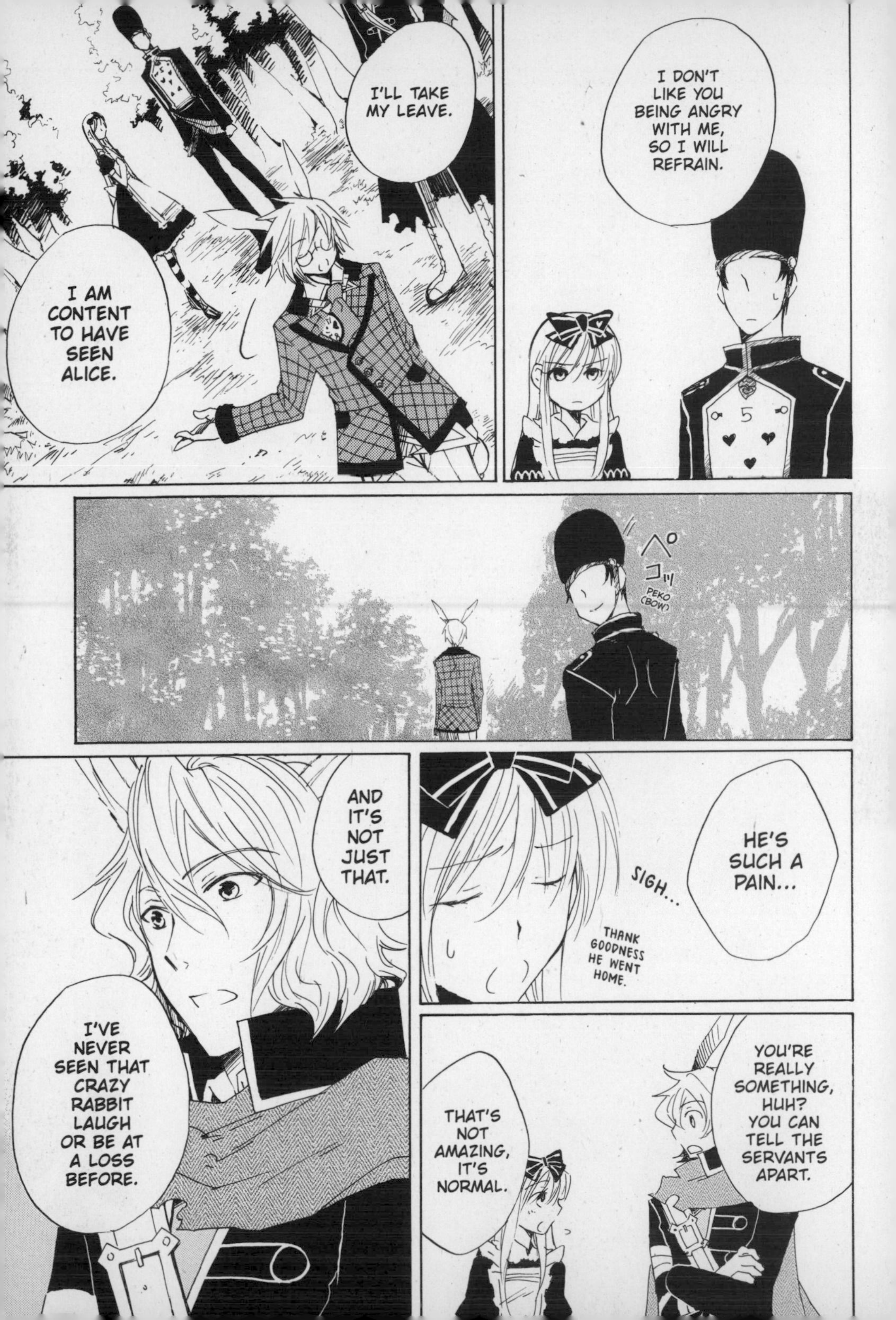
I DON'T LIKE YOU BEING ANGRY WITH ME, SO I WILL REFRAIN.
I'LL TAKE MY LEAVE.
I AM CONTENT TO HAVE SEEN ALICE.
ペコッ
PEKO (BOW)
HE'S SUCH A PAIN...
SIGH...
THANK GOODNESS HE WENT HOME.
YOU'RE REALLY SOMETHING, HUH? YOU CAN TELL THE SERVANTS APART.
THAT'S NOT AMAZING, IT'S NORMAL.
AND IT'S NOT JUST THAT.
I'VE NEVER SEEN THAT CRAZY RABBIT LAUGH OR BE AT A LOSS BEFORE.

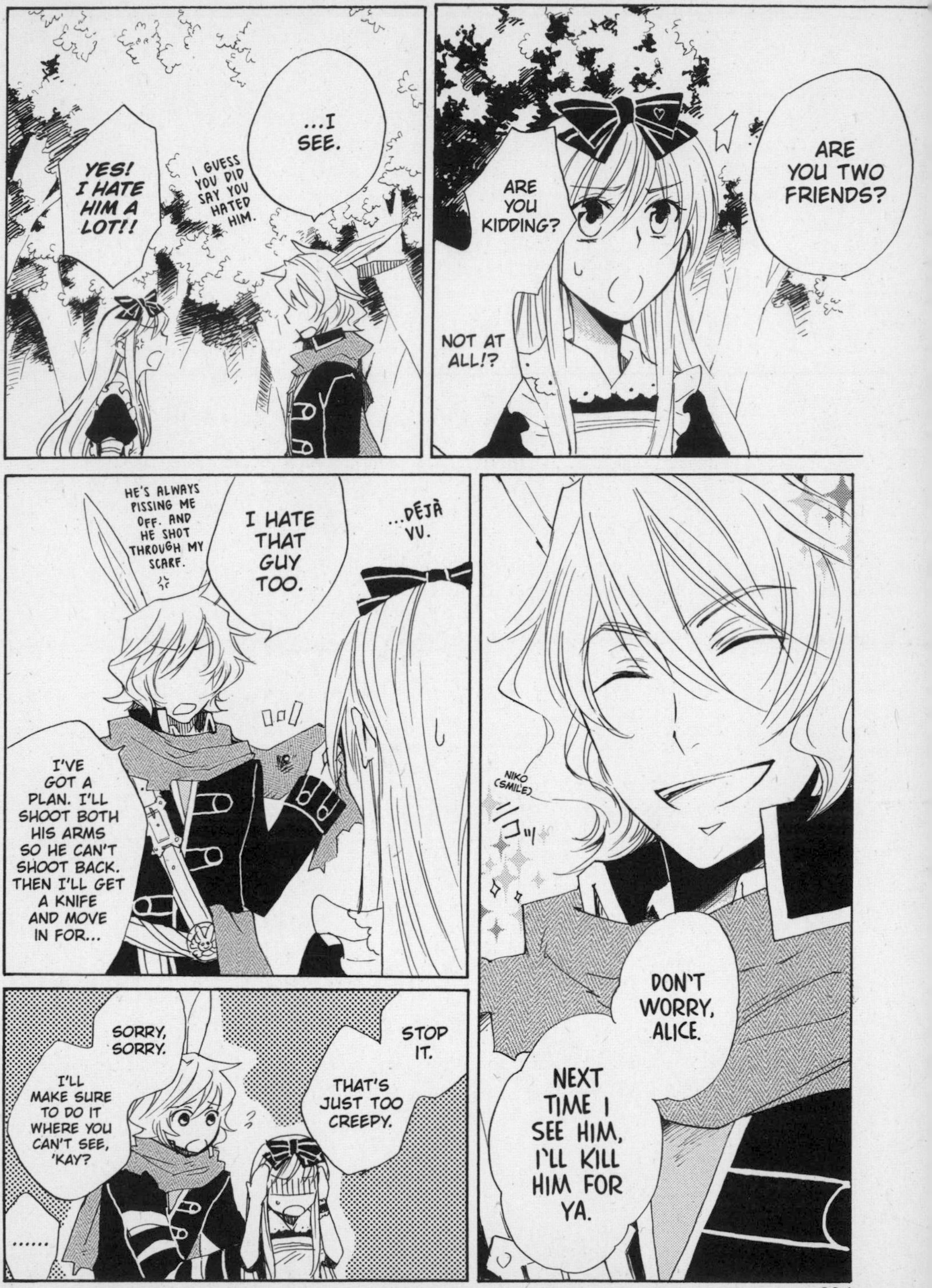

ARE YOU TWO FRIENDS?
ARE YOU KIDDING?
NOT AT ALL!?
...I SEE.
I GUESS YOU DID SAY YOU HATED HIM.
YES! I HATE HIM A LOT!!
NIKO (SMILE)
DON'T WORRY, ALICE.
NEXT TIME I SEE HIM, I'LL KILL HIM FOR YA.
...DÉJÀ VU.
I HATE THAT GUY TOO.
HE'S ALWAYS PISSING ME OFF. AND HE SHOT THROUGH MY SCARF.
I'VE GOT A PLAN. I'LL SHOOT BOTH HIS ARMS SO HE CAN'T SHOOT BACK. THEN I'LL GET A KNIFE AND MOVE IN FOR...
STOP IT.
THAT'S JUST TOO CREEPY.
SORRY, SORRY.
I'LL MAKE SURE TO DO IT WHERE YOU CAN'T SEE, 'KAY?
......

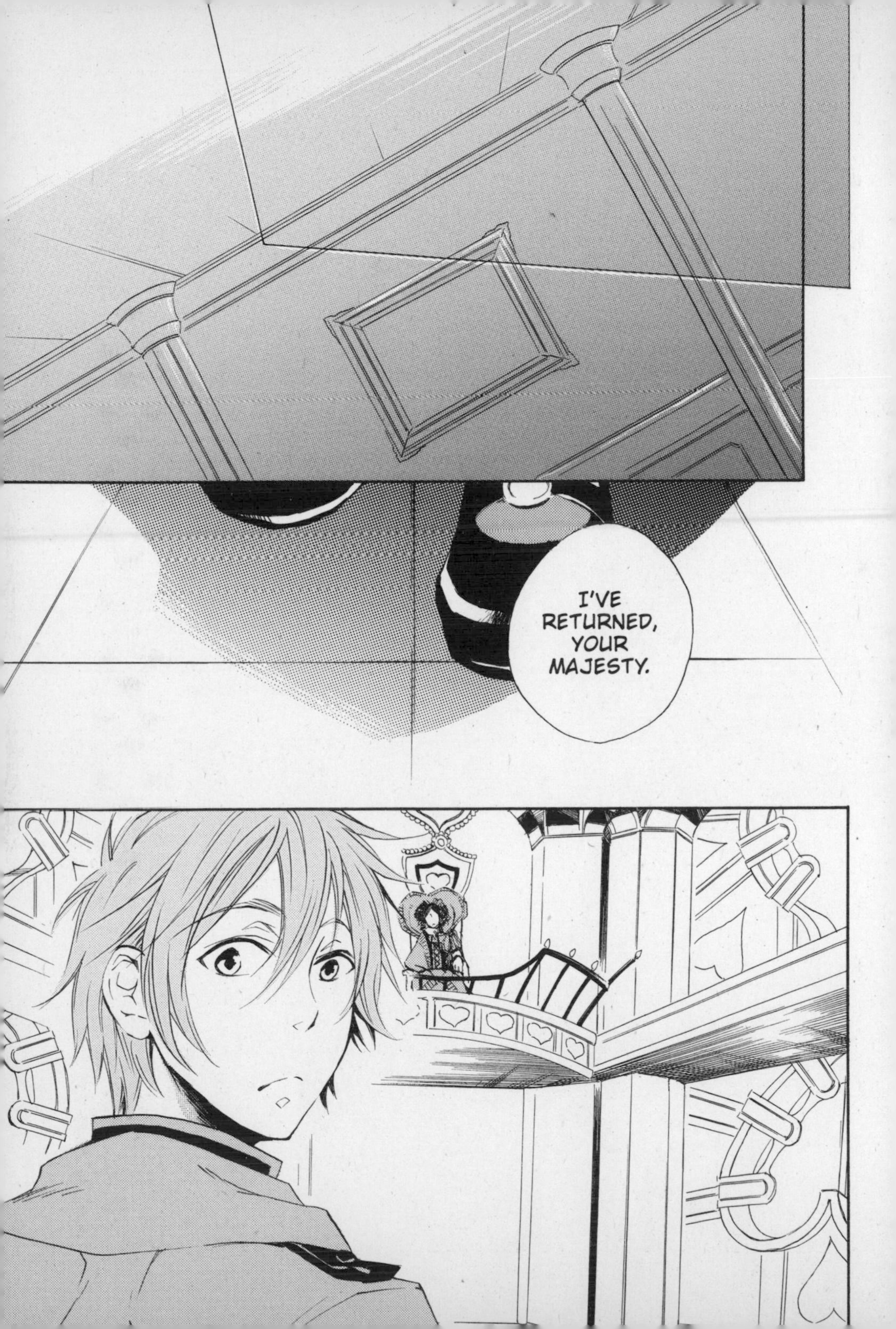
I'VE RETURNED, YOUR MAJESTY.

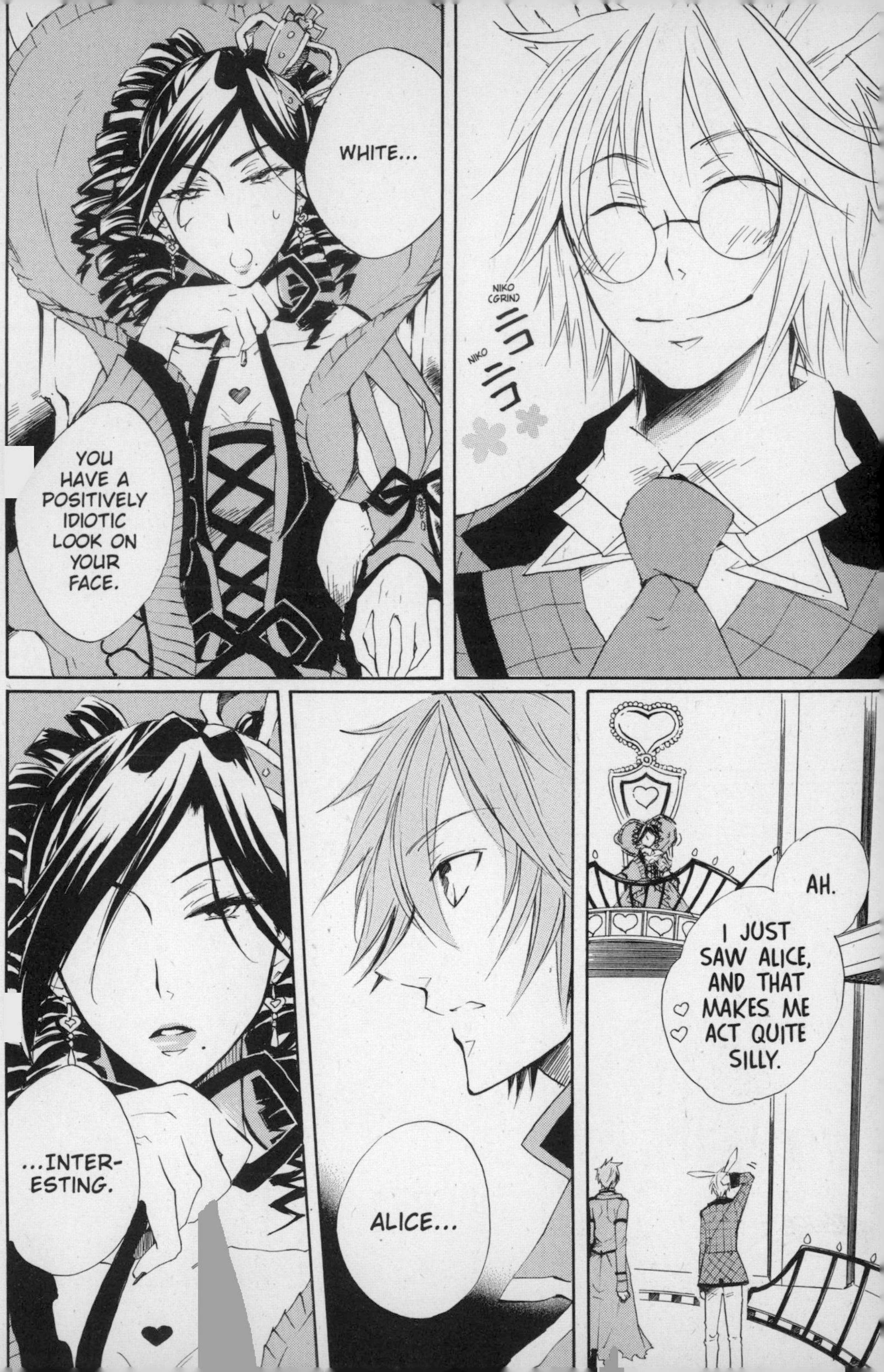

NIKO (GRIN)
ニコ
NIKO
ニコ
WHITE...
YOU HAVE A POSITIVELY IDIOTIC LOOK ON YOUR FACE.
AH.
I JUST SAW ALICE, AND THAT MAKES ME ACT QUITE SILLY.
ALICE...
...INTER-ESTING.

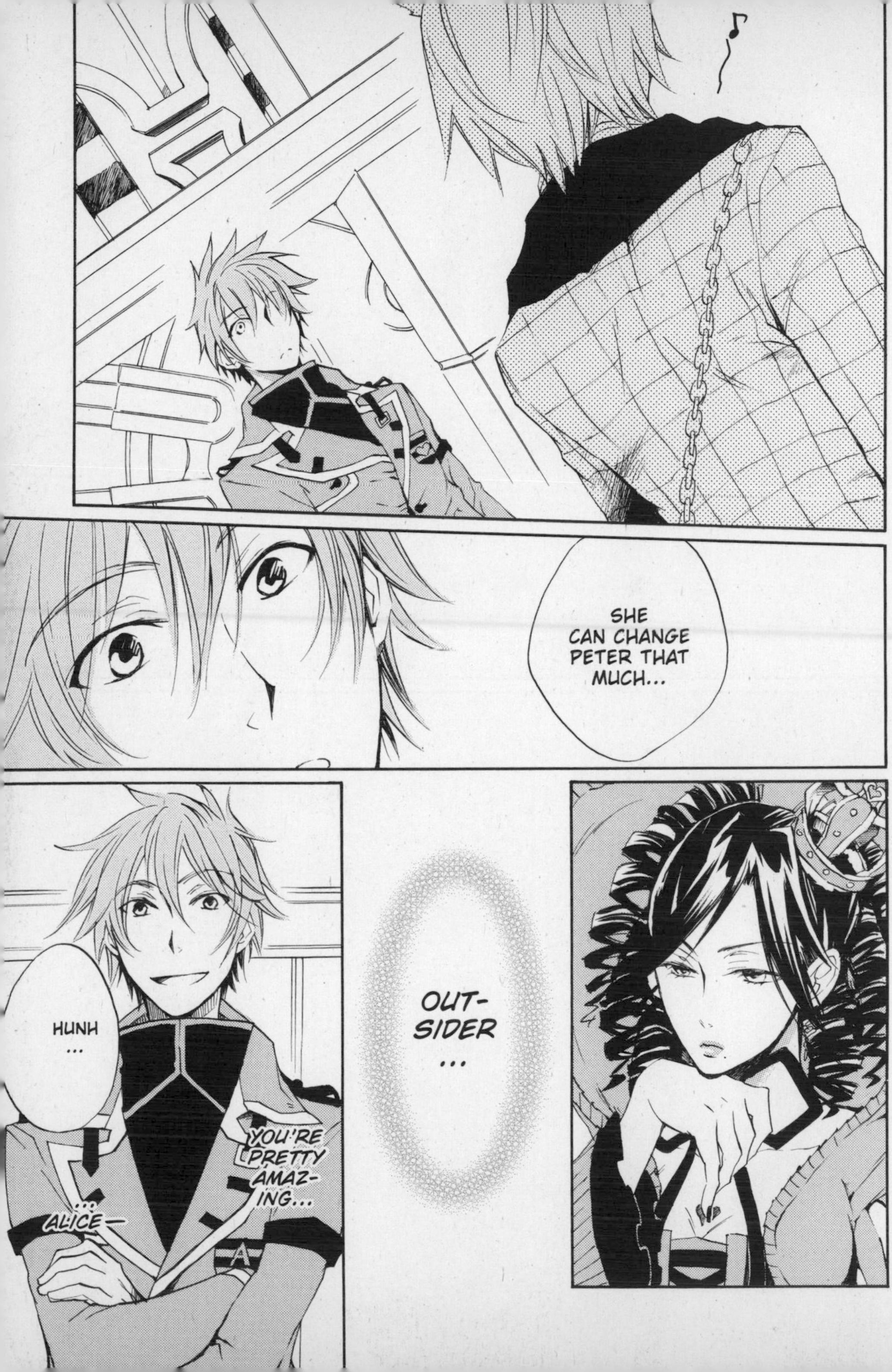
SHE CAN CHANGE PETER THAT MUCH...
OUT-SIDER...
HUNH...
YOU'RE PRETTY AMAZ-ING...
...ALICE—

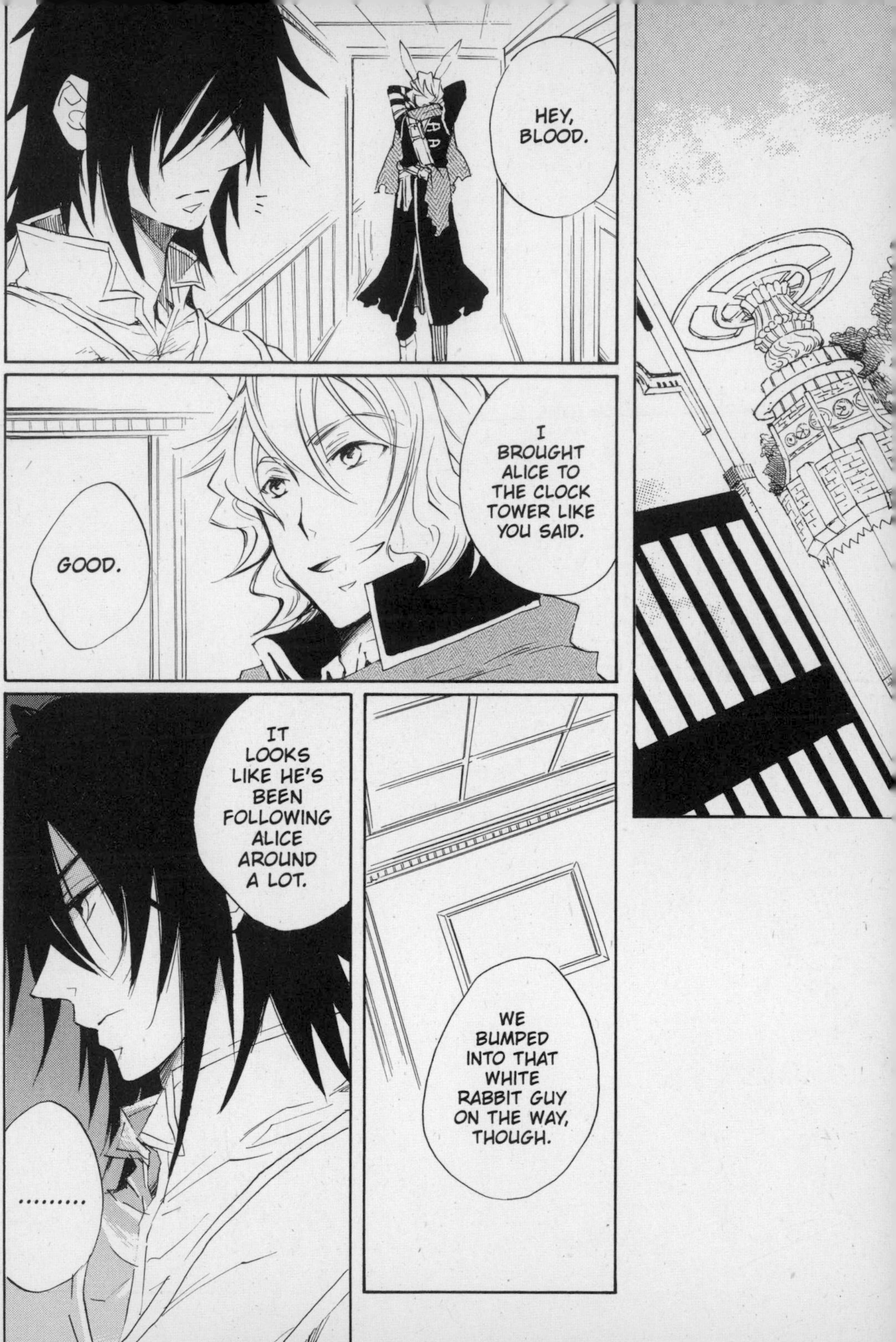
HEY, BLOOD.
I BROUGHT ALICE TO THE CLOCK TOWER LIKE YOU SAID.
GOOD.
WE BUMPED INTO THAT WHITE RABBIT GUY ON THE WAY, THOUGH.
IT LOOKS LIKE HE'S BEEN FOLLOWING ALICE AROUND A LOT.
....

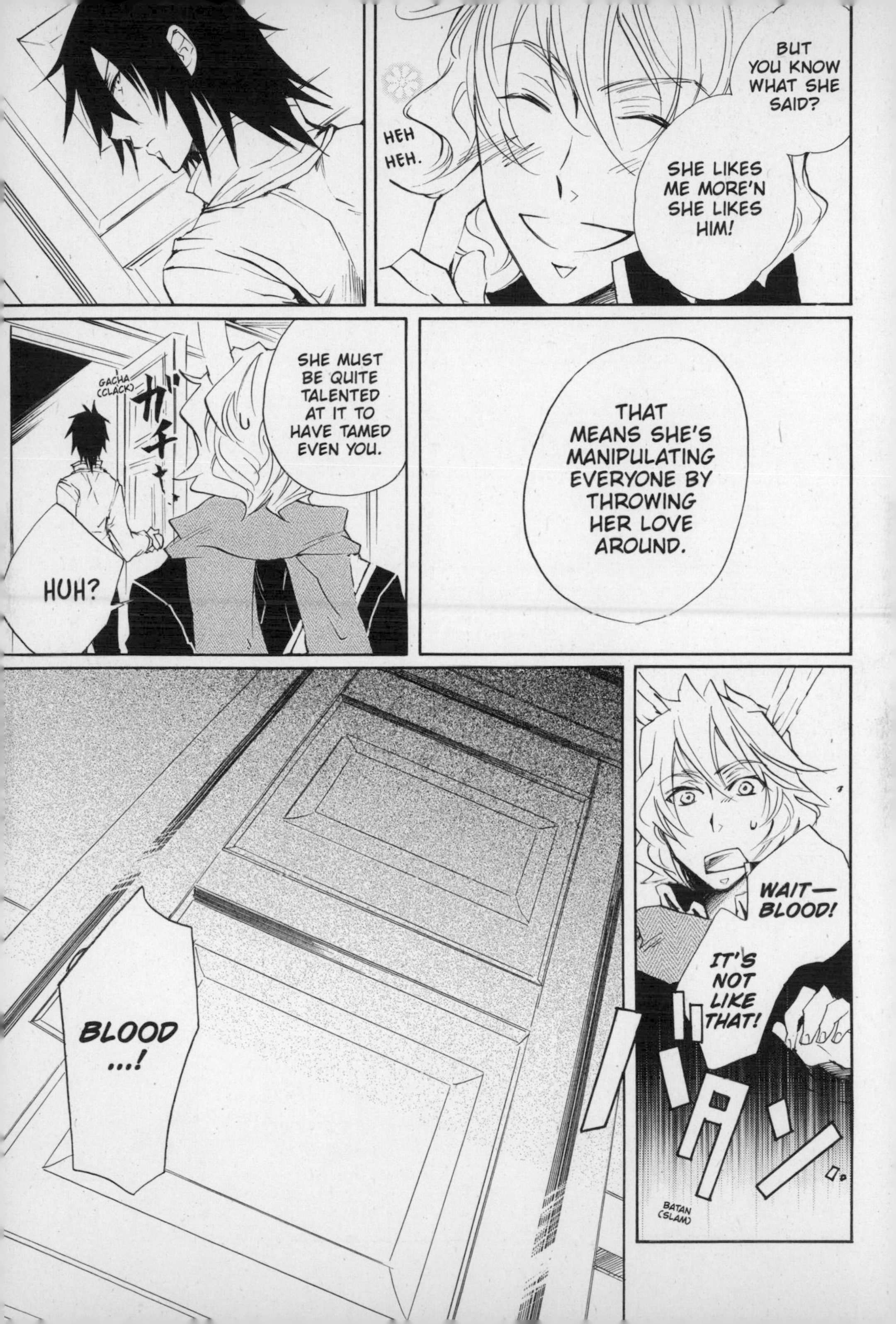
BUT YOU KNOW WHAT SHE SAID?
SHE LIKES ME MORE'N SHE LIKES HIM!
HEH HEH.
THAT MEANS SHE'S MANIPULATING EVERYONE BY THROWING HER LOVE AROUND.
SHE MUST BE QUITE TALENTED AT IT TO HAVE TAMED EVEN YOU.
GACHA (CLACK)
ガチャ
HUH?
WAIT— BLOOD!
IT'S NOT LIKE THAT!
バタン
BATAN (SLAM)
BLOOD ...!

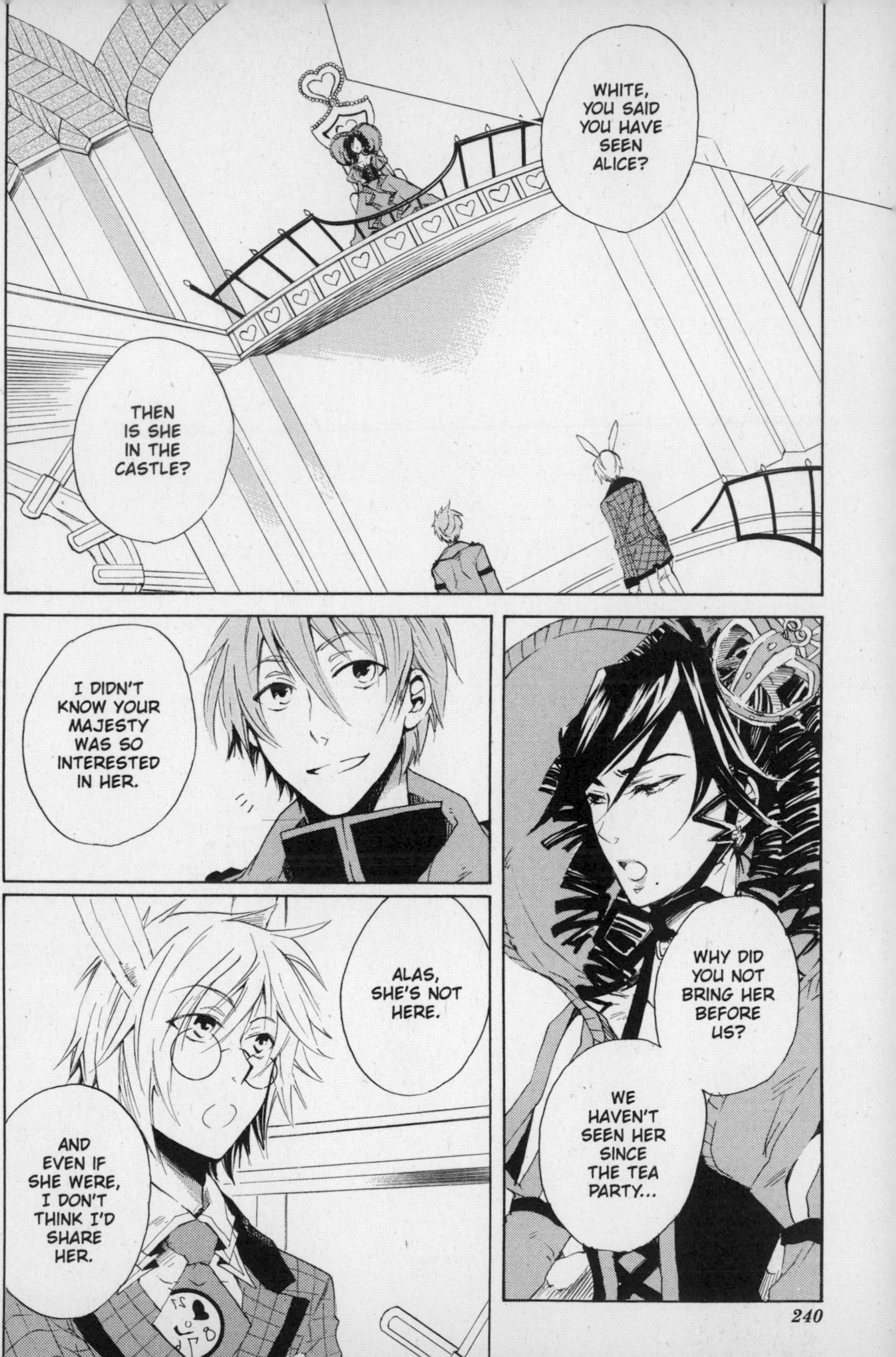
WHITE, YOU SAID YOU HAVE SEEN ALICE?
THEN IS SHE IN THE CASTLE?
WHY DID YOU NOT BRING HER BEFORE US?
WE HAVEN'T SEEN HER SINCE THE TEA PARTY...
I DIDN'T KNOW YOUR MAJESTY WAS SO INTERESTED IN HER.
ALAS, SHE'S NOT HERE.
AND EVEN IF SHE WERE, I DON'T THINK I'D SHARE HER.

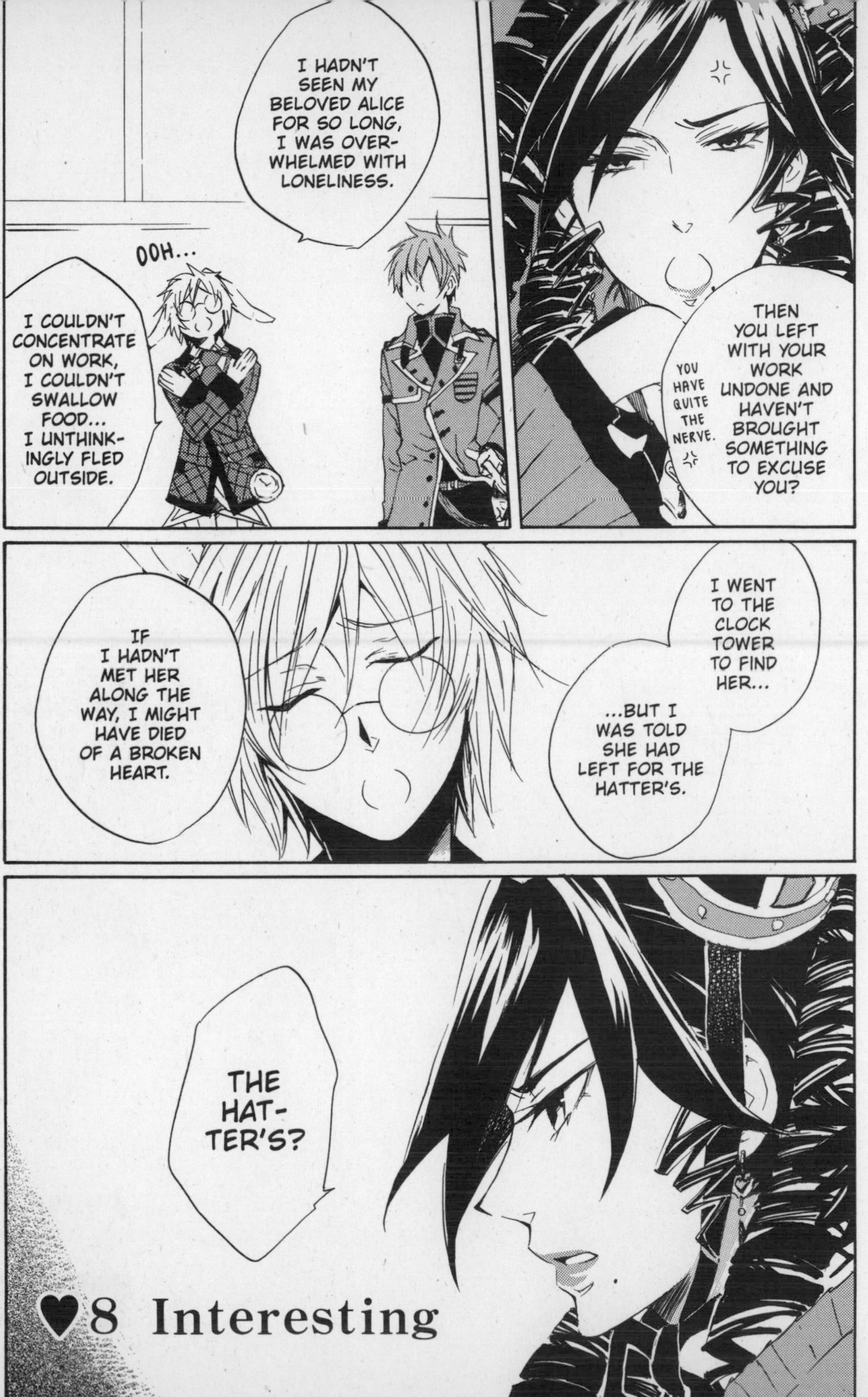
THEN YOU LEFT WITH YOUR WORK UNDONE AND HAVEN'T BROUGHT SOMETHING TO EXCUSE YOU?
YOU HAVE QUITE THE NERVE.
I HADN'T SEEN MY BELOVED ALICE FOR SO LONG, I WAS OVER-WHELMED WITH LONELINESS.
OOH...
I COULDN'T CONCENTRATE ON WORK, I COULDN'T SWALLOW FOOD... I UNTHINK-INGLY FLED OUTSIDE.
I WENT TO THE CLOCK TOWER TO FIND HER...
...BUT I WAS TOLD SHE HAD LEFT FOR THE HATTER'S.
IF I HADN'T MET HER ALONG THE WAY, I MIGHT HAVE DIED OF A BROKEN HEART.
THE HAT-TER'S?

♥8 Interesting

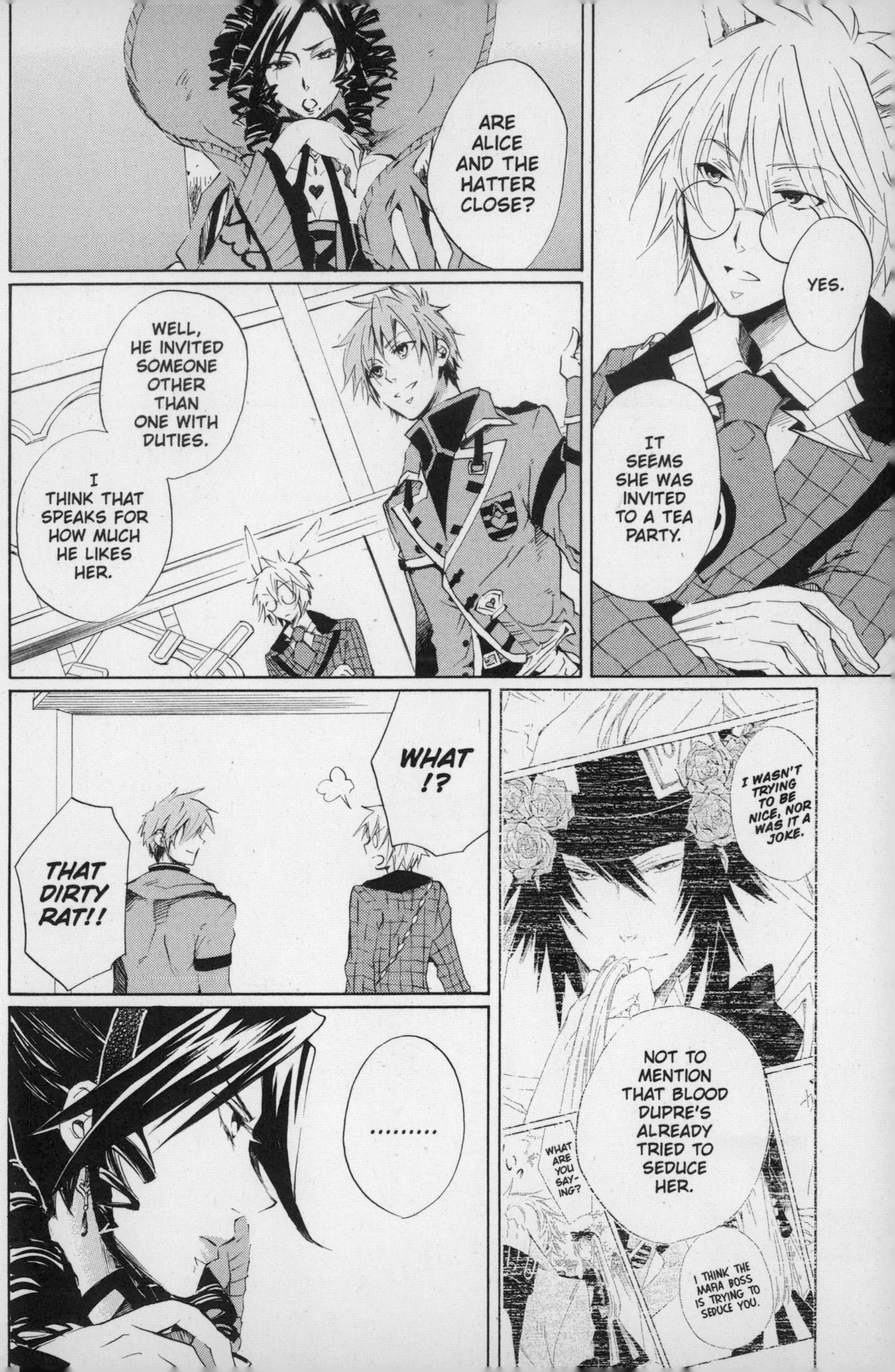
ARE ALICE AND THE HATTER CLOSE?
YES.
IT SEEMS SHE WAS INVITED TO A TEA PARTY.
WELL, HE INVITED SOMEONE OTHER THAN ONE WITH DUTIES.
I THINK THAT SPEAKS FOR HOW MUCH HE LIKES HER.
I WASN'T TRYING TO BE NICE, NOR WAS IT A JOKE.
NOT TO MENTION THAT BLOOD DUPRE'S ALREADY TRIED TO SEDUCE HER.
WHAT ARE YOU SAYING?
I THINK THE MAFIA BOSS IS TRYING TO SEDUCE YOU.
WHAT!?
THAT DIRTY RAT!!
....

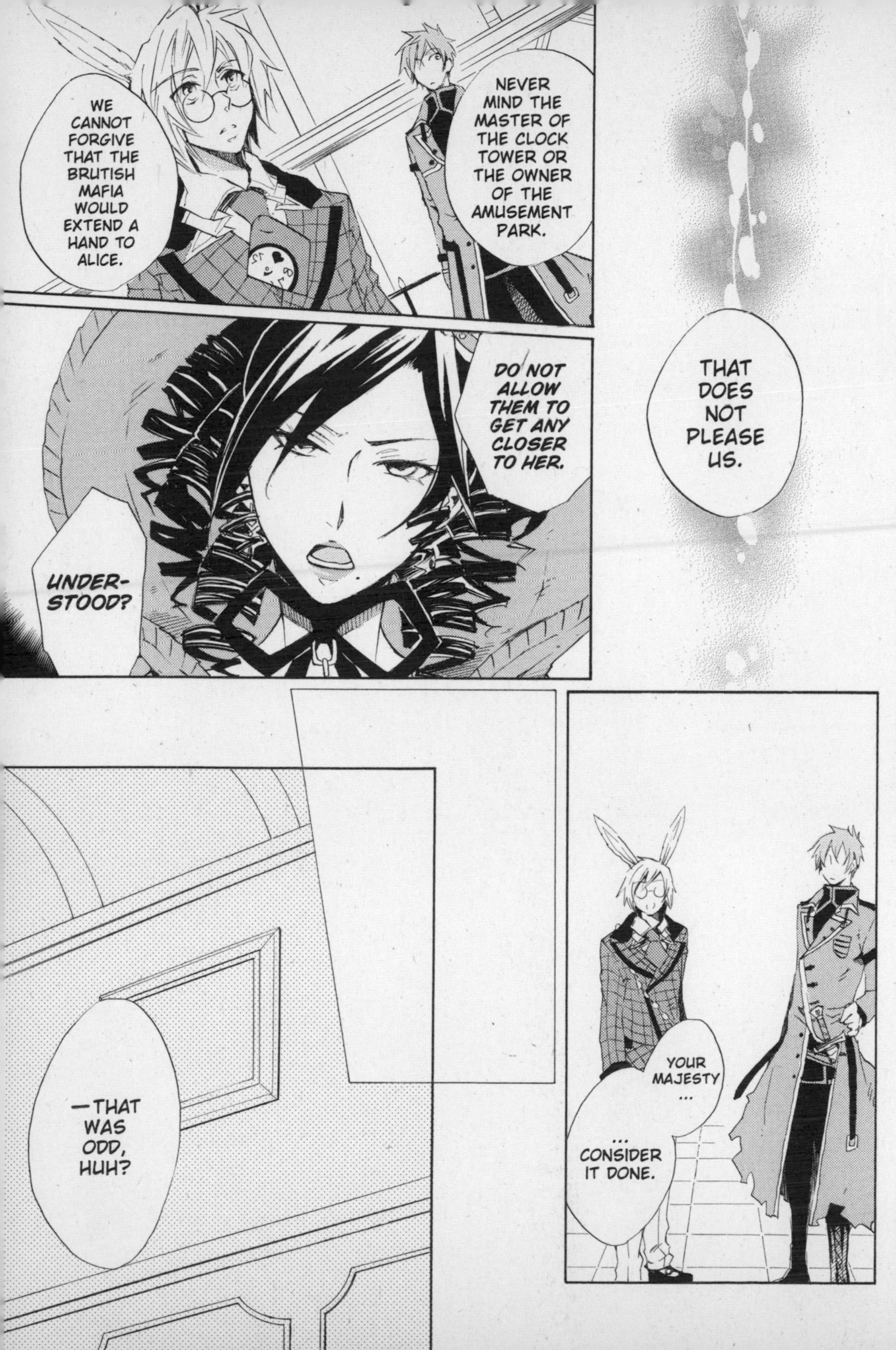
THAT DOES NOT PLEASE US.
NEVER MIND THE MASTER OF THE CLOCK TOWER OR THE OWNER OF THE AMUSEMENT PARK.
WE CANNOT FORGIVE THAT THE BRUTISH MAFIA WOULD EXTEND A HAND TO ALICE.
DO NOT ALLOW THEM TO GET ANY CLOSER TO HER.
UNDER-STOOD?
YOUR MAJESTY ...
... CONSIDER IT DONE.
—THAT WAS ODD, HUH?

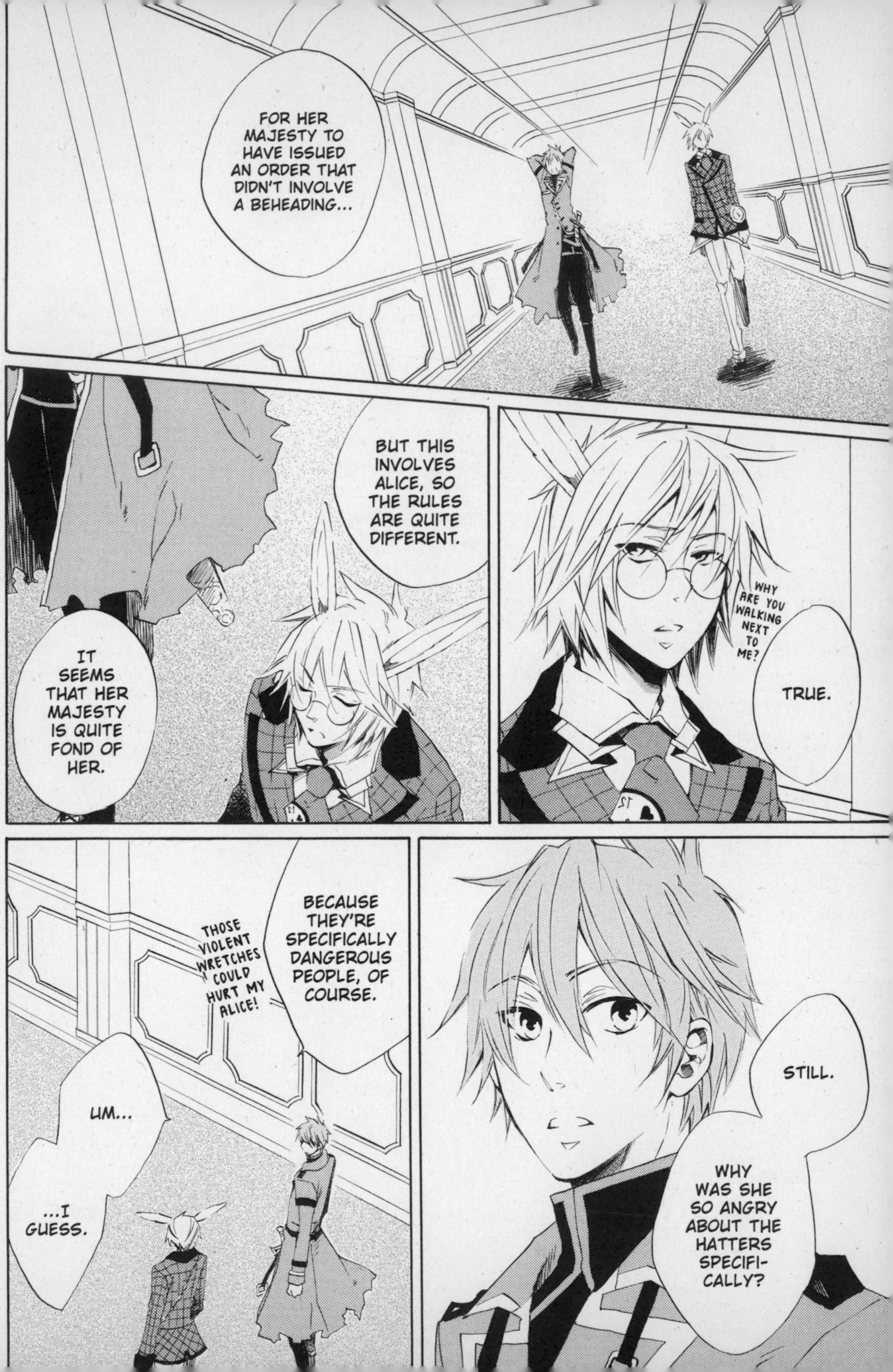
FOR HER MAJESTY TO HAVE ISSUED AN ORDER THAT DIDN'T INVOLVE A BEHEADING...
TRUE.
WHY ARE YOU WALKING NEXT TO ME?
BUT THIS INVOLVES ALICE, SO THE RULES ARE QUITE DIFFERENT.
IT SEEMS THAT HER MAJESTY IS QUITE FOND OF HER.
STILL.
WHY WAS SHE SO ANGRY ABOUT THE HATTERS SPECIFI-CALLY?
BECAUSE THEY'RE SPECIFICALLY DANGEROUS PEOPLE, OF COURSE.
THOSE VIOLENT WRETCHES COULD HURT MY ALICE!
UM...
...I GUESS.

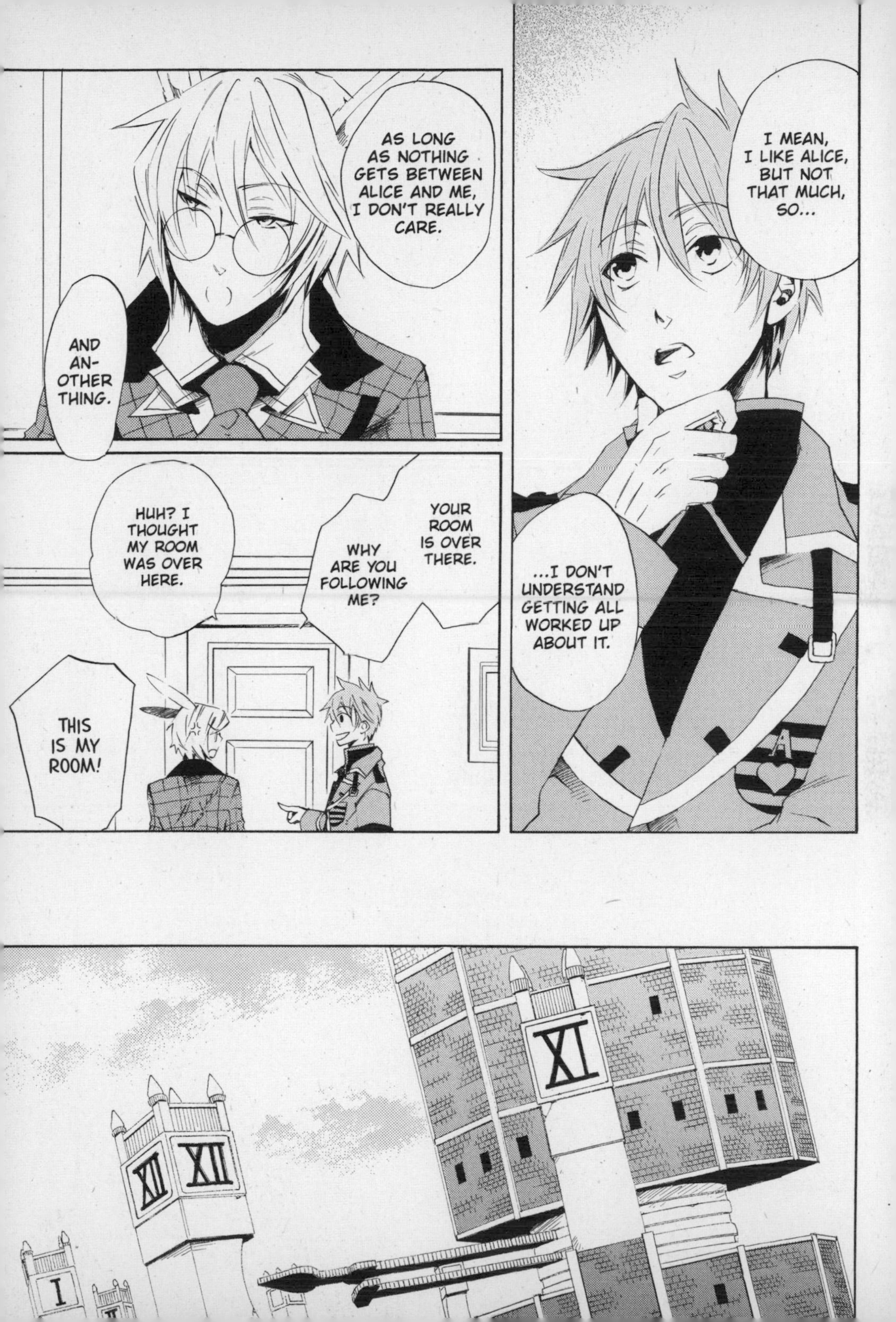
I MEAN, I LIKE ALICE, BUT NOT THAT MUCH, SO...
...I DON'T UNDERSTAND GETTING ALL WORKED UP ABOUT IT.
AS LONG AS NOTHING GETS BETWEEN ALICE AND ME, I DON'T REALLY CARE.
AND AN-OTHER THING.
YOUR ROOM IS OVER THERE.
WHY ARE YOU FOLLOWING ME?
HUH? I THOUGHT MY ROOM WAS OVER HERE.
THIS IS MY ROOM!

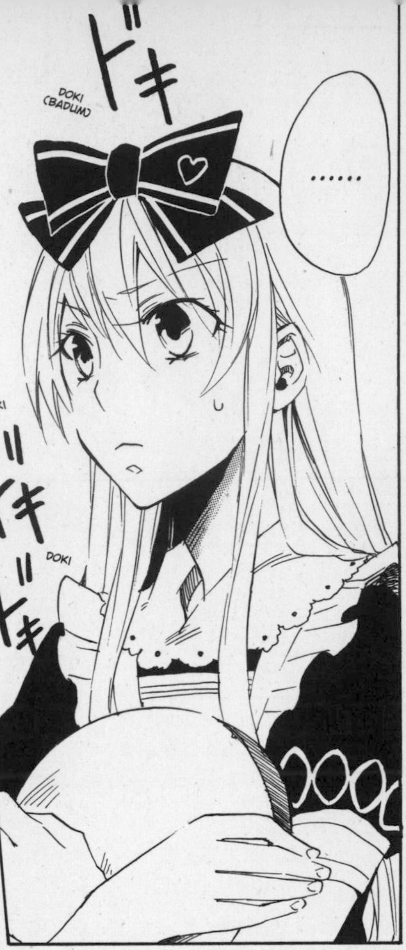
ドキ
DOKI (BADUM)
......
DOKI
ドキ
DOKI
ドキ
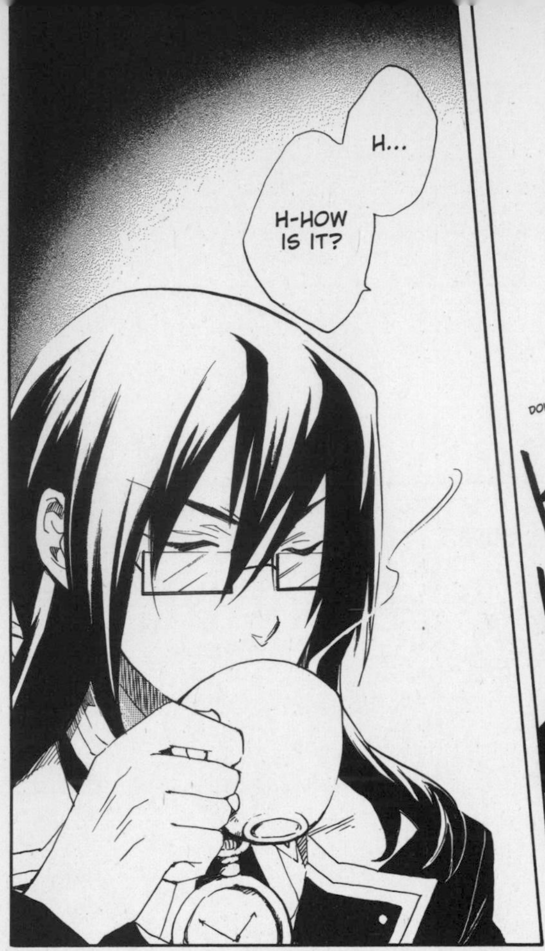
H...
H-HOW IS IT?
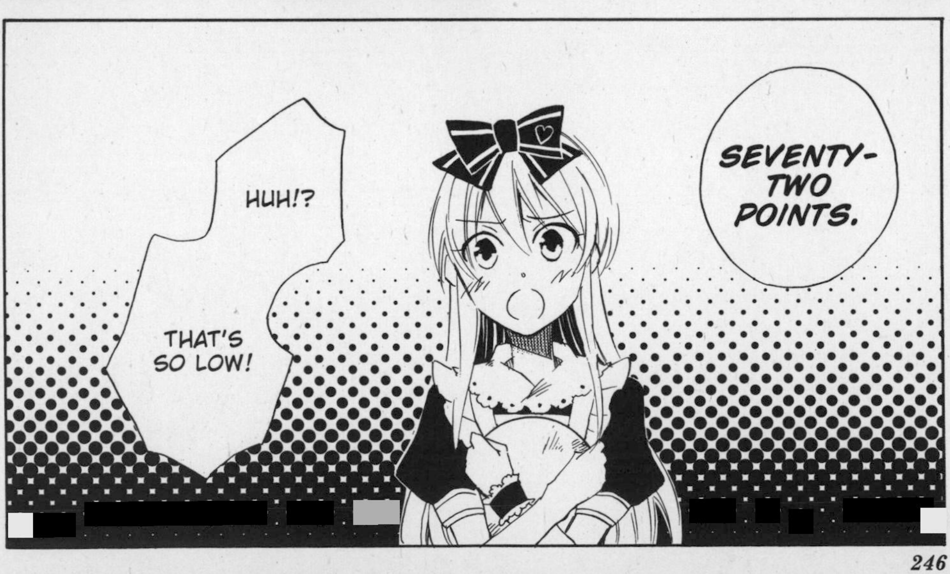
SEVENTY-TWO POINTS.
HUH!?
THAT'S SO LOW!
[redacted]

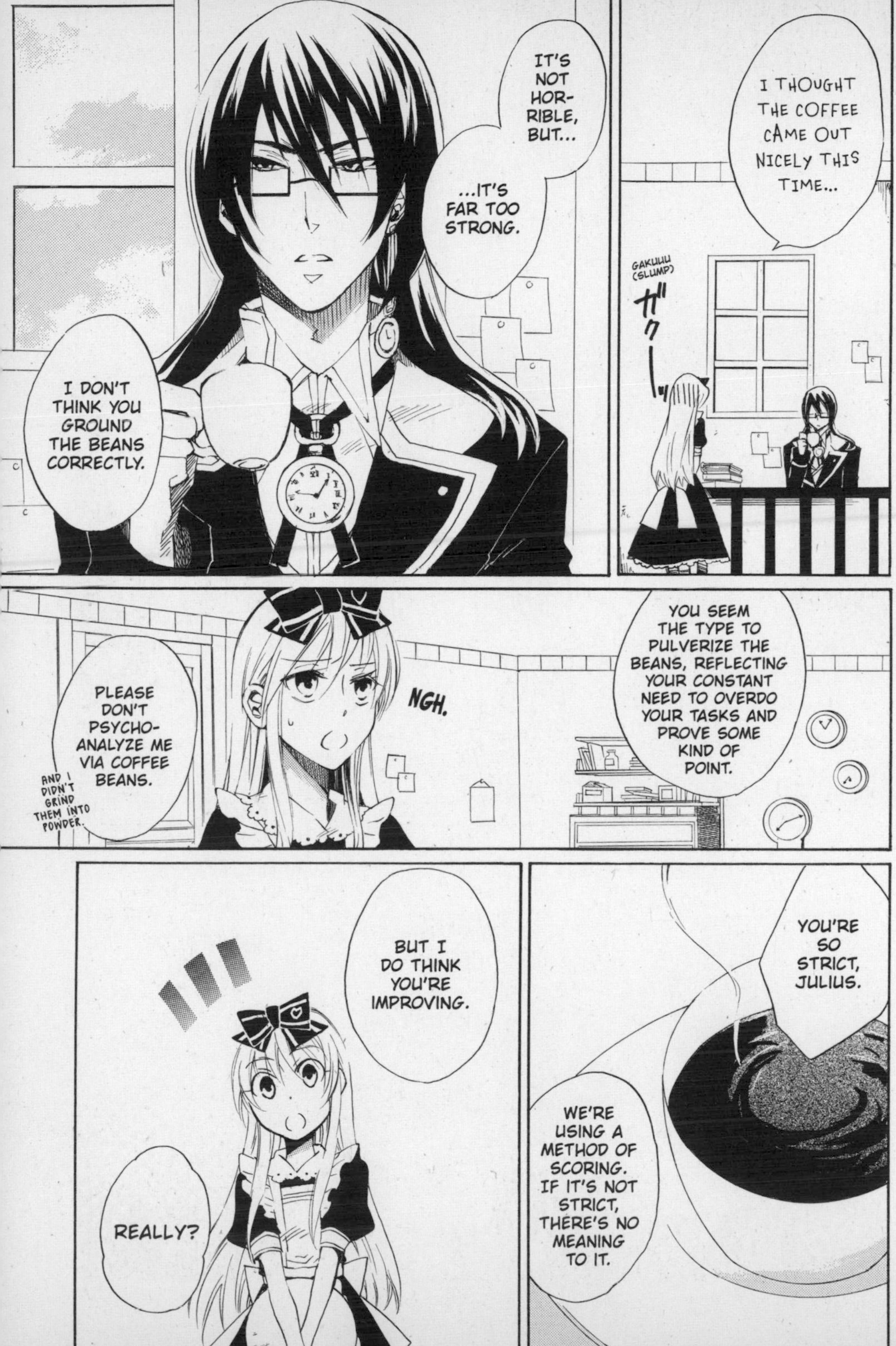
I THOUGHT THE COFFEE CAME OUT NICELY THIS TIME...
GAKUUU (SLUMP)
IT'S NOT HORRIBLE, BUT...
...IT'S FAR TOO STRONG.
I DON'T THINK YOU GROUND THE BEANS CORRECTLY.
YOU SEEM THE TYPE TO PULVERIZE THE BEANS, REFLECTING YOUR CONSTANT NEED TO OVERDO YOUR TASKS AND PROVE SOME KIND OF POINT.
NGH.
PLEASE DON'T PSYCHO-ANALYZE ME VIA COFFEE BEANS.
AND I DIDN'T GRIND THEM INTO POWDER.
YOU'RE SO STRICT, JULIUS.
WE'RE USING A METHOD OF SCORING. IF IT'S NOT STRICT, THERE'S NO MEANING TO IT.
BUT I DO THINK YOU'RE IMPROVING.
REALLY?

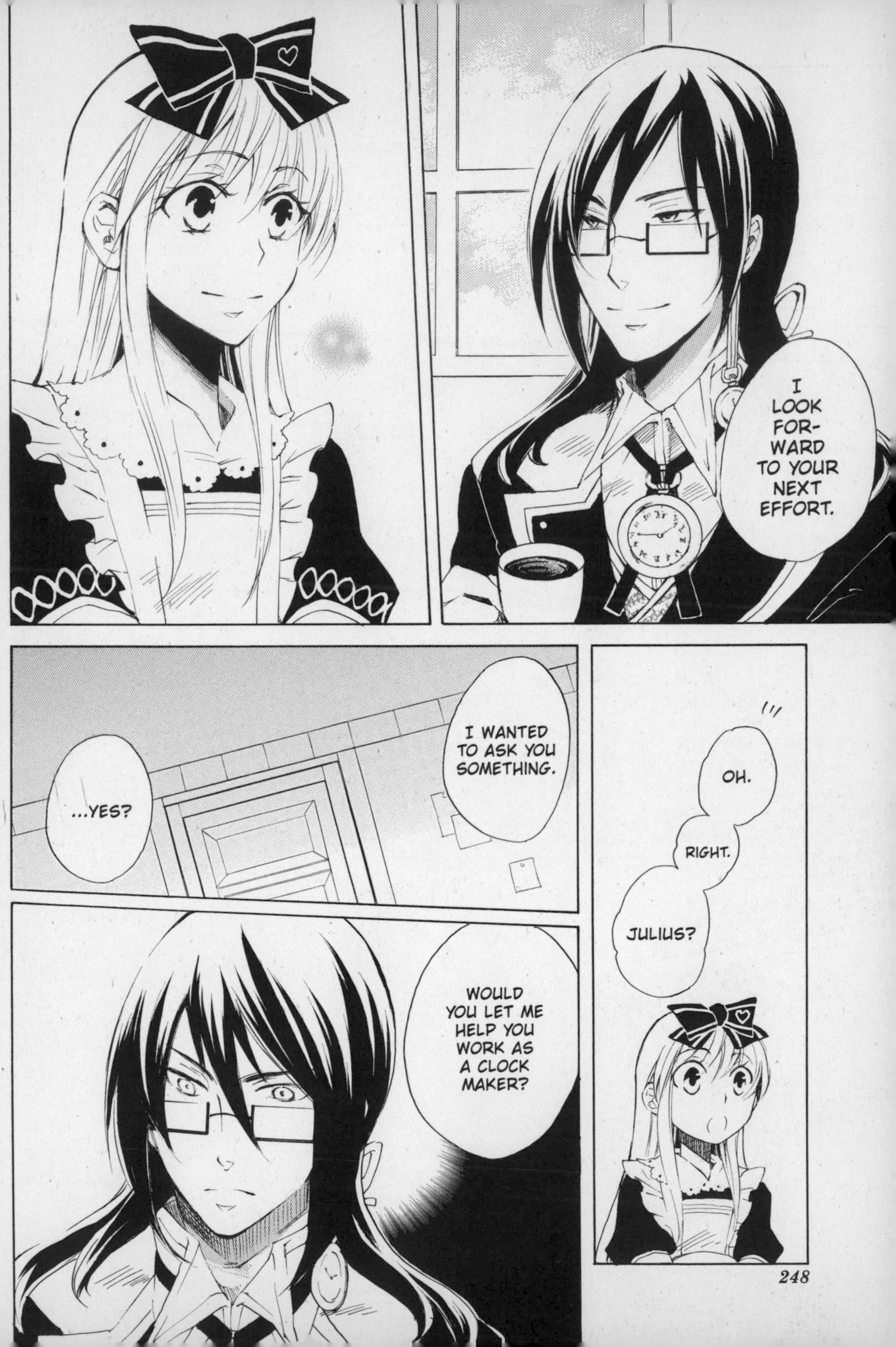
I LOOK FOR-WARD TO YOUR NEXT EFFORT.
OH.
RIGHT.
JULIUS?
I WANTED TO ASK YOU SOMETHING.
...YES?
WOULD YOU LET ME HELP YOU WORK AS A CLOCK MAKER?

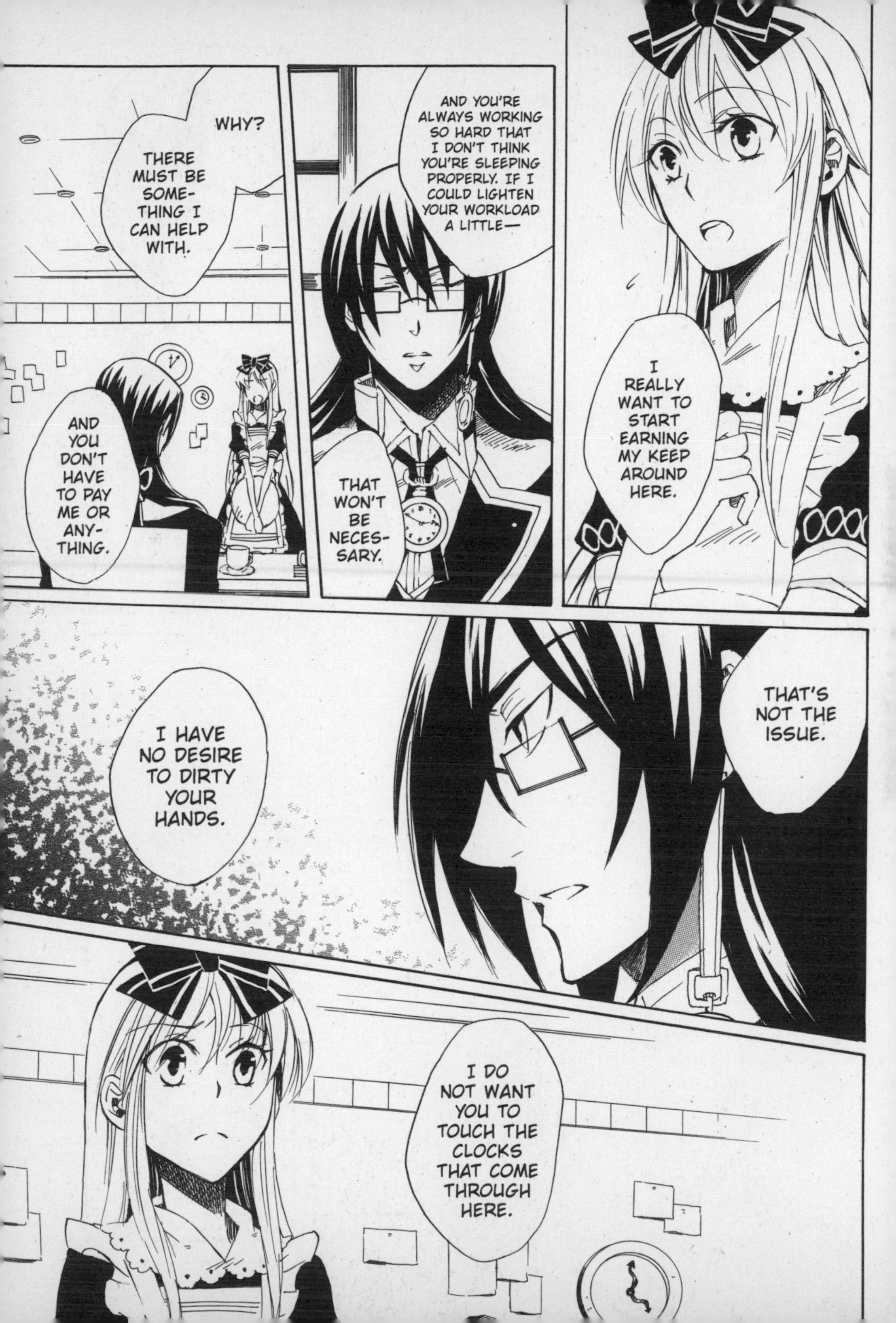
I REALLY WANT TO START EARNING MY KEEP AROUND HERE.
AND YOU'RE ALWAYS WORKING SO HARD THAT I DON'T THINK YOU'RE SLEEPING PROPERLY. IF I COULD LIGHTEN YOUR WORKLOAD A LITTLE—
THAT WON'T BE NECESSARY.
WHY?
THERE MUST BE SOMETHING I CAN HELP WITH.
AND YOU DON'T HAVE TO PAY ME OR ANYTHING.
THAT'S NOT THE ISSUE.
I HAVE NO DESIRE TO DIRTY YOUR HANDS.
I DO NOT WANT YOU TO TOUCH THE CLOCKS THAT COME THROUGH HERE.

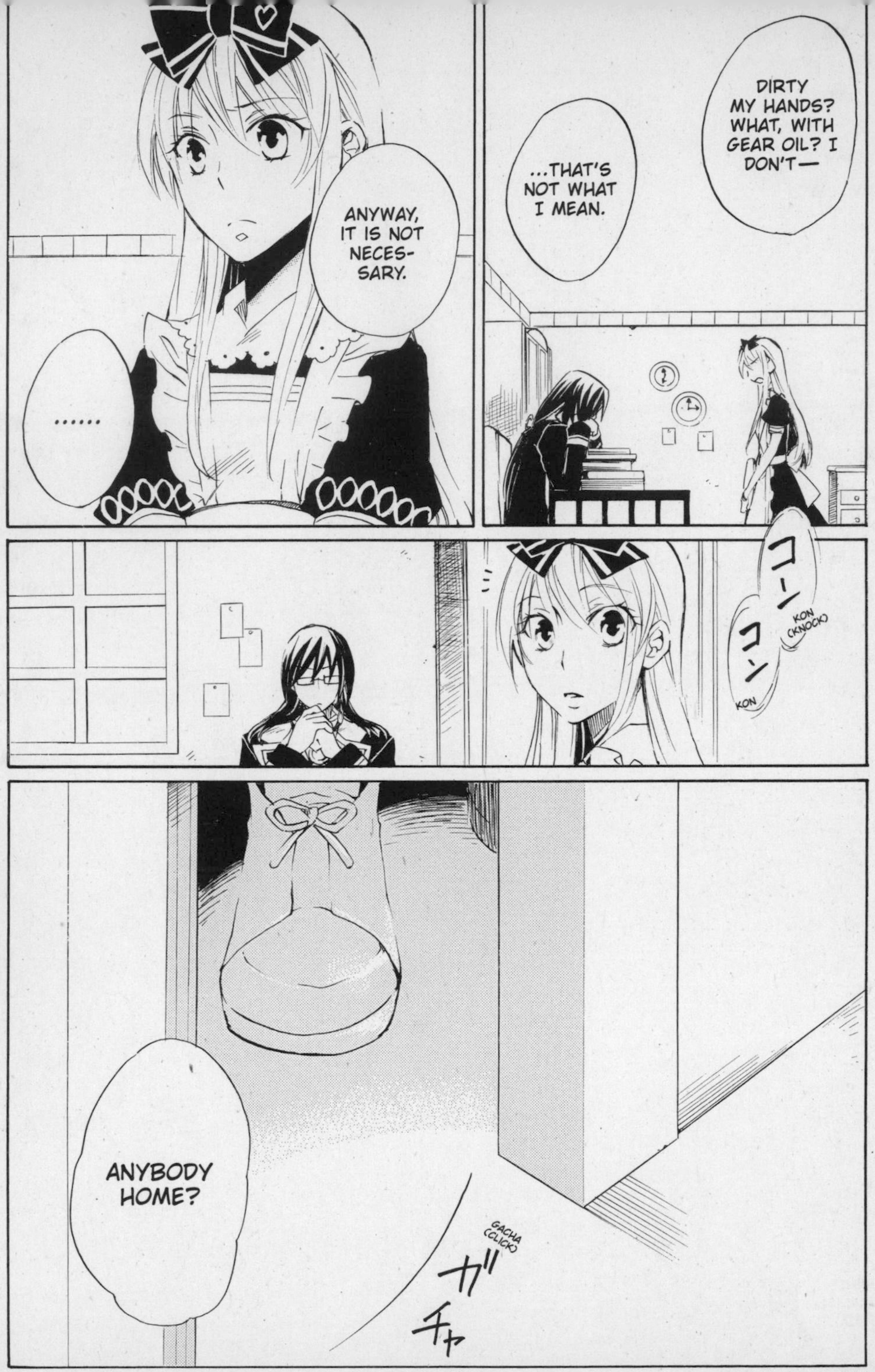
DIRTY MY HANDS? WHAT, WITH GEAR OIL? I DON'T—
...THAT'S NOT WHAT I MEAN.
ANYWAY, IT IS NOT NECES-SARY.
......
コンコン
KON (KNOCK)
KON
ANYBODY HOME?
ガチャ
GACHA (CLICK)

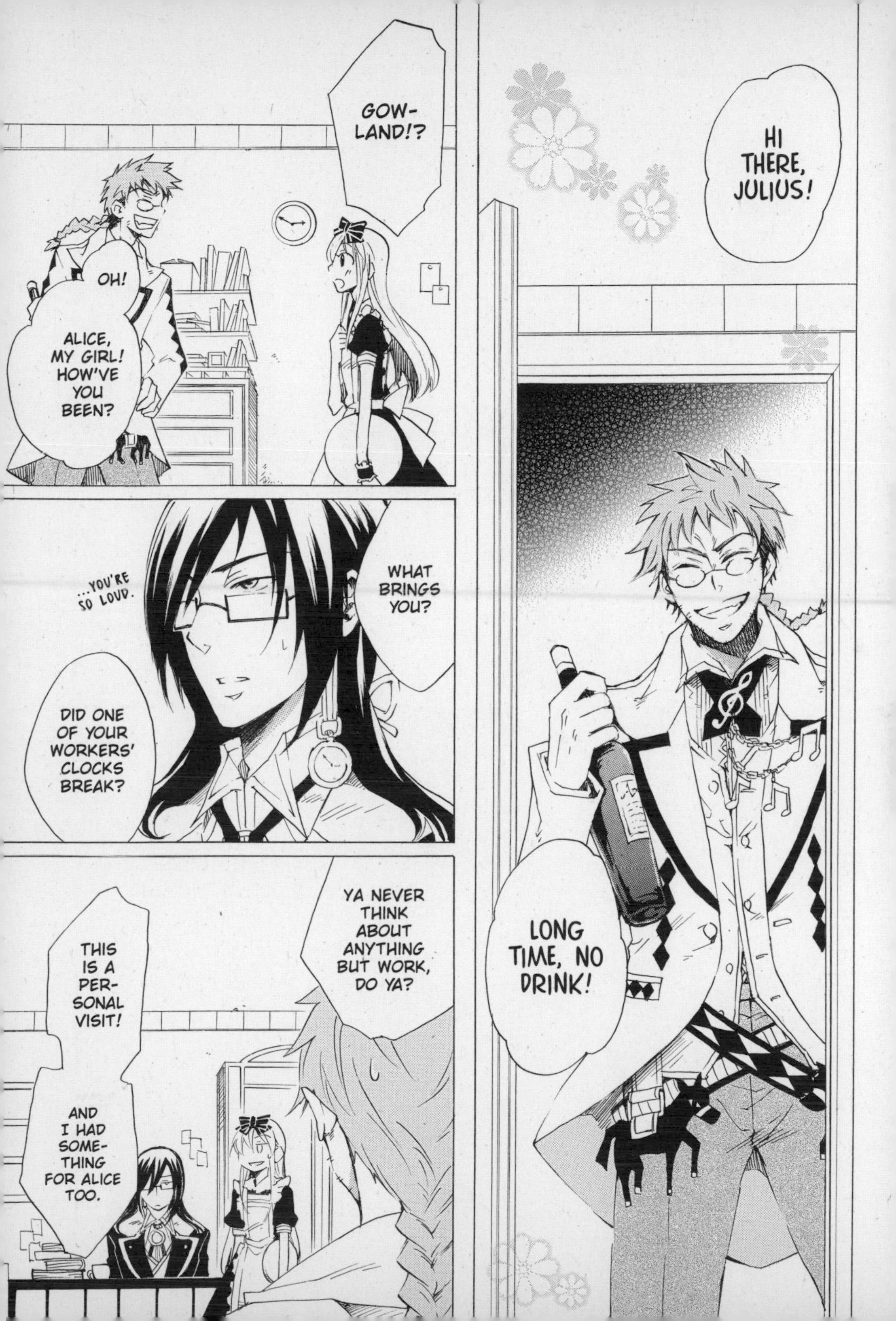
HI THERE, JULIUS!
LONG TIME, NO DRINK!
GOW-LAND!?
OH!
ALICE, MY GIRL! HOW'VE YOU BEEN?
WHAT BRINGS YOU?
...YOU'RE SO LOUD.
DID ONE OF YOUR WORKERS' CLOCKS BREAK?
YA NEVER THINK ABOUT ANYTHING BUT WORK, DO YA?
THIS IS A PERSONAL VISIT!
AND I HAD SOMETHING FOR ALICE TOO.

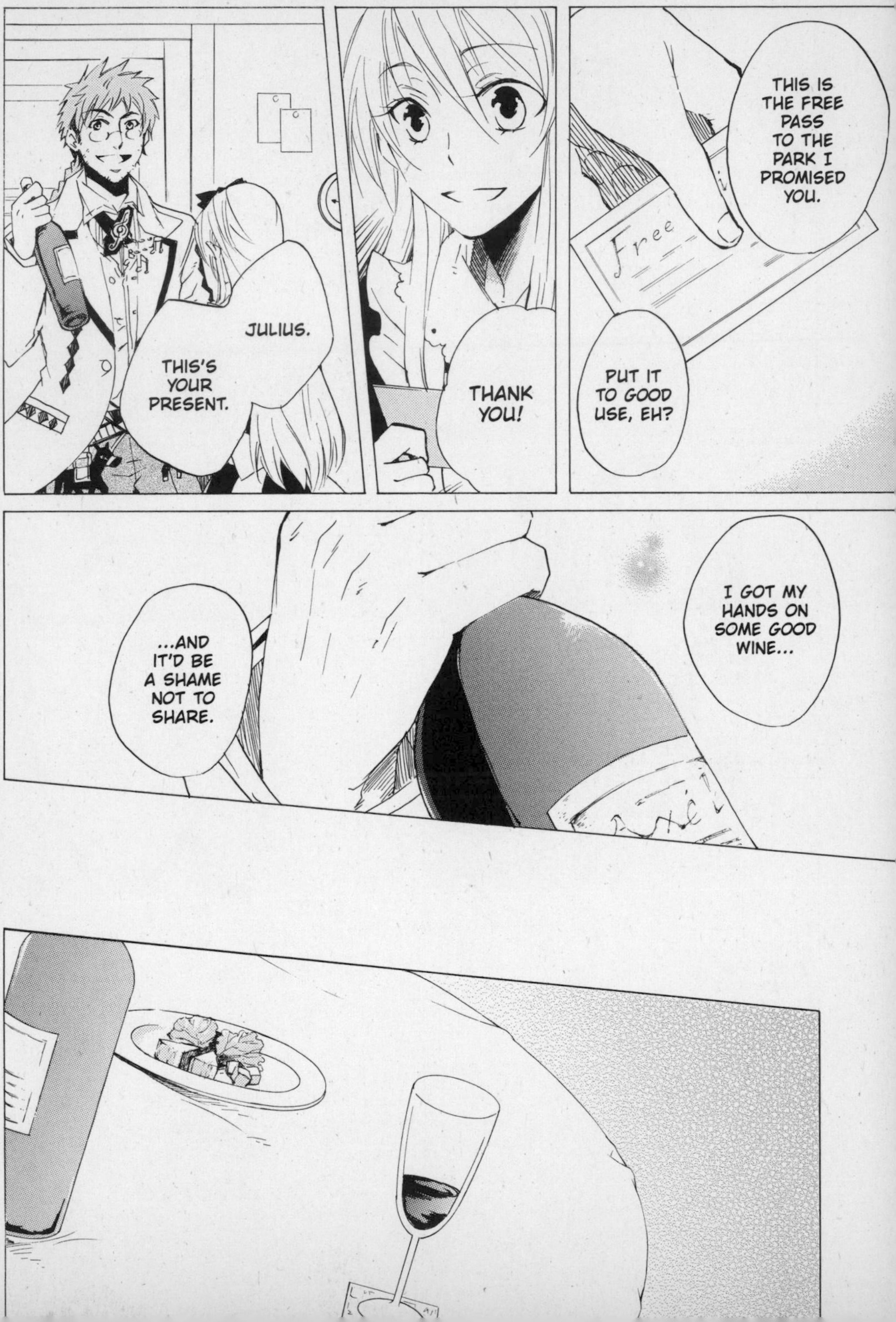
THIS IS THE FREE PASS TO THE PARK I PROMISED YOU.
Free
PUT IT TO GOOD USE, EH?
THANK YOU!
JULIUS.
THIS'S YOUR PRESENT.
I GOT MY HANDS ON SOME GOOD WINE...
...AND IT'D BE A SHAME NOT TO SHARE.

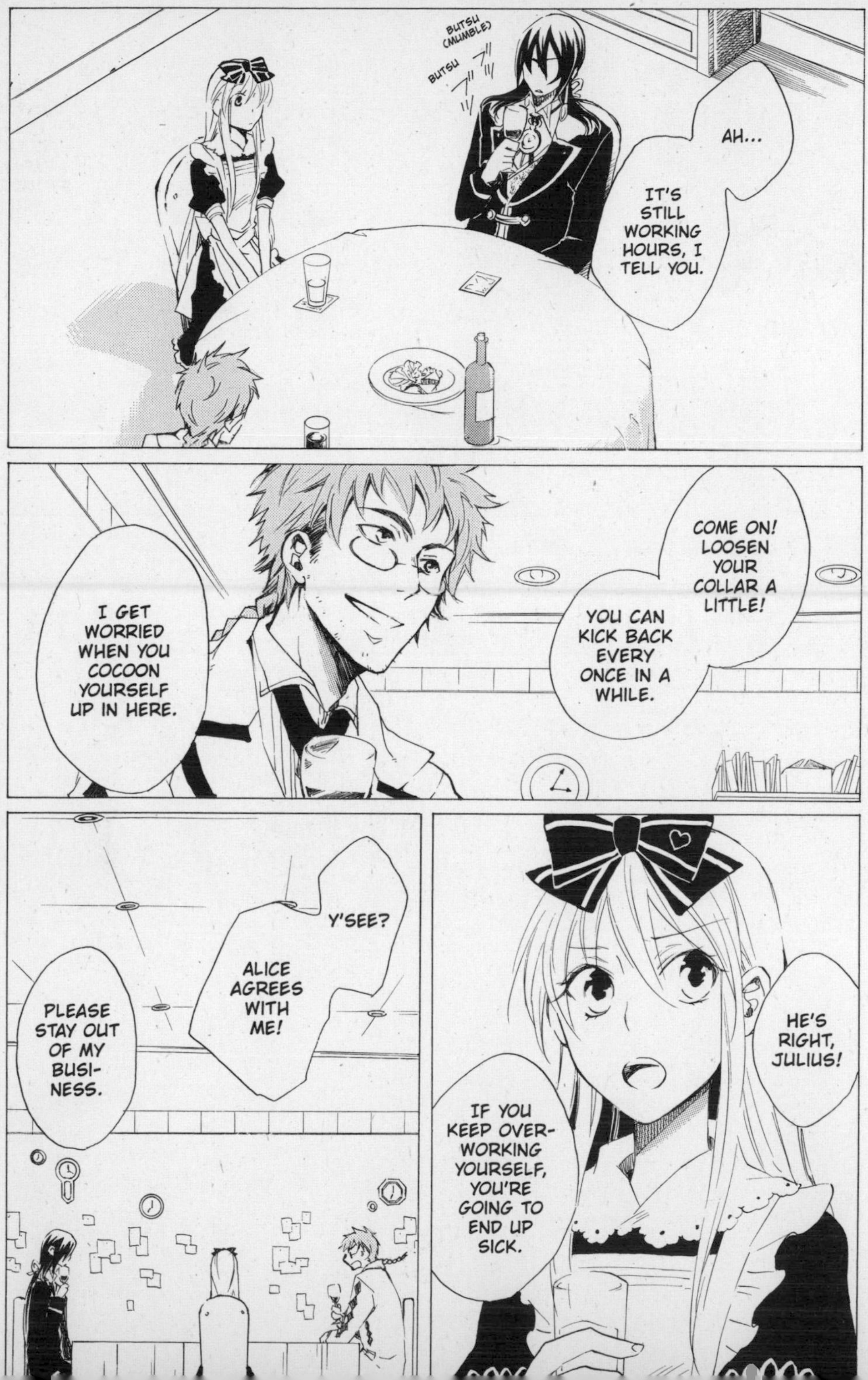
BUTSU (MUMBLE)
BUTSU
AH...
IT'S STILL WORKING HOURS, I TELL YOU.
COME ON! LOOSEN YOUR COLLAR A LITTLE!
YOU CAN KICK BACK EVERY ONCE IN A WHILE.
I GET WORRIED WHEN YOU COCOON YOURSELF UP IN HERE.
HE'S RIGHT, JULIUS!
IF YOU KEEP OVER-WORKING YOURSELF, YOU'RE GOING TO END UP SICK.
Y'SEE?
ALICE AGREES WITH ME!
PLEASE STAY OUT OF MY BUSI-NESS.

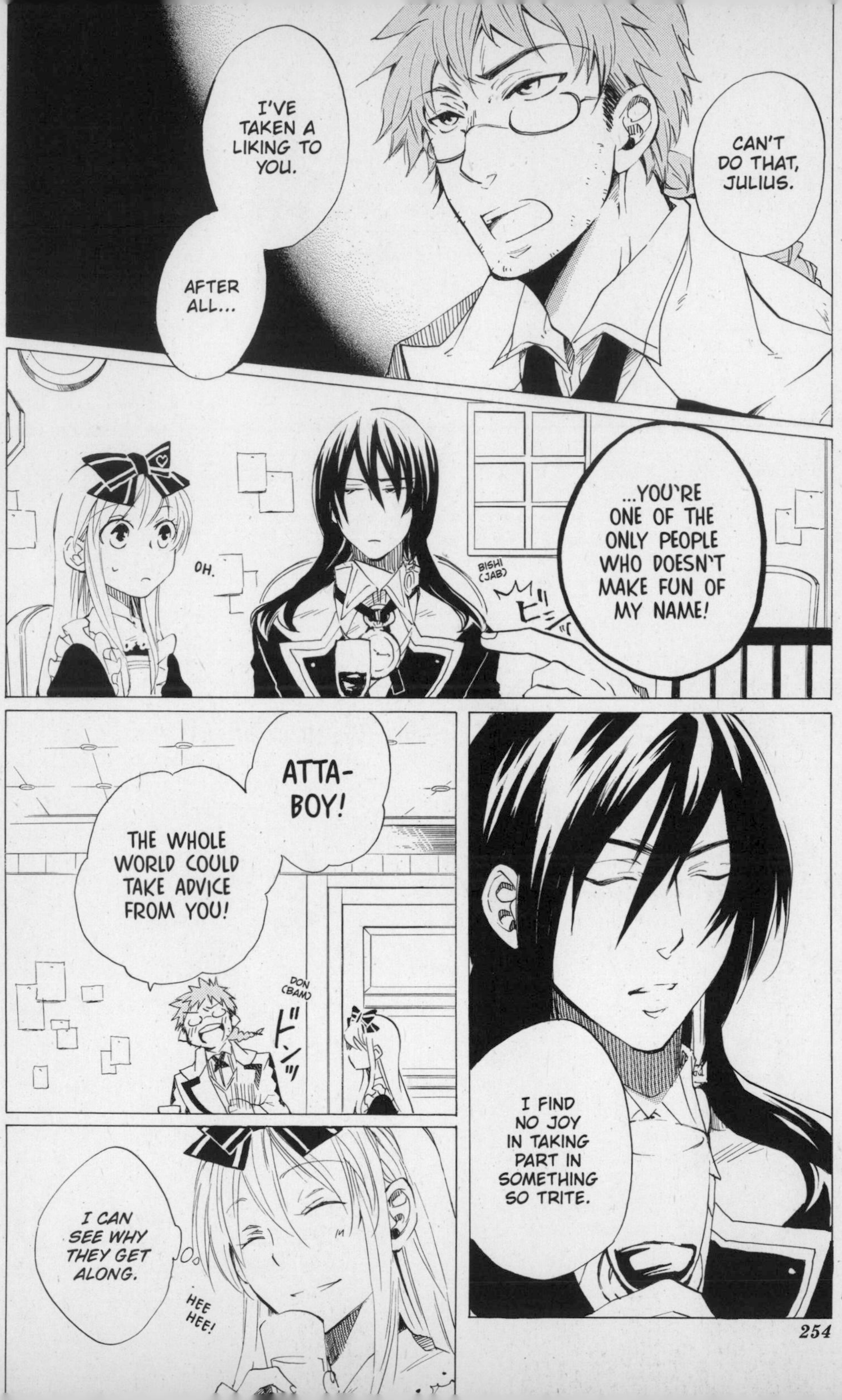
CAN'T DO THAT, JULIUS.
I'VE TAKEN A LIKING TO YOU.
AFTER ALL...
...YOU'RE ONE OF THE ONLY PEOPLE WHO DOESN'T MAKE FUN OF MY NAME!
BISHI (JAB)
OH.
I FIND NO JOY IN TAKING PART IN SOMETHING SO TRITE.
ATTA-BOY!
THE WHOLE WORLD COULD TAKE ADVICE FROM YOU!
DON (BAM)
I CAN SEE WHY THEY GET ALONG.
HEE HEE!

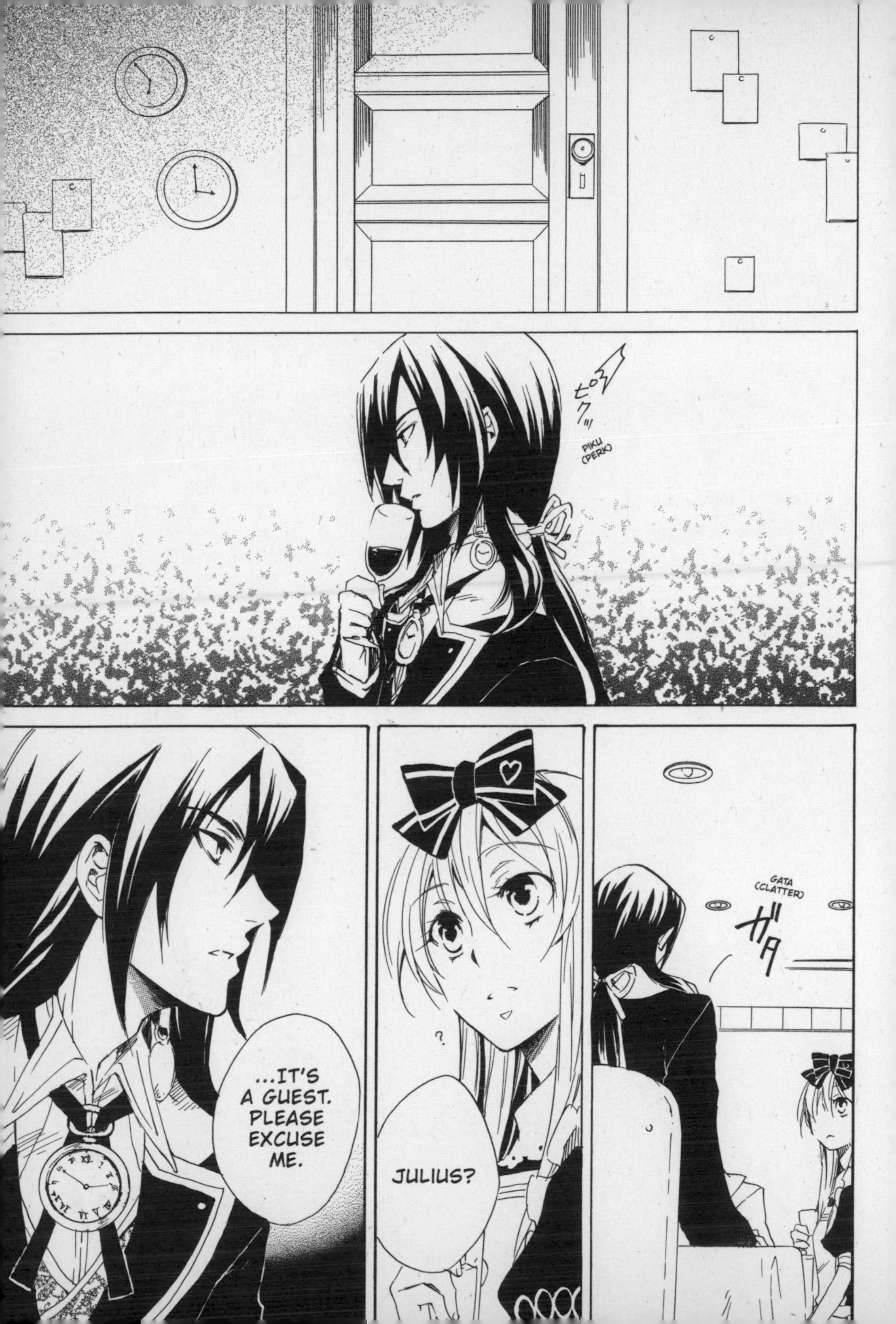
ピクッ
PIKU (PERK)
GATA (CLATTER)
ガタ
JULIUS?
...IT'S A GUEST. PLEASE EXCUSE ME.

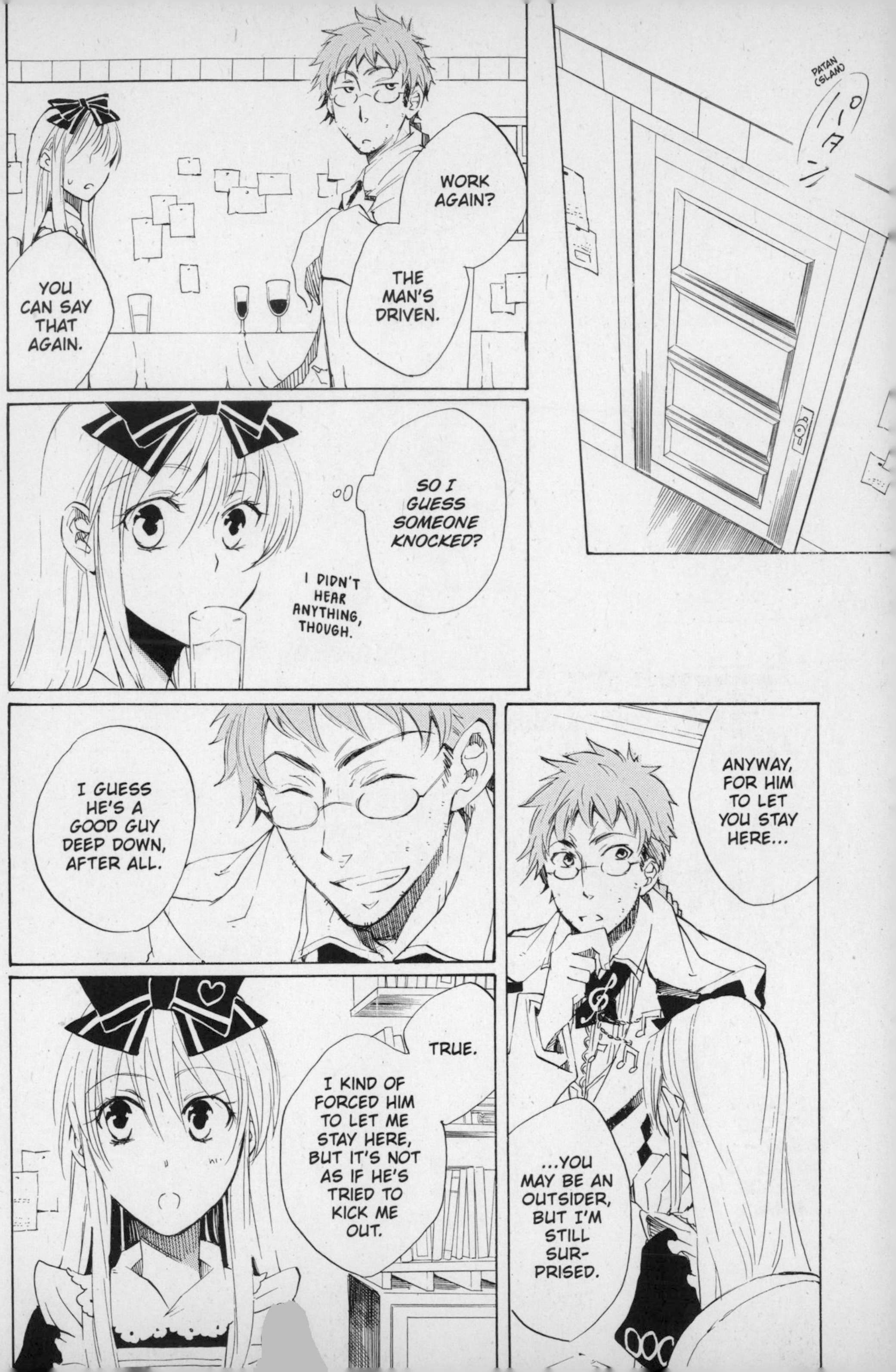
PATAN (SLAM)
パタン
WORK AGAIN?
THE MAN'S DRIVEN.
YOU CAN SAY THAT AGAIN.
SO I GUESS SOMEONE KNOCKED?
I DIDN'T HEAR ANYTHING, THOUGH.
ANYWAY, FOR HIM TO LET YOU STAY HERE...
...YOU MAY BE AN OUTSIDER, BUT I'M STILL SUR-PRISED.
I GUESS HE'S A GOOD GUY DEEP DOWN, AFTER ALL.
TRUE.
I KIND OF FORCED HIM TO LET ME STAY HERE, BUT IT'S NOT AS IF HE'S TRIED TO KICK ME OUT.

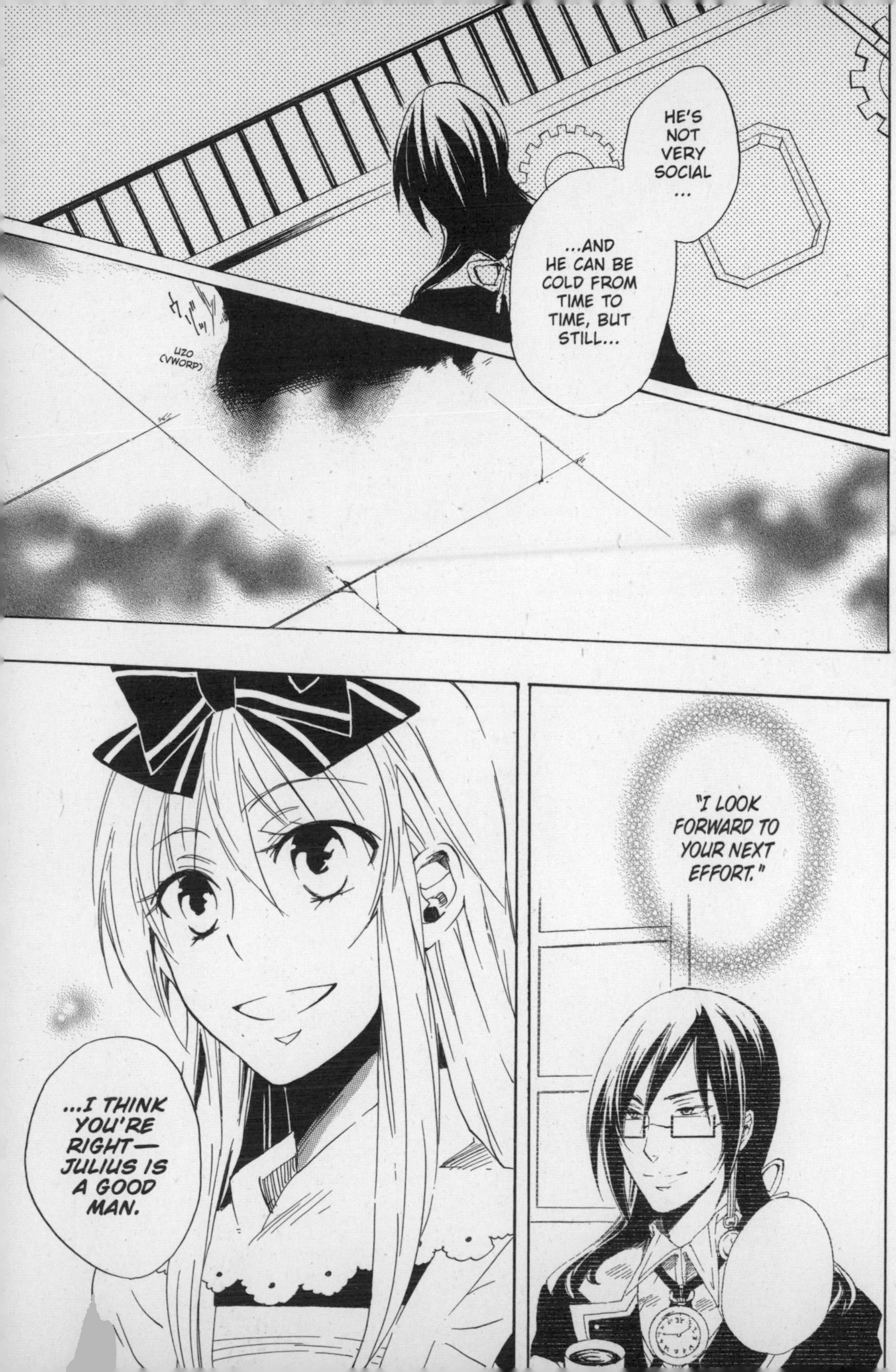
HE'S NOT VERY SOCIAL ...
...AND HE CAN BE COLD FROM TIME TO TIME, BUT STILL...
UZO (VWORP)
"I LOOK FORWARD TO YOUR NEXT EFFORT."
...I THINK YOU'RE RIGHT—JULIUS IS A GOOD MAN.

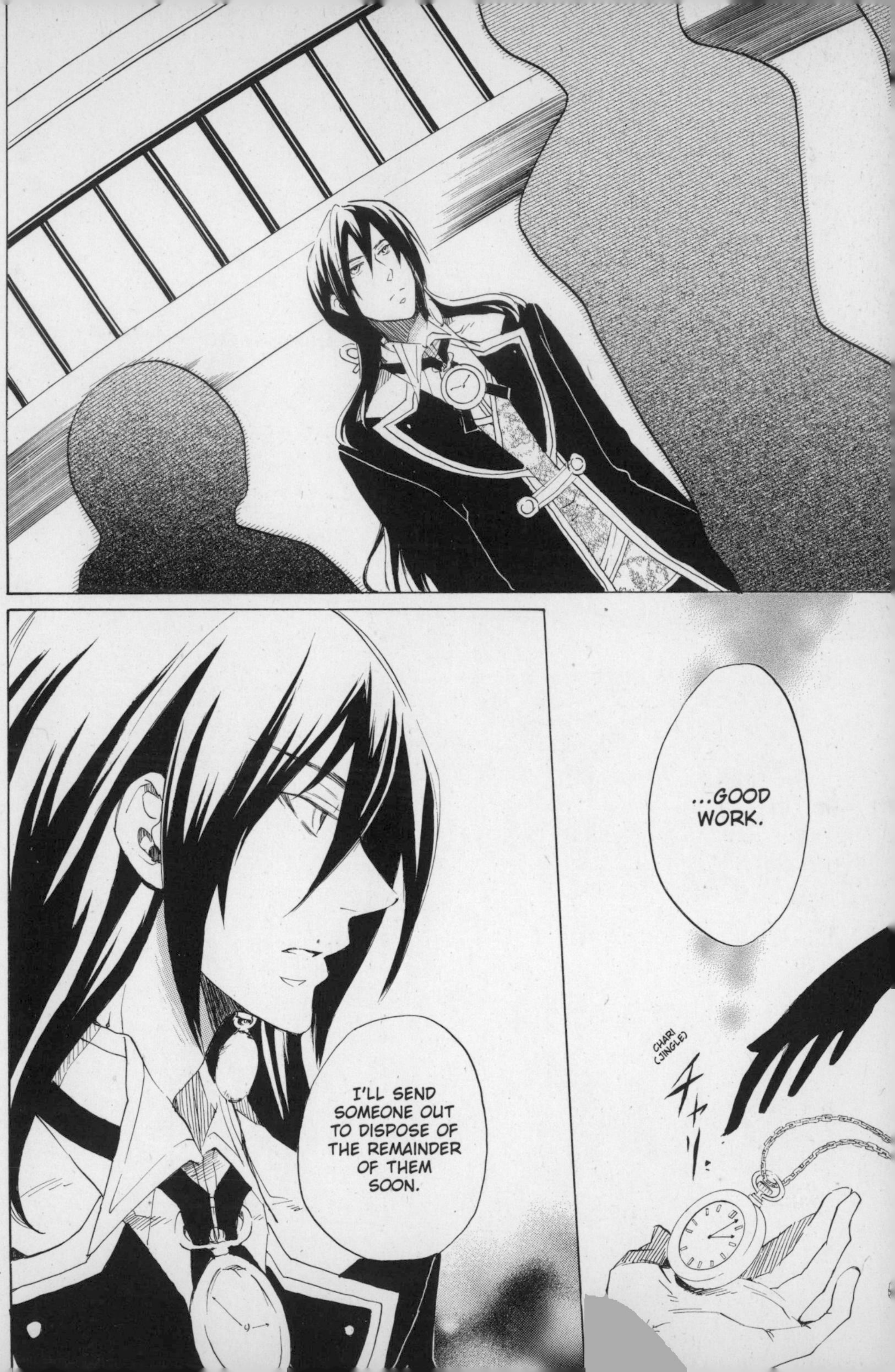
...GOOD WORK.
CHARI (JINGLE)
I'LL SEND SOMEONE OUT TO DISPOSE OF THE REMAINDER OF THEM SOON.

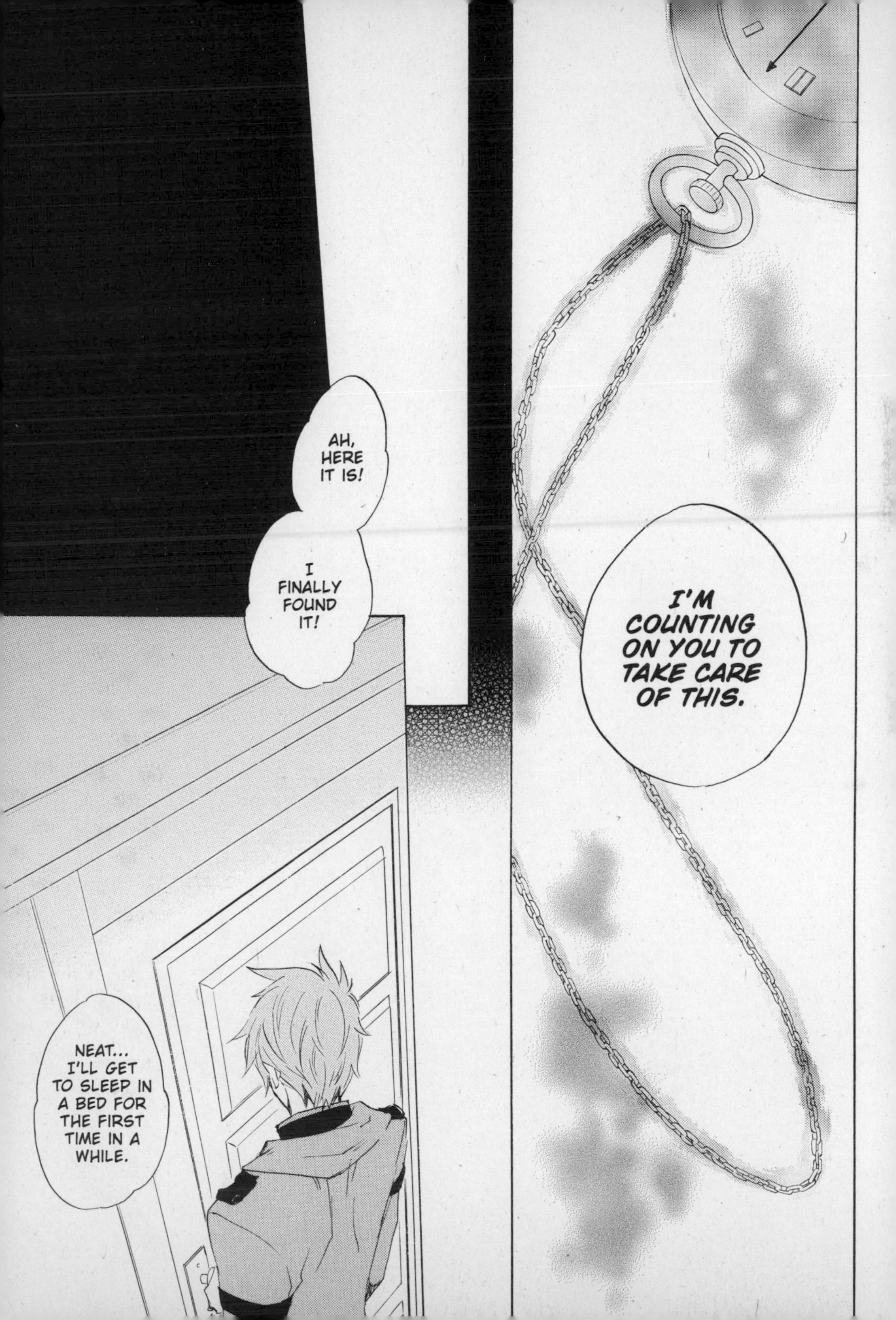
I'M COUNTING ON YOU TO TAKE CARE OF THIS.
AH, HERE IT IS!
I FINALLY FOUND IT!
NEAT... I'LL GET TO SLEEP IN A BED FOR THE FIRST TIME IN A WHILE.

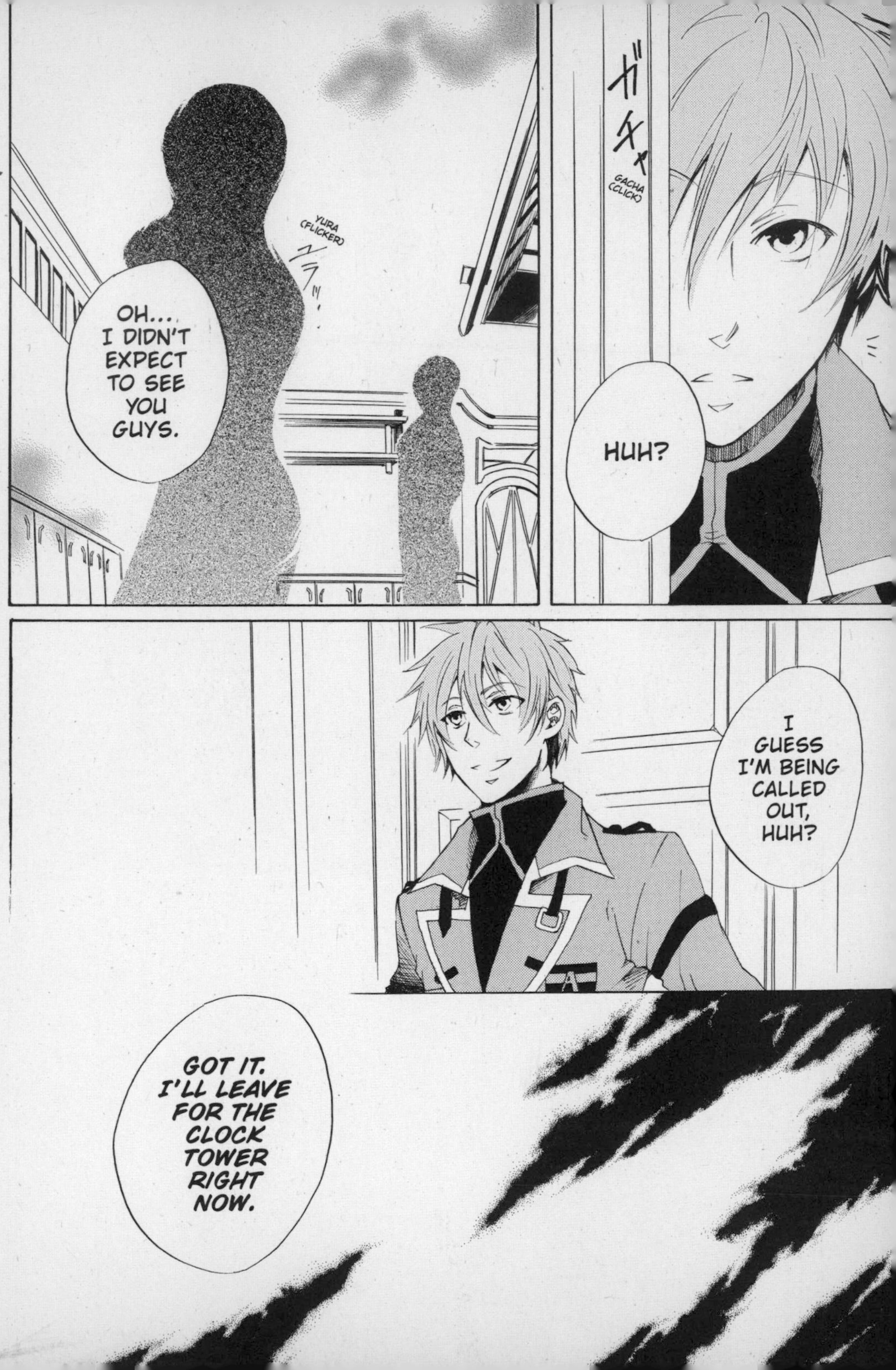
ガチャ
GACHA (CLICK)
HUH?
YURA (FLICKER)
OH... I DIDN'T EXPECT TO SEE YOU GUYS.
I GUESS I'M BEING CALLED OUT, HUH?
GOT IT. I'LL LEAVE FOR THE CLOCK TOWER RIGHT NOW.

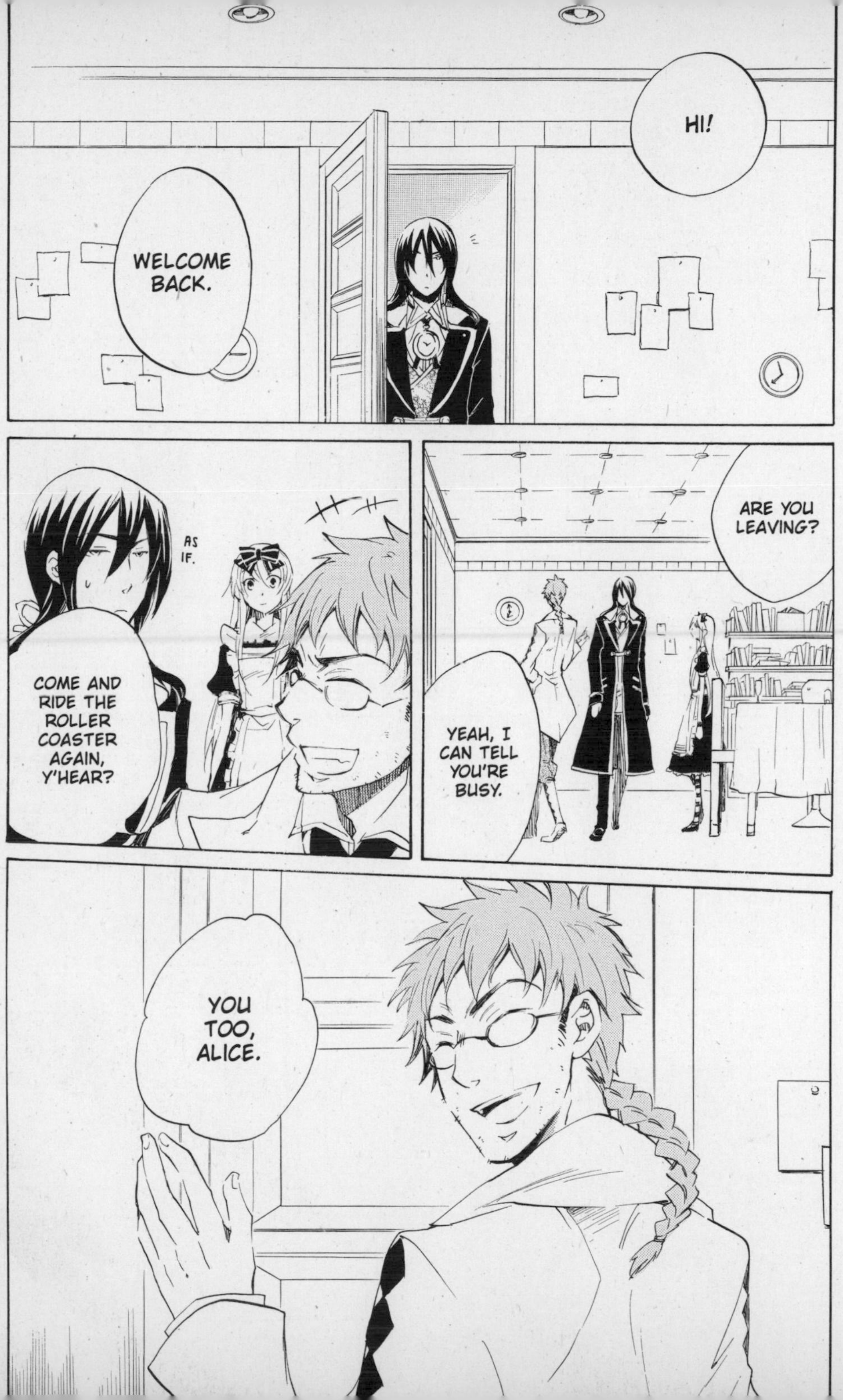
HI!
WELCOME BACK.
ARE YOU LEAVING?
YEAH, I CAN TELL YOU'RE BUSY.
AS IF.
COME AND RIDE THE ROLLER COASTER AGAIN, Y'HEAR?
YOU TOO, ALICE.

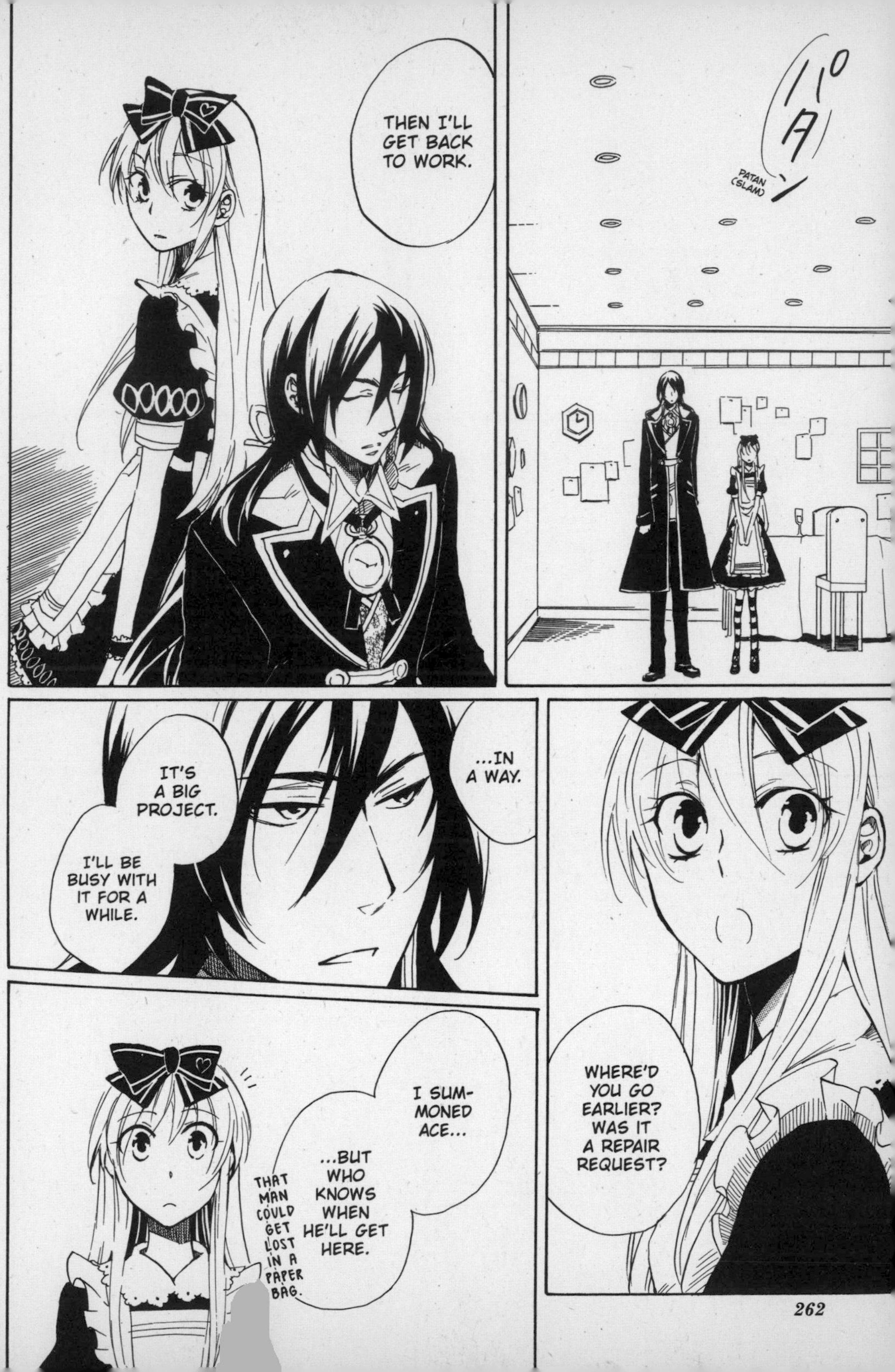
パタン
PATAN (SLAM)
THEN I'LL GET BACK TO WORK.
WHERE'D YOU GO EARLIER? WAS IT A REPAIR REQUEST?
...IN A WAY.
IT'S A BIG PROJECT.
I'LL BE BUSY WITH IT FOR A WHILE.
I SUMMONED ACE...
...BUT WHO KNOWS WHEN HE'LL GET HERE.
THAT MAN COULD GET LOST IN A PAPER BAG.

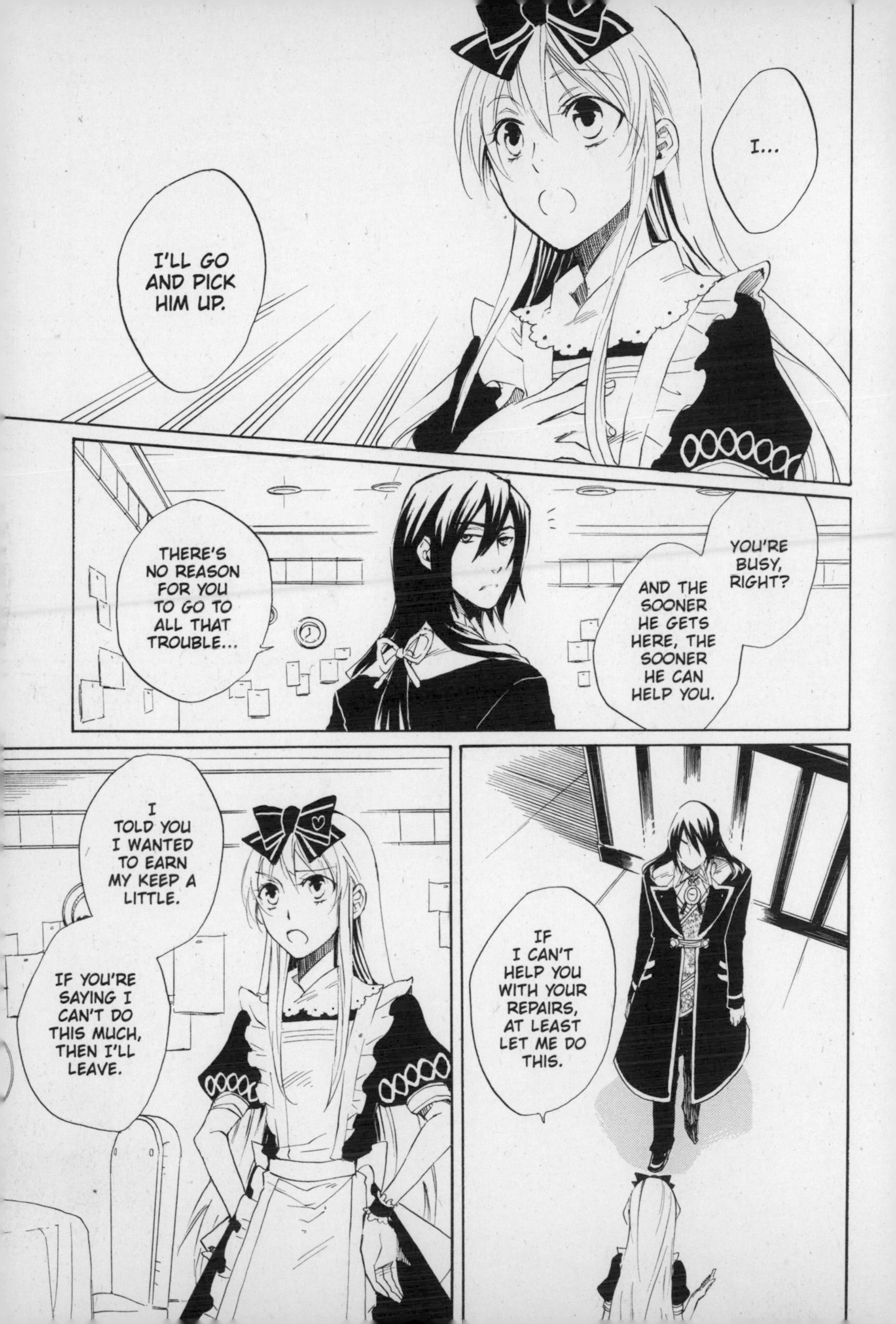
I...
I'LL GO AND PICK HIM UP.
THERE'S NO REASON FOR YOU TO GO TO ALL THAT TROUBLE...
YOU'RE BUSY, RIGHT?
AND THE SOONER HE GETS HERE, THE SOONER HE CAN HELP YOU.
IF I CAN'T HELP YOU WITH YOUR REPAIRS, AT LEAST LET ME DO THIS.
I TOLD YOU I WANTED TO EARN MY KEEP A LITTLE.
IF YOU'RE SAYING I CAN'T DO THIS MUCH, THEN I'LL LEAVE.

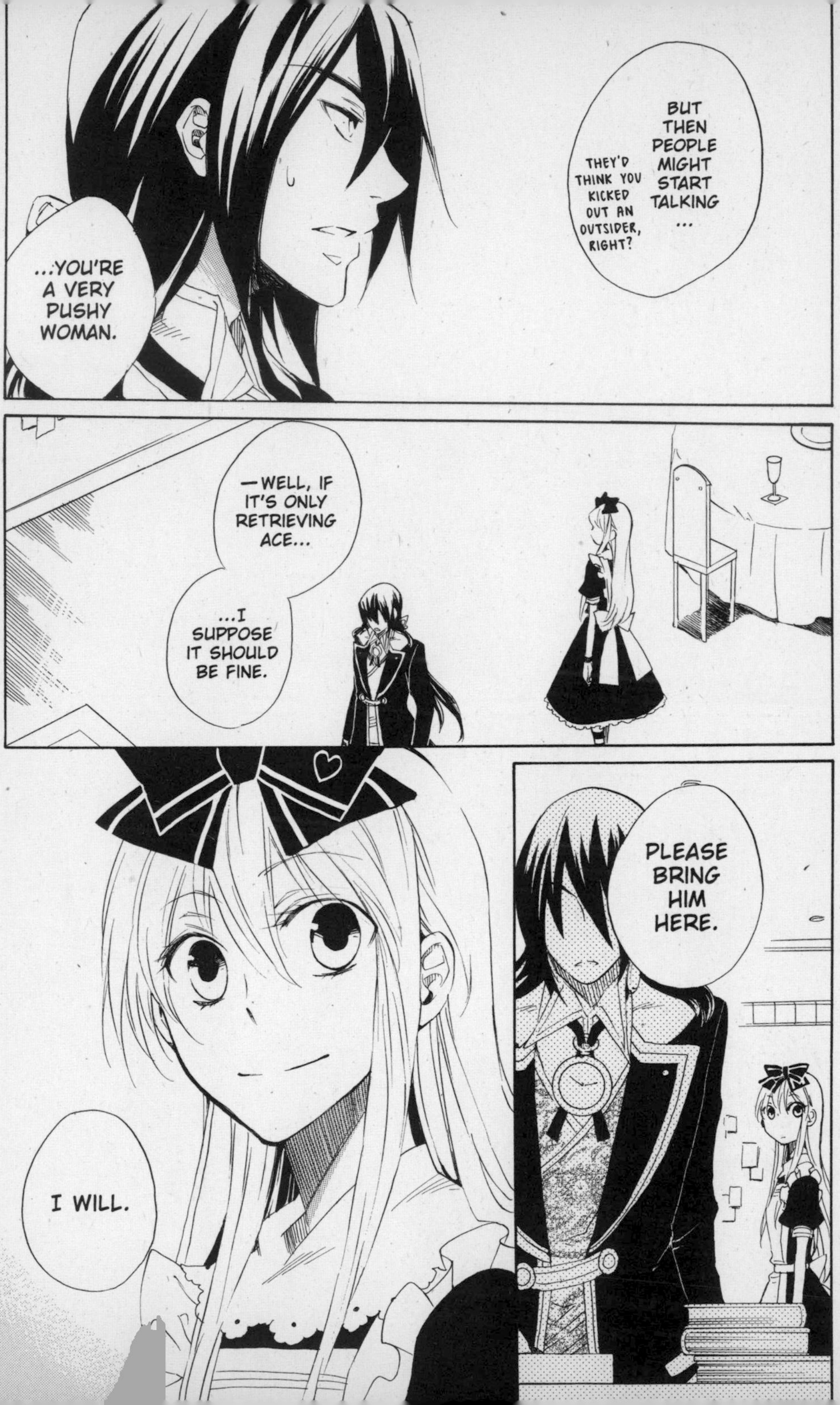
BUT THEN PEOPLE MIGHT START TALKING...
THEY'D THINK YOU KICKED OUT AN OUTSIDER, RIGHT?
...YOU'RE A VERY PUSHY WOMAN.
—WELL, IF IT'S ONLY RETRIEVING ACE...
...I SUPPOSE IT SHOULD BE FINE.
PLEASE BRING HIM HERE.
I WILL.

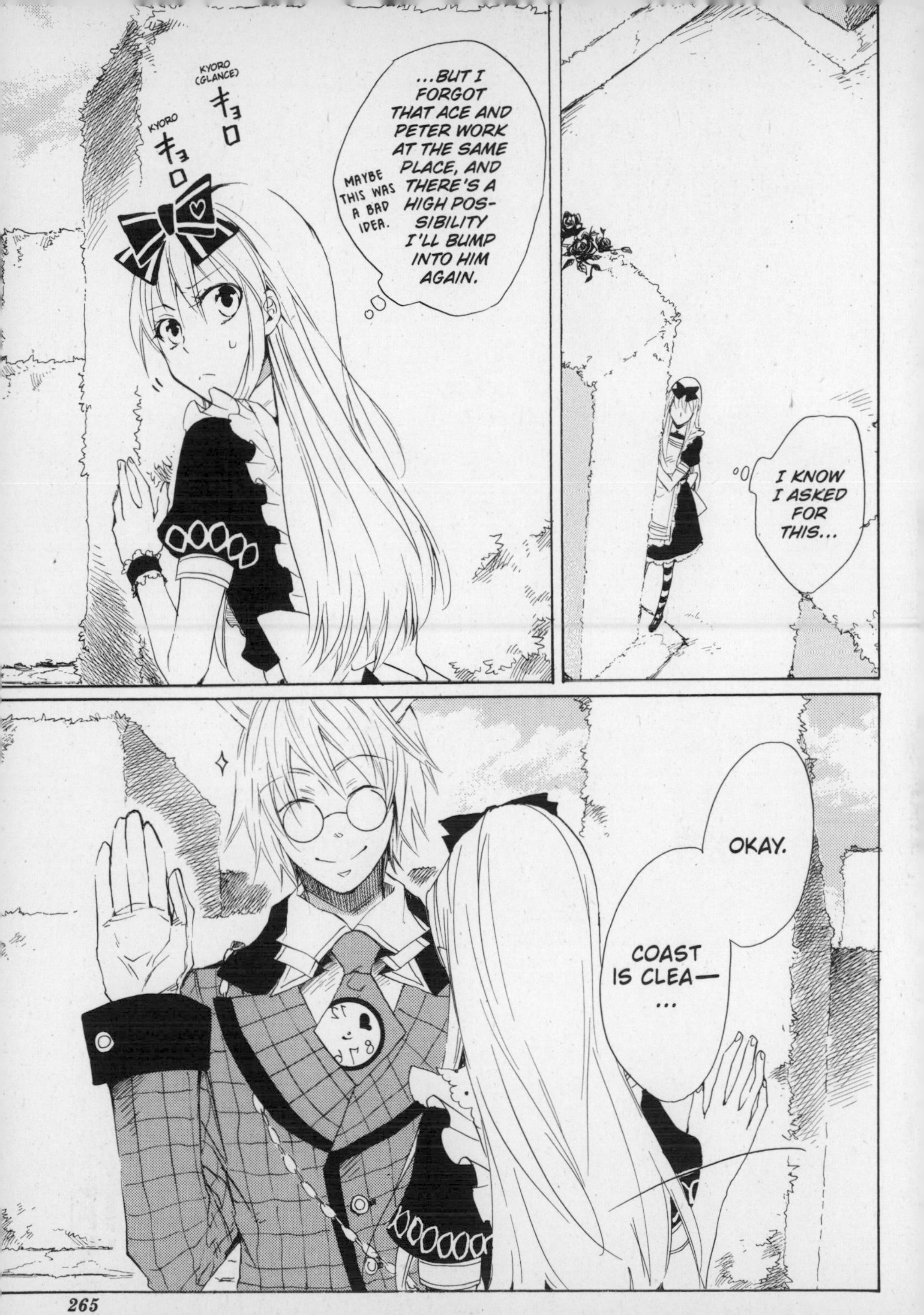
I KNOW I ASKED FOR THIS...
...BUT I FORGOT THAT ACE AND PETER WORK AT THE SAME PLACE, AND THERE'S A HIGH POS-SIBILITY I'LL BUMP INTO HIM AGAIN.
MAYBE THIS WAS A BAD IDEA.
KYORO (GLANCE)
キョロ
KYORO
キョロ
OKAY.
COAST IS CLEA—
...

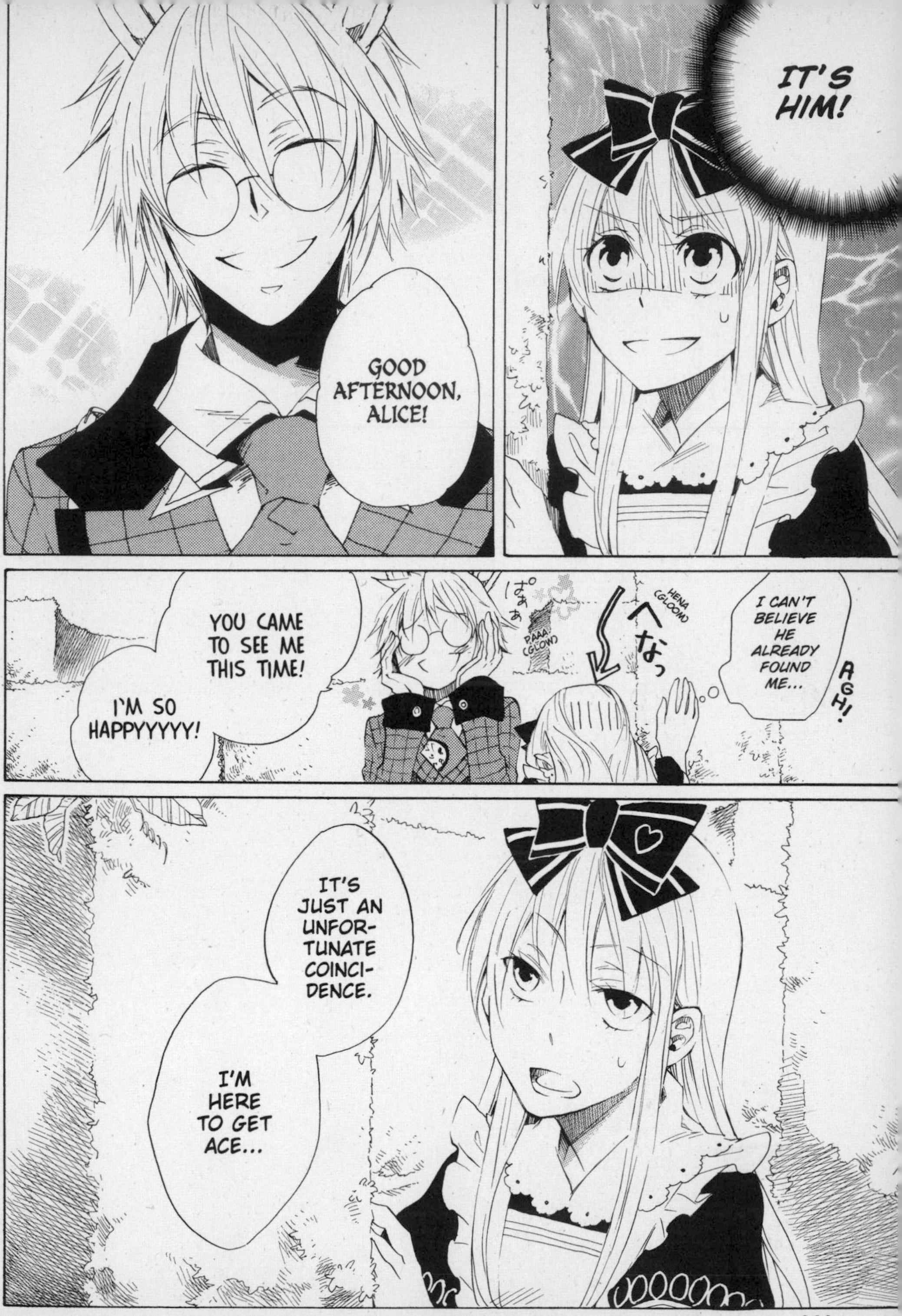
IT'S HIM!
GOOD AFTERNOON, ALICE!
I CAN'T BELIEVE HE ALREADY FOUND ME...
AGH!
HENA (GLOOM)
PAAA (GLOW)
YOU CAME TO SEE ME THIS TIME!
I'M SO HAPPYYYYY!
IT'S JUST AN UNFOR-TUNATE COINCI-DENCE.
I'M HERE TO GET ACE...

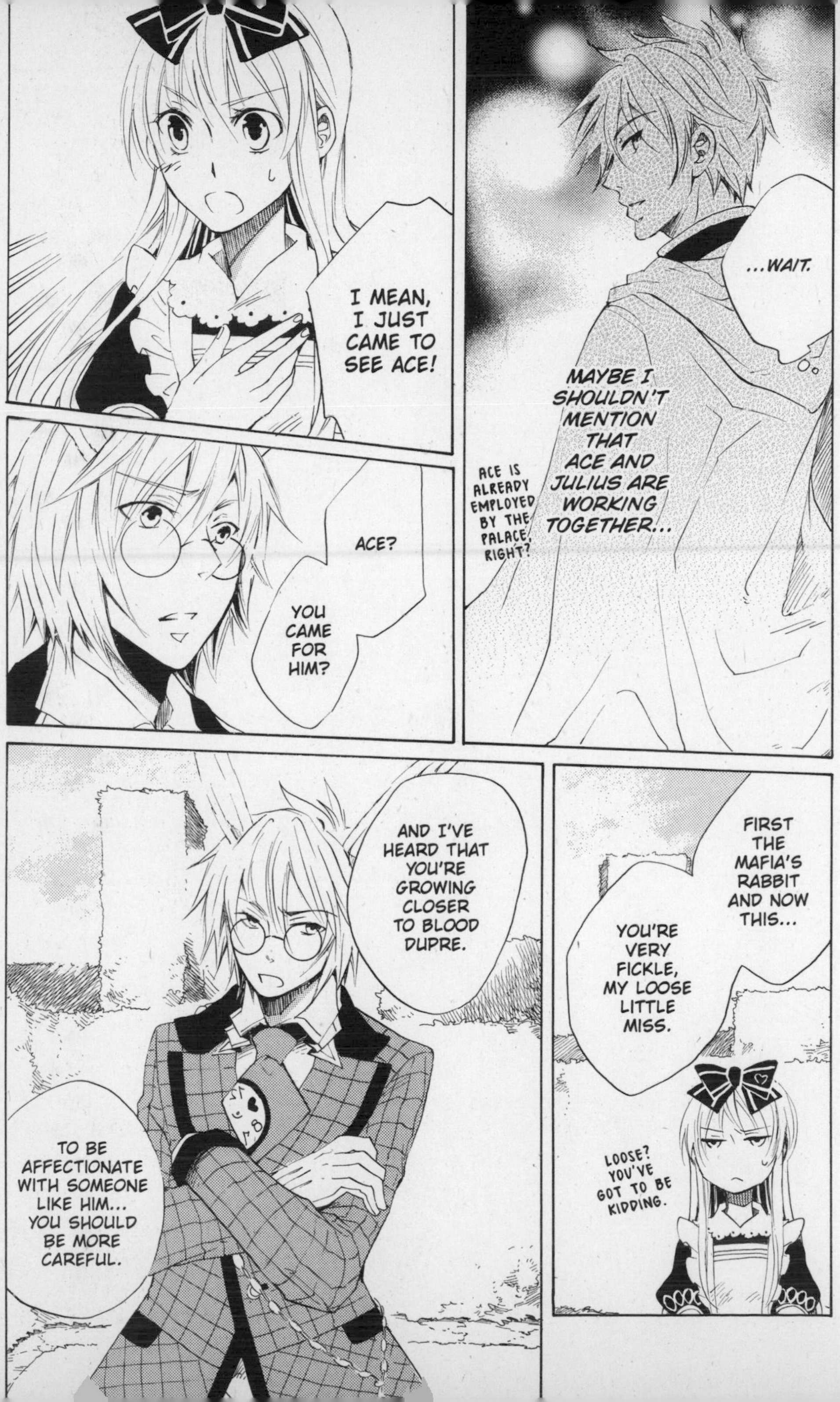
...WAIT.
MAYBE I SHOULDN'T MENTION THAT ACE AND JULIUS ARE WORKING TOGETHER...
ACE IS ALREADY EMPLOYED BY THE PALACE, RIGHT?
I MEAN, I JUST CAME TO SEE ACE!
ACE?
YOU CAME FOR HIM?
FIRST THE MAFIA'S RABBIT AND NOW THIS...
YOU'RE VERY FICKLE, MY LOOSE LITTLE MISS.
LOOSE? YOU'VE GOT TO BE KIDDING.
AND I'VE HEARD THAT YOU'RE GROWING CLOSER TO BLOOD DUPRE.
TO BE AFFECTIONATE WITH SOMEONE LIKE HIM... YOU SHOULD BE MORE CAREFUL.

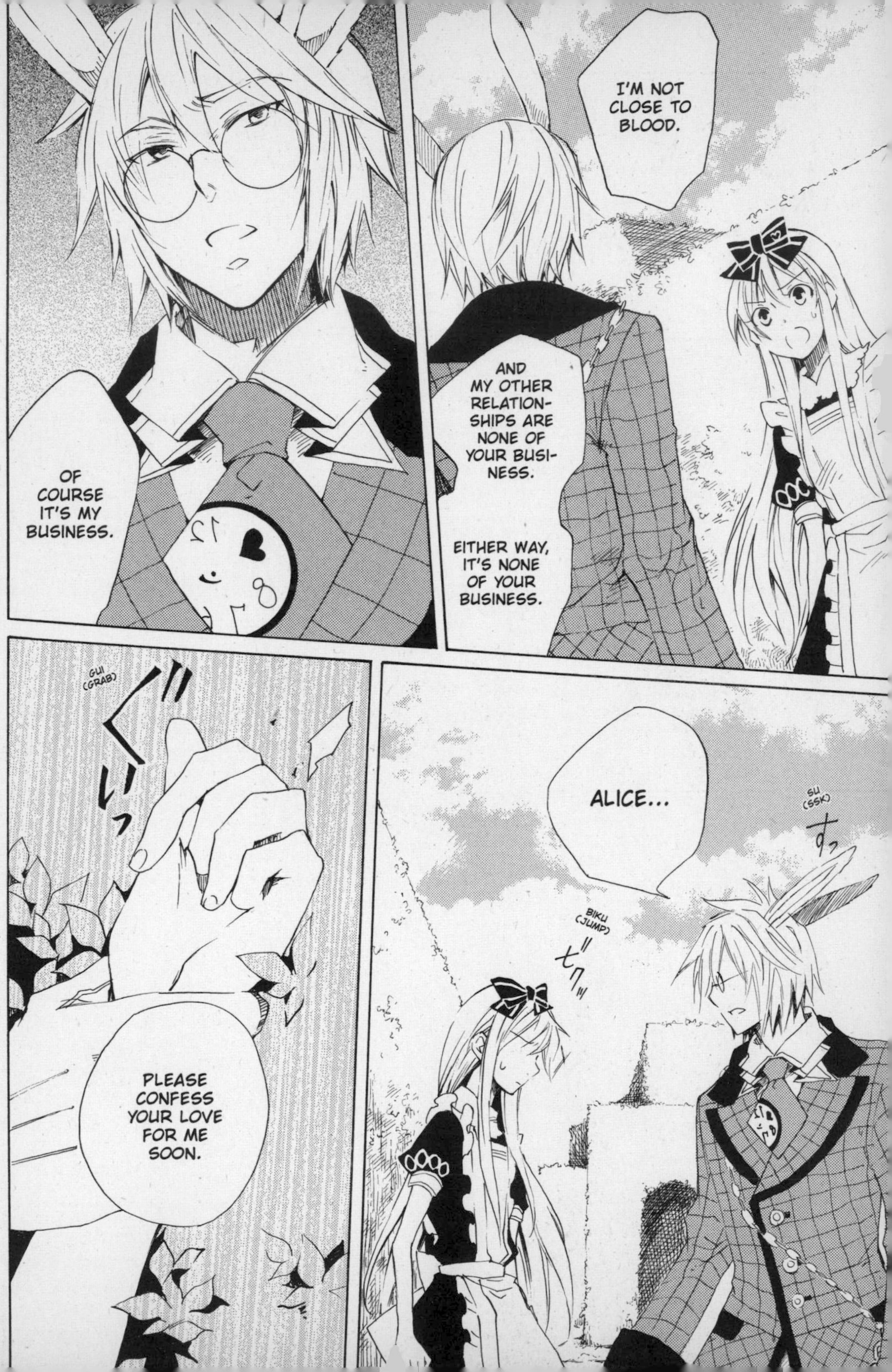
I'M NOT CLOSE TO BLOOD.
AND MY OTHER RELATIONSHIPS ARE NONE OF YOUR BUSINESS.
EITHER WAY, IT'S NONE OF YOUR BUSINESS.
OF COURSE IT'S MY BUSINESS.
ALICE...
SU (SSK)
すっ
BIKU (JUMP)
ビクッ
GUI (GRAB)
ぐいっ
PLEASE CONFESS YOUR LOVE FOR ME SOON.

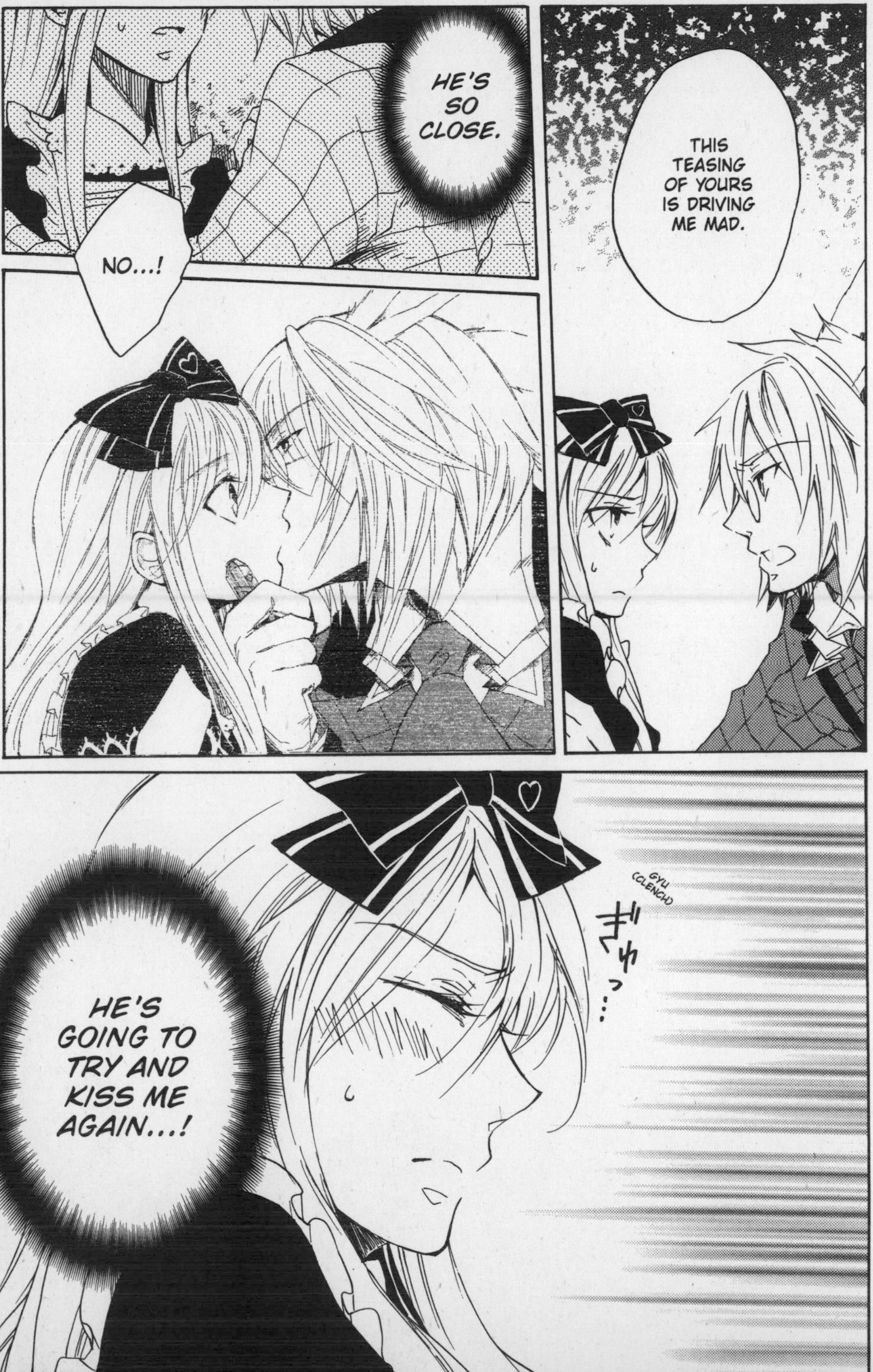
THIS TEASING OF YOURS IS DRIVING ME MAD.
HE'S SO CLOSE.
NO...!
GYU (CLENCH)
ぎゅっ...
HE'S GOING TO TRY AND KISS ME AGAIN...!

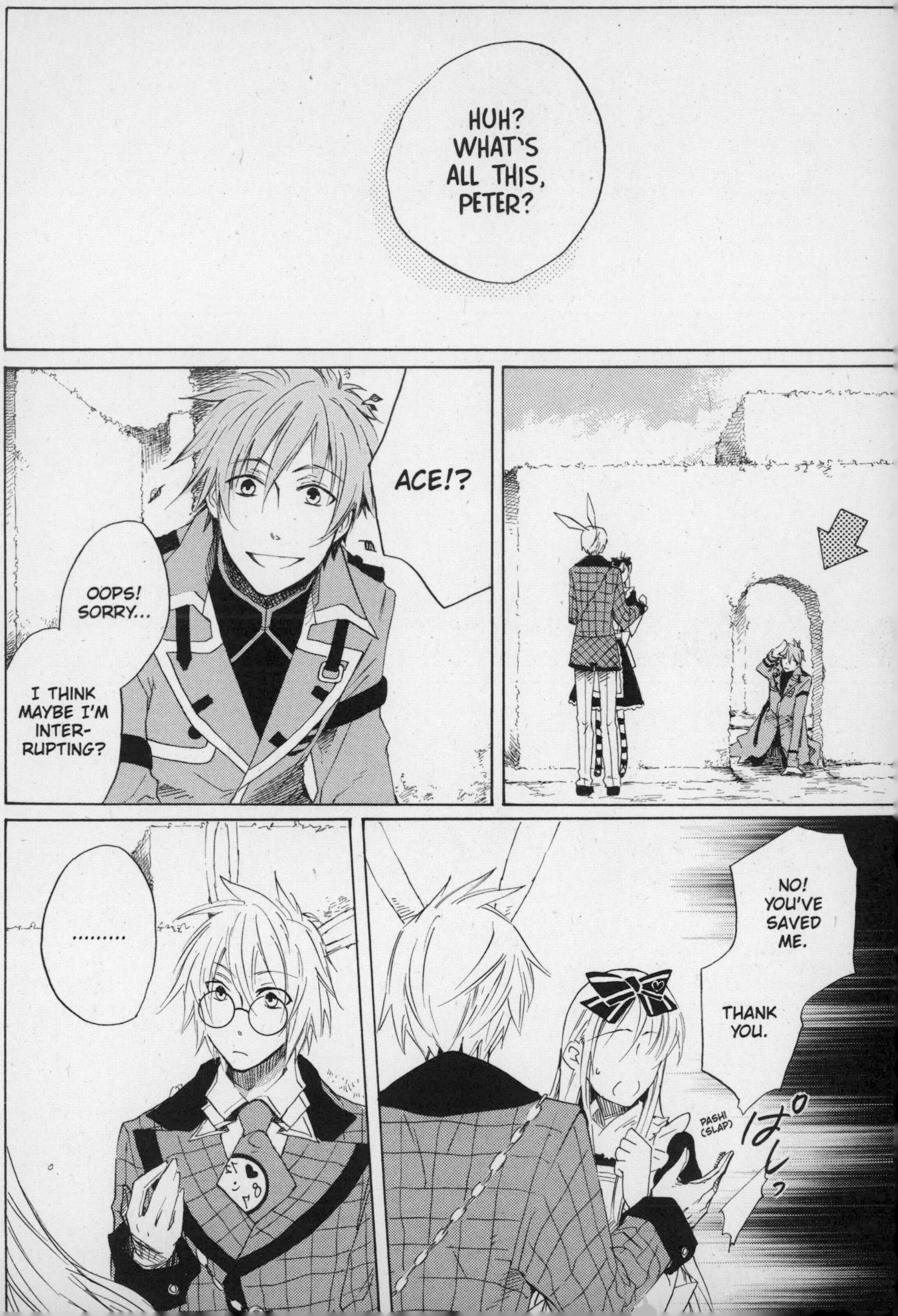

HUH? WHAT'S ALL THIS, PETER?
ACE!?
OOPS! SORRY...
I THINK MAYBE I'M INTER-RUPTING?
NO! YOU'VE SAVED ME.
THANK YOU.
PASHI (SLAP)
ぱしっ
....

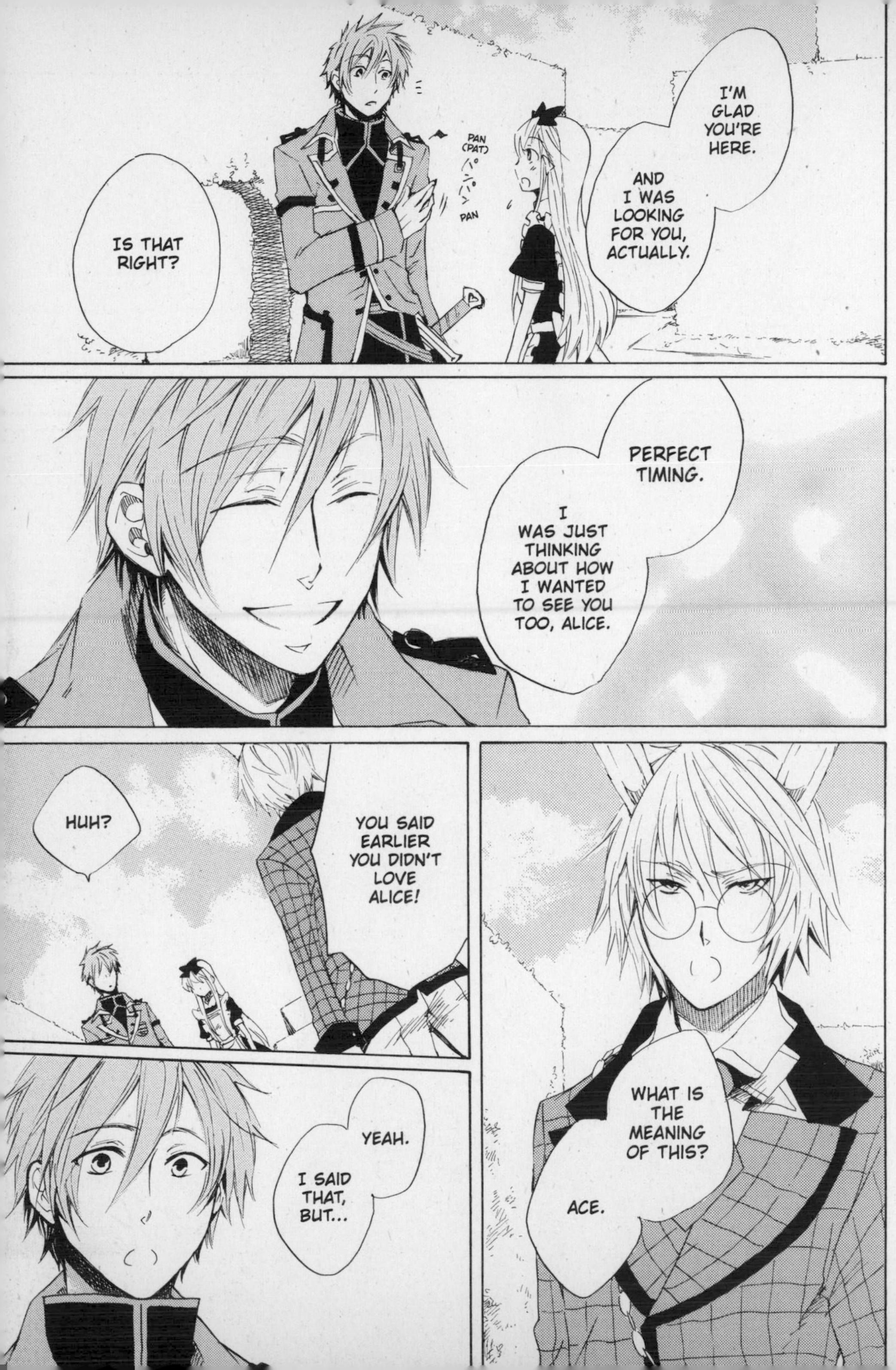
I'M GLAD YOU'RE HERE.
AND I WAS LOOKING FOR YOU, ACTUALLY.
PAN (PAT) パン パン PAN
IS THAT RIGHT?
PERFECT TIMING.
I WAS JUST THINKING ABOUT HOW I WANTED TO SEE YOU TOO, ALICE.
WHAT IS THE MEANING OF THIS?
ACE.
YOU SAID EARLIER YOU DIDN'T LOVE ALICE!
HUH?
YEAH.
I SAID THAT, BUT...

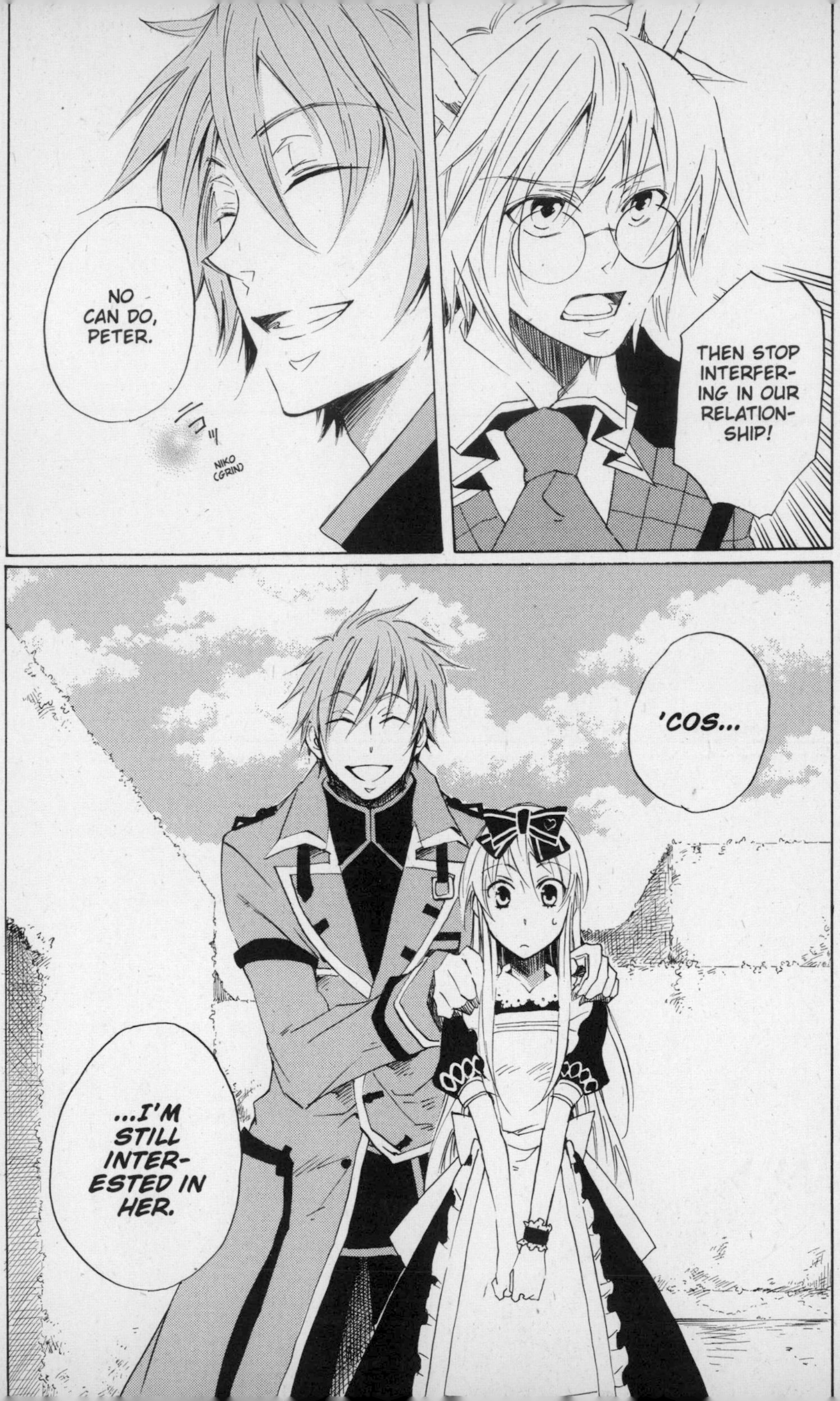
THEN STOP INTERFERING IN OUR RELATIONSHIP!
NO CAN DO, PETER.
NIKO (GRIND)
'COS...
...I'M STILL INTERESTED IN HER.

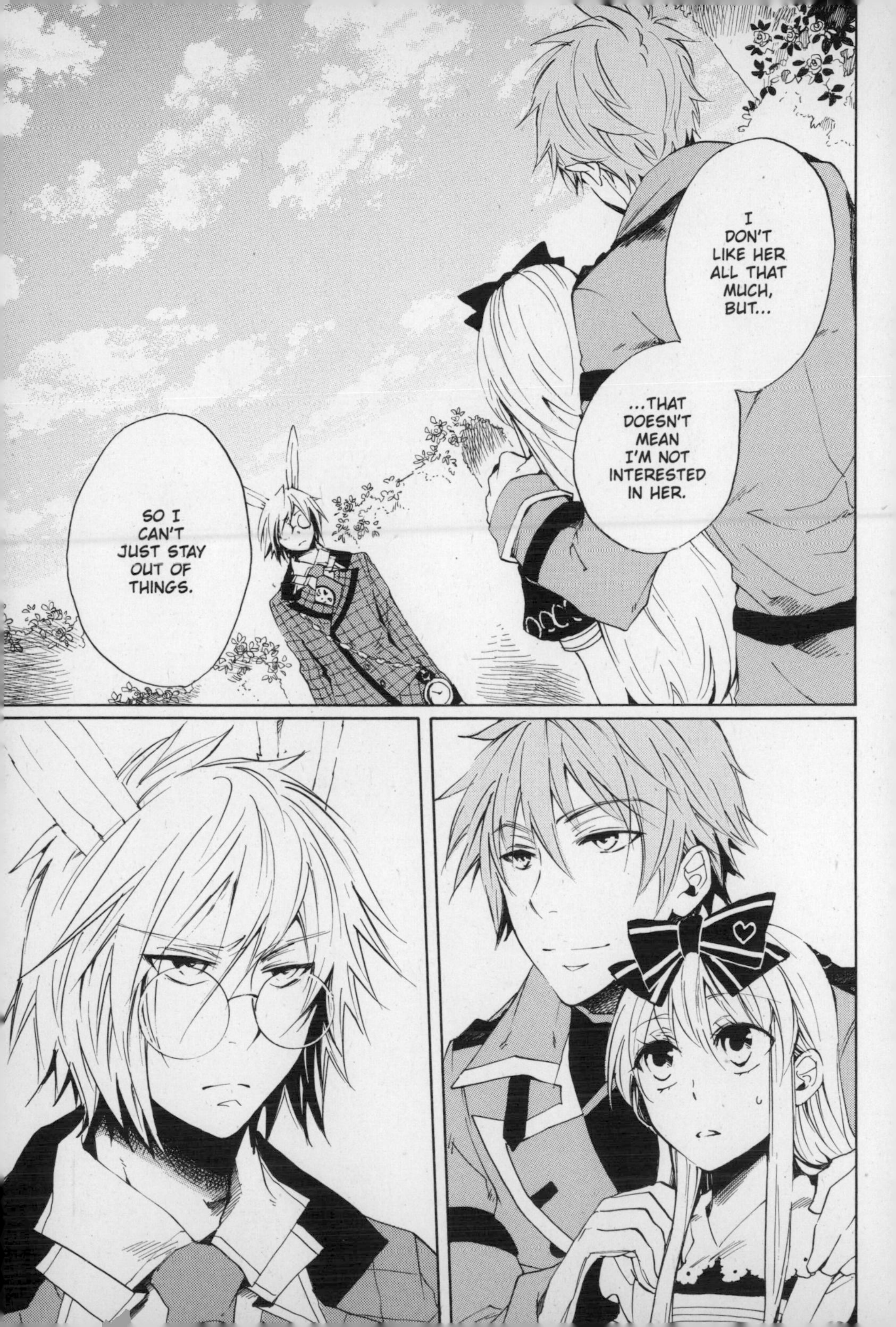
I DON'T LIKE HER ALL THAT MUCH, BUT...
...THAT DOESN'T MEAN I'M NOT INTERESTED IN HER.
SO I CAN'T JUST STAY OUT OF THINGS.

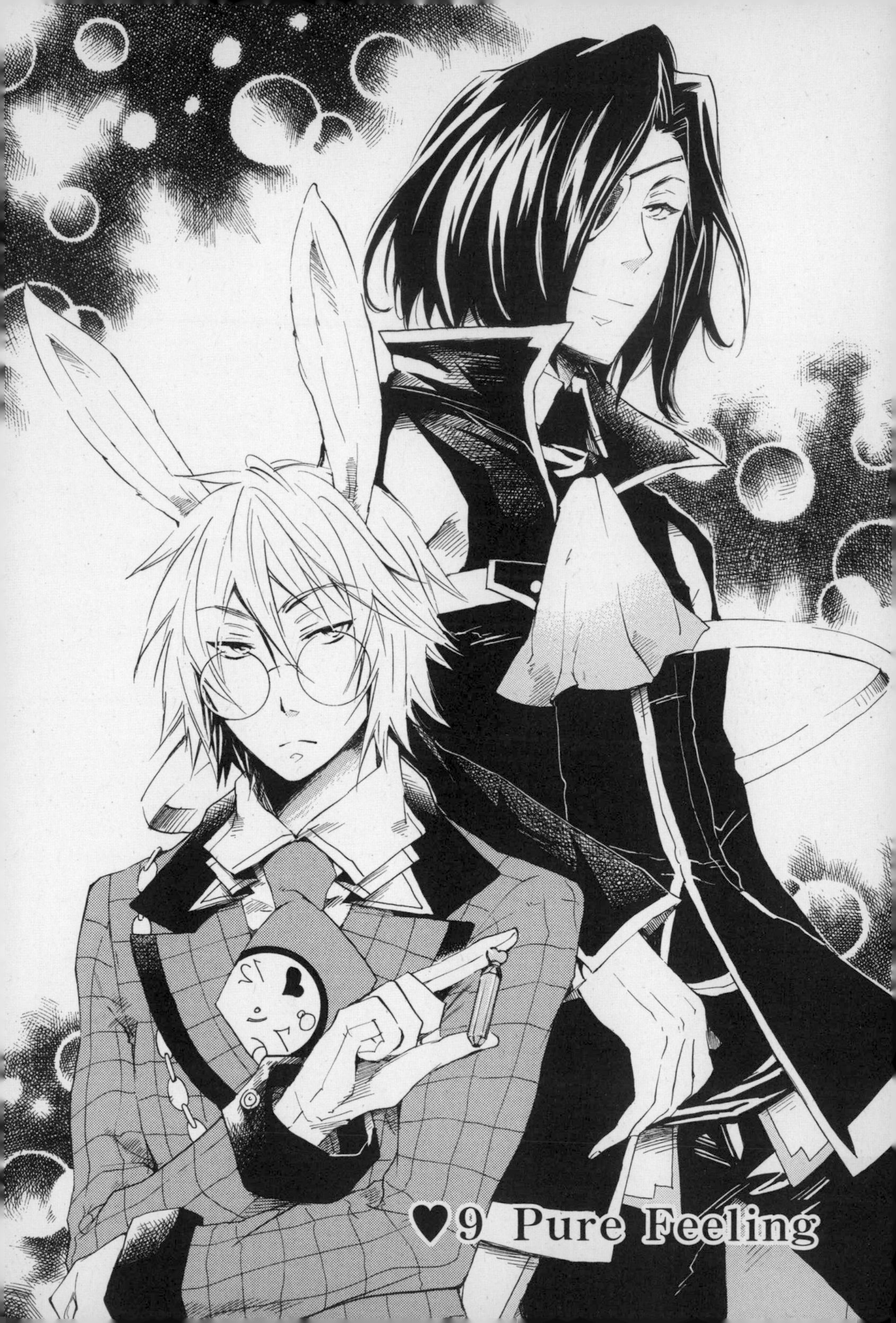

♥9 Pure Feeling

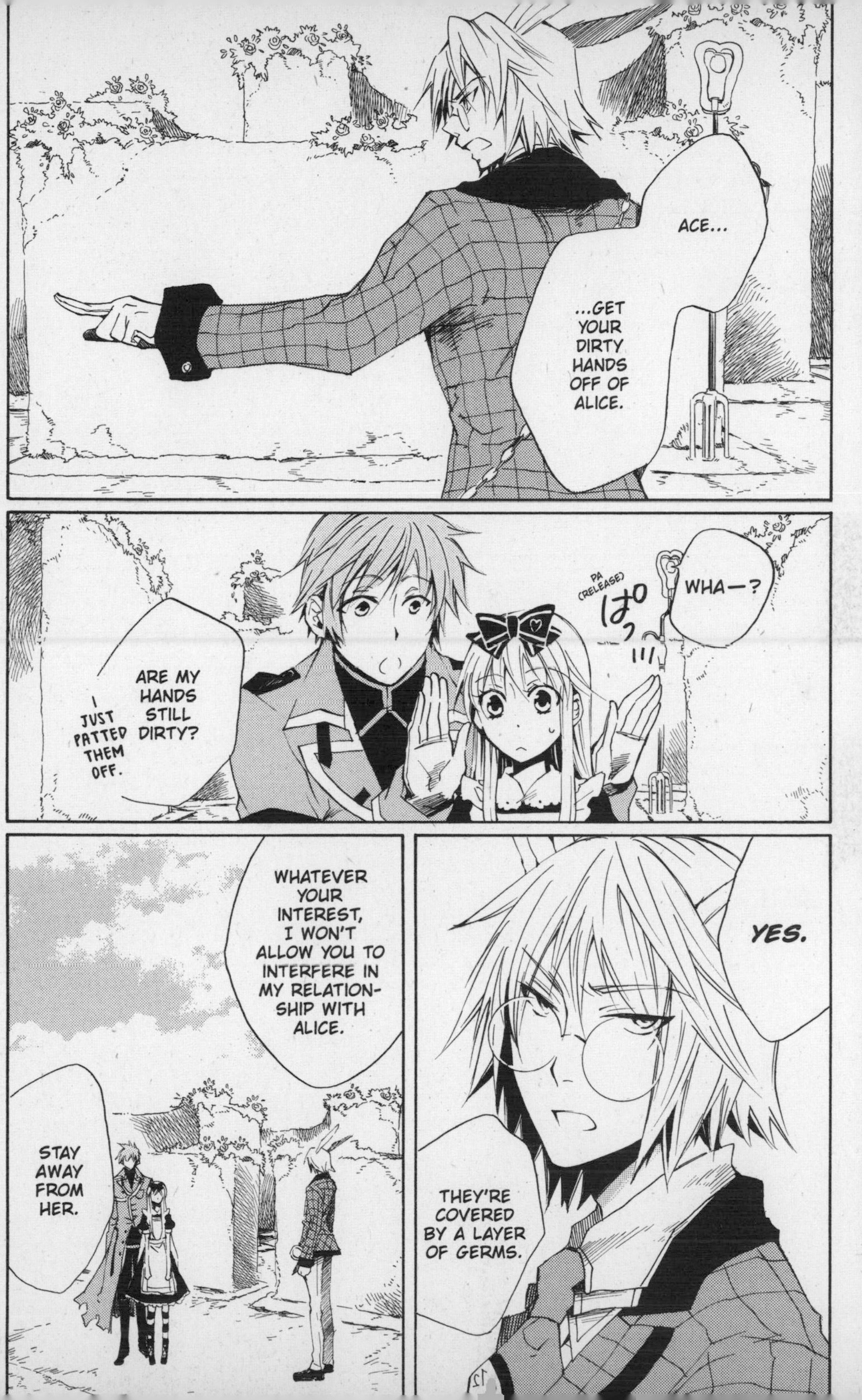
ACE...
...GET YOUR DIRTY HANDS OFF OF ALICE.
WHA—?
PA (RELEASE)
ぱっ
ARE MY HANDS STILL DIRTY?
I JUST PATTED THEM OFF.
YES.
THEY'RE COVERED BY A LAYER OF GERMS.
WHATEVER YOUR INTEREST, I WON'T ALLOW YOU TO INTERFERE IN MY RELATIONSHIP WITH ALICE.
STAY AWAY FROM HER.

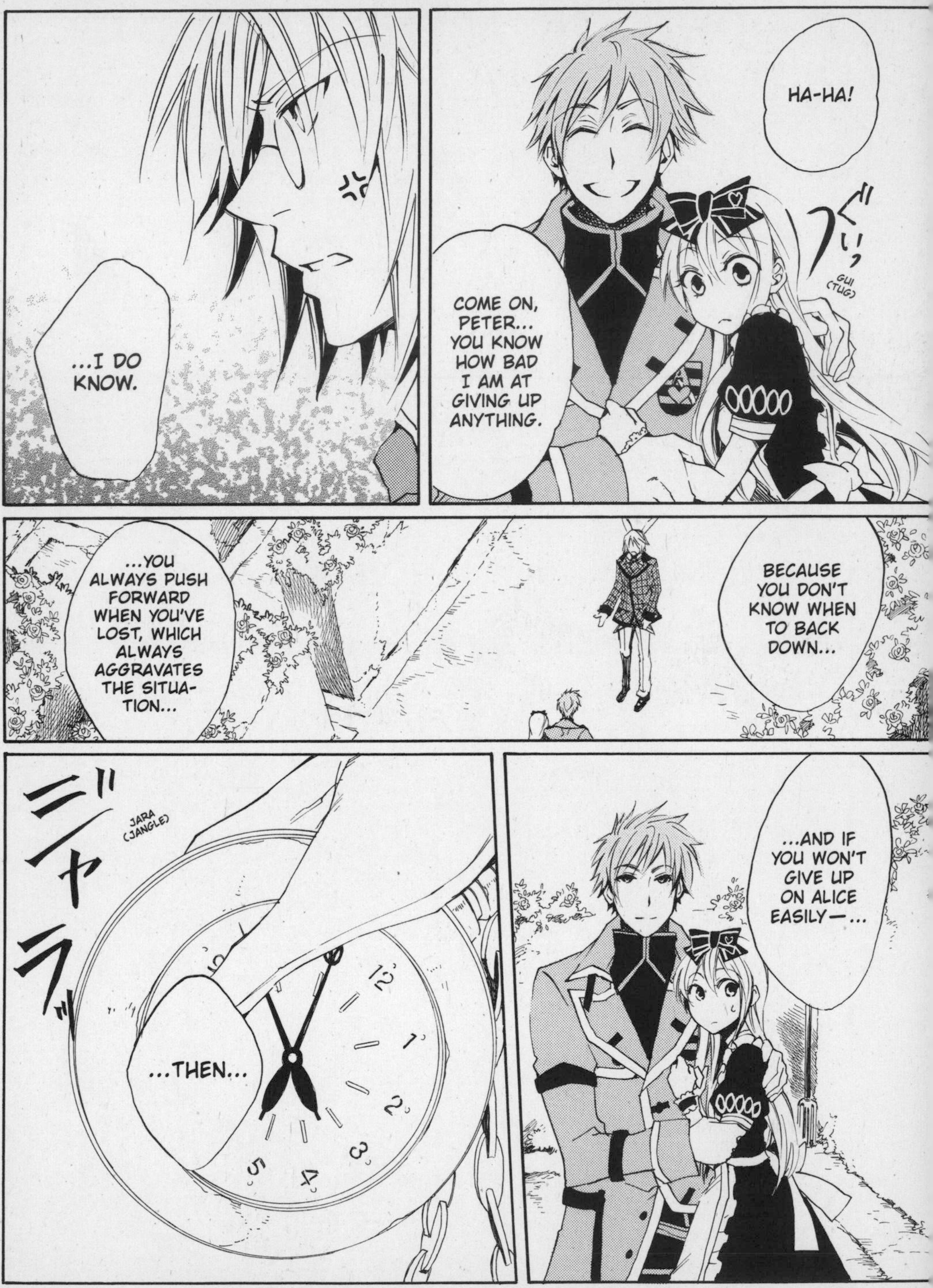
HA-HA!
COME ON, PETER... YOU KNOW HOW BAD I AM AT GIVING UP ANYTHING.
GUI (TUG)
...I DO KNOW.
BECAUSE YOU DON'T KNOW WHEN TO BACK DOWN...
...YOU ALWAYS PUSH FORWARD WHEN YOU'VE LOST, WHICH ALWAYS AGGRAVATES THE SITUATION...
...AND IF YOU WON'T GIVE UP ON ALICE EASILY—...
JARA (JANGLE)
...THEN...

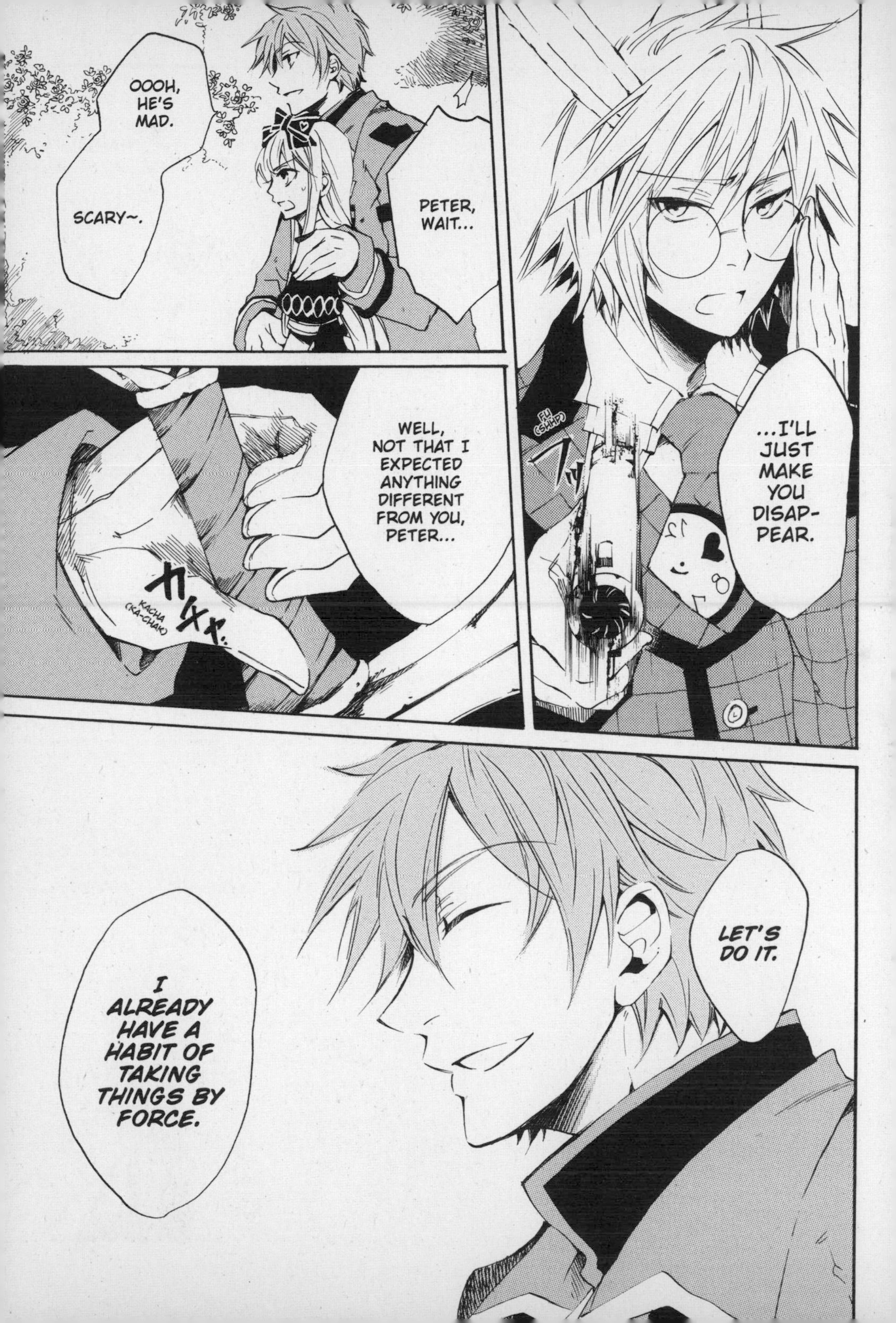
FU
(SHAP)
...I'LL JUST MAKE YOU DISAP-PEAR.
PETER, WAIT...
OOOH, HE'S MAD.
SCARY~.
WELL, NOT THAT I EXPECTED ANYTHING DIFFERENT FROM YOU, PETER...
KACHA
(KA-CHAK)
LET'S DO IT.
I ALREADY HAVE A HABIT OF TAKING THINGS BY FORCE.

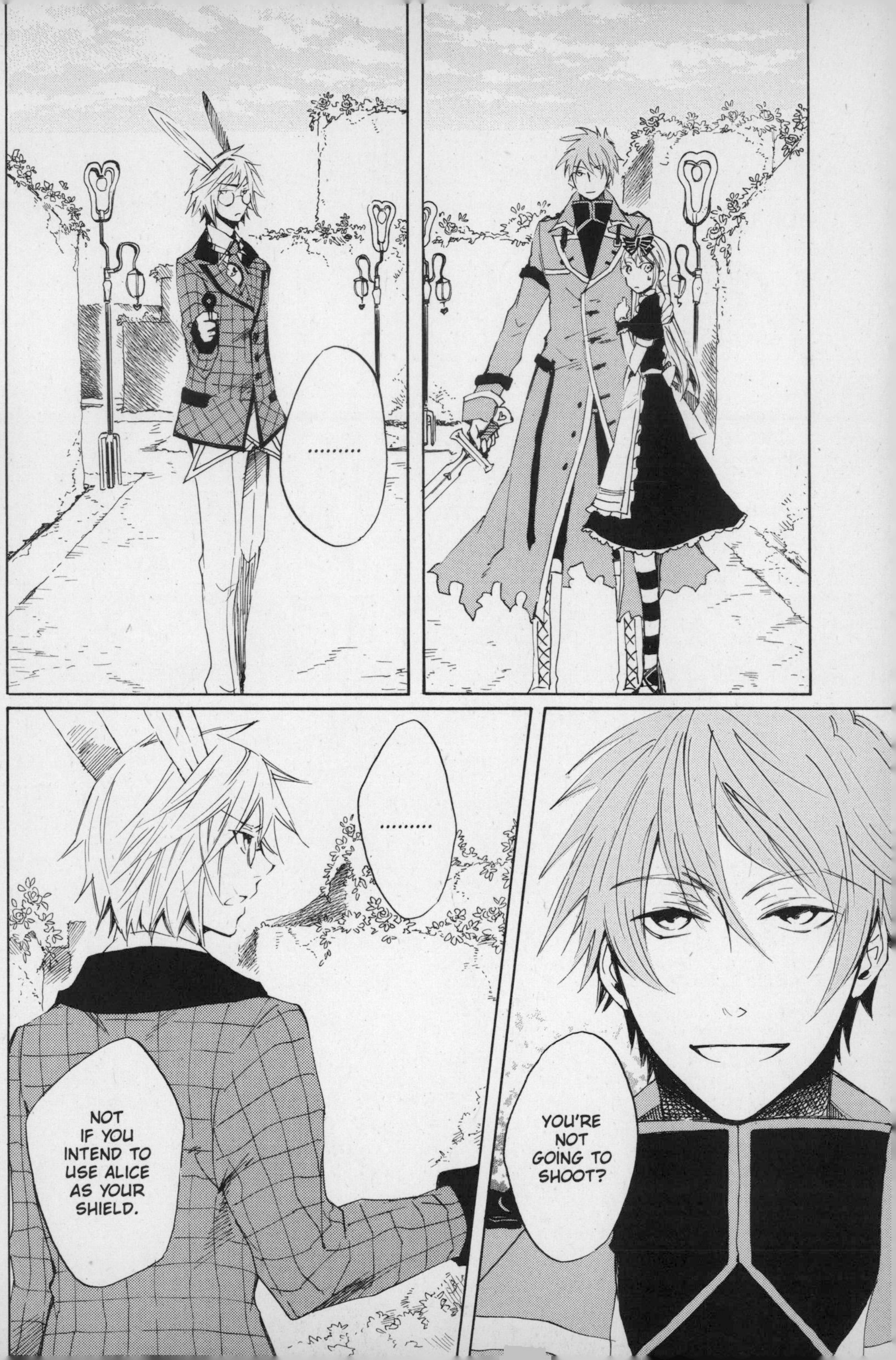
....
YOU'RE NOT GOING TO SHOOT?
....
NOT IF YOU INTEND TO USE ALICE AS YOUR SHIELD.

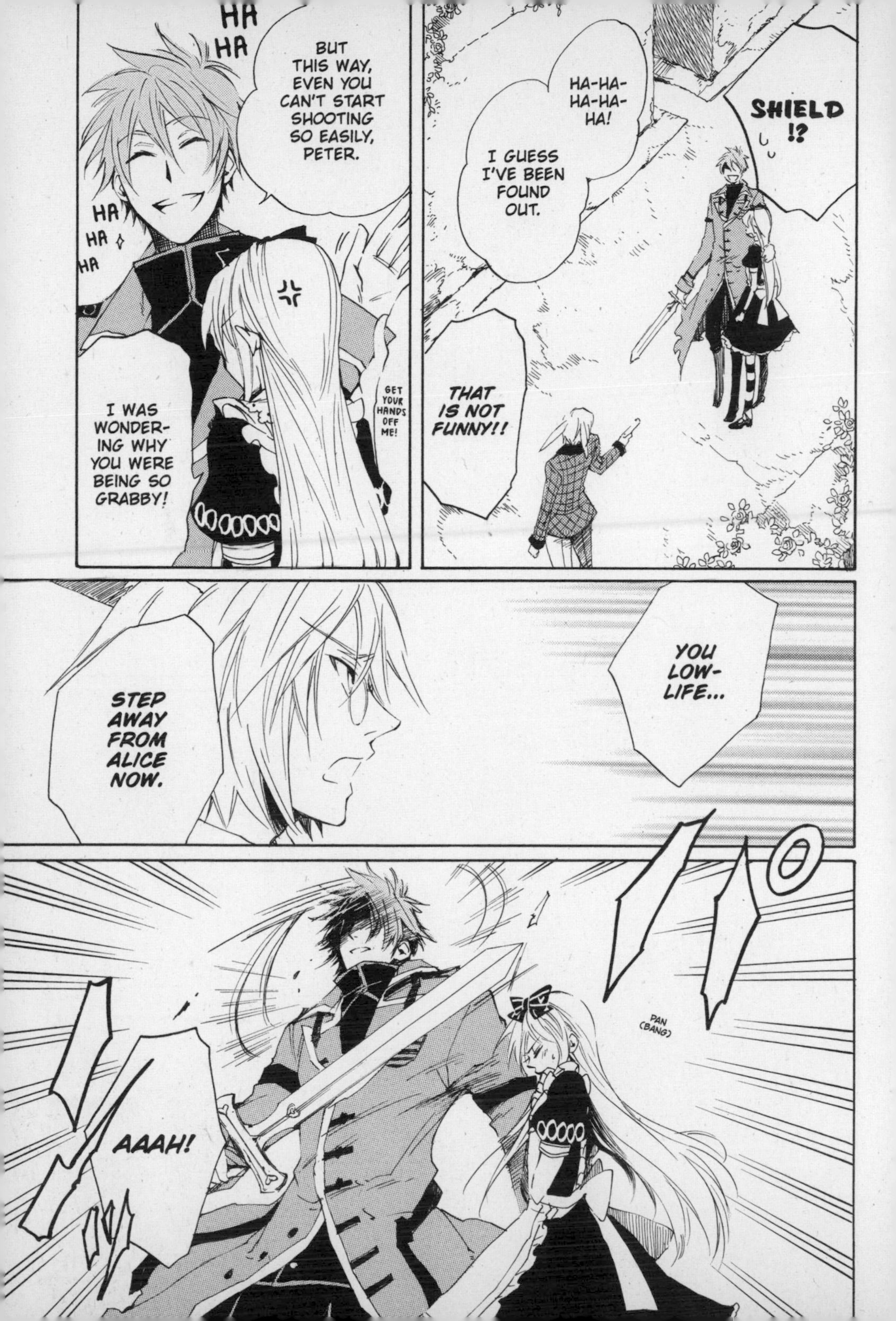
SHIELD !?
HA-HA-HA-HA-HA!
I GUESS I'VE BEEN FOUND OUT.
THAT IS NOT FUNNY!!
HA HA
BUT THIS WAY, EVEN YOU CAN'T START SHOOTING SO EASILY, PETER.
HA HA HA
GET YOUR HANDS OFF ME!
I WAS WONDERING WHY YOU WERE BEING SO GRABBY!
YOU LOW-LIFE...
STEP AWAY FROM ALICE NOW.
PAN (BANG)
AAAH!

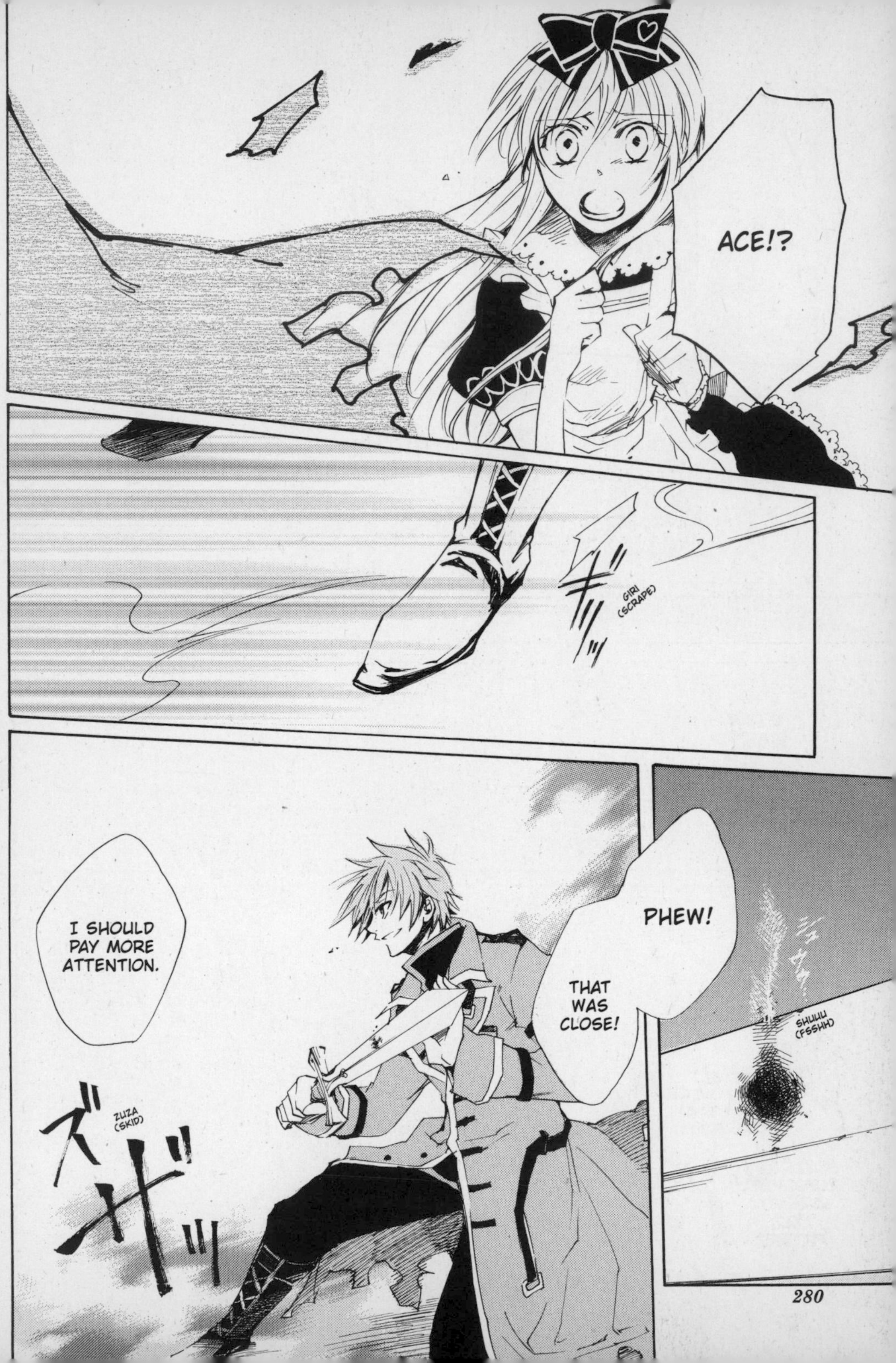
ACE!?
GIRI (SCRAPE)
SHUUU (FSSHH)
PHEW!
THAT WAS CLOSE!
I SHOULD PAY MORE ATTENTION.
ZUZA (SKID)

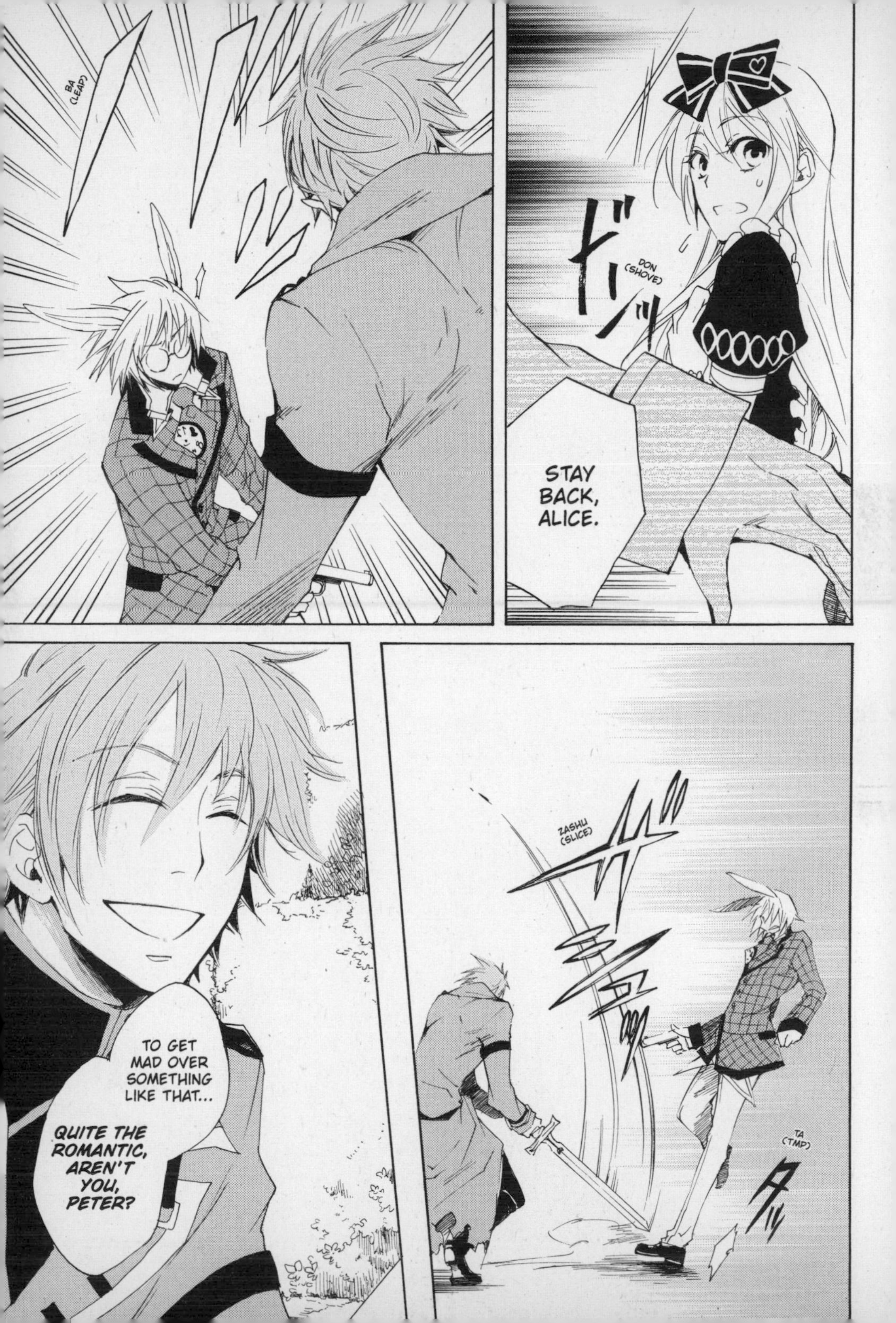
DON (SHOVE)
STAY BACK, ALICE.
BA (LEAP)
ZASHU (SLICE)
TA (TMP)
TO GET MAD OVER SOMETHING LIKE THAT...
QUITE THE ROMANTIC, AREN'T YOU, PETER?

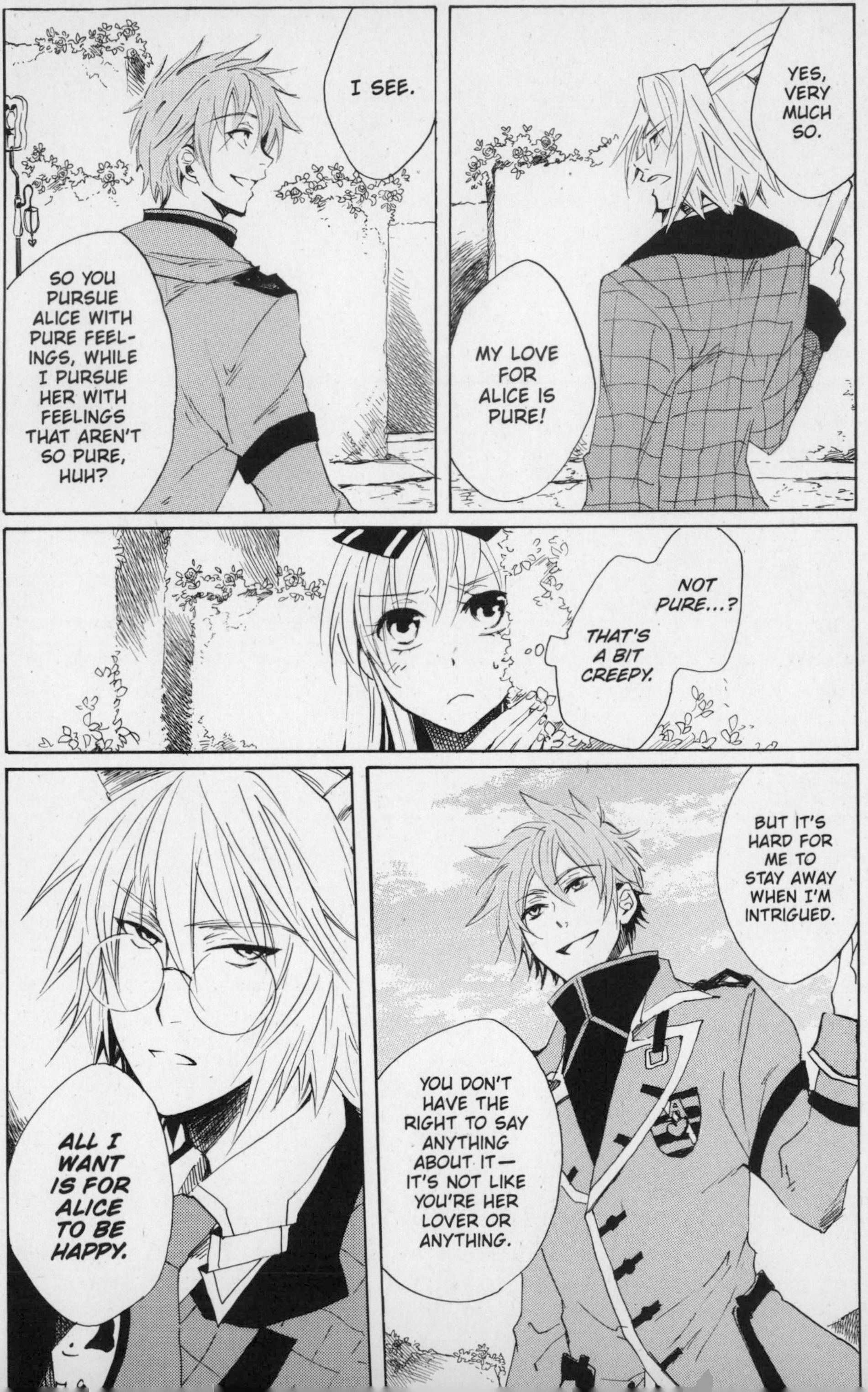
I SEE.
SO YOU PURSUE ALICE WITH PURE FEEL-INGS, WHILE I PURSUE HER WITH FEELINGS THAT AREN'T SO PURE, HUH?
YES, VERY MUCH SO.
MY LOVE FOR ALICE IS PURE!
NOT PURE...?
THAT'S A BIT CREEPY.
ALL I WANT IS FOR ALICE TO BE HAPPY.
BUT IT'S HARD FOR ME TO STAY AWAY WHEN I'M INTRIGUED.
YOU DON'T HAVE THE RIGHT TO SAY ANYTHING ABOUT IT—IT'S NOT LIKE YOU'RE HER LOVER OR ANYTHING.

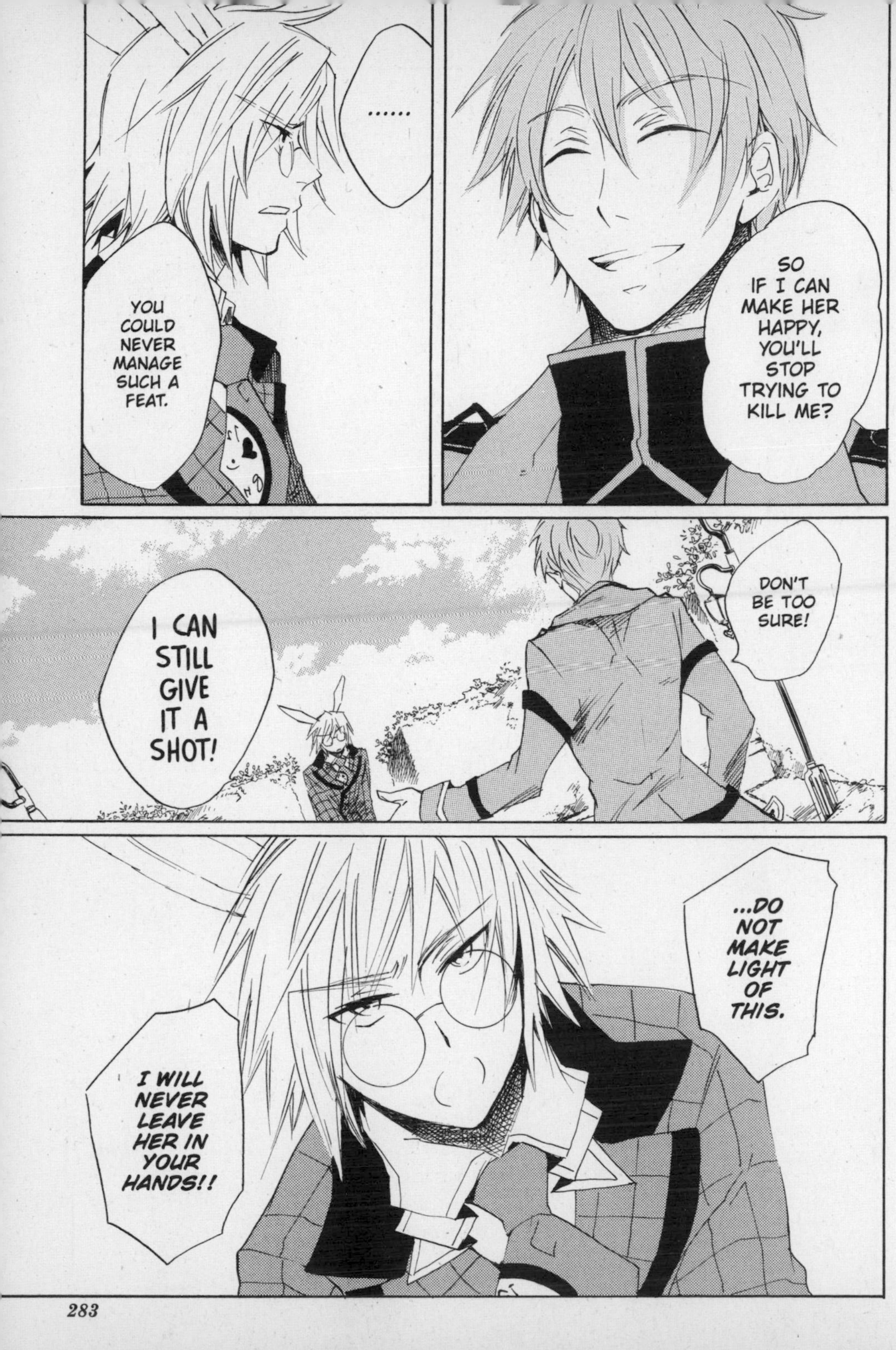

SO IF I CAN MAKE HER HAPPY, YOU'LL STOP TRYING TO KILL ME?
......
YOU COULD NEVER MANAGE SUCH A FEAT.
DON'T BE TOO SURE!
I CAN STILL GIVE IT A SHOT!
...DO NOT MAKE LIGHT OF THIS.
I WILL NEVER LEAVE HER IN YOUR HANDS!!

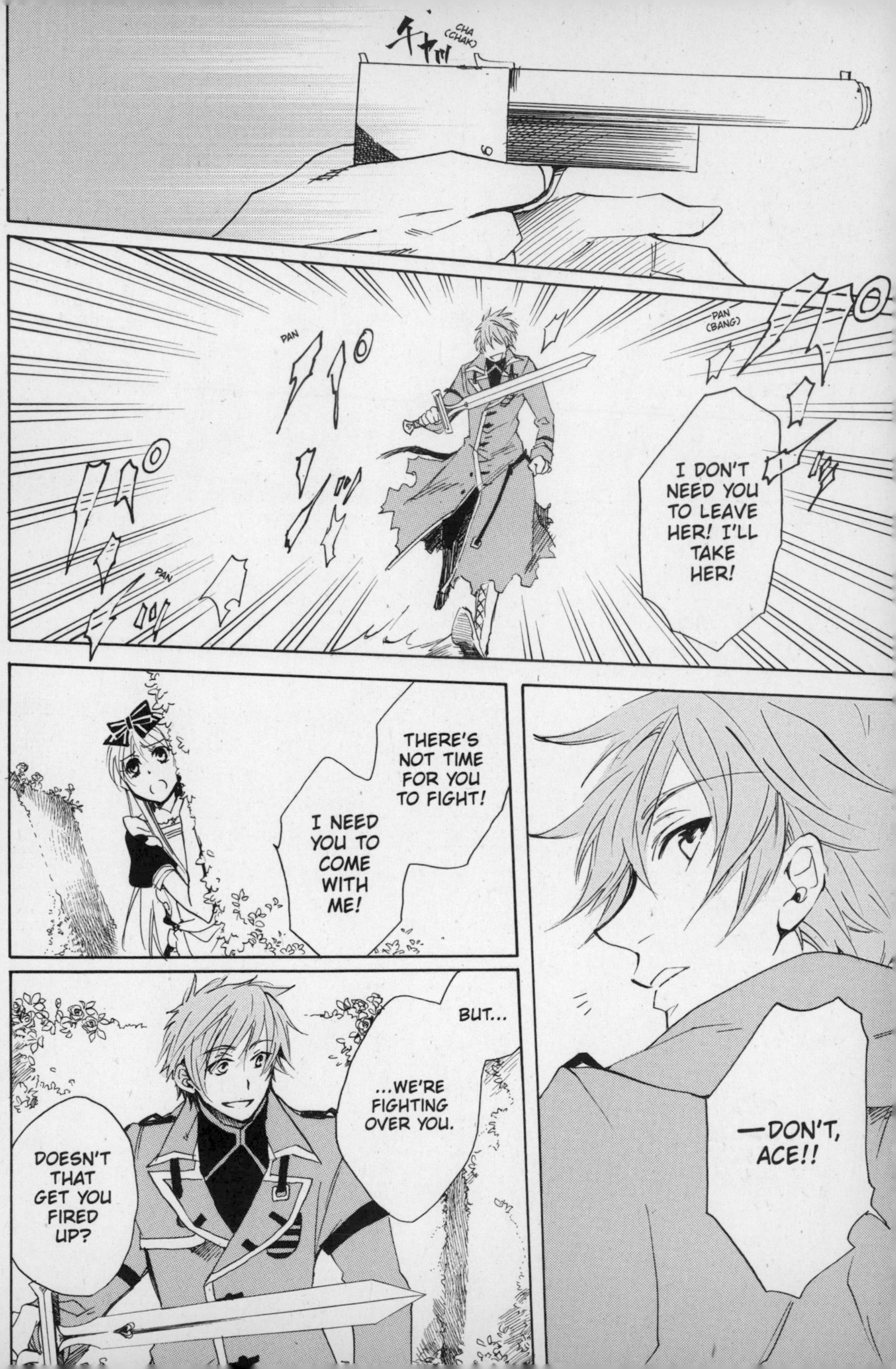
チャッ
CHA (CHAK)
PAN (BANG)
I DON'T NEED YOU TO LEAVE HER! I'LL TAKE HER!
PAN
PAN
—DON'T, ACE!!
THERE'S NOT TIME FOR YOU TO FIGHT!
I NEED YOU TO COME WITH ME!
BUT...
...WE'RE FIGHTING OVER YOU.
DOESN'T THAT GET YOU FIRED UP?

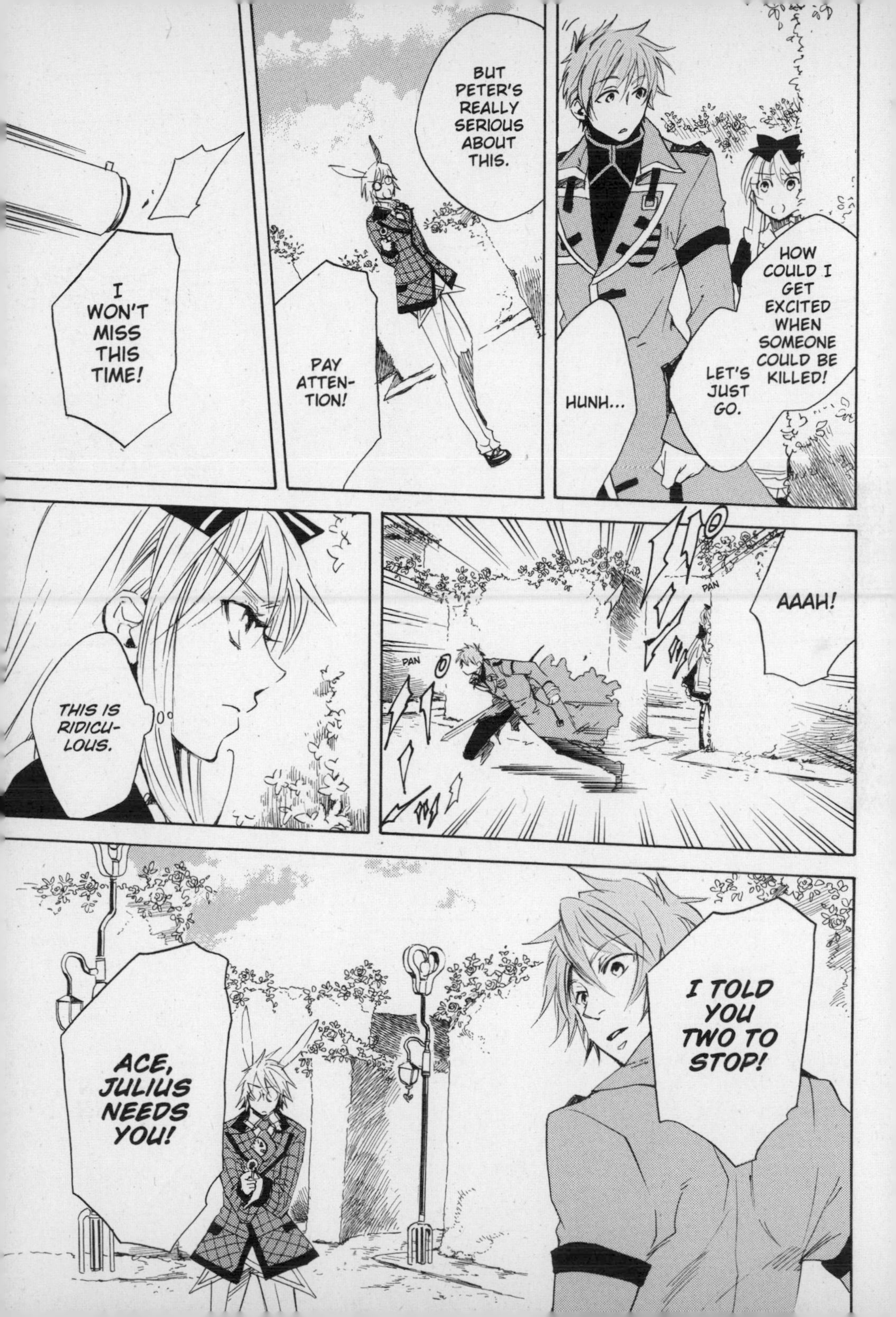
HOW COULD I GET EXCITED WHEN SOMEONE COULD BE KILLED!
LET'S JUST GO.
HUNH...
BUT PETER'S REALLY SERIOUS ABOUT THIS.
PAY ATTENTION!
I WON'T MISS THIS TIME!
PAN
AAAH!
PAN
THIS IS RIDICULOUS.
I TOLD YOU TWO TO STOP!
ACE, JULIUS NEEDS YOU!

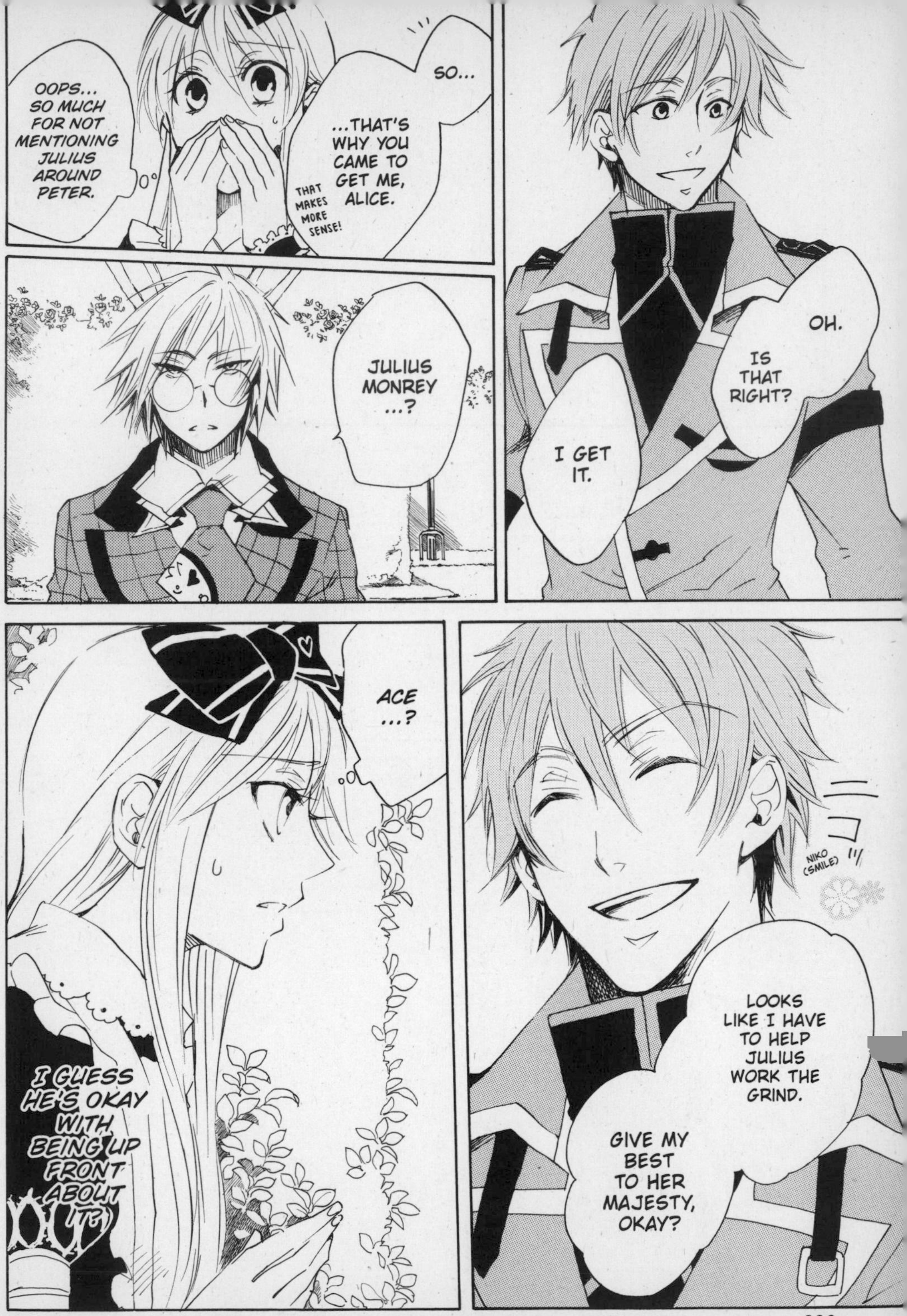
OH.
IS THAT RIGHT?
I GET IT.
SO...
...THAT'S WHY YOU CAME TO GET ME, ALICE.
THAT MAKES MORE SENSE!
OOPS... SO MUCH FOR NOT MENTIONING JULIUS AROUND PETER.
JULIUS MONREY ...?
LOOKS LIKE I HAVE TO HELP JULIUS WORK THE GRIND.
GIVE MY BEST TO HER MAJESTY, OKAY?
NIKO (SMILE)
ACE ...?
I GUESS HE'S OKAY WITH BEING UP FRONT ABOUT IT?

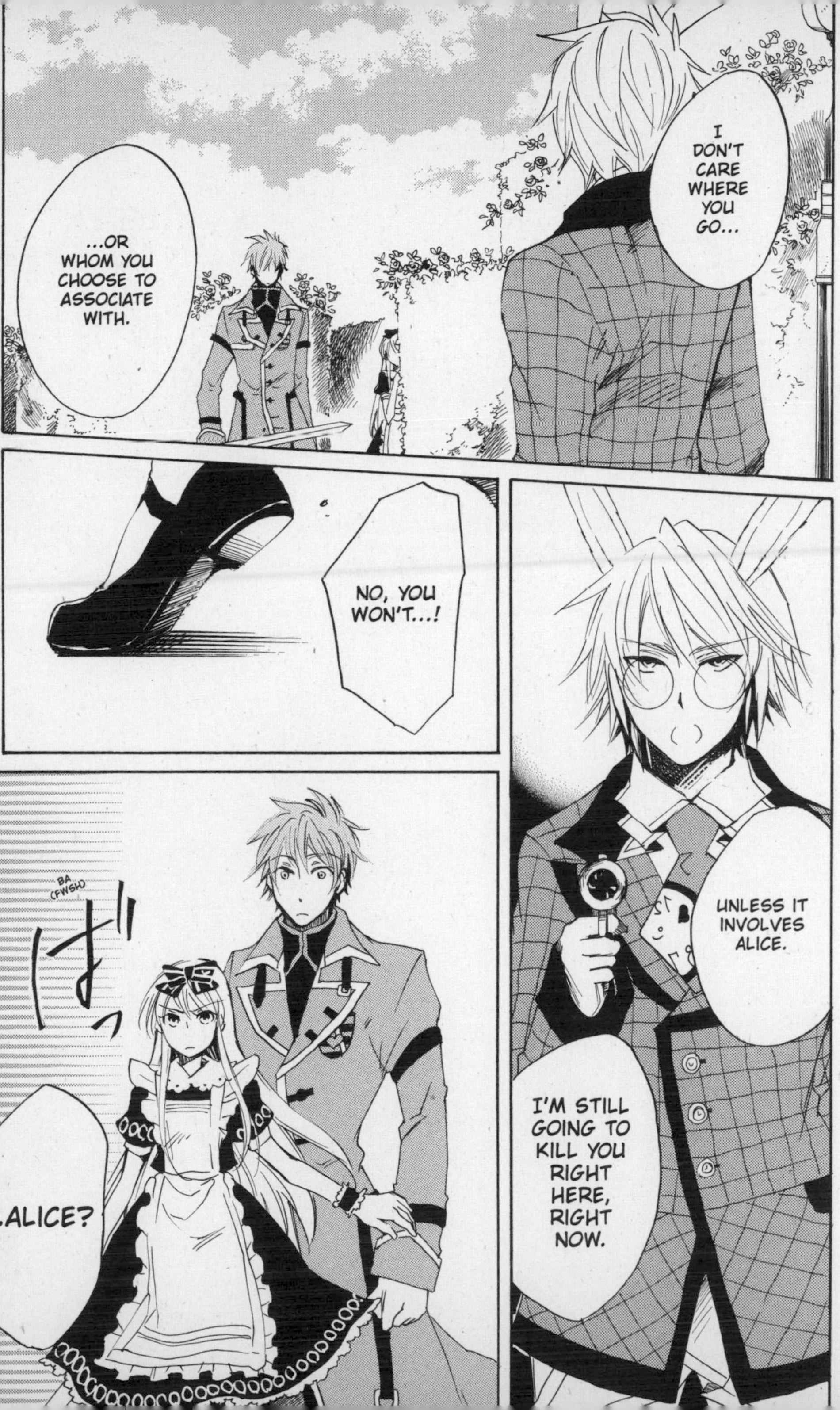
I DON'T CARE WHERE YOU GO...
...OR WHOM YOU CHOOSE TO ASSOCIATE WITH.
UNLESS IT INVOLVES ALICE.
I'M STILL GOING TO KILL YOU RIGHT HERE, RIGHT NOW.
NO, YOU WON'T...!
ばっ
BA (FWSH)
...ALICE?

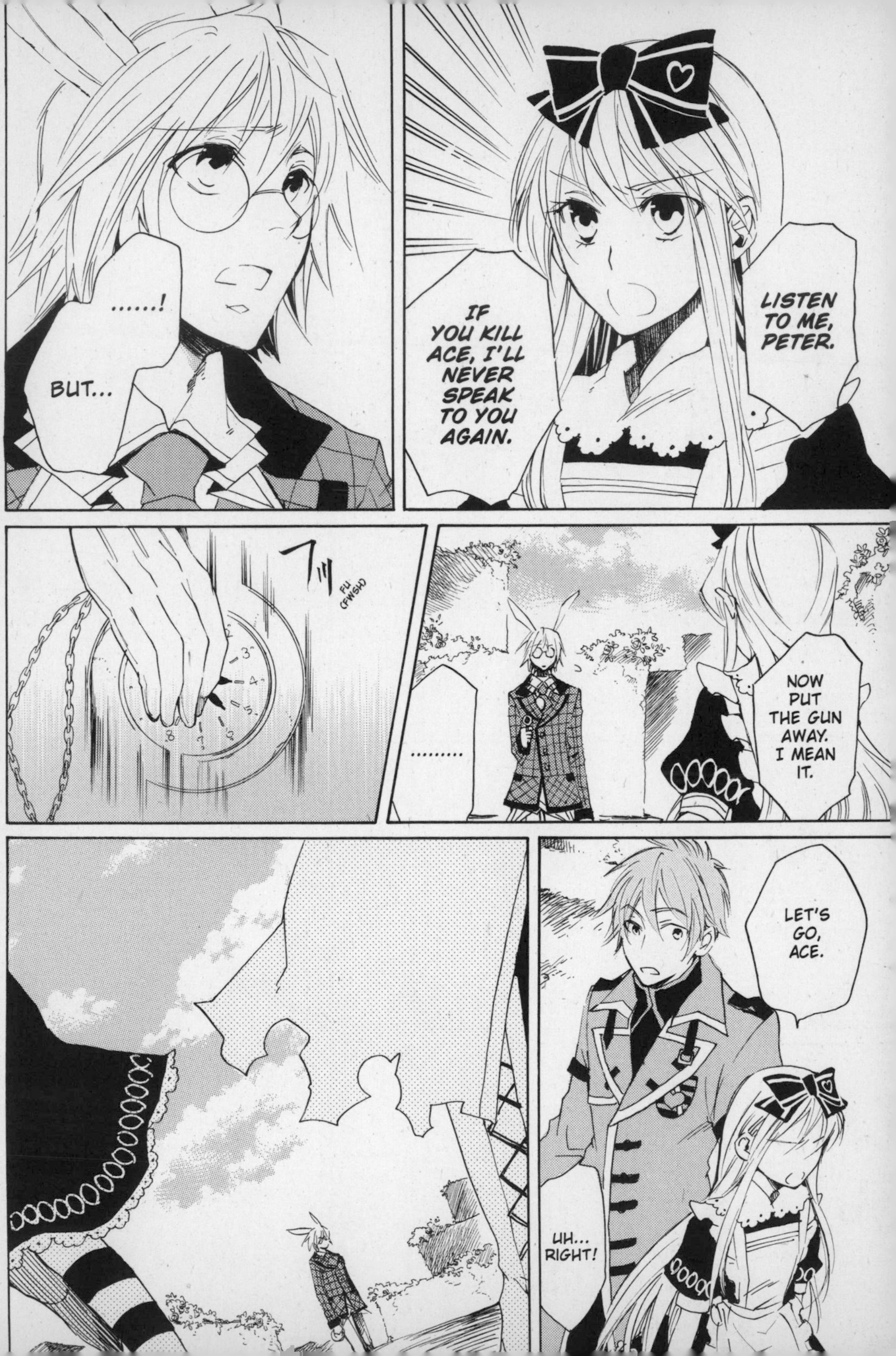
LISTEN TO ME, PETER.
IF YOU KILL ACE, I'LL NEVER SPEAK TO YOU AGAIN.
......!
BUT...
NOW PUT THE GUN AWAY. I MEAN IT.
....
フッ
FU (FWSH)
LET'S GO, ACE.
UH... RIGHT!

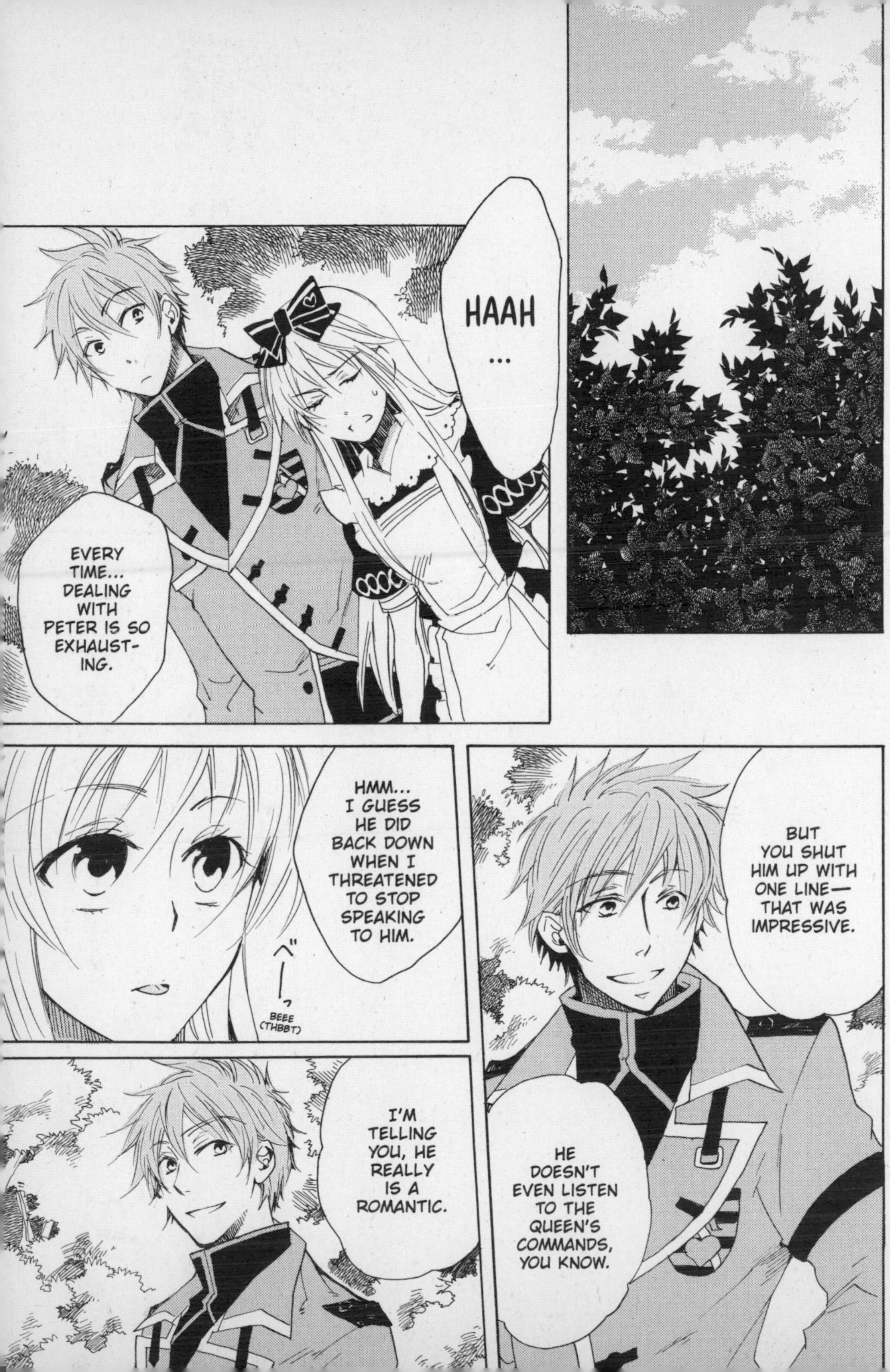
HAAH...
EVERY TIME... DEALING WITH PETER IS SO EXHAUST-ING.
BUT YOU SHUT HIM UP WITH ONE LINE—THAT WAS IMPRESSIVE.
HE DOESN'T EVEN LISTEN TO THE QUEEN'S COMMANDS, YOU KNOW.
HMM... I GUESS HE DID BACK DOWN WHEN I THREATENED TO STOP SPEAKING TO HIM.
べー
BEEE (THBBT)
I'M TELLING YOU, HE REALLY IS A ROMANTIC.

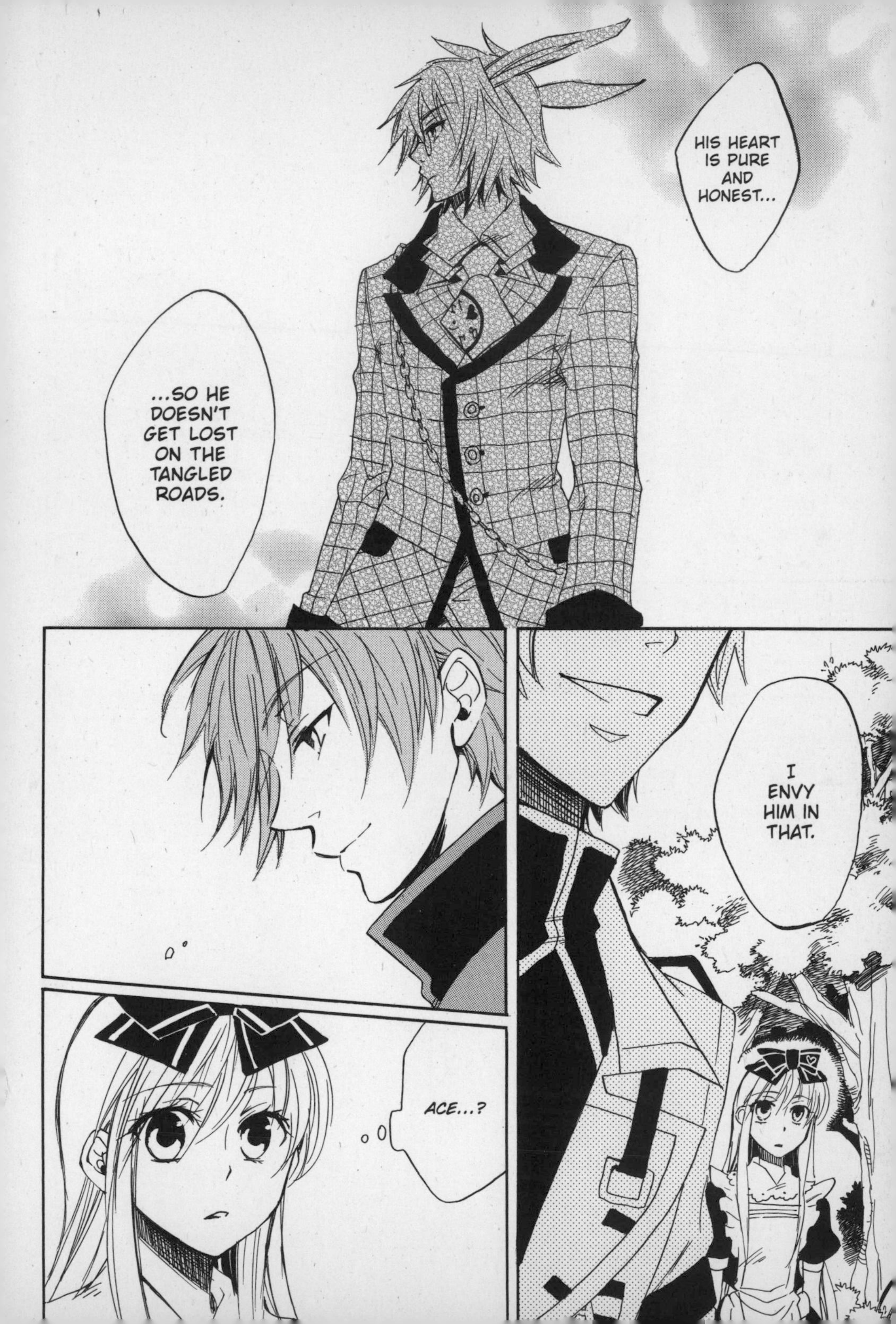
HIS HEART IS PURE AND HONEST...
...SO HE DOESN'T GET LOST ON THE TANGLED ROADS.
I ENVY HIM IN THAT.
ACE...?

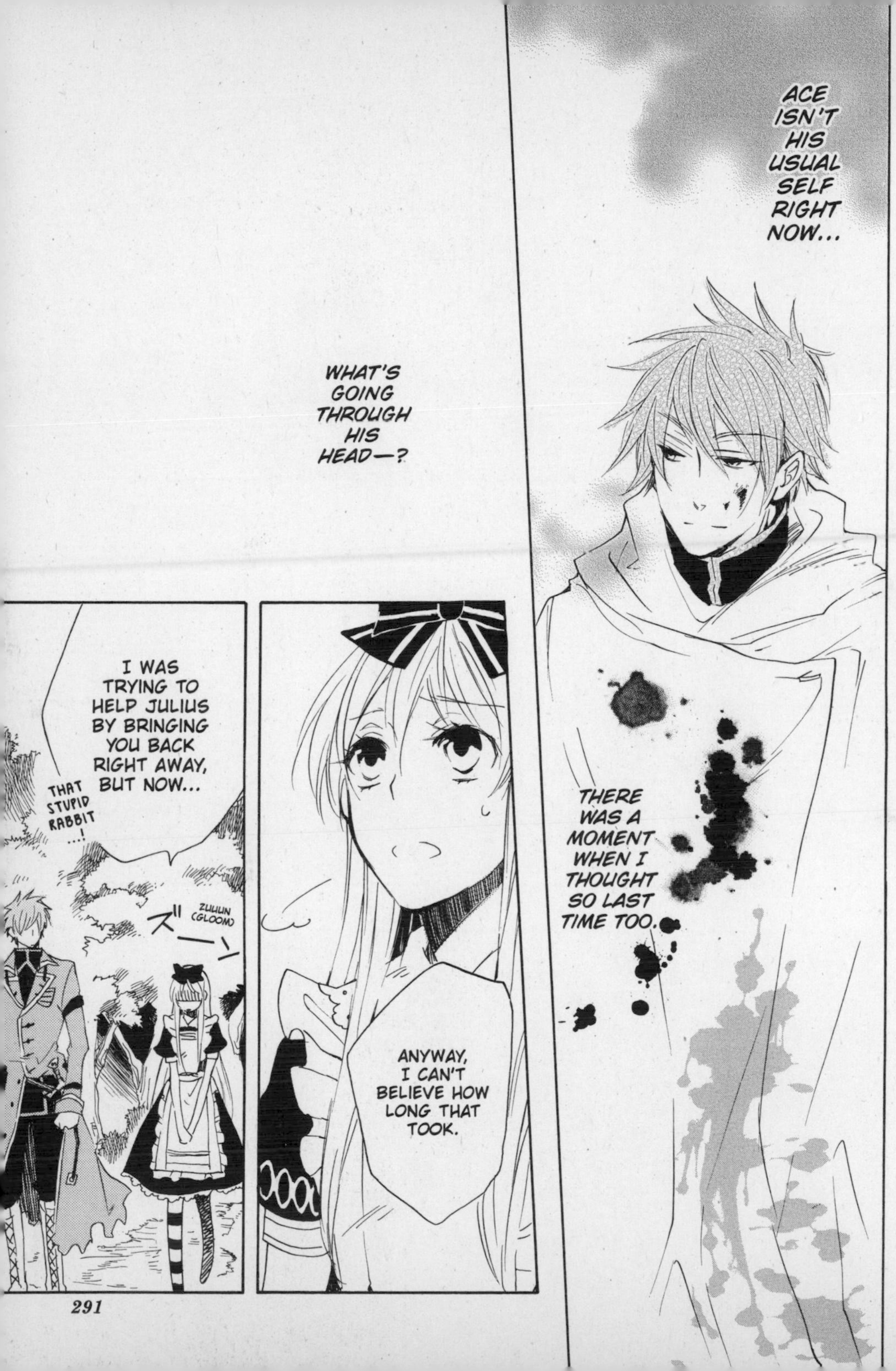

ACE ISN'T HIS USUAL SELF RIGHT NOW...
THERE WAS A MOMENT WHEN I THOUGHT SO LAST TIME TOO.
WHAT'S GOING THROUGH HIS HEAD—?
ANYWAY, I CAN'T BELIEVE HOW LONG THAT TOOK.
I WAS TRYING TO HELP JULIUS BY BRINGING YOU BACK RIGHT AWAY, BUT NOW...
THAT STUPID RABBIT ...!
ZUUUN (GLOOM)

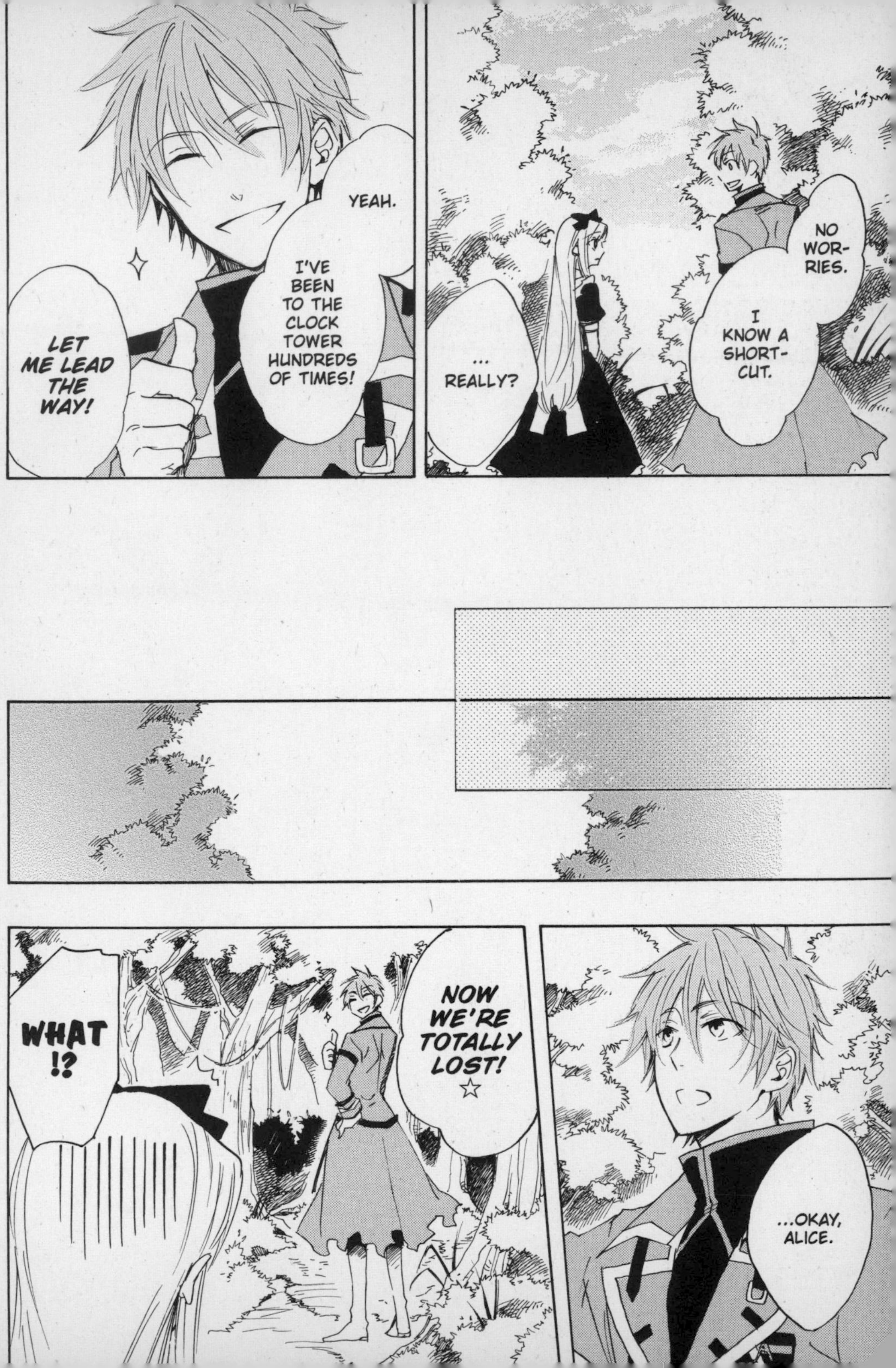
NO WORRIES.
I KNOW A SHORTCUT.
...REALLY?
YEAH.
I'VE BEEN TO THE CLOCK TOWER HUNDREDS OF TIMES!
LET ME LEAD THE WAY!
...OKAY, ALICE.
NOW WE'RE TOTALLY LOST! ☆
WHAT!?

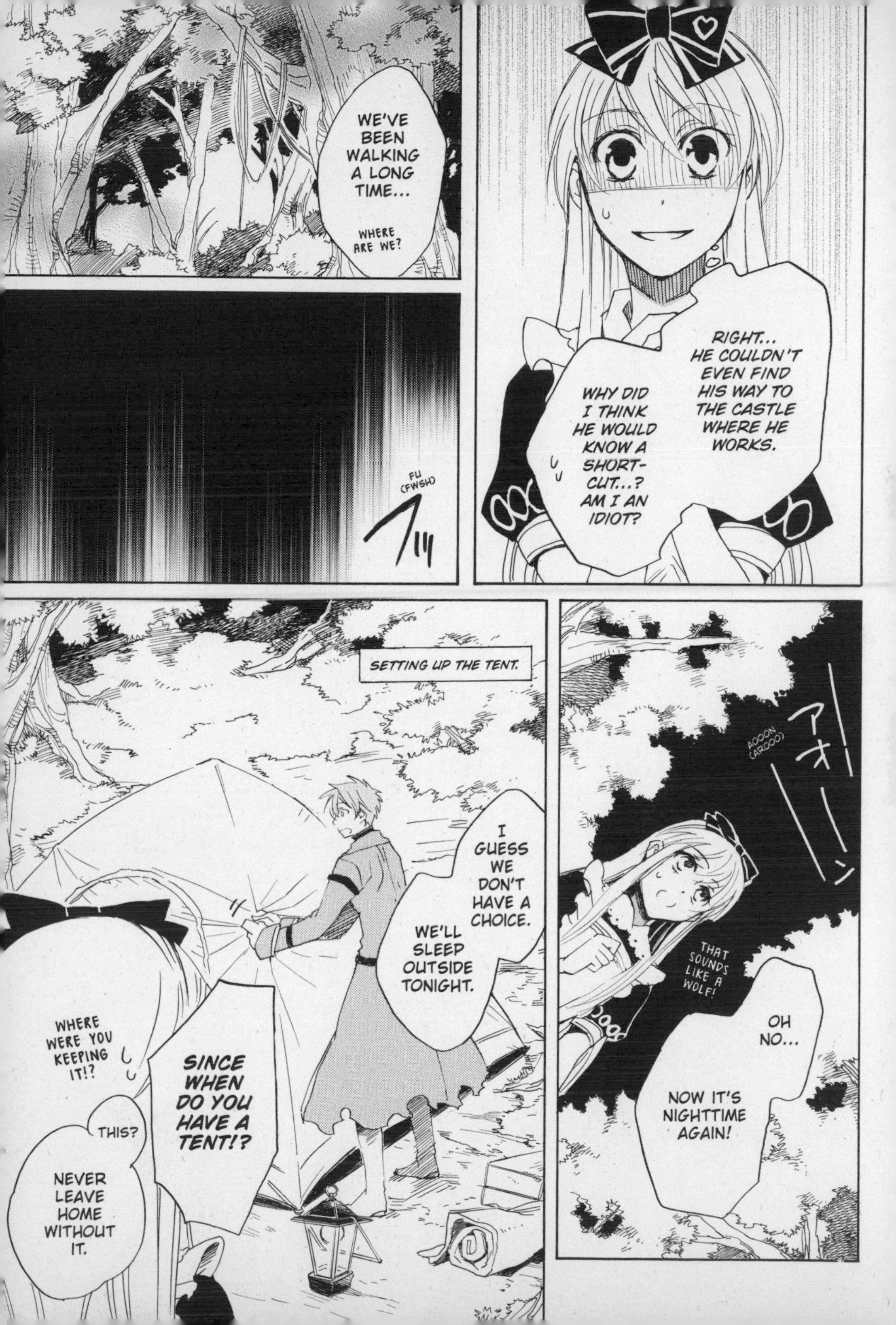
RIGHT... HE COULDN'T EVEN FIND HIS WAY TO THE CASTLE WHERE HE WORKS.
WHY DID I THINK HE WOULD KNOW A SHORT-CUT...? AM I AN IDIOT?
WE'VE BEEN WALKING A LONG TIME...
WHERE ARE WE?
FU (FWSH)
AOOON (AROOO)
THAT SOUNDS LIKE A WOLF!
OH NO...
NOW IT'S NIGHTTIME AGAIN!
SETTING UP THE TENT.
I GUESS WE DON'T HAVE A CHOICE.
WE'LL SLEEP OUTSIDE TONIGHT.
SINCE WHEN DO YOU HAVE A TENT!?
WHERE WERE YOU KEEPING IT!?
THIS?
NEVER LEAVE HOME WITHOUT IT.

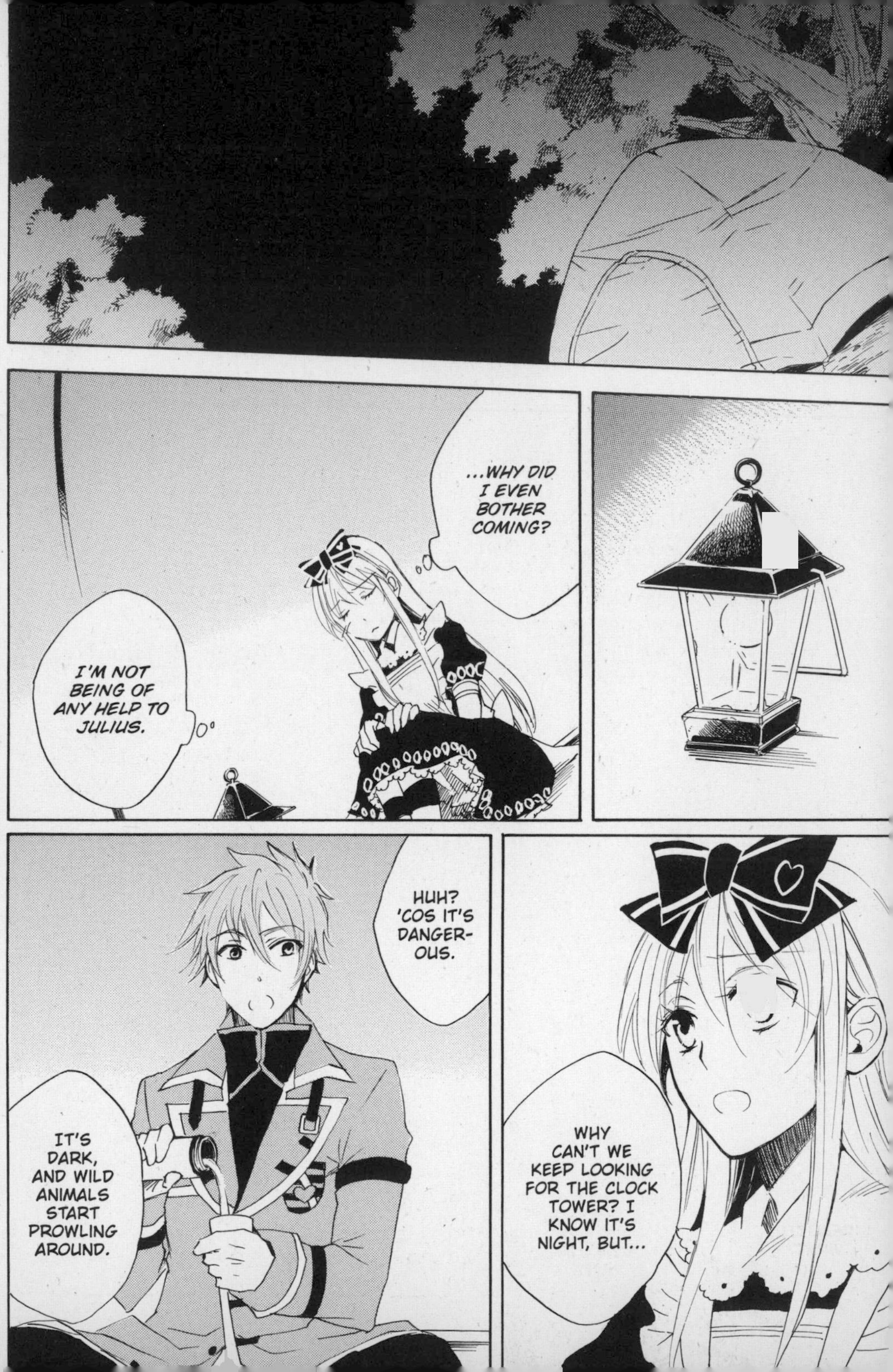
...WHY DID I EVEN BOTHER COMING?
I'M NOT BEING OF ANY HELP TO JULIUS.
WHY CAN'T WE KEEP LOOKING FOR THE CLOCK TOWER? I KNOW IT'S NIGHT, BUT...
HUH? 'COS IT'S DANGER-OUS.
IT'S DARK, AND WILD ANIMALS START PROWLING AROUND.

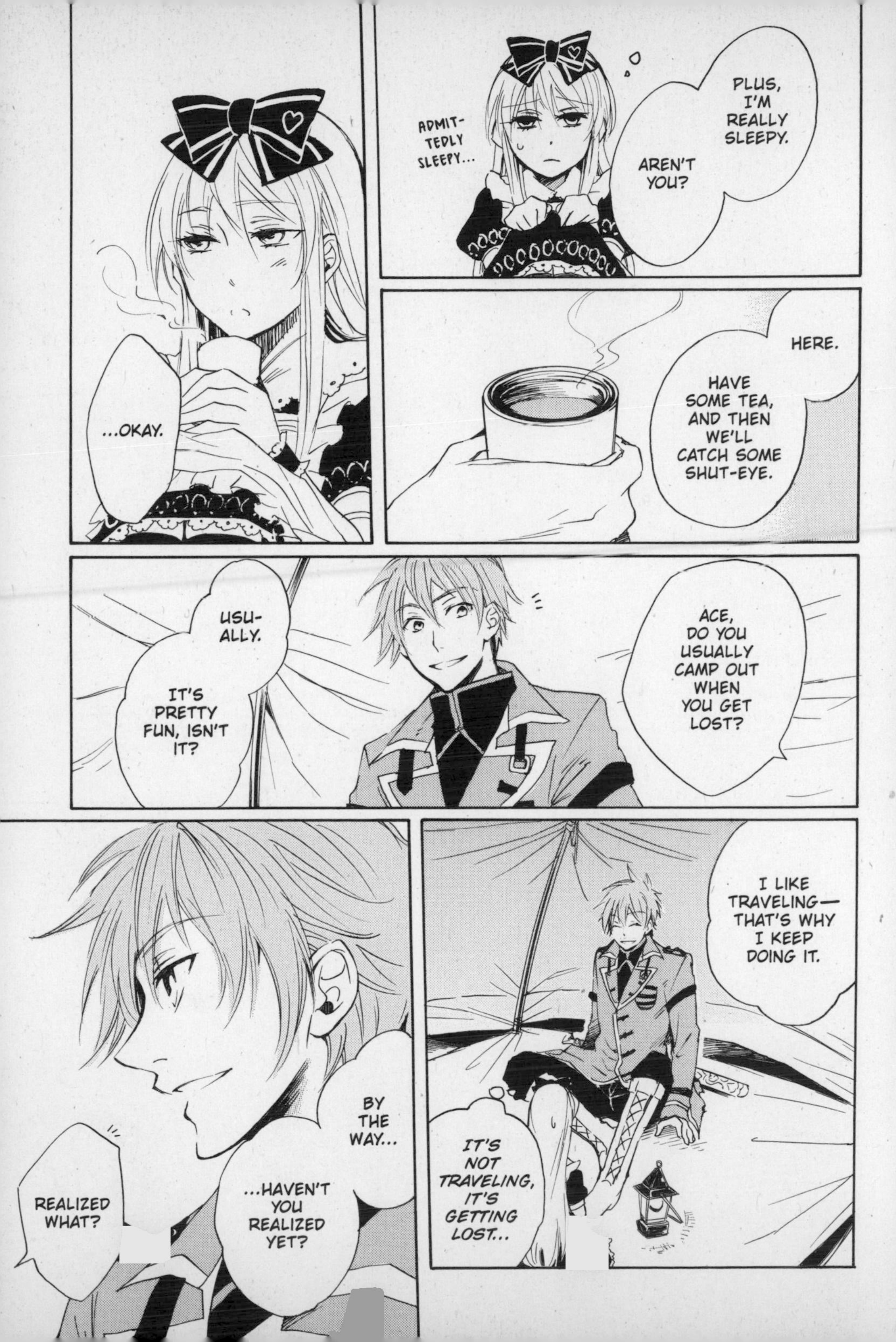
PLUS, I'M REALLY SLEEPY.
AREN'T YOU?
ADMIT-TEDLY SLEEPY...
HERE.
HAVE SOME TEA, AND THEN WE'LL CATCH SOME SHUT-EYE.
...OKAY.
ACE, DO YOU USUALLY CAMP OUT WHEN YOU GET LOST?
USU-ALLY.
IT'S PRETTY FUN, ISN'T IT?
I LIKE TRAVELING—THAT'S WHY I KEEP DOING IT.
IT'S NOT TRAVELING, IT'S GETTING LOST...
BY THE WAY...
...HAVEN'T YOU REALIZED YET?
REALIZED WHAT?

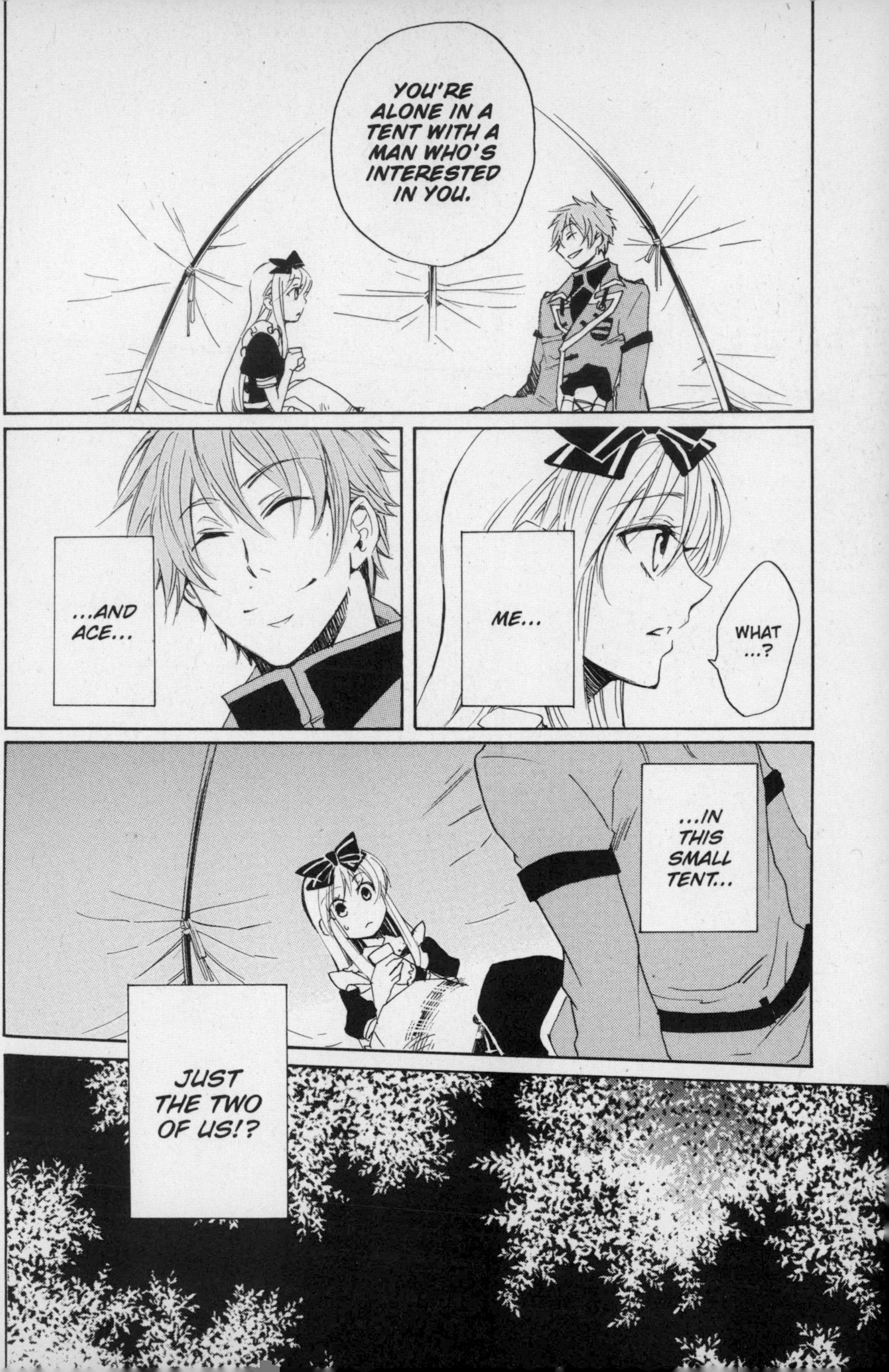
YOU'RE ALONE IN A TENT WITH A MAN WHO'S INTERESTED IN YOU.
WHAT ...?
ME...
...AND ACE...
...IN THIS SMALL TENT...
JUST THE TWO OF US!?

♥10 Heart Sound

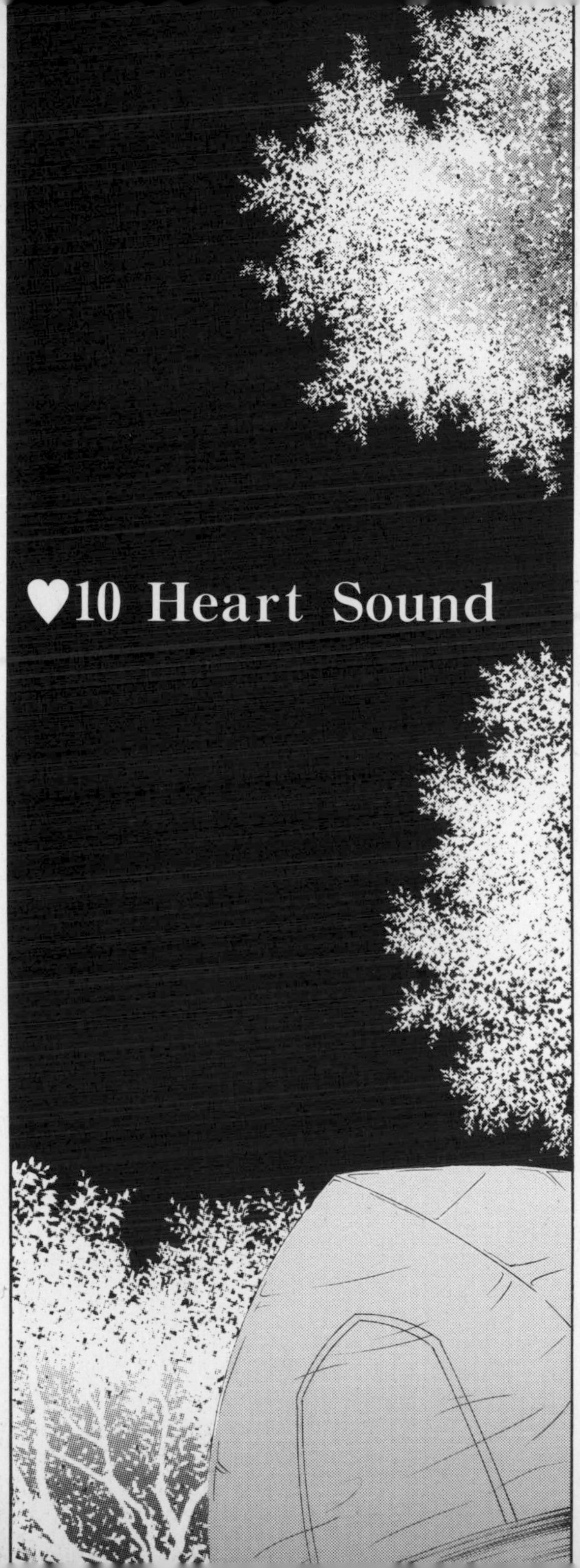

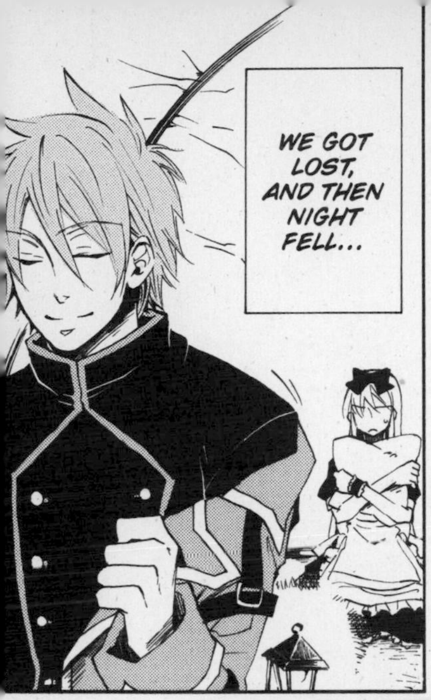
WE GOT LOST, AND THEN NIGHT FELL...

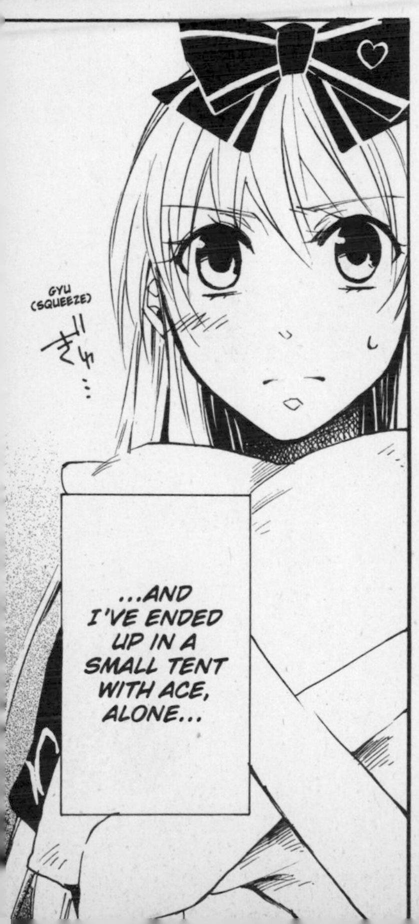
GYU (SQUEEZE)
ぎゅ…
...AND I'VE ENDED UP IN A SMALL TENT WITH ACE, ALONE...

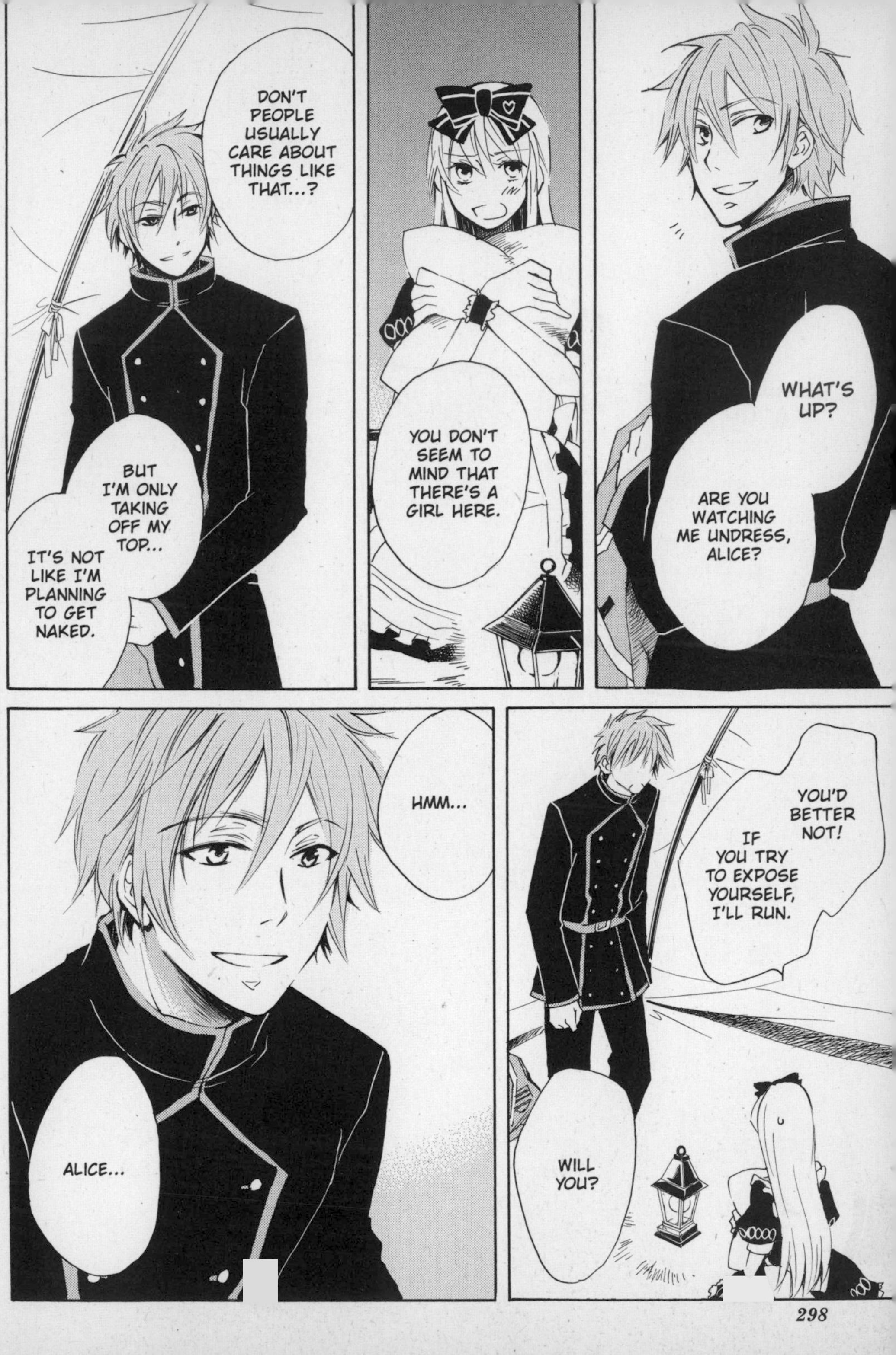
WHAT'S UP?
ARE YOU WATCHING ME UNDRESS, ALICE?
YOU DON'T SEEM TO MIND THAT THERE'S A GIRL HERE.
DON'T PEOPLE USUALLY CARE ABOUT THINGS LIKE THAT...?
BUT I'M ONLY TAKING OFF MY TOP...
IT'S NOT LIKE I'M PLANNING TO GET NAKED.
YOU'D BETTER NOT!
IF YOU TRY TO EXPOSE YOURSELF, I'LL RUN.
WILL YOU?
HMM...
ALICE...

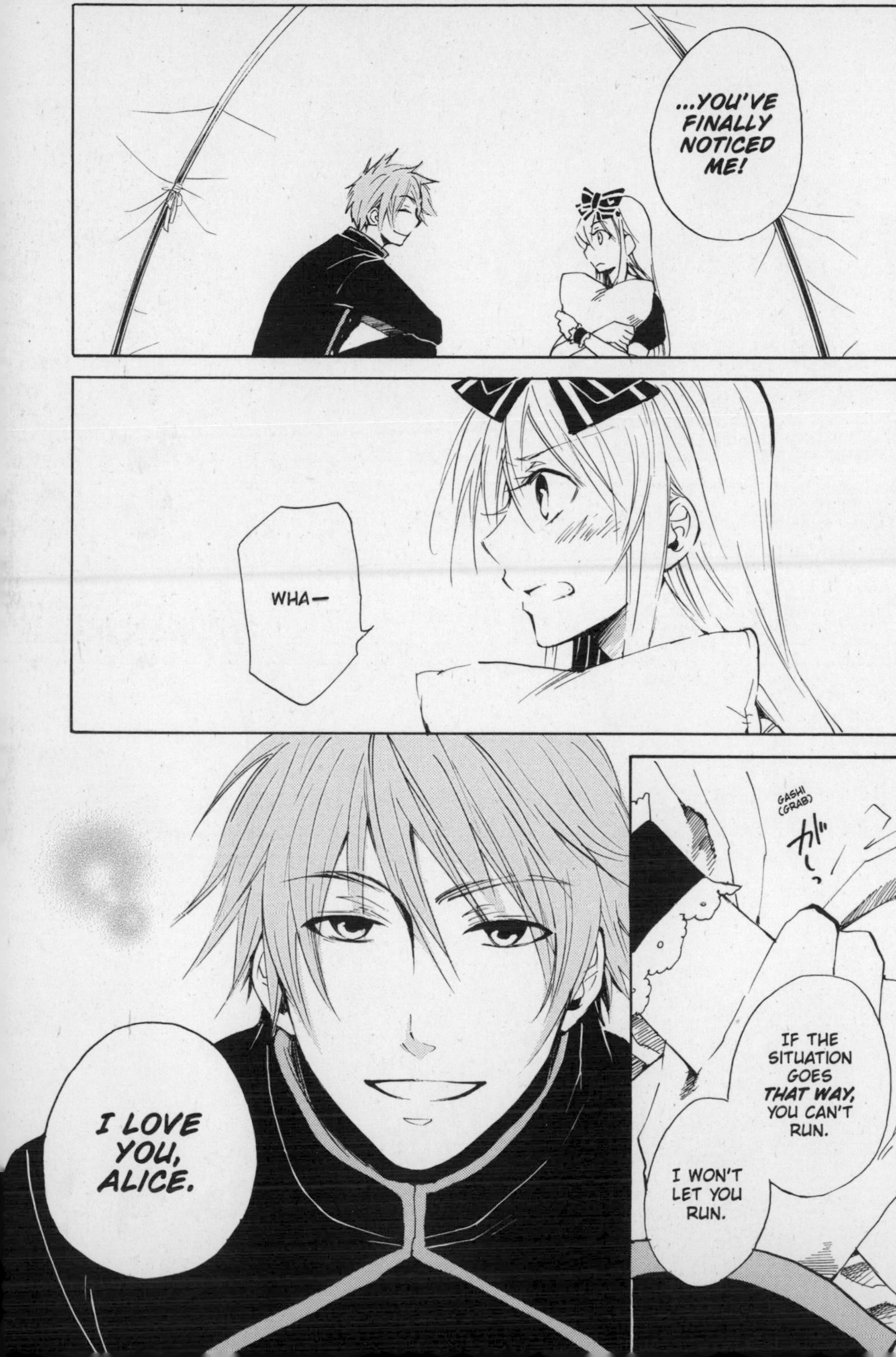
...YOU'VE FINALLY NOTICED ME!
WHA—
GASHI (GRAB)
がしっ
IF THE SITUATION GOES *THAT WAY,* YOU CAN'T RUN.
I WON'T LET YOU RUN.
I LOVE YOU, ALICE.

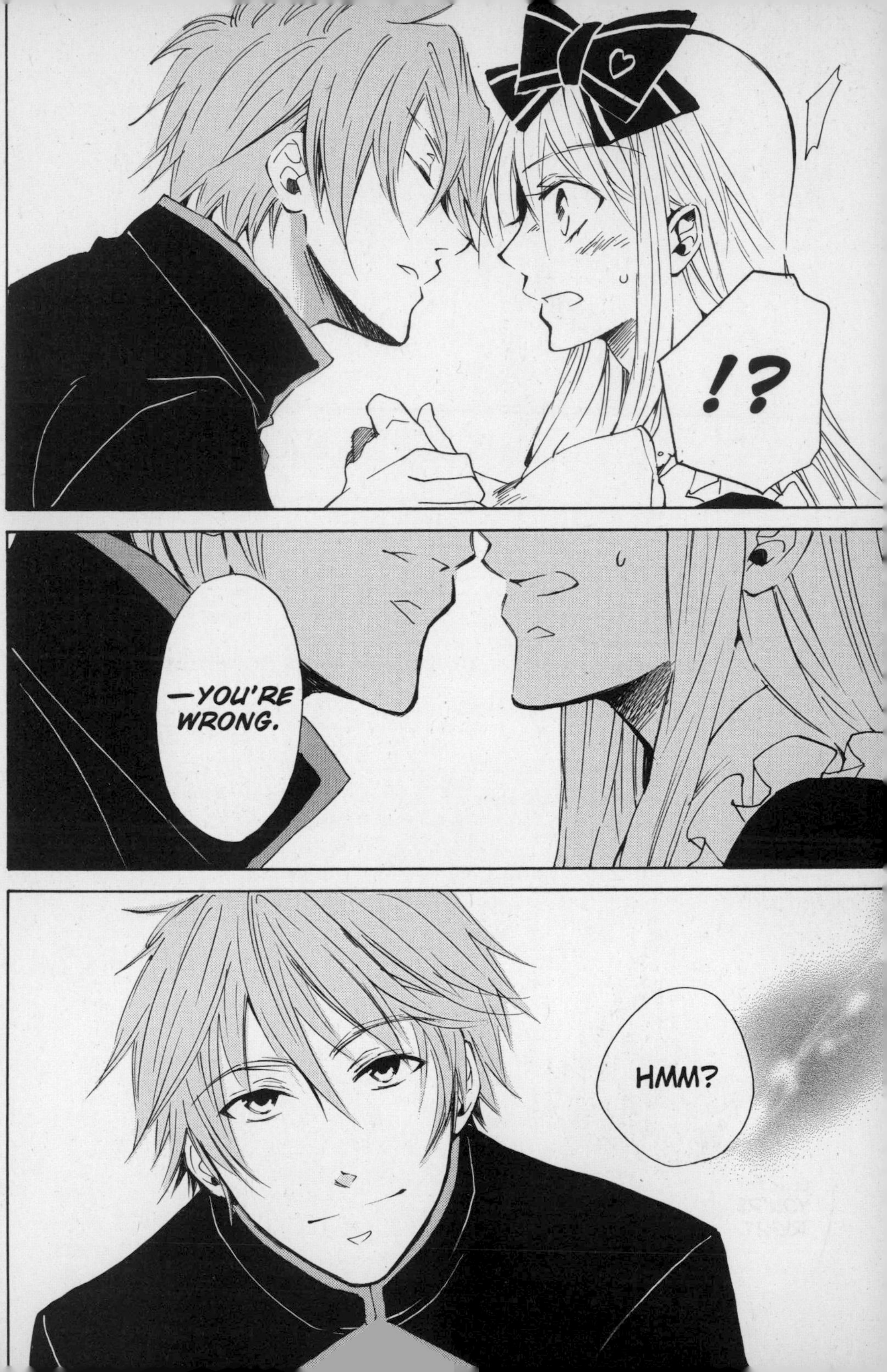
!?
—YOU'RE WRONG.
HMM?

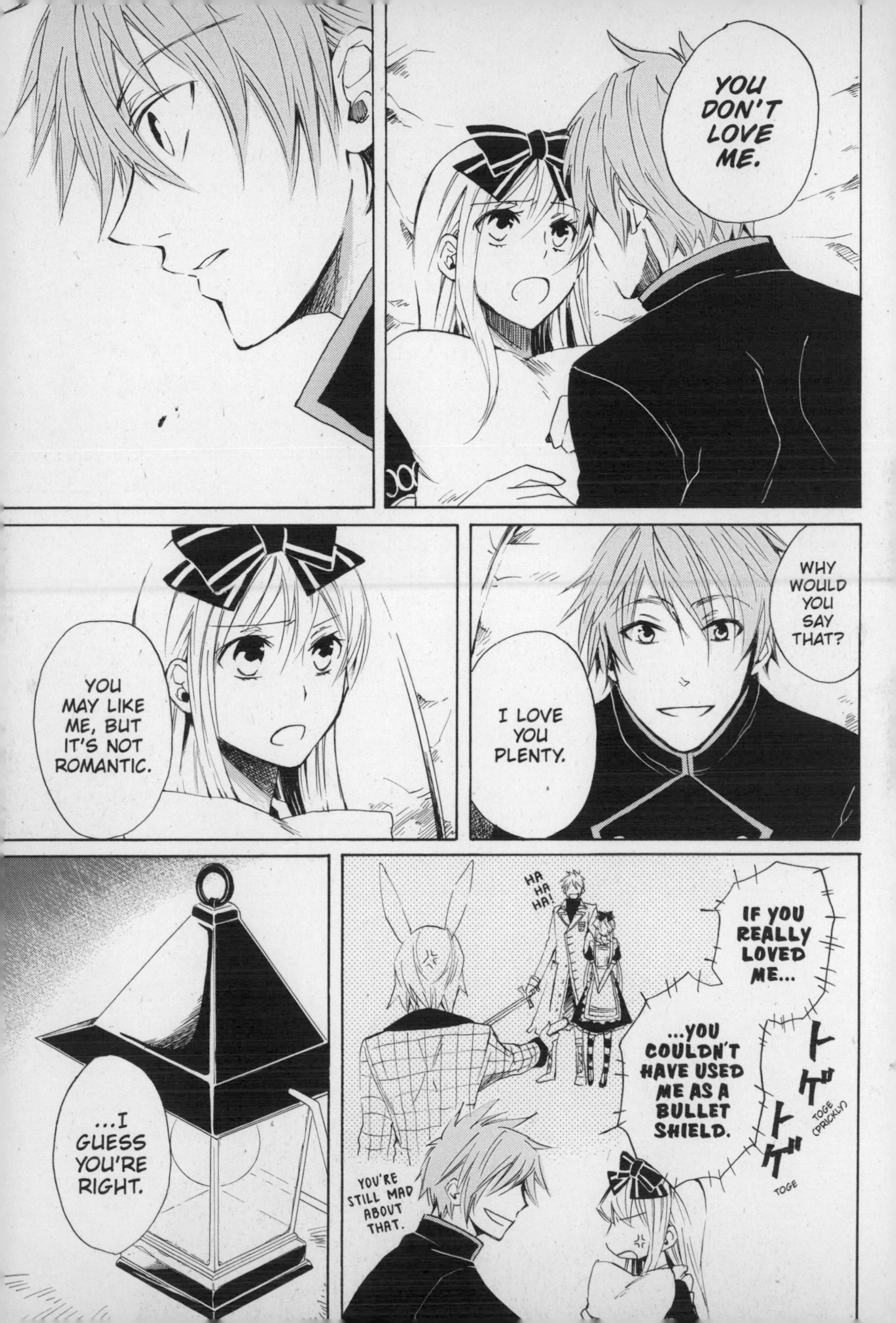
YOU DON'T LOVE ME.
WHY WOULD YOU SAY THAT?
I LOVE YOU PLENTY.
YOU MAY LIKE ME, BUT IT'S NOT ROMANTIC.
IF YOU REALLY LOVED ME...
HA HA HA!
...YOU COULDN'T HAVE USED ME AS A BULLET SHIELD.
トゲ
TOGE (PRICKLY)
トゲ
TOGE
YOU'RE STILL MAD ABOUT THAT.
...I GUESS YOU'RE RIGHT.

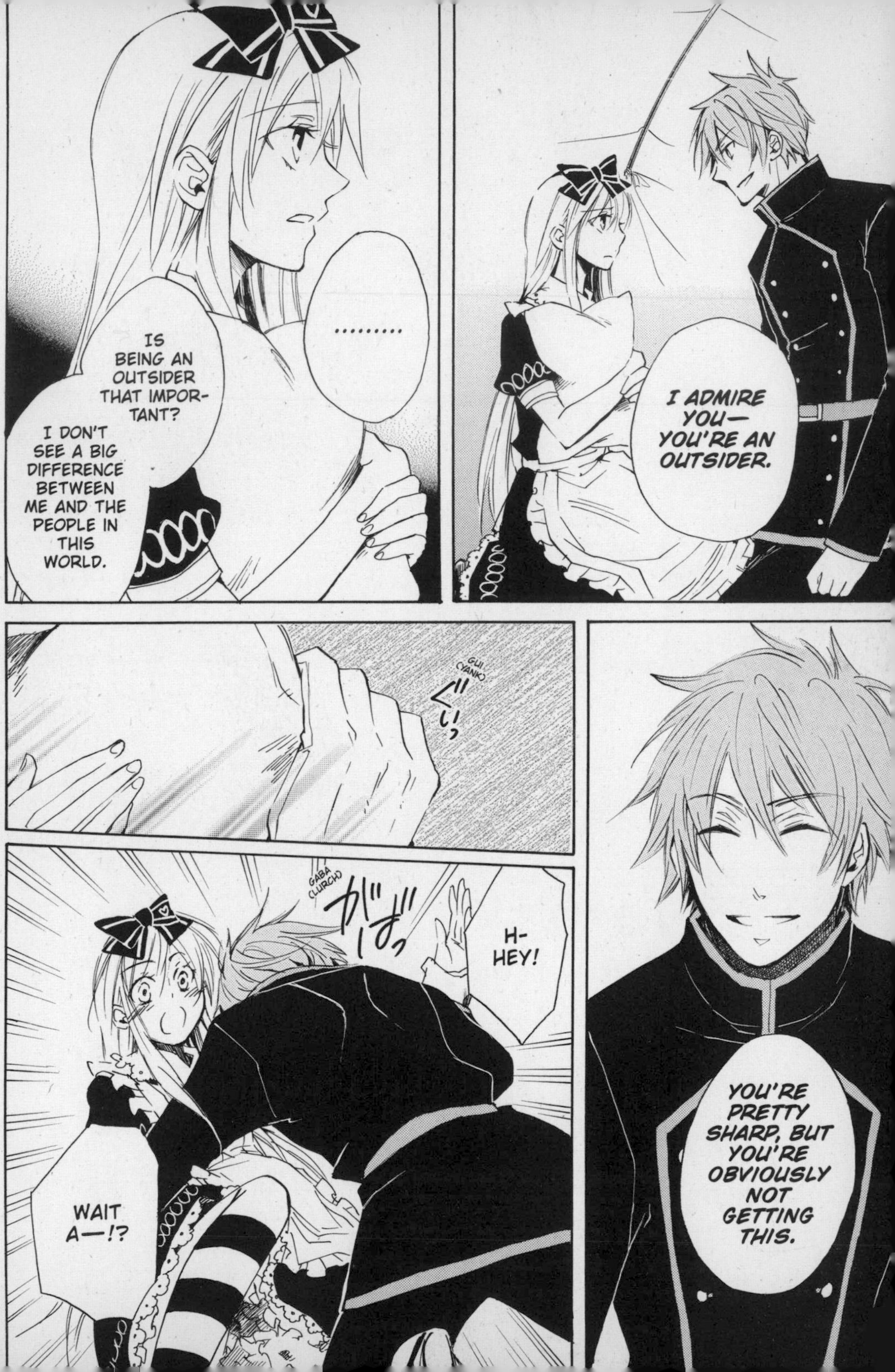
I ADMIRE YOU—YOU'RE AN OUTSIDER.
....
IS BEING AN OUTSIDER THAT IMPORTANT?
I DON'T SEE A BIG DIFFERENCE BETWEEN ME AND THE PEOPLE IN THIS WORLD.
YOU'RE PRETTY SHARP, BUT YOU'RE OBVIOUSLY NOT GETTING THIS.
GUI (YANK)
ぐいっ
GABA (LURCH)
がばっ
H-HEY!
WAIT A—!?

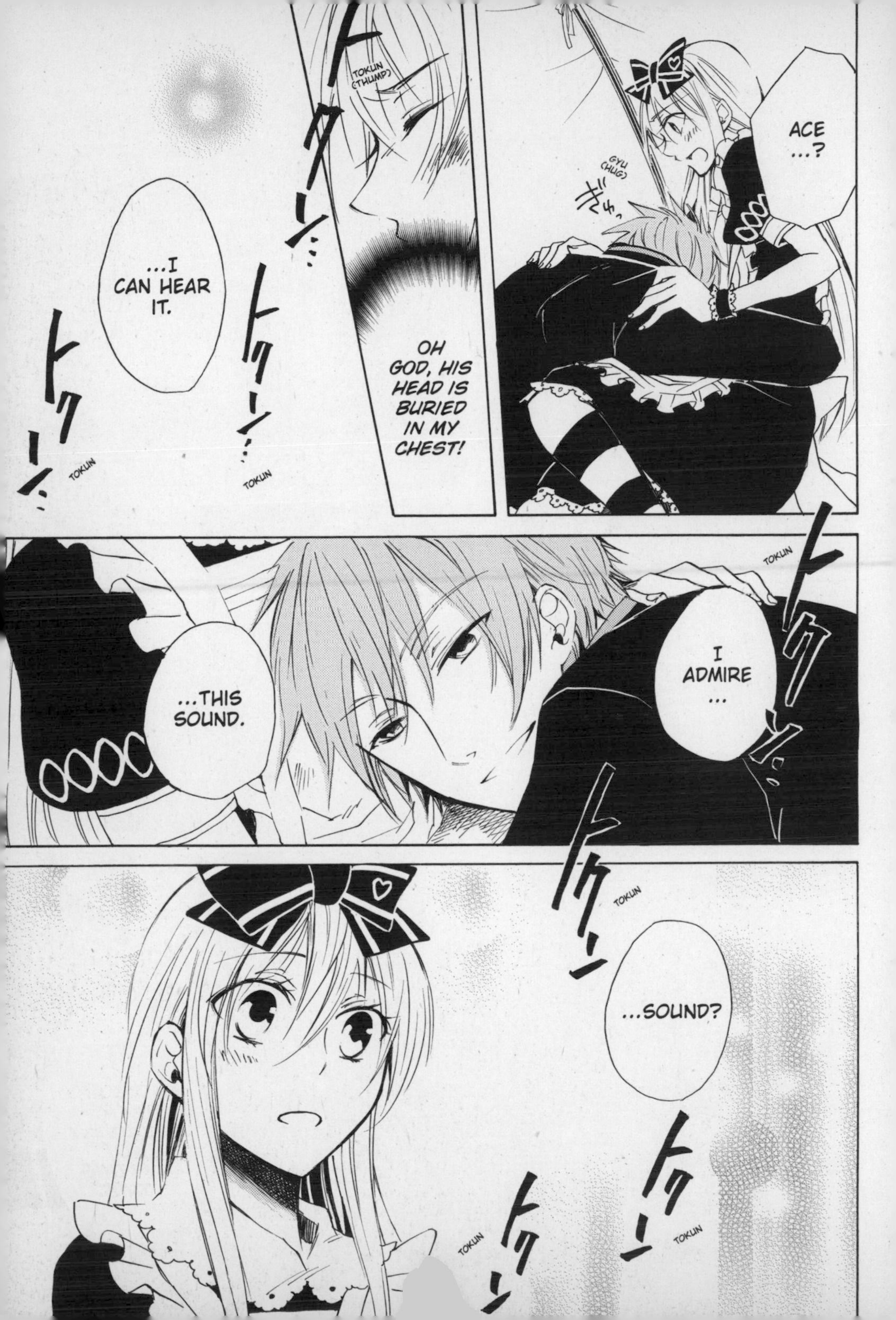
ACE ...?
GYU (HUG)
TOKUN (THUMP)
OH GOD, HIS HEAD IS BURIED IN MY CHEST!
TOKUN
...I CAN HEAR IT.
TOKUN
TOKUN
I ADMIRE ...
...THIS SOUND.
TOKUN
...SOUND?
TOKUN
TOKUN

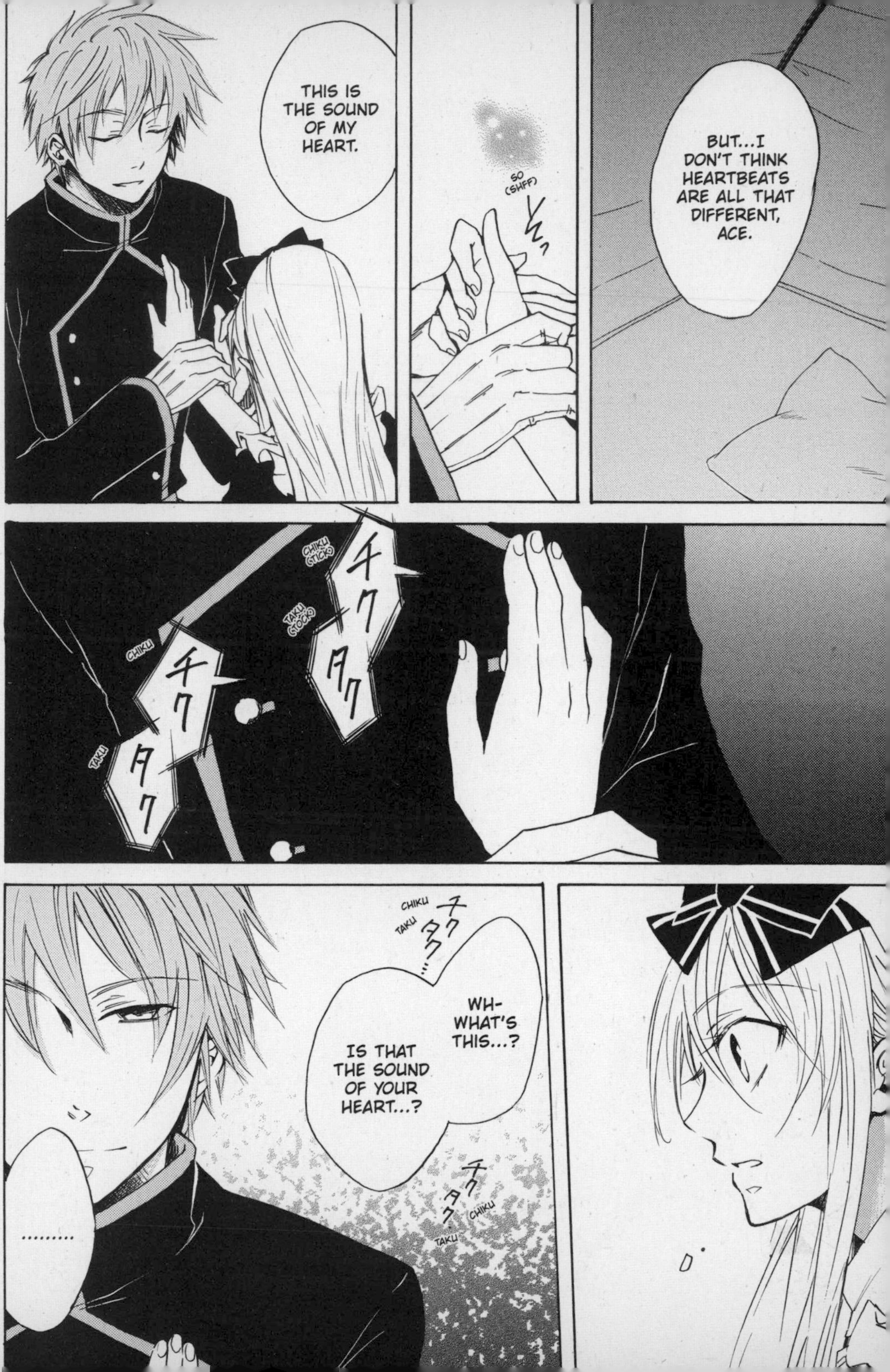
BUT...I DON'T THINK HEARTBEATS ARE ALL THAT DIFFERENT, ACE.
SO (SHFF)
THIS IS THE SOUND OF MY HEART.
CHIKU (TICK)
チク
TAKU (TOCK)
タク
CHIKU
チク
TAKU
タク
WH-WHAT'S THIS...?
IS THAT THE SOUND OF YOUR HEART...?
CHIKU
TAKU
チクタク...
CHIKU
TAKU
チクタク
....

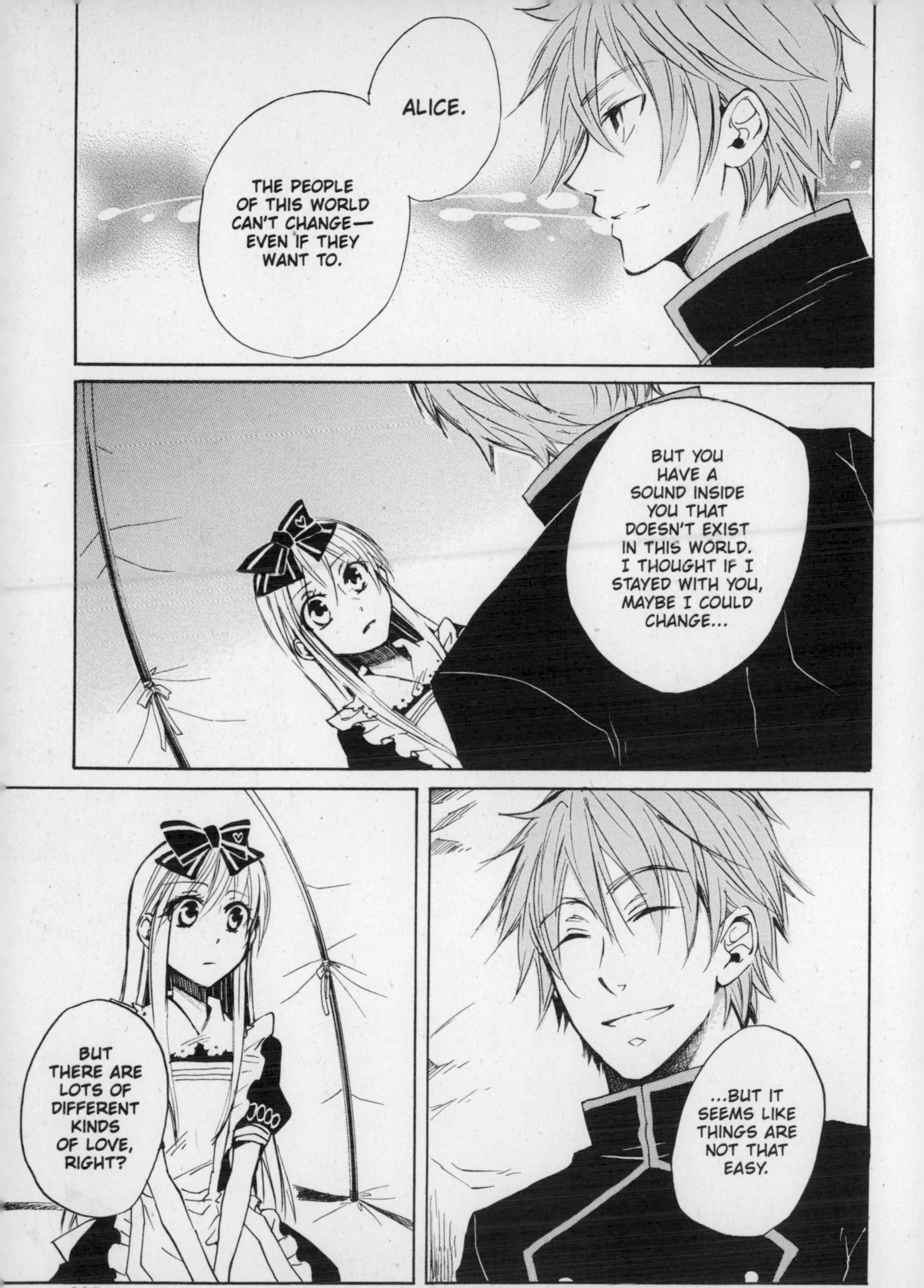
ALICE.
THE PEOPLE OF THIS WORLD CAN'T CHANGE—EVEN IF THEY WANT TO.
BUT YOU HAVE A SOUND INSIDE YOU THAT DOESN'T EXIST IN THIS WORLD. I THOUGHT IF I STAYED WITH YOU, MAYBE I COULD CHANGE...
...BUT IT SEEMS LIKE THINGS ARE NOT THAT EASY.
BUT THERE ARE LOTS OF DIFFERENT KINDS OF LOVE, RIGHT?

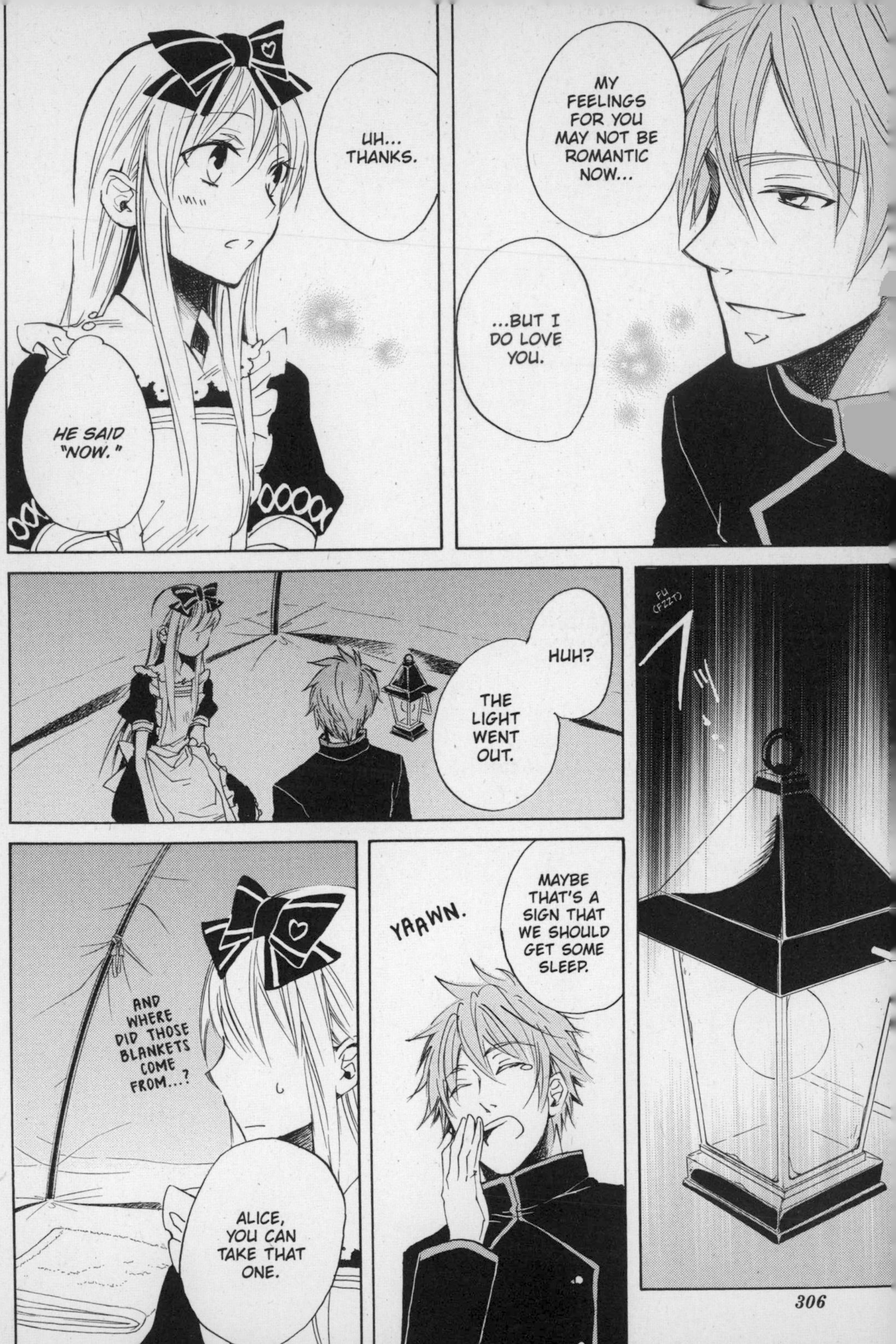
MY FEELINGS FOR YOU MAY NOT BE ROMANTIC NOW...
...BUT I DO LOVE YOU.
UH... THANKS.
HE SAID "NOW."
FU (FZZT)
HUH?
THE LIGHT WENT OUT.
MAYBE THAT'S A SIGN THAT WE SHOULD GET SOME SLEEP.
YAAWN.
AND WHERE DID THOSE BLANKETS COME FROM...?
ALICE, YOU CAN TAKE THAT ONE.

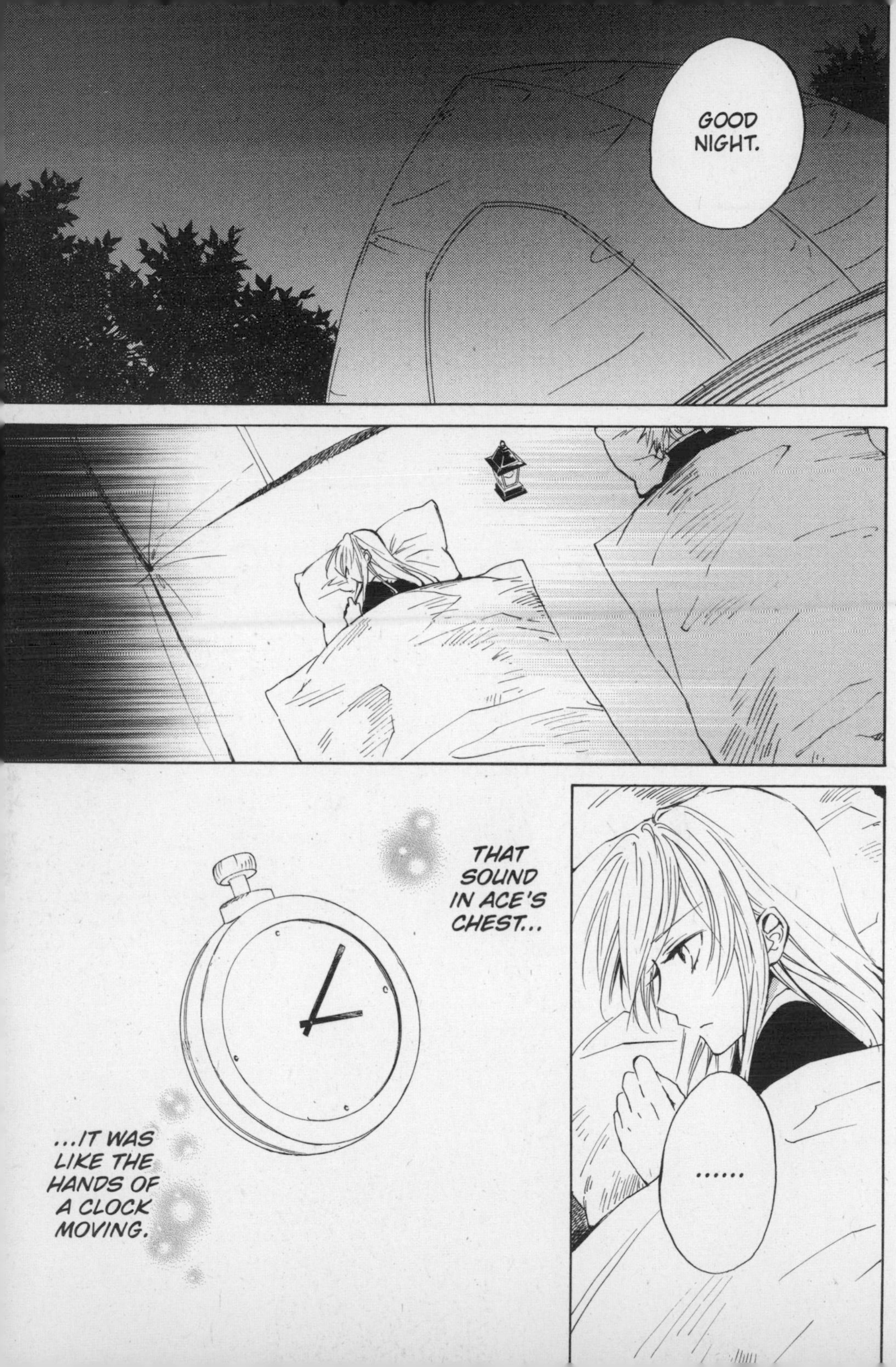
GOOD NIGHT.
......
THAT SOUND IN ACE'S CHEST...
...IT WAS LIKE THE HANDS OF A CLOCK MOVING.

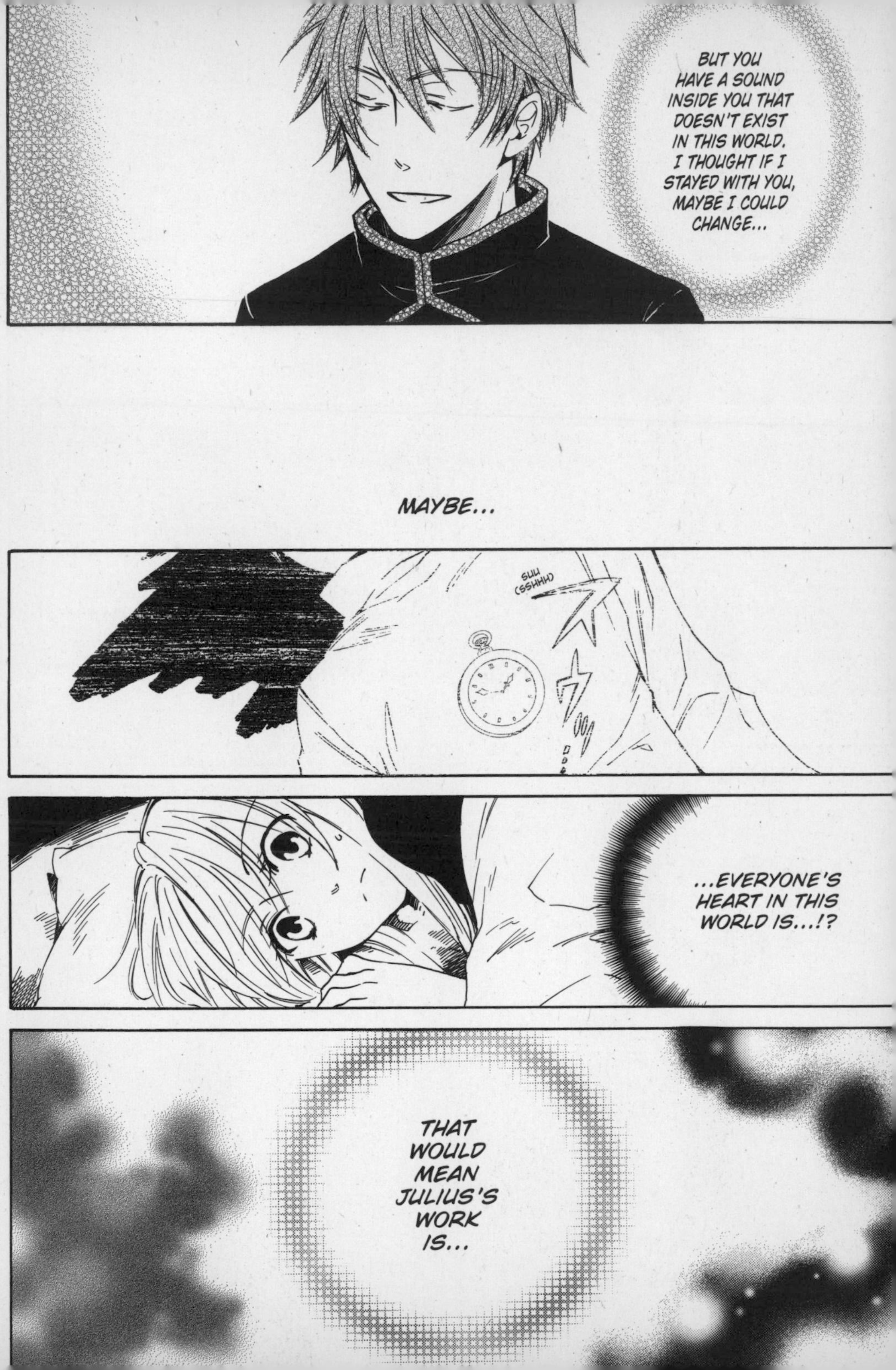
BUT YOU HAVE A SOUND INSIDE YOU THAT DOESN'T EXIST IN THIS WORLD. I THOUGHT IF I STAYED WITH YOU, MAYBE I COULD CHANGE...
MAYBE...
SUU (SSHHH)
...EVERYONE'S HEART IN THIS WORLD IS...!?
THAT WOULD MEAN JULIUS'S WORK IS...

YOU ARRIVE AT LAST...

SINCE YOU DIDN'T SAVE TIME...

...THERE WAS NO POINT IN YOU GOING AT ALL.

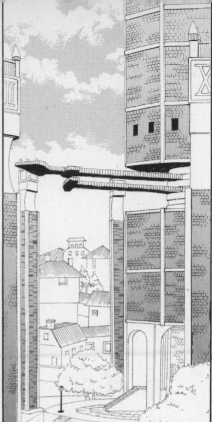

YES, SIR!

......

SORRY, SORRY.

HMPH.

HURRY UP AND GET TO WORK.

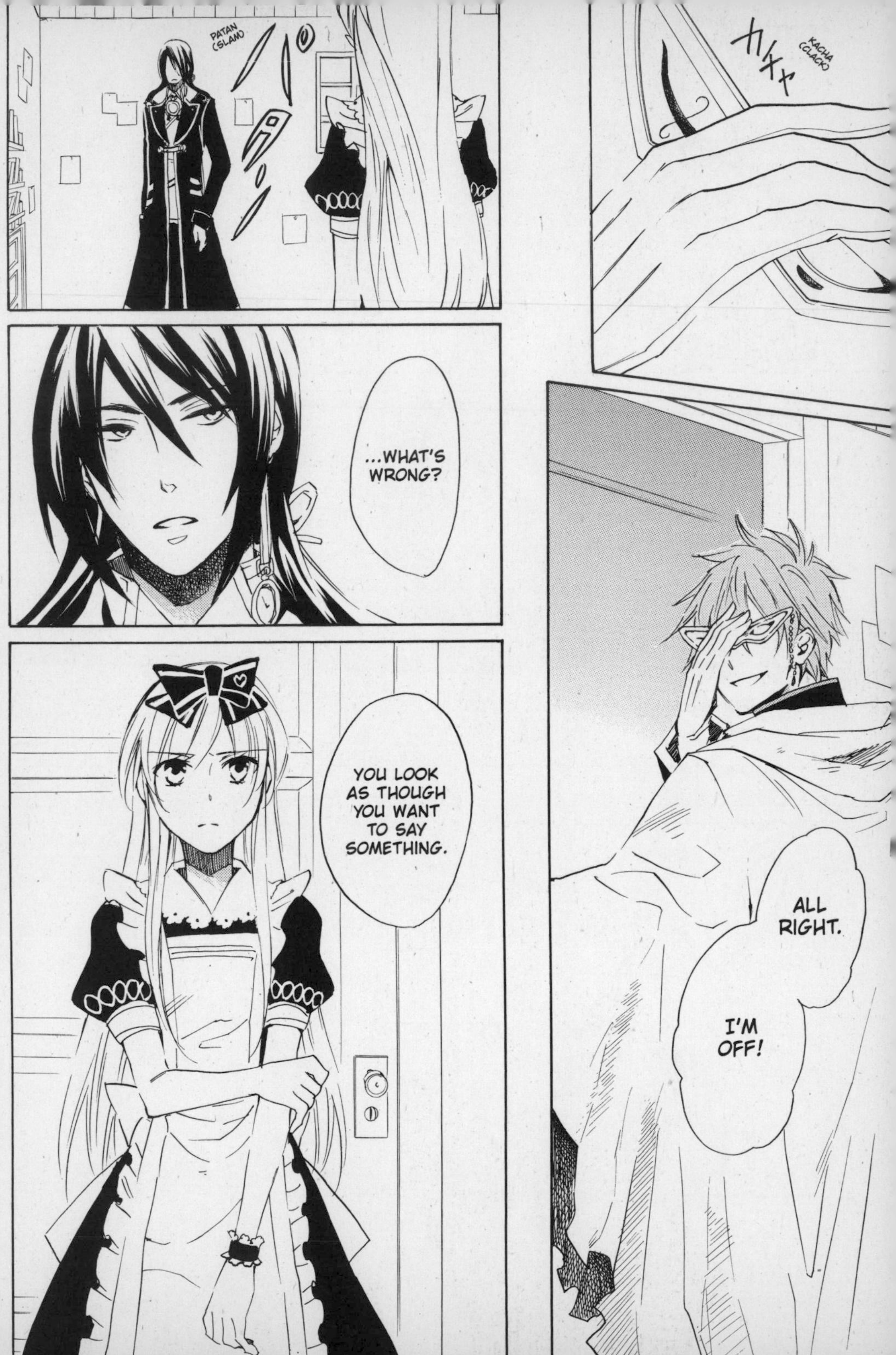

カチャ
KACHA (CLACK)
ALL RIGHT.
I'M OFF!
PATAN (SLAM)
...WHAT'S WRONG?
YOU LOOK AS THOUGH YOU WANT TO SAY SOMETHING.

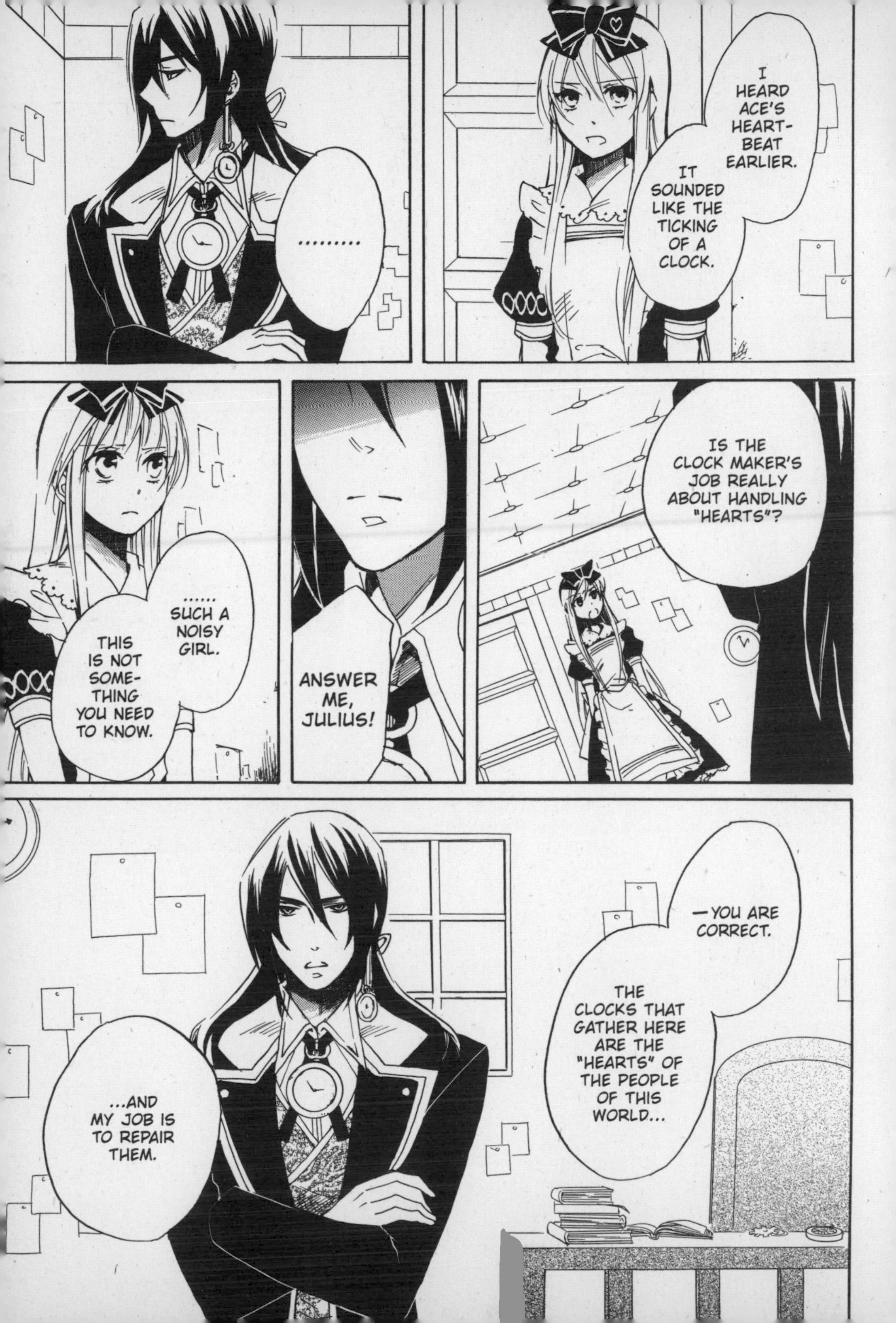
I HEARD ACE'S HEART-BEAT EARLIER.
IT SOUNDED LIKE THE TICKING OF A CLOCK.
....
IS THE CLOCK MAKER'S JOB REALLY ABOUT HANDLING "HEARTS"?
ANSWER ME, JULIUS!
......SUCH A NOISY GIRL.
THIS IS NOT SOME-THING YOU NEED TO KNOW.
—YOU ARE CORRECT.
THE CLOCKS THAT GATHER HERE ARE THE "HEARTS" OF THE PEOPLE OF THIS WORLD...
...AND MY JOB IS TO REPAIR THEM.

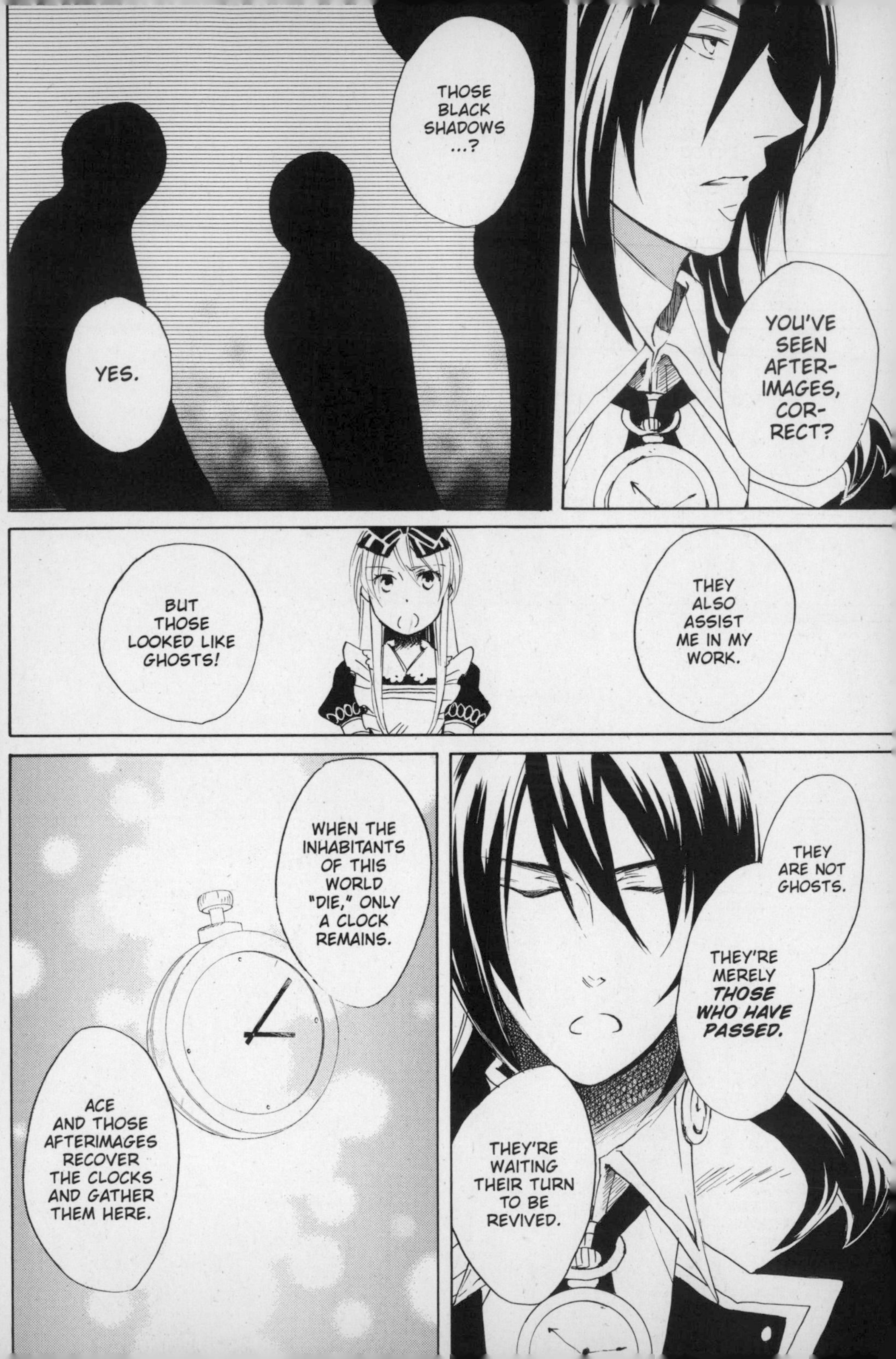
YOU'VE SEEN AFTER-IMAGES, COR-RECT?
THOSE BLACK SHADOWS ...?
YES.
THEY ALSO ASSIST ME IN MY WORK.
BUT THOSE LOOKED LIKE GHOSTS!
THEY ARE NOT GHOSTS.
THEY'RE MERELY *THOSE WHO HAVE PASSED.*
THEY'RE WAITING THEIR TURN TO BE REVIVED.
WHEN THE INHABITANTS OF THIS WORLD "DIE," ONLY A CLOCK REMAINS.
ACE AND THOSE AFTERIMAGES RECOVER THE CLOCKS AND GATHER THEM HERE.

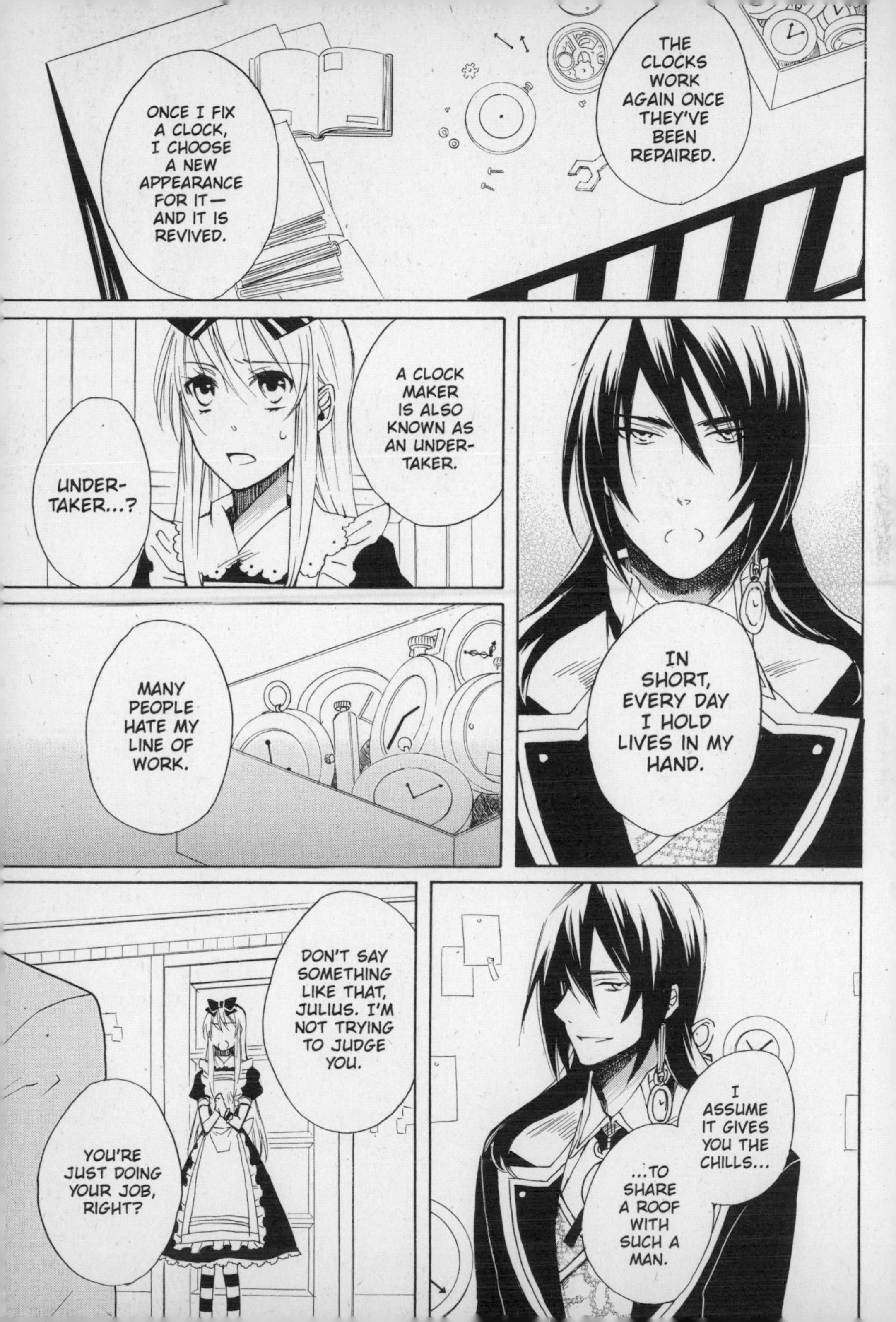
THE CLOCKS WORK AGAIN ONCE THEY'VE BEEN REPAIRED.
ONCE I FIX A CLOCK, I CHOOSE A NEW APPEARANCE FOR IT— AND IT IS REVIVED.
IN SHORT, EVERY DAY I HOLD LIVES IN MY HAND.
A CLOCK MAKER IS ALSO KNOWN AS AN UNDER-TAKER.
UNDER-TAKER...?
MANY PEOPLE HATE MY LINE OF WORK.
I ASSUME IT GIVES YOU THE CHILLS...
...TO SHARE A ROOF WITH SUCH A MAN.
DON'T SAY SOMETHING LIKE THAT, JULIUS. I'M NOT TRYING TO JUDGE YOU.
YOU'RE JUST DOING YOUR JOB, RIGHT?

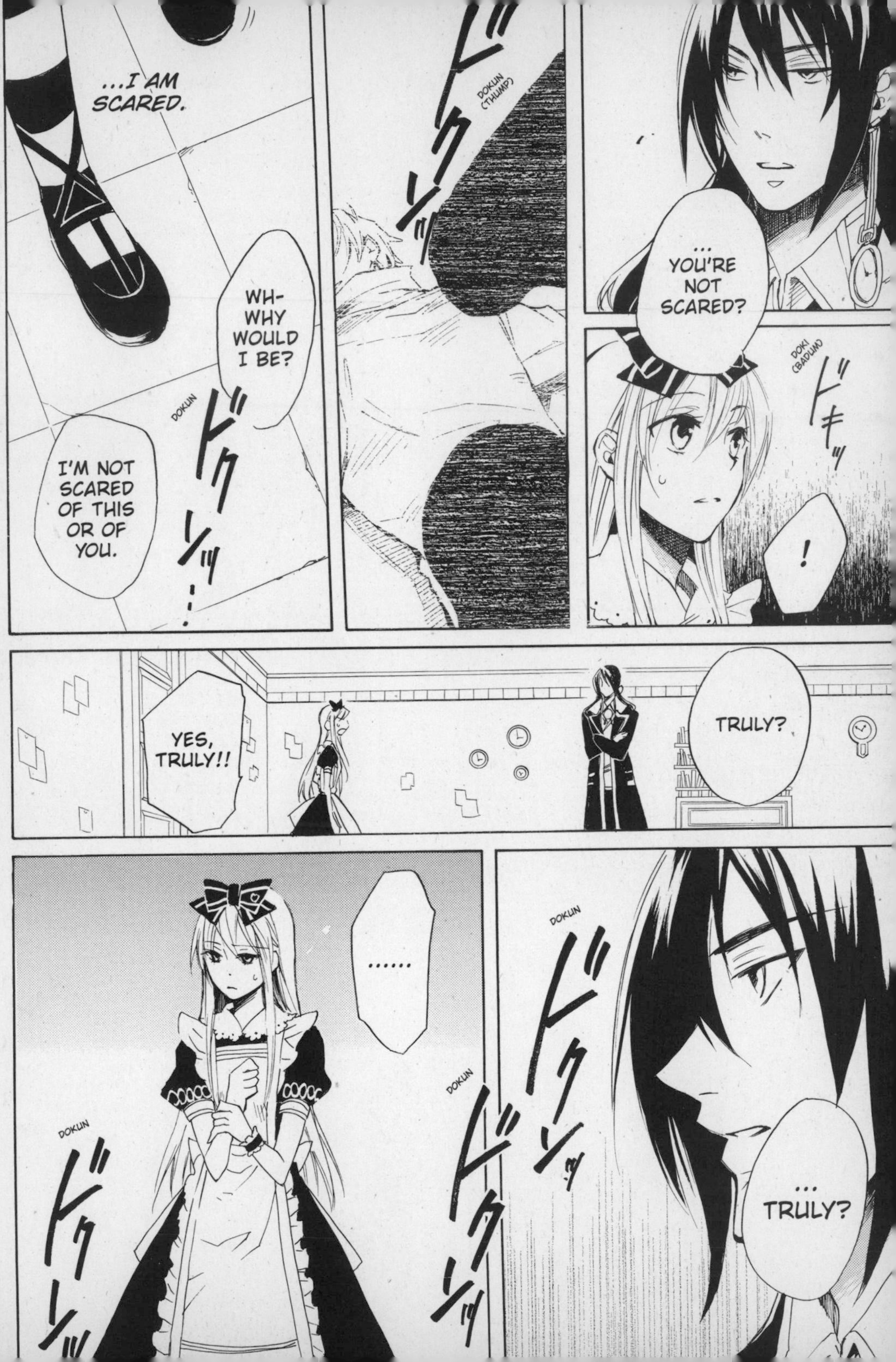
... YOU'RE NOT SCARED?
DOKI (BADUM)
!
DOKUN (THUMP)
WH- WHY WOULD I BE?
DOKUN
I'M NOT SCARED OF THIS OR OF YOU.
...I AM SCARED.
TRULY?
YES, TRULY!!
DOKUN
DOKUN
... TRULY?
......
DOKUN

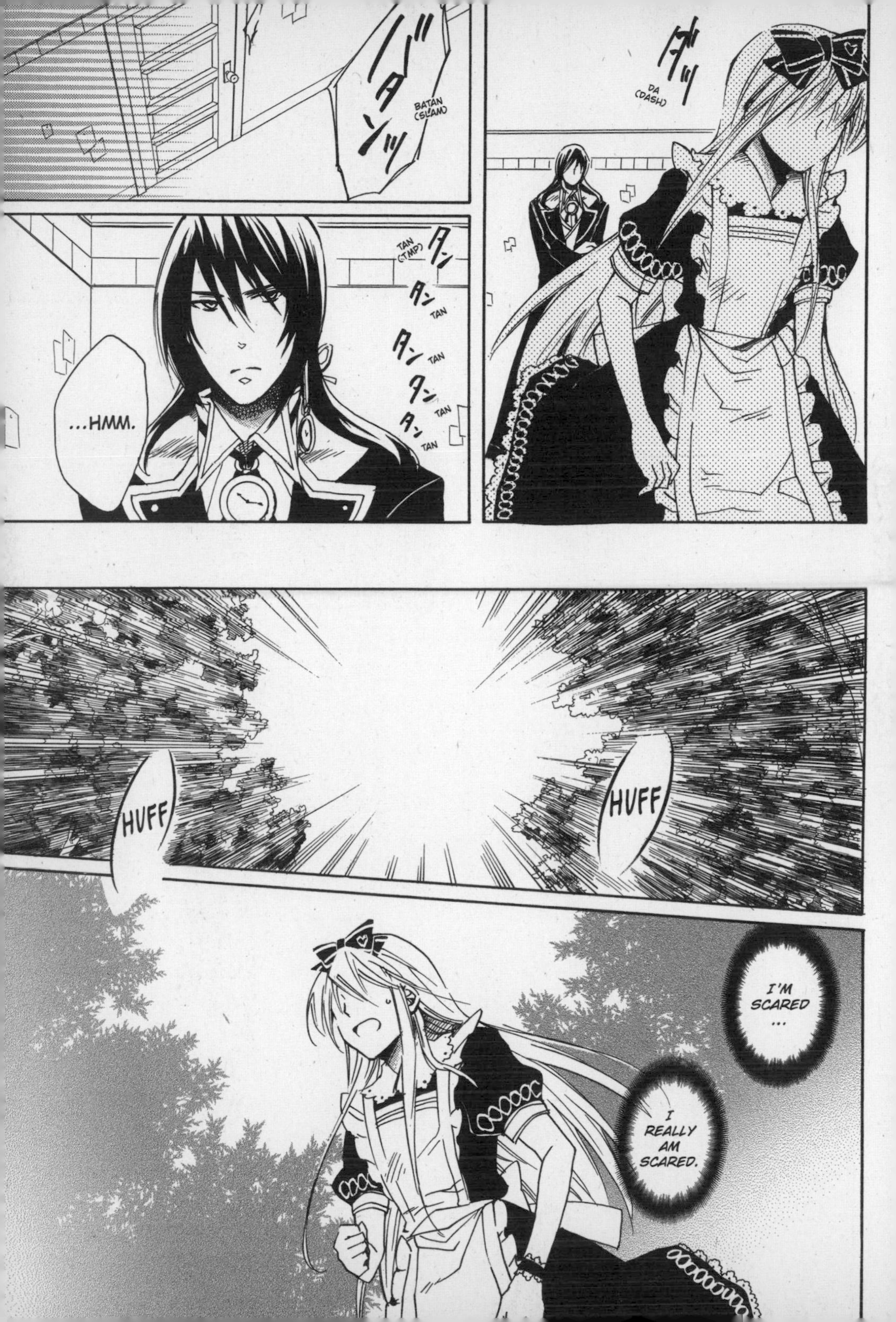
ダッ
DA (DASH)
バタンッ
BATAN (SLAM)
タン
TAN (TMP)
タン
TAN
タン
TAN
タン
TAN
タン
TAN
...HMM.
HUFF
HUFF
I'M SCARED...
I REALLY AM SCARED.

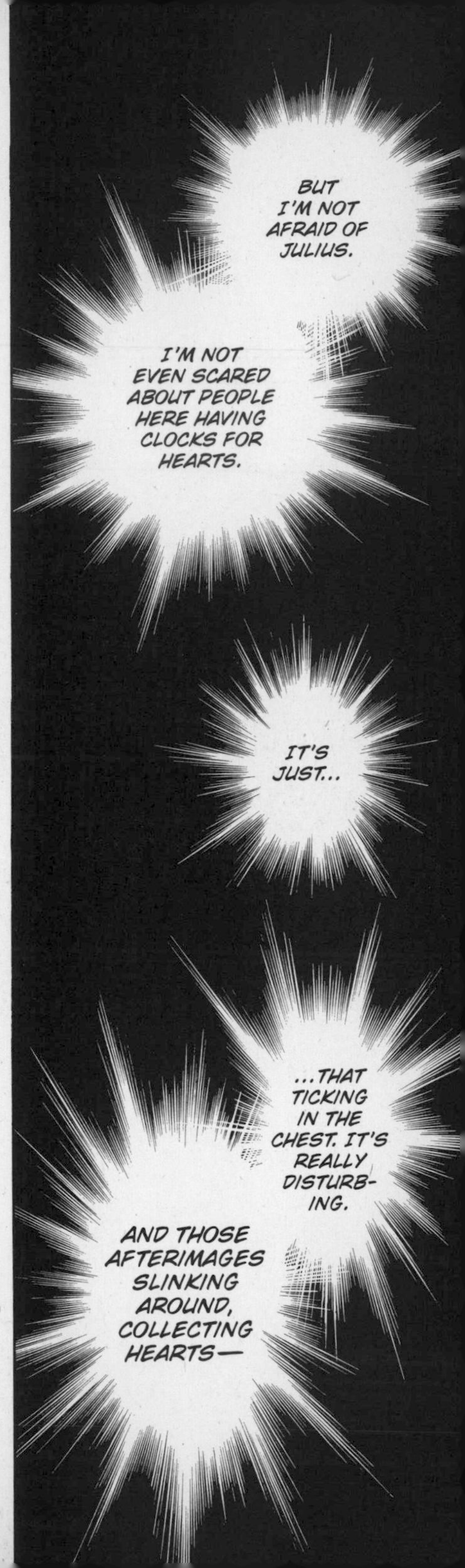
BUT I'M NOT AFRAID OF JULIUS.
I'M NOT EVEN SCARED ABOUT PEOPLE HERE HAVING CLOCKS FOR HEARTS.
IT'S JUST...
...THAT TICKING IN THE CHEST. IT'S REALLY DISTURB-ING.
AND THOSE AFTERIMAGES SLINKING AROUND, COLLECTING HEARTS—
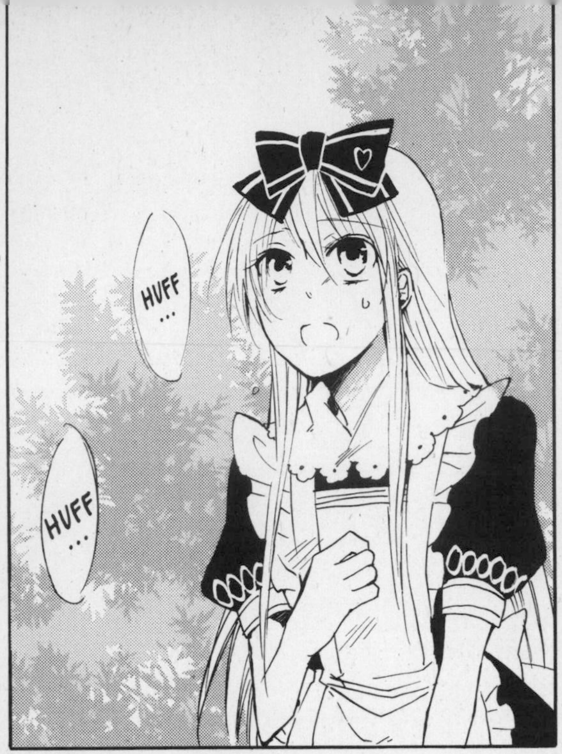
HUFF...
HUFF...
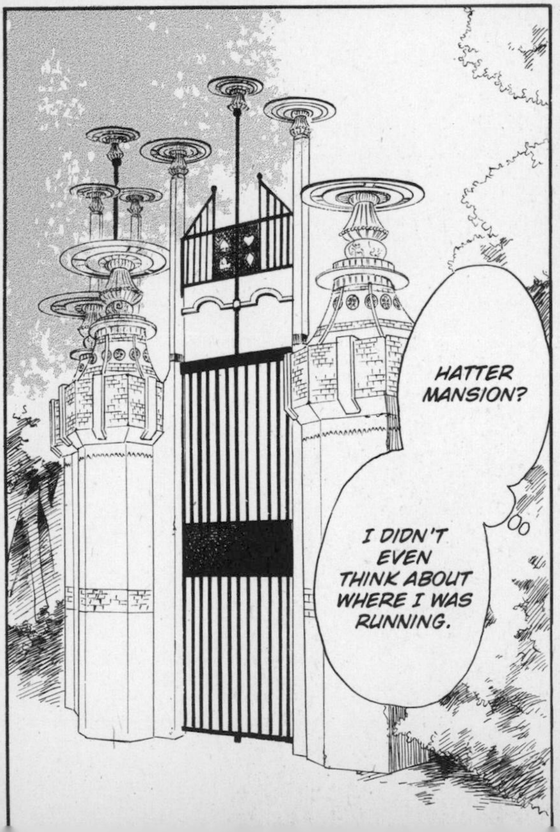
HATTER MANSION?
I DIDN'T EVEN THINK ABOUT WHERE I WAS RUNNING.

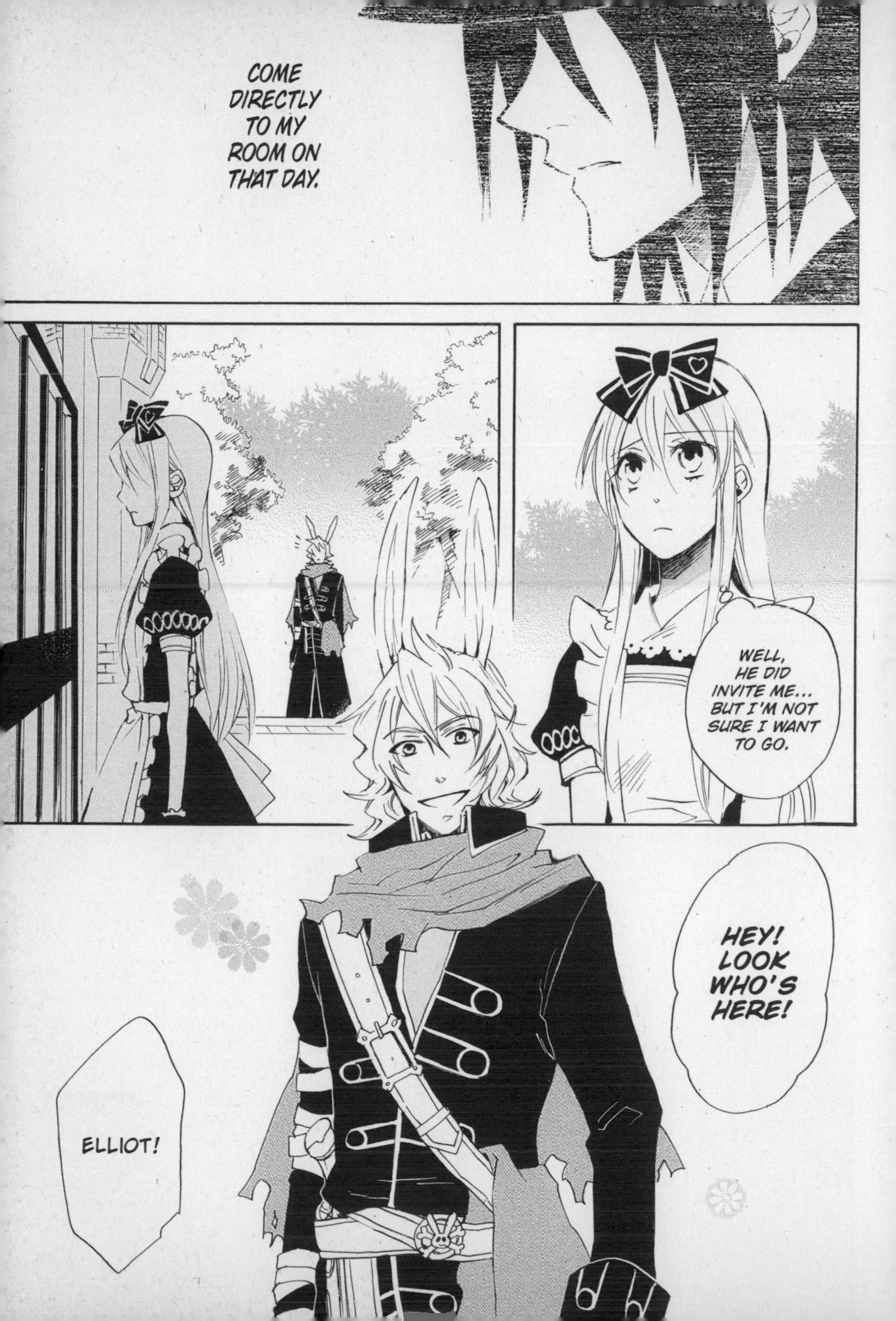
COME DIRECTLY TO MY ROOM ON THAT DAY.
WELL, HE DID INVITE ME... BUT I'M NOT SURE I WANT TO GO.
HEY! LOOK WHO'S HERE!
ELLIOT!

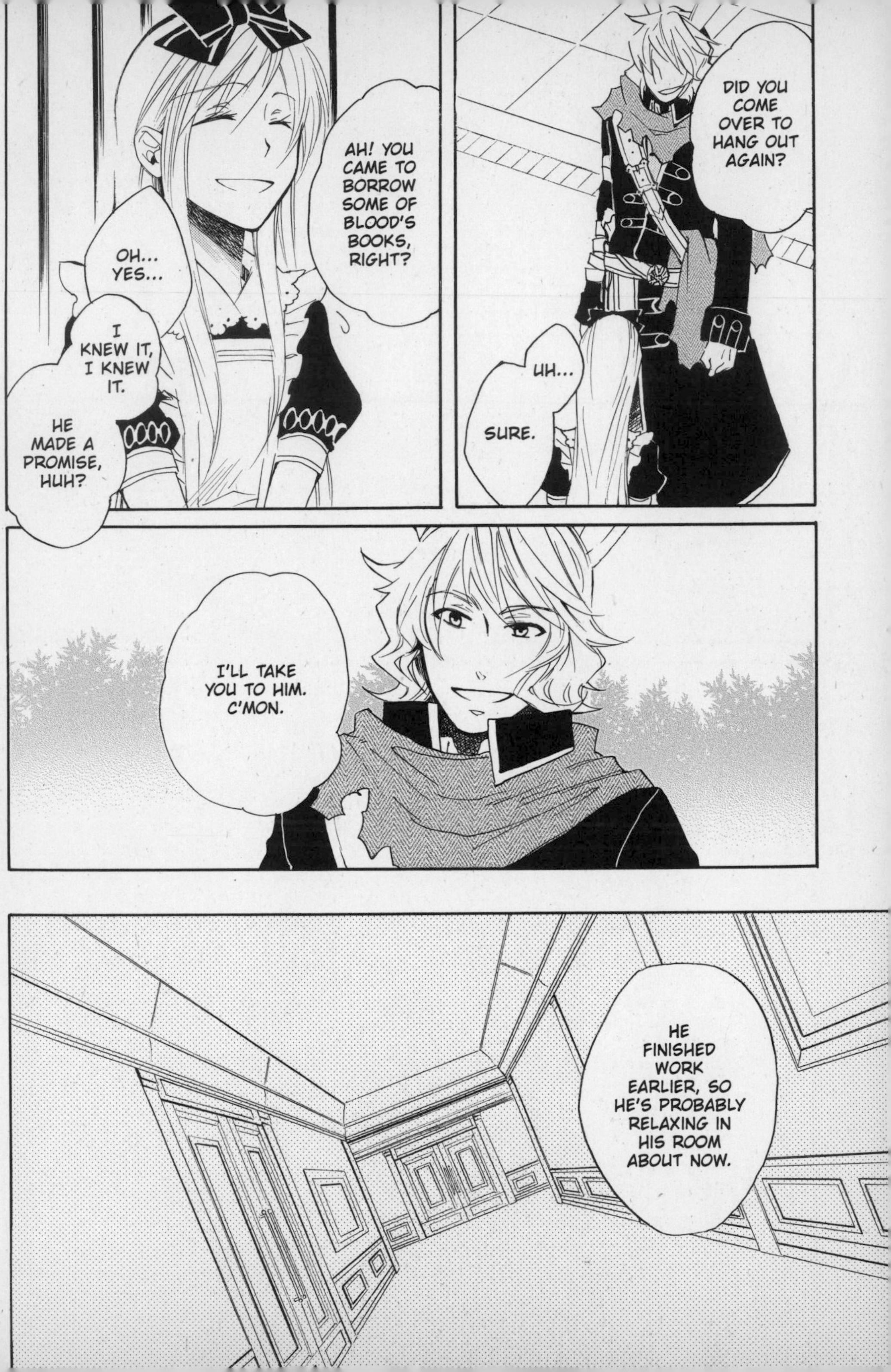
DID YOU COME OVER TO HANG OUT AGAIN?
UH...
SURE.
AH! YOU CAME TO BORROW SOME OF BLOOD'S BOOKS, RIGHT?
OH... YES...
I KNEW IT, I KNEW IT.
HE MADE A PROMISE, HUH?
I'LL TAKE YOU TO HIM. C'MON.
HE FINISHED WORK EARLIER, SO HE'S PROBABLY RELAXING IN HIS ROOM ABOUT NOW.

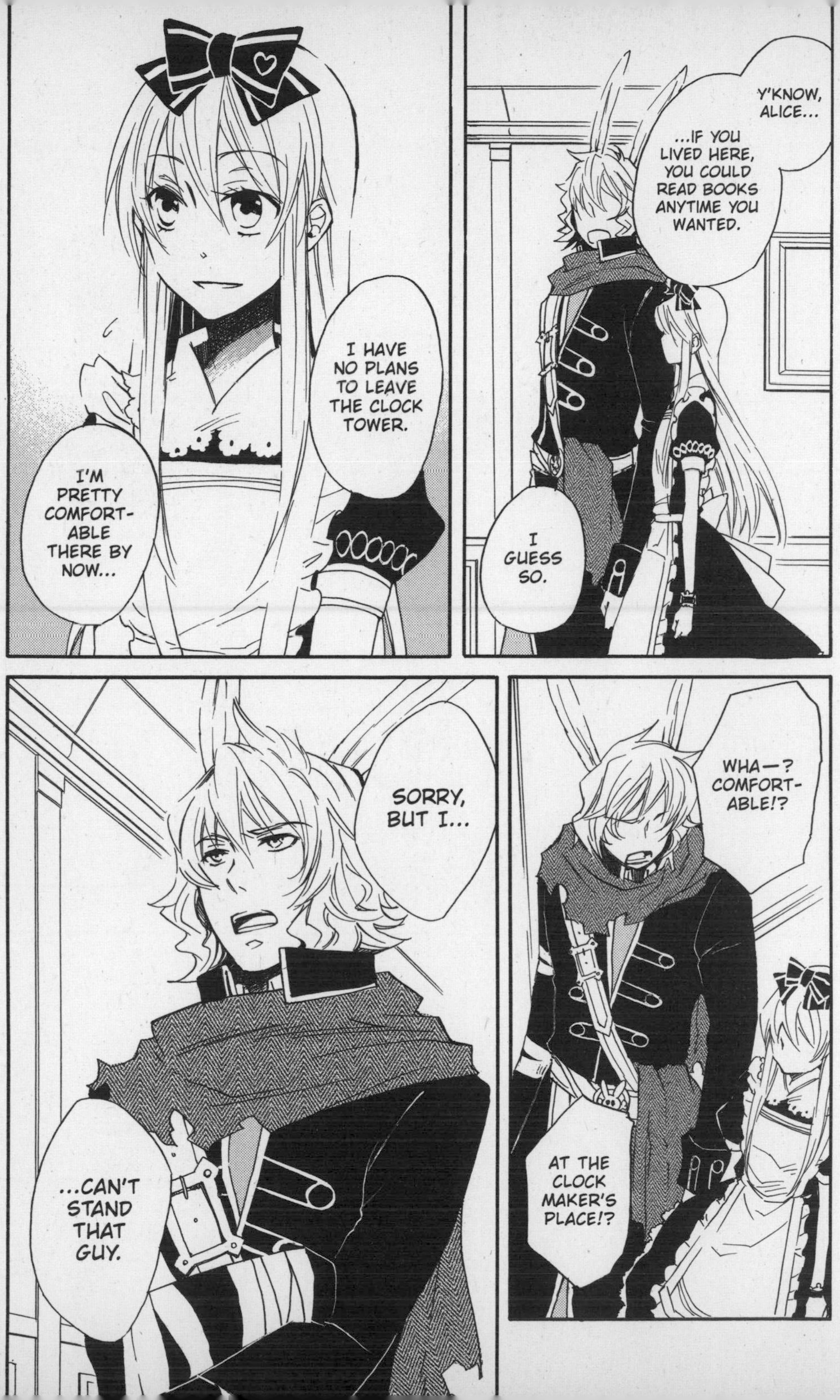
Y'KNOW, ALICE...
...IF YOU LIVED HERE, YOU COULD READ BOOKS ANYTIME YOU WANTED.
I GUESS SO.
I HAVE NO PLANS TO LEAVE THE CLOCK TOWER.
I'M PRETTY COMFORT-ABLE THERE BY NOW...
WHA—? COMFORT-ABLE!?
AT THE CLOCK MAKER'S PLACE!?
SORRY, BUT I...
...CAN'T STAND THAT GUY.

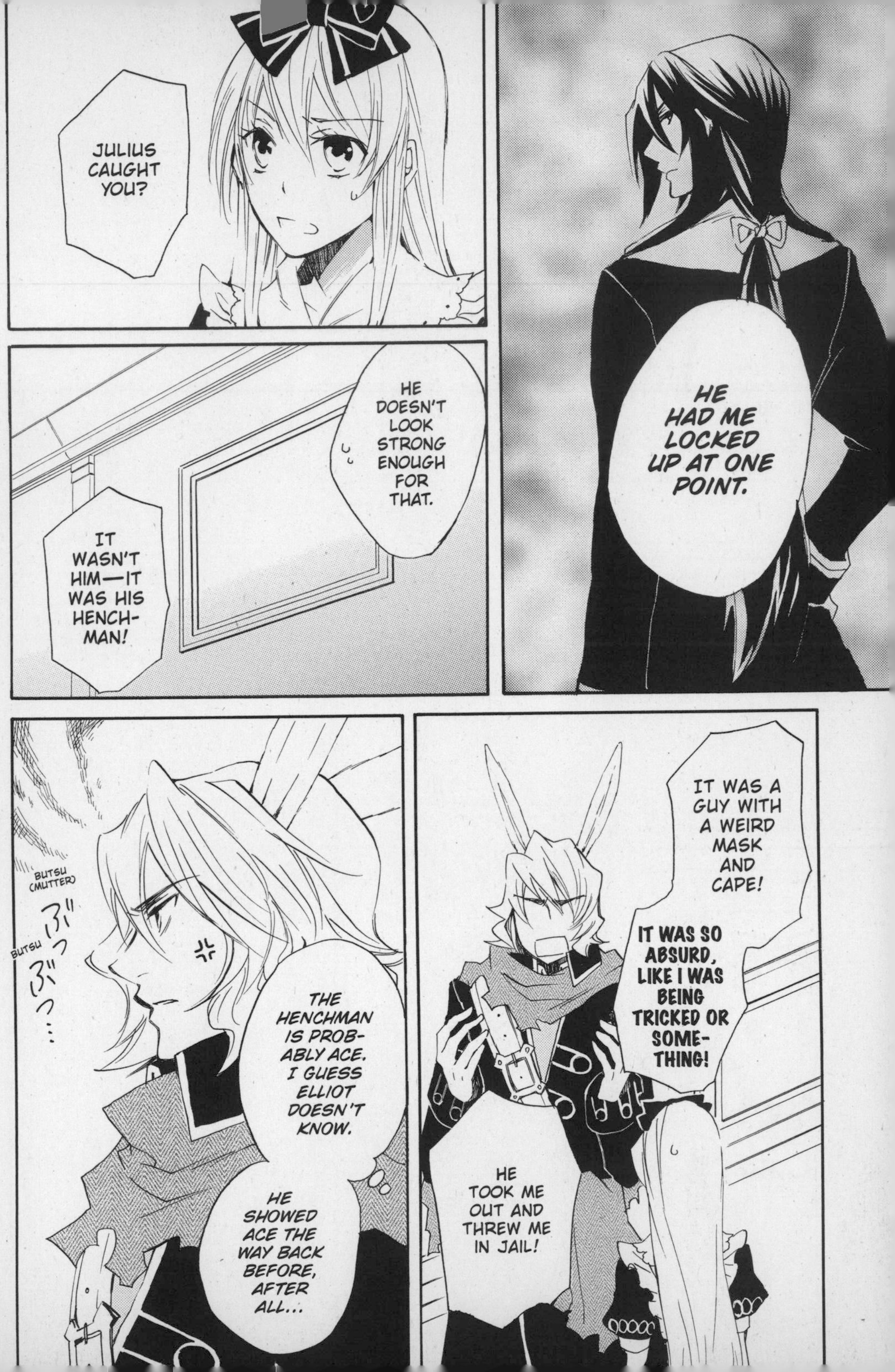
HE HAD ME LOCKED UP AT ONE POINT.
JULIUS CAUGHT YOU?
HE DOESN'T LOOK STRONG ENOUGH FOR THAT.
IT WASN'T HIM—IT WAS HIS HENCH-MAN!
IT WAS A GUY WITH A WEIRD MASK AND CAPE!
IT WAS SO ABSURD, LIKE I WAS BEING TRICKED OR SOME-THING!
HE TOOK ME OUT AND THREW ME IN JAIL!
BUTSU (MUTTER)
BUTSU
ぶつぶつ…
THE HENCHMAN IS PROB-ABLY ACE. I GUESS ELLIOT DOESN'T KNOW.
HE SHOWED ACE THE WAY BACK BEFORE, AFTER ALL...

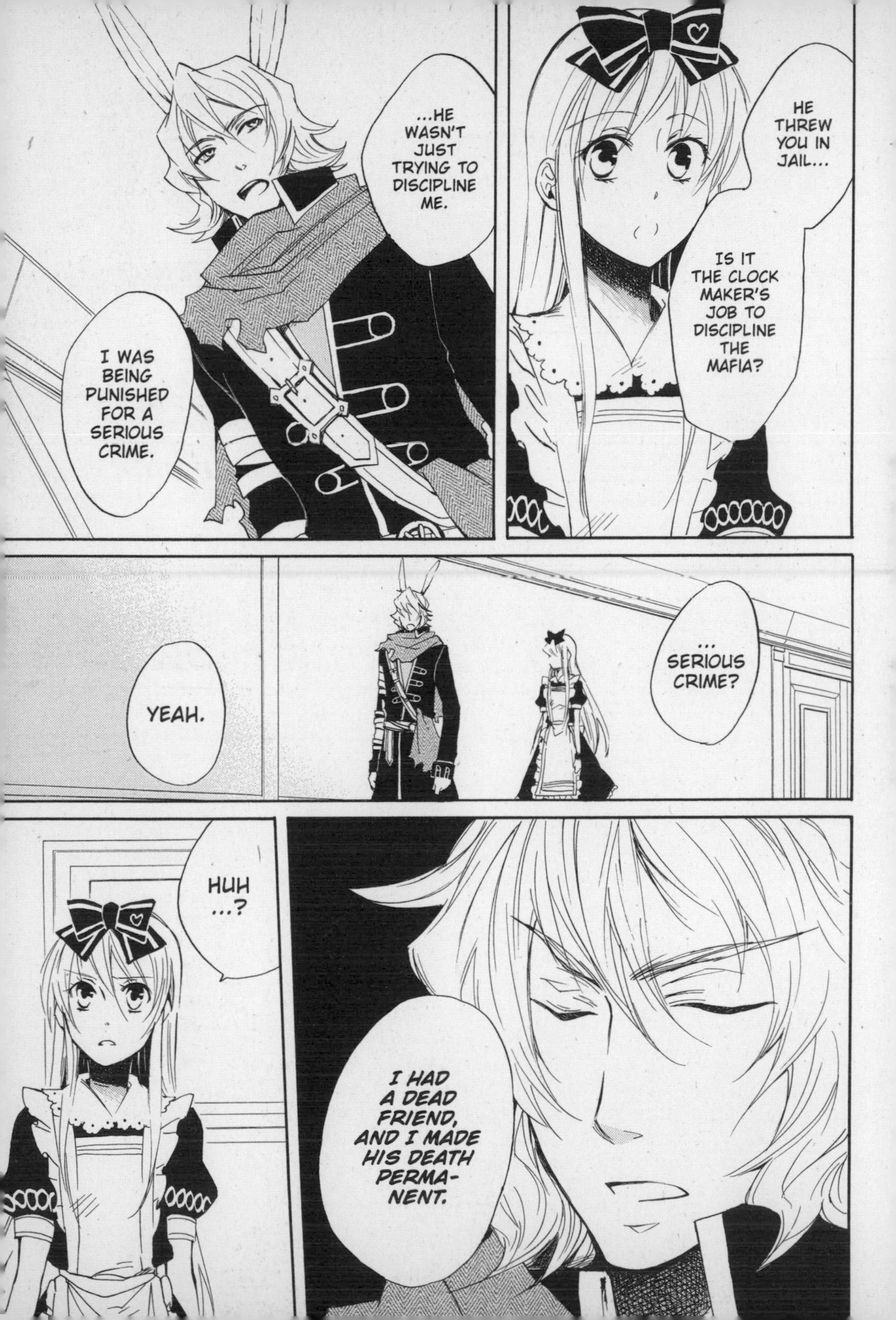
HE THREW YOU IN JAIL...
IS IT THE CLOCK MAKER'S JOB TO DISCIPLINE THE MAFIA?
...HE WASN'T JUST TRYING TO DISCIPLINE ME.
I WAS BEING PUNISHED FOR A SERIOUS CRIME.
... SERIOUS CRIME?
YEAH.
I HAD A DEAD FRIEND, AND I MADE HIS DEATH PERMA-NENT.
HUH ...?

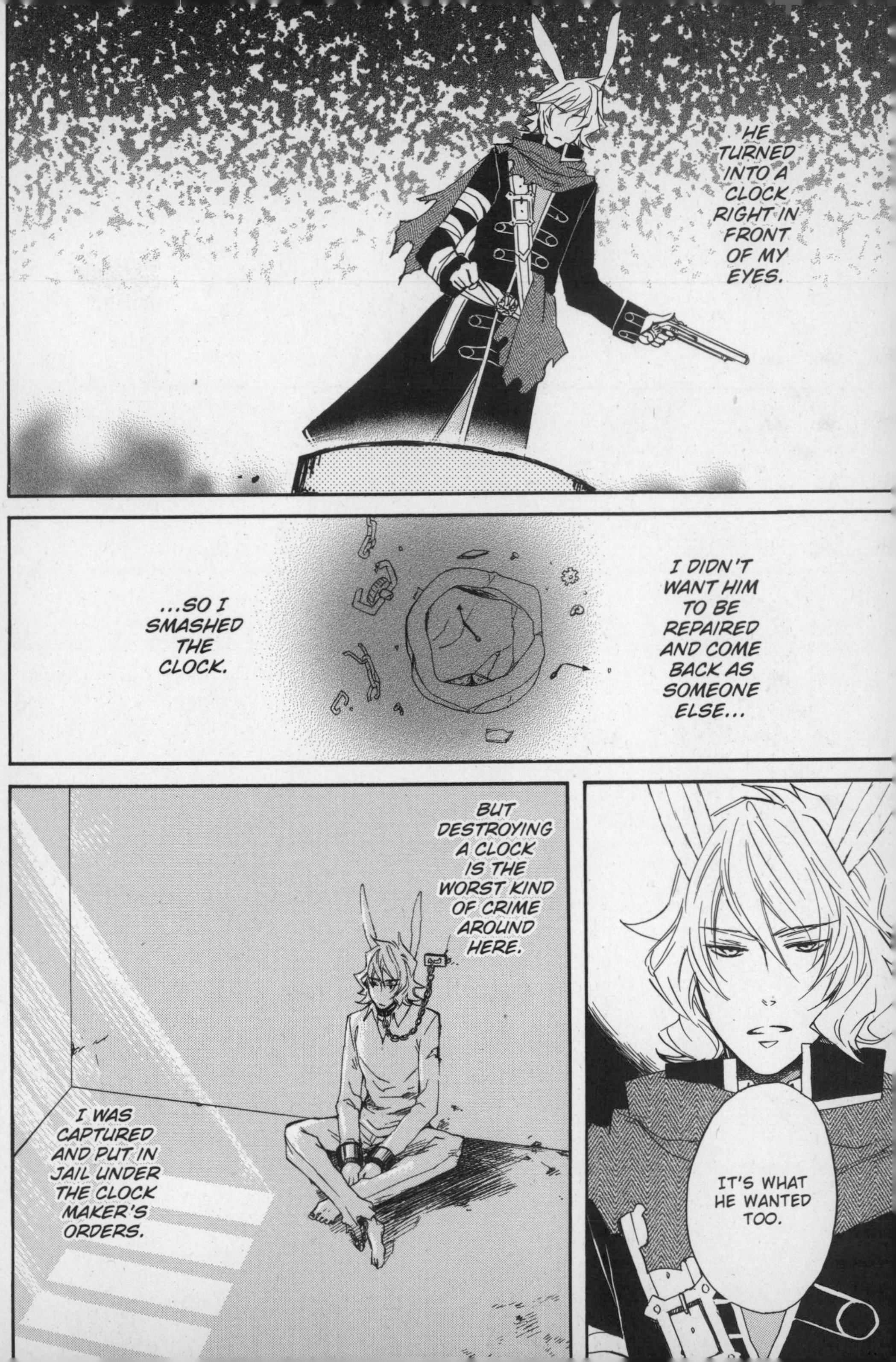
HE TURNED INTO A CLOCK RIGHT IN FRONT OF MY EYES.
I DIDN'T WANT HIM TO BE REPAIRED AND COME BACK AS SOMEONE ELSE...
...SO I SMASHED THE CLOCK.
IT'S WHAT HE WANTED TOO.
BUT DESTROYING A CLOCK IS THE WORST KIND OF CRIME AROUND HERE.
I WAS CAPTURED AND PUT IN JAIL UNDER THE CLOCK MAKER'S ORDERS.

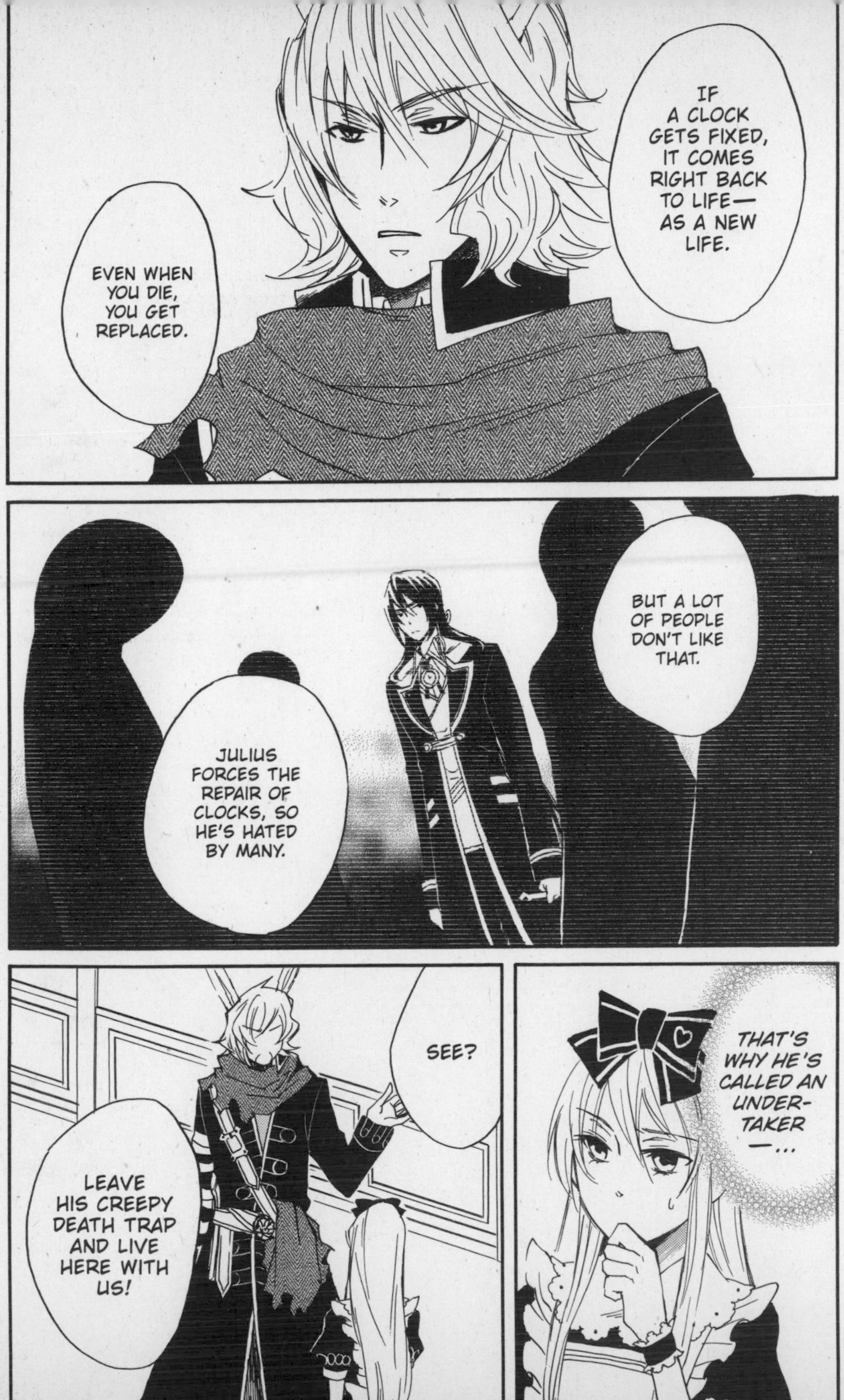
IF A CLOCK GETS FIXED, IT COMES RIGHT BACK TO LIFE— AS A NEW LIFE.
EVEN WHEN YOU DIE, YOU GET REPLACED.
BUT A LOT OF PEOPLE DON'T LIKE THAT.
JULIUS FORCES THE REPAIR OF CLOCKS, SO HE'S HATED BY MANY.
THAT'S WHY HE'S CALLED AN UNDER-TAKER —...
SEE?
LEAVE HIS CREEPY DEATH TRAP AND LIVE HERE WITH US!

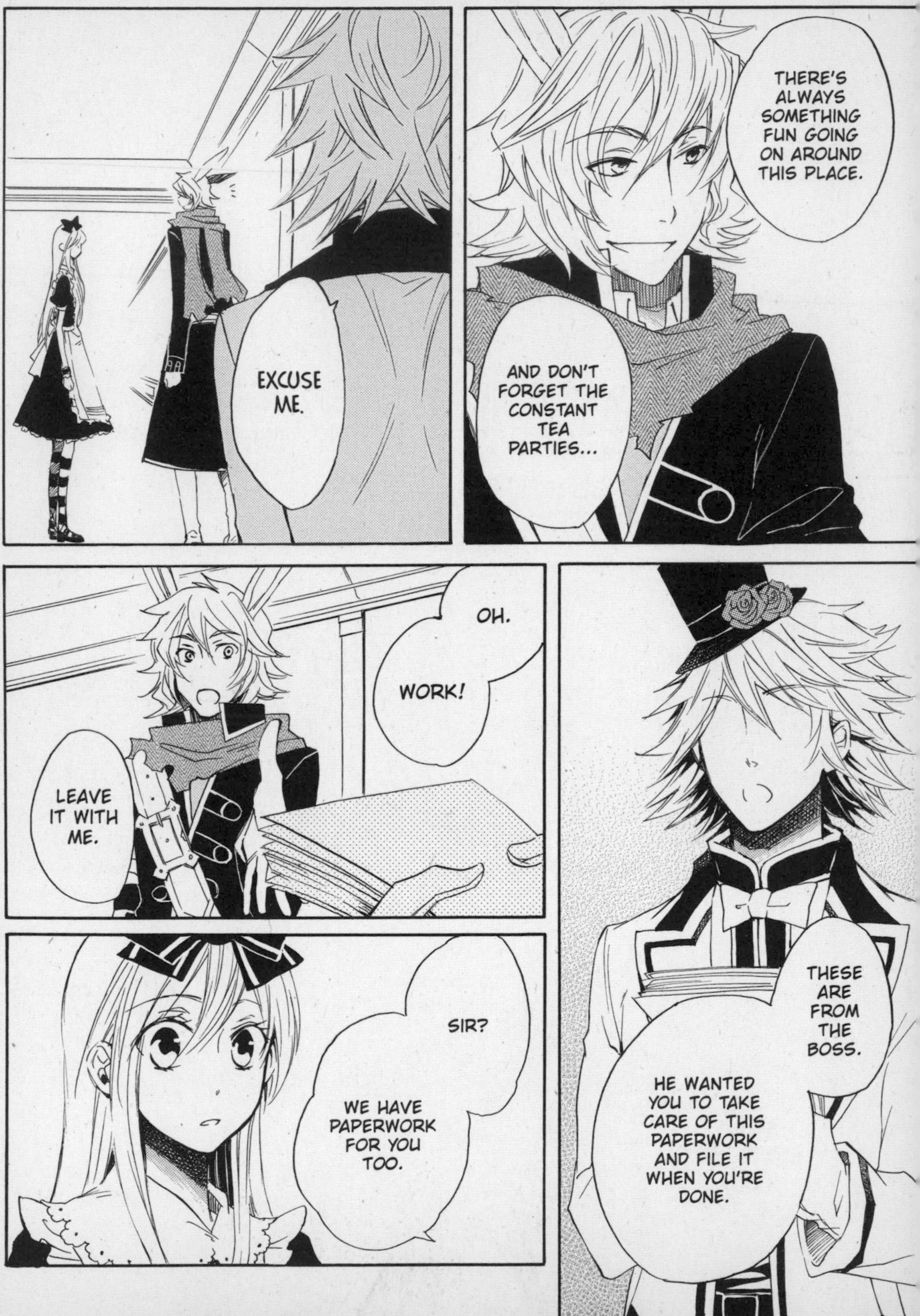
THERE'S ALWAYS SOMETHING FUN GOING ON AROUND THIS PLACE.
AND DON'T FORGET THE CONSTANT TEA PARTIES...
EXCUSE ME.
THESE ARE FROM THE BOSS.
HE WANTED YOU TO TAKE CARE OF THIS PAPERWORK AND FILE IT WHEN YOU'RE DONE.
OH.
WORK!
LEAVE IT WITH ME.
SIR?
WE HAVE PAPERWORK FOR YOU TOO.

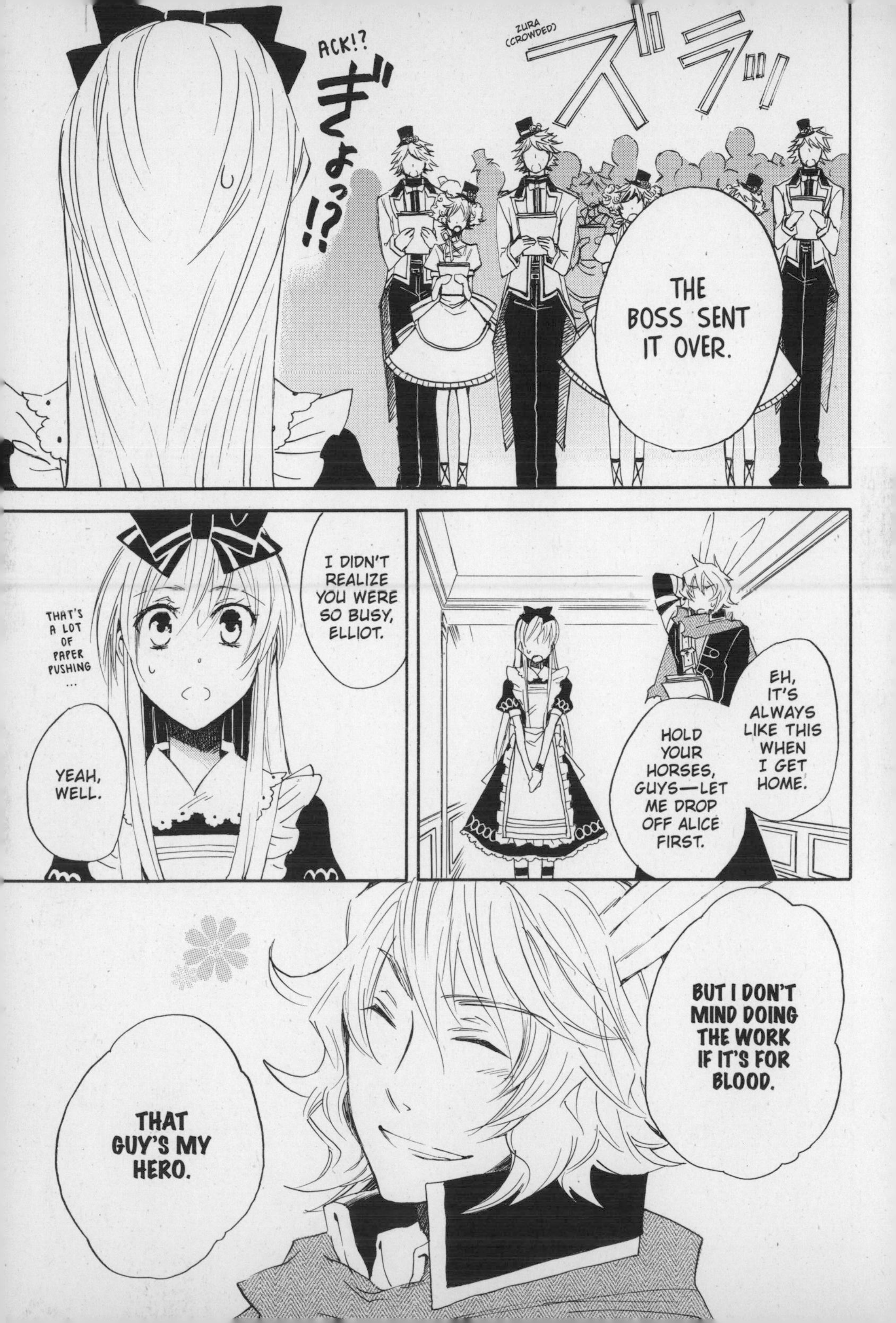
ZURA (CROWDED)
ズラッ!
ACK!?
ぎょっ!?
THE BOSS SENT IT OVER.
EH, IT'S ALWAYS LIKE THIS WHEN I GET HOME.
HOLD YOUR HORSES, GUYS—LET ME DROP OFF ALICE FIRST.
I DIDN'T REALIZE YOU WERE SO BUSY, ELLIOT.
THAT'S A LOT OF PAPER PUSHING...
YEAH, WELL.
BUT I DON'T MIND DOING THE WORK IF IT'S FOR BLOOD.
THAT GUY'S MY HERO.

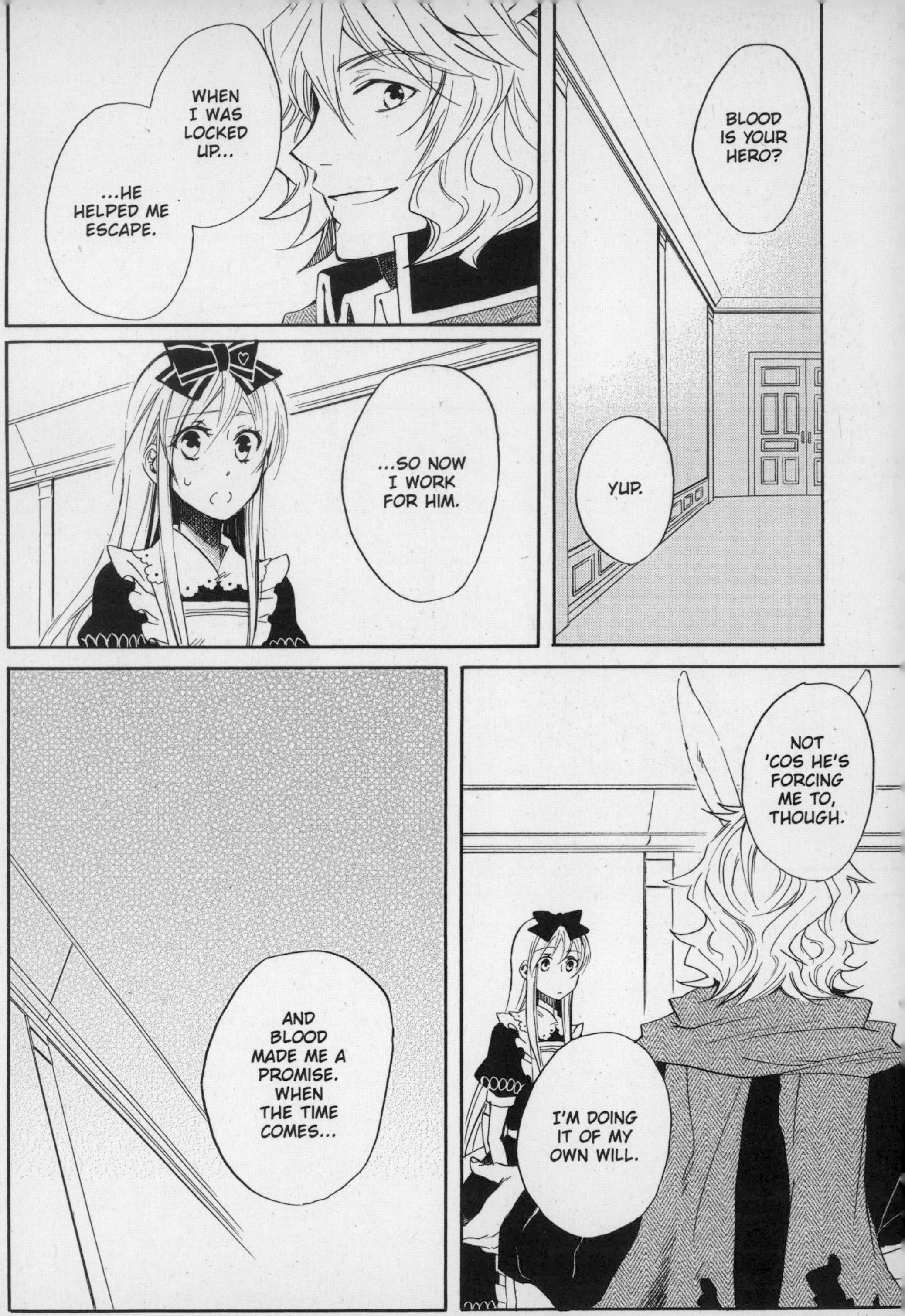
BLOOD IS YOUR HERO?
YUP.
WHEN I WAS LOCKED UP...
...HE HELPED ME ESCAPE.
...SO NOW I WORK FOR HIM.
NOT 'COS HE'S FORCING ME TO, THOUGH.
I'M DOING IT OF MY OWN WILL.
AND BLOOD MADE ME A PROMISE. WHEN THE TIME COMES...

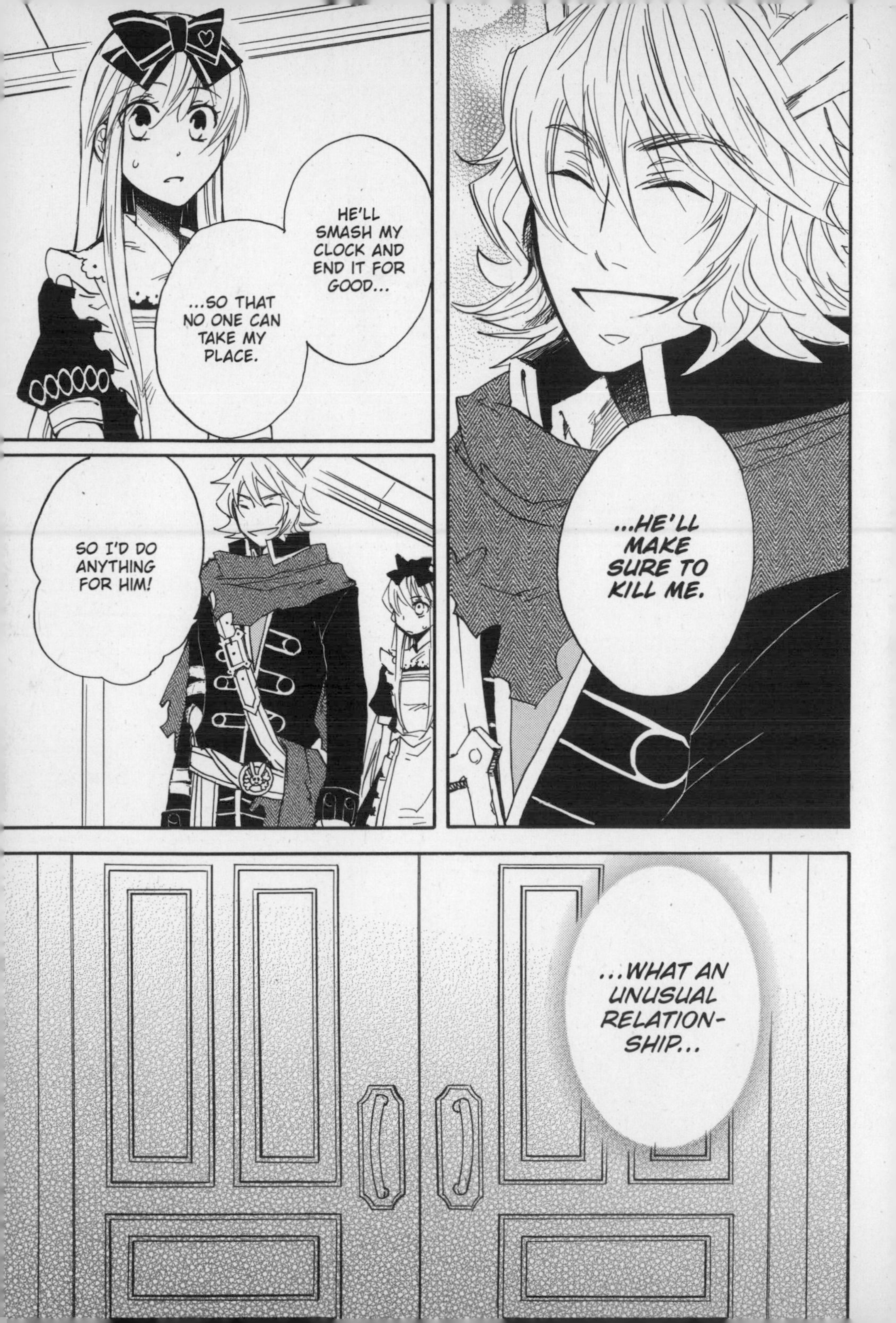

...HE'LL MAKE SURE TO KILL ME.
HE'LL SMASH MY CLOCK AND END IT FOR GOOD...
...SO THAT NO ONE CAN TAKE MY PLACE.
SO I'D DO ANYTHING FOR HIM!
...WHAT AN UNUSUAL RELATION-SHIP...

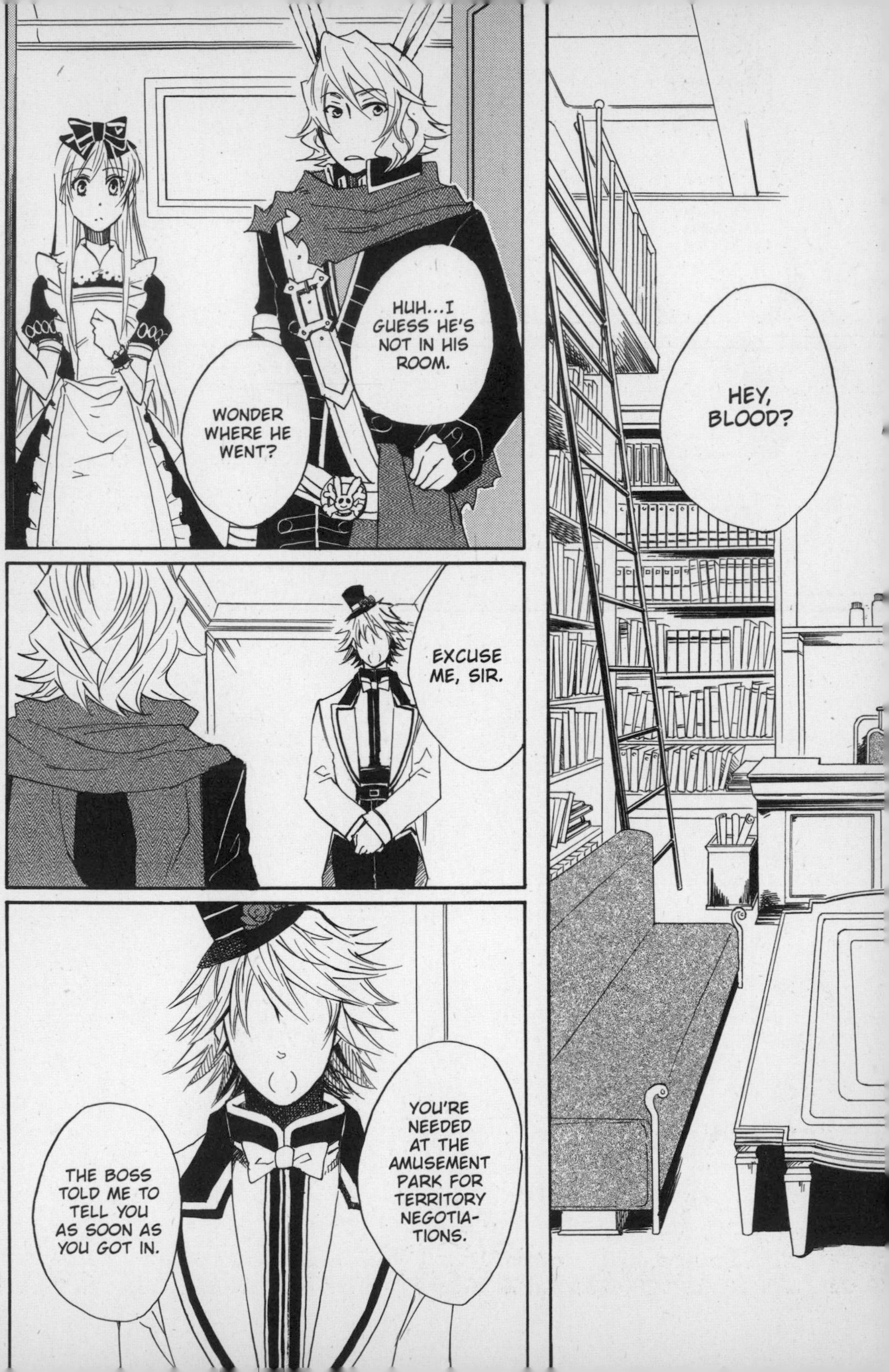
HEY, BLOOD?
HUH...I GUESS HE'S NOT IN HIS ROOM.
WONDER WHERE HE WENT?
EXCUSE ME, SIR.
YOU'RE NEEDED AT THE AMUSEMENT PARK FOR TERRITORY NEGOTIA-TIONS.
THE BOSS TOLD ME TO TELL YOU AS SOON AS YOU GOT IN.

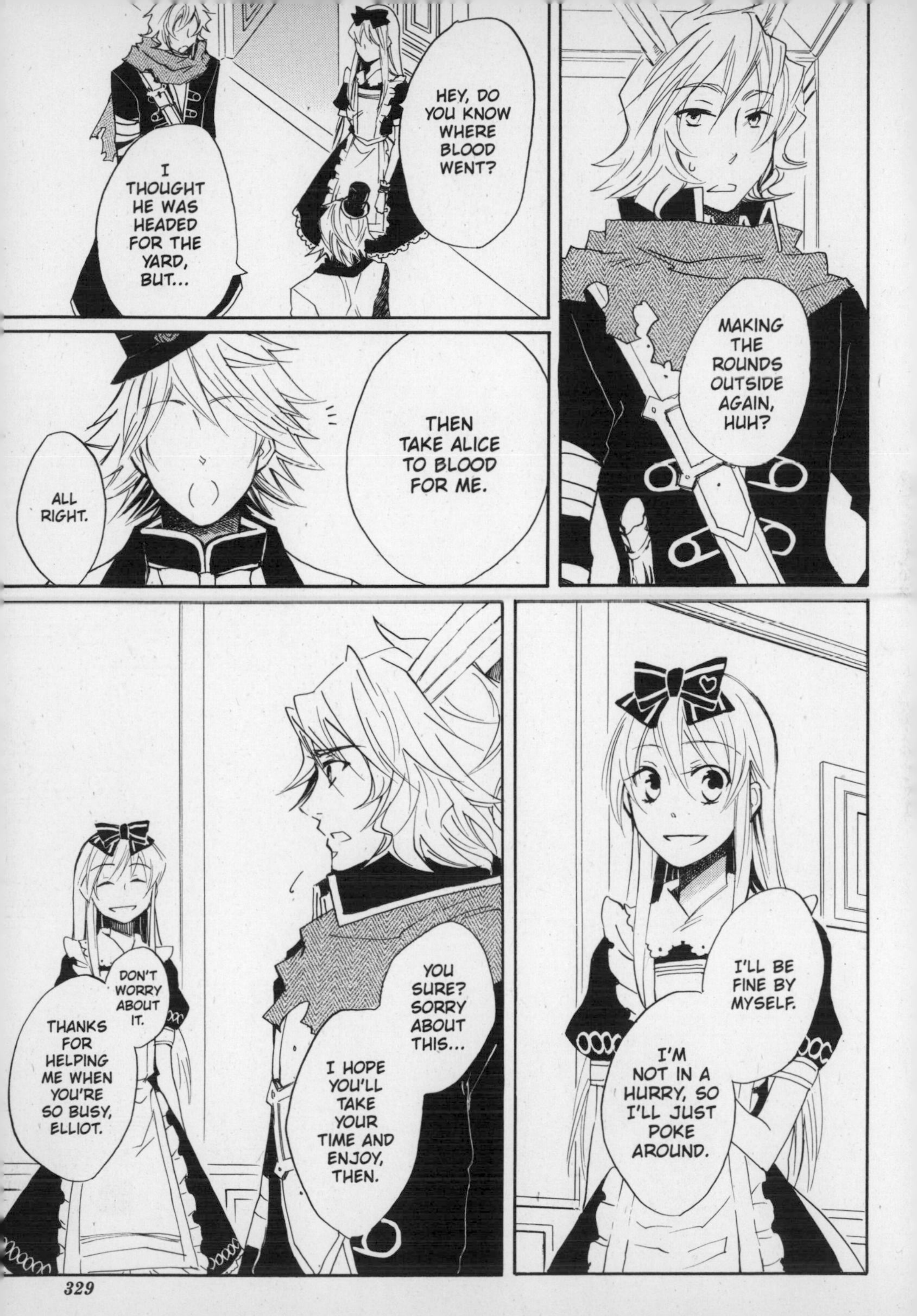
MAKING THE ROUNDS OUTSIDE AGAIN, HUH?
HEY, DO YOU KNOW WHERE BLOOD WENT?
I THOUGHT HE WAS HEADED FOR THE YARD, BUT...
THEN TAKE ALICE TO BLOOD FOR ME.
ALL RIGHT.
I'LL BE FINE BY MYSELF.
I'M NOT IN A HURRY, SO I'LL JUST POKE AROUND.
YOU SURE? SORRY ABOUT THIS...
I HOPE YOU'LL TAKE YOUR TIME AND ENJOY, THEN.
DON'T WORRY ABOUT IT.
THANKS FOR HELPING ME WHEN YOU'RE SO BUSY, ELLIOT.

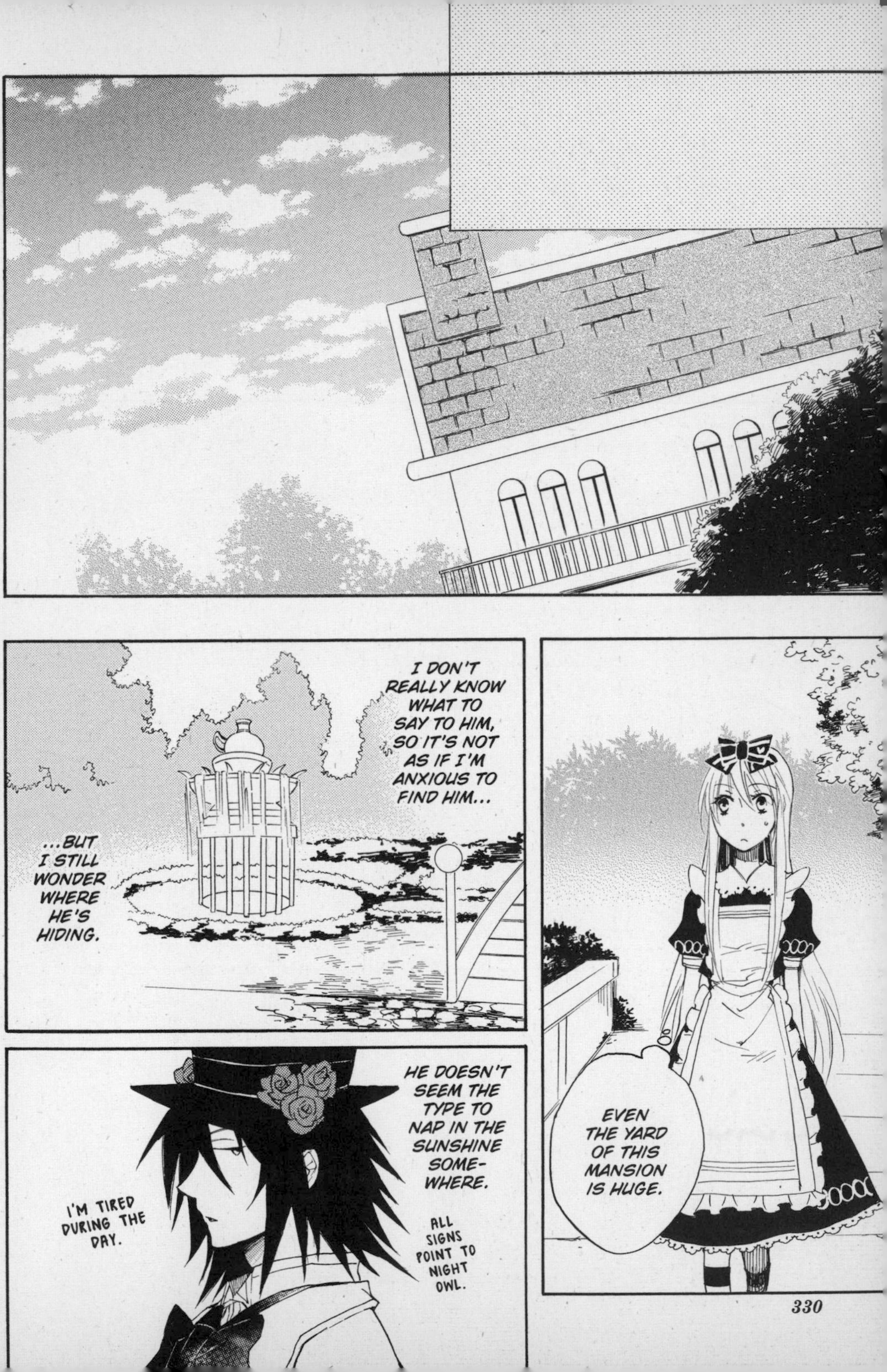
EVEN THE YARD OF THIS MANSION IS HUGE.
I DON'T REALLY KNOW WHAT TO SAY TO HIM, SO IT'S NOT AS IF I'M ANXIOUS TO FIND HIM...
...BUT I STILL WONDER WHERE HE'S HIDING.
HE DOESN'T SEEM THE TYPE TO NAP IN THE SUNSHINE SOME-WHERE.
ALL SIGNS POINT TO NIGHT OWL.
I'M TIRED DURING THE DAY.

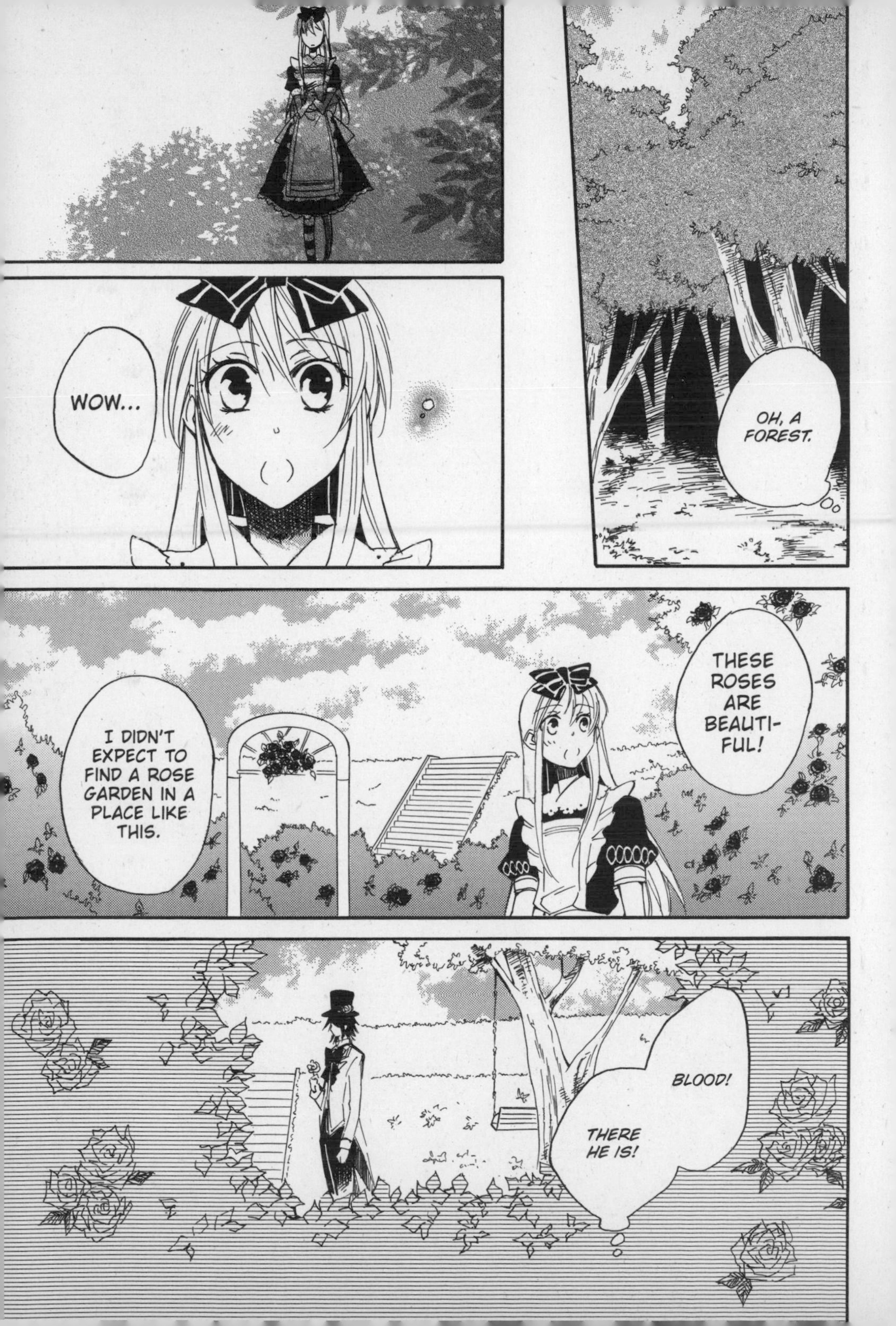
OH, A FOREST.
WOW...
THESE ROSES ARE BEAUTI-FUL!
I DIDN'T EXPECT TO FIND A ROSE GARDEN IN A PLACE LIKE THIS.
BLOOD!
THERE HE IS!

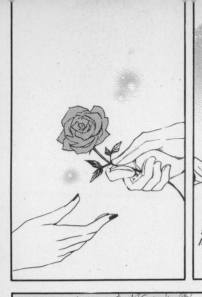

HE'S SMIL-ING...?

HUH?

VIVALDI ...!?

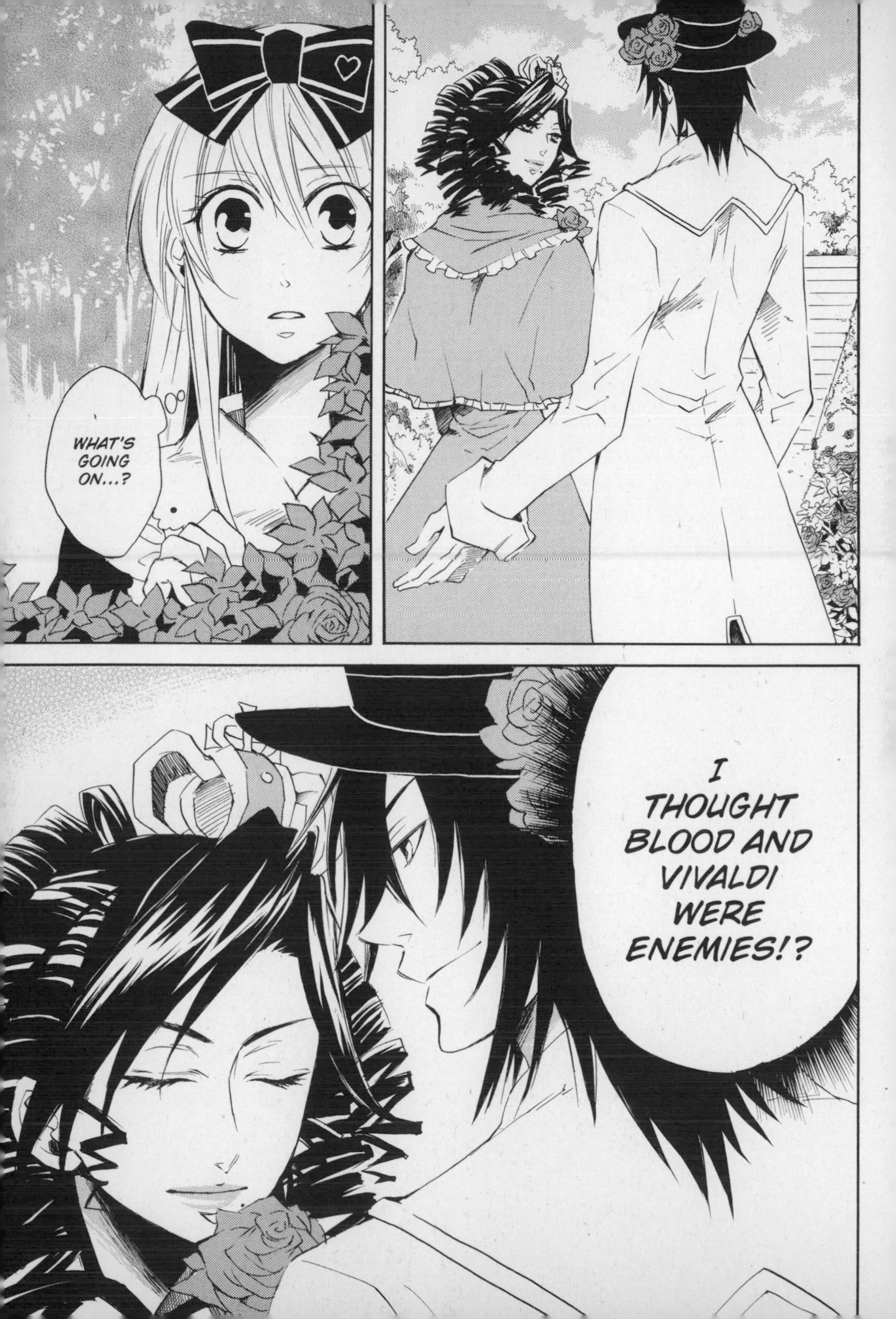
WHAT'S GOING ON...?
I THOUGHT BLOOD AND VIVALDI WERE ENEMIES!?

♥11 Light Weight

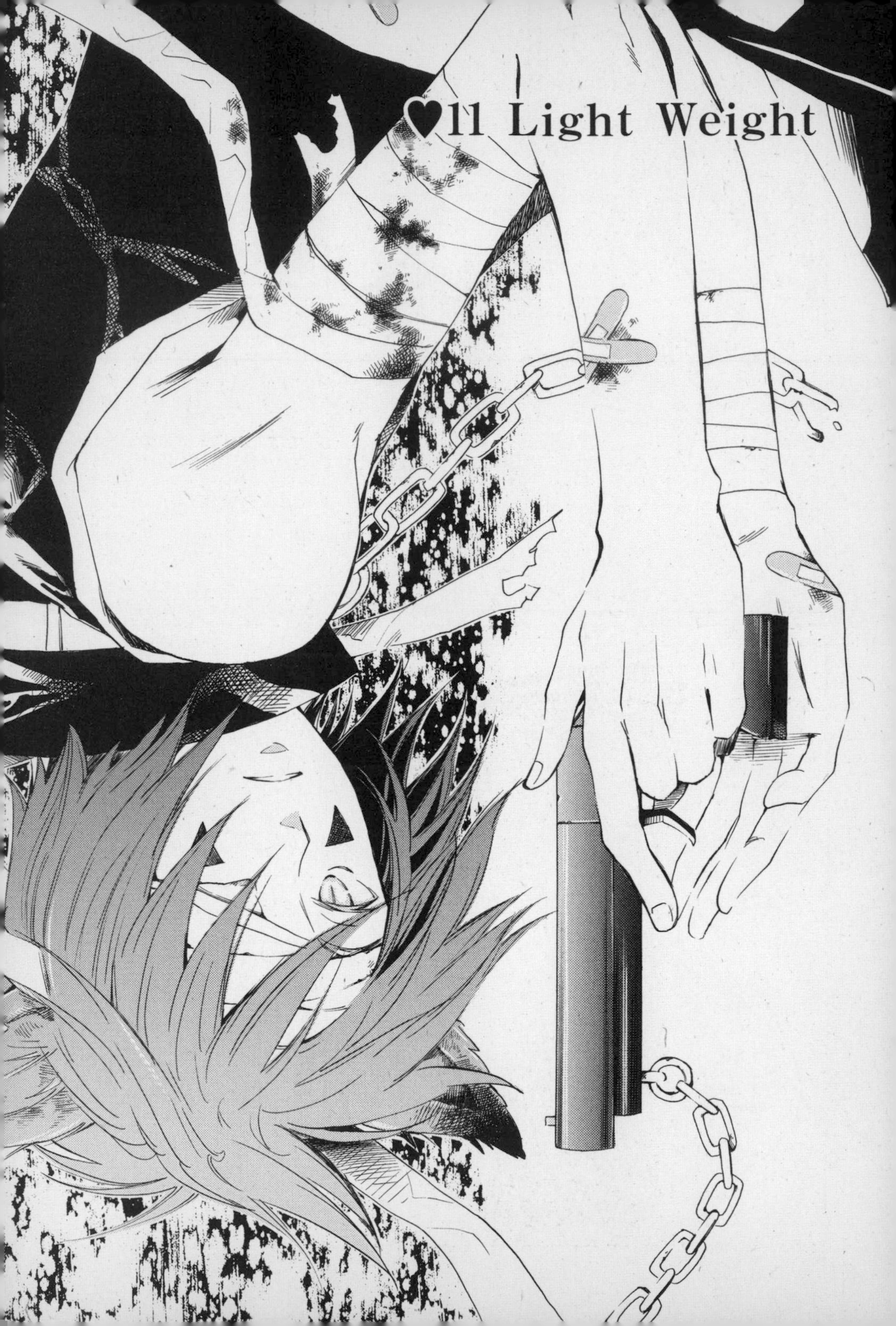

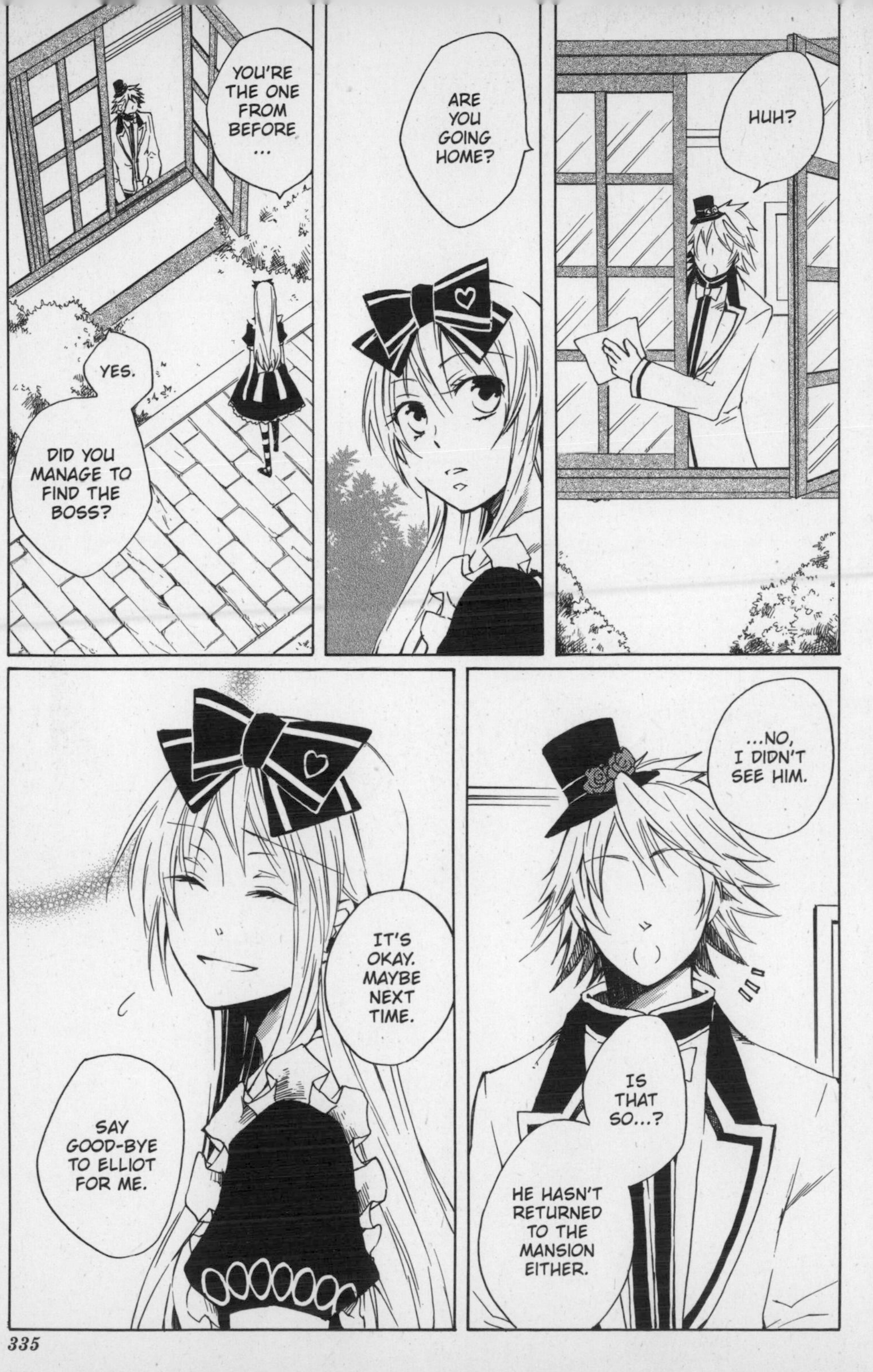
HUH?
ARE YOU GOING HOME?
YOU'RE THE ONE FROM BEFORE ...
YES.
DID YOU MANAGE TO FIND THE BOSS?
...NO, I DIDN'T SEE HIM.
IS THAT SO...?
HE HASN'T RETURNED TO THE MANSION EITHER.
IT'S OKAY. MAYBE NEXT TIME.
SAY GOOD-BYE TO ELLIOT FOR ME.

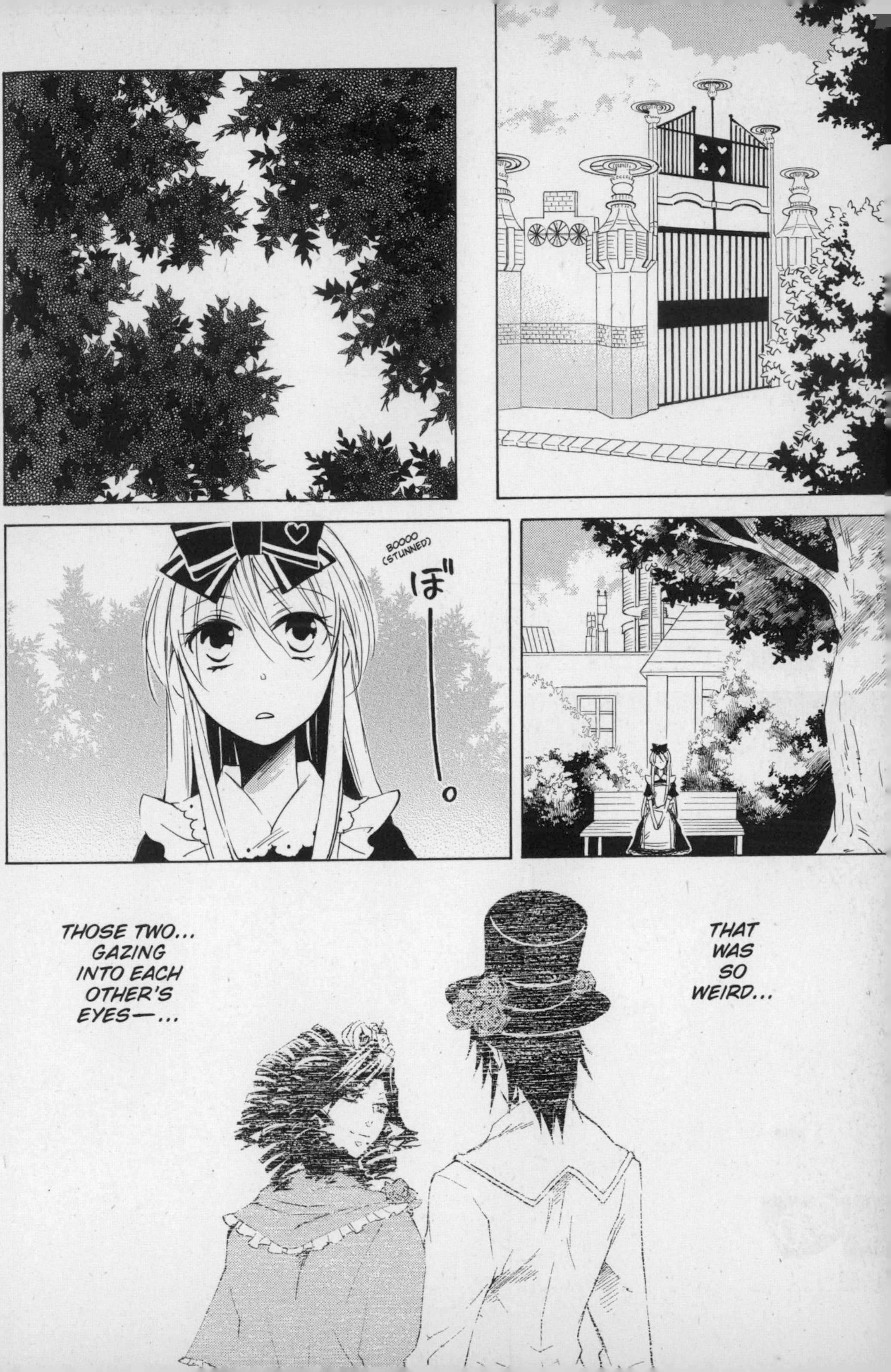
BOOOO (STUNNED)
ぼー。
THAT WAS SO WEIRD...
THOSE TWO... GAZING INTO EACH OTHER'S EYES—...

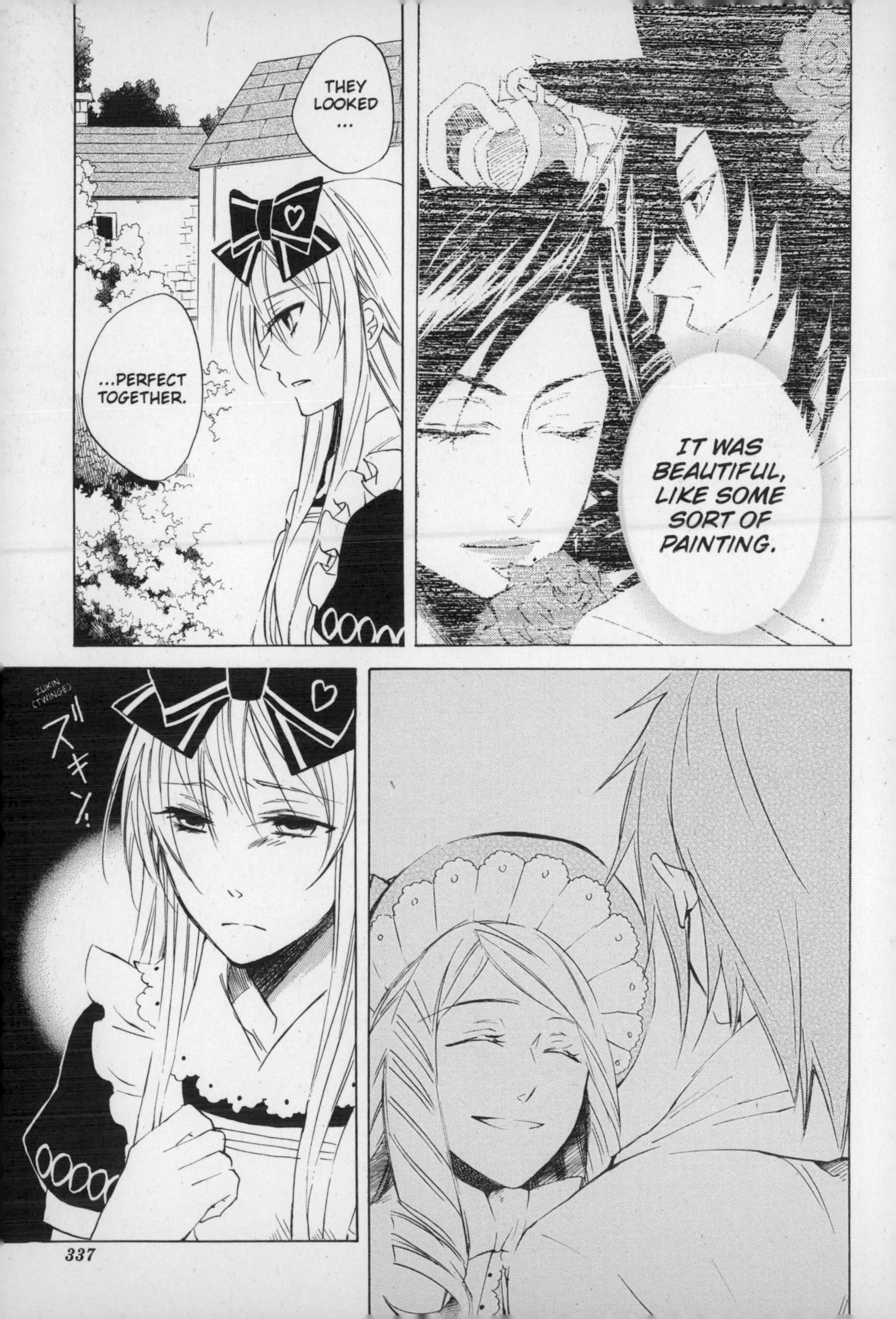
IT WAS BEAUTIFUL, LIKE SOME SORT OF PAINTING.
THEY LOOKED ...
...PERFECT TOGETHER.
ZUKIN (TWINGE)
ズキン!

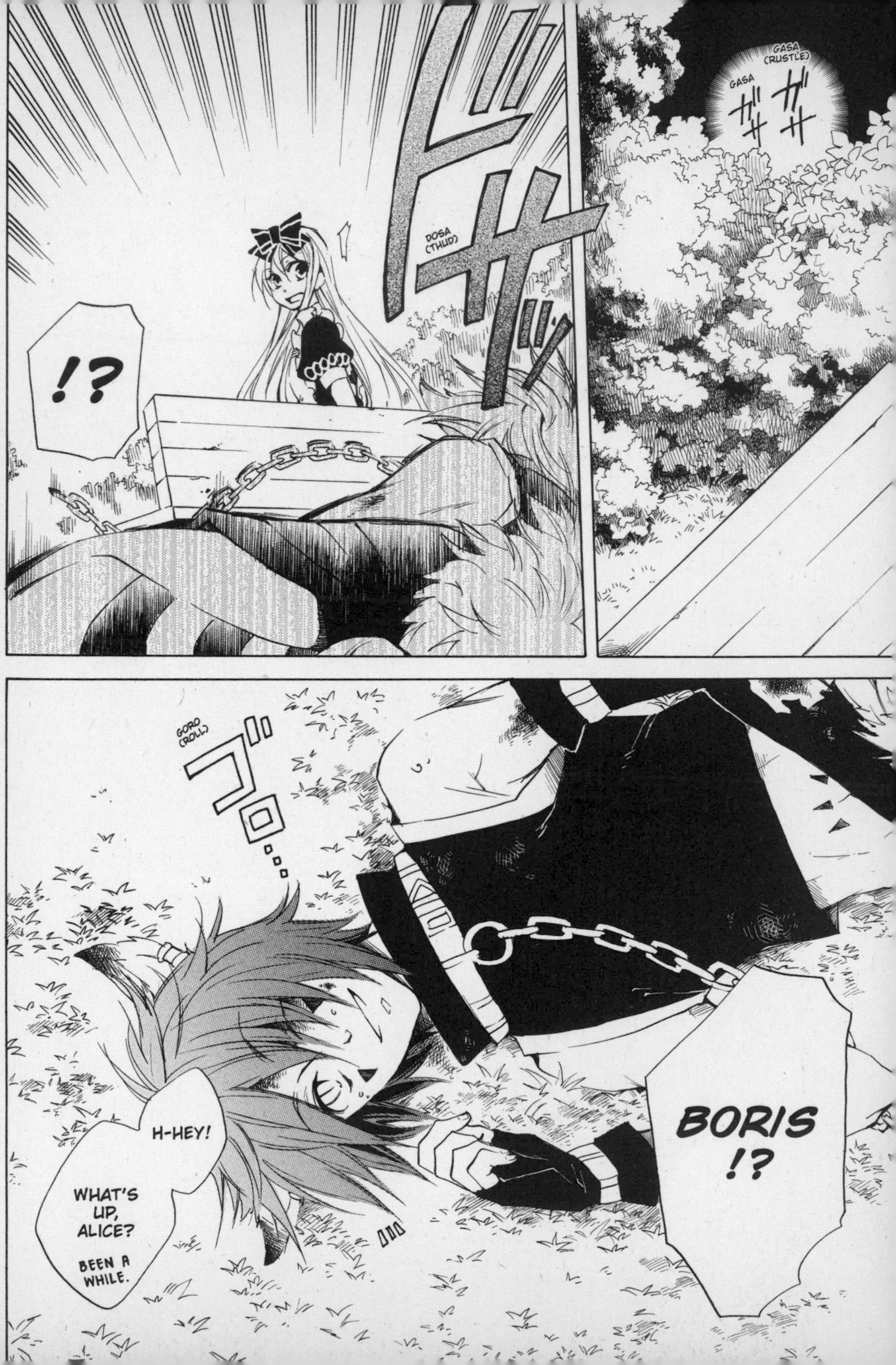
GASA
GASA (RUSTLE)
DOSA (THUD)
!?
BORIS !?
GORO (ROLL)
H-HEY!
WHAT'S UP, ALICE?
BEEN A WHILE.

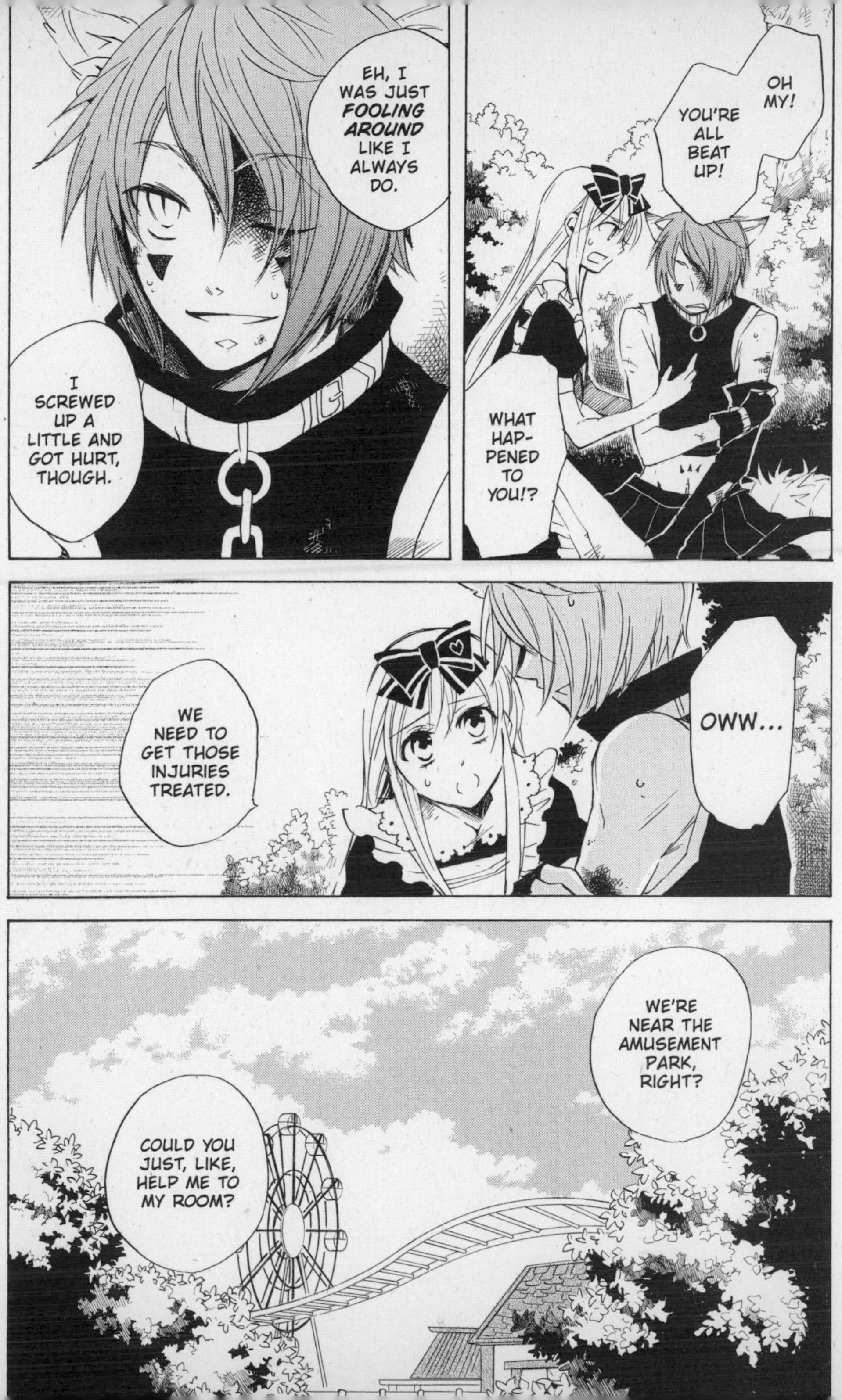

OH MY!
YOU'RE ALL BEAT UP!
WHAT HAP-PENED TO YOU!?
EH, I WAS JUST FOOLING AROUND LIKE I ALWAYS DO.
I SCREWED UP A LITTLE AND GOT HURT, THOUGH.
OWW...
WE NEED TO GET THOSE INJURIES TREATED.
WE'RE NEAR THE AMUSEMENT PARK, RIGHT?
COULD YOU JUST, LIKE, HELP ME TO MY ROOM?

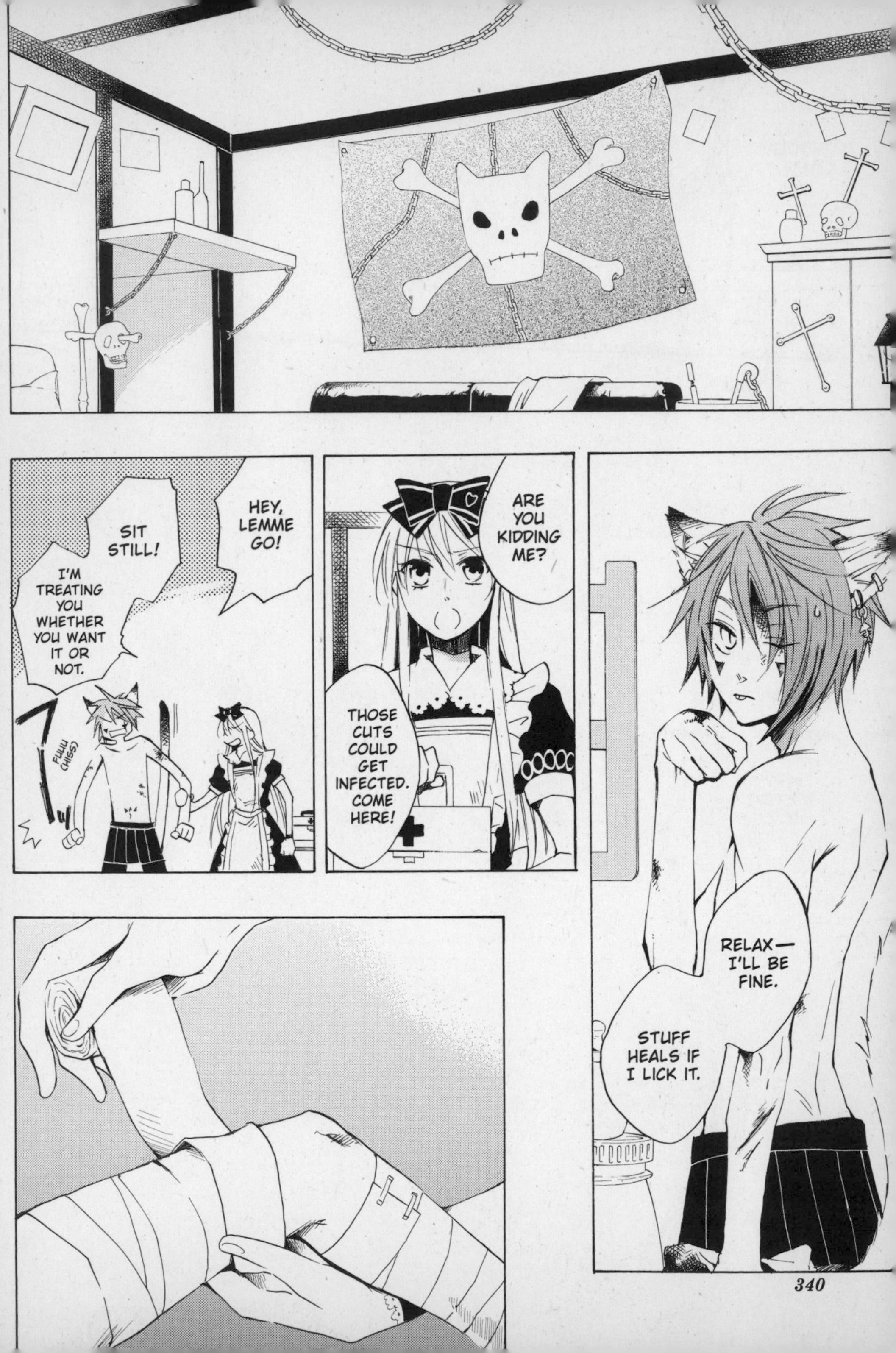
RELAX— I'LL BE FINE.
STUFF HEALS IF I LICK IT.
ARE YOU KIDDING ME?
THOSE CUTS COULD GET INFECTED. COME HERE!
HEY, LEMME GO!
SIT STILL!
I'M TREATING YOU WHETHER YOU WANT IT OR NOT.
FUUU (HISS)

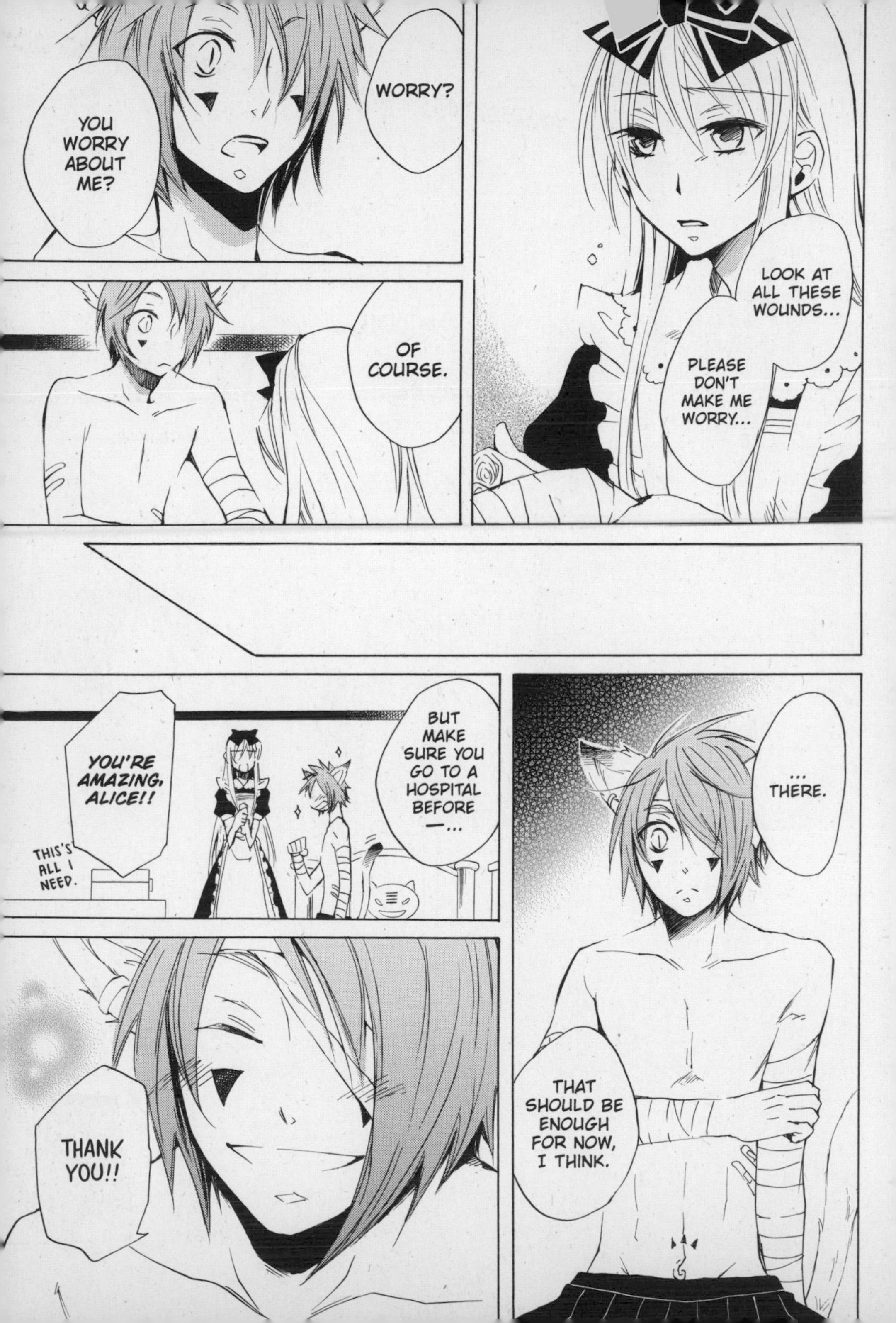
LOOK AT ALL THESE WOUNDS...
PLEASE DON'T MAKE ME WORRY...
WORRY?
YOU WORRY ABOUT ME?
OF COURSE.
... THERE.
THAT SHOULD BE ENOUGH FOR NOW, I THINK.
BUT MAKE SURE YOU GO TO A HOSPITAL BEFORE —...
YOU'RE AMAZING, ALICE!!
THIS'S ALL I NEED.
THANK YOU!!

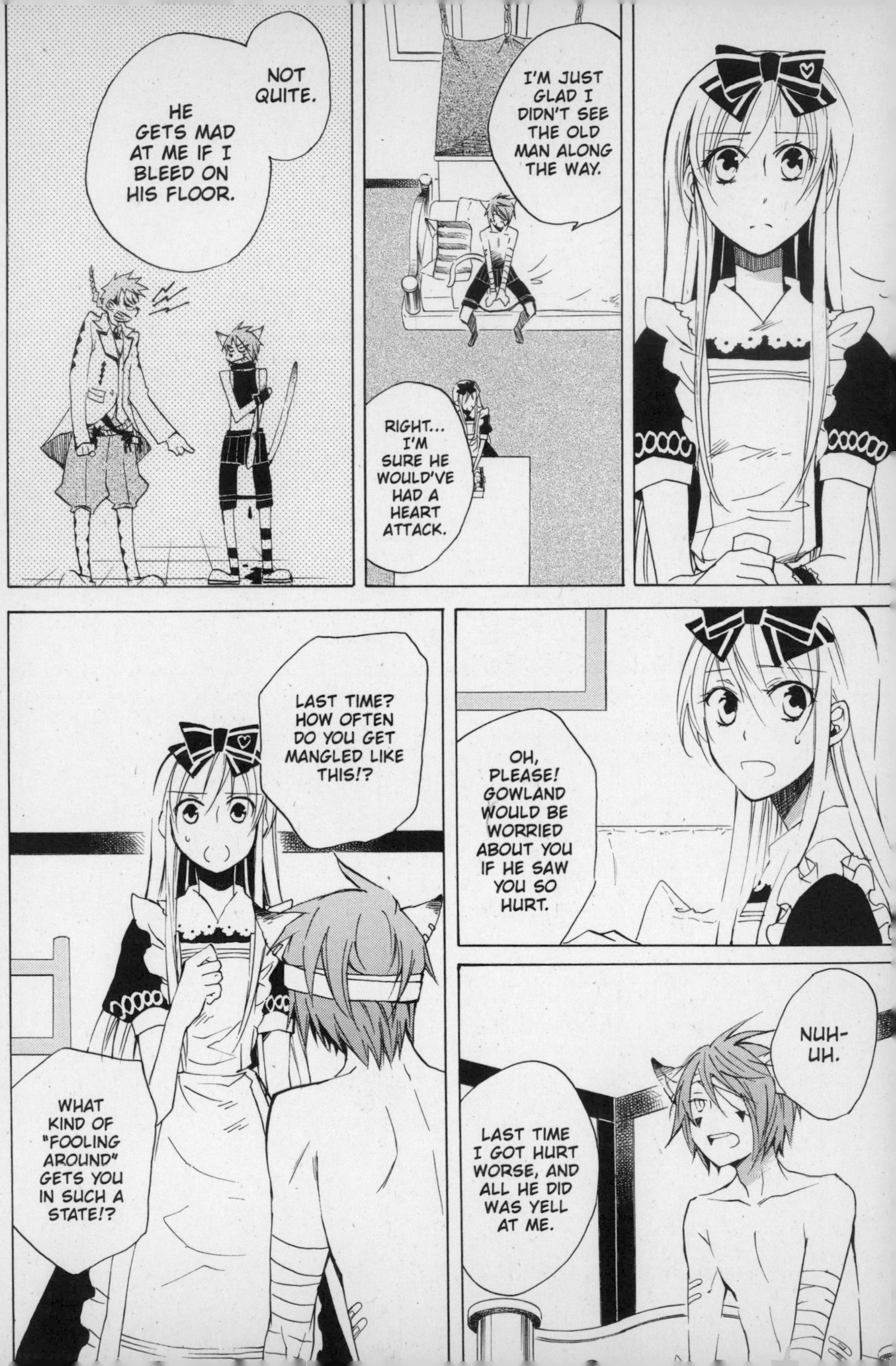
I'M JUST GLAD I DIDN'T SEE THE OLD MAN ALONG THE WAY.
RIGHT... I'M SURE HE WOULD'VE HAD A HEART ATTACK.
NOT QUITE.
HE GETS MAD AT ME IF I BLEED ON HIS FLOOR.
OH, PLEASE! GOWLAND WOULD BE WORRIED ABOUT YOU IF HE SAW YOU SO HURT.
NUH-UH.
LAST TIME I GOT HURT WORSE, AND ALL HE DID WAS YELL AT ME.
LAST TIME? HOW OFTEN DO YOU GET MANGLED LIKE THIS!?
WHAT KIND OF "FOOLING AROUND" GETS YOU IN SUCH A STATE!?

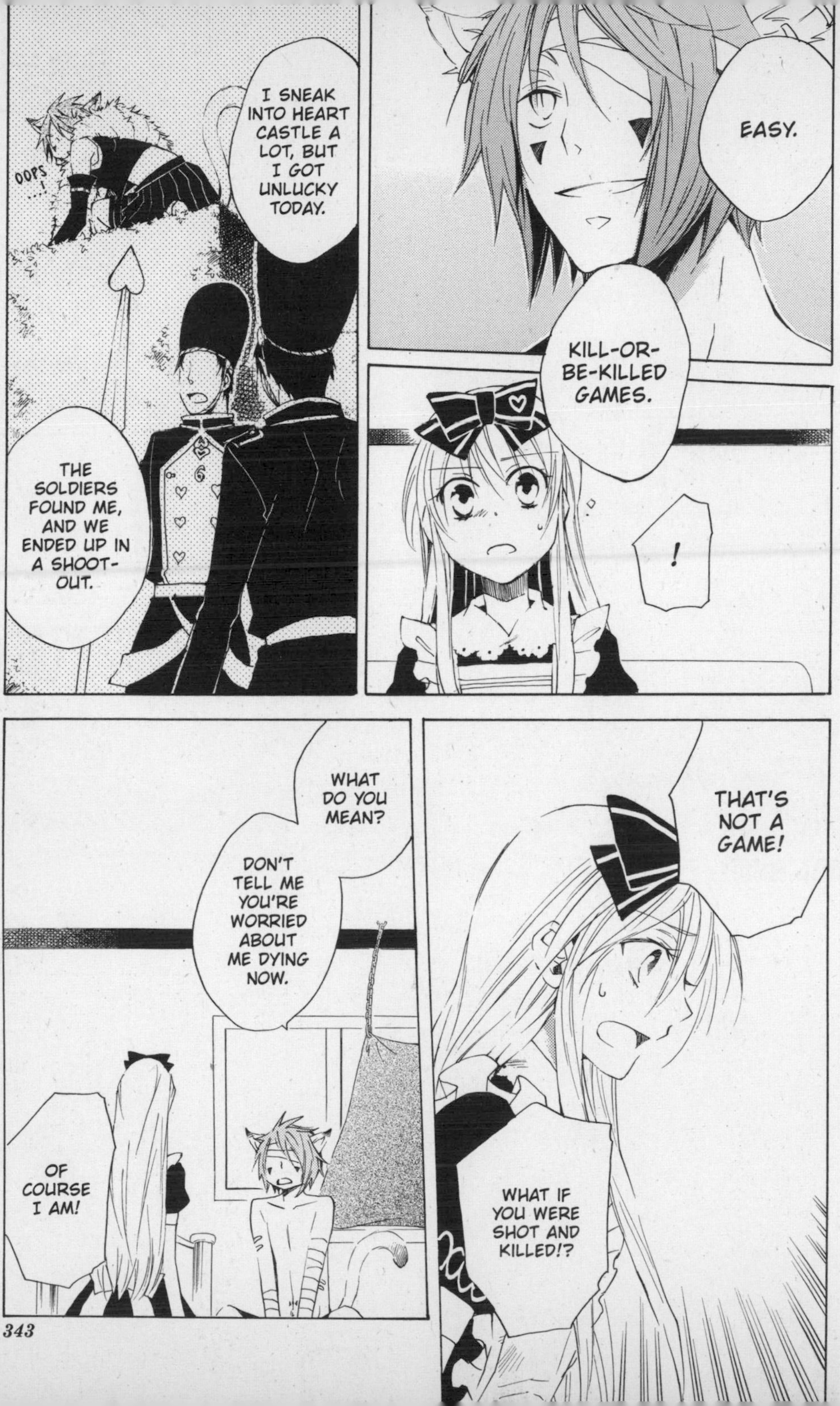
EASY.
KILL-OR-BE-KILLED GAMES.
!
I SNEAK INTO HEART CASTLE A LOT, BUT I GOT UNLUCKY TODAY.
OOPS...!
THE SOLDIERS FOUND ME, AND WE ENDED UP IN A SHOOT-OUT.
THAT'S NOT A GAME!
WHAT IF YOU WERE SHOT AND KILLED!?
WHAT DO YOU MEAN?
DON'T TELL ME YOU'RE WORRIED ABOUT ME DYING NOW.
OF COURSE I AM!

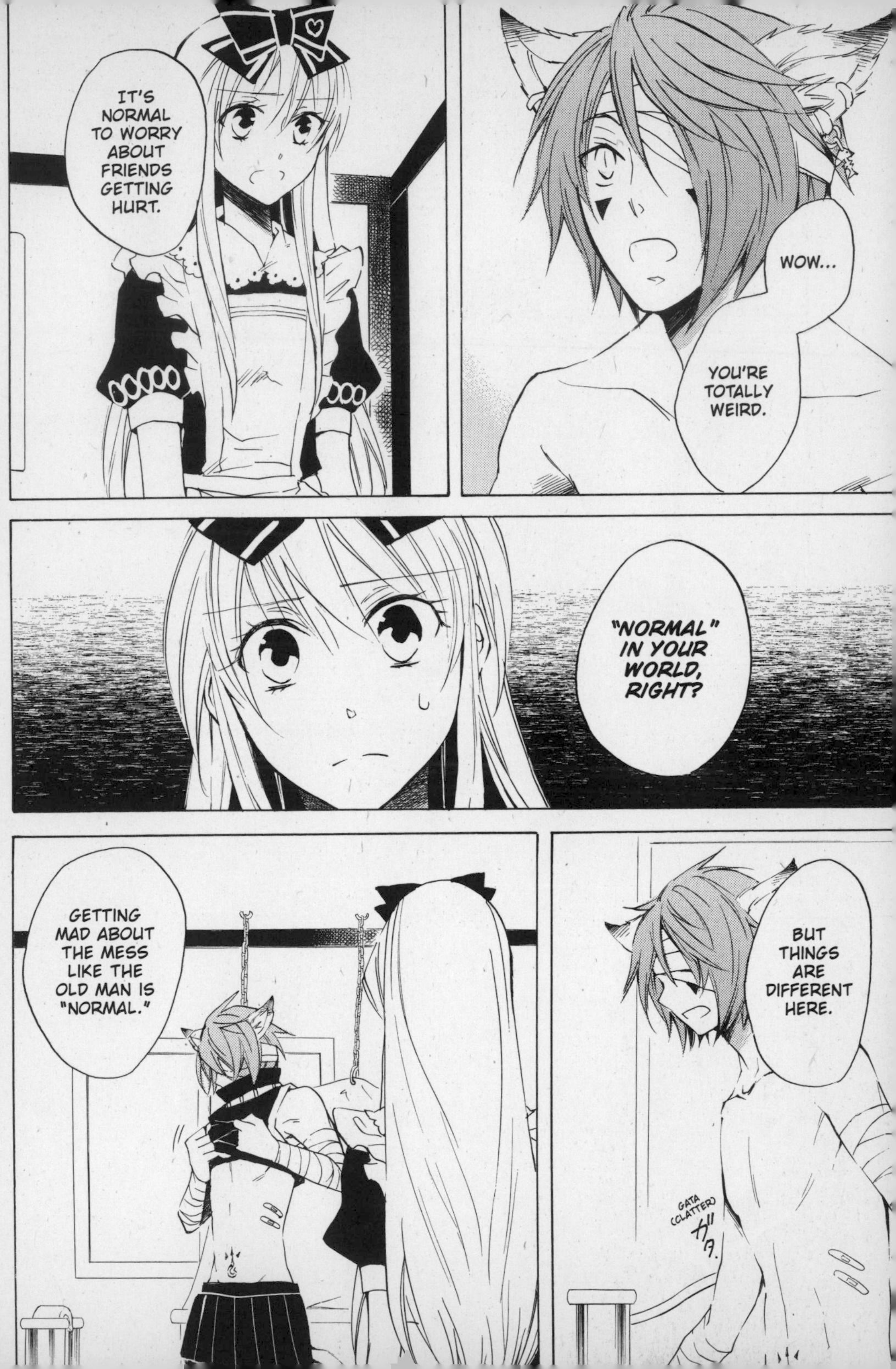
WOW...
YOU'RE TOTALLY WEIRD.
IT'S NORMAL TO WORRY ABOUT FRIENDS GETTING HURT.
"NORMAL" IN YOUR WORLD, RIGHT?
BUT THINGS ARE DIFFERENT HERE.
GATA (CLATTER)
GETTING MAD ABOUT THE MESS LIKE THE OLD MAN IS "NORMAL."

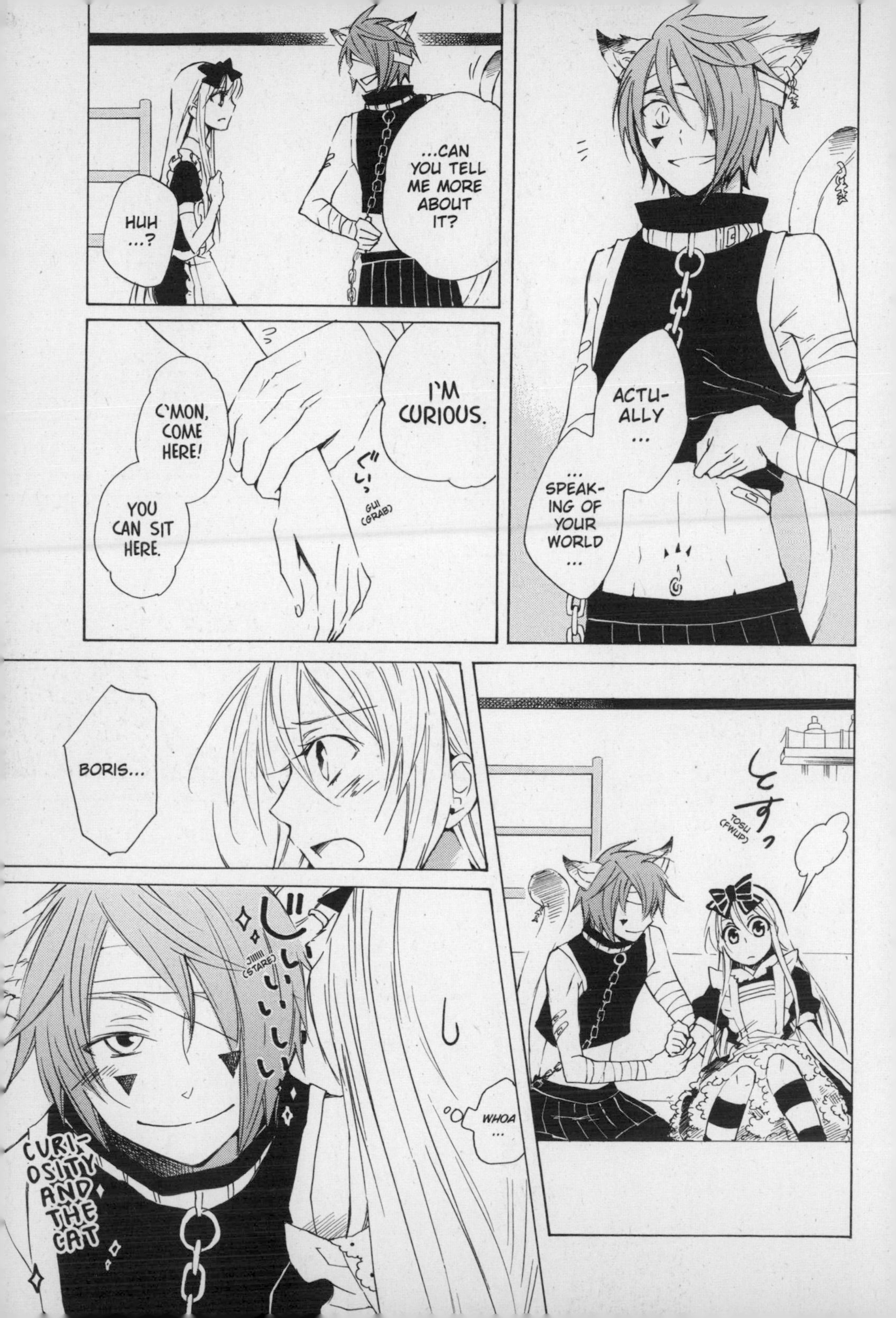
ACTUALLY...
...SPEAKING OF YOUR WORLD...
...CAN YOU TELL ME MORE ABOUT IT?
HUH...?
I'M CURIOUS.
ぐいっ
GUI (GRAB)
C'MON, COME HERE!
YOU CAN SIT HERE.
とすっ
TOSU (FWUP)
WHOA...
BORIS...
JIIIII (STARE)
CURIOSITY AND THE CAT

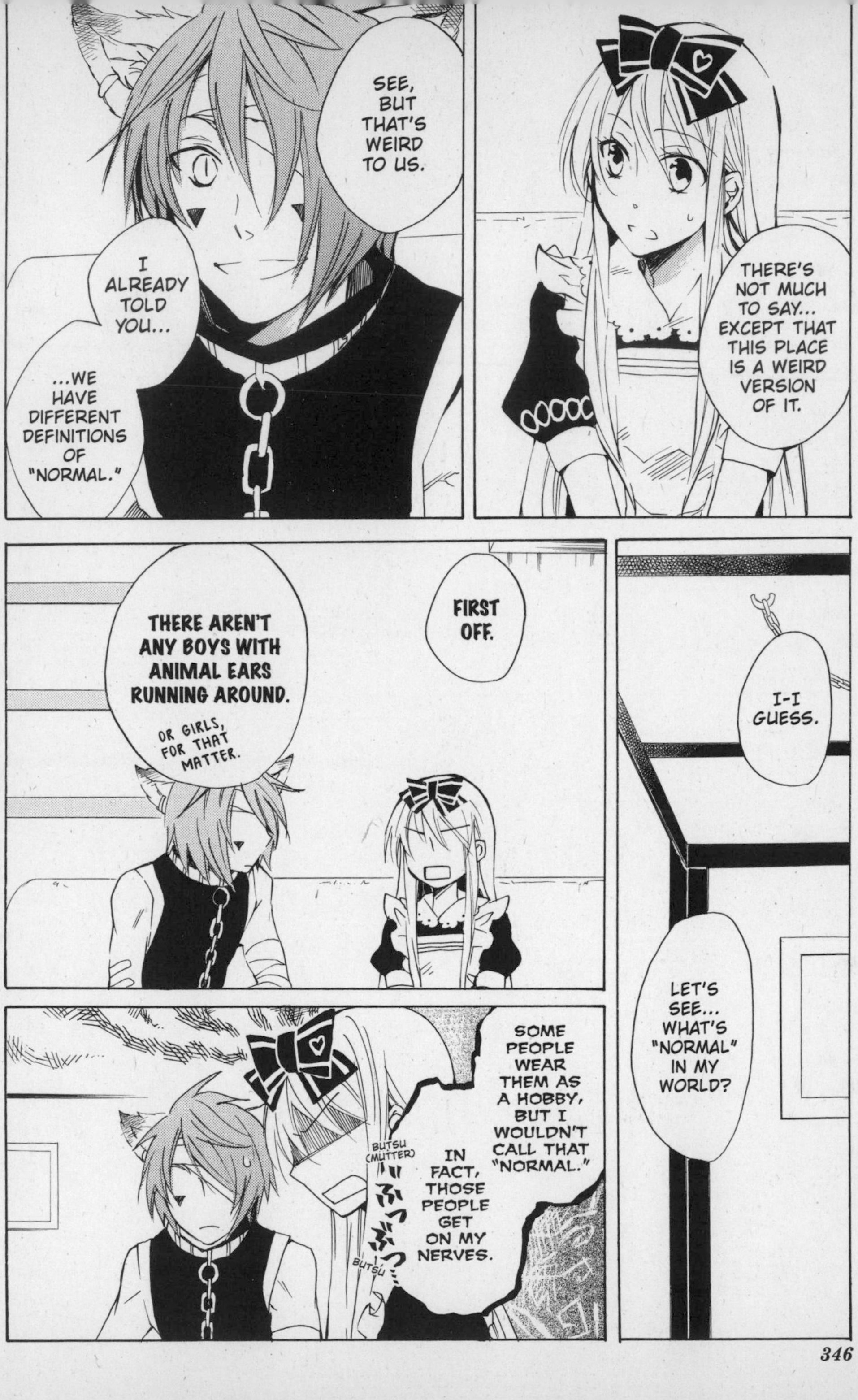
THERE'S NOT MUCH TO SAY... EXCEPT THAT THIS PLACE IS A WEIRD VERSION OF IT.
SEE, BUT THAT'S WEIRD TO US.
I ALREADY TOLD YOU...
...WE HAVE DIFFERENT DEFINITIONS OF "NORMAL."
I-I GUESS.
LET'S SEE... WHAT'S "NORMAL" IN MY WORLD?
FIRST OFF.
THERE AREN'T ANY BOYS WITH ANIMAL EARS RUNNING AROUND.
OR GIRLS, FOR THAT MATTER.
SOME PEOPLE WEAR THEM AS A HOBBY, BUT I WOULDN'T CALL THAT "NORMAL."
IN FACT, THOSE PEOPLE GET ON MY NERVES.
BUTSU (MUTTER)
BUTSU

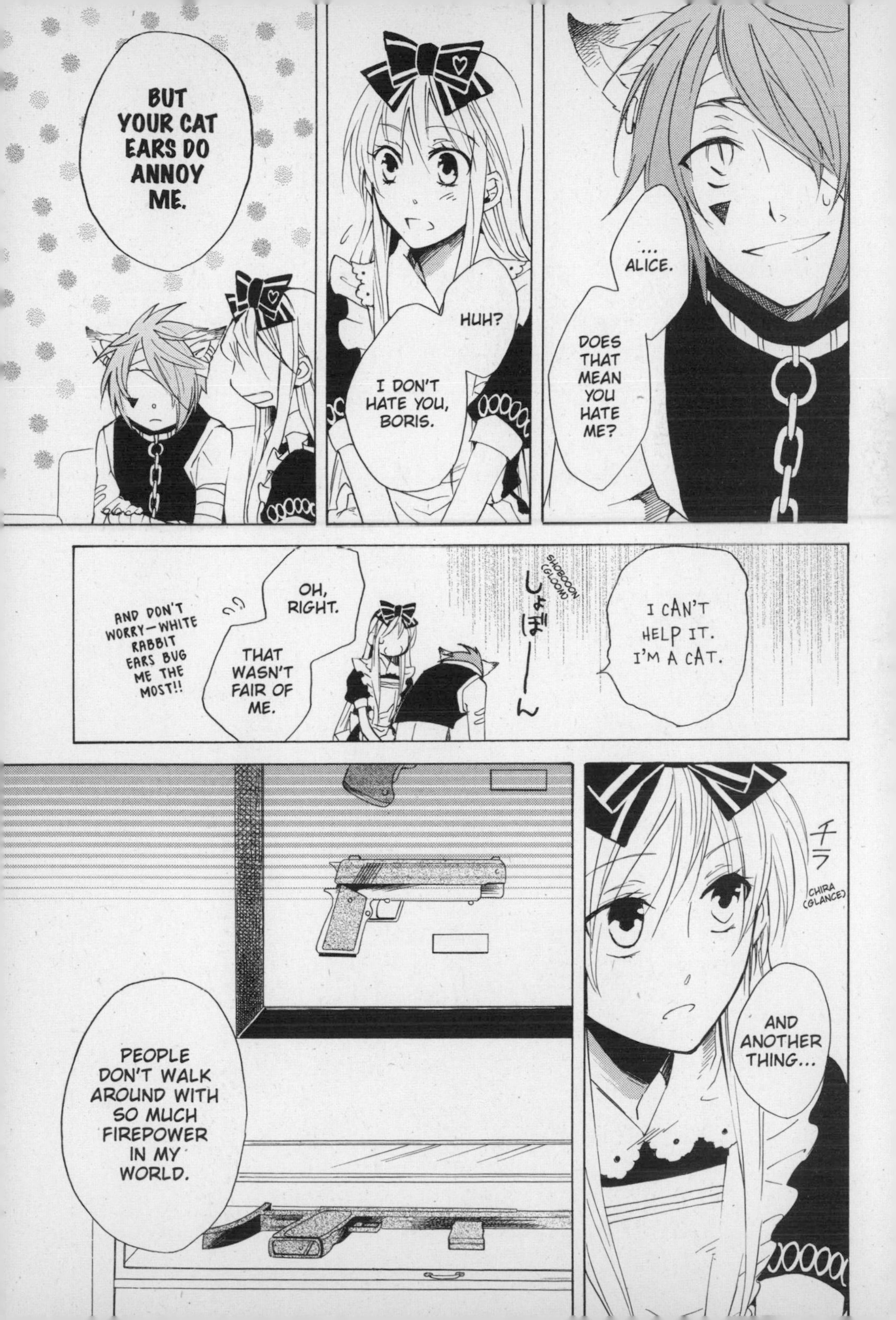
...
ALICE.
DOES THAT MEAN YOU HATE ME?
HUH?
I DON'T HATE YOU, BORIS.
BUT YOUR CAT EARS DO ANNOY ME.
I CAN'T HELP IT. I'M A CAT.
しょぼーん
SHOBOOON (GLOOM)
OH, RIGHT.
THAT WASN'T FAIR OF ME.
AND DON'T WORRY—WHITE RABBIT EARS BUG ME THE MOST!!
チラ
CHIRA (GLANCE)
AND ANOTHER THING...
PEOPLE DON'T WALK AROUND WITH SO MUCH FIREPOWER IN MY WORLD.

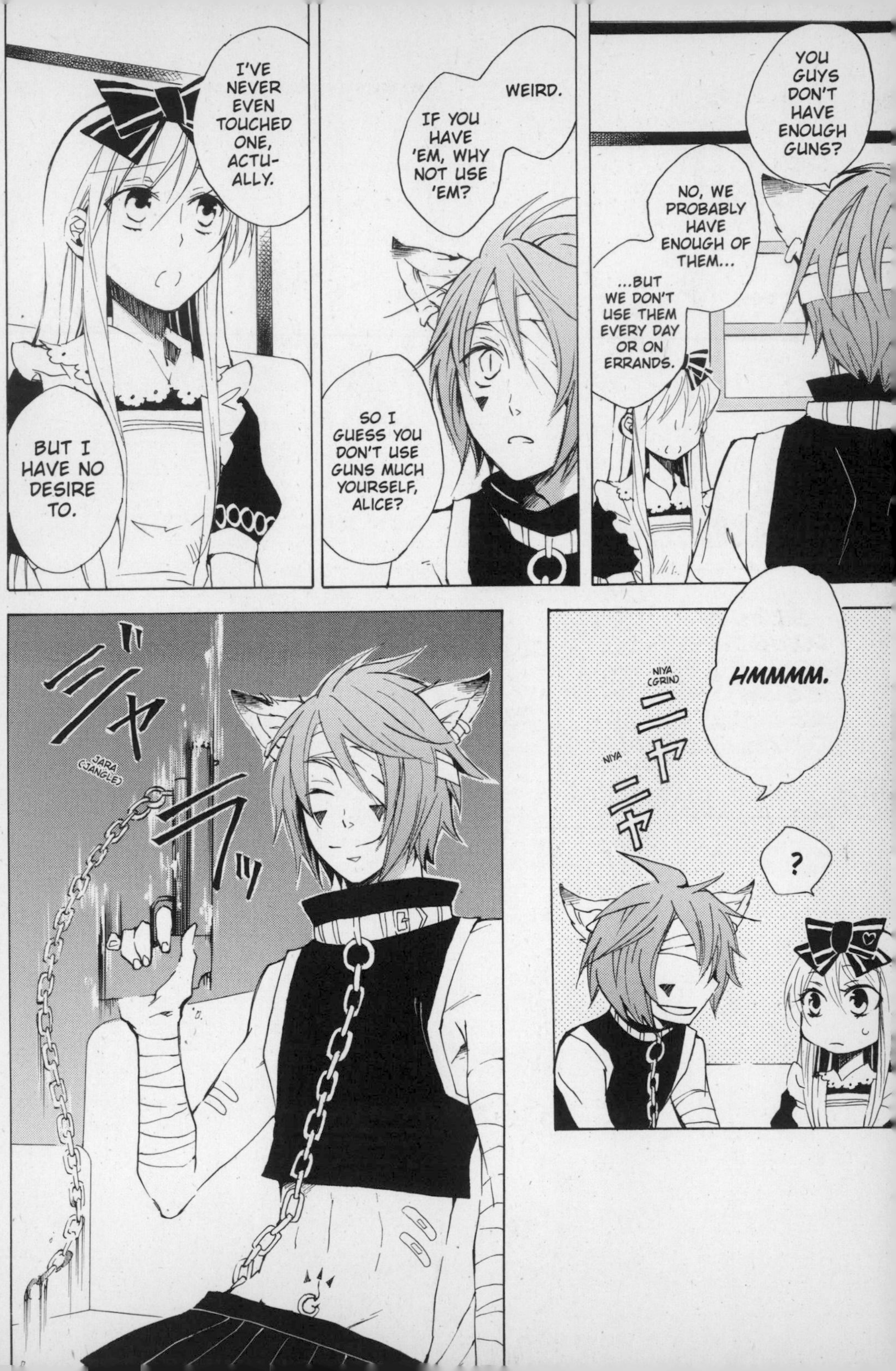
YOU GUYS DON'T HAVE ENOUGH GUNS?
NO, WE PROBABLY HAVE ENOUGH OF THEM...
...BUT WE DON'T USE THEM EVERY DAY OR ON ERRANDS.
WEIRD.
IF YOU HAVE 'EM, WHY NOT USE 'EM?
SO I GUESS YOU DON'T USE GUNS MUCH YOURSELF, ALICE?
I'VE NEVER EVEN TOUCHED ONE, ACTU-ALLY.
BUT I HAVE NO DESIRE TO.
HMMMM.
ニヤ
NIYA (GRIND)
ニヤ
NIYA
?
ジャラッ
JARA (JANGLE)

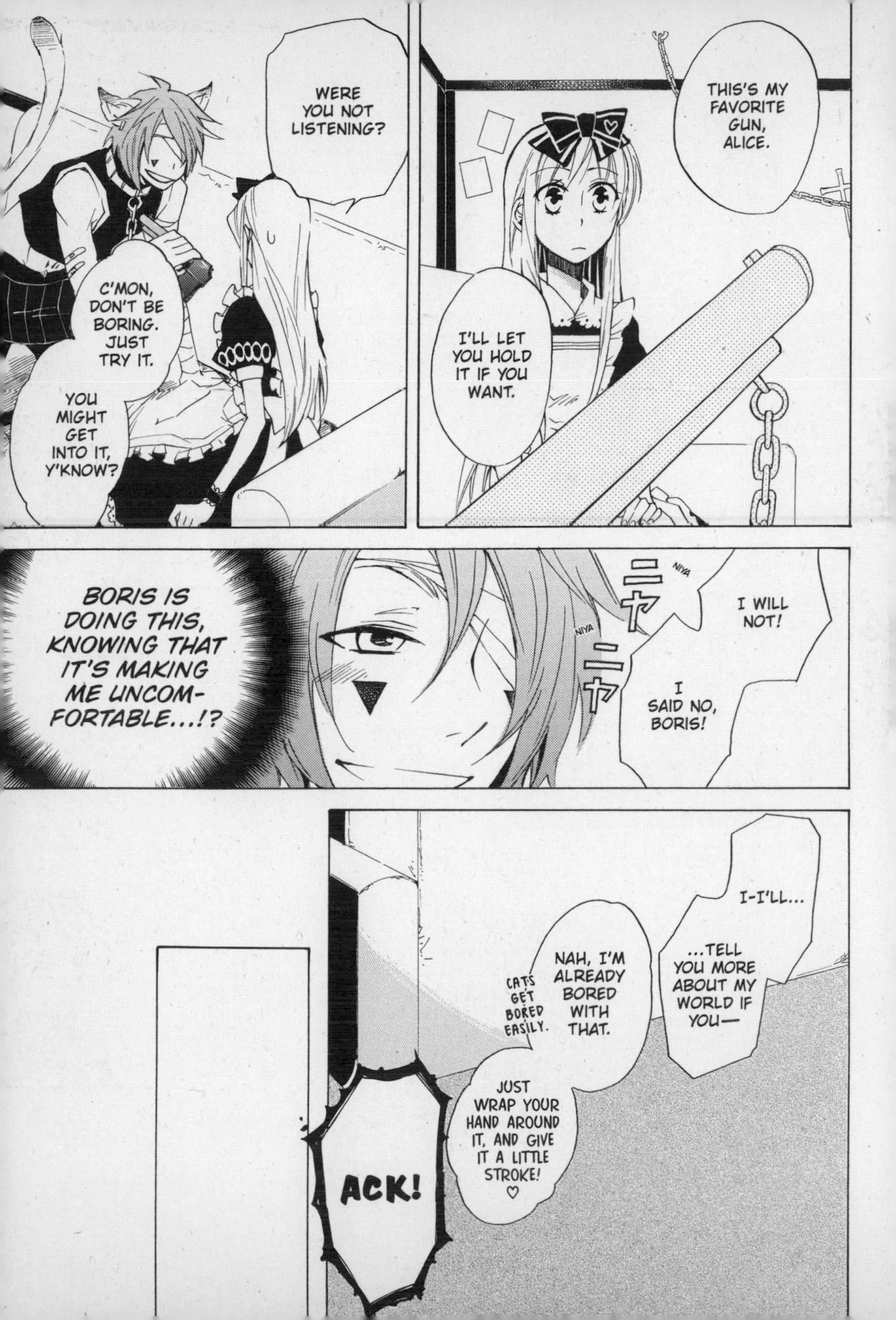
THIS'S MY FAVORITE GUN, ALICE.
I'LL LET YOU HOLD IT IF YOU WANT.
WERE YOU NOT LISTENING?
C'MON, DON'T BE BORING. JUST TRY IT.
YOU MIGHT GET INTO IT, Y'KNOW?
I WILL NOT!
I SAID NO, BORIS!
ニヤ NIYA
ニヤ NIYA
BORIS IS DOING THIS, KNOWING THAT IT'S MAKING ME UNCOMFORTABLE...!?
I-I'LL...
...TELL YOU MORE ABOUT MY WORLD IF YOU—
NAH, I'M ALREADY BORED WITH THAT.
CATS GET BORED EASILY.
JUST WRAP YOUR HAND AROUND IT, AND GIVE IT A LITTLE STROKE! ♡
ACK!

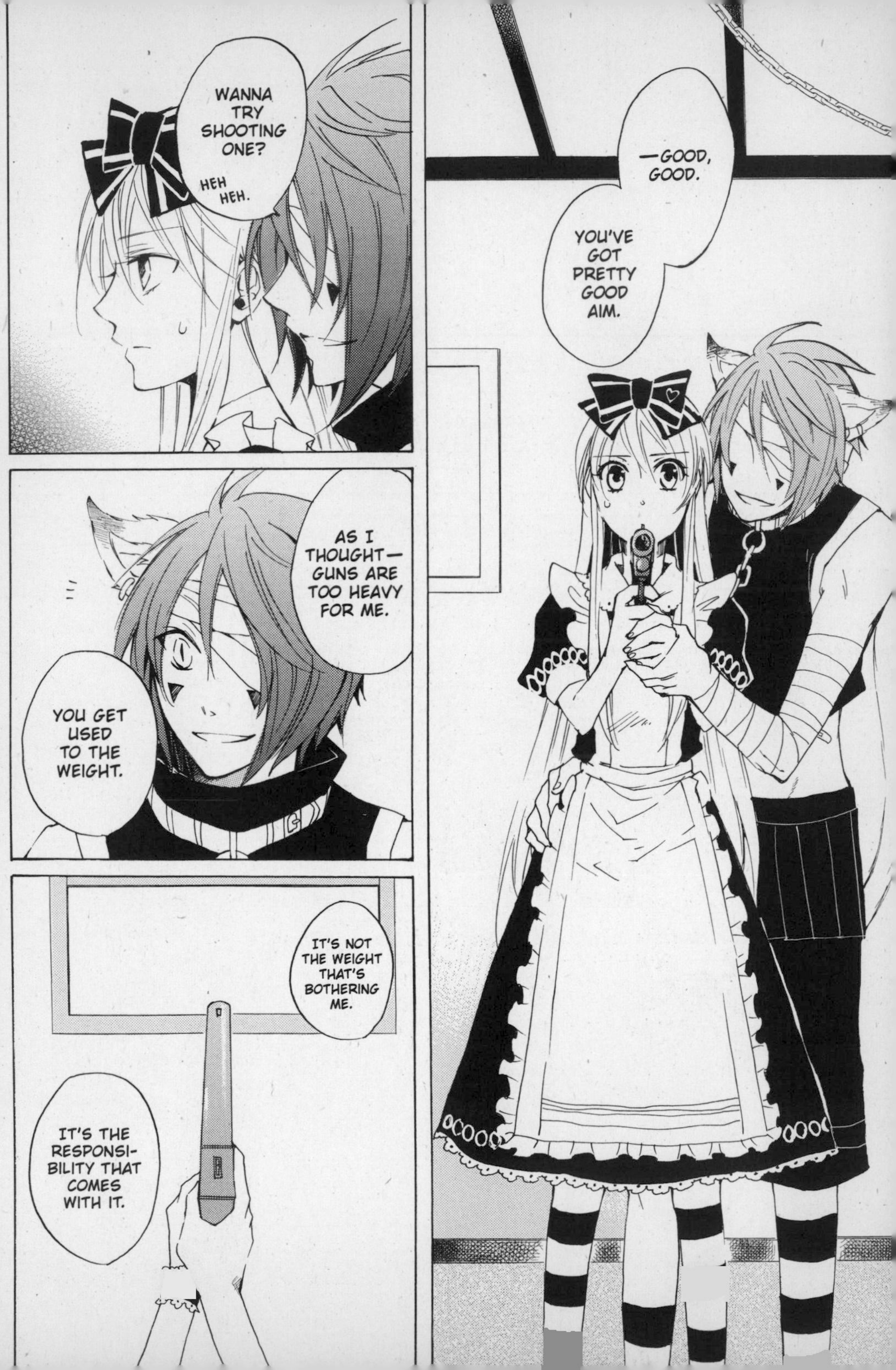
—GOOD, GOOD.
YOU'VE GOT PRETTY GOOD AIM.
WANNA TRY SHOOTING ONE?
HEH HEH.
AS I THOUGHT—GUNS ARE TOO HEAVY FOR ME.
YOU GET USED TO THE WEIGHT.
IT'S NOT THE WEIGHT THAT'S BOTHERING ME.
IT'S THE RESPONSIBILITY THAT COMES WITH IT.

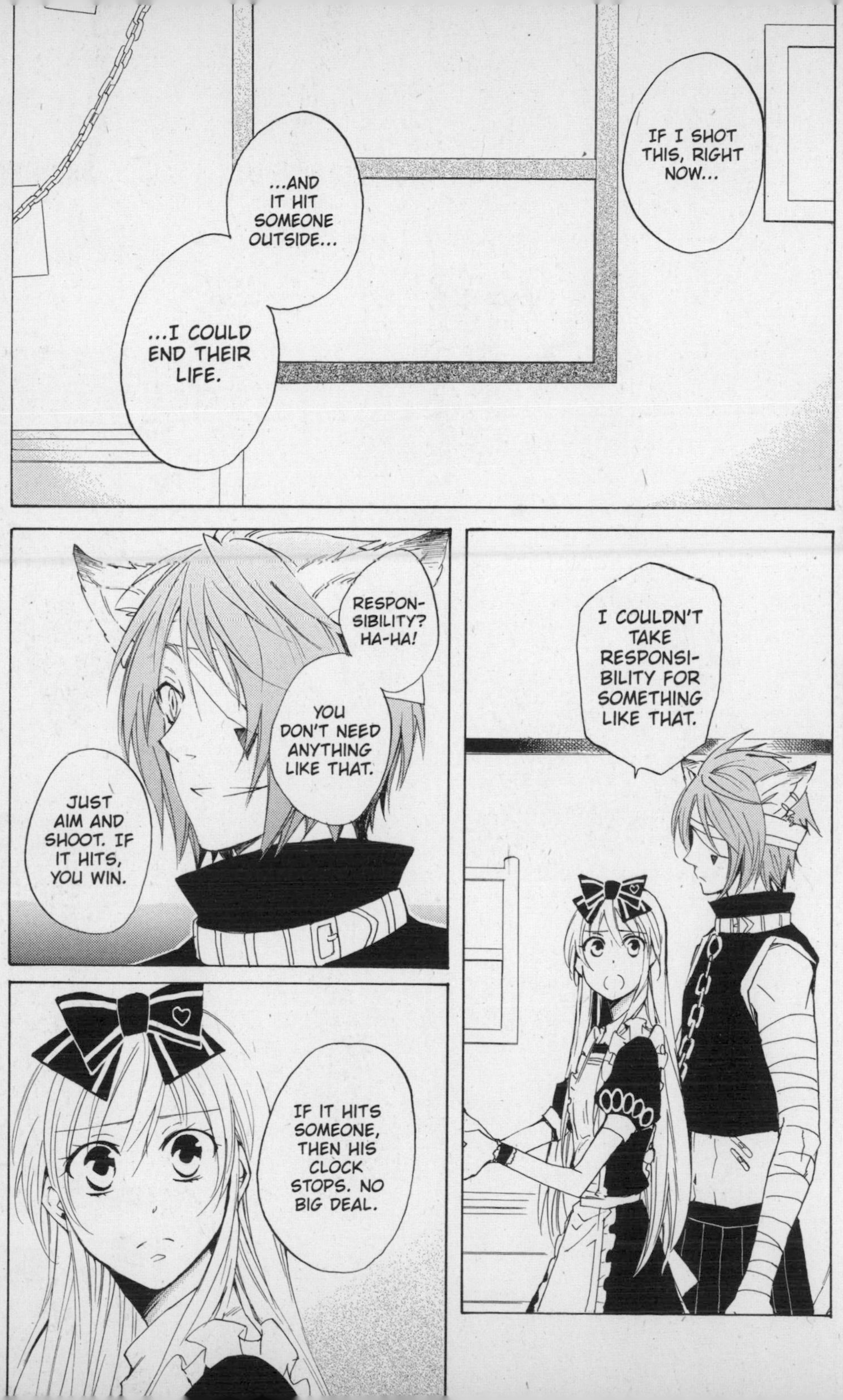
IF I SHOT THIS, RIGHT NOW...
...AND IT HIT SOMEONE OUTSIDE...
...I COULD END THEIR LIFE.
I COULDN'T TAKE RESPONSI-BILITY FOR SOMETHING LIKE THAT.
RESPON-SIBILITY? HA-HA!
YOU DON'T NEED ANYTHING LIKE THAT.
JUST AIM AND SHOOT. IF IT HITS, YOU WIN.
IF IT HITS SOMEONE, THEN HIS CLOCK STOPS. NO BIG DEAL.

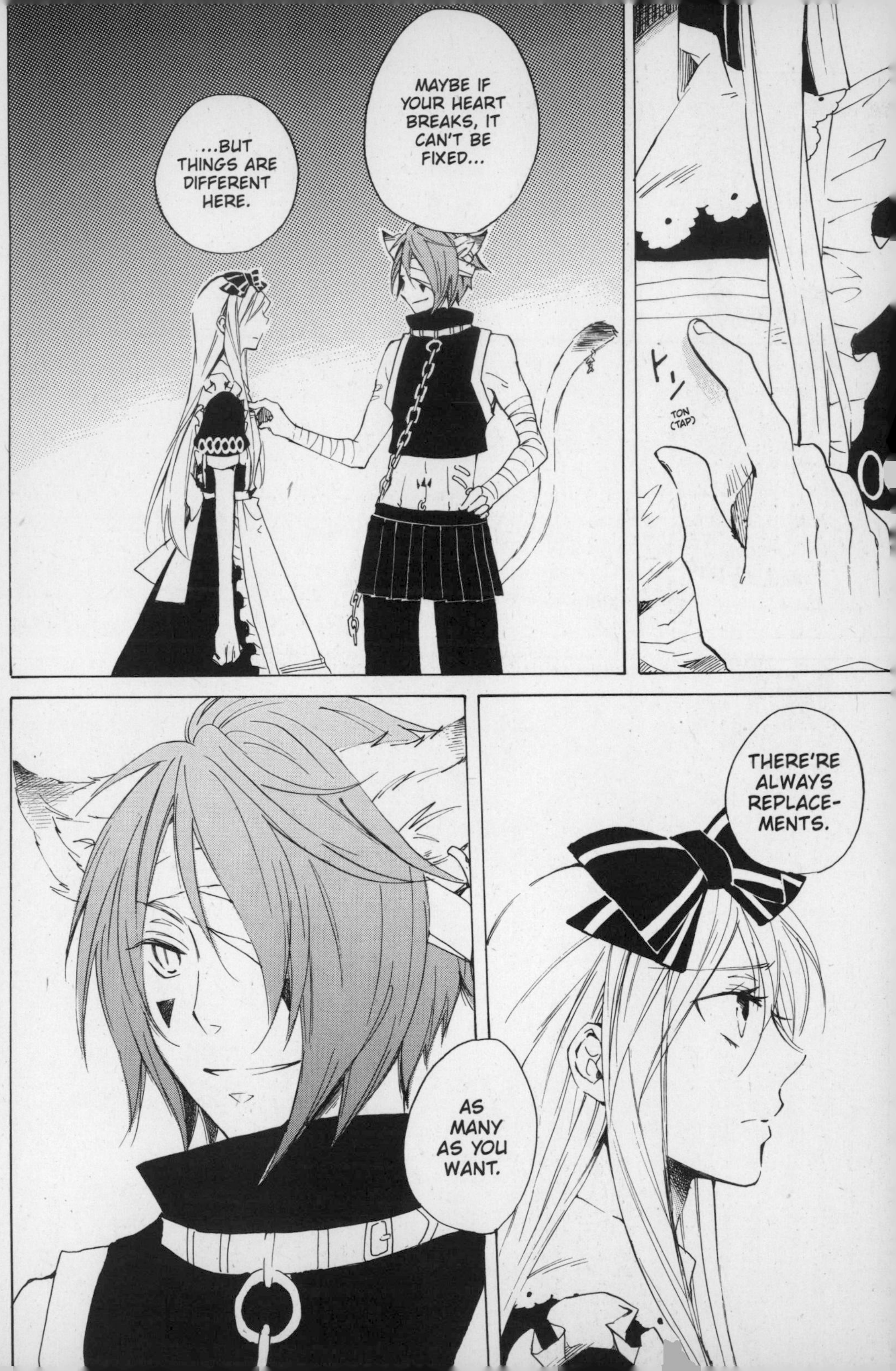
トン
TON (TAP)
MAYBE IF YOUR HEART BREAKS, IT CAN'T BE FIXED...
...BUT THINGS ARE DIFFERENT HERE.
THERE'RE ALWAYS REPLACEMENTS.
AS MANY AS YOU WANT.

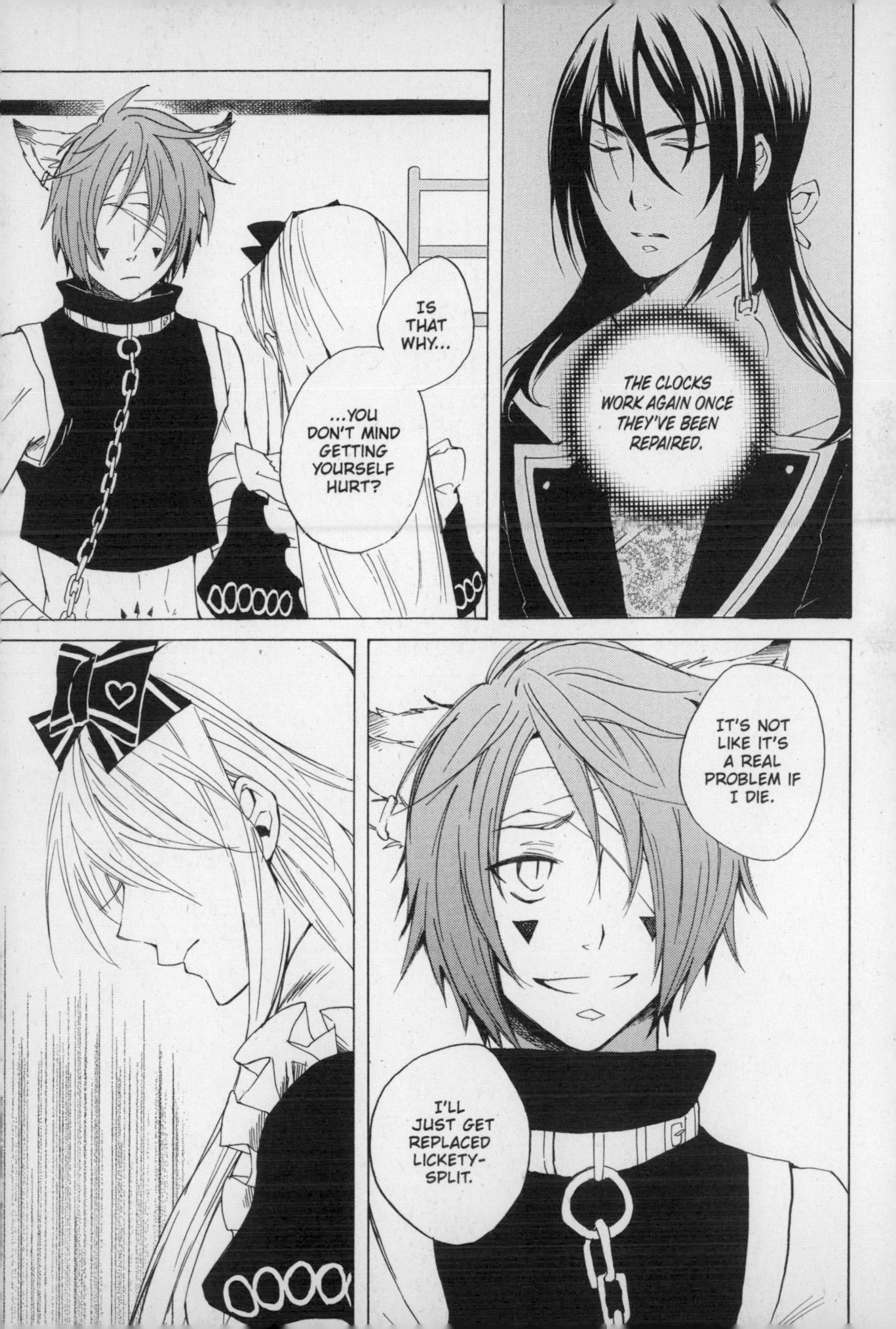
THE CLOCKS WORK AGAIN ONCE THEY'VE BEEN REPAIRED.
IS THAT WHY...
...YOU DON'T MIND GETTING YOURSELF HURT?
IT'S NOT LIKE IT'S A REAL PROBLEM IF I DIE.
I'LL JUST GET REPLACED LICKETY-SPLIT.

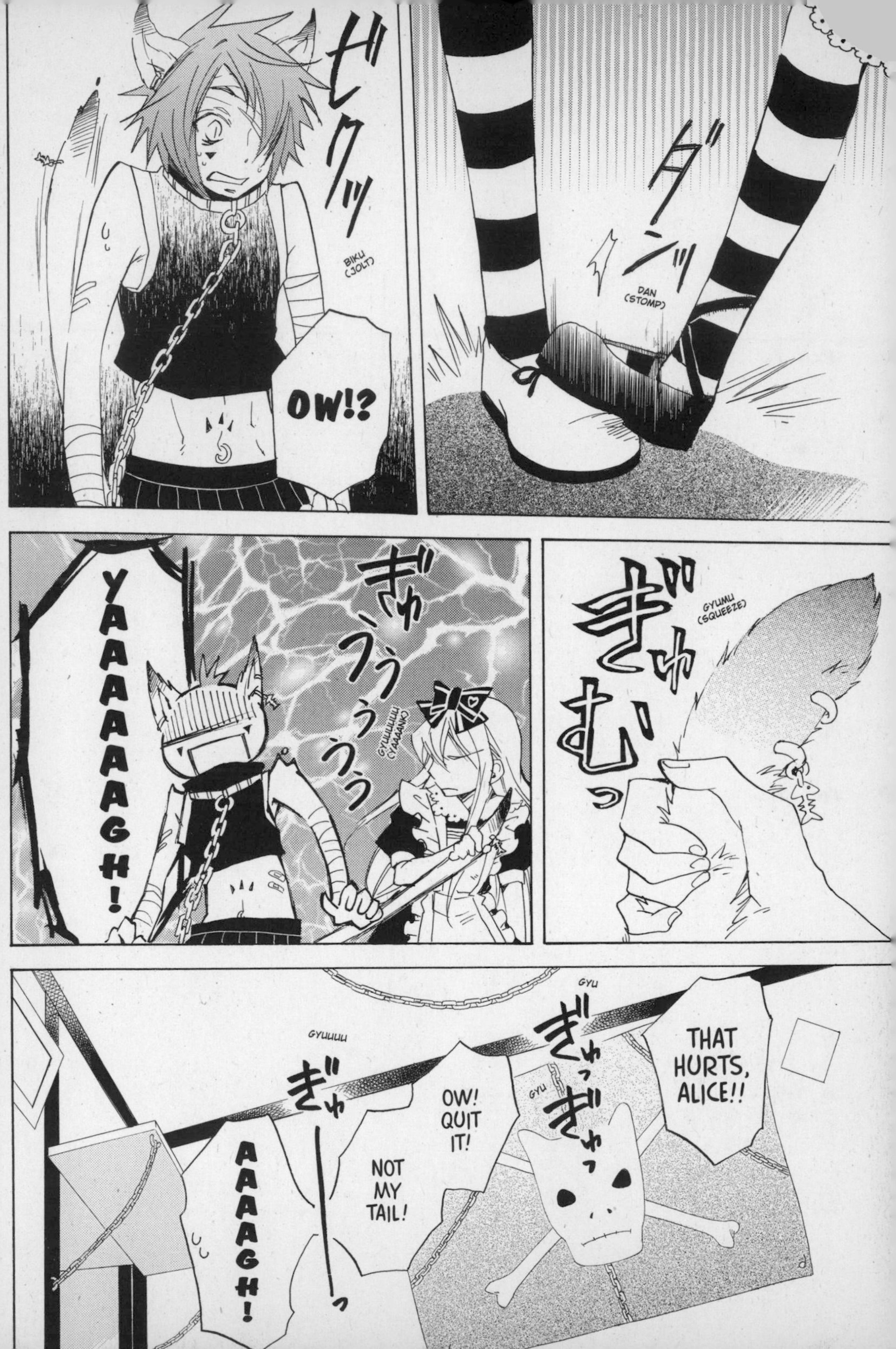
ダンッ
DAN (STOMP)
ビクッ
BIKU (JOLT)
OW!?
ぎゅむっ
GYUMU (SQUEEZE)
ぎゅううううう
GYUUUUUU (YAAAANK)
YAAAAAAGH!
THAT HURTS, ALICE!!
GYU
ぎゅっ
GYU
ぎゅっ
OW! QUIT IT!
NOT MY TAIL!
GYUUUUU
ぎゅー
AAAAGH!

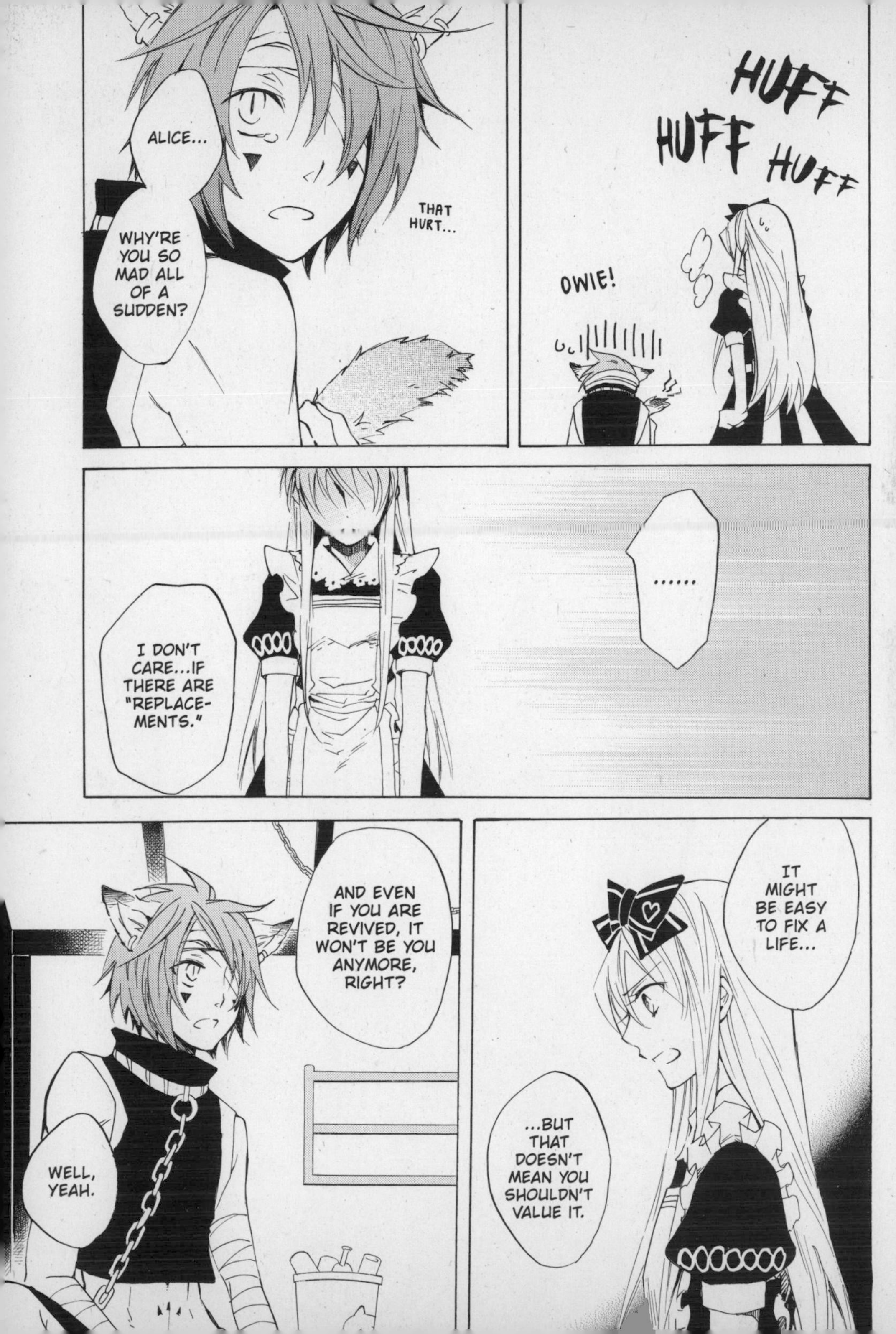
HUFF
HUFF
HUFF
OWIE!
ALICE...
THAT HURT...
WHY'RE YOU SO MAD ALL OF A SUDDEN?
......
I DON'T CARE...IF THERE ARE "REPLACEMENTS."
IT MIGHT BE EASY TO FIX A LIFE...
...BUT THAT DOESN'T MEAN YOU SHOULDN'T VALUE IT.
AND EVEN IF YOU ARE REVIVED, IT WON'T BE YOU ANYMORE, RIGHT?
WELL, YEAH.

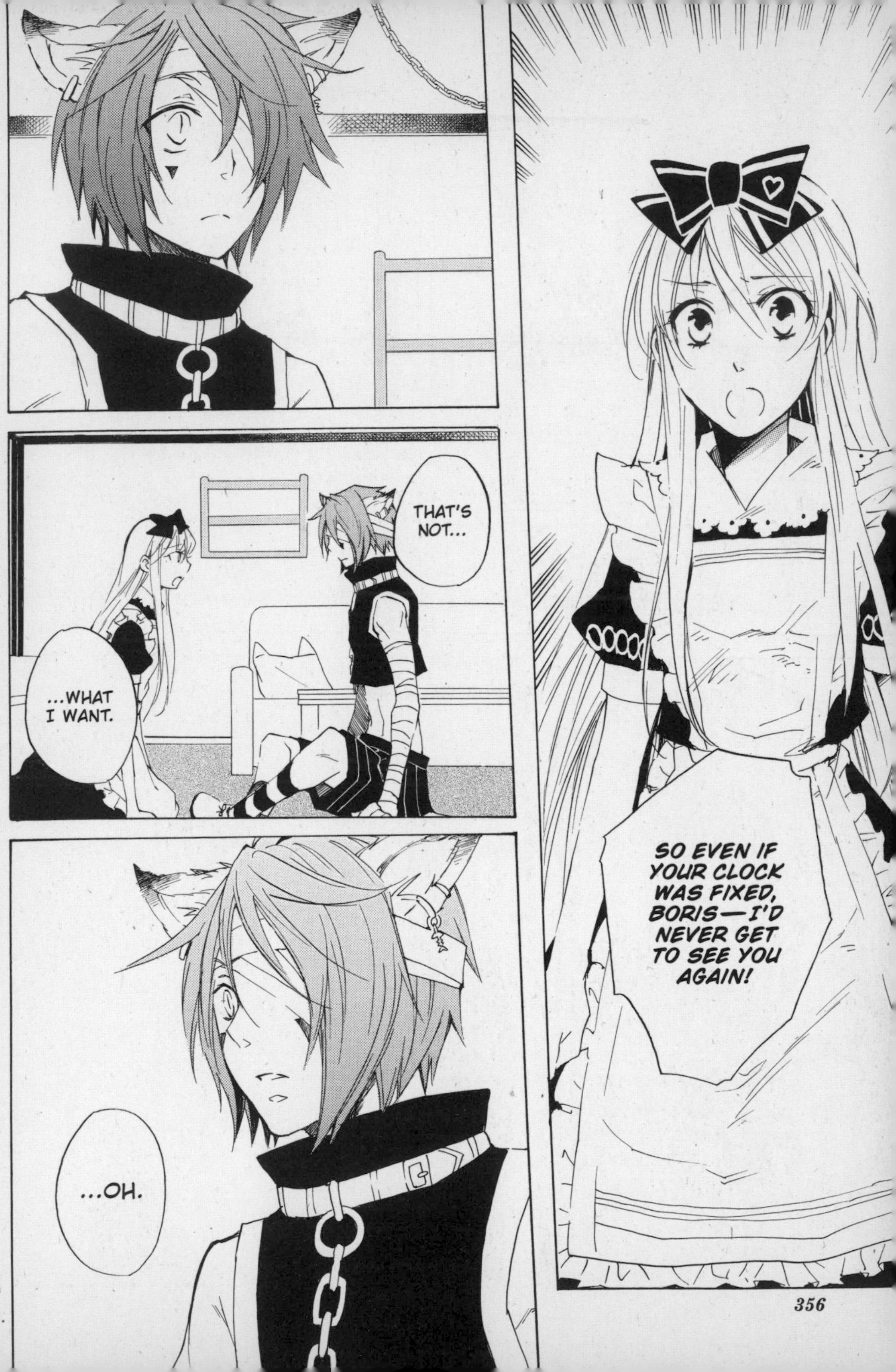
SO EVEN IF YOUR CLOCK WAS FIXED, BORIS—I'D NEVER GET TO SEE YOU AGAIN!
THAT'S NOT...
...WHAT I WANT.
...OH.

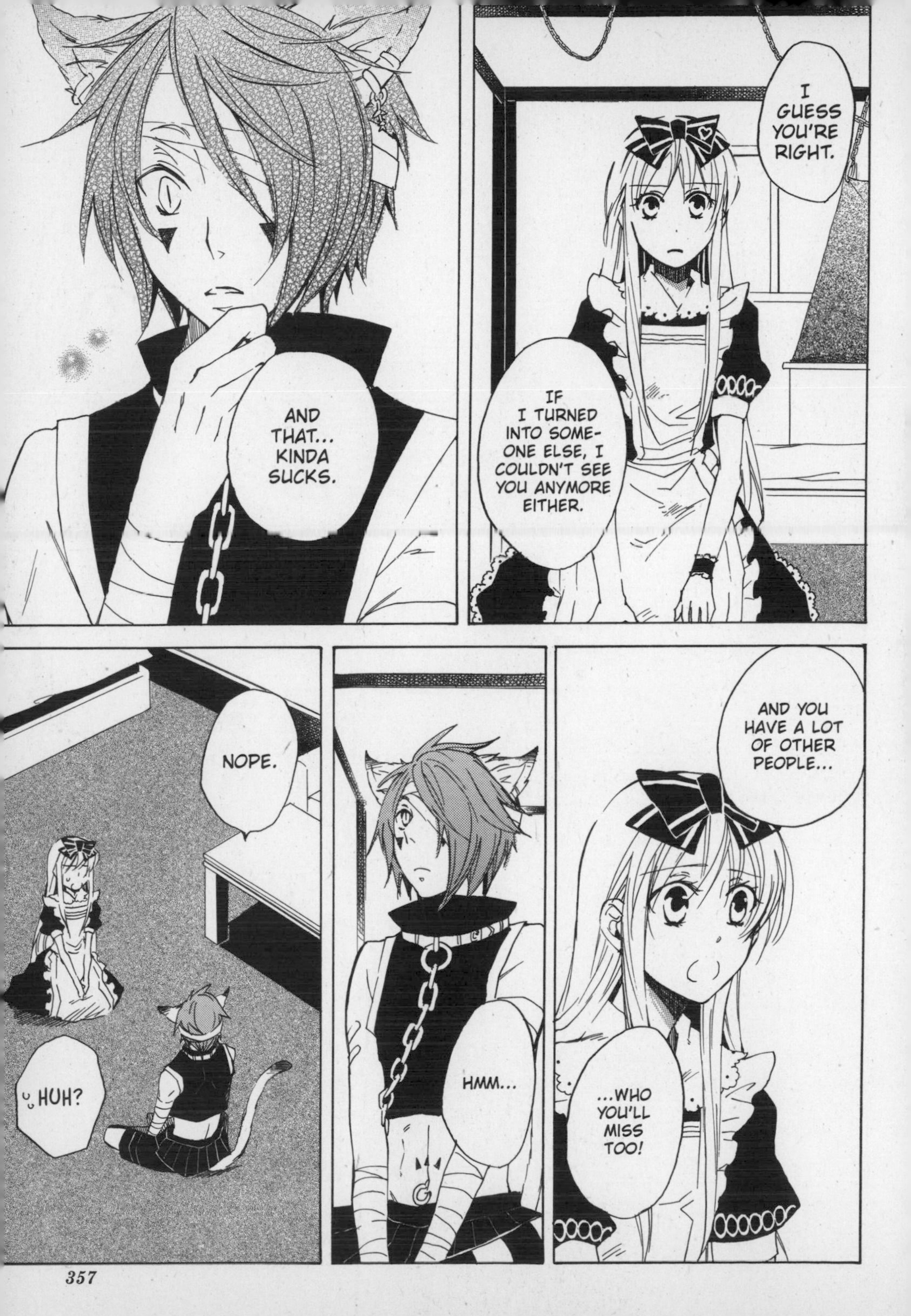
I GUESS YOU'RE RIGHT.
IF I TURNED INTO SOME-ONE ELSE, I COULDN'T SEE YOU ANYMORE EITHER.
AND THAT... KINDA SUCKS.
AND YOU HAVE A LOT OF OTHER PEOPLE...
...WHO YOU'LL MISS TOO!
HMM...
NOPE.
HUH?

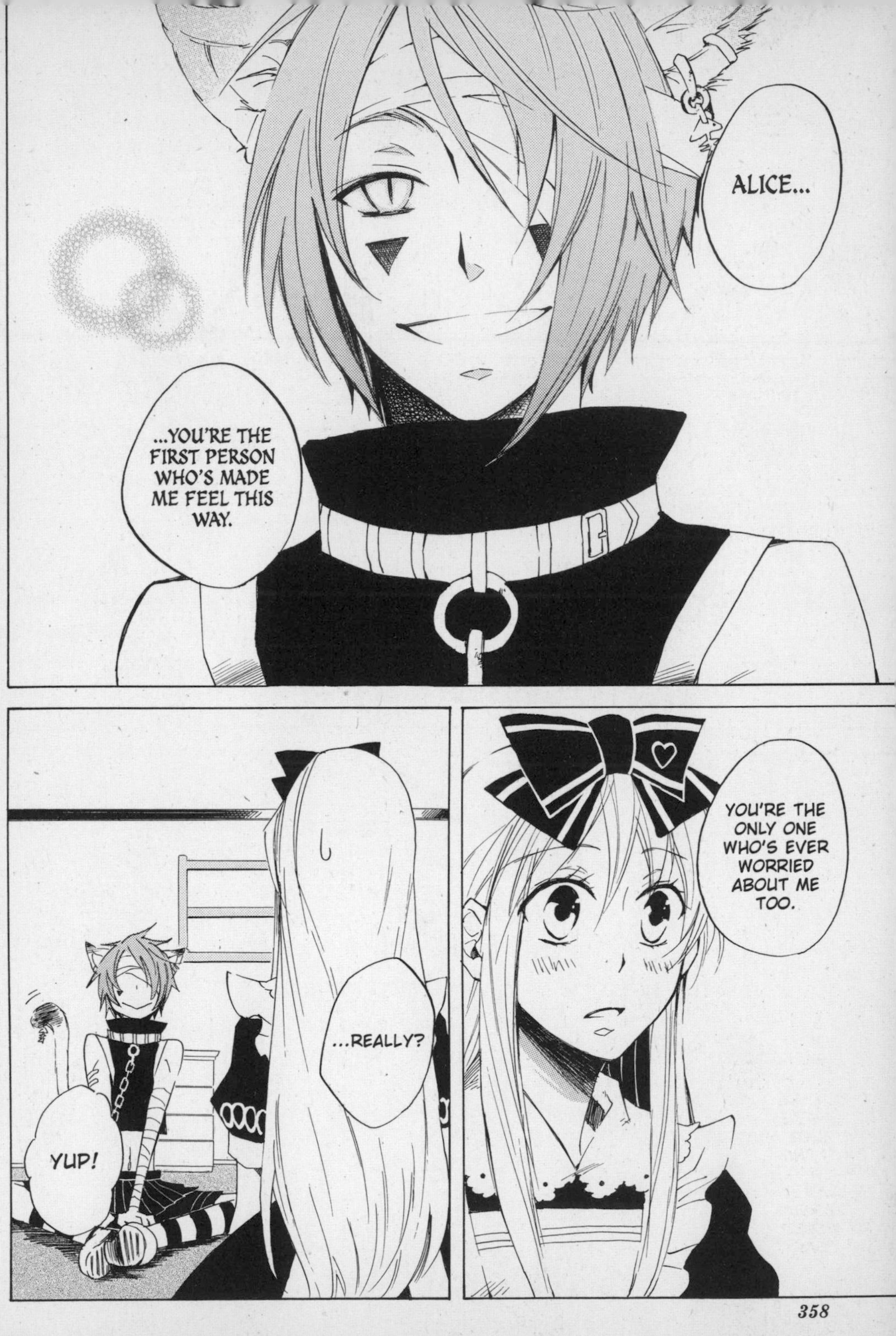
ALICE...
...YOU'RE THE FIRST PERSON WHO'S MADE ME FEEL THIS WAY.
YOU'RE THE ONLY ONE WHO'S EVER WORRIED ABOUT ME TOO.
...REALLY?
YUP!

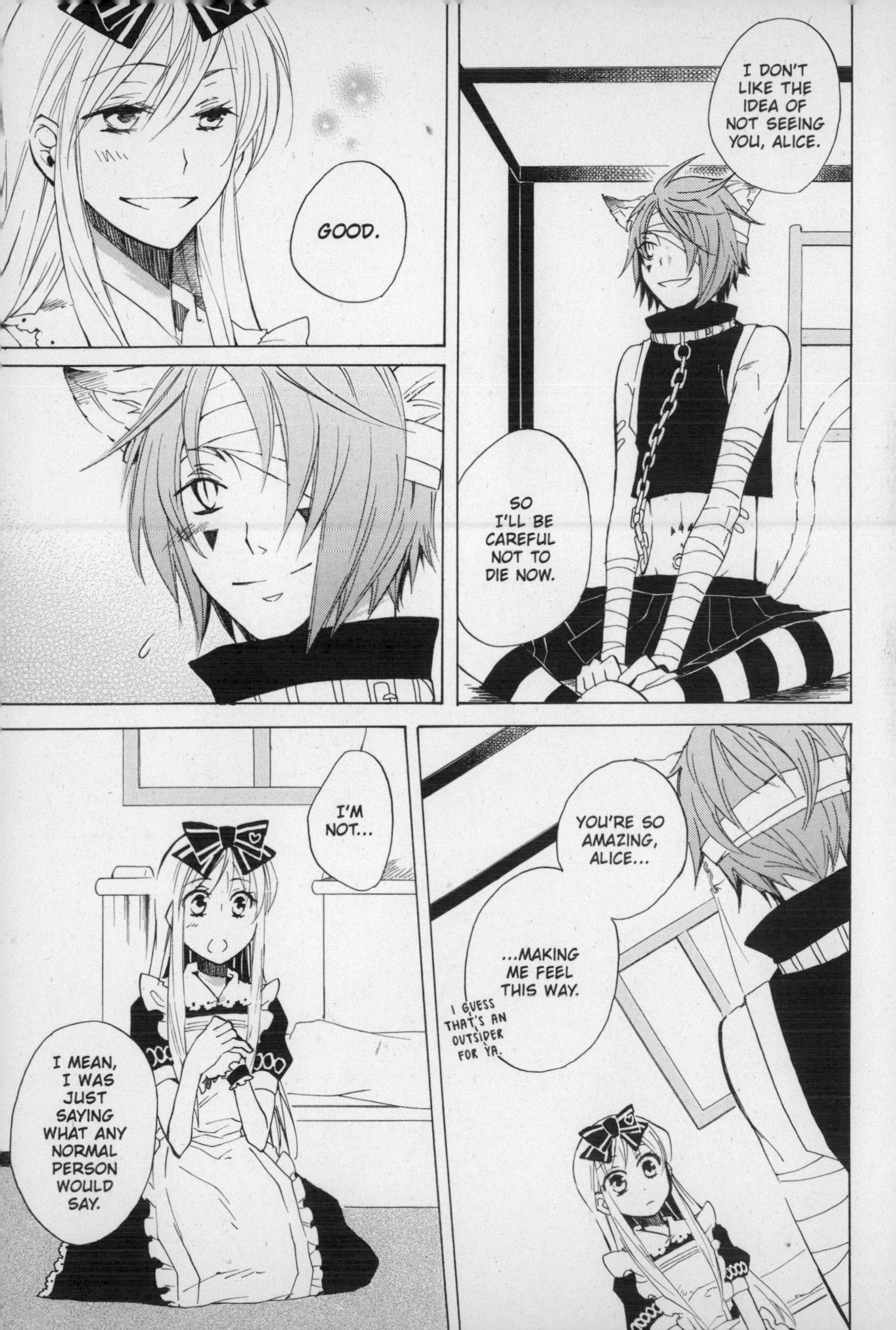
I DON'T LIKE THE IDEA OF NOT SEEING YOU, ALICE.
SO I'LL BE CAREFUL NOT TO DIE NOW.
GOOD.
YOU'RE SO AMAZING, ALICE...
...MAKING ME FEEL THIS WAY.
I GUESS THAT'S AN OUTSIDER FOR YA.
I'M NOT...
I MEAN, I WAS JUST SAYING WHAT ANY NORMAL PERSON WOULD SAY.

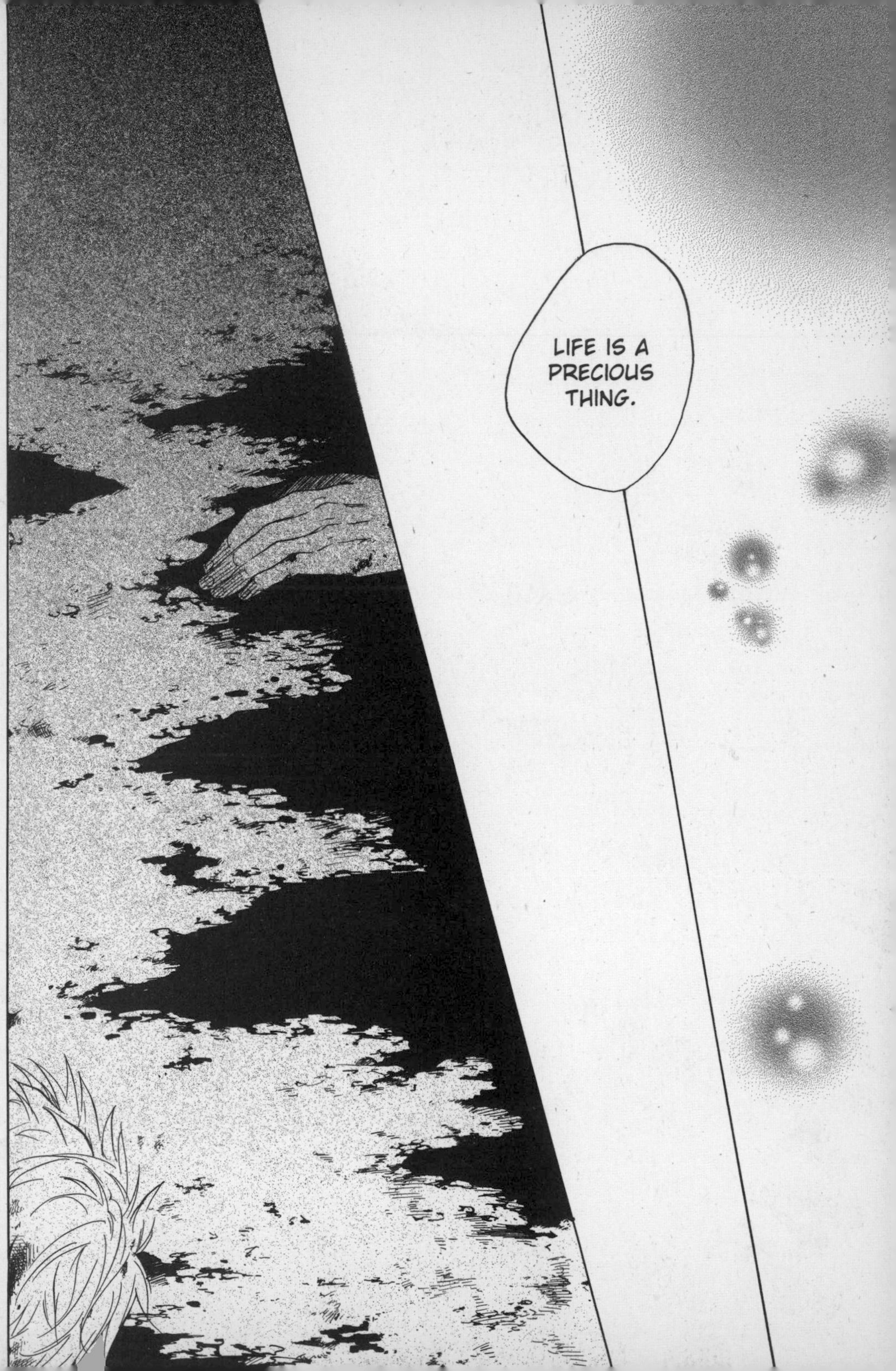
LIFE IS A PRECIOUS THING.

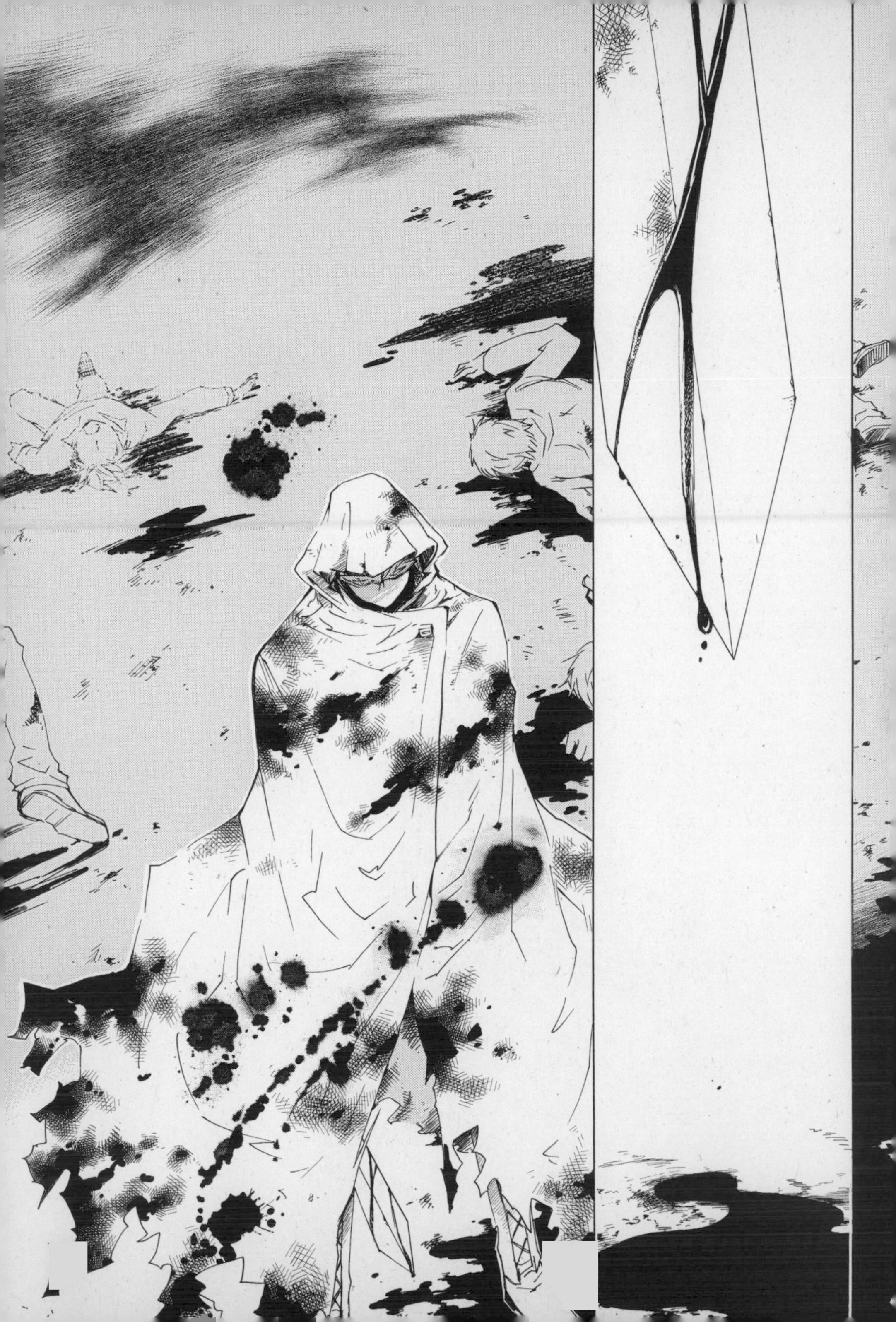

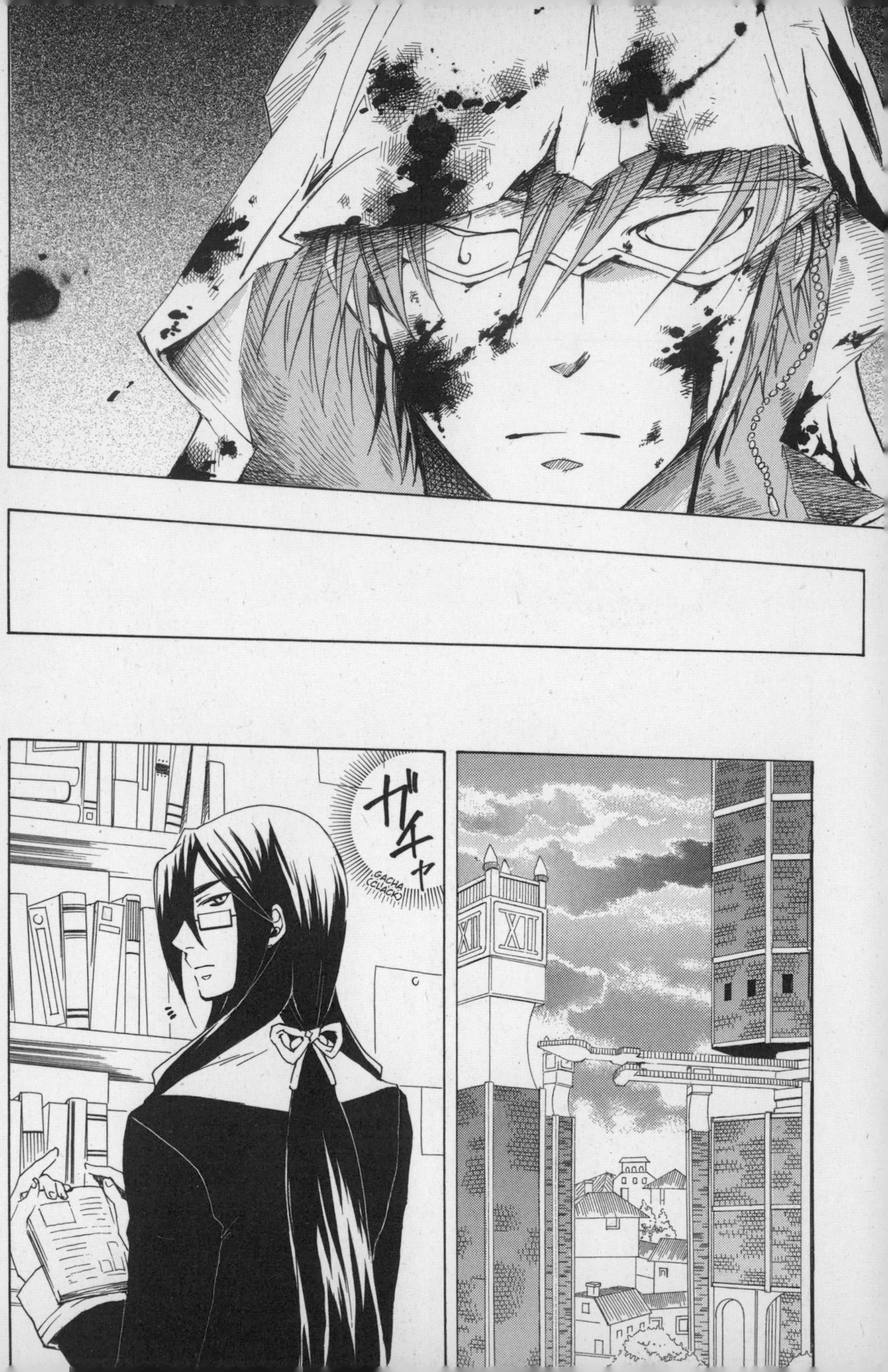
ガチャ
GACHA (CLACK)

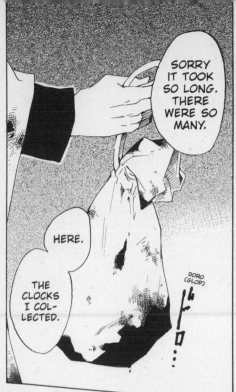

SORRY IT TOOK SO LONG. THERE WERE SO MANY.

HERE.

THE CLOCKS I COLLECTED.

DORO (GLOP)

ロ
ロ
ロ...

I'M HOME!

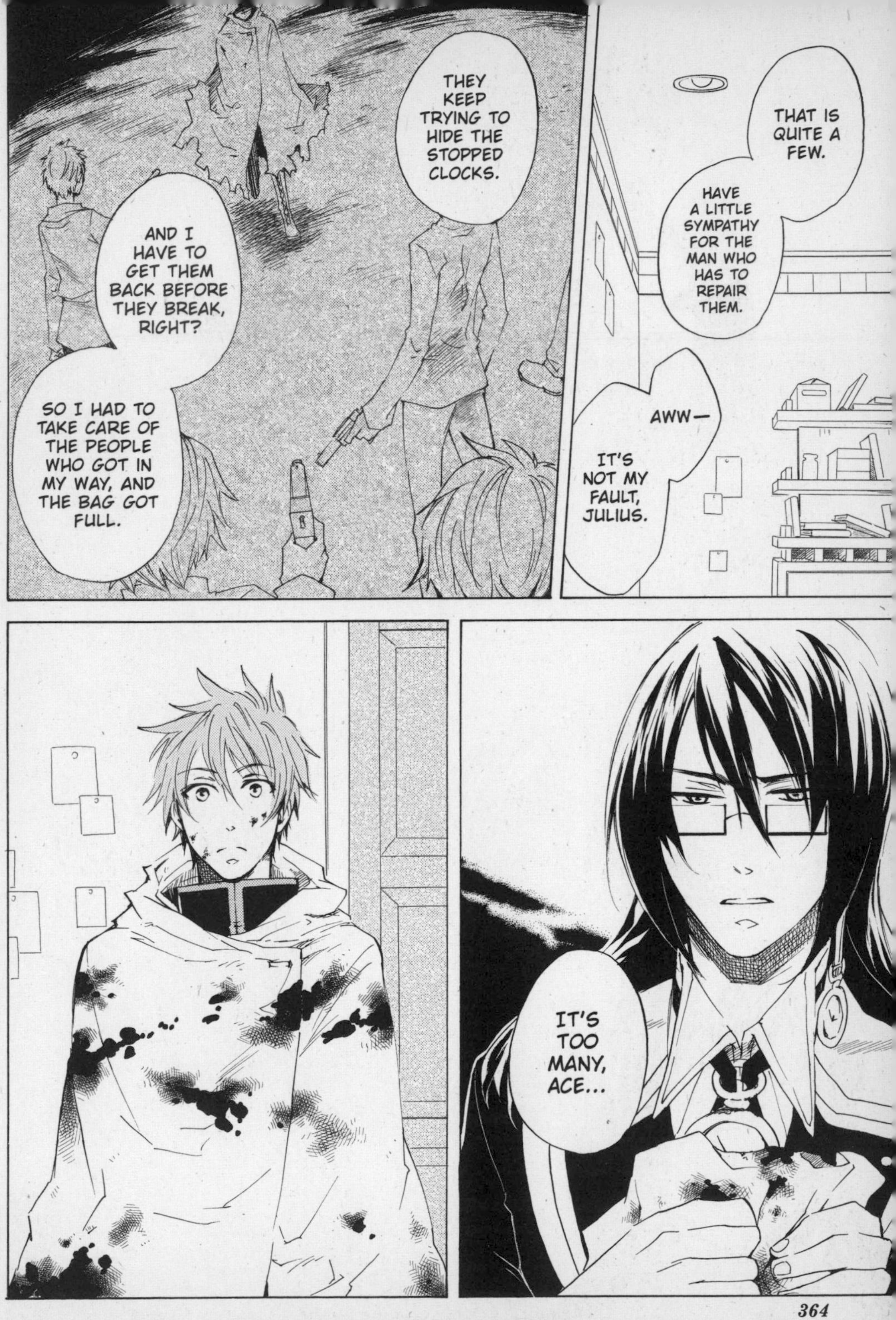
THAT IS QUITE A FEW.
HAVE A LITTLE SYMPATHY FOR THE MAN WHO HAS TO REPAIR THEM.
AWW—
IT'S NOT MY FAULT, JULIUS.
THEY KEEP TRYING TO HIDE THE STOPPED CLOCKS.
AND I HAVE TO GET THEM BACK BEFORE THEY BREAK, RIGHT?
SO I HAD TO TAKE CARE OF THE PEOPLE WHO GOT IN MY WAY, AND THE BAG GOT FULL.
IT'S TOO MANY, ACE...

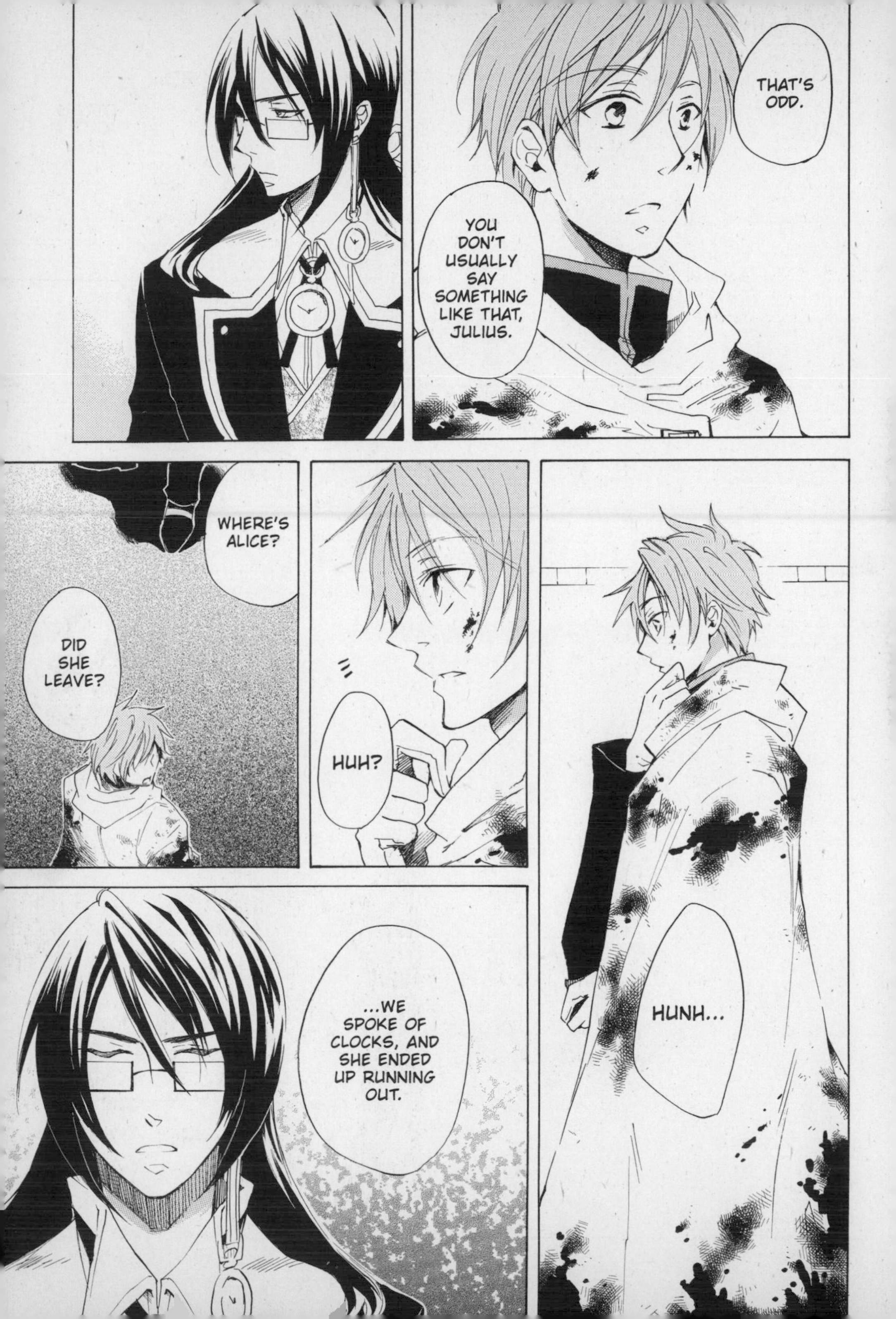
THAT'S ODD.
YOU DON'T USUALLY SAY SOMETHING LIKE THAT, JULIUS.
HUNH...
HUH?
WHERE'S ALICE?
DID SHE LEAVE?
...WE SPOKE OF CLOCKS, AND SHE ENDED UP RUNNING OUT.

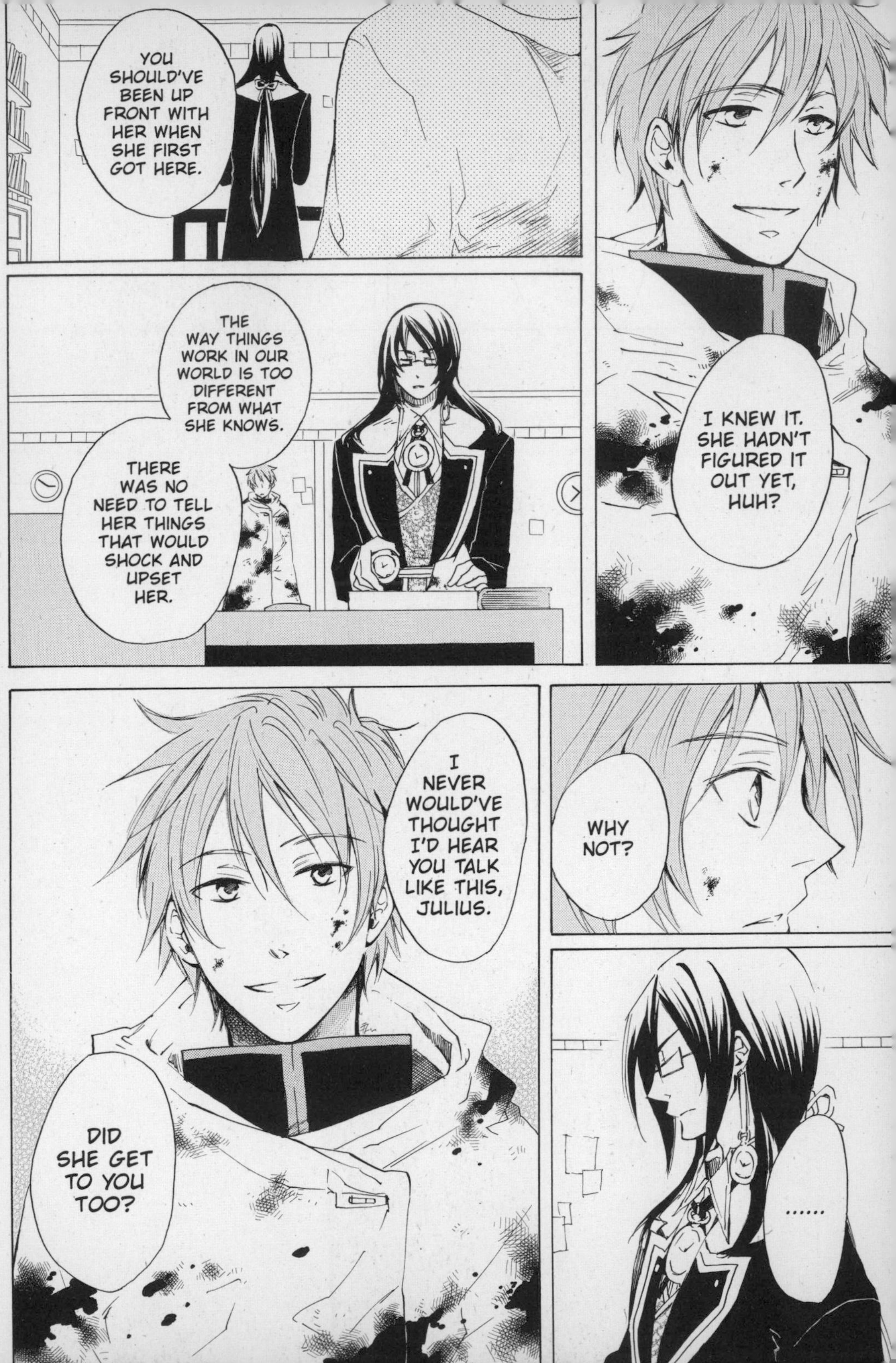
I KNEW IT. SHE HADN'T FIGURED IT OUT YET, HUH?
YOU SHOULD'VE BEEN UP FRONT WITH HER WHEN SHE FIRST GOT HERE.
THE WAY THINGS WORK IN OUR WORLD IS TOO DIFFERENT FROM WHAT SHE KNOWS.
THERE WAS NO NEED TO TELL HER THINGS THAT WOULD SHOCK AND UPSET HER.
WHY NOT?
......
I NEVER WOULD'VE THOUGHT I'D HEAR YOU TALK LIKE THIS, JULIUS.
DID SHE GET TO YOU TOO?

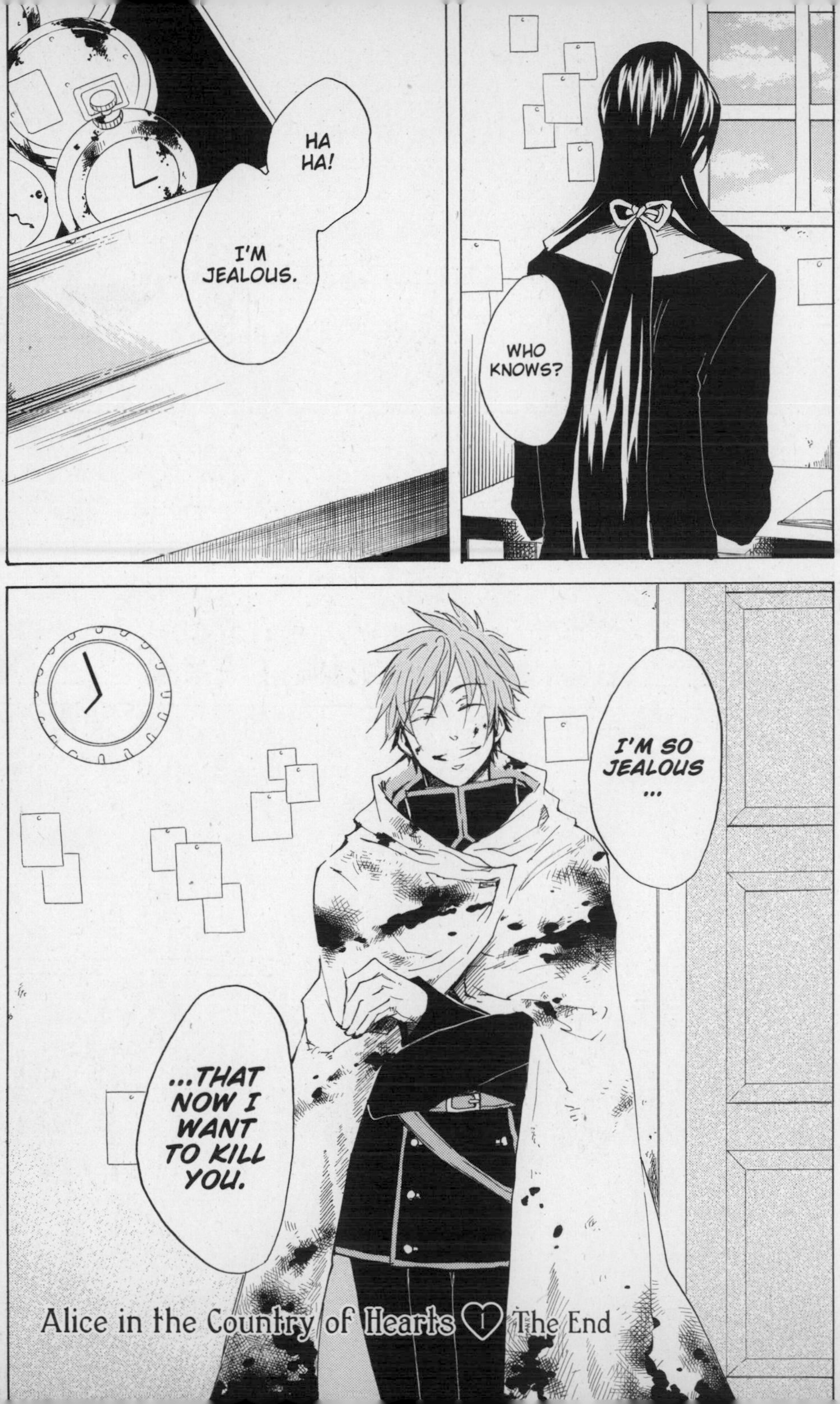
WHO KNOWS?
HA HA!
I'M JEALOUS.
I'M SO JEALOUS ...
...THAT NOW I WANT TO KILL YOU.
Alice in the Country of Hearts 1 The End

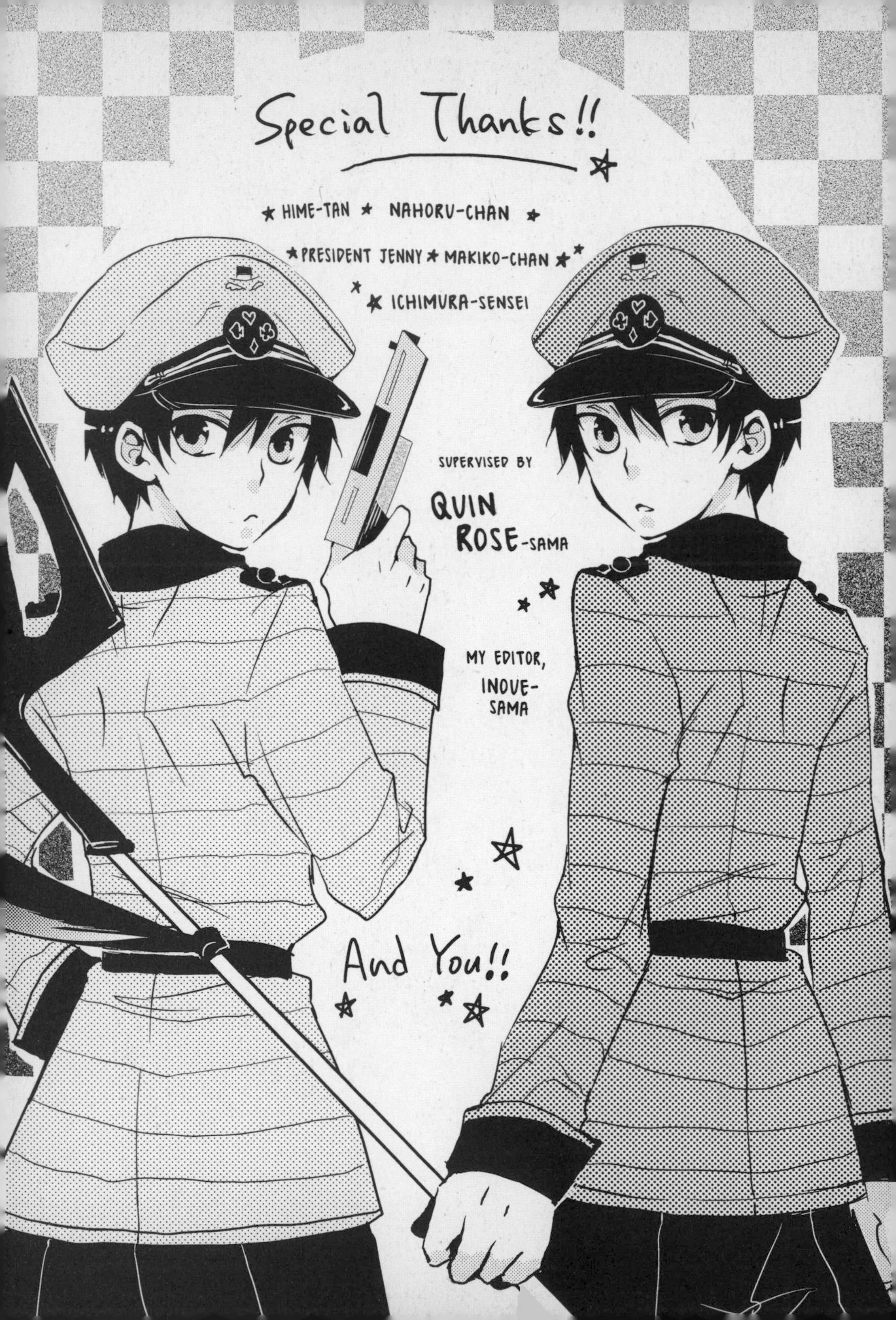
Special Thanks!!
★ HIME-TAN ★ NAHORU-CHAN ★
★ PRESIDENT JENNY ★ MAKIKO-CHAN ★
★ ICHIMURA-SENSEI
SUPERVISED BY
QUIN ROSE-SAMA
MY EDITOR, INOUE-SAMA
And You!!

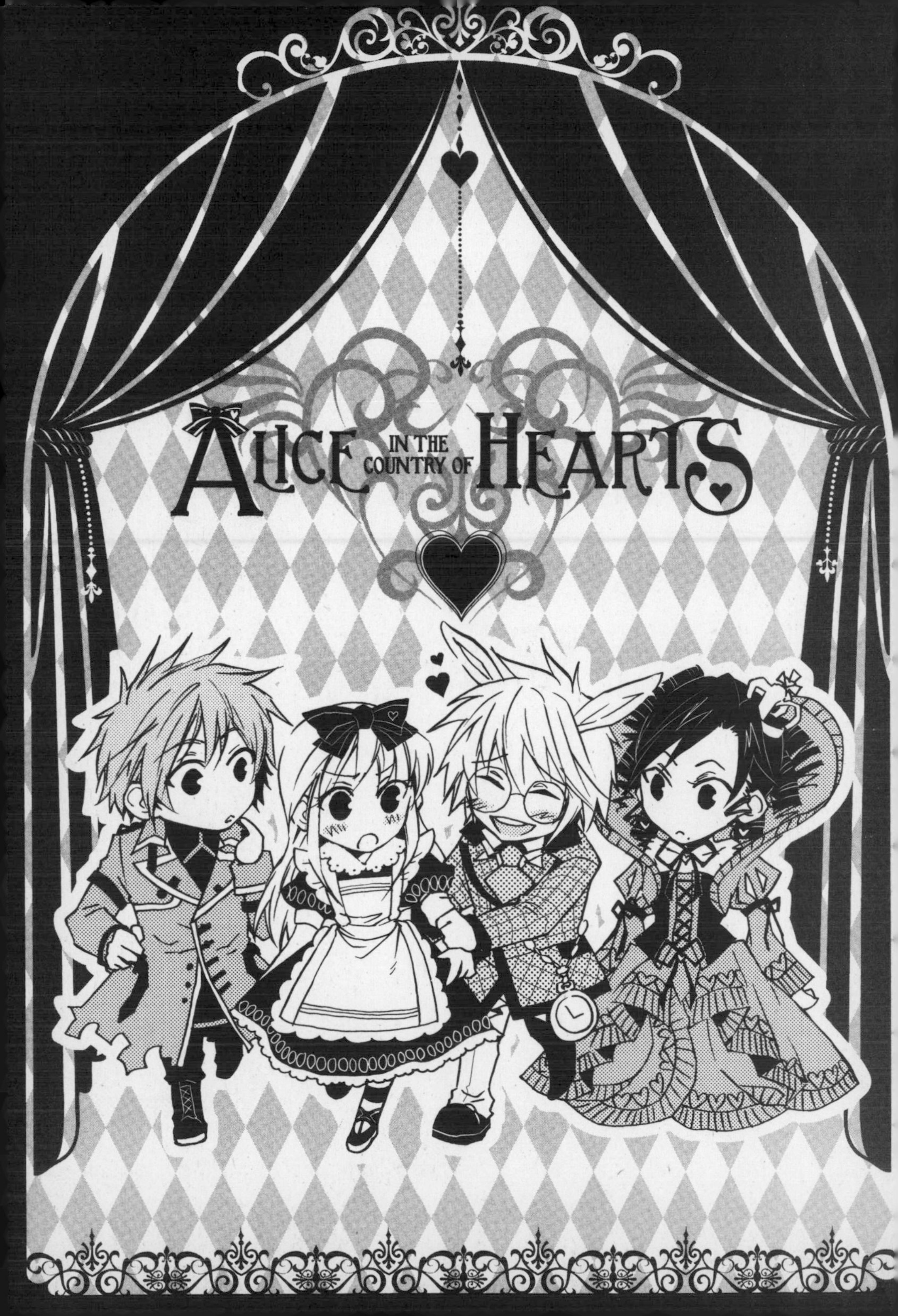
ALICE IN THE COUNTRY OF HEARTS

ALICE IN THE COUNTRY OF HEARTS 1

QUINROSE
SOUMEI HOSHINO

Lettering: Lys Blakeslee
English Adaptation (Omnibus Edition): JuYoun Lee

Translation: Beni Axia Conrad
English Adaptation Vol. 1: Lianne Sentar
English Adaptation Vol. 2: Magda Erik-Soussi

ALICE IN THE COUNTRY OF THE HEART ~Wonderful Wonder World~ Vol. 1, 2
© QuinRose. All rights reserved. © Soumei Hoshino 2008, 2009. First published in Japan in 2008, 2009 by MAG Garden Corporation. English translation rights arranged with MAG Garden Corporation through Tuttle-Mori Agency, Inc., Tokyo.

English translation © 2012 Hachette Book Group, Inc.

Yen Press
Hachette Book Group
237 Park Avenue, New York, NY 10017

www.HachetteBookGroup.com
www.YenPress.com

Yen Press is an imprint of Hachette Book Group, Inc.
The Yen Press name and logo are trademarks of Hachette Book Group, Inc.

First Yen Press Edition: June 2012

ISBN: 978-0-316-21269-4

10 9 8 7 6 5

BVG

Printed in the United States of America